Time Out

Barcelona

timeout.com/barcelona

Penguin Books

PENGUIN BOOKS

Published by the Penguin Group
Penguin Books Ltd, 80 Strand, London WC2R ORL, England
Penguin Books USA Inc., 375 Hudson Street, New York, New York 10014, USA
Penguin Books Australia Ltd, 250 Camberwell Road, Camberwell, Victoria 3124, Australia
Penguin Books Canada Ltd, 10 Alcorn Avenue, Toronto, Ontario, Canada M4V 3B2
Penguin Books (NZ) Ltd, cnr Rosedale and Airborne Roads, Albany, Auckland, New Zealand

Penguin Books Ltd, Registered Offices: Harmondsworth, Middlesex, England

First published 1996
Second edition 1998
Third edition 2000
Fourth edition 2001
Fifth edition 2002
10 9 8 7 6 5 4 3 2 1

Colour reprographics by Icon, Crown House, 56-58 Southwark Street, London SE1
and Precise Litho, 34-35 Great Sutton Street, London EC1
Printed and bound by Cayfosa-Quebecor, Ctra. de Caldes, Km 3 08 130 Sta, Perpètua de Mogoda, Barcelona, Spain

Edited and designed by
Time Out Guides Limited
Universal House
251 Tottenham Court Road
London W1T 7AB
Tel + 44 (0)20 7813 3000
Fax + 44 (0)20 7813 6001
Email guides@timeout.com
www.timeout.com

Editorial

Editor Sally Davies
Deputy Editor Cath Phillips
Consultant Editor William Truini
Listings Researcher Aitziber de la Quintana
Proofreader John Pym
Indexer Anna Raikes

Editorial Director Peter Fiennes
Series Editor Ruth Jarvis
Deputy Series Editor Jonathan Cox
Guides Co-ordinator Jenny Noden

Design

Group Art Director John Oakey
Art Director Mandy Martin
Art Editor Scott Moore
Designers Benjamin de Lotz, Lucy Grant
Scanning/Imaging Dan Conway
Ad Make-up Glen Impey
Picture Editor Kerri Littlefield
Deputy Picture Editor Kit Burnet
Picture Librarian Sarah Roberts

Advertising

Group Commercial Director Lesley Gill
Sales Director/Sponsorship Mark Phillips
International Sales Co-ordinator Ross Canadé
Advertisement Sales (Barcelona) Creative Media Group
Advertising Assistant Sabrina Ancilleri

Administration

Publisher Tony Elliott
Managing Director Mike Hardwick
Group Financial Director Kevin Ellis
Marketing Director Christine Cort
Marketing Manager Mandy Martinez
US Publicity & Marketing Associate Rosella Albanese
Group General Manager Nichola Coulthard
Production Manager Mark Lamond
Production Controller Samantha Furniss
Accountant Sarah Bostock

Features in this guide were written and researched by:
Introduction Sally Davies. **History** Nick Rider, Jeffrey Swartz, William Truini. **Barcelona Today** Richard Schweid (*State of the nation* Matthew Tree). **Architecture** David Howel Evans, Jane Opher, William Truini. **Modernisme** Lluis Bosch, Nick Rider. **Accommodation** Amanda August, Anne Heverin. **Sightseeing** Jonathan Bennett, Eamon Butterfield, Sally Davies, John O'Donovan, Nick Rider, Jeffrey Swartz. **Restaurants** Sally Davies, Nadia Feddo. **Cafés & Bars** Amber Ockrassa. **Shops & Services** Juliet King. **By Season** Jonathan Bennett. **Children** Sally Davies. **Film** Jonathan Bennett. **Galleries** Jeffrey Swartz. **Gay & Lesbian** Eric Goode. **Music** *Classical & Opera* Jonathan Bennett; *Rock, Roots & Jazz* Kirsten Foster, Jack Recasens. **Nightlife** Nick Chapman. **Sport & Fitness** Doug Andrews (*On the ball* Rob Jones). **Theatre & Dance** Jeffrey Swartz. **Trips Out of Town** Sally Davies, Amy Egan. **Directory** Robert Southon.

The Editor would like to thank:
Àngel Uzqueda at Foment de Ciutat Vella, Carles Puig and Steven Guest at Ajuntament de Barcelona, Charo Canal at the Col.lecíó Thyssen-Bornemisza, Ferran Salvador at the Port de Barcelona, Mireia Berenguer at the MNAC, Montse Planas at Turisme de Barcelona, Ernesto Milá, Silvia Pares, Eduardo Berché, David Noguer, Jenny Brickman, Henry O'Donnell, Niall O'Flynn, Gustavo Petrie and, most of all, Cath and John.

Maps by Mapworld, 71 Blandy Road, Henley on Thames, Oxon RG9 1QB, and JS Graphics, 17 Beadles Lane, Old Oxted, Surrey RH8 9JG. Girona and Tarragona street plans are based on material supplied by Thomas Cook Publishers.

Photography by Oriol Tarridas except: pages 7, 10, 17, 19, 38, 81, 284, 291, 292, 299 Godo Foto; pages 9, 66 Ingrid Morato; page 20 Archivo Iconografico, S.A./CORBIS; page 23 Hulton-Deutsch Collection/CORBIS; page 24 Image Bank; page 26 Associated Press/Cesar Rangel; page 35 Tony Bernad/courtesy MBM Architects; page 96 Sucession Picasso/DACS 2002; page 212 Patricia Esteve; page 219 Tony Gibson; page 270 Arenalimages.com/Richard Mildenhall; page 277 Jonathan Cox; pages 275, 281, 294 Nick Inman; page 285 Sally Davies; pages 297, 298 Fergus Stothart.

The following pictures were supplied by the featured establishments: pages 109, 125, 134, 222, 225, 272 (photo Ros Ribas), 287.

Contents

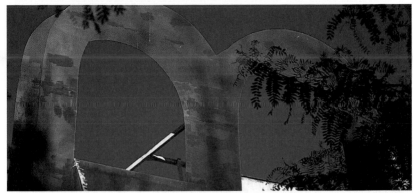

Introduction

Time and again Barcelona is ranked as one of the European cities with the highest quality of life. Whoever decides these things has doubtless never held a bank account, wanted a non-smoking table or tried to park a car here, and has probably never brushed with the tax system. But take a night in June. Maybe, just maybe, they were here when, throughout the night in shady medieval patios, a hollowed-out egg danced on a jet of water rising from a fountain garlanded with flowers; that same magical night when on the other side of town 80,000 young, half-naked Europeans twisted in rapture to mind-warping sets from Aphex Twin and Jeff Mills, while elsewhere a non-stop, theatrical maelstrom of high-octane performances from around the world raged until dawn. A glimpse such as that would almost certainly clinch the deal.

Not that the city hides its light under a bushel. It's a wonder, really, that there hasn't been a backlash against Barcelona's relentless self promotion. Aware that it cannot trade on Olympic glories for much longer, City Hall is constantly finding new projects to put through the star-maker machinery, the current one being 2002's International (no less) Year of Gaudí. Then we have the hugely ambitious Forum of Cultures in 2004. Its objectives? Setting the world to rights. Its

methods? Well, details have remained sketchy, but one thing's for sure; it will be bigger and better than anybody else's parade.

Of course, the lure of the tourist or commercial dollar is largely behind all this, as is the need to show the world that this aspirant capital is serious, and these too lurk behind the constant drive to beautify the city and fill its public spaces with art. Barely has the cement dried on the lamp posts when they're being ripped out and replaced with a fresher, funkier design. Benches, bins and pavements – all are subject to the vagaries of fashion. The raven-haired seductress from the demi-monde that was pre-Olympic Barcelona has tirelessly reinvented herself over the past decade, running the gamut from high-gloss power dresser to boho art maven, thwarting her chroniclers' best attempts at description. Catalan poet Joan Maragall once famously called Barcelona *la gran encisera* – 'the great enchantress'. A century and several face-lifts later, the council has prosaically announced it wants the city to become *la gran amfitriona* – 'the great hostess'. But this is to deny the very essence of the city and all that makes it unique; with all her sultry glamour and sleaze, and capricious, fiery nature, Barcelona is perhaps not quite ready for doilies and small talk.

ABOUT THE TIME OUT CITY GUIDES

The *Time Out Barcelona Guide* is one of an expanding series of Time Out City Guides, now numbering over 35, produced by the people behind London and New York's successful listings magazines. Our guides are all written and updated by resident experts who have striven to provide you with all the most up-to-date information you'll need to explore the city or read up on its background, whether you're a local or a first-time visitor.

THE LOWDOWN ON THE LISTINGS

Above all, we've tried to make this guide as useful as possible. Addresses, telephone numbers, websites, transport information, opening times, admission prices and credit card details are all included in our listings. And, as far, as possible, we've given details of facilities, services and events, all checked and correct as we went to press. However, owners and managers can change their arrangements at any time. Also, in Barcelona, small shops and bars

often do not keep precise opening hours, and may close earlier or later than stated. Similarly, arts programmes are often finalised very late. Before you go out of your way, we'd advise you whenever possible to phone and check opening times, ticket prices and other particulars.

While every effort has been made to ensure the accuracy of the information contained in this guide, the publishers cannot accept responsibility for any errors it may contain.

PRICES AND PAYMENT

Prices throughout this guide are given in euros. At the time of going to press, many Barcelona businesses had not yet confirmed their euro rates for 2002; where this is the case we have converted the price from pesetas into euros (1 euro = 166.386 pesetas) and then rounded the figure to the nearest ten cents. For more on the euro, *see p317.* The prices we've supplied should be treated as guidelines, not gospel. If prices vary wildly from those we've quoted, please write and let us know. We aim to give

TELEPHONE NUMBERS

It is necessary to dial provincial area codes with all numbers in Spain, even for local calls. Hence all normal Barcelona numbers begin 93, whether you're calling from inside or outside the city. From abroad, you must dial 34 (the international dialing code for Spain) followed by the number given in the book – which includes the intial 93. For more information on telephones and codes, *see p319*.

ESSENTIAL INFORMATION

For all the practical information you might need for visiting Barcelona, including emergency phone numbers, visa and customs information, advice on facilities for the disabled, useful websites and details of local transport, turn to the **Directory** chapter at the back of the guide. It starts on page 303.

LANGUAGE

Barcelona is a bilingual city; street signs, tourist information and menus can be in either Catalan or Spanish, and this is reflected in this guide. We have tried to use whichever is more commonly used or appropriate in each case.

MAPS

The map section at the back of this book includes an overview of the greater Barcelona area; detailed street maps of the Eixample, the Raval, Gràcia and other districts, and a small-scale map of the Old City, with a comprehensive street index; a large-scale locality map for planning trips out of town and maps of the local rail and metro networks. The maps start on page 334.

LET US KNOW WHAT YOU THINK

We hope you enjoy the *Time Out Barcelona Guide*, and we'd like to know what you think of it. We welcome tips for places that you consider we should include in future editions and take note of your criticism of our choices. There's a reader's reply card at the back of this book for your feedback, or you can email us at barcelonaguide@timeout.com.

the best and most up-to-date advice, so we always want to know if you've been badly treated or overcharged.

We have noted where shops, restaurants, hotels and so on accept the following credit cards: American Express (**AmEx**), Diners Club (**DC**), MasterCard (**MC**) and Visa (**V**). Many businesses also accept other cards, including Switch, Delta and JCB. Some shops, restaurants and attractions take major travellers' cheques.

THE LIE OF THE LAND

We have divided the city into areas – simplified, for convenience, from the full complexity of Barcelona's geography – and the relevant area name is given with each venue listed in this guide. For a map showing the different city areas and how they relate to our sightseeing chapters, *see p74*. Wherever possible, a map reference is provided for every venue listed, indicating the page and grid reference at which it can be found on the street maps.

There is an online version of this guide, as well as weekly events listings for 35 international cities, at www.timeout.com.

Sponsors & advertisers

We would like to stress that no venue or establishment has been included in this guide because it has advertised in any of our publications and no payment of any kind has influenced any review. The opinions given in this book are those of *Time Out* writers and entirely independent.

Targasys.

A world of services.

Targasys is always with you, ready to assure you all the tranquillity and serenity that you desire for your journeys, 24 hours a day 365 days a year.

Roadside assistance always and everywhere, infomobility so not to have surprises, insurance... and lots more.

To get to know us better contact us at the toll-free number **00-800-55555555**.

...and to discover Targa Connect's exclusive and innovative integrated infotelematic services onboard system visit us at:

www.targaconnect.com

In Context

History

The fraught and often bloody tale of Barcelona's life.

IN THE BEGINNING

Barcelona, unlike many other European cities, did not follow a consistent pattern of growth during its early history. The city see-sawed between periods of relative stability and severe decline over its first 1,000 years, an existence made all the more precarious by a series of invasions from both north and south. This long and unstable beginning left the people of the city and surrounding region with traditions and characteristics quite distinct from those found elsewhere on the Iberian peninsula.

The Romans founded Barcelona in about 15 BC, on the Mons Taber, a small hill between two streams that provided a good view of the Mediterranean, and which today is crowned by the cathedral. The plain around it was sparsely inhabited by the Laetani, an agrarian Iberian people known for producing grain and honey and gathering oysters. Named Barcino, the town was much smaller than Tarraco (Tarragona), the capital of the Roman province of Hispania Citerior, but had the only harbour, albeit a poor one, between there and Narbonne.

Like virtually every other Roman new town in Europe, Barcino was a fortified rectangle with a crossroads at its centre (where the Plaça Sant Jaume is today). It was a decidedly unimportant provincial town, but the rich plain provided it with a produce garden, and the sea gave it an incipient maritime trade. It acquired a Jewish community very soon after its foundation, and was associated with some Christian martyrs, notably Barcelona's first patron saint, Santa Eulàlia. She was supposedly executed at the end of the third century via a series of revolting tortures, including being rolled naked in a sealed barrel full of glass shards down the alley now called Baixada (descent) de Santa Eulàlia.

Barcino accepted Christianity shortly afterwards, in AD 312, together with the rest of the Roman Empire, which by then was under growing threat of invasion. In the fourth century, the town's rough defences were replaced with massive stone walls, many sections of which can still be seen today. It was these ramparts that ensured Barcelona's continuity, making it a stronghold much desired by later warlords (for more on the relics of Roman Barcelona, *see below* **Do as the Romans did**).

These and other defences did not prevent the empire's disintegration. In 415, Barcelona (as it became known) briefly became capital of the kingdom of the Visigoths, under their chieftain Ataülf. He brought with him as a prisoner Gala Placidia, the 20-year-old daughter of a Roman emperor, whom he forced into marriage. She is famous as a woman of strong character, and is credited with converting the barbarian king to Christianity. She was also perhaps fortunate in that Ataülf died shortly afterwards, whereupon Gala Placidia left, married her relative, Emperor Constantius I, and for a time became the most powerful figure in the court of Byzantium. Meanwhile, back in Barcelona, the Visigoths soon moved on southwards to extend their control over the whole of the Iberian peninsula, and for the

next 400 years the town was a neglected backwater. It was in this state when the Muslims swept across the peninsula after 711, easily crushing Goth resistance. They made little attempt to settle Catalonia, but much of the Christian population retreated into the Pyrenees, the first Catalan heartland.

Then, at the end of the eighth century, the Franks began to drive southwards against the Muslims from across the mountains. In 801, Charlemagne's son, Louis the Pious, took Barcelona and made it a bastion of the Marca Hispanica (Spanish March), the southern buffer of his father's empire. This gave Catalonia a trans-Pyrenean origin entirely different from that of the other Christian states in Spain; equally, it is for this reason that the closest relative of the Catalan language is Provençal, not Castilian.

When the Frankish princes returned to their main business further north, loyal counts were left behind to rule sections of the Catalan lands.

Do as the Romans did

Medieval Barcelona and all subsequent buildings in the Barri Gòtic were constructed on top of the Roman settlement of Barcino, founded in 15 BC, and many a local resident has set out to make over a bathroom and turned up a bit of ancient masonry. The original Roman city was only a second-rank outpost, covering just ten hectares (24 acres). Some of its street plan can be seen in the extensive remains beneath the **Museu d'Història de la Ciutat** (*pictured*), the largest underground excavation of a Roman site in Europe. Barcino has had an unappreciated impact on every subsequent era: many of Barcelona's most familiar streets – C/Hospital, even Passeig de Gràcia – follow the line of Roman roads. The best way to get an idea of the Roman town is to walk the line of its walls. Along the route all kinds of Roman remains can be found, poking out from where they were re-used or built over by medieval and later builders (this walk is marked in pink on *pp342-3*).

Barcino's central axis was the junction of C/Llibreteria and C/Bisbe, now a corner of Plaça Sant Jaume. **Llibreteria** began life as the Cardus Maximus, the main road to Rome; walk down it, and at **C/Tapineria** turn left to reach **Plaça Ramon Berenguer el Gran** and the largest surviving stretch of ancient wall, incorporated into the medieval Palau Reial. Continue on along Tapineria, where there

are many sections of Roman building, to **Avda Catedral**. The massive twin-drum gate on C/Bisbe, while often retouched, in its basic shape has not changed since it was the main gate of the Roman town. To its left are fragments of an aqueduct. If you take a detour up C/Capellans to **C/Duran i Bas**, you can see another four arches of an aqueduct; nearby in **Plaça Vila de Madrid** are tombs from the ancient cemetery, which in accordance with Roman custom had to be outside the city walls.

Returning to the cathedral, turn right into **C/Palla**. A little way along, a large chunk of wall is visible, only discovered when a building was demolished in the 1980s. Palla runs into **C/Banys Nous**, where at No.16 there is a centre for disabled children, which inside contains a piece of wall with a relief of legs and feet (try to phone ahead, 93 318 14 81, for a viewing time). Beyond there is the junction with **C/Call**, the other end of the Cardus, and so the opposite side of the Roman town from Llibreteria-Tapineria. The owners of the shoe shop at C/Call 1 are used to people wandering in to examine their piece of Roman tower.

Carry on across C/Ferran and down **C/Avinyó**, next continuation of the perimeter. At the back of the Pakistani restaurant at No.19 there is a cave-like space that once again incorporates portions of Roman wall.

One of these, Count Guifré el Pilós, Wilfred 'the Hairy' (c860-98), succeeded in gaining title to several of the Catalan territories and his successors made Barcelona their capital, thereby setting the seal on the city's future (*see also p10* **Top Cat: Wilfred the Hairy**).

A century after Wilfred, in 985, a Muslim army attacked and sacked Barcelona. The hairy count's great-grandson, Count Borrell II, requested aid from his theoretical feudal lord, the Frankish king. He received no reply, and so repudiated all Frankish sovereignty over Catalonia. From then on – although the name was not yet in use – Catalonia was effectively independent, and the Counts of Barcelona were free to forge its destiny.

FROM COUNTS TO KINGS

In the first century of the new millennium, Catalonia was consolidated as a political entity. The Catalan counties retained from their Frankish origins a French system of aristocratic feudalism – another difference from the rest of Iberia – but also had a peasantry who were notably independent and resistant to noble demands. In the 1060s, the Usatges, the country's distinctive legal code, was established.

The Counts of Barcelona and lesser nobles also endowed monasteries throughout Catalonia. This provided the background to the years of glory of Romanesque art, with the building of the great monasteries and churches of northern Catalonia, such as Sant Pere de Rodes near Figueres, and the painting of the superb murals now in the Museu Nacional on Montjuïc. There was also a flowering of scholarship, reflecting Catalan contacts with both Islamic and Carolingian cultures. In Barcelona, shipbuilding and commerce in grain and wine all expanded, and a new trade developed in textiles. The city grew both inside its old Roman walls and outside them, where *vilanoves* (new towns) appeared at Sant Pere and La Ribera.

From **C/Milans**, turn left on to **C/Gignás**: by the junction with **C/Regomir** there are remains of the fourth sea gate of the town, which would have faced the beach, and the Roman shipyard. On C/Regomir there is also one of the most important relics of Barcino, the **Pati Llimona** (*see below*). After visiting there, walk up **C/Correu Vell**, where there are more fragments of wall, to reach one of the most impressive relics of Roman Barcelona in the small, shady **Plaça Traginers**: a Roman tower, one corner of the ancient wall, in a remarkable state of preservation, despite having had a medieval house built on top

of it. Turn up **C/Sots-Tinent Navarro** – with a massive stretch of Roman rampart – to complete the circuit back at Llibreteria, and perhaps head back to Barcino's centre and the **Temple d'August** (*see below*).

Pati Llimona

C/Regomir 3 (93 268 47 00). Metro Jaume I/17, 40, 45 bus. **Open** *9am-10pm Mon-Fri; 10am-2pm Sat, Sun.* **Exhibitions** *10am-2pm, 4-8pm Mon-Fri; 10am-2pm Sat, Sun. Closed Aug.* **Admission** free. **Map** p340 D5.
One of the oldest continuously occupied sites in Barcelona, incorporating part of a round tower that dates from the first Roman settlement, and later Roman baths. The excavated foundations are visible from the street. Most of the building above is a 15th-century residence, converted into a social centre in 1988.

Temple d'August

C/Paradís 10 (information Museu d'Història de la Ciutat 93 315 11 11). Metro Jaume I/17, 19, 40, 45 bus. **Open** *10am-2pm, 4-8pm Tue-Sat; 10am-2pm Sun.* **Admission** free. **Map** p340 D5.
The Centre Excursionista de Catalunya (a hiking club) contains four fluted Corinthian columns that formed the rear corner of the Temple of Augustus, built in the first century BC as the hub of the town's Forum.

Top Cat: Wilfred the Hairy

Count Guifré el Pilós, also known as Wilfred 'the Hairy', was a real-life ninth-century count and also a semi-mythical figure considered to be the founding father of Catalonia.

Wilfred was one of several loyal counts left behind on the southern side of the Pyrenees, entrusted by Frankish princes with defending lands recently won back from the Saracens. From his base in the mountain valleys near Ripoll, Wilfred managed to extend and unite a territory that would later form the basis of the Catalan state. He is also credited with founding the dynasty of the Counts of Barcelona, a remarkably successful house that would reign in an unbroken line until 1410.

In particular, he is linked with the creation of the Catalan national flag, the Quatre Barres (Four Bars), which is also called La Senyera. The flag's origins lie wrapped in medieval legend and later romantic embellishments, but the most popular account (and one which every Catalan child learns at school) tells the tale of hirsute Wilfred.

The story goes that one day, Wilfred was called to serve his lord (none other than Charles 'the Bald', though some accounts say Louis 'the Pious') and was mortally wounded in a battle against the Moors. In recognition of his vassal's heroism, the emperor dipped his fingers into Wilfred's

bloody wounds and ran them down the count's golden shield, thereby creating La Senyera, a name claimed by some to be derived from *sang i or*, 'blood and gold'.

Contemporary historians have set about to disprove this tale, noting among other things that heraldic devices didn't become fashionable until some two centuries after Wilfred's day. But whatever the true origins of the flag may be, the Quatre Barres is first reliably recorded on the tomb of Count Ramon Berenguer II in 1082. This makes the four-red-stripes-on-yellow symbol the oldest national flag in Europe, predating its nearest competitor, that of Denmark, by some 100 years.

Catalonia – a name that gained currency in Latin in the 11th century – was also gaining more territory from the Muslims to the south, beyond the Penedès. For a long time, though, the realm of the Counts of Barcelona continued to look just as much to the north, across the Pyrenees. After 1035, during the reigns of the four Counts Ramon Berenguer, large areas of what is now southern France were acquired, either through marriage or with Arab booty. In 1112, the union of Ramon Berenguer III 'the Great' (1093-1131) with Princess Dolça of Provence extended his authority as far as the Rhône.

A more significant marriage occurred in 1137, when Ramon Berenguer IV (1131-62) wed Petronella, heir to the throne of Aragon. This would, in the long term, bind Catalonia into Iberia. The uniting of the two dynasties created a powerful entity known as the Crown of Aragon, each element retaining its separate institutions, and ruled by monarchs known as the Count-Kings. Since Aragon was already a kingdom, it was given precedence and its name was often used to refer to the state, but the court language was Catalan and the centre of government remained in Barcelona. Ramon Berenguer IV also extended Catalan territory to its current frontiers in the Ebro valley. At the beginning of the following century, however, the dynasty lost virtually all its lands north of the Pyrenees to France, when Count-King Pere I 'the Catholic' was killed at the battle of Muret in 1213. This was a blessing in disguise. In future, the Catalan-Aragonese state would be oriented decisively towards the Mediterranean and the south, and was able to embark on two centuries of imperialism equalled in vigour only by Barcelona's burgeoning commercial enterprise.

ALL THE KINGS' MED

Pere I's successor was the most expansionist of the Count-Kings. Jaume I 'the Conqueror' (1213-76) abandoned any idea of further adventures in Provence and joined decisively in the campaign against the Muslims to the south, taking Mallorca in 1229, Ibiza in 1235 and then, at much greater cost, Valencia in 1238. He made it another separate kingdom, the third part of the Crown of Aragon.

Barcelona became the centre of an empire extending across the Mediterranean. The city grew tremendously under Jaume I, and in the mid 13th century he ordered the building of a new, second wall, along the line of the Rambla and roughly encircling the area between there and the modern Parc de la Ciutadella, thus bringing La Ribera and the other *vilanoves* within the city. In 1274 he also gave Barcelona a form of representative self-government, the Consell de Cent, a council of 100 chosen citizens, an institution that would last for more than 400 years. In Catalonia as a whole, royal powers were limited by a parliament, the Corts, with a permanent standing committee, known as the Generalitat.

Catalan imperialism advanced by conquest and marriage well beyond the Balearic Islands. The Count-Kings commanded a powerful fleet and a mercenary army, the Catalan Companies (Almogàvers). For decades they were led by two great commanders, the fleet by Roger de Llúria and the army by Roger de Flor. The stuff of another set of heroic legends – such as their sword-in-hand battle cry '*Desperta ferro!*' ('Awaken, iron!') – the Almogàvers made themselves feared equally by Christians and Muslims as they travelled the Mediterranean conquering, plundering and enslaving in the name of God and the Crown of Aragon.

In 1282, Pere II 'the Great' annexed Sicily; Catalan domination over the island would last for nearly 150 years. The Catalan empire reached its greatest strength under Jaume II 'the Just' (1291-1327). Corsica (1323) and Sardinia (1324) were added to the possessions

of the Crown of Aragon, although the latter would never submit to Catalan rule and would be a constant focus of revolt.

GOLDEN TOWN

The Crown of Aragon was often at war with Arab rulers, but its capital flourished through commerce with every part of the Mediterranean, Christian and Muslim. Catalan ships also sailed into the Atlantic, to England and Flanders. Their ventures were actively supported by the Count-Kings and burghers of Barcelona, and regulated by the first-ever code of maritime law, the Llibre del Consolat de Mar (written 1260-70), an early example of the Catalans' tendency to legalism, the influence of which extended far beyond their own territories. By the late 13th century, nearly 130 consulates ringed the Mediterranean, engaged in a complex system of trade that involved spices, coral, grain, slaves, metals, wool and other textiles, olive oil, salt fish and leather goods.

> '**Catalonia was one of the first areas in Europe to use its vernacular language in written form and as a language of culture.**'

Not surprisingly, this age of power and prestige was also the great era of building in medieval Barcelona. The Catalan Gothic style reached its peak between the reigns of Jaume 'the Just' and Pere III 'the Ceremonious' (1336-87). The Count-Kings' imperial conquests may have been ephemeral, but their talent for permanence in building can still be admired today. Between 1290 and 1340, the construction of most of Barcelona's major Gothic buildings was initiated. Religious edifices such as the cathedral, Santa Maria del Mar and Santa Maria del Pi were matched by civil buildings such as the Saló de Tinell and the Llotja, the old market and stock exchange. As a result, Barcelona today contains the most important nucleus of Gothic civil architecture anywhere in Europe.

The ships of the Catalan navy were built in the monumental Drassanes (shipyards), begun by Pere II and completed under Pere III, in 1378. In 1359, Pere III also built the third, final city wall, along the line of the modern Paral.lel, Ronda Sant Pau and Ronda Sant Antoni. This gave the 'old city' of Barcelona its definitive shape. La Ribera, 'the waterfront', was the centre of trade and industry in 14th-century Barcelona. Once unloaded at

the beach, wares were taken to the Llotja. Just inland, the Carrer Montcada was the street par excellence where newly enriched merchants could display their wealth in opulent Gothic palaces. All around were the workers of the various craft guilds, grouped together in their own streets.

Women's domains in this Barcelona were initially limited to home, market, convent or brothel, although in 1249 they won the right to inherit property, and women were at one time the main textile workers. At the very top of society some women became very powerful, as it was quite common – unusually for that era – for Catalan Count-Kings to delegate their authority to their queens when they went on campaigns, as happened with Eleanor of Sicily, wife of Pere III.

The Catalan 'Golden Age' was also an era of cultural greatness. Catalonia was one of the first areas in Europe to use its vernacular language, as well as Latin, in written form and as a language of culture. The oldest written texts in Catalan are the *Homílies d'Organyà*, translations from the Bible dating from the 12th century. Not just monks, but also the court and the aristocracy seem very early to have attained an unusual level of literacy, and Jaume I wrote his own autobiography, the *Llibre dels Feits* or 'Book of Deeds', dramatically recounting his achievements and conquests.

Incipient Catalan literature was given a vital thrust by the unique figure of Ramon Llull (1235-1316). After a debauched youth, he turned to more serious pursuits after he experienced a series of religious visions, and became the first man in post-Roman Europe to write philosophy in a vernacular language. Steeped in Arabic and Hebrew writings, he brought together Christian, Islamic, Jewish and classical ideas, and also wrote a vast amount on other subjects – from theories of chivalry to poetry and visionary tales.

In doing so Llull effectively created Catalan as a literary language. Catalan translations from Greek and Latin were also undertaken at this time. In the very twilight of the Golden Age, in 1490, the Valencian Joanot Martorell published *Tirant Lo Blanc*, the bawdy story that is now considered to be the first true European novel.

REVOLT AND COLLAPSE

Barcelona was not, however, a peaceful and harmonious place during its Golden Age, especially as the 14th century wore on. Social unrest and violence in the streets was common: grain riots, popular uprisings, attacks on Jews and gang warfare. An ongoing struggle took place between two political factions,

the Biga (roughly representing the most established merchants) and the Busca (roughly composed of smaller tradesmen).

The extraordinary prosperity of the medieval period was not to last. The Count-Kings had overextended Barcelona's resources, and overinvested in far-off ports. By 1400, the effort to maintain their conquests by force, especially Sardinia, had exhausted the spirit and the coffers of the Catalan imperialist drive. The Black Death, which had arrived in the 1340s, had also had a devastating impact on Catalonia. This only intensified the bitterness of social conflicts between the aristocracy, merchants, peasants and the urban poor.

In 1410, Martí I 'the Humane' died without an heir, bringing to an end the line of Counts of Barcelona unbroken since Guifré el Pilós. After much deliberation between church and aristocracy the Crown of Aragon was passed to a member of a Castilian noble family, the Trastámaras: Fernando de Antequera (1410-16).

His son, Alfons V 'the Magnanimous' (1416-58), undertook one more conquest, of Naples, but the empire was under ever greater pressure, and Barcelona merchants were unable to compete with the Genoese and Venetians. At home, in the 1460s, the effects of war and catastrophic famine led to a collapse into civil war and peasant revolt. The population was depleted to such an extent that Barcelona would not regain the numbers it had had in 1400 (40,000) until the 18th century.

In 1469, an important union for Spain initiated another woeful period in Barcelona's history, dubbed by some Catalan historians the Decadència, which would lead to the end of Catalonia as a separate entity. In that year, Ferdinand of Aragon (reigned 1479-1516) married Isabella of Castile (1476-1506), and so united the different Spanish kingdoms, even though they would retain their separate institutions for another two centuries.

As Catalonia's fortunes had declined, so those of Castile had risen. While Catalonia was impoverished and in chaos, Castile had become larger, richer, had a bigger population and was on the crest of a wave of expansion. In 1492, Granada, the last Muslim foothold in Spain, was conquered, Isabella decreed the expulsion of all Jews from Castile and Aragon, and Columbus discovered America.

It was Castile's seafaring orientation towards the Atlantic, rather than the Mediterranean, that confirmed Catalonia's decline. The discovery of the New World was a disaster for Catalan commerce: trade shifted decisively away from the Mediterranean, and Catalans were officially barred from participating in the exploitation of the new empire until the

1770s. The weight of Castile within the monarchy was increased, and it very soon became the clear seat of government.

In 1516, the Spanish crown passed to the House of Habsburg, in the shape of Ferdinand and Isabella's grandson, Emperor Charles V. His son, Philip II of Spain, established Madrid as the capital of all his dominions in 1561. Catalonia was managed by appointed viceroys, the power of its institutions increasingly restricted, with a down-at-heel aristocracy and a meagre cultural life.

GRIM REAPERS

While Castilian Spain went through its 'Golden Century', Catalonia was left more and more on the margins. Worse was to come, however, in the following century, with the two national revolts, both heroic defeats, that have since acquired a central role in Catalan nationalist mythology.

The problem for the Spanish monarchy was that, whereas Castile was an absolute monarchy and so could be taxed at will, in the former Aragonese territories, and especially Catalonia, royal authority kept coming up against a mass of local rights and privileges. As the Habsburgs' empire became bogged down in endless wars and expenses that not even American gold could meet, the Count-Duke of Olivares, the formidable great minister of King Philip IV (1621-65), resolved to extract more money and troops from the non-Castilian dominions of the crown. The Catalans, however, felt they were taxed quite enough already.

In 1640, a mass of peasants, later dubbed Els Segadors (the Reapers), gathered on the Rambla in Barcelona, outside the Porta Ferrissa (Iron Gate) in the second wall. They rioted against royal authority, surged into the city and seized and murdered the viceroy, the Marqués de Santa Coloma. This began the general uprising known as the Guerra dels Segadors, the Reapers' War. The authorities of the Generalitat, led by its president, Pau Claris, were fearful of the violence of the poor and, lacking the confidence to declare Catalonia independent, appealed for protection from Louis XIII of France. French armies, however, were unable to defend Catalonia adequately, and in 1652 a destitute Barcelona capitulated to the equally exhausted army of Philip IV. In 1659, France and Spain made peace with a treaty that gave the Catalan territory of Roussillon, around Perpignan, to France. After the revolt, Philip IV and his ministers were surprisingly magnanimous, allowing the Catalans to retain what was left of their institutions despite their disloyalty. This war provided the Catalan national anthem, *Els Segadors*.

Fifty years later came the second of the great national rebellions, in the War of the Spanish Succession, the last time Catalonia sought to regain its national freedom by force. In 1700, Charles II of Spain died without an heir. Castile accepted the grandson of Louis XIV of France, Philip of Anjou, as King Philip V of Spain (1700-46). However, the alternative candidate, Archduke Charles of Austria, promised to restore the traditional rights of the former Aragonese territories, and so won their allegiance. He also had the support, in his fight against France, of Britain, Holland and Austria.

'After a 13-month siege, Barcelona fell to the French and Spanish armies on 11 September 1714.'

Once again, though, Catalonia backed the wrong horse, and was let down in its choice of allies. In 1713, Britain and the Dutch made a separate peace with France and withdrew their aid, leaving the Catalans stranded with no possibility of victory. After a 13-month siege in which every citizen was called to arms, Barcelona fell to the French and Spanish armies on 11 September 1714.

The most heroic defeat of all, this date marked the most decisive political reverse in Barcelona's history, and is now commemorated as Catalan National Day, the Diada. Some of Barcelona's resisters were buried next to the church of Santa Maria del Mar in the Born in the Fossar de les Moreres (Mulberry Graveyard), now a memorial.

In 1715, Philip V issued his decree of Nova Planta, abolishing all the remaining separate institutions of the Crown of Aragon and so, in effect, creating 'Spain' as a single, unitary state. Large-scale 'Castilianisation' of the country was initiated, and Castilian replaced the Catalan language in all official documents.

In Barcelona, extra measures were taken to keep the city under firm control. The crumbling medieval walls and the castle on Montjuïc were refurbished with new ramparts, and a massive new citadel was built on the eastern side of the old city, where the Parc de la Ciutadella is today. To make space for it, thousands of people had to be expelled from La Ribera and forcibly rehoused in the Barceloneta, Barcelona's first-ever planned housing scheme, with its barrack-like street plan unmistakably provided by French military engineers. This citadel became the most hated symbol of the city's subordination.

RETAIL THERAPY

Politically subjugated and without a significant native ruling class, following the departure of many of its remaining aristocrats to serve the monarchy in Madrid, Catalonia nevertheless revived in the 18th century. Catalans continued speaking their language, and developed independent commercial initiatives. Ironically, the Bourbons, by abolishing legal differences between Catalonia and the rest of Spain, also removed the earlier restrictions on Catalan trade, especially with the colonies. The strength of Barcelona's guilds had enabled it to maintain its artisan industries, and the city revived in particular after the official authorisation to trade with the Americas by King Charles III in 1778.

Shipping picked up again, and in the last years of the 18th century Barcelona had a booming export trade to the New World in wines and spirits from Catalan vineyards, and textiles, wool and silk. In 1780, a merchant called Erasme de Gómina opened Barcelona's first true factory, a hand-powered weaving mill in C/Riera Alta with 800 workers. In the next decade, Catalan trade with Spanish America had quadrupled; Barcelona's population had grown from around 30,000 in 1720 to close to 100,000 by the end of the century.

This prosperity was reflected in a new wave of building in the city. Neo-classical mansions appeared, notably on C/Ample and the Rambla. The greatest transformation, though, was in the Rambla itself. Until the 1770s, it had been no more than a dusty, dry riverbed where country people came to sell their produce, lined on the Raval side mostly with giant religious houses and on the other with Jaume I's second wall. In 1775, the Captain-General, the Marqués de la Mina, embarked on an ambitious scheme to demolish the wall and turn the Rambla into a paved promenade. Beyond the Rambla, the previously semi-rural Raval was becoming densely populated.

Barcelona's expansion was briefly interrupted by the French invasion of 1808. Napoleon sought to appeal to Catalans by offering them national recognition within his empire, but, curiously, met with very little response. After six years of turmoil, Barcelona's growing business class resumed their projects in 1814, with the restoration of the Bourbon monarchy in the shape of Ferdinand VII.

GETTING UP STEAM

The upheaval of the Napoleonic occupation ushered in 60 years of conflict and political disorder in Spain, as new and traditional forces in society – reactionaries, conservatives, reformists and revolutionaries – struggled with

Dope on a rope

Medieval Barcelona was dense with the noise, smell and colour of craftsmen at work: knifegrinders, weavers, tanners, shoemakers, mirror makers and more. Belonging to a craft guild provided a powerful sense of identity and it's not hard to imagine the inevitable rivalry, friendly or not, that must have existed among the various trades. One group, however, the ropemakers, was definitely at the bottom of the pole and its members were oddly shunned by just about everyone else.

The ropemakers' guild was officially established in 1404, although records of its activity can be found 300 years earlier. With the city's success in trade as the Catalan empire expanded, the quality of rope from Barcelona became famous around the Mediterranean – but this did nothing to raise the standing of the ropemakers' guild, which was subdivided into various groups depending on whether they made rope for navigation, domestic use or punishment and hangings.

The role of ropemakers in the system of punishment helps explain their social ostracism, but does not tell the whole story. Not only was it believed that they could craft a special hangman's rope that appeared strong but would break under the right tension (at which point the condemned man was free to go), but they also sold all manner of string charms to use against illness and evil-doers. In short, they were a weird bunch and generally held to possess supernatural powers.

The secret to the ropemakers' standing may have something to do with the fact that they used hemp, or cannabis, to make their ropes. Not all hemp is psychoactive, but the plant used in this corner of the Mediterranean was intoxicating. The cannabis was harvested when the plant was in flower and ropemakers spent all day stripping off leaves and buds. They then soaked and dried the stems before shredding them for their fibre, which was used to make rope. It's quite probable that this lengthy, hands-on process led to the absorption of the plant's psychoactive elements. In other words, being stoned most of the time, ropemakers enjoyed a unique view of the medieval world. And the rest of society just didn't get it.

A week of rage and rampage

Barcelona at the turn of the 20th century was a city plagued with contradictions. On the one hand, the metropolis, like the rest of Catalonia, was enjoying a period of cultural rebirth, the artisan-based, bourgeoisie-financed *Modernista* movement being the most remarkable example of this. On the other hand, the life expectancy for the city's poor – less than 40 years – was among the lowest in Europe, with the numbers of the 'new' poor, unskilled factory workers living and working in horrendous conditions, steadily on the increase.

Not surprisingly, ideological beliefs took firm root on either side of this social divide. Factory owners and the bourgeoisie sought refuge in an ever more conservative Catholicism, one exceptional symbol of which was Gaudí's Sagrada Família. Anarchism, meanwhile, found a ready home among the working classes, so much so that by the first decade of the 1900s, Barcelona had more self-proclaimed anarchists than anywhere else in the world.

Class tensions finally exploded in July 1909, with the full-scale revolt that later became known as the Setmana Tràgica, or Tragic Week. By the last day of the rebellion, more than a hundred people were dead, thousands wounded, and more than half the city's religious buildings, some 80 in all, were destroyed. The immediate cause of upheaval came from outside the city, in a nakedly cynical abuse of power by the Spanish government. Earlier in the month, conservative leaders in Madrid had blundered into and lost a colonial battle in Morocco for control of an iron mine. To remedy matters, the government decided to muster some 40,000 Catalans, most of them married, working-class residents of Barcelona, to go off and fight.

Protests against the so-called 'bankers' war' began almost immediately and on 26 July, workers' organisations called a general strike. Everyone but tram workers heeded the call, and it was in blocking the trams from running that the first full-blown street battles between workers and the forces of order took place. Over the following days, matters swiftly degenerated as the government lost all control of the situation and was forced to declare a state of war.

The rebellion, however, was really more of a sustained riot; instead of trying to implement a strategy, workers simply wreaked as much

one other to establish a viable system of government. Even so, Barcelona was still able to embark upon the transformations of the industrial revolution, Catalonia, with Lombardy, being one of only two areas in southern Europe to do so before the end of the 19th century.

On his restoration, Ferdinand VII (1808-33) attempted to reinstate the absolute monarchy of his youth and reimpose his authority over Spain's American colonies, but failed to do either. On his death he was succeeded by his three-year-old daughter Isabel II (1833-68), but the throne was also claimed by his brother Carlos, who was backed by the most reactionary sectors in the country.

To defend Isabel's rights, the Regent, Ferdinand's widow Queen Maria Cristina, was obliged to seek the support of liberals, and so granted a very limited form of constitution. Thus began Spain's Carlist Wars, which had a powerful impact in conservative rural Catalonia, where Don Carlos's faction won a considerable following, in part because of its support for traditional local rights and customs.

While this see-saw struggle went on around the country, in Barcelona a liberal-minded local administration, freed from subordination to the military, was able to engage in some city planning, opening up the soon-to-be fashionable C/Ferran and Plaça Sant Jaume in the 1820s, and later adding the Plaça Reial. A fundamental change came in 1836, when a liberal government in Madrid decreed the Desamortació (disentailment) of Spain's monasteries. In Barcelona, where convents and religious houses still took up great sections of the Raval and the Rambla, a huge area was freed for development.

The Rambla took on the appearance it roughly retains today, while the Raval, the main district for new industry in a Barcelona still contained within its walls, rapidly filled up with tenements and textile mills several storeys high. In 1832, the first steam-driven factory in Spain was built on C/Tallers, sparking resistance from hand-spinners and weavers.

Most of the city's factories were still relatively small, however, and Catalan manufacturers were very aware that they

havoc as they could, with the Church, viewed as the refuge of power, being the prime target. In the frenzy of destruction, bands of men sacked and burned churches, convents, monasteries and religious schools around the city, including the now vanished 16th-century Jerònimes convent in the Raval. At times, the rioters even emptied crypts of the long-dead corpses of priests and nuns and left these to stand like ghastly puppets on street corners (pictured). Gaudí was terrified that his temple would be a target, but the Sagrada Família, miraculously or not, was spared any damage.

After government troops finally restored order on 1 August, a group of prime suspects was rounded up and tried, among them the anarchist educator, Francesc Ferrer. Although no real evidence was ever produced against him and, in fact, he wasn't even in Barcelona during the revolt, Ferrer was found to be 'morally responsible' for the event and summarily executed. This tragic finale of a savage seven days had at least one hopeful outcome: Ferrer's death raised a cry of protest both in Spain and around Europe, and within a few months the government in Madrid was forced to fold.

were at a disadvantage in competing with the industries of Britain and other countries to the north. For decades, their political motto would emphasise protectionism rather than nationalism, as they incessantly demanded of Madrid that the textile markets of Spain and its remaining colonies be sealed against all foreign competition.

Also, they did not have the city to themselves. Not only did the anti-industrial Carlists threaten from the countryside, but Barcelona soon became a centre of radical ideas. Its people were notably rebellious, and liberal, republican, free-thinking and even utopian socialist groups proliferated between sporadic bursts of repression. In 1842, a liberal revolt, the Jamancia, took over Barcelona, and barricades went up around the city. This was the last occasion Barcelona was bombarded from the castle on Montjuïc, as the army struggled to regain control.

The Catalan language, by this time, had been relegated to secondary status, spoken in every street but rarely written or used in cultured discourse. Then, in 1833, Bonaventura Carles Aribau published his *Oda a la Pàtria*, a romantic eulogy in Catalan of the country, its language and its past. This poem had an extraordinary impact, and is traditionally credited with initiating the Renaixença (rebirth) of Catalan heritage and culture. The year 1848 was a high point for Barcelona and Catalonia, with the inauguration of the first railway in Spain, from Barcelona to Mataró, and the opening of the Liceu opera house.

SETTING AN EIXAMPLE

The optimism of Barcelona's new middle class was counterpointed by two persistent obstacles: the weakness of the Spanish economy as a whole, and the instability of their own society, reflected in atrocious labour relations. No consideration was given to the manpower behind the industrial surge: the underpaid, overworked men, women and children who lived in appalling conditions in high-rise slums within the cramped city. In 1855, the first general strike took place in Barcelona. The Captain-General, Zapatero, inaugurating a long cycle of conflict, refused to permit any workers' organisations, and bloodily suppressed all resistance.

One response to the city's problems that had almost universal support in Barcelona was the demolition of the city walls, which had imposed a stifling restriction on its growth. For years, however, the Spanish state refused to relinquish this hold on the city. To find space, larger factories were established in villages around Barcelona, such as Sants and Poblenou. In 1854, permission finally came for the demolition of the citadel and the walls. The work began with enthusiastic popular participation, crowds of volunteers joining in at weekends. Barcelona at last broke out of the space it had occupied since the 14th century and spread outward into its new *eixample* (extension), to a plan by Ildefons Cerdà.

In 1868, Isabel II, once a symbol of liberalism, was overthrown by a progressive revolt. During the six years of upheaval that followed, power in Madrid would be held by a provisional government, a constitutional monarchy under an Italian prince and then a federal republic. Workers were free to organise, and in November 1868 Giuseppe Fanelli, an Italian emissary of Bakunin, brought the ideas of anarchism to Madrid and Barcelona, finding a ready response in Catalonia. In 1870, the first-ever Spanish workers' congress was held, in Barcelona. The radical forces, however, were divided between multiple factions, while the established classes of society, increasingly threatened, called for the restoration of order. The Republic proclaimed in 1873 was unable to establish its authority, and succumbed to a military coup.

In 1874, the Bourbon dynasty was restored to the Spanish throne in the person of Alfonso XII, son of Isabel II. Workers' organisations were again suppressed. The middle classes, however, felt their confidence renewed. The 1870s saw a frenzied boom in stock speculation, the *febre d'or* (gold fever), and the real take-off of building in the Eixample. From the 1880s, *Modernisme* became the preferred style of the new district, the perfect expression for the self-confidence, romanticism and impetus of the industrial class. The first modern Catalanist political movement was founded by Valentí Almirall.

Barcelona felt it needed to show the world all that it had achieved, and that it was more than just a 'second city'. In 1885, an exhibition promoter named Eugenio Serrano de Casanova proposed to the city council the holding of an international exhibition, such as had been held successfully in London, Paris and Vienna. Serrano proved to be a highly dubious character, who eventually made off with large amounts of public funds, but by the time this became clear the city fathers had fully committed themselves. The Universal Exhibition of 1888 was used as a pretext for the final conversion of the Ciutadella into a park; giant efforts had to be made to get everything ready in time, a feat that led the mayor, Francesc Rius i Taulet, to exclaim that 'the Catalan people are the yankees of Europe'. The first of Barcelona's three great efforts to demonstrate its status to the world, the 1888 Exhibition signified the consecration of the *Modernista* style, the end of provincial, dowdy Barcelona and its establishment as a modern-day city on the international map.

THE CITY OF THE NEW CENTURY

The 1888 Exhibition left Barcelona with huge debts, a new look and reasons to believe in itself as a paradigm of progress. As 1900 approached, there were few cities where the new century was regarded with greater anticipation than in Barcelona. The Catalan Renaixença continued, and acquired a more political tone. In 1892, the Bases de Manresa were drawn up, a draft plan for Catalan autonomy. Middle-class opinion was becoming more sympathetic to political Catalanism. A decisive moment came in 1898, when the underlying weakness of the Spanish state was abruptly made plain, despite the superficial prosperity of the first years of the Bourbon restoration.

> 'Barcelona had some of the worst overcrowding and highest mortality rates of any city in Europe.'

Spain was manoeuvred into a short war with the United States, in which it very quickly lost its remaining empire in Cuba, the Philippines and Puerto Rico. Catalan industrialists, horrified at losing the lucrative Cuban market, despaired of the ability of the state ever to reform itself. Many swung behind a conservative nationalist movement founded in 1901, the Lliga Regionalista (Regionalist League), led by Enric Prat de la Riba and the politician-financier Francesc Cambó. It promised both national revival and modern, efficient government.

Barcelona continued to grow, fuelling Catalanist optimism. The city officially incorporated most of the surrounding smaller communities in 1897, reaching a population of over half a million, and in 1907 initiated the 'internal reform' of the old city with the cutting through it of the Via Laietana, intended to allow in more air and so make the streets less unhealthy.

Public execution after the 1893 anarchist bombings, painted by Ramón Casas.

Catalan letters were thriving: the Institut d'Estudis Catalans (Institute of Catalan Studies) was founded in 1906, and Pompeu Fabra set out to create the first Catalan dictionary. Literature had acquired a new maturity, and in 1905 Victor Català (a pseudonym for a woman, Caterina Albert) shocked the country with *Solitud*, a darkly modern novel of a woman's sexual awakening. Above all, Barcelona had a vibrant artistic community, centred on *Modernisme*, consisting of great architects and established, wealthy painters such as Rusiñol and Casas, and the penniless bohemians who gathered round them, like the young Picasso.

Barcelona's bohemians were also drawn to the increasingly wild nightlife of the Raval. The area had already been known for very downmarket entertainments in the 1740s, but cabarets, bars and brothels multiplied at the end of the 19th century.

Around the cabarets, though, were also the poorest of the working class, whose conditions had continued to decline. Barcelona had some of the worst overcrowding and highest mortality rates of any city in Europe. Most exploited were women and children, toiling for a pittance for 15 hours a day. A respectable feminist movement undertook philanthropic projects aimed at educating the female masses. Barcelona, however, was more associated internationally with revolutionary politics and violence than gradual reform. In 1893, more than 20 people were killed

in a series of anarchist bombings, the most notorious of them when a bomb was thrown into the stalls of the Liceu during a performance of *William Tell*. The perpetrators were individuals acting alone, but the authorities took the opportunity to carry out a general round-up of anarchists and radicals, several of whom were tortured and executed in the castle above Barcelona. In retaliation, in 1906 a Catalan anarchist tried to assassinate King Alfonso XIII on his wedding day in Madrid.

Anarchism was still only in a fledgling stage among Barcelona workers in the 1900s, but, in general, rebellious attitudes, growing republican sentiment and a fierce hatred of the Catholic Church united the underclasses and predisposed them to take to the barricades with little provocation. In 1909 came the explosive outburst of the Setmana Tràgica (Tragic Week), a citywide riot that resulted in the destruction of more than half the city's religious buildings (*see p16* **A week of rage and rampage**).

These events dented the optimism of the Catalanists of the Lliga, but in 1914 they secured from Madrid the Mancomunitat, or administrative union, of the four Catalan provinces, the first joint government of any kind in Catalonia in 200 years. Its first president was Prat de la Riba, who would be succeeded on his death in 1917 by the architect Puig i Cadafalch. However, the Lliga's many other projects for respectable Catalonia were to be obstructed by a further surge in social tensions.

YOU SAY YOU WANT A REVOLUTION

Spain's neutral status during World War I gave a huge boost to the Spanish, and especially Catalan, economy. Exports soared as Catalonia's manufacturers made millions supplying uniforms to the French army. Barcelona's industry was at last able to diversify from textiles into engineering, chemicals and other more modern sectors.

Barcelona also became the most amenable place of refuge for anyone in Europe who wished to avoid the war. It acquired an international refugee community, among them avant-garde artists Sonia and Robert Delaunay, Francis Picabia, Marie Laurencin and Albert Gleizes, and was a bolt-hole for all kinds of low-life from around Europe. The Raval area would shortly be dubbed the Barrio Chino, 'Chinatown', definitively identifying it as an area of sin and perdition, and the city acquired a reputation similar to that of Marseille in the 1970s as the primary centre of drug trafficking and just about every other kind of illegal trade in the Mediterranean.

Some of the most regular patrons of the lavish new cabarets were industrialists, for many of the war profits were spent immediately in very conspicuous consumption. The war also set off massive inflation, driving people in their thousands from rural Spain into the cities. Barcelona doubled in size in 20 years to become the largest city in Spain, and the fulcrum of Spanish politics.

Workers' wages, meanwhile, had lost half their real value. The chief channel of protest in Barcelona was the anarchist workers' union, the Confederació Nacional del Treball (CNT), constituted in 1910, which gained half a million members in Catalonia by 1919. The CNT and the socialist Union General de Trabajadores (UGT) launched a joint general strike in 1917, roughly coordinated with a campaign by the Lliga and other liberal politicians for political reform. However, the politicians quickly withdrew at the prospect of serious social unrest. Inflation continued to intensify, and in 1919 Barcelona was paralysed for two months by a CNT general strike over union recognition. Employers refused to recognise the CNT, and the most intransigent among them hired gunmen to get rid of union leaders, often using a gang organised by an ex-German spy known as the 'Baron de Koening'. Union activists replied in kind, and virtual guerrilla warfare developed between the CNT, the employers and the state. More than 800 people were killed on the city's streets in the space of five years.

In 1923, in response both to the chaos in Barcelona and a crisis in the war in Morocco, the Captain-General of Barcelona, Miguel Primo

SOCORS ROIG
DE CATALUNYA
S. R. I.
FRONT UNIC de la SOLIDARITAT

Civil War poster calling for aid for refugees.

de Rivera, staged a coup and established a military dictatorship under King Alfonso XIII. The CNT, already exhausted, was suppressed. Conservative Catalanists, longing for an end to disorder and the revolutionary threat, initially supported the coup, but were rewarded by the abolition of the Mancomunitat and a vindictive campaign by the Primo regime against the Catalan language and national symbols.

This, however, achieved the opposite of the desired effect, helping to radicalise and popularise Catalan nationalism. After the terrible struggles of the previous years, the 1920s were actually a time of notable prosperity for many in Barcelona, as some of the wealth recently accumulated filtered through the economy. This was also, though, a highly politicised society, in which new magazines and forums for discussion – despite the restrictions of the dictatorship – found a ready audience.

A prime motor of Barcelona's prosperity in the 1920s was the International Exhibition of 1929, the second of the city's great showcase events. It had been proposed by Cambó and Catalan business groups, but Primo de Rivera saw that it could also serve as a propaganda event for his regime. A huge number of public projects were undertaken in association with the main event, including the post office in Via Laietana, the Estació de França and Barcelona's first Metro line, from Plaça Catalunya to Plaça d'Espanya. Thousands of migrant workers came from southern Spain to build them, many living in decrepit housing or shanty towns on the city fringes. By 1930, Barcelona was very different from the place it had been in 1910; it contained more than a million people, and its urban sprawl had crossed into neighbouring towns such as Hospitalet and Santa Coloma.

For the Exhibition itself, Montjuïc and Plaça d'Espanya were comprehensively redeveloped, with grand halls by Puig i Cadafalch and other local architects in the style of the Catalan neo-classical movement *Noucentisme*, a backward-looking reaction to the excesses of *Modernisme*. They contrasted strikingly, though, with the German pavilion by Mies van der Rohe (the Pavelló Barcelona), emphatically announcing the international trend toward rationalism.

STRIKING TIMES
Despite the Exhibition's success, in January 1930 Primo de Rivera resigned, exhausted. The King appointed another soldier, General Berenguer, as prime minister, with the mission of restoring stability. The dictatorship, though, had fatally discredited the old regime, and a protest movement spread across Catalonia against the monarchy. In early 1931, Berenguer called local elections as a first step towards a restoration of constitutional rule. The outcome was a complete surprise, for republicans were elected in all of Spain's cities. Ecstatic crowds poured into the streets, and Alfonso XIII abdicated. On 14 April 1931, the Second Spanish Republic was proclaimed.

The Republic came in amid real euphoria. This was especially true in Catalonia, where it was associated with hopes for both social change and national reaffirmation. The clear winner of the elections in the country had been the Esquerra Republicana, a leftist Catalanist group led by Francesc Macià. A raffish, elderly figure, Macià was one of the first politicians in Spain to win genuine affection from ordinary people. He declared Catalonia independent, but later agreed to accept autonomy within the Spanish Republic.

The Generalitat was re-established as a government that would, potentially, acquire wide powers. All aspects of Catalan culture were then in expansion, and a popular press in Catalan achieved a wide readership. Barcelona was a small but notable centre of the avant-garde. Miró and Dalí had already made their mark in painting; under the Republic, the Amics de l'Art Nou (ADLAN, Friends of New Art), group worked to promote contemporary art, while the GATCPAC architectural collective sought to work with the new authorities to bring rationalist architecture to Barcelona.

In Madrid, the Republic's first government was a coalition of republicans and socialists led by Manuel Azaña. Its overriding goal was to modernise Spanish society through liberal-democratic reforms, but as social tensions intensified the coalition collapsed, and a conservative republican party, with support from the traditional Spanish right, secured power after new elections in 1933. For Catalonia, the prospect of a return to right-wing rule prompted fears that it would immediately abrogate the Generalitat's hard-won powers. On 6 October 1934, while a general strike was launched against the central government in Asturias and some other parts of Spain, Lluis Companys, leader of the Generalitat since Macià's death the previous year, declared Catalonia independent. This 'uprising', however, turned out to be something of a farce, for the Generalitat had no means of resisting the army, and the 'Catalan Republic' was rapidly suppressed.

> ## 'Barcelona was the chief centre of the revolution in republican Spain, the only truly proletarian city.'

The Generalitat was suspended and its leaders imprisoned. Over the following year, fascism seemed to become a real threat for the left, as political positions became polarised throughout Spain. Then, in February 1936, fresh Spain-wide elections were won by the Popular Front of the left. The Generalitat was reinstated, and in Catalonia the next few months were, surprisingly, relatively peaceful. In the rest of Spain, though, tensions were reaching bursting point, and right-wing politicians, refusing to accept the loss of power, talked openly of the need for the military to intervene. In July, the 1929 stadium on Montjuïc was to be the site of the Popular Olympics, a leftist alternative to the main Olympics of that year in Nazi Germany. On 18 July, the day of their inauguration, however, army generals launched a coup against the Republic and its left-wing governments, expecting no resistance.

UP IN ARMS
In Barcelona, militants from the unions and leftist parties, on alert for weeks, poured into the streets to oppose the troops in fierce fighting. Over the course of 19 July the military were gradually worn down, and finally surrendered in the Hotel Colón on Plaça Catalunya (by the corner with Passeig de Gràcia, the site of which is now occupied by the Radio Nacional de España building). Opinions have always

differed as to who could claim most credit for this remarkable popular victory: workers' militants have claimed it was the 'people in arms' who defeated the army, while others stress the importance of the police remaining loyal to the Generalitat. A likely answer is that they actually encouraged each other.

Tension released, the city was taken over by the revolution. People's militias of the revived CNT, different Marxist parties and other left-wing factions marched off to Aragon, led by streetfighters such as the anarchists Durruti and García Oliver, to continue the battle. The army rising had failed in Spain's major cities but won footholds in Castile, Aragon and the south, although in the heady atmosphere of Barcelona in July 1936 it was often assumed that their resistance could not last long, and that the people's victory was near-inevitable.

Far from the front, Barcelona was the chief centre of the revolution in republican Spain, the only truly proletarian city. Its middle class avoided the streets, where, as Orwell recorded in his *Homage to Catalonia*, workers' clothing was all there was to be seen. Barcelona became a magnet for leftists from around the world, including writers such as André Malraux, Hemingway and Octavio Paz. Industries and public services were collectivised, including cinemas, the phone system and food distribution. Ad hoc 'control patrols' of the revolutionary militias roamed the streets supposedly checking for suspected right-wing agents and sometimes carrying out summary executions, a practice that was condemned by many leftist leaders.

The alliance between the different left-wing groups was unstable and riddled with tensions. The Communists, who had extra leverage because the Soviet Union was the only country prepared to give the Spanish Republic arms, demanded the integration of the loosely organised militias into a conventional army under a strong central authority. The following months saw continual political infighting between the discontented CNT, the radical-Marxist party Partido Obrero de Unificación Marxista (POUM), and the Communists. Co-operation broke down totally in May 1937, when republican and Communist troops seized the telephone building in Plaça Catalunya (on the corner of Portal de l'Angel) from a CNT committee, sparking off the confused war-within-the-civil-war witnessed by Orwell from the roof of the Teatre Poliorama. A temporary agreement was patched up, but shortly afterwards the POUM was banned, and the CNT excluded from power. A new republican central government was formed under Dr Juan Negrín, a Socialist allied to the Communists.

The war became more of a conventional conflict. This did little, however, to improve the Republic's position, for the Nationalists, under General Francisco Franco, and their German and Italian allies had been continually gaining ground. Madrid was under siege, and the capital of the Republic was moved to Valencia, and then to Barcelona, in November 1937.

'Barcelona would not regain the standard of living of 1936 until the mid 1950s.'

Catalonia received thousands of refugees, and food shortages and the lack of armaments ground down morale. Barcelona also had the sad distinction of being the first major city in Europe to be subjected to sustained intensive bombing – to an extent that has rarely been appreciated – with heavy raids throughout 1938, especially by Italian bombers based in Mallorca. The Basque Country and Asturias had already fallen to Franco, and in March 1938 his troops reached the Mediterranean near Castellón, cutting the main Republican zone in two. The Republic had one last throw of the dice, in the Battle of the Ebro in summer 1938, when for months the Popular Army struggled to retake control of the river. After that, the Republic was exhausted. Barcelona fell to the Francoist army on 26 January 1939. Half a million refugees fled to France, to be interned in barbed-wire camps along the beaches.

THE FRANCO YEARS

In Catalonia the Franco regime was iron-fisted and especially vengeful. Thousands of Catalan republicans and leftists were executed, Generalitat President Lluís Companys among them; exile and deportation were the fate of thousands more. Publishing, teaching and any other public cultural expression in Catalan, including even speaking it in the street, were prohibited, and every Catalanist monument in the city was dismantled. All independent political activity was suspended: censorship and the secret police were a constant presence, and the resulting atmosphere of fear and suspicion was to mark many who lived through it. The entire political and cultural development of the country during the previous century and a half was thus brought to an abrupt halt.

The epic of the Spanish Civil War is known worldwide; more present in the collective memory of Barcelona, though, is the long *posguerra* or post-war period, which lasted nearly two decades after 1939. The Barcelona of these years is best recorded in the novels of Juan Marsé; a grimy, pinched city full of the smell of drains and casual cruelty, in which any high idealistic expectations had given way to a fatalistic concern for getting by from one day to the next.

Barcelona was impoverished, and food and electricity rationed; it would not regain the standard of living of 1936 until the mid 1950s. Nevertheless, migrants in flight from the still more brutal poverty of the south flowed into the city, occupying precarious shanty towns around Montjuïc and other areas in the outskirts. Reconstruction of the nearly 2,000 buildings destroyed by bombing was slow, for the regime built little during its first few years in power other than monumental showpieces and the vulgarly ornate basilica on top of Tibidabo, completed to expiate Barcelona's 'sinful' role during the war.

Some underground political movements were able to operate. Anarchist urban guerrillas such as the Sabaté brothers attempted to carry on armed resistance, and March 1951 saw the last gasp of the pre-war labour movement in a general tram strike, the only major strike during the harshest years of the regime. It was fiercely repressed, but also achieved some of its goals. Clandestine Catalanist groups undertook small acts of resistance and rebellion, including underground publications and secret theatre performances. Some Catalan high

culture was tolerated: the poet Salvador Espriu promoted a certain resurgence of Catalan literature, and the young Antoni Tàpies held his first solo exhibition in 1949. For a great many people, though, the only remaining public focus of national sentiment – of any collective excitement – was Barcelona football club, which took on an extraordinary importance at this time, above all in its biannual meetings with the 'team of the regime', Real Madrid.

As a fascist survivor, the Franco regime was subject to a UN embargo after World War II. Years of international isolation and attempted self-sufficiency came to an end in 1953, when the United States and the Vatican saw to it that this anti-communist state was at least partially re-admitted to the western fold. Even a limited opening to the outside world meant that foreign money began to enter the country, and the regime relaxed some control over its population. In 1959, the Plan de Estabilización (Stabilisation Plan), drawn up by Catholic technocrats of the Opus Dei, brought Spain definitively within the western economy, throwing its doors wide open to tourism and foreign investment.

Two years earlier, in 1957, José Maria de Porcioles was appointed Mayor of Barcelona, a post he would retain until 1973. Porcioles has since been regarded as the personification of the damage inflicted on the city by the

Anarchist militia in Barcelona during the Spanish Civil War.

The Jewry's out

Long before the interfaith movement sat down folks from different spiritual walks of life in the pursuit of mutual understanding, Christians and Jews in medieval Europe would every so often settle in for an old-style argument. Usually this involved making local rabbis defend themselves against the accusations of the priests, such as happened in the notorious set-to in Paris in 1240 where Christian theologians ended up burning copies of the Talmud. Slightly more civilised was the famous Disputation of Barcelona held in July 1263: under the impartial eye of King Jaume I of Aragon, a group of Dominican monks faced off against the spiritual leader of the Jews of Catalonia, Rabbi Moshe ben Nahman.

Born in Girona in 1194, the seasoned rabbi was no easy opponent. Known today in Jewish circles as Nahmanides or just Ramban, or in Catalan as Bonastruc ça Porta, he was one of medieval Judaism's most important thinkers. His commentary on the Torah is one of the most read and studied in history, and his mystical bent was no less renowned: the Girona circle he guided was among the first to delve into cabbala as a means of illuminating the esoteric meaning of the Torah and the concealed order of the universe.

During the Disputation, which lasted three days, Nahmanides and his rival, Pablo Christiani, a converted Jew turned evangelising monk, battled it out over questions of Messianic proportions. On the second day, the rabbi tried to cut short the debate, fearful that certain Christians might use his words as a justification to attack the Jewish community in Barcelona, but a fascinated Jaume I gave him assurances to proceed. The contrasting accounts of the dispute written afterwards by the two opponents, each claiming victory, made the event notorious for centuries. A few years later, Nahmanides moved to Jerusalem, where he died in 1270.

In some ways, the Disputation was the swansong of Jewish life in Catalonia. Thriving since Roman times, the *calls*, or Jewish quarters, of cities like Barcelona, Girona and Tortosa then came to foster an important Jewish population in medieval times, its fate shifting with the vicissitudes of each political moment. The Visigoths had decreed the Jews slaves in 694, then, under the Count-Kings, their status improved, and eventually they gained the right to be civil servants. Proselytising pressure eventually led to Jaume I passing a law in 1243 requiring them to wear identifiable clothing. Around the time of the Disputation, the inhabitants of the Barcelona *call* were mostly artisans and farmers, yet many more were fiscal agents and traders, doctors, Arabic translators and many even became Catalan-language poets. Others served the Catalan nobility and advised the monarchy, drafting Catalan documents in Hebrew lettering for the Crown of Aragon.

Eventually, however, the Dominicans were to have their way; in August 1391, the Barcelona *call* was sacked in the wave of pogroms that tragically affected every Jewish quarter in Catalonia, Valencia and Mallorca. A fanatical mob, incited by the monks, massacred scores of Jews. The *calls* of Catalonia never really recovered, and very few Jews were left in Barcelona when the official ban was signed in 1424, a prelude to the eventual expulsion of all Jews from Spain in 1492.

Franco regime during its 1960s boom, accused of covering it with drab high-rises and road schemes without any concern for its character. Many valuable historic buildings – such as the grand cafés of the Plaça Catalunya – were torn down to make way for bland modern business blocks, and minimal attention was paid to collective amenities.

After the years of repression and the years of development, 1966 marked the beginning of what became known as *tardofranquisme*, 'late Francoism'. Having made its opening to the outside world, the regime was losing its grip, and labour, youth and student movements began to emerge from beneath the shroud of repression. Nevertheless, the Franco regime never hesitated to show its strength. Strikes and demonstrations were dealt with savagely, and just months before the dictator's death the last person to be executed in Spain by the traditional method of the garrotte, a Catalan anarchist named Puig Antich, went to his death in Barcelona.

'When Franco died on 20 November 1975, the people of Barcelona took to the streets in celebration.'

In 1973, however, Franco's closest follower, Admiral Carrero Blanco, had been assassinated by a bomb planted by the Basque terrorist group ETA, leaving no one to guard over the core values of the regime. Change was in the air.

GENERALISSIMO TO GENERALITAT

When Franco died on 20 November 1975, the people of Barcelona took to the streets in celebration, and not a bottle of cava was left in the city by evening. However, no one knew quite what was about to happen. The Bourbon monarchy was restored, under King Juan Carlos, but his attitudes and intentions were not clear. In 1976, he made a little-known Francoist bureaucrat, Adolfo Suárez, prime minister, charged with leading the country to democracy.

The first months and years of Spain's 'transition' were still a difficult period. Nationalist and other demonstrations continued to be repressed by the police with considerable brutality, and far-right groups threatened less open violence. However, political parties were legalised, and June 1977 saw the first democratic elections since 1936. They were won across Spain by Suárez's own new party, the Union de Centro Democratico (UCD), and in Catalonia by a mixture of Socialists, Communists and nationalist groups.

It was, again, not clear how Suárez expected to deal with the demands of Catalonia, but shortly after the elections he surprised everyone by going to visit the president of the Generalitat in exile, a veteran pre-Civil War politician, Josep Tarradellas. His office was the only institution of the old Republic to be so recognised, perhaps because Suárez astutely identified in the old man a fellow conservative. Tarradellas was invited to return as provisional president of a restored Generalitat, and arrived amid huge crowds in October 1977.

The following year, the first free local elections took place, won by the Socialist Party, with Narcis Serra as mayor. They have retained control of the Barcelona Ajuntament ever since. 1980 saw yet another set of elections, to the restored Generalitat, won by Jordi Pujol and his party Convergència i Unió. Again, they have kept power throughout the 1980s and '90s. Imprisoned for Catalanist activities in 1960, Pujol represents a strain of conservative nationalism that goes back to Prat de la Riba. Facing each other across Plaça Sant Jaume, the Generalitat and Ajuntament are the two constants of modern Catalan politics.

CITY OF DESIGN

Inseparable from the restoration of democracy was a complete change in the city's atmosphere in the late 1970s. New freedoms – in culture, in sexuality, in work – were explored, and newly released energies expressed in a multitude of ways. Barcelona soon began to look different too, as the inherent dowdiness of the Franco years was swept away by a new Catalan style for the new Catalonia: postmodern, high-tech, punkish, comic strip, minimalist and tautly fashionable. For a time, street culture was still highly politicised, but simultaneously it was also increasingly hedonistic. In the 1980s, design mania struck the city, a product of unbottled energies and a rebirth of Barcelona's artistic, artisan and architectural traditions.

This emphasis on a slick, fresh style began on a street and underground level, but the special feature of Barcelona was the extent to which it was taken up by public authorities, and above all the Ajuntament, as a central part of their drive to reverse the policies of the previous regime. The highly educated technocrats who led the Socialist city administration began, gradually at first, to 'recover' the city from its neglected state, and in doing so enlisted the elite of the Catalan intellectual and artistic community in their support. No one epitomises this more than Oriol Bohigas, the architect and writer who was long the city's head of culture and chief planner (*see p34* **Top Cat: Oriol Bohigas**). A rolling programme of urban renewal was initiated, beginning with the open spaces and public art programme and low-level initiatives, such as the campaign in which hundreds of historic façades were given an overdue facelift.

This ambitious, emphatically modern approach to urban problems acquired much greater focus after Barcelona's bid to host the 1992 Olympic Games was accepted, in 1986. Far more than just a sports event, the Games were to be Barcelona's third great effort to cast aside suggestions of second-city status and show the world its wares. The exhibitions of 1888 and 1929 had seen developments in the Ciutadella and on and around Montjuïc; the Olympics provided an

Current Catalan President Jordi Pujol.

opening for work on a citywide scale. Taking advantage of the public and private investment they would attract, Barcelona planned an all-new orientation of itself toward the sea, in a programme of urban renovation of a scope unseen in Europe since the years of reconstruction after World War II.

Along with the creation of the new Barcelona in bricks and mortar went the city-sponsored promotion of Barcelona-as-concept, a seductive cocktail of architecture, imagination, tradition, style, nightlife and primary colours. This was perhaps the most spectacular – certainly the most deliberate – of Barcelona's many reinventions of itself; it also succeeded in good part because this image of creativity and vivacity fitted an idea many of Barcelona's citizens had always had of their town, as if the drab decades had been just a bad dream.

Inseparable from all this was Pasqual Maragall, mayor of Barcelona from 1982 to 1997, a tireless 'Mr Barcelona' who appeared in every possible forum to expound his vision of the role of cities, and intervened personally to set the guidelines for projects or secure the participation of major international architects. In the process, Barcelona, like all Spanish cities a byword for modern blight only a few years before, became an international reference point in urban affairs. Maragall also established a personal popularity well beyond that of his Catalan Socialist Party.

ENDGAMES

The Games were finally held in July-August 1992 and universally hailed an outstanding success. The city held its breath to see what would happen next, and 1993 was a difficult year. From 1994 onwards, however, confidence picked up again, the city's relentless self-promotion seemed actually to be attracting investment, and Barcelona and Catalonia rode out Spain's post-1992 recession better than any other part of the country. The Ajuntament announced still more large-scale projects, such as the Old Port and the Raval. Maragall's own popularity meant he was able to stand aside from the corruption scandals that dragged down his Socialist allies in the central government of Felipe González after 13 years in office, and enabled the right-wing Partido Popular (PP) to take power in Madrid after the elections of 1996.

From 1993 to 1999, the support of the Catalan nationalists in the Madrid parliament was essential to keep minority Socialist (till 1996) and then PP central governments in power, a situation that enabled Jordi Pujol and his Convergència party to build up a pivotal role in all-Spanish affairs. In return for this support, Pujol won more concessions for the Generalitat, and a reputation for being the most artful operator in Spanish politics. Though this agility reinforced his popularity among his core support in Catalonia, it intensified the aversion felt towards him in other parts of Spain. Since the spectacular absolute majority won by the PP in national elections in 2000, though, Pujol has been forced to retreat, somewhat ignominiously, from his power-broker status.

In the Barcelona Ajuntament, Pasqual Maragall caused general surprise by standing down in 1997, after winning a fifth term. He was succeeded as mayor by his deputy, Joan Clos, previously a somewhat anonymous figure, who, however, held on to the post with an increased majority in the next city elections in June 1999. Maragall declared his intention to stand as the next Socialist candidate for President of the Generalitat and big changes seemed on the cards: then, in the October 1999 elections, the Socialists won more votes than Convergència, but fewer seats in the Catalan Parliament. To stay in power, Pujol was obliged to call on the local PP to return the favour he had done their government in Madrid. Change was coming, but not fast enough to stop Jordi Pujol from entering the third decade of his reign. In 2001, however, Pujol himself recognised that enough was enough, and declared that his current term would be his last. By all accounts, the next elections in 2003 will be fought over by his deputy in Convergència, Artur Mas, and the ever-determined Maragall.

Key events

c15 BC Barcino founded by Roman soldiers.
cAD 350 Roman stone city walls built.
415 Barcelona briefly capital of Visigoths.
719 Muslims attack and seize Barcelona.
801 Barcelona taken by Franks.
985 Muslims sack Barcelona; Count Borrell II renounces Frankish sovereignty.
1035-76 Count Ramon Berenguer I of Barcelona extends his possessions into southern France
1137 Count Ramon Berenguer IV marries Petronella of Aragon, uniting the two states in the Crown of Aragon.
c1160 *Homílies d'Organyà*, first Catalan texts, written.
1213 Pere I is killed and virtually all his lands north of the Pyrenees are seized by France.
1229 Jaume I conquers Mallorca, then Ibiza (1235) and Valencia (1238); second city wall built in Barcelona.
1274 Consell de Cent, municipal government of Barcelona, established.
1282 Pere II conquers Sicily.
1298 Gothic cathedral begun. Population of city c40,000.
1323-4 Conquest of Corsica and Sardinia.
1347-8 Black Death cuts population by half.
1462-72 Catalan civil war.
1479 Ferdinand II inherits Crown of Aragon, and with his wife Isabella unites the Spanish kingdoms.
1492 Final expulsion of Jews, and discovery of America.
1522 Catalans refused permission to trade in America.
1640 Catalan national revolt, the Guerra dels Segadors.
1652 Barcelona falls to Spanish army.
1702 War of Spanish Succession begins.
1714 Barcelona falls to Franco-Spanish army after siege.
1715 Nova Planta decree abolishes Catalan institutions; new ramparts and citadel built around Barcelona. Population c33,000.
1808-13 French occupation.
1814 Restoration of Ferdinand VII.
1833 Aribau publishes *Oda a la Pàtria*, beginning of Catalan cultural renaissance. Carlist wars begin.
1836-7 Dissolution of Barcelona monasteries.
1839 First workers' associations formed in Barcelona.
1842-4 Barcelona bombarded for the last time from Montjuïc, to quell Jamancia revolt.

1854 Demolition of Barcelona city walls.
1855 First general strike is violently suppressed.
1859 Cerdà plan for the Eixample approved.
1868 September: revolution overthrows Isabel II. November: first anarchist meetings held in Barcelona.
1873 First Spanish Republic.
1874 Bourbon monarchy restored under Alfonso XII.
1882 Work begins on the Sagrada Família.
1888 Barcelona Universal Exhibition.
1899 FC Barcelona founded; first electric trams.
1900 Population of Barcelona 537,354.
1909 Setmana Tràgica, anti-church and anti-army riots.
1910 CNT anarchist workers' union founded.
1921 First Barcelona Metro line opened.
1923 Primo de Rivera establishes dictatorship in Spain.
1929 Barcelona International Exhibition.
1930 Population 1,005,565. Fall of Primo de Rivera.
1931 14 April: Second Spanish Republic.
1934 October: Generalitat attempts revolt against new right-wing government in Madrid, and is then suspended.
1936 February: Popular Front wins Spanish elections; Catalan Generalitat restored. 19 July: military uprising against left-wing government is defeated in Barcelona.
1937 May: fighting within the republican camp in Barcelona.
1939 26 January: Barcelona taken by Franco's army.
1959 Stabilisation Plan opens up Spanish economy.
1975 20 November: Franco dies.
1977 First democratic general elections in Spain since 1936; provisional Catalan Generalitat re-established.
1978 First democratic local elections in Barcelona won by Socialists.
1980 Generalitat fully re-established under Jordi Pujol.
1982 Pasqual Maragall becomes mayor.
1992 Olympics Games held in Barcelona.
1996 Partido Popular wins Spanish elections.
1997 Joan Clos replaces Maragall as mayor.
1999 Jordi Pujol wins sixth term as president of the Generalitat.
2000 Partido Popular wins absolute majority in the Madrid parliament.

Barcelona Today

Amid ambitious projects and political wrangling, life goes quietly on under the plane trees.

A telling feature of life in Barcelona is the fact that most shops still shut down at two in the afternoon on Saturday and don't reopen again until Monday morning. For owners of small, independent shops this has become a matter of choice, after a recent change in the law allowed them, and only them, to open when they like. Keeping Sunday a day of rest has been the feat of this sizeable and particularly vocal voting block, who have fought tooth and nail over the past decade to stop larger department stores and malls from encroaching on their day off.

While perhaps seemingly a mundane matter, the issue of opening hours and days epitomises certain fundamental tensions in Barcelona: its desire to grow and embrace change while simultaneously maintaining a traditional identity; to be a city on the economic fast track as well as a relaxed place to live; its desire to open up further to the world in terms of immigration and foreign investment, but knowing how to control that expansion.

Traditional Barcelona, while still on show in certain pockets of the old city, truly resides in the wide, orderly streets of the Eixample, that 575-square-block grid designed in the middle of the 19th century by Ildefons Cerdà. The area is divided into 'left' and 'right' by two famous shopping boulevards, the Passeig de Gràcia and the Rambla Catalunya, both lined with expensive, elegant stores. The rest of the Eixample, however, is the redoubt of the small shop owner. Here in the long, high-ceilinged flats typical of the area, people live lives that set the tone for Barcelona; these are the city's burghers, the ordinary hard-working citizens who keep their shops running, their families afloat and their taxes paid.

The streets of the Eixample are full of small shops offering different components of a meal: the vegetable shop; the *bodega* with its casks of everything from red wine to *moscatell*; the pork butcher with ten varieties of ham, from the daily table variety to black-foot *jabugo* selling at €50 a kilo. There are also florists and pharmacies, bars and hardware stores: everything required to serve the needs of a residential *barri*. One other feature of the Eixample is that it is not very ethnically diverse, in marked contrast to the recent massive arrival of non-Europeans in the Old City.

Neighbourhood mercantile life, both in the Eixample and elsewhere, is not only an economic tradition, but a political one. A municipal regulation requires that 13 per cent of any new residential unit in Barcelona must be used as commercial space. Much of this space, throughout the city, is occupied by small shops and businesses. Large shopping complexes have had a hard time gaining a foothold in Barcelona, and mall equivalents are few and far between, mostly scattered in the suburbs.

The 21st century, however, does not promise to be particularly friendly toward small shop owners, and a *bodega* or butcher's shop do not always bring in enough money to keep a family financially afloat, let alone at a level to finance a city where long-term economic fortunes look more to the global marketplace than to the neighbourhood as a sphere of activity. Small business is not enough to feed the budget of a modern, growing, attractive city, which is what Barcelona became during the 1980s.

> **'A report in *Newsweek* in spring 2001 listed Barcelona as one of the top nine "cities of the future" for its digital economy.'**

Then, the strip of coastal land along where the Vila Olímpica now stands was changed from industrial to commercial, residential and recreational. Now, in an effort to keep the momentum generated by those changes, the Poblenou neighbourhood north of the Vila Olímpica is being developed, promoted as a new centre of digital technology that the Ajuntament has dubbed District 22@. Some €100 million will be spent renovating the *barri* with high-tech infrastructure and construction of 2,500 new apartments. A report in *Newsweek* in spring 2001 listed Barcelona as one of the top nine 'cities of the future' for its digital economy, primarily represented by the 22@ area. In addition, the city continues to draw ever-growing numbers of tourists. The Ajuntament estimates that one in every 12 jobs is related to tourism.

Another big project that will alter the city is being built around an event, Fòrum 2004 – just as the expansion in the late 1980s and early 1990s was related to the 1992 Summer Olympics. Or, at least, that's what planners are hoping. Mayor Joan Clos, closely following the trail blazed by his predecessor, mentor and fellow Socialist party member, Pasqual Maragall, has overseen the extension of the Avenida Diagonal north to the mouth of the Besòs river, an area abandoned to heroin addicts and run-down buildings for many years, and now being vigorously reclaimed.

The area is called Diagonal Mar and will include residential buildings, a new beach, a new park, fancy hotels and nine new skyscrapers, and will drastically alter the city's skyline. In a city where taxi drivers have their favourite architects and follow urban development as closely as they follow the football fortunes of Barça or Espanyol, there has been particular controversy over one of the new buildings, the Torre Agbar, a tubular (some say phallic) edifice designed by Jean Nouvel as the new headquarters for Aigües de Barcelona, the city's water company.

However, there are some serious differences between Fòrum 2004 and the 1992 Olympics. Fòrum 2004 has suffered from a lack of identity

Catalonia: a nation of shopkeepers?

since it was first announced in the late '90s. Initially, it was to be a heavy-duty intellectual gathering; the best minds of the world getting together in a new place to come up with new and better strategies to resolve the world's great dilemmas. This was ambitious and worthy, but not very sexy, a far cry from the sweat, competition and patriotic hot air of an Olympics. Instead of concentrating on attracting weighty minds, some seemed to feel that perhaps Sting or Madonna would be more appropriate to inaugurating a new, upscale neighbourhood.

There also was a regular turnover of planning personnel, and by the end of 2001 the Fòrum had yet to capture the public's imagination. In time, the Fòrum may prove to have served an important purpose by simply highlighting the debate about how the city sees itself, its own culture, sustainability, reconciling its urban identity to the global marketplace and the quick-buck shuffle – which, ironically, is reflected in the real-estate gamble of Diagonal Mar and the Fòrum itself.

Unfortunately, in terms of sharing Spain's revenues and attracting funds from the central government in Madrid, this is not the best of times for Catalonia. The government of José María Aznar is strongly oriented towards Madrid, where public spending on the capital has reached an all-time high. Aznar's Partido Popular (PP) enjoys an absolute Congressional majority until at least the 2003 elections, and has no need to negotiate with Catalonia to court its votes.

This has left Catalan president Jordi Pujol, at the autonomous region's helm since 1980, with somewhat pinched and colourless prospects for what he has announced will be his last term. Whether or not his designated political heir, Artur Mas, will be strong enough to lead the nationalist coalition Convergencia i Unio (CiU) to another term in office is uncertain, meaning that for the first time since 1978, the Partit dels Socialistes de Catalunya (PSC), Catalonia's socialist party, might have a go at governing the Generalitat. The PSC will run hot favourite Pasqual Maragall, popular four-term mayor of Barcelona during the Olympics, against Mas. When he ran against Pujol in 1999, he actually won more votes, although the PSC lost to the CiU, and Pujol was installed for another term.

There is plenty of change on Barcelona's horizon. The skyline will feature nine skyscrapers at one end. City Hall may change hands. On the other hand, the plane trees will continue to leaf out and people will carry on sitting at café tables beneath them, sipping their coffees, talking about how things aren't what they used to be.

State of the nation

Go to Scotland – one of the European areas with a level of political autonomy comparable to Catalonia's – and ask where you are and the majority will answer 'Scotland'. Come to Catalonia with the same question, however, and you'll get as many answers as there are people who happen to hear the question. They might tell you that you're in Spain, period, or a country called Catalonia, which finds itself inside Spain, or in a place called the 'Països Catalans' (the Catalan-speaking areas, including Catalonia, Valencia and the Balearics), which together are bearing the full brunt of Spanish oppression.

These viewpoints will be determined by a series of shifting factors that reflect the complex mosaic of Catalan society: where a person was born (around 30 per cent of the Catalan population of just over six million comes from other parts of Spain); who they vote for (a Catalan party or a Spanish party); the media they consume; the people they hang out with (60 per cent of the population speaks Catalan as well as Spanish) and so on. The only thing that can be said for sure is that Catalonia emerged from the forced hibernation of the Francoist dictatorship screaming and kicking, and full of beans, but also slightly confused as to its own identity.

Today, it is a country permanently sitting on the fence, torn between accepting its current lot as a Spanish autonomous community (46 per cent of Catalans want this, according to a 2001 survey), or pushing for a referendum and becoming a small free state, a kind of Holland by the Med (38 per cent desire independence, according to the same source). The latter option is not just about achieving international recognition for Catalonia, but also about ending a long-standing financial feud with Madrid (at a total of over €7 billion a year, Catalonia pays the highest per capita taxes in Spain). Many Catalans, however, believe Madrid would never give up Catalonia without a fight – and a fight (graffiti has recently appeared in Madrid saying 'Catalans, remember Sarajevo!') is the last thing anybody wants.

Be that as it may, although Catalonia now runs its own schools, hospitals, prisons and a local police force, not to mention its own national lottery, there is a general consensus, reflected in a 2000 survey, that it still deserves, at the very least, more autonomy within Spain, including control of its ports and airports, a 100 per cent return on local income tax, and greater control over the judicial system.

For many Catalans, the existence of the Catalan language is living proof that Catalonia is something more than just another Spanish region, and is therefore justified in making these demands. To this day, full cultural integration into Catalonia is impossible without learning Catalan. It is believed that if Catalan were to go – that is, if it vanished from mainstream use on all levels, from scientific treatises to conversations on the street – then Catalonia would go with it. By the same reasoning, if the language keeps its pecker up, then Catalonia will always be a centre in its own right – will be *catalanocentric* – and not merely a satellite of Madrid.

Little wonder then, that a whole flock of hawk-eyed sociolinguists are forever monitoring the progress of Catalan. As with most things, there is good news and bad news. The good news, at least for Catalans, is that in the electronic media, Catalan is thriving: TV3, the main Catalan language channel, has been the most viewed for the past five years; the number of radio stations in Catalan has tripled in the past two years; and Catalan is the 19th most used language on the Internet.

The bad news is that the central government in Madrid is doing its best to keep Catalonia as invisible as possible. It has banned Catalan national identification decals ('CAT') on numberplates; has kept Catalan out of the EU European Year of Languages campaign (although languages with fewer speakers, such as Irish and Danish, have been included); has banned the use of the words 'Made in Catalonia' on Catalan products; and has refused to produce multilingual stamps or euro banknotes.

More worryingly, on the street Catalan is losing ground among two vital sectors of the population: young people and foreign immigrants, especially in the Barcelona Metropolitan Area, in which more than a third of the Catalan population is concentrated. Young people – adolescents, in particular – have divided themselves into *quillos* (who refuse to speak Catalan) and *catalanufos*

(who use it regularly) and ne'er the twain shall meet. The question of the immigrants is far thornier and, indeed, leads us to the main challenge Catalonia is now facing in terms of preserving its identity.

Early in 2001, an ageing ex-president of the Catalan parliament, Heribert Barrera, made inflammatory statements to the effect that the area was being swamped by North Africans and Subsaharans – none of whom, he incorrectly claimed, spoke Catalan – and that the result would be the end of Catalonia as we know it. His remarks opened a debate that is still raging between those who believe that these immigrants are the Catalans of the future and those who are afraid or intolerant of people with different skin colour, clothes and traditions. So far, Catalonia has always been what the Catalans themselves call a *terra de pas*, that is, a place subject to constant migratory movements (the massive French immigration of the 16th century, for example, or that from other parts of Spain in the 20th). The question now remains whether they will be able to welcome and integrate the new Catalans of the 21st century, or whether they will succumb to the racism so prevalent in the rest of Europe.

● Matthew Tree's book, *CAT. Un anglès viatja per Catalunya per veure si existeix* (An Englishman travels around Catalonia to see if it exists), is published by Columna Edicions in Catalan.

Architecture

From Gothic to Gaudí, get to grips with Barcelona's buildings.

Architecture has a very special importance among all the arts in Catalonia. It has frequently taken on the role of the most appropriate medium – ahead of painting, music or any other art form – through which to express national identity. Periods when architecture flourished have paralleled eras of increased Catalan freedom of action and self-expression, greater wealth and a reinforcement of collective civic pride.

A clear line of continuity, of recurring characteristics, can be traced between generations of Catalan architects. Ideas, attitudes and trends are taken in from abroad, but are assimilated into this strong local culture. Catalan builders have always shown interest in decorating surfaces, and a concern with texture and the use of fine materials and finishes. This is combined with a simplicity of line and sense of sobriety often seen as distinguishing Catalan character from that of the rest of Spain. Other common elements are references to the traditional architecture of

rural Catalonia – the large *masia* farmhouses, with chalet-type tile roofs, massive stone walls and round-arched doorways, a style maintained by anonymous builders for centuries – and to the powerful constructions of Catalan Romanesque and Gothic. There has also long been a close relationship between architects and craftsmen in the production of buildings, especially in the working of metal and wood.

The revival and renewed vigour of Catalan culture and the city of Barcelona since 1975 have once again been accompanied by dynamic expansion in architecture, as is now world-famous. Modern Catalans have a sense of contributing to their architectural heritage in the present day, rather than preserving it as a relic. Contemporary buildings are daringly constructed alongside (or even within) old

▶ For details of buildings mentioned in this chapter, *see section* **Sightseeing**.

ones, and this mix of old and new is a major characteristic of many spectacular projects seen in Barcelona over the past two decades.

The importance of architecture is also reflected in public attitudes. Barcelona's citizens cherish their buildings, and form a critical audience. There is a range of architectural guides, some in English (*see p325*) and informative leaflets on different building styles are also available (in English) at the tourist offices (*see p320*).

FROM ROMAN TO GOTHIC
The Roman citadel of Barcino was founded on the hill of Mons Taber, just behind the cathedral, which to this day remains the religious and civic heart of the city. It left an important legacy in the shape of the fourth-century city wall, fragments of which are visible at many points around the Old City.

'Catalan Gothic has very particular characteristics that distinguish it clearly from more northern, classic Gothic.'

Barcelona's next occupiers, the Visigoths, left little in the city, although a trio of fine Visigothic churches survives nearby in **Terrassa**. When the Catalan state began to form under the Counts of Barcelona from the ninth century, the dominant architecture of this new community was massive, simple Romanesque. In the Pyrenean valleys there are hundreds of fine Romanesque buildings, notably at **Sant Pere de Rodes**, **Ripoll**, **Sant Joan de les Abadesses** and **Besalú** . There is, however, relatively little in Barcelona. On the right-hand side of the cathedral, looking at the main façade, is the 13th-century chapel of **Santa Llúcia**, incorporated into the later building; tucked away near Plaça Catalunya is the church of **Santa Anna**; and in La Ribera there is the tiny travellers' chapel, the **Capella d'en Marcús**. The city's greatest Romanesque monument, though, is the beautifully plain 12th-century church and cloister of **Sant Pau del Camp**, built as part of a larger monastery.

By the 13th century, Barcelona was the capital of a trading empire, and was growing rapidly. The settlements called *ravals* or *vilanoves* that had sprung up outside the Roman walls were brought within the city by the building of Jaume I's second set of walls, which extended Barcelona west to the Rambla, then just an often dry riverbed.

This commercial growth and political eminence formed the background to the great flowering of Catalan Gothic, and the construction of many of Barcelona's most important civic and religious buildings to replace Romanesque equivalents. The **cathedral** was begun in 1298, in place of an 11th-century building. Work commenced on the **Ajuntament** (Casa de la Ciutat) and **Palau de la Generalitat** – later subject to extensive alteration – in 1372 and 1403 respectively. Major additions were made to the **Palau Reial** of the Catalan-Aragonese kings, especially the **Saló del Tinell** of 1359-62, and the great hall of the Llotja or trading exchange was finished in 1380-92. Many of Barcelona's finest buildings were built or completed in these years, in the midst of the crisis that followed the Black Death.

Catalan Gothic has very particular characteristics that distinguish it clearly from more northern, classic Gothic. It is simpler, and gives more prominence to solid, plain walls between towers and columns, rather than the empty spaces between intricate flying buttresses of the great French cathedrals. Buildings thus appear much more massive. In façades, as much emphasis is given to horizontals as to verticals; and in the latter, octagonal towers end in cornices and flat roofs, not spires. Decorative intricacies are mainly confined to windows, portals, arches and gargoyles. Many churches have no aisles but only a single nave, the classic example of this design being the beautiful **Santa Maria del Pi** in Plaça del Pi, which was built between 1322 and 1453.

This style has ever since provided the historic benchmark for Catalan architecture. It is simple and robust, yet elegant and practical. Innovative, sophisticated techniques were developed: the use of transverse arches supporting timber roofs allowed the spanning of great halls uninterrupted by columns, a system used in the Saló del Tinell. Designed by Pere III's court architect Guillem Carbonell, it has some of the largest pure masonry arches in Europe, the elegance and sheer scale of which give the space tremendous splendour. The **Drassanes**, built from 1378 as the royal shipyards (and now the **Museu Marítim**), is really just a very beautiful shed, but the enormous parallel aisles make it one of the most exciting spaces in the city.

La Ribera, the Vilanova del Mar, was the commercial centre of the city, and gained the great masterpiece of Catalan Gothic, **Santa Maria del Mar**, built between 1329 and 1384. Its superb proportions are based on a series of squares imposed on one another, with three aisles of, unusually, almost equal height. The interior is staggering in its austerity and spareness of structure.

The domestic architecture of medieval Barcelona, at least that of its noble and merchant residences, can be seen at its best in the line of palaces along **Carrer Montcada**, next to Santa Maria. Built by the city's merchant elite at the height of their confidence and wealth, they all conform to a very Mediterranean style of urban palace, making maximum use of space. A plain exterior is presented to the street, with heavy doors opening into an imposing patio, on one side of which a grand external staircase leads to the main rooms on the first floor (*planta noble*), which often have elegant open loggias. Many of these palaces now house some of Barcelona's most visited cultural institutions.

FORGOTTEN CENTURIES

By the beginning of the 16th century, political and economic decline meant there were far fewer patrons for new building in the city. In the next 300 years a good deal was still built in Barcelona, but rarely in any distinctively Catalan style, with the result that these structures have often been disregarded. In the 1550s, the **Palau del Lloctinent** was built for the royal viceroys on one side of Plaça del Rei, and in 1596 the present main façade was added to the **Generalitat**, in an Italian Renaissance style. The Church built lavishly, with baroque convents and churches along La Rambla, of which the **Betlem** (1680-1729), at the corner of C/Carme, is the most important survivor. Later baroque churches include **Sant Felip Neri** (1721-52) and **La Mercè** (1765-75).

Another addition, after the siege of Barcelona in 1714, was new military architecture, since the city was encased in ramparts and fortresses. Examples remain in the **Castell de Montjuïc**, the buildings in the **Ciutadella** – one, curiously, the Catalan parliament – and the **Barceloneta**.

A more positive 18th-century alteration was the conversion of the Rambla into an urbanised promenade, begun in 1775 with the demolition of Jaume I's second wall. Neo-classical palaces were built alongside: **La Virreina** and the **Palau Moja** (at the corner of Portaferrisa) both date from the 1770s. Also from that time but in a less classical style is the **Gremial dels Velers** (Candlemakers' Guild) at Via Laietana 50, with its two-coloured stucco decoration.

Top Cat: Oriol Bohigas

Architect, urban planner, writer, editor, educator and politician, Oriol Bohigas has been described as a kind of Catalan Thomas Jefferson, a ubiquitous and crucial figure in the so-called 'reconstruction' of Barcelona since 1975. Along with Josep Martorell and David Mackay, Bohigas all but stamped the city with a new identity, being responsible for – among other things – the design of the vast 1992 residential and leisure zone of the Vila Olímpica.

During the grey years of the 1950s and '60s, Bohigas was a frenetically busy young man, forming architecture and design groups (the Grup R with Moragas, Sostres, Coderch and others, and FAD, Spain's first industrial design association), editing (as member of the board at Edicions 62, the main publisher of books in Catalan), teaching and protesting against the regime. In 1966, he was fired from his post as professor of architecture at the University of Barcelona after participating in a pro-democracy sit-in, while a few years later, the Ministry of Education rescinded his appointment as director of the university's architecture school after he refused to swear allegiance to the principles of Franco's dictatorship

(in 1977, he was finally able to accept the post without betraying his principles).

Probably Bohigas's most important achievement has been his capacity to culturally reconnect the city with its pre-civil war past. In 1969, he published the first general study of *Modernista* architecture, a work that has since become an indispensable point of reference. Another work written shortly afterwards, *Spanish Architecture in the Second Republic*, has also done much to patch up the holes in historical memory.

Bohigas himself claims to be a proponent of architectural 'realism'. In 1980, after being asked to lead the city's urban planning department, he had a chance to put his philosophy into action, demonstrating his aversion to utopian visions by instituting a programme of urban renewal whose fundamentals were firmly in touch with city life. One idea, to 'monumentalise the periphery', supplied the city with nearly 100 entirely new squares and parks, many of which are located in the outlying neighbourhoods that had sprung up chaotically in the 1950s and '60s. This same initiative also brought first-rate sculpture to city streets.

It was not, however, until the closure of the monasteries in the 1820s and '30s that major rebuilding on the Rambla could begin. Most of the first constructions that replaced them were still in international, neo-classical styles. The site that is now the **Mercat de la Boqueria** was first remodelled in 1836-40 as Plaça Sant Josep to a design by Francesc Daniel Molina, based on the English Regency style of John Nash. It is now buried beneath the 1870s market building, but its Doric colonnade can still be detected.

Molina also designed the **Plaça Reial**, begun in 1848. Other fine examples from the same era are the collonaded **Porxos d'en Xifré**, the 1836 blocks opposite the Llotja on Passeig Isabel II, by the Port Vell.

THE BUILDING OF THE EIXAMPLE

In the 1850s, Barcelona was able to expand physically, with the demolition of the walls, and psychologically, with economic expansion and the cultural reawakening of the Catalan Renaixença. The stage was set for it to spread into the great grid of Ildefons Cerdà's **Eixample**, which would connect

the city with Gràcia and other outlying towns. An engineer by trade, Cerdà (1815-75) had surveyed and drawn the city's first accurate plans in 1855. He was also a radical influenced by utopian socialist ideas, concerned with the cramped, unhealthy conditions of workers' housing in the old city.

With its love of straight lines and uniform grid, Cerdà's plan, begun in 1859, is very much related to visionary rationalist ideas of its time, as was the idea of placing two of its main avenues along a geographic parallel and a meridian. His central aim was to alleviate overpopulation problems while encouraging social equality by using quadrangular blocks of a standard size, with strict building controls to ensure that they were built up on only two sides, to a limited height, leaving a garden in between. Each district would be of 20 blocks, containing all community necessities.

In the event, though, this idealised use of urban space was scarcely ever achieved, for the private developers who actually built the Eixample regarded Cerdà's restrictions on their property as pointless interference.

Bohigas's more successful creations are a happy balance between the practical and functional, on the one hand, and existing local conditions and traditions on the other. The overall layout of the Vila Olímpica, for example, completes one corner of Cerdà's 19th-century grid, while echoes of *Modernisme* can be seen in the ironwork of the lamps along the port boardwalk. What reigns throughout the area, however, is the cleanly functional aesthetic of the area's residential buildings.

Not all Bohigas's creations have met with praise. One job, the remodelling of El Corte Inglés on the Plaça Catalunya, is frankly dubious, with the building's curved grey form looking more like a huge alien battleship than a temple of consumerism. Despite scattered criticism, however, one thing that cannot be denied is Bohigas's unflinching commitment to the city. In 1986, he bought a large, semi-derelict flat in the Plaça Reial, the heart of the then still exceedingly seedy old city. To this day, he lives there still, braving the occasional hassle (he was mugged on La Rambla two years ago), to witness the city's remarkable ongoing rejuvenation.

Buildings went up to much more than the planned heights, and in practice all the blocks from Plaça Catalunya to the Diagonal have been enclosed, with very few inner gardens withstanding the onslaught of construction.

However, the construction of the Eixample saw the refinement of a specific type of building: the apartment block, with giant flats on the *principal* floor (first above the ground), often with large glassed-in galleries for the drawing room, and small flats above. The area's growth also provided perfect conditions for the pre-eminence of the most famous of Catalan architectural styles, *Modernisme*. This branch of art nouveau that developed so vigorously in Catalonia was quite distinct in its ideas and products. For more information on the movement and its proponents, the most famous of whom is Antoni Gaudí, *see chapter* **Modernisme**.

THE 20TH CENTURY

By the 1900s, *Modernisme* had become too extreme for the Barcelona middle class, and the later buildings of Gaudí, for example, were met with derision. The new 'proper' style for Catalan architecture was *Noucentisme*, which stressed the importance of classical proportions. However, it failed to produce anything of much note: the main buildings that survive are those of the 1929 Exhibition – also the excuse for the bizarre, neo-baroque **Palau Nacional**.

The 1929 Exhibition also brought to Barcelona one of the most important buildings of the century: Mies van der Rohe's German Pavilion, the **Pavelló Barcelona**. Even today it is modern in its challenge to conventional ideas of space, and its impact at the time was extraordinary. The famous Barcelona chair was designed for this building, which was rebuilt to its original design in 1986.

Mies had a strong influence on the main new trend in Catalan architecture of the 1930s, which, reacting against *Modernisme* and nearly all earlier Catalan styles, was emphatically functionalist. Its leading figures were Josep Lluís Sert and the GATCPAC collective, who struggled to introduce the ideas of their friend Le Corbusier and the International Style. Under the Republic, Sert built a sanatorium off C/Tallers, and the **Casa Bloc**, a workers' housing project at Passeig Torres i Bages 91-105 in Sant Andreu. In 1937, he also built the Spanish Republic's pavilion for that year's Paris Exhibition, since rebuilt in Barcelona as the **Pavelló de la República** in Vall d'Hebron. Sert's finest work, however, came much later, in the **Fundació Joan Miró**, built in the 1970s after he had spent years in exile in the United States.

Santa Maria del Mar. *See p33.*

BARCELONA'S THIRD STYLE

The Franco years had an enormous impact on the city: as the economy expanded at breakneck pace in the 1960s, Barcelona received a massive influx of migrants, in a context of unchecked property speculation and minimal planning controls. The city was thus surrounded by numerous high-rise suburbs. Another legacy of the era are some ostentatiously tall office blocks, especially on the Diagonal and around Plaça Francesc Macià.

> **'The 1992 Olympic Games were to provide a focus for a sweeping renovation of the city.'**

Hence, when an all-new democratic city administration finally took over the reins of Barcelona at the end of the 1970s, there was a great deal for them to do. Budgets were limited, so it was decided that resources should initially be concentrated not on buildings as such, but on the gaps in between them, the public spaces, with a string of fresh, contemporary parks and squares, many of them incorporating original artwork. From this beginning, Barcelona placed itself in the forefront of international urban design.

Barcelona's renewal programme took on a far more ambitious shape with the award of the 1992 Olympics, helped by a booming economy in the late 1980s. The Barcelona Games were intended to be stylish and innovative, but most of all to provide a focus

Part of Cerdà's revolutionary street plan for the **Eixample**. *See p35.*

See p35.

for a sweeping renovation of the city, with emblematic new buildings and infrastructure projects linked by clear strategic planning. The three main Olympic sites – **Vila Olímpica**, **Montjuïc** and **Vall d'Hebron** – are quite different. The Vila Olímpica had the most comprehensive masterplan, which sought to extend Cerdà's grid down to the seafront. The main project on Montjuïc was the transformation of the existing 1929 stadium, but alongside it there is also Arata Isozaki's **Palau Sant Jordi**, with its space-frame roof. Vall d'Hebron is the least successful of the three sites, but Esteve Bonell's **Velòdrom** is one of the finest (and earliest) of the sports buildings, built before the Olympic bid in 1984.

Not content with all the projects completed up to 1992, the city has continued to expand over the past decade, as one major scheme has followed another. Post-1992, the main focus of activity shifted to the Raval and the Port Vell (old port), and is now moving on to the Diagonal-Mar area in the north of the city. Many striking buildings are by local architects, such as Helio Piñón and Albert Viaplana, whose work combines fluid, elegant lines with a strikingly modern use of materials, from the controversial 1983 **Plaça dels Països Catalans** through daring transformations of historic buildings such as the Casa de la Caritat, now the **Centre de Cultura Contemporània**, and on to all-new projects

like **Maremàgnum** in the port. Others are by international names: Richard Meier's bold white **MACBA**, or Norman Foster's **Torre de Collserola** on Tibidabo, which, with the skyscrapers in the Vila Olímpica, has provided new emblems for Barcelona's skyline. Another major acquisition, the giant, box-like **Auditori**, is by a Madrid-based Spanish architect (a rare thing in Barcelona), Rafael Moneo.

The polemical and ambitious **Fórum Universal de las Culturas**, a combination development scheme and gathering of the entire world's cultures planned for 2004, is bringing a new set of major urban changes to the city. The main stage is the shoreline of the Diagonal-Mar, where classy seaside high-rises are already springing up and a huge new landfill is under way to create the city's second largest park. Various internationally famous architects have been invited to endow the city with yet more wonders, including the Fórum's main building, a flat, glittering triangle by Jacques Herzog. Nearby at the Plaça de les Glòries, work has begun on a blatantly phallic-shaped, 142-metre (466-foot) high skyscraper by Jean Nouvel, which should nicely complement Herzog's wedge. All this dynamic new architecture has come to represent a 'third style' incorporated into the city's identity, alongside Gothic and *Modernisme* – but far more diffuse and eclectic than either.

Modernisme

More than just architecture and more than just Gaudí.

The late 19th century was a time of uncertainty in the arts and architecture across Europe. The huge expansion of cities, dramatic social upheavals, the rise of new nationalisms and new political pressures all created special tensions, while the introduction of new materials such as iron and steel demanded a new architectural language. As the end of the century approached, the movement known in French and English as art nouveau emerged, encompassing some of these concerns and contradictions.

The influence of art nouveau spread quickly all over Europe, to the Americas and even to the European colonies in Africa and Asia. From approximately 1890 to 1914, art nouveau – its main characteristic form being the undulating *coup de fouet* or whiplash shape – became the leading movement of the decorative and fine arts, all of which integrated spectacularly in architecture. In Catalonia, the influence of art nouveau merged with the cultural and political movement of the Catalan Renaixença to produce what became known as *Modernisme* (always confusing, since 'modernism' in English usually refers to 20th-century functional styles).

Influenced, like other forms of art nouveau, by Viollet-le-Duc, Ruskin, William Morris and the Arts and Crafts movement, French symbolism and other international currents, *Modernisme* was nevertheless a passionately nationalist and self-consciously indigenous expression that made use of – and in many cases revived – Catalan traditions of design and craftwork. Artists strove to revalue the best of Catalan art, showing enormous interest in the Romanesque and Gothic of the Catalan Golden Age. *Modernistes* sought to integrate fine and decorative arts, and gave as much weight to furniture and glasswork as to painting, sculpture and architecture. But *Modernisme* (as the name suggests) was primarily concerned with the modern world and therefore looked

---

▶ Many of the buildings mentioned in this chapter are described in more detail in the **Sightseeing** chapters.
▶ For some lesser-known *Modernista* creations, *see* **Walk 3: *Modernisme*** in chapter **The Eixample**.

---

towards Europe and North America, rather than towards the rest of Spain, which Catalans saw as backward and unenlightened: the dark Spain still sulking over its lost empire.

Modernista architects, even as they constructed a nostalgic and legendary vision of the ideal Catalan motherland, plunged into experimentation with the new technologies of the age. Encouraged by their wealthy patrons, they designed works of iron and glass, introduced electricity, water and gas piping to their building plans, were the first to tile bathroom and kitchen walls, made a point of allowing natural light and fresh air into all rooms, and toyed with the most advanced, revolutionary expressionism.

Catalan *Modernista* creativity was at its peak for about 20 years, from 1888 to 1908. The Eixample is the style's foremost display case, with the greatest concentration of art nouveau in Europe (the Ajuntament's *Quadrat d'Or* book is a good architectural guide, though currently out of print), but *Modernista* buildings and details can be found in innumerable other locations around Barcelona and Catalonia: in streets behind the Paral.lel or villas on Tibidabo, in shop interiors or dark hallways, in country town halls or the cava cellars of the Penedès.

International interest in Gaudí has often eclipsed the fact that there were many other remarkable architects and designers, for the style caught on with extraordinary vigour throughout Catalonia. Even less known is the fact that *Modernisme* was much more than an architectural style. The movement enlisted painters such as Ramón Casas, Santiago Rusinyol and Isidre Nonell, forerunners of and an inspiration to Miró, Dalí and Picasso; sculptors such as Josep Llimona, Miquel Blay, and Eusebi Arnau; joiners, notably the superb Mallorcan, Gaspar Homar; writers, composers, journalists and philosophers. *Modernisme* was an artistic movement in the fullest sense of the word, yet it is in architecture that it found its most splendid and lasting expression.

GAUDÍ

Seen as the genius of the *Modernista* movement, Antoni Gaudí i Cornet was really a one-off, an unclassifiable figure. His work was a product of the social and cultural context of the time, but also of his own unique perception of the world, together with a deep patriotic devotion to anything Catalan. Unlike Domènech i Montaner and Puig i Cadafalch, who were public figures taking an active part in politics and other fields, Gaudí, after being fairly sociable as a youth, became increasingly eccentric, leading a semi-monastic existence lost in his own obsessions.

Sagrada Família. Nearly there.

Born in Reus in 1852, he qualified as an architect in 1878. His first architectural work was as assistant to Josep Fontseré on the building of the **Parc de la Ciutadella** in the 1870s. The gates and fountain of the park are attributed to him, and around the same time he also designed the lamp-posts in the **Plaça Reial**. His first major commission was for the **Casa Vicens**, built between 1883 and 1888 for Manuel Vicens, a tile manufacturer. An orientalist fantasy, it is structurally fairly conventional, but Gaudí's control of the use of surface material already stands out in the building's exuberant neo-Moorish decoration, multicoloured tiling and superbly elaborate ironwork on the gates. The house, originally half its current size, was enlarged in the 1920s by a lesser-known architect, who had the decency to respect the original Gaudí design at a time when *Modernisme* had lost ground to the next neo-classical wave, *Noucentisme*. Gaudí's **Col.legi de les Teresianes** convent school (1888-9) is more restrained, but the clarity and fluidity of the building, with its simple finishes and use of light, is very appealing.

An event of crucial importance in Gaudí's life came in 1878, when he met Eusebi Güell, heir to one of the largest industrial fortunes in Catalonia (*see p42* **Sugar daddies**). Güell had been impressed by some of Gaudí's early furniture, and the pair also discovered that they shared many ideas on religion, philanthropy and the socially redemptive role of architecture. Güell placed utter confidence in his architect, allowing him to work with complete liberty. He produced several buildings for Güell, the first being the **Palau Güell** (1886-8), a darkly impressive, historicist building that established Gaudí's reputation, as well as the crypt at **Colònia Güell** outside Barcelona, one of Gaudí's most structurally experimental and surprising buildings.

In 1883, Gaudí became involved in the design of the **Sagrada Família**, begun the previous year. He would eventually devote himself entirely to this work. Gaudí was profoundly religious, and an extreme Catholic conservative; part of his obsession with the building was a belief that it would help redeem Barcelona from the sins of secularism and the modern era (some conservative Catalan Catholics are currently campaigning for him to be made a saint). From 1908 until his death he worked on no other projects, often sleeping on site, a shabby, white-haired hermit, producing visionary ideas that his assistants had to 'interpret' into drawings (on show in the museum alongside).

The Sagrada Família became the testing ground for Gaudí's ideas on structure and form. However, he would see the completion of only the crypt, apse and nativity façade, with its representation of 30 different species

of plants. As his work matured he abandoned historicism and developed free-flowing, sinuous expressionist forms. His boyhood interest in nature began to take over from more architectural references, and what had previously provided external decorative motifs became the inspiration for the actual structure of his buildings.

In his greatest years, Gaudí combined other commissions with his cathedral. **La Pedrera**, also known as **Casa Milà**, begun in 1905, was his most complete project. In a prime location on a corner of Passeig de Gràcia, it has an aquatic feel about it: the balconies resemble seaweed, and the undulating façade the sea or rocks washed by it. Interior patios are in blues and greens, and the roof resembles an imaginary landscape inhabited by mysterious figures. The **Casa Batlló**, on the other side of Passeig de Gràcia, was an existing building that Gaudí remodelled in 1905-7; the roof looks like a reptilian creature perched high above the street. The symbolism of the façade is the source of endless speculation. Some link it to the myth of St George and the dragon; others maintain it is a celebration of Carnival, with its Harlequin hat roof, its wrought-iron balcony 'masks' and the cascading, confetti-like tiles – this last element an essential contribution of Josep Maria Jujol, more skilled than his master as a mosaicist.

Gaudí's later work has a uniquely dreamlike quality. His fascination with natural forms found full expression in the **Parc Güell**

Casa Batlló: here be dragons?

(1900-14), where he blurs the distinction between natural and artificial forms in a series of colonnades winding up the hill. These paths lead up to the large central terrace projecting over a hall; a forest of distorted Doric columns planned as the marketplace for Güell's proposed 'garden city'. The terrace benches are covered in some of the finest examples of *trencadís*

(broken mosaic work), again mostly by Jujol. This was meant to a be an upmarket housing development along the lines of the suburban garden-cities that Ebenezer Howard and others were then promoting in England (it was originally known as Park Güell, in English). However, the park turned out to be a financial flop: only two buyers signed up for houses,

Sugar daddies

For all their genius, Gaudí, Domènech and the rest of the *Modernista* architects could not have built their masterpieces if there hadn't been wealthy patrons ready to pay for them. If *Modernisme* was the fruit of the international art nouveau movement espousing the Catalan Renaixença, it was also the product of a booming economy. By the end of the 19th century, Catalans had developed a thriving commercial activity with the Americas, importing cotton, sugar, cocoa, rum and tobacco, with a less wholesome sideline in African slaves. Once home from their travels, enriched Catalans – known as *indianos* – spent ostentatiously, building residences to boast of their success and competing frenziedly to have the most astounding palace – as seen in the Mansana de la Discòrdia.

Three men were to play pivotal roles in financing *Modernista* buildings. Pere Milà i Camps was the developer behind Gaudí's

La Pedrera (*pictured*). Something of a bon viveur, whose intense social life left him little time for business, he married Roser, widow of a wealthy *indiano*, Josep Guardiola. The building of La Pedrera was a painful process for Gaudí: Milà encouraged him to outdo himself with no regard for cost, while Roser kept a tight grip on expenditure and a critical eye on the architect's decorative elements.

According to one story, the morning after the housewarming party, Gaudí found scores of empty champagne bottles lying about: in a bout of inspiration, he ordered his assistants to carry the bottles up to the roof, break them and set the broken pieces in the fresh mortar of the chimneys. Shortly afterwards,

Roser Guardiola arrived home; when she saw the workers smashing the empties which she had planned to sell to make up for her husband's extravagance of the previous night, she had the decoration process stopped.

Another of Gaudí's patrons was Eusebi Güell. His business acumen was legendary, but his dealings were not entirely honest. When the anarchists confiscated his mansions on the Rambla during the Spanish Civil War, they discovered that Palau Güell had hidden galleries running the length of the main halls; during dinner parties, Güell would hide in these and eavesdrop on his guests' conversation.

Güell's brother-in-law was Antoni López i López, the head of a truly self-made *indiano* family. His father had risen from impoverished peasantry to transatlantic commerce in 20 years of Cuban enterprise; Antoni went one step further by acquiring the title of Marquis of Comillas. Together with the Güells, the Comillas family became one of the most influential clans of the Barcelonan bourgeoisie. López commissioned Gaudí to build El Capricho ('The Whim') in Comillas, his father's home village in northern Spain, where he held high-society parties and entertained his mistresses. Gaudí carried out the commission, but refused to look his employer in the eye or shake his hand.

The statue of the first Marquis of Comillas, known popularly as 'El Negro Domingo' thanks to his unashamed activity in slave-trading to Cuba and Santo Domingo, still stands at the end of Via Laietana across from the main post office.

and Güell's misfortune later became a leafy blessing for the cramped city of Barcelona.

In June 1926, Antoni Gaudí was run over by a tram on the Gran Via. Nobody recognised the down-at-heel old man, and he was taken to a public ward in the old Hospital de Santa Creu in the Raval. When his identity was discovered, Barcelona gave its most famous architect almost a state funeral.

DOMÈNECH I MONTANER

Modernista architecture was given a decisive boost by the buildings commissioned for the Universal Exhibition of 1888, many of which were planned by Lluís Domènech i Montaner (1850-1923). Most of them no longer exist, but one that remains is the **Castell dels Tres Dragons** in the Ciutadella, designed to be the exhibition restaurant and now the **Museu de Zoologia**. It already demonstrated many key features of *Modernista* style: the use of structural ironwork allowed greater freedom in the creation of openings, arches and windows; and plain brick, instead of the stucco usually applied to most buildings in Barcelona, was used in an exuberantly decorative manner.

Domènech was one of the first *Modernista* architects to develop the idea of the 'total work', working closely with large teams of craftsmen and designers on every aspect of a building. Not in vain was he dubbed 'the great orchestra conductor' by his admirers. His greatest creations are the **Hospital de Sant Pau**, built as small 'pavilions' within a garden to avoid the usual effect of a monolithic hospital, and the fabulous **Palau de la Música Catalana**, an extraordinary display of outrageous decoration.

Domènech also left a series of impressive constructions in Reus (about 115 kilometres/ 71 miles south-west of Barcelona). **Casa Navàs** and **Casa Rull** are worth a visit, as are the spectacularly ornate pavilions of the **Institut Pere Mata**, a former pyschiatric hospital and forerunner of the Hospital de Sant Pau.

PUIG I CADAFALCH

Third in the trio of leading *Modernista* architects was Josep Puig i Cadafalch (1867-1957), who showed a strong neo-Gothic influence in such buildings as the **Casa de les Punxes** ('House of Spikes', officially the **Casa Terrades**) in the Diagonal, combined with many traditional Catalan touches. Nearby on the Passeig de Sant Joan is another of his masterpieces, the **Casa Macaya**, its inner courtyard inspired by the late medieval palaces that still line C/Montcada. The Fundació La Caixa's cultural centre is due to move from Casa Macaya to another of Puig i Cadafalch's striking creations, the **Fábrica Casaramona**

at Montjuïc, in mid 2002. His best-known work is the **Casa Amatller** (*pictured on p39*), sitting between Domènech's **Casa Lleó Morera** and Gaudí's Casa Batlló in the **Mansana de la Discòrdia**.

Puig was also a renowned art historian and archaeologist, whose position as president of the Mancomunitat (the semi-autonomous government of Catalonia) from 1917 to 1923, was crucial in the establishment of basic modern public services such as the telephone network, sewage systems and technical schools. Unlike Domènech, however, Puig never allowed ethics to get in the way of his success, as he unashamedly used his influence as president to extort architectural contracts from the city council. Most of the plans for the urbanisation of Montjuïc were drawn up by him in this way.

These are the famous names of *Modernista* architecture, but there were many others. Some of the most engaging architects are the least known internationally, such as Gaudí's assistant **Josep Maria Jujol** (1879-1949), who built some remarkable, sinuous buildings in Sant Joan Despí, to the west of Barcelona. Not to be missed are **Can Negre**, a dizzying re-interpretation of the traditional Catalan country house, and Torre de la Creu, popularly known as **Torre dels Ous** ('Tower of the Eggs') because of its five oval-shaped minarets. North from Barcelona is La Garriga, Catalonia's Baden-Baden, where **JM Raspall** built exuberant summer houses for the rich and fashionable families of the time. Some of the best of *Modernista* industrial architecture, by **Lluís Moncunill** (1868-1931), can be seen in the nearby town of Terrassa, while the 'wine cathedrals' by **Cèsar Martinell** still stand proud in many villages in southern Catalonia.

Domenèch's ornate **Palau de la Música.**

Accommodation

Accommodation 46

Features

Accommodation

The rush is on to provide sufficient pillow space for the increasing numbers of visitors to Barcelona.

Brand-new construction, improvements, modernisations or complete makeovers of older hotels have not ceased since the 1992 Olympic Games, which provided the first big catalyst for recent hotel building in Barcelona, with dozens of new places opening in just a couple of years. Barcelona has grown massively in popularity as a city to visit – and more recently as a centre of commerce – and hotels have been tripping over themselves to provide adequate facilities to satisfy both business travellers and tourists.

The city no longer has a true low season (although January and February are perhaps relatively slack), and is hard to find rooms at certain times, especially in midsummer and during trade fairs or important festivals. During the past few years, the city has been working to realise a 49 per cent increase (by 2004) in the number of hotel beds; not only with new construction, but also expansion of many hotels and hostels. However, it is always advisable to book a room well in advance of travel. Many of the cheaper hotels, particularly in the Barri Gòtic, will not accept reservations, although this is beginning to change.

The rapid growth in demand has also pushed up prices very noticeably. In particular, mid-range hotel rates have shot up, and the once-traditional cheaper weekend rates have disappeared almost completely. Not surprisingly, the events of 11 September 2001 and the aftermath have had an impact on occupancy rates. The city saw a drop of 30 per cent in the month after the tragedy and, although it is not known what the longer-term effect will be, many travellers have cancelled trips for 2002.

Barcelona's first real hotels were all built along the Rambla and a great number of places are still concentrated in the Old City, which is still the best area to find cheaper accommodation. Hotels on or very near the Rambla itself are convenient, but have tended to bring in the most swingeing price hikes; they're also often noisy, and this is where you most need to be streetwise about petty crime. The other main hotel area is the Eixample, where there are many mid-range places and some good-value hostals. As the centre has filled up, mid-range and budget hotels have also been opening in districts a bit further afield, such as Horta and Zona Alta. They offer greater tranquillity and, thanks to Barcelona's high density and good transport links, are never more than 20 minutes or so from the centre of the city.

STARS, HOTELS, *PENSIONS*, PRICES

All Catalonia's accommodation is regulated by the regional government, the Generalitat. There are now only two official categories, hotels (H) and *pensions* (P), although many places still use older names (*fondes, residències, hostals*), which can be confusing. To be a hotel, star-rated one to five, a place must have en suite bathrooms in every room. Ratings are given on the basis of general quality and services rather than price. *Pensions*, star-rated one or two and usually cheaper, do not have to have en suite bathrooms throughout, nor restaurants. However, most have been renovated in the past few years, and many now have bathrooms in at least some rooms. In short, star ratings are not an automatic guide to cost or facilities.

All hotel bills are subject to seven per cent IVA (value added tax) on top of the basic price; this is normally quoted separately on bills. Hotels and *pensions* listed here are divided according to the basic price of a double room including tax, according to the official weekday rates in high season. Expect to pay, for a double room per night, €30-€55 for a budget *pension*, €50 to over €100 in a mid-range establishment and from €150 to more than €400 in a luxurious, top-of-the-range hotel.

This should be taken as a guideline only, as prices can still vary by sizeable amounts at different times of year and depending on demand. Also, although far fewer hotels now offer weekend and other short-term discounts (usually in January and August), it's still worth asking whether any such deals are available.

Breakfast is not included in rates given below unless stated. Hotel breakfasts are often poor and overpriced, and you'll frequently do better at a café. If you make use of a hotel car park, this will also add to the bill, and you should reserve a parking space when booking.

BOOKING A ROOM

You are strongly advised to book well in advance, but if you do arrive in the city without a room, the tourist offices in Plaça Catalunya and Plaça Sant Jaume (*see p320*) have hotel booking desks that can usually find somewhere.

There's no commission, but a deposit is requested. Four private booking services are also listed below. None covers all accommodation in Barcelona, but tourist offices can provide a complete local hotel list.

When booking, to be sure of light or a view, ask for an outside room (*habitación exterior*), usually facing the street. Many of Barcelona's buildings are constructed around a central patio or air shaft, and the inside rooms (*habitación interior*) around them can be gloomy, albeit quieter. There are some cases where an inward-facing room is the best option because they look on to large, open-air patios or gardens; we have tried to mention these where possible.

For flat rental agencies, *see p67*; for student and youth accommodation services, *see p318*.

Europerator

Gran Via de les Corts Catalanes 561, Eixample (93 451 03 32/fax 93 451 14/www.europerator.org). Metro Urgell/9, 14, 50, 56, 59 bus. **Open** 9.30am-2pm, 4-8pm Mon-Fri; 9.30am-2pm Sat. **Credit** AmEx, MC, V. **Map** p340 C5.
This company offers a search service, which is very useful at problem times – when there's a big trade fair, festival or sports event, for instance. It deals in hotels, *pensions* and private apartments, and you can sometimes get special prices (usually for three- and four-star hotels). English, French, German, Italian, Spanish and Catalan are spoken. No booking fees and no commission.

Halcón Viajes

C/Aribau 34, Eixample (93 454 59 95/902 30 06 00/ www.halconviajes.com). Metro Universitat/bus all routes to Plaça Universitat. **Open** 9.30am-1.30pm, 4.30-8pm Mon-Fri; 10am-1.30pm Sat. **Credit** AmEx, DC, MC, V. **Map** p340 C5.
This giant travel agency, which has about 700 offices across Spain, can also book rooms in many hotels (often with car rental deals included). Commission is charged.

Hotel Connect

Berkeley House, 18-24 High Street, Edgware, London HA8 7RP (00 44 (0)208 381 2233/ fax 00 44 (0)208 381 1155/www.hotelconnect.co.uk). **Open** 8am-8pm Mon-Fri. **Credit** MC, V.
A London-based hotel booking agency that deals in two- to five-star hotels. Discount rates are offered to regular clients. No booking fees and no commission.

Ultramar Express

Vestibule, Estació de Sants, Sants (93 491 44 63/ www.uex.es). Metro Sants Estació/bus all routes to Estació de Sants. **Open** 8am-9.30pm daily. **Credit** MC, V. **Map** p339 A4.
An office in the hall at Sants train station. When booking, you will be asked to pay a deposit (which will be incorporated into your final hotel bill), plus a small fee of about €3. You will be given a map and directions to the hotel.

Barri Gòtic & La Rambla

Expensive

Hotel Catalonia Albinoni

Avda Portal de l'Àngel 17 (93 318 41 41/ fax 93 301 26 31/www.hoteles-catalonia.es). Metro Catalunya/bus all routes to Plaça Catalunya. **Rates** single €121.80-€160.50; double €154-€173.30. **Credit** AmEx, DC, MC, V. **Map** p342 B2.
Formerly called the Allegro, this smart, 74-room hotel opened in 1998 and is a favourite with tourists despite its corporate air. The former mansion of the Rocamora family, it dates back to 1872 and retains a great deal of its original structure. The public spaces, such as the internal courtyard and marble staircase, are impressive, but many of the rooms are small, impersonal and disappointing. The 18 rooms with private terraces over the back patio are slightly smaller than those facing the pedestrian street, Portal de l'Àngel. A good Spanish breakfast is served in an attractive marquee structure (with heat or air-con) in the back patio.
Hotel services *Air-conditioning. Bar. Disabled: adapted rooms (2). Garden. Laundry. Multilingual staff. Ticket agency.* **Room services** *Minibar. Room service (7-11am). Safe. Telephone. TV: pay movies/ satellite.*

Hotel Colón

Avda de la Catedral 7 (93 301 14 04/fax 93 317 29 15/www.hotelcolon.es). Metro Jaume I/ 17, 19, 40, 45 bus. **Rates** single €161; double €230; suite €364. **Credit** AmEx, DC, MC, V. **Map** p342 B2.

Catalonia Albinoni.

Hotels

The best

Accommodation

For spotting celebrities

The **Hotel Condes de Barcelona** (*see p61*) has hosted Isabel Allende, John Malkovich, Catherine Denueve, Lenny Kravitz and Pedro Almodóvar. Garbage, Eric Clapton and Michael Jackson prefer **Le Meridien** (*see p48*), while Travis like the **Duc de la Victòria** (*see p61* **Hotel Podium**).

For making four-legged friends

At the **Hostal Fontanella** (*see p64*), meet Benji, a big fluffy chow who must be the most internationally photographed dog in town. Mini, a *really* miniature poodle at the **Hostal San Remo** (*see p63*), likes to think of herself as hotel security.

For scrubbing up nice

Hotels Podium, **Duc de la Victòria** (for both, *see p61*) and **Sant'Àngelo** (*see p64*) – all part of the NH chain – have special rooms for women, with cosmetics by Spanish designer Jesús del Pozo. Bvlgari provides a specially designed luxury bathroom kit in the *habitaciones superiores* at the **Hotel Arts** (*pictured –see p59*).

For a kitsch fix

Try **Hotel Barcelona House** (*see p51*). Rooms 306 and 406 have antique double beds and huge headboards with attached lamps, in bright, clashing colours. Or maybe you'd prefer the fondant-fancy pastel colours of the paintwork in your room at the **Hostal Plaza** (*see p63*).

For taking the plunge

Enjoy an oh-so-cool dip in the rooftop pool at **Hotel Claris** (*see p61*) and then a hearty lunch at the poolside restaurant. At the **Barcelona Plaza** (*see p65*), take breathers between laps in the pool to admire the imposing beauty of the Palau Nacional, with Montjuïc behind it.

With touches of old-world luxury, this 147-room hotel has a superb location opposite the cathedral, with matchless views of the Sunday *sardana* dancing or Thursday's antique market. There's a good restaurant and relaxing piano bar, and staff are friendly and efficient. Guests at the not-as-luxurious sister hotel around the corner, the Regencia Colón (€90 double), can use the Colón's facilities.
Hotel services *Air-conditioning. Babysitting. Bar. Disabled: adapted rooms (2). Laundry. Limousine service. Multilingual staff. Restaurant.* **Room services** *Minibar. Room service (24hrs). Safe. Telephone. TV: pay movies/satellite.*
Branch: Hotel Regencia Colón C/Sacristans 13, Barri Gòtic (93 318 98 58).

Hotel Hesperia Metropol

C/Ample 31 (93 310 51 00/fax 93 319 12 76/ www.hoteles-hesperia.es). Metro Jaume I/14, 17, 19, 36, 40, 45, 57, 59, 64, 157, N6, N8 bus. **Rates** single €132.20; double €132.20-€145.70. **Credit** AmEx, DC, MC, V. **Map** p339 B4.
This 19th-century hotel was given a makeover in 1992, but maintains its old charm. It also pays homage to some of the city's artistic alumni with a replica of a Gaudí chair, and Dalí prints on the walls. Half the 71 rooms look on to C/Ample and C/Gignàs, which are surprisingly quiet and tranquil for old-city streets near the port. Interior rooms can be gloomy unless they are on the top floor.
Hotel services *Air-conditioning. Disabled: rooms currently being adapted (3). Laundry. Multilingual staff.* **Room services** *Minibar. Safe. Telephone. TV: satellite.*

Hotel Laietana Palace

Via Laietana 17 (93 268 79 40/fax 93 319 02 45). Metro Jaume I/17, 19, 40, 45 bus. **Rates** single €116-€154.70; double €167.60-€225.60; suite €261. **Credit** AmEx, DC, MC, V. **Map** p342 A2.
A brand new hotel on one of the city's main thoroughfares, the Laietana Palace sits between Port Vell and the cathedral. Its neo-classical façade makes it a suitable neighbour to the remains of the Roman wall that are clearly visible in the small street running alongside it. The lobby has classical features, too, including mosaic floors, busts and golden pillars. The hotel's 62 rooms are stylish and tasteful, with marble-tiled floors. All have TVs set up for Internet access, with keyboards.
Hotel services *Air-conditioning. Bar. Disabled: adapted rooms (1). Laundry. Multilingual staff. Restaurant.* **Room services** *Dataport. Safe. Telephone. TV: satellite.*

Hotel Le Meridien Barcelona

La Rambla 111 (93 318 62 00/fax 93 301 77 76/ www.lemeridien-barcelona.com). Metro Liceu/ 14, 38, 59, 91, N9, N12 bus. **Rates** single €321-€508; double €353-€540; suite €631-€1,926. **Credit** AmEx, DC, MC, V. **Map** p342 A2.
An ultra-central location right on the Rambla and luxurious accommodation have made this 206-room hotel a first choice for celebs such as the Stones,

Hotel Hesperia Metropol: pretty as a picture. *See p48.*

Accommodation

Garbage and Oasis (although in recent years the Hotel Arts – *see p59* – has stolen its thunder). Its fine restaurant, Le Patio, serves Mediterranean food and its intimate bar offers live music nightly. Some rooms have terraces with a panoramic view over Barcelona's rooftops, from Montjuïc to Vila Olímpica. A substantial facelift has been in progress, which will (though no one knows when) reposition the hotel into the five-star category.
Hotel services *Air-conditioning. Babysitting. Bar. Car park. Car rental. Disabled: adapted rooms (4). Fitness centre (gym). Laundry. Limousine service. Multilingual staff. Non-smoking rooms. Restaurant. Safe. Ticket agency.* **Room services** *Minibar. Room service (24hrs). Telephone. TV: satellite/VCR.*

Hotel Rivoli Ramblas

La Rambla 128 (93 302 66 43/reservations 93 412 09 88/fax 93 317 50 53/www.rivolihotels.com). Metro Catalunya or Liceu/bus all routes to Plaça Catalunya. **Rates** single €209; double €273; suite €355. **Credit** AmEx, DC, MC, V. **Map** p342 A2.
Rebuilt in the early 1990s, the peaceful Rivoli is a world apart from the bustle on La Rambla outside. The 89 rooms have interesting colour schemes, and the Blue Moon piano bar is a relaxing place to end the evening. It's a popular choice for tourists and business people.
Hotel services *Air-conditioning. Babysitting. Bar. Car park. Fitness centre (gym/sauna/solarium). Laundry. Limousine service. Multilingual staff. Restaurant. Terrace. Ticket agency.* **Room services** *Minibar. Room service (7am-11pm). Safe. Telephone. TV: satellite.*
Branch: Hotel Ambassador C/Pintor Fortuny 13, Raval (93 412 05 30).

Mid-range

Hostal Jardí

Plaça Sant Josep Oriol 1 (93 301 59 00/fax 93 318 36 64). Metro Liceu/14, 38, 59, 91, N9, N12 bus. **Rates** single €60.20; double €72.30. **Credit** AmEx, DC, MC, V. **Map** p343 A3.
Always one of the most popular budget options in Barcelona, the Jardi is located on Plaça Sant Josep Oriol, just next to Plaça del Pi. It has recently been renovated, so prices have gone up a notch. A special new feature is the sunny breakfast room with balconies overlooking the square. Rooms vary in size; the ones to go for are those with a view over the leafy *plaças*. All have bathrooms, with either a bath (big or small) or a shower. The decor is fresh and crisp with lots of white. Book well in advance.
Hotel services *Air-conditioning. Safe.* **Room services** *Telephone. TV.*

Hostal Rey Don Jaime I

C/Jaume I 11 (tel/fax 93 310 62 08). Metro Jaume I/ bus 17, 19, 40, 45, N8. **Rates** single €38.70; double €58; triple €77.30. **Credit** AmEx, DC, MC, V. **Map** p343 B3.
The Don Jaime sits on the main artery through the centre of the Old City; it's noisy but handy for both the Barri Gòtic and La Ribera. The small reception is deceptive, as the hotel is spacious and has quite a few large rooms suitable for groups and families. Basic but clean, all 30 rooms have new bathrooms. Some of the inside rooms can be gloomy, so it's best to go for an outside one (though those on C/Jaume I can be noisy). Pets are welcome.
Hotel services *Lounge. Multilingual staff. Safe. TV.* **Room services** *Telephone.*

UNIVERSITAT DE BARCELONA

ESTUDIOS HISPÁNICOS
Spanish for foreigners

Diploma in Hispanic Studies
Spanish Language Course (one year or four months)
Spanish Culture (one year or four months)
Intensive Spanish Language Courses
Spanish Language Course (D.E.L.E.) preparation
Business Spanish
Spanish Conversation and Writing Course
Spanish Language and Culture (summer)
Spanish Grammar for Teachers of Spanish as a Second Language (summer)

For more information: Estudios Hispánicos, Universitat de Barcelona
Gran Via de les Corts Catalanes, 585. 08007 Barcelona (Spain).
Tel. 93 403.55.19 Fax 93 403.54.33
E-mail: est-hispa@d1.ub.es. http://www.ub.es/ieh

The Spanish Studies Centre is part of the University of Barcelona and is dedicated to the teaching of Spanish as a foreign language. It also dedicates a part of its courses to Spanish culture. The Centre was founded in 1952 and is celebrating its fiftieth anniversary this year. Over the last five decades it has received students from all the five continents. At this moment in time it has over thirty courses and more than 2000 students annually.

The Spanish Studies Centre office is located in the heart of Barcelona, in a building that forms part of the University of Barcelona, which was declared a historic monument in 1970.

Spanish Studies students have access to the libraries, study rooms, computer rooms, bookshops and sports facilities.

Hotel Barcelona House

C/Escudellers 19 (93 301 82 95/fax 93 412 41 29/
www.hbhouse@interplanet.es). Metro Drassanes/
14, 38, 59, 91, N9, N12 bus. **Rates** (incl breakfast)
single €25.20-€32.30; double €48.50-€64.60;
triple €74.50-€84.10. **Credit** AmEx, DC, MC, V.
Map p343 A3-B3.

The smart reception of Barcelona House gives no
clue to the unique decor of its 70 rooms. High kitsch
works well with old, chunky, porcelain sinks and
baths, 1950s-style furniture and antique beds.
Rooms vary in style and facilities; most have complete bathrooms, all have showers. Some have a
telephone and TV. The hotel bar-restaurant provides a cold buffet breakfast (included in the price)
and does good tapas. Barcelona House has direct
access to the popular bar-club Café Royale (*see
p248*) and hotel guests have priority getting in
there before 12.30am. A fun place to stay.
Hotel services *Bar. Laundry. Multilingual staff.
Restaurant. Safe.*

Hotel Cortés

*C/Santa Ana 25 (93 317 91 12/fax 93 412 66 08).
Metro Catalunya/bus all routes to Plaça Catalunya.*
Rates (incl breakfast) single €50-€65; double €84.
Credit AmEx, MC, V. **Map** p342 B2.

With a useful location and friendly service, the small
and comfortable Hotel Cortés (43 rooms in all) is a
good choice. It has a typical, Barcelona-style bar-
restaurant right next door, where breakfast is
served. If the Cortés is booked up, its sister hotel,
the Cataluña, is directly opposite it on the same
pedestrian shopping street.
Hotel services *Air-conditioning. Bar. Laundry.
Multilingual staff. Restaurant.* **Room services**
Safe. Telephone. TV.
Branch: Hotel Cataluña C/Santa Ana 24,
Barri Gòtic (93 301 91 20).

Hotel Internacional

*La Rambla 78-80 (93 302 25 66/fax 93 317
61 90/ www.husa.es). Metro Liceu/14, 38, 59,
91, N9, N12 bus.* **Rates** (incl breakfast) single
€53.50-€55.60; double €93.10-€96.30; triple
€120.90-€126.30. **Credit** AmEx, DC, MC, V.
Map p343 A3.

An institution on the Rambla, presiding over the
Plaça de la Boqueria, and popular with visiting foreign football fans, who drape their colours along
the balconies. Built in 1894, the 60-room hotel has
been fully refurbished. It's always full, so book way
ahead. It's also noisy. Note that the Internacional
has brought in some of the biggest recent price
hikes of any Barcelona hotel.
Hotel services *Bar. Multilingual staff. TV.*
Room services *Telephone.*

Hotel Suizo

*Plaça de l'Àngel 12 (93 310 61 08/fax 93 315
04 61/ www.gargallo-hotels.com). Metro Jaume I/
17, 19, 40, 45 bus.* **Rates** single €103.80; double
€125.20; triple €167.60. **Credit** AmEx, DC, MC, V.
Map p343 B3.

The entrance and reception of the Suizo are quite
oppressive, with lots of dark wood, but its corridors
and rooms are brighter. All rooms look out over the
streets; the ones above Plaça de l'Àngel and C/Jaume
I are noisier than those over C/Llibreteria. For its
location – near the Rambla, the cathedral and the
Born – the Suizo is good value.
Hotel services *Air-conditioning. Coffee bar. Disabled:
adapted rooms (1). Laundry. Multilingual staff.*
Room services *Minibar. Safe. Telephone. TV.*

Ramblas Hotel

*La Rambla 33 (93 301 57 00/fax 93 412 25 07/
www.ramblashotels.com). Metro Liceu/14, 38, 59,
91, N9, N12 bus.* **Rates** (incl breakfast) single
€100.60-€138.60; double €128.90-€154.70; triple
€167.60-€193.40; quadruple €167.60-€232. **Credit**
AmEx, MC, V. **Map** p343 A3-4.

The Ramblas occupies an attractive 18th-century
building with a tiled *Modernista* façade. Rooms are
spacious and comfortable; those on the eighth and
ninth floors have large terraces. The front rooms
have views of the Rambla and the port, while those
at the back look out towards Montjuïc and the roof
of Gaudí's Palau Güell.
Hotel services *Air-conditioning. Bar. Laundry.*
Room services *Minibar. Room service (breakfast
only). Safe. Telephone. TV: satellite.*

Budget

Hostal Fina

*C/Portaferrissa 11, entro (tel/fax 93 317 97 87).
Metro Liceu/14, 38, 59, N9, N12 bus.* **Rates** single
€24-€30; double €36-€51. **No credit cards.**
Map p342 A2.

Set on one of the main shopping streets in the old
town and just off the Rambla, the two-floor Fina is
a basic, comfortable and clean *pension*. Most rooms
have their own bathrooms, and the only communal
bathroom can be a schlep from some of the non-en
suite rooms. Of the outward-facing rooms, those on
the side of C/Bot are quieter.
Hotel services *Lounge. Safe. Telephone. TV.*

Hostal Lausanne

*Avda Portal de l'Àngel 24 (93 302 11 39). Metro
Catalunya/bus all routes to Plaça Catalunya.* **Rates**
single €21.50; double €34.90-€46.40; triple €49.90-
€64.20. **No credit cards. Map** p342 B2.

This 17-room, family-run *pension* is on the first
floor of a fine old building. It has high ceilings and
ample rooms, some of which have balconies overlooking the wide, pedestrian Portal de l'Àngel. It's
clean, bright and basic, with a big sitting room. The
reception is open 24 hours.
Hotel services *Lounge. Multilingual staff.
Safe. Telephone. Terrace. TV.*

Hostal Maldà

*C/del Pi 5, 1° 1ª (93 317 30 02). Metro Liceu/
14, 38, 59, 91, N9, N12 bus.* **Rates** single €12.60;
double €13-€23.80; triple €23.80. **No credit cards.**
Map p342 B2.

This comfortable *pension* in the heart of the Barri Gòtic is a find in every sense: access is through one of the entrances (open 24 hours) to the Galeries Maldà shopping arcade, but even the hike up the stairs (there's no lift) is forgotten when you meet the friendly lady who runs it. There are no en suite facilities, but the four communal bathrooms are impeccably clean. All 22 rooms face on to the street or a large, sunny patio. A genuine bargain.
Hotel services *Laundry. Lounge. Refrigerator. Telephone. TV: satellite.*

Hostal Noya

La Rambla 133, 1° (93 301 48 31). Metro Catalunya/ bus all routes to Plaça Catalunya. **Rates** single €19; double €34.90. **No credit cards.** **Map** p342 A2.
This modest *pension* is in an excellent position on the Rambla right by Plaça Catalunya, and is good value for its location. It's basic and clean, and 11 of the 15 rooms have balconies overlooking the crowds or a bright patio, while the rest are inward-facing and quite dark. There is only one communal bathroom to serve all rooms.
Hotel services *Telephone.*

Hostal Palermo

C/Boqueria 21 (tel/fax 93 302 40 02). Metro Liceu/ 14, 38, 59, 91, N9, N12 bus. **Rates** single €36.10; double €42.20; triple €72.30. **Credit** DC, MC, V. **Map** p343 A3.
A cheerful place with 34 impeccably clean, recently refurbished rooms, most of which have en suite

bathrooms. Of the interior rooms, one looks on to a dark air shaft; the rest overlook a brighter patio, which is used by a bar beneath, so these can be noisy. English-speaking staff.
Hotel services *Laundry.*

Hostal Parisien

La Rambla 114 (tel/fax 93 301 62 83). Metro Liceu/ 14, 38, 59, 91, N9, N12 bus. **Rates** single €21.10-€30.10; double €45.20-€51.20. **No credit cards.** **Map** p342 A2.
A student favourite, the Parisien has a great mid-Rambla location opposite the Virreina. The 13 rooms are well kept, and eight have bathrooms. The rooms overlooking the Rambla are noisy but fun for people-watching; others are darker but quieter. Renovations over the past few years have included new bathrooms and new flooring.
Hotel services *Lounge. Multilingual staff. Safe. Telephone. TV: satellite.*

Hostal Rembrandt

C/Portaferrissa 23, pral 1° (tel/fax 93 318 10 11). Metro Liceu/14, 38, 59, 91, N9, N12 bus. **Rates** single €24-€33; double €39-€53; triple €60-€63. **No credit cards.** **Map** p342 B2.
Popular with backpackers, the cheerful Rembrandt is spotlessly clean, with 29 pleasantly decorated rooms. The foyer opens on to an attractive communal patio. The owners will accommodate up to five people in a room at reasonable prices.
Hotel services *Multilingual staff. Refrigerator. Safe. Telephone. TV.*

The brand-new **Hostal Gat Raval**.
See p53.

Hostal Victòria

*C/Comtal 9, 1° 1ª (93 318 07 60/93 317 45 97/
victoria@atriumhotels.com). Metro Catalunya
or Urquinaona/bus all routes to Plaça Catalunya.*
Rates single €25.80-€29; double €38.70-€41.90;
triple €51.60-€54.80. **No credit cards.**
Map p342 B2.
This spacious, 30-room *pension* offers communal
cooking and washing facilities. Rooms are basic,
clean and light; most have balconies, but none has
an en suite bathroom. Discounts are available in
winter (Nov-Mar) for stays of more than 20 days.
You should book in advance.
Hotel services *Kitchen. Laundry. Lift. Lounge.
Telephone. Terrace. TV.*

Hotel El Cantón

*C/Nou de Sant Francesc 40 (93 317 30 19).
Metro Drassanes/14, 36, 38, 57, 59, 64, 157 bus.*
Rates single €26.70-€39.50; double €55.60-€42.80;
triple €75. **Credit** AmEx, DC, MC, V.
Located in a quiet street that has recently been
cleaned up, and just two minutes' walk from the
attractive Plaça del Duc de Medinaceli on C/Ample,
where Pedro Almodóvar shot scenes in *All About
My Mother*, the El Cantón is a bright little hotel in
the heart of the Old City. It is in the process of being
renovated to meet hotel standards; at the moment,
not all rooms have bathrooms. It's basic but good
for the price and location. The best rooms are those
that face the street.
Hotel services *Air-conditioning. Disabled: adapted
rooms (1). Multilingual staff.* **Room services** *Safe.
TV: satellite.*

Hotel Toledano

*La Rambla 138, 4° (93 301 08 72/fax 93 412 31 42/
www.hoteltoledano.com). Metro Catalunya/bus all
routes to Plaça Catalunya.* **Rates** single €31; double
€53.50; triple €67.40. **Credit** AmEx, DC, MC, V.
Map p342 A2.
Very near Plaça Catalunya, the Hotel Toledano may
be handily placed, but it can be rather noisy – the
interior rooms that have views of the cathedral are
the quietest. The 28 rooms are basic, but some have
air-con and all have bathrooms, and there is a
chintzy lounge area with a balcony overlooking the
Rambla. There's another *pension*, Hostal Residencia
Capitol, in the same building; the reception for both
is on the fourth floor.
Hotel services *Multilingual staff. Safe.*
Room services *Telephone. TV: satellite.*

Pensión-Hostal Mari-Luz

*C/Palau 4 (93 317 34 63/fax 93 412 23 63).
Metro Liceu/14, 38, 59, N9, N12 bus.* **Rates** double
€30-€36; 4-8-person rooms €11.40-€13.20 per
person. **Credit** AmEx, DC, MC, V. **Map** p343 B3.
Mari-Luz takes great care of her lodgers in this spotlessly clean *pension*, a few streets' walk from the
main Plaça Reial drag. The 15 rooms – five with en
suite showers – are plain but quiet, and the old building is atmospheric and affordable. The family also
own the similarly cheap Pensión Fernando nearby.

Hotel services *Bar-restaurant. Lockers. Safe.*
Room services *Telephone.*
Branch: Pensión Fernando C/Ferran 31,
Barri Gòtic (93 301 79 93).

Pensión Vitoria

*C/Palla 8, pral (tel/fax 93 302 08 34). Metro Liceu/
14, 38, 59, 91, N9, N12 bus.* **Rates** single €9.70-
€12; double €27.10-€33.10; triple €30.10-€39.20.
Credit MC, V. **Map** p342 B2.
Close to the Plaça del Pi, the Vitoria has ten light and
airy double rooms with balconies and two dark,
inward-facing single rooms. Two of the doubles
have en suite bathrooms with showers, while the
rest of the rooms share one bathroom. The best room
in the house is the corner double, which has three
balconies and a bathroom. Despite the basic facilities, the *pension* has a loyal bunch of repeat guests,
so it's a good idea to book early.
Hotel services *Multilingual staff. Telephone. TV.*

Raval

Mid-range

Hostal Gat Raval

*C/Joaquín Costa 44, 2ª (93 481 66 70/www.
gataccommodation.com). Metro Universitat/
bus all routes to Plaça Universitat.* **Rates** single
€30-€36; double €41.90-€67.70; triple €81.30.
Credit AmEx, MC, V. **Map** p340 C5.
A brand new *hostal*, with good facilities and a great
location, Gat Raval has filled a niche in this accommodation bracket. With its funky green doors and
woodwork, and crisp white walls, it's a fun and
bright place to stay. Most of the 24 rooms – including seven singles – don't have bathrooms, but the
communal facilities are excellent. Some interior
rooms get lots of light and have great views of Plaça
dels Àngels and the MACBA, while those looking
on to C/Joaquín Costa can be noisy.
Hotel services *Internet access. Safe. Telephone.*
Room services *TV.*

Hostal-Residencia Ramos

*C/Hospital 36 (93 302 07 23/fax 93 302 04 30).
Metro Liceu/14, 38, 59, 91, N9, N12 bus.*
Rates single €38-€42; double €58-€62; triple
€78-€81. **Credit** AmEx, DC, MC, V.
Map p342-3 A2-3.
Another off-Rambla hotel, the Ramos occupies the
first and second floors of a charming old building
with a tiled entrance and elegant staircase. Renovated
in the past few years, the *pension* is in excellent condition. All rooms are a good size and have bathrooms,
and those at the front (€4 supplment) overlook the
church and trees of Plaça Sant Agustí (two outside
corner rooms have two balconies). It's excellent
value for money and, not surprisingly, attracts a
string of regular guests.
Hotel services *Air-conditioning. Multilingual staff.
Safe. Terrace.* **Room services** *Room service
(10am-6pm). Telephone. TV.*

Accommodation

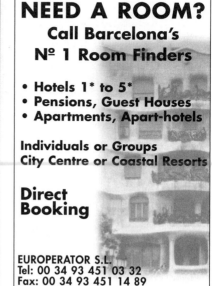

Hotel Aneto

*C/Carme 38 (93 301 99 89/fax 93 301 98 62/
www.hotelpelayo.com). Metro Liceu/14, 38, 59,
N9, N12 bus.* **Rates** single €48; double €72.
Credit AmEx, MC, V. **Map** p342 A2.
With the MACBA, the Boqueria market and the
Rambla almost on its doorstep, this small hotel is
ideally located. Its 15 rooms – all with bathrooms –
are basic and comfortable. The best rooms are the
exterior ones at the front on C/Carme, with their view
of the Antic Hospital.
Hotel services *Air-conditioning.* **Room services**
Telephone. TV.

Hotel España

*C/Sant Pau 9-11 (93 318 17 58)/fax 93 317 11 34/
hotelespanya@tresnet.com). Metro Liceu/14, 38,
59, 91, N9, N12 bus.* **Rates** (incl breakfast) single
€43.50; double €83. **Credit** AmEx, DC, MC, V.
Map p343 A3.
The España is a *Modernista* landmark, with lower
floors designed by Domènech i Montaner in 1902.
The main restaurant (good for lunch) is decorated
with floral tiling and elaborate woodwork, and the
larger dining room beyond it features extravagant
murals of river nymphs by Ramon Casas. The rooms
can come as a disappointment after all this; they
vary in size and some are bare and rather gloomy,
although several open on to a bright interior patio.
Hotel services *Air-conditioning. Multilingual staff.
Restaurant. Safe. TV room.* **Room services**
Telephone. TV.

Hotel Gaudí

*C/Nou de la Rambla 12 (93 317 90 32/fax 93 412
26 36/www.hotelgaudi.es). Metro Liceu/14, 38, 59,
91, N9, N12 bus.* **Rates** single €82.40-€98.40;
double €103.80-€125.20; triple €129.50-€156.20;
quadruple €142.30-€163.70. **Credit** AmEx, DC,
MC, V. **Map** p343 A3.
The Gaudí's great selling point is its convenience as
the main mid-range hotel in a central, much-visited
area. True to its name, it has a Gaudí-inspired lobby
and café-bar. Some of the 73 rooms, which are all
simply decorated, look directly on to Gaudí's Palau
Güell on the other side of the road. Rooms with large
terraces are also available. This is a popular choice
for British travellers.
Hotel services *Air-conditioning. Babysitting.
Bar. Car park. Disabled: adapted rooms (2).
Fitness centre (gym). Multilingual staff. Restaurant.*
Room services *Room service (noon-midnight).
Telephone. TV: satellite.*

Hotel Mesón Castilla

*C/Valldonzella 5 (93 318 21 82/fax 93 412 40 20/
hmesoncastilla@teleline.es). Metro Universitat/
bus all routes to Plaça Catalunya or Plaça
Universitat.* **Rates** (incl breakfast) single €86;
double €103-€121; triple €146; quadruple €175.
Credit AmEx, DC, MC, V. **Map** p342 A1.
This old-world-style hotel could be a museum of
artisan antiques with its murals and assorted furniture. It has 57 individually decorated rooms, some

Tables indoor and out at **Mesón Castilla**.

furnished with handpainted wardrobes, beds and bedside tables. Some rear rooms have terraces, and the three large rooms, with up to four beds, are great for families with children. Most rooms have mini-bars. A hearty buffet breakfast is served in a bright dining room or on the beautifully tiled patio, which has a lovely view of the MACBA.
Hotel services *Air-conditioning. Car park. Laundry. Multilingual staff. Safe. Terrace.* **Room services** *Telephone. TV: satellite.*

Hotel Peninsular

C/Sant Pau 34-36 (93 302 31 38/fax 93 412 36 99). Metro Liceu/14, 38, 59, 91, N9, N12 bus. **Rates** (incl breakfast) single €43.40; double €62; triple €74.50; quadruple €93; quintuple €99.30. **Credit** MC, V. **Map** p342 A3.

Like the Oriente (*see p66* **A taste of the Oriente**), the Peninsular was built inside the shell of a former monastery, which had a passageway connecting it to Sant Agusti church. The hotel was modernised in the early 1990s, but wicker furniture imparts a colonial feel and a sense of tranquillity remains, thanks to its bright, fresh, plant-lined inner courtyard. All 85 rooms are off the courtyard, and are clean and comfortable with en suite baths or showers.
Hotel services *Air-conditioning. Multilingual staff. Safe. Terrace. TV room.* **Room services** *Telephone.*

Hotel Principal

C/Junta de Comerç 8 (93 318 89 74/fax 93 412 08 19/www.hotelprincipal.es). Metro Liceu/14, 38, 59, 91, N9, N12 bus. **Rates** (incl breakfast) single €63.30; double €80.60; triple €106.40; quadruple €132. **Credit** AmEx, DC, MC, V. **Map** p343 A3.

One of a few hotels and *pensions* on this quiet street near the Rambla, the Principal distinguishes itself by the ornate furniture in its 58 bedrooms, all of which have modernised bathrooms. The same owners also run the slightly cheaper – and completely renovated – Joventut along the street (work is currently under way to connect the two hotels, making them into one). The hotel is open 24 hours, and travellers who arrive in the night have the option of waiting in a comfortable lounge with toilet facilities for a room to be vacant in the morning.
Hotel services *Air-conditioning. Babysitting. Bar. Disabled: adapted rooms (3). Multilingual staff. Restaurant.* **Room services** *Safe. Telephone. TV.*
Branch: Hotel Joventut C/Junta de Comerç 12, Raval (93 301 84 99).

Hotel Sant Agusti

Plaça Sant Agusti 3 (93 318 16 58/fax 93 317 29 28/www.hotelsa.com). Metro Liceu/14, 38, 59, 91, N9, N12 bus. **Rates** (incl breakfast) single €90.20; double €119.20-€128.90; triple €148.30. **Credit** AmEx, DC, MC, V. **Map** p343 A3.

One of the oldest continuously functioning hotels in Barcelona, the Sant Agusti has been owned and run by the Tura-Monistrol family for well over 100 years. It has had two major facelifts in the past decade but retains some old-world charm: top-floor

rooms have oak-beamed ceilings and romantic views over the city's rooftops. Rooms are comfortable, and three big ones have two bathrooms each and sleep up to six. The interior rooms are surprisingly bright, thanks to a large central patio (not easy to find in this part of the city). Situated on the recently done-up Plaça Sant Agusti and next to the commanding church of the same name, this is one of the most attractive options in the Rambla area.
Hotel services *Air-conditioning. Babysitting. Bar. Disabled: adapted rooms (2). Laundry. Multilingual staff. Restaurant (dinner only).* **Room services** *Safe. Telephone. TV: satellite.*

Budget

Hostal La Terrassa

C/Junta de Comerç 11 (93 302 51 74/fax 93 301 21 88). Metro Liceu/14, 38, 59, 91, N9, N12 bus. **Rates** single €15.60; double €23.50-€30; triple €33-€39. **Credit** DC, MC, V. **Map** p343 A3.

Under the same ownership as the hugely popular Hostal Jardi (*see p49*), La Terrassa is one of Barcelona's most likeable cheap *pensions*, and great value. About half the rooms have bathrooms, and the best have balconies overlooking the street or an attractive interior patio that backs on to the Sant Agusti church. A peaceful, friendly place.
Hotel services *Lounge. Multilingual staff. Safe. Telephone. Terrace. TV.*

Hostal Opera

C/Sant Pau 20 (93 318 82 01). Metro Liceu/14, 38, 59, 91, N9, N12 bus. **Rates** single €23.40-€34.90; double €39-€49; triple €69. **No credit cards. Map** p343 A3.

As you might expect from the name, this *pension* is right beside the Liceu opera house, just off the Rambla. It's been totally renovated in the past few years and now has a total of 69 rooms, all with bathrooms and air-conditioning.
Hotel services *Air-conditioning. Disabled: adapted rooms (6). Lift. Multilingual staff. Safe.*

Hosteria Grau

C/Ramelleres 27 (93 301 81 35/fax 93 317 68 25/ www.intercom.es/grau). Metro Catalunya/bus all routes to Plaça Catalunya. **Rates** single €28.90; double €43.80-€63.10; triple €64.20-€83.50; apartment €73.80-€128.40. **Credit** AmEx, DC, MC, V. **Map** p342 A1.

This pleasant *pension* has been in the family Grau for more than 50 years. It has an artisan charm about it, with its beautifully tiled spiral staircase and low ceilings. Rooms are clean and pleasant, but inside rooms (all singles) are dark. The *hostal* has direct access to a funky little café (Café-Bar Centric) next door, where breakfast is served. The family also owns six apartments, each big enough for six people, in another building along the street. It has a 24-hour reception.
Hotel services *Bar. Multilingual staff. Telephone. TV lounge.*

Sant Pere, La Ribera & Born

Mid-range

Hostal Orleans

*Avda Marquès de l'Argentera 13 (93 319 73 82/
fax 93 319 22 19). Metro Barceloneta/14, 39,
51 bus.* **Rates** single €27; double €51.20-
€54.20; triple €63.30. **Credit** AmEx, DC, MC, V.
Map p336 C4.

This family-run hostel near the Port and the Parc de
la Ciutadella has 17 good-sized rooms with en suite
facilities, including some with balconies (which can
be noisy). All are clean, but the upper-floor rooms
are more modern. There are special rates for triples
or quadruples; weekly rates can also be negotiated.
Not all rooms have telephones.
Hotel services *Laundry. Multilingual staff.
Telephone.* **Room services** *TV.*

Hotel Triunfo

*Passeig Picasso 22 (tel/fax 93 315 08 60). Metro
Arc de Triomf/39, 40, 41, 42, 51, 141 bus.* **Rates**
single €42.70; double €66.70; triple €90.40. **Credit**
MC, V. **Map** p341 E6.

Located in a quiet area of the Born overlooking the
Parc de la Ciutadella, the Hotel Triunfo changed
hands very recently. All 15 rooms have bathrooms.
Six have balconies overlooking the park, while the
others are bright and airy interior rooms.
Hotel services *Air-conditioning. Safe.*
Room services *Telephone. TV.*

Hotel Urquinaona

*Ronda de Sant Pere 24 (93 268 13 36/fax 93
295 41 37/www.barcelonahotel.com/urquinaona).
Metro Urquinaona/19, 39, 40, 41, 45, 55, 141 bus.*
Rates single €73; double €93; triple €119. **Credit**
MC, V. **Map** p342 B1.

This spick-and-span modern hotel (remodelled from
a *pension* in 1999) offers the kind of comfort and
facilities that usually cost more, including large
beds. All 18 rooms are spacious and brightly decorated, and have bathrooms. Book early.
Hotel services *Air-conditioning. Laundry.
Multilingual staff.* **Room services** *Minibar.
Room service (breakfast only). Safe. Telephone.
TV: satellite.*

Pensió 2000

*C/Sant Pere Més Alt 6, 1º (93 310 74 66/fax 93 319
42 52/www.pensio2000.com). Metro Urquinaona/17,
19, 40, 45, N8 bus.* **Rates** single €33.50-€43.80;
double €41.90-€54.80; triple €61.20-€74.10;
quadruple €74.10-€87. **Credit** MC, V. **Map** p342 B2.

This spacious *pension*, run by the friendly Orlando
and Manuela, is perfect for classical music lovers as
it's located directly in front of the stunning Palau de
la Mùsica and in the same building as a school full
of music students. Three of the seven spacious,
yellow-walled rooms have balconies looking on to
the Palau, and these share a bathroom. Six different
menus are offered for breakfast, which is served at
tables in the rooms or on the outdoor patio.
Hotel services *Laundry. Safe.* **Room services**
Room service (8-10.30am). TV.

Hotel Barcelona House. *See p51.*

Budget

Pensión Francia

C/Rera Palau 4 (93 319 03 76). Metro Barceloneta/ 36, 57, 59, 64, 157, N6 bus. **Rates** single €19.30; double €32-€51.60; triple €52-€58. **Credit** AmEx, DC, MC, V. **Map** p343 C4.

Just off Plaça Ollés, in the Born, the Francia is a friendly, peaceful, 15-room *pension*. Exceptionally clean and bright (even the woodwork is painted white), it has a comfortable lounge in which to read one of the many books kept at reception. Rooms vary in size and most have showers or baths. Being off the main Born-nightlife route, it's generally quiet (especially the larger rooms looking over the tiny Passatge Palau), and, unusually for this price range, all rooms have TVs. Excellent value.
Hotel services *Telephone.* **Room services** *TV.*

Vila Olímpica – Port Olímpic

Expensive

Hotel Arts

C/Marina 19-21 (93 221 10 00/fax 93 221 10 70/ www.ritzcarlton.com). Metro Ciutadella-Vila Olímpica/10, 36, 71, 92, N6, N8 bus. **Rates** standard room €332-€428; suite €444-€578; club €482-€621; apartment €1,177-€4,815. **Credit** AmEx, DC, MC, V. **Map** p341 F7.

Designed by US architects Skidmore, Owings and Merrill, the first Ritz-Carlton hotel in Europe towers 44 storeys above the beachfront and Port Olímpic. Fountains play by the entrance, and palm-fringed gardens surround modern sculptures and the city's only beachfront pool. The Arts offers matchless service, stunning interiors (specially commissioned artwork is scattered throughout the building) and staggering views, and has impressed even seasoned world travellers. Three upper floors form the Club, for guests desiring still more comfort and service, and the top six floors house magnificent luxury duplex apartments with contemporary decor by Catalan designer Jaume Treserra.
Hotel services *Air-conditioning. Babysitting. Bar. Beauty salon. Car park. Disabled: adapted rooms (3). Fitness centre (gym/sauna/massage). Garden. Laundry. Limousine service. Multilingual staff. Non-smoking floor. Pool (outdoor). Restaurants. Ticket agency.* **Room services** *CD player. Minibar. Room service (24hrs). Safe. Telephone. TV: satellite.*

Poble Sec

Mid-range

Hotel Nuevo Triunfo

C/Cabanes 34 (93 442 59 33/fax 93 443 21 10). Metro Paral.lel/20, 36, 57, 64, 91, 157 bus. **Rates** single €52; double €95. **Credit** AmEx, MC, V. **Map** p340 C6.

Located off a quiet residential street at the base of Montjuïc, the Nuevo Triunfo is central, but away from the hustle and bustle. A private hotel, it's owned by Ramon and Maria, who used to run the popular Hotel Triunfo (*see p58*). Its 40 rooms are all simply decorated, with good bathrooms; some have private terraces. A continental breakfast is available.
Hotel services *Air-conditioning. Disabled: adapted rooms (1). Multilingual staff. Safe.* **Room services** *Telephone. TV: satellite.*

Hotel Paral.lel

C/Poeta Cabanyes 5 (93 329 11 04/www.nnhotels.es). Metro Paral.lel/20, 57, 64, 157 bus. **Rates** single €65.30; double €101.70. **Credit** AmEx, DC, MC, V. **Map** p339 B6.

Although this hotel looks more like an office building with its black and grey colour scheme, it's comfortable and has friendly, multilingual staff. It's popular with business people, but is useful for tourists, too, being reasonably central, and there are a couple of family suites.
Hotel services *Air-conditioning. Babysitting. Bar. Disabled: adapted rooms (1). Laundry. Multilingual staff.* **Room services** *Safe. Telephone. TV: satellite.*

Eixample

Expensive

Hilton Barcelona

Avda Diagonal 589-91 (93 495 77 77/fax 93 495 77 00/www.hilton.com). Metro Maria Cristina/ 6, 7, 33, 34, 63, 66, 67, 68, N12 bus. **Rates** single €270-€325; double €300-€355; single suite €325-€825; double suite €370-€870. **Credit** AmEx, DC, MC, V. **Map** p335 B2-3.

Opened in 1990, the steel-and-glass, 286-room Hilton is in the heart of Barcelona's modern business district and concentrates on providing a comprehensive range of business services. It lacks the array of facilities of some of its competitors, but its rooms are a little more intimate.
Hotel services *Air-conditioning. Babysitting. Bar. Car park. Disabled: adapted rooms (4). Fitness centre (gym). Laundry. Limousine service. Multilingual staff. Non-smoking rooms. Restaurants. Safe. Terrace.* **Room services** *Minibar. Room service (24hrs). Telephone. TV: satellite.*

Hotel Balmes

C/Mallorca 216 (93 451 19 14/fax 93 451 00 49/ www.derbyhotels.es). FGC Provença/7, 16, 17, 20, 43, 44, 67, 68, N7 bus. **Rates** single €166.90; double €186. **Credit** AmEx, DC, MC, V. **Map** p336 C4.

This 100-room hotel in the middle of the Eixample offers all-round comfort and a high standard of service. Rooms at the rear get the morning sun and look on to the interior garden, solarium and pool; some of the ground-floor rooms have terraces. The tranquillity of the patio contrasts greatly with the bustle of the street outside.
Hotel services *Air-conditioning. Babysitting (24hrs notice). Bar (Mon-Fri). Car park. Garden. Laundry.*

Lifts. Limousine service. Multilingual staff. Pool (outdoor). Restaurant (Mon-Fri). Ticket agency.
Room services *Minibar. Room service (8am-11pm Mon-Fri). Safe. Telephone. TV: satellite.*

Hotel Caledonian

Gran Via de les Corts Catalanes 574 (93 453 02 00/ fax 93 451 77 03/www.hotel-caledonian.com). Metro Universitat/9, 14, 50, 56, 59, N1, N2, N13, N14, N15 bus. **Rates** (incl breakfast) single €115.80; double €180.10; suite €192.90. **Credit** AmEx, DC, MC, V. **Map** p314 C5.

This small, modern hotel was constructed for the 1992 Olympic Games, and couples style with warmth. It's centrally located yet sufficiently far from the crowds of the Plaça Catalunya/Rambla area, which gives it a relatively peaceful feel. It has 50 rooms, a small bar and garage parking.
Hotel services *Air-conditioning. Bar. Laundry.* **Room services** *Minibar. Safe. Telephone. TV: satellite.*

Hotel Claris

C/Pau Claris 150 (93 487 62 62/fax 93 215 79 70/ www.derbyhotels.es). Metro Passeig de Gràcia/ 7, 16, 17, 20, 22, 24, 28, 43, 44, N6, N7 bus. **Rates** single €318.80; double €354. **Credit** AmEx, DC, MC, V. **Map** p336 D4.

This refined, 120-room hotel is the perfect place for lovers of ancient art, modern design, the latest technology and *la dolce vita*. Artworks, antiques and archaeological relics are distributed around the hotel, in the bedrooms and in the small museum, making everything that bit more personal. All the works are part of the private collection of the hotel's owner, Jordi Clos, whose archaeological foundation maintains the city's Museu Egipci. Another find is the roof, with its open-air swimming pool, giant cacti, bar and terrace. The hotel is part of the same chain as Hotel Balmes (*see p59*).
Hotel services *Air-conditioning. Babysitting. Bar. Car park. Disabled: adapted rooms (4). Fitness centre (gym/sauna). Laundry. Limousine service. Multilingual staff. Non-smoking floor. Pool (outdoor). Restaurants. Ticket agency.* **Room services** *Minibar. Room service (24hrs). Safe. Telephone. TV: satellite.*

Hotel Condes de Barcelona ✓

C/Passeig de Gràcia 73-75 (93 467 47 86/ fax 93 467 47 85/www.condesdebarcelona.com). Metro Passeig de Gràcia/7, 16, 17, 20, 22, 24, 28, 43, 44, N6, N7 bus. **Rates** single €212.10-€289.40; double €228.30-€308.60; suite €514.50. **Credit** AmEx, DC, MC, V. **Map** p336 D4.

The Condes is made up of two hotels sitting on opposite sides of C/Mallorca at the intersection with Passeig de Gràcia. The one on the south side is more modern, but what it loses in character it makes up for with the spectacular views of La Pedrera and the Sagrada Família from outside rooms (especially those on the top floor with terraces). The building on the north side maintains elements of the 19th-century palace it once was in its façade, roof-terrace balustrade and foyer. Rooms vary in size. They are

decorated simply in cream and white, with parquet flooring and wood-panelled headboards. Facilities differ in the two sections of the hotel, but guests are free to move between the two to take advantage of everything the Condes has to offer.
Hotel services *Air-conditioning. Bar. Disabled: adapted rooms (2). Laundry. Multilingual staff. Pool (outdoor) Restaurant. Solarium.* **Room services** *Minibar. Room service (7am-midnight). Safe. Telephone. TV: satellite.*

Hotel Inglaterra

C/Pelai 14 (93 505 11 00/fax 93 505 11 09/ www.hotel-inglaterra.com). bus all routes to Plaça Universitat. **Rates** single €130.70; double €201.10; triple €241.30. **Credit** AmEx, DC, MC, V. **Map** p342 A1.

The Hotel Inglaterra opened in 1999 when all but the façade and tiled staircase of the original building was rebuilt. It's aimed mainly at a business clientele, but couldn't be better located for seeing the major sights. The rooms are impressively comfortable. On the sixth floor, as well as a rooftop terrace, there is only a very large junior suite, ideal if you're looking for extra space and privacy – it's recommended for honeymooners. Pets are welcome.
Hotel services *Air-conditioning. Bar. Disabled: adapted rooms (1). Laundry. Multilingual staff. Safe. Ticket agency.* **Room services** *Minibar. Room service (7.30am-10.45pm). Telephone. TV: satellite.*

Hotel Podium

C/Bailèn 4 (93 265 02 02/reservations 902 11 51 16/fax 93 265 05 06/www.nh-hotels.com). Metro Arc de Triomf/19, 39, 40, 41, 42, 55, 141, N4, N11 bus. **Rates** single €109-€117.70; double €126.20-€207.50; suite €283.50. **Credit** AmEx, DC, MC, V. **Map** p315 E5.

Housed in a refurbished, turn-of-the-20th-century building, this 145-room hotel is part of the reliable NH chain. Tastefully decorated throughout, it has a very cheerful restaurant with walls covered in small paintings. For views, the inward-facing rooms beat the outside-facing ones as they look over an old convent and its cloisters. With its rooftop pool, sauna and outdoor pool, the Podium is a favourite with visiting national football teams. Lower weekend rates are available. There is also a smaller, stylish, more central branch, the **Duc de la Victòria** (C/Duc de la Victòria 15, Barri Gòtic; 93 270 34 10).
Hotel services *Air-conditioning. Babysitting. Bar. Car park. Disabled: adapted rooms (6). Fitness centre (gym/sauna). Laundry. Limousine service. Multilingual staff. Pool (outdoor). Restaurant. Safe.* **Room services** *Minibar. Room service (24hrs). Telephone. TV: satellite.*

Hotel Regente

Rambla Catalunya 76 (93 487 59 89/reservations 902 102 120/93 481 73 50/fax 93 487 32 27/ www.hoteles-centro-ciudad.es). Metro Passeig de Gràcia/FGC Provença/7, 16, 17, 22, 24, 28, N4 bus. **Rates** single €109.10-€198; double €128.40-€240.80. **Credit** AmEx, DC, MC, V. **Map** p336 D4.

Hidden away in Barcelona's hotels are some fabulous artistic features, which are worth checking out even if you're not staying in the hotel.

Hotel Claris

Clock the Andy Warhol originals in the bar-restaurant, East 47. *See p61.*

Hotel Mesón Castilla

An elaborate mural depicts all the regions of Spain. *See p55.*

Hotel Sant Agustí

The breakfast buffet is laid out on an antique oven – and the view's good too (*pictured*). *See p57.*

Hostal-Residencia Oliva

The lift is a wonderful museum piece. *See p63.*

Hotel España

The marble fireplace in the dining room was created by *Modernista* sculptor Eusebi Arnau. *See p55.*

The 79-room Regente occupies a renovated 1913 *Modernista* mansion designed by Evarist Juncosa. It has a finely restored façade and the stained-glass decoration imparts distinctive charm, while double glazing shields guests from the Eixample's street noise down below. The sixth- and seventh-floor rooms have terraces with stunning views, and many of the lower rooms open on to grand, wrought-iron balconies. There's a rooftop pool, too – a perfect place to enjoy the sunset.
Hotel services *Air-conditioning. Babysitting. Bar. Disabled: adapted rooms (2). Fitness centre (gym/ sauna/solarium). Laundry. Limousine service.*
Multilingual staff. Pool (outdoor). Ticket agency.
Room services *Minibar. Room service (7am-11pm). Safe. Telephone. TV: satellite.*

Ritz Hotel

Gran Via de les Corts Catalanes 668 (93 318 52 00/ fax 93 317 36 40/www.ritzbcn.com). Metro Passeig de Gràcia/7, 39, 45, 47, 50, 54, 56, 62 bus. **Rates** double €386; suite €482. **Credit** AmEx, DC, MC, V. **Map** p340 D5.

If you're feeling flush, the Ritz is a good choice, where emblematic luxury is still the order of the day. The 19th-century building has been finely renovated, but it still qualifies as the most elegant hotel in town, offering old-fashioned style in quantities that its rivals can only envy. The celebrity guest list has included Orson Welles and Woody Allen, as well as Salvador Dalí, who spent months here at a stretch (he stayed in suite 108). The sumptuous restaurant is open to non-guests.
Hotel services *Air-conditioning. Babysitting. Bar. Garden. Fitness centre (gym/massage/sauna). Laundry. Limousine service. Multilingual staff. Non-smoking floor. Restaurant. Ticket agency.*
Room services *Minibar. Room service (24hrs). Safe. Telephone. TV.*

Mid-range

Hostal Ciudad Condal

C/Mallorca 255, pral (93 215 10 40/fax 93 487 04 59). Metro Passeig de Gràcia/FGC Provença/ 20, 21, 28, 43, 44, N7 bus. **Rates** single €74.90; double €96.30-€107; triple €125.40. **Credit** MC, V. **Map** p336 D4.

The Ciudad Condal occupies part of the Casa Àngel Batlló, an 1891 *Modernista* block of three houses with one single façade, which was designed by Josep Vilaseca i Casanovas (not to be confused with Gaudí's Casa Batlló). The *hostal* has been recently renovated and all its 15 clean, basic rooms have new bathrooms. Many of the rooms are interior-facing and can be a little dark, but there are others that overlook a beautiful, lush garden – though they cost a bit more, they're better value for money.
Hotel services *Bar. Car park. Laundry. Safe.*
Room services *Telephone. TV.*

Hostal Girona

C/Girona 24, 1° 1ª (93 265 02 59/fax 93 265 85 32). Metro Urquinaona/19, 39, 40, 41, 42, 55, 141, N4, N11 bus. **Rates** single €21.10; double €39.20-€45.20. **Credit** MC, V. **Map** p342 C1.

A grand entrance with a double marble staircase is the perfect indicator of what to expect from this family-run, nine-room *hostal*; *Modernista* furniture, rugs, heavy doors and original floor tiles, all making up a characterful decor that is warm and inviting. Four single rooms and one double share a bathroom; the four other doubles have showers. Refreshments are served in a tiny breakfast area.
Hotel services *Telephone.*
Room services *TV.*

Hostal Plaza

C/Fontanella 18 (tel/fax 93 301 01 39/www.plaza hostel.com). Metro Urquinaona or Plaça Catalunya/ bus all routes to Plaça Urquinaona or Plaça Catalunya. **Rates** single €51.60-€58; double €58-€64.50; triple €77.40-€83.80. **Credit** AmEx, DC, MC, V. **Map** p342 B1.

Run by Hispanic Americans, the Hostal Plaza is an unusual, fun place. It offers a raft of services including a communal fridge, freezer and microwave. The reception and a new cocktail-style bar, with bamboo furniture, are down a floor from the 14 rooms, which are clean, with brightly painted woodwork and ceilings. All rooms have showers. Simple tapas are available in the bar in the afternoons.

Hotel services *Laundry. Microwave. Multilingual staff. Safe. TV room.*
Branch: Hotel **Duques de Bergara** C/Bergara 11, Eixample (93 301 51 51/fax 93 317 34 42).

Hostal-Residencia Oliva

Passeig de Gràcia 32, 4° (93 488 01 62/fax 93 487 04 97). Metro Passeig de Gràcia/7, 16, 17, 22, 24, 28, N1, N4, N6 bus. **Rates** single €24; double €45-€52; triple €72. **No credit cards.** Map p340 D5.

The family-run Oliva shares building space with designer Adolfo Dominguez's Passeig de Gràcia store, and yet is surprisingly reasonable. The *hostal* is found at the top of a beautiful, oval-shaped entrance patio, with a museum-piece lift bound to have guests taking photos before they even set their luggage down. Rooms are off a corridor decorated Laura Ashley style, and are light and airy. The six rooms facing Passeig de Gràcia have splendid views, but can be noisy in summer. Note that not all rooms have televisions.

Hotel services *Lounge. Telephone.*

Hostal San Remo

C/Ausiàs Marc 19, 1° 2ª (93 302 19 89/fax 93 301 07 74). Metro Urquinaona/bus all routes to Plaça Urquinaona. **Rates** single €27.10-€39.20; double €42.20-€51.20; triple €51.20-€63.30. **Credit** MC, V. **Map** p342 C1.

This friendly, family-run *pension* takes full advantage of its position on the bevelled corner of an Eixample building, offering four sunny exterior rooms with balconies. All the seven rooms are clean, basic and of a good size, and most have new en suite bathrooms. An exceptionally large triple/quadruple room has its own separate bathroom. The attentive owner, Roser, and her son speak some English.

Hotel services *Air-conditioning. Safe. Telephone. TV.*

Hotel Catalonia Roma

Avda de Roma 31 (93 410 66 33/reservations 900 301 078/fax 93 410 13 52/www.hoteles-catalonia.es). Metro Entença or Sants/27, 30, 32, 43, 44, 78, 215, N7 bus. **Rates** single €87-€121.80; double €106-€141. **Credit** AmEx, DC, MC, V. **Map** p339 B4.

Located near the main Sants station and Plaça d'Espanya, the Roma is a warm, comfortable and elegantly decorated hotel. Some rooms have antique furniture; others are modern. A good breakfast is served in the dining room, which has a pleasant patio coming off it.

Hotel services *Air-conditioning. Bar. Car park. Disabled: adapted rooms (1). Laundry. Restaurant. Safe.* **Room services** *Minibar. Room service (7-10am). Telephone. TV: pay movies/satellite.*

Hotel Ginebra

Rambla Catalunya 1, 3° 1ª (93 317 10 63/fax 93 317 55 65). Metro Catalunya/all buses to Plaça Catalunya. **Rates** single €38.50; double €60.90. **Credit** DC, MC, V. **Map** p342 B1.

As centrally located as can be, this small hotel is housed on the third floor of a gracious old building overlooking Plaça Catalunya and is pleasant and cosy. All rooms have air-conditioning, a TV, telephone and private baths, and the double-glazed windows help keep out the noise. A few rooms have balconies with views over the *plaça*.

Hotel services *Air-conditioning. Car park. Safe. Snack bar.* **Room services** *Telephone. TV: satellite.*

Hotel Gran Vía

Gran Via de les Corts Catalanes 642 (93 318 19 00/ fax 93 318 99 97/www.nnhotels.es). Metro Passeig de Gràcia/7, 16, 17, 22, 24, 28, 42, 47, 50, 54, 56, 62, N1, N2, N3, N9 bus. **Rates** single €70-€80.20; double €107; triple €144.50. **Credit** AmEx, DC, MC, V. **Map** p340 D5.

Amid the renovation fever of 1990s Barcelona, the Gran Via, with its splendid Victorian-rococo interiors, counts as a remarkable survivor. The mansion was built for a wealthy banker in 1873, and has been a hotel since 1936. The bedrooms have been modernised, but no changes have marred the lounge area and mirrored breakfast room with their paintings, chandeliers and gilt frames. To match this look of fading grandeur, the atmosphere is suitably sedate, but the hotel has real charm. There's also a pleasant outdoor patio with a fountain and plants. It's part of the same chain as the Hotel Paral.lel (*see p59*).

Hotel services *Air-conditioning. Garden.*
Room services *Minibar. Room service (8-11am). Safe. Telephone. TV: satellite.*

Hotel Paseo de Gracia

Passeig de Gràcia 102 (93 215 58 24/fax 93 215 06 03). Metro Diagonal/22, 24, 28, 100, 101, N4 bus. **Rates** single €58; double €64. **Credit** V. **Map** p336 D4.

This small, family-run hotel is a monument to several eras, with an 1875 tapestry in reception, 1970s fake-leather, padded furniture, and '60s-style wood-panelled walls – in fact, a more successful blend than it sounds. Lucky guests who get room 307 have a private terrace over Passeig de Gràcia, with the rooftop of La Pedrera and the sea to the left and Tibidabo to the right. Unfortunately, the management will not reserve specific rooms.

Hotel services *Air-conditioning. Safe.*
Room services *Telephone. TV.*

Hotel Pelayo

*C/Pelai 9 (93 302 37 27/fax 93 412 31 68/
www.hotelpelayo.com). Metro Universitat/
bus all routes to Plaça Universitat.* **Rates** (incl
breakfast) single €48; double €72; triple €90.
Credit MC, V. **Map** p342 A1.
This family-run hotel is between Plaça Universitat
and Plaça Catalunya, and is surprisingly quiet for
such a central location. All its 14 rooms are a good
size and have bathrooms, and there is one spacious
and airy exterior room big enough for a family or
group. The interior rooms are set around a patio that
is larger than most, so they get plenty of light. The
owners are friendly and accommodating.
Hotel services *Air-conditioning. Laundry.
Multilingual staff.* **Room services** *Safe.
Telephone. TV.*

Hotel Sant'Àngelo

*C/Consell de Cent 74 (93 423 46 47/fax 93 423
88 40/www.nh-hoteles.es). Metro Rocafort or
Tarragona/27, 109, N0 bus.* **Rates** single
€110.20-€141.20; double €132.70-€170.10; junior
suite €184-€236.50. **Credit** AmEx, DC, MC, V.
Map p339 B5.
A member of the NH hotel chain, the Sant'Àngelo is
located beside the unusual Joan Miró park. The
small, 48-room hotel offers all the comforts of more
expensive places. A notable feature is the lounge
area that gives on to an interior garden.
Hotel services *Air-conditioning. Bar. Car park.
Disabled: adapted rooms (1). Laundry. Restaurant.
Safe.* **Room services** *Minibar. Room service
(7-11am). Telephone. TV; satellite.*

Hotel Splendid

*C/Muntaner 2 (93 451 21 42/fax 93 323 16 84/
www.hotel-splendid.com). Metro Universitat/
24, 41, 55, 64, 91, 141, N6 bus.* **Rates** single
€105.90; double €141.20-€160.50; junior suite
€192.60. **Credit** AmEx, DC, MC, V.
Map p340 C5.
Small, functional and central (just next to Plaça
Universitat), this cheerfully decorated Best Western
hotel has 43 rooms that vary in size, but all have a
minibar, TV and Internet access. A hot and cold
buffet breakfast is available, and there is a little bar.
Hotel services *Air-conditioning. Bar. Car park.
Disabled: adapted rooms (1). Laundry. Multilingual
staff. Non-smoking rooms.* **Room services**
*Minibar. Room service (7am-11pm). Safe. Telephone.
TV: satellite/VCR.*

Budget

Hostal Eden

*C/Balmes 55 (93 454 73 63/fax 93 452 66 21/
www.barcelona-on-line.es/hostaleden). Metro
Passeig de Gràcia/7, 16, 17, 63, 67, 68 bus.*
Rates single €23-€39; double €32-€55; triple
€75-€60. **Credit** AmEx, MC, V. **Map** p336 D4.
The Eden occupies three floors of an old Eixample
building. Right uptown, it's in a good situation for
visiting some of Gaudí's works. Its 33 rooms vary

in facilities; not all have bathrooms, while some have
luxury or whirlpool baths, and others have fridges.
Avoid interior rooms around the small patio and try
for those around the larger patio, which have plenty
of light. The exterior rooms can be noisy.
Hotel services *Internet access. Multilingual
staff. Telephone. Ticket agency.* **Room services**
Safe. TV.

Hostal Fontanella

*Via Laietana 71, 2° (tel/fax 93 317 59 43). Metro
Urquinaona/bus all routes to Plaça Urquinaona.*
Rates single €22.50-€29; double €35.50-€44;
triple €42.80-€62; quadruple €44.40-€66.80.
Credit AmEx, DC, MC, V. **Map** p335 B1.
A beautiful *Modernista* entrance with its original lift
prepares guests for the homely feel of this *pension*,
run by Encarna (with the help of her pet chow,
Benji). Most of the 11 rooms have either a shower or
bath. Clean, cosy and centrally located, it attracts
tourists and business travellers, young and old.
Hotel services *Laundry. Safe.*

Hostal Goya

*C/Pau Claris 74, 1° (93 302 25 65/fax 93 412
04 35/goya@cconline.es). Metro Urquinaona/
41, 55, 141, N4, N8 bus.* **Rates** single €23;
double €48-€39. **Credit** MC, V. **Map** p314 D5.
Just off Plaça Urquinaona, this friendly *pension*
couldn't be better located for visiting the sights and
getting some shopping done. It has recently undergone renovation and expansion, resulting in new
bathrooms, parquet flooring and some rooms having direct access to an attractive, communal patio.
However, some of the original rooms still don't have
bathrooms. Prices vary according to the changes.
Hotel services *Safe. TV room.*

Hostal de Ribagorza

*C/Trafalgar 39 (93 319 19 68/fax 93 319 19 68)
Metro Urquinaona/19, 39, 40, 41, 42, 55, 141, N4
bus.* **Rates** double €38-€50.80; triple €45.20-€54.20.
Credit AmEx, MC, V. **Map** p342 C2.
A peaceful, family-run *pension* in a central area near
the Palau de la Música and the Arc de Triomf. It's
simply decorated throughout, with a pale blue and
white panelled passageway and original floor tiles.
Rooms – all basic and clean – vary in size, but all
have TVs and most have bathrooms. A drinks
machine provides refreshments.
Hotel services *Safe. Telephone.*
Room services *TV.*

Hostal Sofia

*Avda de Roma 1-3, entl (93 419 50 40/fax 93 430
69 43). Metro Sants Estació/27, 30, 32, 43, 44,
78, 215, N7 bus.* **Rates** single €24-€42.20; double
€36.10-€60.20; triple €48.20-€72.30. **Credit** MC, V.
Map p339 B4.
This *pension*, located beside Sants railway station,
is clean and functional and a good base from which
to explore the Plaça d'Espanya-Montjuïc area. Some
of the 18 rooms have TVs; all have baths.
Hotel services *Telephone.*

Pensión Cortés

Gran Vía de les Corts Catalanes 540, pral 2ª (93 454 84 83). Metro Urgell/9, 20, 50, 56, N1, N2, N13, N14, N15 bus. **Rates** €18.10; double €36.10-€42.20; triple €48.20. **No credit cards. Map** p340 C5.

This typically ornate Eixample building – once the mansion of the Count of Rocamora – has been declared of historical and artistic interest by city authorities. The entrance is magnificent, but the part occupied by this simple *pension* has seen better days. However, the metro is on the doorstep and the airport bus stop is nearby.

Hotel services *Telephone. TV.*

Pensión Rondas

C/Girona 4, 3º 2ª (tel 93 232 51 02/fax 93 232 12 25). Metro Urquinaona/19, 39, 40, 41, 42, 55, 141, N4, N11 bus. **Rates** single €21; double €35-€43. **No credit cards. Map** p342 C1.

Here you'll find 11 basic, clean rooms on the third floor of an old Eixample building, in a central but unusually quiet location. Brother-and-sister team David and Sonia run the place, and are exceptionally friendly and helpful. Most rooms have baths or showers, and two of the interior rooms look on to an enormous open-air patio.

Hotel services *Telephone.*

Sants

Expensive

Hotel Catalonia Barcelona Plaza

Plaça Espanya 6-8 (93 426 26 00/fax 93 426 04 00/ plaza@hoteles-catalonia.es). Metro Plaça Espanya/ bus all routes to Plaça Espanya. **Rates** single €141-€212; double €177-€244; suite €257.80-€322. **Credit** AmEx, DC, MC, V. **Map** p339 A5.

The bunker-like façade of this 347-room hotel, looming up beside the Plaça Espanya, hides a splendid and charming interior. The guest rooms at the front (although not very spacious) and the nine tower suites have breathtaking views over the plaça and Montjuïc and its fountains. The ornate breakfast room is magnificently over the top, and the many leisure facilities include a truly stunning rooftop pool. The Plaza is often booked up; November-December and July-August are the easiest times to get in, and lower rates may be available.

Hotel services *Air-conditioning. Babysitting. Bar. Car park. Disabled: adapted rooms (4). Fitness centre (gym/massage/sauna). Laundry. Limousine service. Multilingual staff. Pool (outdoor). Restaurant. Terrace.* **Room services** *Minibar. Room service (24hrs). Safe. Telephone. TV: satellite.*

Mid-range

Hotel Onix

C/Llançà 30 (93 426 00 87/fax 93 426 19 81/ hotelonix@icyesa.es). Metro Espanya/bus all routes to Plaça d'Espanya. **Rates** single €96.30-€127.30; double €119.80-€159.40. **Credit** AmEx, DC, MC, V. **Map** p339 B5.

A comfortable, if functional business hotel off Plaça d'Espanya, close to Sants railway station and with easy access to the airport. The quiet outside rooms have views of the old Arenas bullring on one side, and Parc Joan Miró on the other. All rooms have balconies. The Onix also has a tiny rooftop pool and sundeck, as well as underground parking.

Hotel services *Air-conditioning. Bar. Car park. Disabled: adapted rooms (3). Laundry. Multilingual staff. Pool (outdoor). Ticket agency.* **Room services** *Minibar. Refrigerator. Room service (8am-11pm). Safe. Telephone. TV: satellite.*

Budget

Hostal Béjar

C/Béjar 36-38, 1º-3º, esc B (93 325 59 53). Metro Espanya, Tarragona or Sants Est/27, 127, 109 bus. **Rates** single €24; double €42-€48. **Credit** MC, V. **Map** p339 A4.

Located in the Hostafrancs district, the Béjar is only a five-minute walk from Sants station and the Plaça d'Espanya. Its 22 rooms (six with bathrooms) are in two buildings, with one reception area, and guests have use of a fridge. The owners speak English.

Hotel services *Laundry.*

Pensión Sants

C/Antoni de Capmany 82 (93 331 37 00/ fax 93 421 68 64). Metro Plaça de Sants/ 30, 215, N7 bus. **Rates** single €18-€20; double €29-€30. **Credit** MC, V. **Map** p339 A4.

This large, recently renovated *pension* occupies a seven-storey building just a stone's throw from Sants station. The 76 rooms are bright – including those at the rear – and impeccably clean. Almost all have en suite baths and some have balconies. To avoid street noise and get a spectacular view, ask for a room on the upper floors (all singles are on the seventh floor), preferably with a balcony.

Hotel services *Safe. TV.*
Room services *Telephone.*

Zona Alta

Expensive

Hotel Alimara

C/Berruguete 126 (tel/fax 93 427 00 00/fax 93 427 92 92/www.alimarahotel.com). Metro Montbau/ 10, 27, 60, 73, 76, 85, 173, N4 bus. **Rates** (incl breakfast) single €83.50-€144.40; double €99.90-€166.30; suite €161.80-€235.90. **Credit** AmEx, DC, V.

In an unusual location in the hills of Vall d'Hebron and very near the magical Parc del Laberint, the Alimara is still only 20 minutes by metro from Passeig de Gràcia. It was built in 1992 near the Olympic velodrome and tennis courts, but, unlike many hotels of the same vintage, has an elegant decor and a comfortable, airy atmosphere to go with its modern exterior. The junior suites on the third floor have large terraces with wonderful views; more spectacular still are the views from the glass lift and La Ronda restaurant. Good weekend rates are offered, and it's also handy for anyone coming to Barcelona by car.

Hotel services *Air-conditioning. Bar. Car park. Disabled: adapted rooms (4). Garden. Laundry. Multilingual staff. Non-smoking rooms. Restaurant. Ticket agency.* **Room services** *Minibar. Room service (7am-1am). Safe. Telephone. TV/VCR.*

Mid-range

Hotel Guillermo Tell

C/Guillem Tell 49 (93 415 40 00/fax 93 217 34 65/info@guillemhotel.com). Metro Fontana or Lesseps/FGC Plaça Molina/16, 17, 27, 31, 32 bus. **Rates** single €106.60-€127.90; double €135-€162; suite €179-€215. **Credit** MC, V. **Map** p336 D2.

The independently owned Hotel Guillermo Tell (William Tell) is located in a residential part of upper Barcelona near Plaça Molina, but is still just three metro stops from Plaça Catalunya. Opened in 2000, the 61-room hotel has warm, colonial-style furnishings throughout, and bright, airy rooms. Of the 46 exterior rooms, those looking on to C/Guillem Tell are more spacious than those on the C/Lincoln side. Lower prices are available at weekends and in some special-offer months (January, mid July to mid September, December).

Hotel services *Air-conditioning. Bar. Car park. Disabled: adapted rooms (2). Laundry. Restaurant. Safe.* **Room services** *Minibar. Telephone. TV.*

Hotel Via Augusta

Via Augusta 63 (93 217 92 50/fax 93 237 77 14/reservas@hotelviaaugusta.com). Metro Fontana/FGC Gràcia/16, 17, 22, 24, 25, 28, 31, 32, N4 bus. **Rates** single €51.70-€67.40; double €80.30-€84.50; triple €105.90. **Credit** AmEx, DC, MC, V. **Map** p336 D3.

In an elegant building in Sant Gervasi, on the edge of Gràcia, this is a pleasant hotel with superior

A taste of the Oriente

Sitting in state like the grande dame of La Rambla, the Hotel Oriente has lived many lives. A Franciscan monastery was built on the site in the 17th century, only to be sold during the divestiture of religious buildings in the 1830s. Parts of the monastery, including the cloisters, are still discernible in what was later to become the ballroom, and to this day some of the first-floor rooms are higher than the corridor, the step having been used originally as a kneeler for night prayer. In the basement are the remains of a crypt, and the entrance to a vaulted tunnel that once led to the Capuchin monastery on the site now occupied by the Plaça Reial.

With the riches that the industrial revolution brought to Barcelona in the mid 19th century, the area around La Rambla saw the inauguration of many great buildings – the Liceu opera house, also built on the site of an old monastery, opened in 1848 – but the Oriente was the first of the 'grand hotels' to open, in 1842. It was a great social event. Such luxury had never been seen. Guests could even have a rudimentary bath – consisting of a wooden tub with shower incorporated (a servant holding the hose).

Over the years, the Oriente has played host to many illustrious travellers, including Hans Christian Andersen, General Grant and, in 1913, ex-Sultan Muley Hafid of Morocco, who was given to leaning over his balcony at midday to toss basketfuls of coins to passers-by, creating great revelry. Four years later, during the 1917 general strike, the same balcony was used as a platform by politicians trying to calm protesters on La Rambla, though even that did not compare to the commotion over the arrival in 1924 of silent-screen star Mary Pickford, and, later, over Errol Flynn. The hotel's proximity to the Liceu also made it a favourite with musicians: Toscanini and Maria Callas both stayed here.

The Oriente was rebuilt in the 1880s, and in 1929, coinciding with the International Exhibition, the cloisters were covered to become a ballroom and banquet hall. After all this historical drama, the bedrooms themselves (142 in total) can come as a disappointment, being rather plain, but many are furnished with antiques, and the brass door plaques naming famous former guests give a sense of past glories.

Hotel Oriente

La Rambla 45-47, Barri Gòtic (93 302 25 58/fax 93 412 38 19/www.husa.es). Metro Drassanes/14, 38, 59, 91, N9, N12 bus. **Rates** single €84.20-€100; double €122.70; triple €169.80. **Credit** AmEx, DC, MC, V. **Map** p343 A3.

Hotel services *Bar. Conference facilities. Fax. Lifts. Multilingual staff. Restaurant.* **Room services** *Room service (7am-10pm). Safe. Telephone. TV.*

facilities. The atmosphere is friendly and its 56 rooms are modern and bright, with en suite bathrooms – although the rooms facing Via Augusta can be a bit noisy. The buffet breakfast is generous.
Hotel services *Air-conditioning. Car park. Disabled: adapted rooms (1). Laundry. Multilingual staff. Ticket agency.* **Room services** *Safe. Telephone. TV: satellite.*

Apartment hotels

Apartment hotels are made up of self-contained small flats with kitchen facilities, plus maid service. They are good for slightly longer stays, and usually offer reduced monthly or longer term rates.

Apartaments Calàbria

C/Calàbria 129, Eixample (93 426 42 28/fax 93 426 76 40/calabria@city-hotels.es). Metro Rocafort/9, 41, 50, 56, N1, N2, N13, N14, N15 bus. **Rates** *Per night* one person €103.40; two people €118.20; each additional person €29.50. *Per month* €1,477.60. **Credit** AmEx, MC, V. **Map** p339 B5.

This Eixample apartment block houses 72 functional, short-term apartments with good kitchen and bathroom facilities, plus separate lounge areas. Office services are available. Book well in advance.
Hotel services *Air-conditioning. Laundry. Multilingual staff.* **Room services** *Safe. Telephone. TV: satellite.*

Aparthotel Bertran

C/Bertran 150, Zona Alta (93 212 75 50/fax 93 418 71 03/www.hotelbertran.com). Metro Vallcarca/ FGC Tibidabo/16, 17, 74 bus. **Rates** single €91; double €112.30. **Credit** AmEx, DC, MC, V.
In the residential Putxet area, near Tibidabo and with good vehicle access to the *rondas*, these 30 apartments are spacious and bright, with good facilities. Most have balconies, some have larger terraces, and there are more extras than at most aparthotels: a gym, cycle rental, a rooftop terrace and a pool.
Hotel services *Air-conditioning. Car park. Fitness centre (gym). Laundry. Multilingual staff. Pool (outdoor). Safe. Ticket agency.* **Room services** *Telephone. TV: satellite.*

Atenea Aparthotel

C/Joan Güell 207-211, Zona Alta (93 490 66 40/ fax 93 490 64 20/www.apartahotelatenea.com). Metro Les Corts/bus all routes to Plaça Maria Cristina. **Rates** *Per night* single studio or apartment €161.10; double studio or apartment €180.50; third person supplement €25.80. *Per month* €3,094. **Credit** AmEx, DC, MC, V. **Map** p335 A3.
A large (105 apartments), 1990s aparthotel offering four-star facilities, including bar, restaurant and conference rooms, in the heart of the business district. Apartments are efficiently organised with first-rate technology, without having any great character. A food shopping service is available on request.
Hotel services *Air conditioning. Bar. Car park. Disabled: adapted rooms (4). Multilingual staff. Restaurant.* **Room services** *Room service (7am-11pm). Safe. Telephone. TV: satellite.*

Apartment/room rentals

Barcelona Allotjament

C/Pelai 12, pral B, Eixample (tel/fax 93 268 43 57/ www.barcelona-allotjament.com). Metro Universitat or Catalunya/bus all routes to Plaça Universitat or Plaça Catalunya. **Open** 10am-2pm, 5-7pm Mon-Thur; 10am-2pm Fri. Closed afternoons July & all Aug. **No credit cards. Map** p342 A1.
Rooms with local families (B&B, half-board or full-board), in shared student flats, aparthotels, hotels or private apartments can be booked through this agency, aimed mainly at students, but catering for business and individual travellers, too. Short-term B&B rates start at €60 per day (for students); long-term (course-length) B&B stays cost €270-€720 per month, plus a €100 agency fee. Courses (in dance, languages, cookery) are also offered.

B&B Norma Agency

C/Ali Bei 11, 3° 2ª, Eixample (tel/fax 93 232 37 66).
Metro Arc de Triomf/19, 39, 40, 41, 42, 55, 141
bus. **Open** 24hr answer machine. **Map** p342 C1.
Rooms booked on a B&B basis in private homes, or
whole apartments, in Barcelona and along the coast,
for short or long-term stays. B&B rates begin at
around €36.10 per night for a single room, or
€48.20-€75.30 for doubles.

Habit Servei

C/Muntaner 200, 2° 3ª, Eixample (93 209 50 45/
fax 93 414 54 25/www.habitservei.com). FGC
Provença/ bus 58, 64, 66, 67, 68. **Open** 10am-
2pm, 4-7pm Mon-Fri. **Credit** DC, MC, V.
Map p336 C3.
This agency can find rooms in flats for anyone
staying in Barcelona for at least two weeks. Rates
are about €322.50 a month for a flatshare, or €253
for a room in a private house. Whole flats are also
available. The agency fee (€108) is payable only
when a suitable place is found, and a deposit is
returned at the end of the stay. English is spoken,
and it's popular with Erasmus students.

Youth hostels

Rates can vary by season. For student and
youth services and websites that can take
reservations for hostels, *see p318.*

Alberg Mare de Déu de Montserrat

Passeig de la Mare de Déu del Coll 41-51, Horta
(93 210 51 51/fax 93 210 07 98/www.tujuca.com).
Metro Vallcarca/25, 28, 87, N4 bus. **Open** *Hostel*
8am-midnight daily (ring for entry after hours).
Reception 8am-3pm, 4.30-11pm daily. **Rates**
€13 under-25s; €16.30 over-25s. **Credit** MC,V.
This 183-bed hostel, in a pleasant old house with a
garden, is some way from the centre, but not far
from a metro station and Parc Güell. Rooms sleep
two to eight people. IYHF cards are required.
Hotel services *Car park. Dining room. Disabled:*
adapted rooms (1). Internet access. Laundry.
Multilingual staff. Safe. TV/video room.

Albergue Kabul

Plaça Reial 17, Barri Gòtic (93 318 51 90/
fax 93 301 40 34/www.kabul-hostel.com).
Metro Liceu/14, 38, 59, 91, N9, N12 bus.
Open 24hrs daily. **Rates** €12-€18.10 per person.
No credit cards. Map p343 A3.
This popular hostel, currently undergoing a complete renovation, is one of the most welcoming in the
city. The large, rustic-style lounge, with games
room, has windows looking on to Plaça Reial, and
the café-restaurant is open 24 hours a day. Rooms
can be cramped but are functional, sleeping four, six
or eight people. The communal washing facilities
are excellent. Reservations are not accepted.
Hotel services *Billiard table. Café-restaurant.*
Laundry. Lounge. Multilingual staff. Safe.
Telephone. TV: satellite/VCR. **Room services**
Lockers.

Hostal Hedy Holiday

C/Buenaventura Muñoz 4, Eixample (93 300 57 85/
fax 93 300 94 44/www.hedyhostal.com). Metro Arc
de Triomf/39, 41, 51 bus. **Rates** (incl breakfast)
€15.10 per person; double €21.10. **No credit cards.**
Map p341 E6.
Located beside the Parc de la Ciutadella, this hostel
is spacious and has good facilities, including a bar-
restaurant with eight Internet-connected computers.
All rooms have central heating, with large, individual lockers. Rooms sleep two, six or ten. It's open 24
hours, and staff are helpful and friendly.
Hotel services *Air-conditioning. Bar. Cafeteria.*
Internet access. Laundry. Lockers. Lounge.
Multilingual staff. Telephone.

Itaca Alberg-Hostel

C/Ripoll 21, Barri Gòtic (93 301 97 51/
www.itaca hostel.com). Metro Urquinaona/
17, 19, 40, 45, N8 bus. **Open** *Reception*
7am-4am daily. **Rates** dormitory €15; twin
€18. **Credit** MC, V. **Map** p342 B2.
This funky, colourful hostel, a stone's throw from
the cathedral, opened in summer 2001 and looks
destined to be a great success. Nuria and Cristina
have made the reception area fabulously welcoming,
with murals, sofas, Internet access and great music,
and the kitchen is also popular meeting spot. There
are 33 beds in five airy dormitories, all with balconies, and one twin-bedded room with bathroom.
Hotel services *Air-conditioning. Internet access.*
Kitchen. Lockers. Café-lounge.

Campsites

For more information on campsites not far from
the city, get the *Catalunya Campings* brochure
from the Palau Robert *(see p321).* As well as the
rates listed below, there are extra charges for
cars, motorbikes, caravans, tents and light.

Estrella de Mar

Autovia de Castelldefels km 16.7, Castelldefels
(93 633 07 84). **Open** *Reception* 9am-1.30pm,
3.30pm-midnight daily. *Campsite* 7.30am-midnight
daily. **Rates** *Per person* €4.50; € 3.50 under-10s.
Per bungalow (5 people) €42.80. **Credit** MC, V.
This campsite is between Barcelona and Sitges, a
good location for a city and beach holiday. Basic
services include a bar, restaurant and supermarket,
and it's open all year.

Masnou

Carretera N2, km 633, El Masnou, Outer Limits
(tel/fax 93 555 15 03). **Open** *Reception Winter* 9am-
1pm, 2.30-7pm daily. *Summer* 8am-1pm, 2.30pm-10pm
daily. *Campsite* 7am-11.30pm daily. **Rates** *Per person*
€4.80; €3.90 under-10s. **No credit cards.**
Near the coast north of Barcelona, this small campsite has a bar, restaurant and supermarket (open
June-September), kids' playground and pools.
There's a sandy beach nearby, with diving and sailing. Bungalows (€16.10-€22.60 per person per day)
and rooms (double €29-€36.70) can also be rented.

Sightseeing

Features

Introduction

An overview of Barcelona's *barris*, and the best ways to get around them.

Over the past 20 years or so, Barcelona has undergone a dramatic transformation from a dusty port, notorious for rowdy sailors, prostitutes and inept waiters, to become one of the world's most celebrated (and ongoing) examples of urban planning, with an incomparable mix of tradition, modernity, style, unique architecture and vivid streetlife. Along with its seaside location and agreeable climate, the city has a compactness that makes it easy to explore, with many sights within enjoyable walking distance of each other. When places are further afield, an excellent transport system makes them readily accessible.

Pick up any map of Barcelona and you will see a tightly packed mass of narrow streets bordered by Avda Paral.lel, the Ciutadella park, Plaça Catalunya and the sea. This is the area that fell within the medieval walls and, until 150 years ago, made up the entire city. At its heart is the **Barri Gòtic** (Gothic Quarter), a body of interconnecting streets and buildings from Barcelona's Golden Age. Its twisting streets grew inside the original Roman wall; then, as Barcelona's wealth increased in the Middle Ages, new communities developed around the Roman perimeter. These areas, **La Mercè**, **Sant Pere** and **La Ribera**, were brought within the city with the building of a second wall in the 13th century. The area south of this wall, on the other side of the riverbed later to become the Rambla, was the **Raval**, enclosed within a third city wall built in the 14th century. All Barcelona's great medieval buildings are within this old walled city, except a very few – most notably the superb Gothic monastery of **Pedralbes** (*see p127*) – which were built in open countryside. Barcelona grew little between 1450 and 1800. The old walls remained standing, and the city's first modern industries developed inside them. Factories also appeared in small towns on the surrounding plain, such as **Gràcia**, **Sants**, **Sant Martí** and **Sant Andreu**. The walls finally came down in the 1850s, and Barcelona extended across the plain following Ildefons Cerdà's plan for the **Eixample** (*see p35*). With its long, straight streets, this became the city's second great characteristic district, and the location for many of the greatest works of *Modernista* creativity between 1880 and 1914 – although there are others to be found in many parts of the city. Beyond the Eixample lie the green mountains of **Montjuïc** and, at the centre of the great ridge of the Serra de Collserola, **Tibidabo**, both towering above Barcelona and providing wonderful views.

Each of Barcelona's traditional districts (*barris*) has its own resilient, often idiosyncratic character. However, since the 1970s the city has undergone an unprecedented physical transformation, in a burst of urban renovation unequalled in Europe. Areas such as Montjuïc (with the main stadium), the **Port Olímpic** and the **beach** were rebuilt or created from next to nothing for the 1992 Olympics; since then the pace of renovation has not let up, with the spectacular reinvention of the old harbour,

The best Places

For idle wandering
La Rambla (*see p79*), Barri Gòtic (*see p74*) and **Montjuïc** (*see p105*).

For art attacks
Fundació Miró (*see p107*), Museu Picasso (*see p97*) and **MACBA** (*see p89*).

For communing with nature
Parc Güell (*see p121*), Parc de la Ciutadella (*see p93*) and Parc del Laberint (*see p131*).

For communing with God
The Catedral (*see p77*), Santa Maria del Mar (*see p98*) and Sagrada Família (*see p118*).

For Gaudí and friends
Palau de la Música (*see p98*), La Mansana de la Discordia (*see p117*) and La Pedrera (*see p116*).

For grown-up kids
Font Màgica (*see p106*), Museu FC Barcelona (*see p133*) and Tibidabo funfair (*see p222*).

For escaping the crowds
Museu Marès (*see p79*), Hospital de Sant Pau (*see p117*) and Monestir de Pedralbes (*see p127*).

The city awaits, so jump to it.

Port Vell, the dramatic urban surgery performed in the Raval, and attention now moving to the Diagonal-Mar project, in the very north of the city. In the process the identities of individual *barris* have been pushed and pulled in many directions, and sometimes changed beyond recognition.

Barcelona has entered squarely into the post-industrial age, as a city with big ambitions. Most of its factories are now in the **Zona Franca**, the industrial zone between Montjuïc and the airport. Within the city, old factories that had not moved out have been encouraged to do so, while the shells of those that did leave have become art spaces, sports centres, studios, clubs or restaurants. The ultimate aim, according to former mayor Pasqual Maragall, has been 'for Barcelona to become a city of services'.

Discount schemes

Barcelona offers a variety of tour facilities and discount schemes that give reduced admission to many attractions. Where discounts apply, this is indicated in the listings below and throughout the guide with the abbreviations **BC** (Barcelona Card), **BT** (Bus Turístic), **RM** (Ruta del Modernisme) and **Articket**. For tourist offices, *see p320*, and for regular city transport, *see p304*.

Articket
Rates €15.
The Articket is a joint-entry ticket for six major arts centres: **MNAC** (*see p108*), which includes the **Museu d'Art Modern** (*see p96*), **MACBA** (*see p89*), the **Fundació Miró** (*see p107*), **Espai Gaudí-La Pedrera** (*see p116*), the **Fundació Tàpies** (*see p116*) and the **CCCB** (*see p89*). With the Articket, admission to each is roughly half the standard price. You can visit them at any time within three months from the date of purchase; the ticket is available from participating venues and via Tel-entrada (*see p210*).

Barcelona Card
Rates *24hrs* €16.25; €13.20 concessions. *48hrs* €19.25; €16.25 concessions. *72hrs* €22.25; €19.25 concessions.
A discount scheme run by the city tourist authority, Barcelona Turisme. For the time stipulated (24, 48 or 72 hours), the Barcelona Card gives you unlimited transport on the metro and city buses, and discounts on the airport bus, Montjuïc funicular and cable cars, as well as discounted entry to a wide variety of museums, theatres and clubs, and discounted prices at several shops and restaurants (a current list comes with the card). It is sold in the airport, at city tourist offices (*see p320*) and at branches of El Corte Inglés (*see p184*).

Ruta del Modernisme
Centre del Modernisme, Casa Amatller, Passeig de Gràcia 41, Eixample (93 488 01 39/www.bcn.es). Metro Passeig de Gràcia/7, 16, 17 22, 24, 28 bus. **Open** 10am-7pm Mon-Sat; 10am-2pm Sun. **Tickets** €3.60; €2.40 concessions; free under-10s. **No credit cards. Map** p340 D5.
Multi-access ticket giving 50% discount on entry to many *Modernista* buildings (and at some restaurants); a guidebook is available, and guided tours are often included. Ticket is valid for 30 days.

Ways to see the city

The 'Bus Gaudí' will run from March to September 2002 for 'International Year of Gaudí', and will include discounts for some buildings. Check with tourist offices for more details.

Barcelona by Bicycle

Un Cotxe Menys, C/Esparteria 3, La Ribera (93 268 21 05). Metro Barceloneta/14, 17, 39, 40, 45, 51 bus. **Tours** 10am Sat, Sun. **Rates** €20. **No credit cards. Map** p343 C3-4.
This bicycle shop offers tours of the city, bike hire included, lasting 2½hrs. Booking essential.

My Favourite Things

93 329 53 51/637 26 54 05/www.myft.net.
Walking tours of the city (€24-€30), with routes based on food, textiles and other themes, or kids' tours including a trip to the Fundació Miró. Phone or check out the funky website for details.

Museu d'Història tours

Museu d'Història de la Ciutat, C/Veguer 2, Barri Gòtic (93 315 11 11/www.bcn.es/icub). Metro Jaume I/17, 19, 40, 45 bus. **Tours** *Nit al Museu* 9pm Tue, Wed June-Sept. *Ruta del Gòtic* 10am Sat (phone to confirm months).* **Tickets** Nit al Museu €5.40; Ruta del Gòtic €6; various concessions. **Advance tickets** Servi-Caixa. **No credit cards. Map** p343 B3.
Several interesting tours, especially Una Nit al Museu, a great night tour around the buildings of Plaça del Rei. Always check timings.

Rodamolls

Tours *Mid June-mid Sept* 11am-9.30pm daily. *Mid Sept-Oct, Apr-mid June* 11am-9.30pm Sat, Sun. Closed Nov-Mar. **Tickets** €1.80; €1.50 concessions; free under-3s. **Discounts** BT. **No credit cards.**
The 'quay wanderer' is a special bus service that follows a route around the port area, from Colom to Port Olímpic and back.

Walking tours

906 301 282/www.barcelonaturisme.com.
Tours 10am (English), noon (Catalan/Spanish) Sat, Sun. **Tickets** €7; €3 4-12s. **Discounts** BC, BT. **No credit cards. Map** p342 B1.
Professional English-speaking guides take visitors around the Barri Gòtic on foot in an informative tour of about 1½hrs. Numbers are limited, so book ahead via the tourist offices.

On the buses

If you want a change from street-pounding, there are a couple of ways to let the sights and the neighbourhoods come to you.

The **Bus Turístic** (*pictured*) is an open-topped tourist bus, with two circular routes, both running through Plaça Catalunya: the northern (red) route passes La Pedrera, Sagrada Família, Parc Güell, Tibidabo and Pedralbes; the southern (blue) route takes in Montjuïc, Port Vell, Vila Olímpica and the Barri Gòtic. Both routes are one-way. Ticket holders get discount vouchers for a large range of attractions, which can be used at any time. The new bus on the block, the orange, open-topped **Barcelona Tours**, has a single one-way route, which covers most of the same attractions, with slightly fewer stops. Where it does stop, no indication is given; the problem being that the city council is dragging its feet over allowing the bus company to erect signs – which may or may not be connected to the fact that the council part-owns the rival fleet.

The main difference between the two is the commentary: on the Bus Turístic this amounts to a rather garbled barking, with the languages difficult to tell apart, while on Barcelona Tours there is an informed recorded commentary via headphones. With both buses, you can buy tickets on board and get on and off as many times as you wish during the day. The entire route (without stopping) takes three hours on Barcelona Tours and 90 minutes on each of the Bus Turístic routes. The former is less frequent, but usually less crowded – perhaps because no one knows where to get on.

Bus Turístic

Tours *Apr-28 Oct* 9am-9pm daily. *29 Oct-Mar* 9am-7pm daily. Approx every 10min. **Tickets** *1 day* €14; €8 4-12s. *2 days* €18. Free under-4s. Available from tourist offices or on board bus. **No credit cards.**

Barcelona Tours

93 317 64 54. **Tours** *May-Sept* 9am-9pm daily. *Oct-Apr* 9am-8pm daily. Approx every 20min. **Tickets** *1 day* €15; €9 7-14s. *2 days* €18.60; €12 7-14s. Free under-7s. Available on board bus. **No credit cards.**
Prices are liable to rise after March 2002.

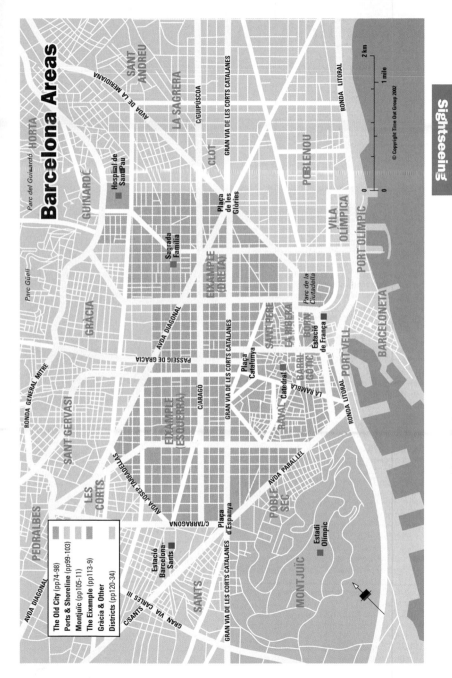

Barcelona Areas

Parc del Guinardó

HORTA

GUINARDÓ

SANT ANDREU

AVDA DE LA MERIDIANA

LA SAGRERA

C/GUIPUSCOA

Hospital de Sant Pau

CLOT

GRAN VIA DE LES CORTS CATALANES

RONDA LITORAL

Parc Güell

Sagrada Família

EIXAMPLE (DRETA)

POBLENOU

© Copyright Time Out Group 2002

GRÀCIA

Plaça de les Glòries

VILA OLÍMPICA

AVDA DIAGONAL

PASSEIG DE GRÀCIA

PORT OLÍMPIC

RONDA GENERAL MITRE

SANT GERVASI

Parc de la Ciutadella

BARCELONETA

EIXAMPLE (ESQUERRA)

C/ARAGÓ

GRAN VIA DE LES CORTS CATALANES

Plaça Catalunya

SANT PERE

LA RIBERA

BORN

Estació de França

PORT VELL

AVDA JOSEP TARRADELLAS

SANT GERVASI

LES CORTS

RAVAL

BARRI GÒTIC

Catedral

LA RAMBLA

RONDA LITORAL

PEDRALBES

AVDA PARAL·LEL

POBLE SEC

AVDA DIAGONAL

Plaça d'Espanya

C/TARRAGONA

Estadi Olímpic

Estació Barcelona-Sants

GRAN VIA DE LES CORTS CATALANES

SANTS

C/SANTS

GRAN VIA CARLES III

MONTJUÏC

The Old City (pp74-98)
Ports & Shoreline (pp99-103)
Montjuïc (pp105-11)
The Eixample (pp113-9)
Gràcia & Other Districts (pp120-34)

2 km
1 mile

The Old City

Lose yourself in medieval labyrinths or find yourself in tranquil parks.

The Old City appears on the map as an elongated hexagon, following the outline of the city's third and final wall, built in the 14th century. The area is divided into three distinct neighbourhoods, with the **Barri Gòtic** separated from the **Raval** by the mile-long, tree-lined **La Rambla**, and from **Sant Pere**, **La Ribera** and **Born** by the noisy thoroughfare of the Via Laietana.

Barri Gòtic

In the first century BC Roman soldiers established a colony on a small hill called the Mons Taber, the precise centre of which was long believed to have been marked by a round millstone set into the paving of C/Paradis, between the cathedral and the Plaça Sant Jaume. The real centre of the Roman city, however, was a road junction that occupied one part of the modern Plaça Sant Jaume. Large sections of the Roman wall can still be seen (*see p8* **Do as the Romans did**).

When Barcelona began to revive under the Catalan Counts, its social and political core stayed where it had been under the Romans. As a result, it became the site of what is now one of the most complete surviving ensembles of medieval buildings – from churches to private residences – in Europe.

The Gothic **cathedral** is the third cathedral to be built on the same site; the first was in the sixth century. Many buildings around here represent history written in stone. In C/Santa Llúcia, just in front of the cathedral, is **Casa de l'Ardiaca**, originally an 15th-century residence with a superb tiled patio, which now houses the city archives. It was renovated recently, and before that in the 1870s, when it acquired its curious letterbox by the *Modernista* architect Domènech i Montaner showing swallows and a tortoise, believed by some to symbolise the contrast between the swiftness of truth and the 'law's delay', or by others, rather more prosaically, to be a reflection on the postal service. On the other side of Plaça Nova from the Casa de l'Ardiaca is the **Col.legi d'Arquitectes**, with architectural exhibitions. In Plaça Sant Iu, on the north side of the cathedral, is **Museu Frederic Marès**; nearby is the **Museu Diocesà**, housing religious art.

Plaça Sant Felip Neri. *See p75.*

Alongside the cathedral the Catalan monarchs built the various sections of the Palau Reial (Royal Palace), clustered around the superbly preserved medieval square, the **Plaça del Rei**. With additions from different periods piled on top of each other, the *plaça* gives a vivid impression of the nature of life in the medieval city, particularly since the square, as well as receiving all the traffic of the court, also served as the main flour and fodder market. It is reasonably certain that Ferdinand and Isabella received Columbus on his first return from America either on the palace steps or in the **Saló del Tinell** behind, although miserable sceptics still place the story in doubt. The square is an acoustically challenged but unbeatably atmospheric venue for summer concerts in the **Grec** festival (*see p217*).

Most of the sections of the Palau Reial now form part of the **Museu d'Història de la Ciutat**. Even after Catalonia lost its indigenous monarchy in the 15th century, this complex was still the seat of the viceroys who then governed the country. To the left of the palace steps is the 16th-century viceroys' palace, with its five-tiered watchtower, the Mirador del Rei Martí. Local civil administration, meanwhile, was centred in nearby Plaça Sant Jaume, the main square of the old city and still the administrative centre of modern Barcelona. It contains both the City Hall (**Ajuntament**) and the seat of the Catalan regional government (**Palau de la Generalitat**), standing opposite each other in occasional rivalry. They have not always done so: the square was only opened up in 1823, after which the present neo-classical façade was added to the Ajuntament. That of the Generalitat is older, from 1398 to 1602. The greater part of both buildings, however, was built in the early 15th century, and both of their original main entrances open on to the street now called Bisbe Irurita on one side of the *plaça*, and Ciutat on the other.

The district's antiquity is genuine, but the idea of it as a 'Gothic Quarter' is a fairly recent invention, from the 1920s. To help the image stick, a few touches were made to enhance the area's 'Gothicness'. One of the most photographed features of the Barri Gòtic, the 'Bridge of Sighs' across C/Bisbe from the Generalitat, is actually a completely new addition, from 1928.

The narrow streets bounded by Carrers Banys Nous, Call and Bisbe once housed a rich Jewish ghetto, or Call. At the corner of C/Sant Domènec del Call and C/Marlet is the medieval **synagogue**, recently restored and due to reopen in early 2002. At C/Marlet 1 is a 12th-century inscription from a long demolished house, on a stone that was placed there in the 1820s. Hebrew inscriptions can also be seen on stones set into the eastern wall of the **Plaça Sant Iu**, across from the cathedral, and at ankle level in the south-west corner of the Plaça del Rei. The area is best known these days, however, for its antique shops. To walk around this area is to delight in what is perhaps the most satisfying and peaceful part of the Barri Gòtic. Near the centre of the Call is the beautiful little **Plaça Sant Felip Neri**, with a fine baroque church and a soothing fountain.

Close by are the leafily attractive **Plaça del Pi** and **Plaça Sant Josep Oriol**, where there are some great pavement bars, and painters exhibit work at weekends. The squares are separated by **Santa Maria del Pi**, one of Barcelona's most distinguished – but least visited – Gothic churches, with a magnificent rose window. Another attraction of the streets between the Rambla and Via Laietana is the wonderful variety of their shops, from the oldest in Barcelona to smart modern arcades to the clubwear shops found on **C/Portaferrissa**.

Despite the expansion of Barcelona into the Eixample, the old centre has remained a hub of cultural, social and political life. In C/Montsió, a narrow street off Portal de l'Angel, is the **Els Quatre Gats** café (*see p172*), legendary haunt of Picasso and other artists and bohemians. Between C/Portaferrissa and Plaça del Pi lies **C/Petritxol**, one of the most charming streets of the Barri Gòtic, known for its traditional *granges* offering coffee and

Café terrace at **Museu Marès**. *See p79.*

Plaça Reial.

cakes, but which also houses the **Sala Parés** (*see p229*), the city's oldest art gallery, where Rusiñol, Casas and the young Picasso all exhibited. On the other side of C/Portaferrissa, heading up C/Bot, you come to the sorely mistreated **Plaça Vila de Madrid**, where there are the excavated remains of a Roman necropolis. Between here and the Plaça Catalunya is the marvellous little Romanesque church of **Santa Anna**, begun in 1141 as part of a monastery then outside the walls, and with an exquisite 14th-century cloister.

Back on the seaward side of the Barri Gòtic, if you walk from Plaça Sant Jaume up C/Ciutat, to the left of the Ajuntament, and turn down the narrow alley of C/Hércules you will come to **Plaça Sant Just**, a fascinating old square with a Gothic water fountain from 1367 and the grand church of **Sants Just i Pastor**, built in the 14th century on the site of a chapel founded by Charlemagne's son Louis the Pious.

The area between here and the port is correctly called La Mercè, and has a different atmosphere from the Barri Gòtic proper – shabbier and with less prosperous shops. Its heart is the **Plaça Reial**, known for its bars and cheap hotels, and a favourite spot for a drink or an outdoor meal – provided you don't mind the odd drunk and are prepared to keep an eye on your bags. An addition from the

1840s, the plaça has the Tres Gràcies fountain in the centre and lamp-posts designed by the young Gaudí. On Sunday mornings a coin and stamp market is held here. Plaça Reial has had a dangerous reputation in the past, but has been made safer by heavy policing, and the opening of new restaurants and clubs. Such are the fickle ways of Barcelona fashion that C/Escudellers, the next street towards the port, once a deeply dubious and shabby prostitutes' alley, is now a trendy place for grungy, hip socialising, with a string of cheap, studenty bars.

It's hard to imagine, but the streets nearest the port, particularly **C/Ample**, were until the building of the Eixample the most fashionable in the city. The grand porticos of some buildings – once wealthy merchants' mansions – still give evidence of former glories. Here too is the church of the **Mercè**, home of Barcelona's patron virgins, and the place where Barça football club has to come to properly dedicate its victories. There are also a dwindling number of lively *tascas*, small traditional tapas bars, on C/Mercè. Most of this area, however, became steadily more run-down throughout the 20th century. The city authorities made huge efforts to change this, particularly in the 1990s, when new squares were opened up: **Plaça George Orwell** on C/Escudellers, known as the 'Plaça del Trippy' by the youthful crowd that hangs out there and the subject of much heated debate when CCTV was introduced in 2001 (the irony of which was lost on no one), and **Plaça Joaquim Xirau**, off the Rambla. Another tactic was the siting of parts of the Universitat Pompeu Fabra on the lower Rambla. Flats in run-down areas of the old city are popular with young foreigners, who don't object to their condition as much as local families do.

Beyond C/Ample and the Mercè you emerge from narrow alleys on to the **Passeig de Colom**, where a few shipping offices and ships' chandlers still recall the dockside atmosphere of former decades. The pretty **Plaça Medinaceli**, off to one side, was the setting for some of the scenes in Almodóvar's *Todo Sobre Mi Madre*. Monolithic on Passeig de Colom is the army headquarters, the **Capitanía General**, with a façade that has the distinction of being the one construction in Barcelona directly attributable to the dictatorship of Primo de Rivera.

Ajuntament de Barcelona

Plaça Sant Jaume (93 402 70 00/special visits 93 402 73 64/ww.bcn.es). Metro Liceu or Jaume I/ 14, 17, 19, 38, 40, 45, 59 bus. **Open** *Office 8.30am-2.30pm Mon-Fri. Visits 10am-2pm Sun.* **Admission** free. **Map** p343 B3.
The centrepiece of the Ajuntament is the stately 15th-century Saló de Cent, flanked by the semi-circular Saló de la Reina Regent, where council

meetings are still held, and the Saló de Cròniques, spectacularly painted with murals by Josep Maria Sert. Visitors can see the main rooms on Sundays. The entrance to the tourist information office and gift shop is on the C/Ciutat side, next to the old entrance; a work of Catalan Gothic contrasting completely with the main entrance.

Catedral de Barcelona

Pla de la Seu (93 315 15 54). Metro Jaume I/17, 19, 40, 45 bus. **Open** *Cathedral* 8am-1.30pm, 4-7.30pm Mon-Fri; 8am-1.30pm, 5-7.30pm Sat. *Cloister* 9am-1.15pm, 4-7pm daily. *Museum* 10am-1pm daily. **Admission** Cathedral & cloister free; museum €1; choir 90¢. **No credit cards. Map** p343 B3.

The first cathedral on this site was founded in the sixth century, but the present one dates from between 1298 and 1430, except for its façade, only completed in a rather un-Catalan Gothic-revival style in 1913 during the 'rediscovery' of medieval Barcelona. Not all is Gothic: in the far right corner of the cathedral, looking at the façade, is the older and simpler Romanesque chapel of Santa Llúcia. The most striking aspect of the cathedral is its volume: it has three naves of near-equal width. It contains many images, paintings and sculptures, and an intricately carved choir built in the 1390s.

The cathedral museum, in the 17th-century chapter house, has paintings and sculptures, including works by the Gothic masters Jaume Huguet, Bernat Martorell and Bartolomé Bermejo. In the crypt is the alabaster tomb of Santa Eulàlia, local Christian martyr and first patron saint of Barcelona. The cloister, bathed in light filtered through arches, palms and fountains, is the most attractive section of the cathedral, and an atmospheric retreat from the city. It contains some white geese, which are said to represent the purity of Santa Eulàlia. Inside the cathedral, there is also a lift to the roof, for a magnificent view of the Old City.

Col.legi d'Arquitectes

Plaça Nova 5, Barri Gòtic (93 301 50 00/ www.coac.net). Metro Jaume I/17, 19, 40, 45 bus. **Open** 10am-9pm Mon-Fri; 10am-2pm Sat. **Admission** free. **Map** p342 B2.

The College of Architects, opposite the cathedral, hosts interesting exhibitions on 20th-century architecture. The façade murals were designed by Picasso in the 1950s, but executed by other artists.

Museu Diocesà

Avda de la Catedral 4 (93 315 22 13). Metro Jaume I/17, 19, 40, 45 bus. **Open** 10am-2pm, 5-8pm Tue-Sat; 11am-2pm Sun. **Admission** €1.90. **Credit** (shop only) V. **Map** p342 B2.

The best of Catalan religious art is in the MNAC on Montjuïc, but this space run by the Diocese of Barcelona has a few strong works, such as a group of sculpted virgins on the top floor, altarpieces by Bernat Martorell and murals from Polinyà. The display is rather confusing and disorganised, but the visit is interesting for the building itself, which

includes the Pia Almoina, a former almshouse, stuck on to a Renaissance canon's residence, which in turn was built inside a Roman tower. An exhibition in mid 2002 will be dedicated to Gaudí, whom the diocese is trying to have canonised on the basis of some unsubstantiated 'miracles' completely unrelated to his architecture.

Museu d'Història de la Ciutat

Plaça del Rei 1 (93 315 11 11). Metro Jaume I/ 17, 19, 40, 45 bus. **Open** *June-Sept* 10am-8pm Tue-Sat; 10am-2pm Sun. *Oct-May* 10am-2pm, 4-8pm Tue-Sat; 10am-2pm Sun. **Guided tours** by appointment. **Admission** €3; €1.80 concessions; free under-12s. Free 1st Sat of the mth. **Discounts** BC. **No credit cards. Map** p343 B3.

The City History Museum had a chance beginning: when the 15th-century Casa Padellàs was being transferred to this site in 1931, remains of the Roman city of Barcino were uncovered while digging the new foundations. They now form a giant labyrinthine cellar beneath the museum, with Roman streets and villa layouts still visible. A visit to the remains takes you right underneath the Plaça del Rei and winds as far as the cathedral itself, beneath which there is a fourth-century baptistery. Busts, monuments and other sculptures found in the excavations are also on display (*see also p8* **Do as the Romans did**). The admission fee also gives you access to sections of the former royal palace such as the extraordinary Saló del Tinell, a medieval

Saló de Cent in the **Ajuntament**. *See p76.*

C

A point of interest

Walking down La Rambla, on the right, quite near the Columbus monument, lies the Cultural Information Point of the Autonomous Government of Catalonia. There you will find addresses, data and information on cultural activities, literary awards, art prizes, museums, the Filmotheque, theatre, exhibitions... and the opportunity to connect to the Internet.

Rambla de Santa Mònica, 7
08001 Barcelona
publinfo@correu.gencat.es
http://cultura.gencat.es
Fax: 93 316 28 11
Telephone for cultural information:
93 316 27 27

Generalitat de Catalunya
Departament de Cultura

banquet hall with massive unadorned arches; a classic example of Catalan Gothic. The Santa Agata chapel has a 15th-century altarpiece by Jaume Huguet, one of the greatest Catalan medieval painters. From here you can usually climb up the Rei Martí tower, although it was closed for an unknown period at the time of writing.

The museum runs an impressive virtual reality presentation, *Barcelona: Una Història Virtual*, on the city's history, with English commentary (shows last approx 30min; book for a time when you arrive). The Casa Padellàs is not large enough to accommodate a permanent chronological display; from March to August 2002 a temporary show will look at Barcelona in the late 19th century through the work of Gaudí and his contemporary, the poet Jacint Verdaguer. There's also a well-stocked bookshop and information centre with leaflets in English. The museum has also added a satellite, in the old Farinera del Clot flour factory in Sant Martí, now a lively cultural centre (Gran Via 837, 93 291 80 80).

Museu Frederic Marès

Plaça Sant Iu 5-6 (93 310 58 00). Metro Jaume I/ 17, 19, 40, 45 bus. **Open** 10am-5pm Tue, Thur; 10am-7pm Wed, Fri, Sat; 10am-3pm Sun. **Admission** €3; €1.50 concessions; free under-16s. Free 3-7pm Wed, 1st Sun of the mth. **Guided tours** 11.30am Sun. **Discounts** BC, BT. **Credit** (shop only) AmEx, MC, V. **Map** p343 B3.

The son of a customs agent in Port Bou on the French border, Frederic Marès possibly learnt his trade by observing how valuable objects were 'collected' from travellers unable to pay import duties in cash. Trained as a sculptor (his figurative bronzes and marbles are found all over Barcelona), Marès dedicated his 97 years to gathering every imaginable type of object. Created for him by the city in the 1940s, the museum contains his personal collection of religious sculpture, with legions of sculpted virgins, crucifixions and saints on the lower floors. Marès even collected clothing for saints. The Museu Sentimental on the top floor contains his more extraordinary collections: everything from iron keys, ceramics and tobacco pipes to pocket watches, early daguerreotypes and Torah pointers. Especially beautiful is the Sala Femenina, in a room once belonging to the medieval royal palace: fans, sewing scissors, nutcrackers and perfume flasks give a charming image of 19th-century bourgeois taste.

The museum has completed the first part of a judicious renovation programme, bringing some coherence to Marès' kleptomaniac collecting and making it possible to appreciate the real quality of the pieces. When the basement is completed, religious sculpture from different periods will be more clearly organised; the renovation has also opened Marès' own study and library upstairs. The museum also hosts interesting and unusual temporary shows; other pluses include unusually good labelling in English, and the fact that the handsome patio contains a great open-air café in summer, the Cafè d'Estiu (*see p169*).

Casa de l'Ardiaca's letterbox. *See p74.*

Palau de la Generalitat

Plaça Sant Jaume (93 402 46 00/www.gencat.es). Metro Liceu or Jaume I/14, 17, 19, 38, 40, 45, 59 bus. **Guided tours** 10.30am-1.30pm 2nd & 4th Sun of the mth; also by appointment. **Admission** free. **Map** p343 B3.

Like the Ajuntament, the Generalitat has a Gothic side entrance, with a beautiful relief of Sant Jordi, patron saint of Catalonia, made by Pere Johan in 1418. Inside, the finest features are the the Pati de Tarongers ('Orange Tree Patio'), and the magnificent chapel of Sant Jordi of 1432-4, the masterpiece of Catalan architect Marc Safont. The Generalitat is traditionally open to the public on Sant Jordi (23 April), when its patios are spectacularly decorated with red roses, and queues are huge; it also opens on 11 September (Catalan National Day) and 24 September (La Mercè) and on some other holidays.

La Rambla

It is the best of streets, it is the worst of streets, as a Catalan Dickens might say. On crisp winter mornings with the weak sun filtering through the leaves, and the sky a washed-out blue, La Rambla – the mile-long walkway that cuts through the middle of the Old City and leads down to the port – is delightful: full of life and colour. On clammy August afternoons it can be wretched: a charmless thoroughfare crammed with tourists in search of some rumoured essence. The truth is that La Rambla has as many guises as the human statues that line its path. It changes by the hour, the day, the season. In fact, Les Rambles (technically plural, composed of one Rambla after another, end to end) is best experienced by day, when everything is in full, vibrant flow.

A *rambla* is an urban feature virtually unique to Catalonia, and there is one in most towns in this area of Spain. Originally, the Rambla of Barcelona, like most of its smaller equivalents, was a seasonal riverbed, running along the western edge of the 13th-century city, the name deriving from *ramla*, an Arabic word for sand. From the Middle Ages to the baroque era a

Sightseeing

great many churches and convents were built along this riverbed, some of which have given their names to sections of it: as one descends from Plaça Catalunya, it is successively called **Rambla de Canaletes**, **Rambla dels Estudis** (or **dels Ocells**), **Rambla de Sant Josep** (or **de les Flors**), **Rambla dels Caputxins** and **Rambla de Santa Mònica**. The Rambla also served as the meeting ground for city and country dwellers, for on the far side of these church buildings lay the still scarcely built-up Raval, 'the city outside the walls', and rural Catalonia. At the fountain on the corner with C/Portaferrissa, once a city gateway, there is an artist's impression in tiles

of this space beside the wall, which became a natural marketplace. From these beginnings sprang La Boqueria, Spain's largest market, and still on the Rambla today.

The Rambla took on its recognisable present form between approximately 1770 and 1860. The second city wall came down in 1775, and the Rambla was gradually paved and turned into a boulevard. Seats were available to strollers for rent in the late 18th century. The avenue acquired its definitive shape after the closure of the monasteries in the 1830s, which made swaths of land available for new building. No longer on the city's edge, the Rambla became a wide path through its heart.

Walk 1: The Chino

Duration: 50 minutes
Map: Walk shown in **orange** on p340.
Barcelona has been famous for many things: Gaudí, the Rambla – and the Barrio Chino, for decades one of the legendary centres of low-life in Europe. The French in particular romanticise the 'Chino' – Jean Genet's *The Thief's Journal* and André Pieyre de Mandiargues' *La Marge* are two classics of Chino literature – and right up until very recently visiting French literati, when asked what most impressed them in Barcelona, regularly used to say the Chino, with its Felliniesque whores and smell of piss.

Barcelona without its Chino used to be inconceivable, but there is no preservation order on it, and today only lipstick traces of this lost world can be seen. This was a harsh, often overwhelming, desperate place, certainly; it was also one of the planet's rarer environments, and before it vanishes entirely it can be thought-provoking to take a last look.

Unless otherwise indicated, all the places mentioned here have disappeared. Another leap of the imagination is required to populate these streets with massed crowds of people, for photos from the 1930s, when the Chino was at its peak, show its alleys packed from one side to the other 24 hours a day. There were brothels, gambling dens, *tavernas*, pawnshops, music halls, drifters, ordinary workers and the very poor, all coexisting side by side, all dedicated to the business of surviving. Today, although the streets may be far quieter, this is still a hard area, and this walk is not one to try after dark.

Near the bottom of the Rambla, at the corner of C/Portal de Santa Madrona and Avda Drassanes, it's impossible not to see

a 1960s skyscraper, the **Edifici Colom**, the product of Franco-era attempt at modernisation. It stands on the site of a celebrated brothel of the 1930s, **Can Manco** ('House of the One-Armed Man'), famous for specialising in cheap and quick *flautes* (flutes) or blow-jobs. On the same site, at what used to be C/Montserrat 20, stood the **Teatro Circo Barcelonés**, known for its *transformistas* or drag queens. This street maintains its traditions, and **El Cangrejo** at No.9 is perhaps the most authentic survivor of old Chino nightlife.

Turning left into **C/Cervelló** and then right and across at Avda Drassanes you enter **C/Cid. C/Peracamps**, which runs across it, was known as a street of ultra-cheap doss houses. In the 1930s, C/Cid was the epicentre of the Chino: No.10, now a more recent block of flats, was the site of **La Criolla**, the most celebrated cabaret of the era, renowned for its drag and female performers and patronised by high and low society. Lesbians also met here in relative safety. It was a gambling joint too, and a centre for drugs and arms dealing; the owner, Pepe, was shot down in the doorway in one of the Chino's most notorious murders, in April 1936.

A turn right into **C/Ramon Berenguer el Vell** takes you to the **Mercat del Carme**, built on the site of **La Mina**, a taverna that had – shades of Dickens – an *academia de lladres* (school for thieves) in its basement. Turn right down C/Arc del Teatre, and cross Avda Drassanes where you enter the **Plaça Jean Genet**, named after Barcelona's most famous rent boy. Genet came to the Chino in the 1930s, selling sex, thieving and begging.

It used to be said that it was an obligation for every true Barcelona citizen to walk down the Rambla and back at least once a day. Nowadays, many locals are blasé about the place, but the avenue remains one of Barcelona's essential attractions. There are many ways of *ramblejant* – a specific verb for going along the Rambla – from a saunter to a purposeful stride, but the best way to get a feel for the place is to take a seat at one of the newly installed public benches at the top of the avenue or in the **Café Zurich** (*see p169*) on Plaça Catalunya, an iconic bar that had all its charm refurbished out of it when the block was rebuilt a couple of years ago, but which is still a key meeting point.

As well as having five names, the Rambla is divided into territories. The first part – at the top, by Plaça Catalunya – has belonged by unwritten agreement to groups of men perpetually engaged in a *tertulia*, a classic Iberian half-conversation, half-argument about anything from politics to football. The **Font de Canaletes** drinking fountain is beside them; if you drink from it, the legend goes, you'll return to Barcelona. Here too is where Barça fans converge to celebrate their triumphs – not such a frequent event these days.

The pet stalls a little further down are as improbable and perplexing as the porn-merchants masquerading as news kiosks that

He robbed clients after servicing them, stole from churches and earned three pesetas a night in La Criolla, dressed as a girl. Continue down C/Arc de Teatre; at No.6, now demolished, was **Madame Petit**, an internationally famous brothel known for answering every need, including sado-masochism and necrophilia.

Turn left into La Rambla and left again into **C/Nou de la Rambla**. This was the more public main avenue of the Chino, especially in the boom years of World War I. The **Hotel Gaudí** at No.12 – opposite the Palau Güell – occupies the site of the **Eden Concert**, Barcelona's most opulent *café concierto*, a combination of music hall, high-class restaurant, gambling den and strip club. Here textile millionaires and their mistresses rubbed shoulders with *pinxos* – the Chino's hard men, part pimps, part bouncers, part gang members.

On the left is **C/Lancaster**; the **Bar Bohemia**, a legendary venue where very aged performers of the old cabarets used to keep their acts going, stood at No.2. It finally closed only in 1997, and remains half-demolished. On the right at C/Nou 34 is

the 1910 **London Bar** (*see p177*), last of the *cafés concierto*, and now a foreigners' favourite. Further towards the end of C/Nou de la Rambla is **C/Estel**, which had at No.2 **La Suerte Loca**, a 1900s brothel frequented by Picasso. At the very end of C/Nou de la Rambla (at No.103), was **El Pompeya**, a cheap cabaret for workers and students. It is now the **Bagdad**, where live porn is available and 'inter-active sex' by Internet is on offer.

If you loop back on to C/Tapies after passing the old **Arnau** music hall on Paral.lel, and carry on along it back towards the Rambla, then turn left at C/Sant Oleguer, go right at C/Marqués de Barberà and left again at C/Sant Ramon, you will enter an area where street prostitution and squalor are still very visible. Be warned that this area can feel quite intimidating. Where C/Sant Ramon hits C/Sant Pau, there is the **Marsella** (*see p177*), a bar that has survived all the district's renovations and still retains its slightly seedy image as an 'absinthe bar'.

Almost opposite it is the **Plaça Salvador Seguí**: Seguí was the greatest of Barcelona's CNT union leaders, and was murdered in 1923 by a gunman hired by wealthy manufacturers, at the nearby corner of C/Cadena (now one border of the new Rambla del Raval and about to be transformed under new plans for the immediate area) and C/Sant Rafael. Along **C/Robador**, across the shabby square, there are still a few *bares de camareras*, shabby 'girly bars' used for prostitution. This last vestige of the Chino, though, is doomed, for these old, decrepit blocks will soon be swept away, to make way for a new complex containing an appropriately phallic-shaped hotel.

**RUTA DEL MODERNISME
DE BARCELONA**

Centre del Modernisme de Barcelona
Casa Amatller, pg. de Gràcia, 41 baixos
Tel. 93 488 01 39 - www.rutamodernisme.com

Ajuntament de Barcelona

Institut del Paisatge Urbà
i la Qualitat de Vida

dot the Ramblas from top to bottom. Both have a range of the exotic, the everyday and the absurd, and it's virtually impossible to catch anyone actually purchasing either pets or porn, though someone out there must. At night the stalls are closed up, and you can hear the occasional melancholy cluck from inside. By day, the chastened roosters, disgruntled guinea fowl and bewildered budgies are no less lugubrious, watching helplessly as piratical feral parrots swoop down to steal their food.

Next comes perhaps the best-loved section of the boulevard, known as Rambla de les Flors for its line of magnificent flower stalls, open into the night. To the right is the **Palau de la Virreina** exhibition and cultural information centre, and the superb **Boqueria** market; don't linger near the entrance, however – the food here is expensive and non-Catalans are liable to be ripped off with rotten fruit and rottener prices. There's more fun to be had inside, where the sheep's heads leer and the crayfish make futile bids for freedom. A little further is the **Pla de l'Os** (or **Pla de la Boqueria**), centrepoint of the Rambla, with a pavement mosaic created in 1976 by Joan Miró. On the left, where more streets run off into the Barri Gòtic, is the extraordinary **Bruno Quadros** building (1883), with umbrellas on the wall and a Chinese dragon protruding over the street.

The lower half of the Ramblas is far more restrained, flowing between the sober façade of the **Liceu** opera house and the rather more fin-de-siècle (architecturally and atmospherically) **Café de l'Opera** (*see p169*), Barcelona's second most famous café after the Zurich. It then brushes the faded grandeur of **Plaça Reial**, by day a palm-filled salon for tramps, tourists and pensioners, by night a meeting point for anyone young, drunk and out for some extra-curricular cultural exchange, as well as the inevitable predators, both economic and sexual, they attract.

On the right is C/Nou de la Rambla (where you'll find Gaudí's Palau Güell), and then the promenade widens into the Rambla de Santa Mònica. Here you hit the stretch that for years was a thriving prostitution belt. You will still see a few lycra-and-furred transvestites, but official clean-up efforts have greatly reduced the visibility (if not the existence) of street soliciting. Renovations, including a 1980s arts centre, the **Centre d'Art Santa Mònica**, have diluted the sleaziness of this part of the Rambla – although this is still one of the areas where you need to be most wary of pickpockets and bag-snatchers (*see p83* **Top ten scams**).

Further towards the port and the Colom column are the **Museu de Cera** (*see p223*) and, at weekends, stalls selling bric-a-brac

Top ten | Scams

Petty crime in Barcelona has reached epidemic proportions. Little of it is violent, however, and most is easily avoided. Just be aware of the following favourites.

Grab it and run
Your basic bag snatch. Money belts are particularly easy to snip and often contain richer pickings.

Cut the mustard
What's that on your shoulder? Can I help you wipe it off while my friend picks your pocket?

Unlucky heather
Beware she of the headscarf and many skirts. Particularly adept at helping you find the change for your smart new nosegay.

Victim support
You will meet many victims of crime; they're the ones waving a photocopied 'police report' and asking you to lend them some cash to help them get home. Don't.

Bag-slashing
Trickier to avoid. Be aware of who's around you and don't wear your bag on your back.

The metro escalator shuffle
The person in front of you bends down to pick something up, and in the ensuing comic domino effect his accomplice behind you steadies himself by thrusting one hand into your pocket.

Please hold my baby
She of the headscarf again. Oh, and that's one of her grown-up babies standing just behind you.

Hunt the lady
Guessing which cup the pea's under may look easy, and my, aren't people winning a lot? But they're all in it together, see.

Snogging
It may be that you are so sexually attractive that fellow clubbers and ladies of the night can't resist a quick tongue sarnie, or it may be that they're interested in what else is in your trousers.

Passport control
Can I see your passport, sir? Can I see your ID, officer?

The flora and fauna of **La Rambla**. *See p79.*

Dancing in the streets

If a national dance says something about a nation's psyche, then the Catalans are in a lot of trouble. The *sardana* is basically difficult to perform, unexciting to watch and mostly practised by the elderly as an alternative to t'ai chi. It's enough to make you nostalgic for Morris dancers. On the plus side, it's open to anyone, doesn't require any special costume and is probably a good way to make Catalan friends. All you have to do is stand in a circle and bob up and down, taking the occasional step to one side, followed almost immediately by another one back again.

It might look extremely simple, but is in fact fiendishly difficult and, apparently, a joy to dance. The music is played by a band called a *cobla*, consisting of 11 musicians playing traditional tubas, trombones and reedy, squeaky wind instruments similar to clarinets and oboes. Anyone can join in the dance – provided you don't break up a couple, so you should move in to the man's

left. And of course it is frowned upon to join a circle above your level. Instead, you should look for the groups of muddlers – there are always a couple.

The origins of the dance are somewhat obscure. Some have traced it back to Ancient Greece, though more, perhaps, on romantic than historical grounds. Others see its origins in the *ballo sardo* of Sardinia: the island was once a Catalan colony. The first written reference to the *sardana* comes in 1552, though early sources all recount the dance being banned in front of, and sometimes inside, various Catalan churches, owing to the noise.

Sardanas are danced at all traditional festivals, including the *festa major* of every neighbourhood and village, as well as every weekend in front of the cathedral (noon-2pm Sun) and in Plaça Sant Jaume (6.30-8.30pm Sat, 6pm-8pm Sun). For details of classes, contact the Federació Sardanista on 93 319 76 37.

and craftwork, alongside fortune tellers and tarot readers catering to an incorrigible local interest in all things astrological. As well as the human statues there are buskers, clowns, puppeteers, dancers and musicians. There's street theatre of another kind in the shape of the three-card sharpers or hustlers with three walnut shells and a pea under one of them, challenging you to a bet. Then finally it's a short skip to the port, where Christopher Columbus points resolutely towards India rather than the Americas – a geographical confusion he never really resolved.

Centre d'Art Santa Mònica

La Rambla 7 (93 316 28 10/www.cultura.gencat.es/ casm/index.htm). Metro Drassanes/14, 38, 59, 91 bus. **Open** 11am-2pm, 5-8pm Mon-Sat; 11am-3pm Sun. **Admission** usually free. **Map** p343 A4.
Since this 17th-century monastery was renovated as a centre for contemporary art in the 1980s it has had its ups and downs, ceding much of its importance to the MACBA in recent years. The redesign, by architects Piñón and Viaplana, is difficult enough for installation artists, and is near impossible when it comes to showing painting. In 2002 there will be two shows for the Photography Spring festival: a view of mid 20th-century Mexican society by Catalan exile Carles Fontserè and another by contemporary photo-based artist Daniel Canogar. In the summer, Santa Mònica director Josep Miquel Garcia will curate a show on Gaudí's influence on Catalan 20th-century art, from Miró and Dalí up to contemporary creators such as Perejaume and designer-architect Oscar Tusquets.

Palau de la Virreina

La Rambla 99 (93 301 77 75/www.bcn.es/icub). Metro Liceu/14, 38, 59, 91 bus. **Open** 11am-8pm Tue-Sat; 11am-2.30pm Sun. **Admission** €3; €1.50 concessions, Wed; free under-16s. **No credit cards.** **Map** p342 A2.
This neo-classical palace takes its name from the wife of a viceroy of Peru, who lived in it after its completion in the 1770s. Once the city council's main exhibition space, the Virreina handed over all significant programming to the MACBA in the late 1990s. Now, under the direction of Cuban critic Ivan de la Nuez, it has made a strong comeback, with the upstairs dedicated to international group shows (such as *Human Park*, in spring 2002) and the smaller downstairs gallery focused on historical and contemporary photography. La Virreina also has information on cultural events in Barcelona.

Raval

On the other side of La Rambla from the Barri Gòtic is the Raval. This is the name currently used for the area bounded by the Rambla, Paral.lel, Ronda Sant Pau and Ronda Sant Antoni, but it has been known by many different names in the past. Raval is the original medieval name, referring to the part of the city

outside the walls. The trades and institutions then confined here were those too dangerous or noxious to be allowed inside the city, such as brickmaking or slaughtering, or the huge **Antic Hospital de la Santa Creu**, which served the needs of the city from the 15th century until it finally closed in 1926. Other institutions located here were those that demanded too much space, such as the line of monasteries that once ran down one side of the Rambla. In the corner of the Raval next to the sea were the **Drassanes** or shipyards, now home to the Museu Marítim.

On the Paral.lel, near the port, there is still a large section of Barcelona's third city wall: the one which brought the Raval within the city in the 14th century. However, Barcelona largely stagnated in the following centuries, and, as late as 1800, much of the Raval had still not been built up, but consisted of small fruit and vegetable gardens and sometimes even vineyards. A trace of this earlier Raval can still be seen in the name of one of the most beautiful pockets of peace in the district, the ancient Romanesque church of **Sant Pau del Camp** (St Paul's in the Field). Iberic remains dating to 200 BC have been found next to the church, making it one of the two oldest known parts of Barcelona, the other being the Plaça del Pi in the Barri Gòtic.

When industry began to develop, it was in this area that most land was available. A great deal more land also came into use when liberal governments dissolved the monasteries in 1836; La Boqueria market, the Plaça Reial, the Liceu theatre and the Hotel Oriente are just some of the places on or around La Rambla to have risen from the ashes. Barcelona's first industry, mainly textile mills, thus had to grow within the cramped confines of the still-walled Raval, making use of every particle of space. Some of the strange, barrack-like factories from that time can still be seen in places, despite recent demolitions. Their workers lived alongside them, often in appalling conditions.

Then known to most people as the *Quinto* or 'Fifth District', this was the area where the dangerous classes of society took refuge, and it became the great centre of revolutionary Barcelona, a perennial breeding ground for anarchists and other radical groups. Numerous conspiracies were hatched here, riots and revolts began on innumerable occasions, and whole streets became no-go areas for the police after dark.

The other aspect of the area (or of that part of it between C/Sant Pau and the port) that made it notorious was its situation as a centre of low-life, drug trafficking and the sex industry, with high-class brothels for the rich and cheap dives for the poor in the so-called Barrio Chino (Barri Xino, in Catalan) or Chinatown. This label was given to the area (which had no Chinese connections) in the 1920s by a journalist, Francesc Madrid, after he saw a film about vice in San Francisco's Chinatown, and swiftly caught on. Barcelona had always had an underworld, centred in the Raval, but it really took off during World War I. The heyday of the Barrio Chino was in the 1920s and '30s, but it managed to survive to a certain extent under Franco. Hundreds of bars and cheap hostals lined streets such as Nou de la Rambla, catering to a floating population (*see p80* **Walk 1: The Chino**).

Today the whole district has changed enormously, perhaps more comprehensively than anywhere else in Barcelona. Its surviving industry consists of a dwindling number of old-fashioned workshops in trades such as printing, bookbinding, furniture repair or building supplies. The hospital now houses cultural and academic institutions. The former hotbed of radical politics is but a shadow of its pre-Franco self. The biggest change of all has been in the Chino, a prime target of the Ajuntament's urban renewal schemes.

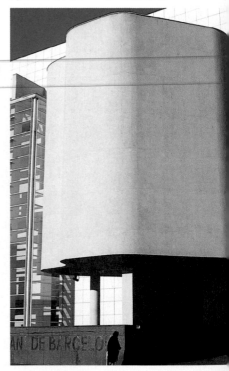

In the late 1970s serious problems were caused in the Chino by the arrival of heroin. The old, semi-tolerated petty criminality became much more threatening, affecting the morale of Barcelona residents and the tourist trade. Spurred on by the approaching Olympics, the authorities set about the problem with their customary clean-sweep approach. Between 1988 and 1992 the cheapest *hostals* were closed, and whole blocks associated with drug dealers or prostitution were demolished to make way for new squares. The people displaced were often transferred to newer flats on the outskirts of town, out of sight and so perhaps out of mind. Student residences and office blocks were constructed, and a new police station was built.

Most dramatic of all was the plan to create a *'Raval obert al cel'* – 'a Raval open to the sky', with far more open space. The most tangible result so far is the **Rambla del Raval**, completed in 2000, which now ranks as one of the city's most sweeping pedestrian spaces. Just below the new *rambla*, Avda Drassanes, by Colom, was actually created in an earlier attempt to 'open up' the Raval, under Franco's mayor Porcioles in the 1960s (one thing that

Franco's administrators and modern planners could agree on is that the Chino must go), but only got as far as C/Nou de la Rambla. The new Rambla now extends the effort far into the district, bulldozing all before it up to C/Hospital. Entire streets have vanished in its wake. The current grand project, situated halfway along it, is the 'Illa de la Rambla del Raval' – a block is slowly being demolished to make way for a complex containing shops, offices and a hotel 11 storeys high.

Some of these changes have undeniably been for the best, but their cumulative effect has been to leave one of the most singular parts of the city looking rather empty. It still has a hard edge, though, and it's advisable to be wary of thieves, especially between Sant Pau and the port. Another, unpredicted change in the Raval has been the appearance of a sizeable Muslim community, mostly from Pakistan and North Africa, who have taken over flats no longer wanted by Spaniards. This is now one of the city's most multicultural areas, where Muslim halal butcher shops serving North Africans sit alongside *carnisseries* selling every part of the pig to Catalans.

MACBA. See p89.

The main thoroughfare of the lower Raval, **C/Nou de la Rambla**, today has only a fraction of its earlier animation, but retains a sometimes surreal selection of shops. It also contains a peculiar addition from the 1880s, the **Palau Güell**, built by Gaudí for Eusebi Güell. It was a very eccentric decision of Güell's to have his new residence located in what was then a deeply unfashionable area, and he often had trouble persuading reluctant dinner guests to take up their invitations. Nearby, in C/Sant Pau, is another *Modernista* landmark, the **Hotel España**.

The upper Raval, towards Plaça Catalunya, has seen large-scale official projects for the rejuvenation of the area in the giant cultural complex that includes the **MACBA (Museu d'Art Contemporani de Barcelona)** and the **CCCB (Centre de Cultura Contemporània de Barcelona)**, built in what was once the workhouse, the Casa de la Caritat. Alongside these new cultural centres, parts of the old Raval are also enjoying a new lease of life thanks to their being (re)discovered as hip places to be, with a plethora of late-night bars and laid-back restaurants, largely free of the hordes of tourists found in the watering holes on the other side of La Rambla.

Antic Hospital de la Santa Creu & La Capella

C/Carme 47-C/Hospital 56 (no phone).
Metro Liceu/14, 18, 38, 59 bus. **Open** 9am-8pm
Mon-Fri; 9am-2pm Sat. *La Capella* noon-2pm,
4-8pm Tue-Sat; 11am-2pm Sun. **Admission** free.
Map p342 A2.

A hospital was founded on this site in 1024. The buildings combine a 15th-century Gothic core – including a beautifully shady colonnaded courtyard – with baroque and classical additions. It remained the city's main hospital until its medical facilities moved across to the new site built by Domènech i Montaner in the 1930s. Gaudí died here in 1926.

Today it houses Catalonia's main library, an arts school and La Capella, an attractive exhibition space in an impressive Gothic building that used to be the hospital's church; the choir balcony and side chapels are still visible, adding character to the shows. La Capella accepts contemporary projects from young Barcelona-based artists, and commissions innovative work able to give a social dimension to the gallery. In 2002, it will continue to emphasise multimedia work, performance and participative projects, including a show on the viewer as work of art. You can enter the hospital from both streets, but C/Hospital 56 is the main entrance.

CCCB (Centre de Cultura Contemporània de Barcelona)

C/Montalegre 5 (93 306 41 00/www.cccb.org).
Metro Catalunya/bus all routes to Plaça Catalunya.
Open *Mid June-mid Sept* 11am-8pm Tue-Sat;

11am-3pm Sun. *Mid Sept-mid June* 11am-2pm, 4-8pm Tue, Thur, Fri; 11am-8pm Wed, Sat; 11am-7pm Sun. **Admission** *1 exhibition* €4; €2.50 concessions. *2 exhibitions* €5; €4 concessions. *Wed* (public holidays only) €2.50. Free under-16s. **Discounts** Articket, BC, BT. **Credit** MC, V. **Map** p342 A1.

This multi-use centre teams up with the adjacent MACBA to form a culture front in the Raval. It occupies part of the Casa de la Caritat, built in 1802 on the site of a medieval monastery to serve as the city's main workhouse. The massive façade and part of the courtyard remain from the old building, while the rest was rebuilt in 1994 by architects Piñón and Viaplana, resulting in a dramatic combination of original elements with the imposing curtain wall in the cloister. As a contemporary culture centre it picks up on whatever falls through the cracks elsewhere in Barcelona, including urban culture (architecture, but also linking writers with their cities – including, in late 2002, Borges' Buenos Aires), early 20th-century art, and thematic shows on TV or cinema.

In spring 2002, *Interior City* will deal with private spaces in North African cities, while *The Harem* (Apr-June) examines western myth and iconography of the harem. In May a show on Gaudí's context and collaborators will be part of the International Year of Gaudí. Other activities include a festival of video art, an alternative cinema festival, the Sónar music festival (*see p214*), dance, concerts and oddities such as an online flyer project (www.cccb.org/flyercenter). There is also a particularly good bookshop specialising in a vast range of urban-related topics.

MACBA (Museu d'Art Contemporani de Barcelona)

Plaça dels Àngels 1 (93 412 08 10/www.macba.es).
Metro Catalunya/bus all routes to Plaça Catalunya.
Open *June-Sept* 11am-8pm Mon, Wed-Fri;
10am-8pm Sat; 10am-3pm Sun. *Oct-May* 11am-7.30pm Mon, Wed-Fri; 10am-8pm Sat; 10am-3pm
Sun. **Guided tours** *Oct-May only* 6pm Wed, Sat;
noon Sun. **Admission** *Museum* €5.10; €3.50
concessions. *1 exhibition* €3.50; €3.30 concessions.
Wed €2.60. Free under-16s, over-65s. **Discounts**
Articket, BC, BT. **Credit** (shop only) MC, V.
Map p342 A1.

With its perky geometry and spanking white façade presiding over the Plaça dels Àngels, Richard Meier's MACBA is finally starting to look comfortable in the middle of the working-class Raval. Chatting Filipino immigrants mix with skateboarders on the hard-paved square in front, while inside visitors find more sublime amusements in the museum's fine-tuned contemporary exhibits, accessed along airy transitional spaces and never-ending ramps between floors. MACBA's content now holds its own on the international stage, largely thanks to director Manuel Borja-Villel, who has enabled MACBA to do what no Barcelona museum has ever done: show contemporary art and collect it with certain criteria. Borja is allied to the current reinterpretation of socio-political art of the 1960s and '70s, giving it a decidedly southern European flavour.

Since the MNAC and Museu d'Art Modern are supposed to take us up to the Civil War, the MACBA begins with the 1940s, although earlier works by Paul Klee, Alexander Calder and Catalan sculptor Leandre Cristòfol are also on display. The work from the 1940s to the '60s is mostly painting, with Spanish expressionists such as Saura, Tàpies and Millares, and Basque abstract sculptors Jorge Oteiza and Eduardo Chillida. Collections from the past 30 years are more international, with work by Joseph Beuys, Robert Rauschenberg, Anselm Kiefer, Mario Merz and Christian Boltanski, along with recent acquisitions of Mike Kelly, Bruce Naumann and Eulàlia Valldosera, one of Spain's most able emerging creators. The Spanish collection includes a review of Catalan painting (Ràfols Casamada, Xavier Grau, Miquel Barceló) and Spanish sculpture (Miquel Navarro, Susana Solano,

Sergi Aguilar), plus conceptual artists Muntadas, Francesc Torres and the unclassifiable ZAJ. In 2002, Spanish-content shows include Basque sculptor Txomin Badiola in the spring and the latest version of *On Translation*, by senior Barcelona media artist Antoni Muntadas, in the autumn. There are also exhibitions by Raymond Pettibon, South African photographer David Goldblatt and one dedicated to acoustic art. At the end of the year, MACBA will finally open a show by Blinky Palermo that it has been working on for years.

Palau Güell

C/Nou de la Rambla 3-5 (93 317 39 74).
Metro Liceu/14, 18, 38, 59 bus. **Guided tours** (subject to change) *Mar-Oct* 10am-8pm Mon-Sat. *Nov-Feb* 10am-6pm Mon-Sat. **Admission** €2.40; €1.20 concessions; free under-6s. **Discount** RM. **No credit cards. Map** p343 A3.

The fine art of anarchy

If you stand still long enough in Barcelona, one of three things is sure to happen: you'll be robbed, pigeoned on or graffitied. Ubiquitous and energetic petty thieves and pigeons do their stuff day and night for everyone to see. The graffiti artists are more cautious, though their handiwork is wherever you look. No wall is left unmarked, no street left unsigned.

At the simple end of the scale, from the foot-soldiers of the movement, comes basic territorial tagging – the rushed, illegible scrawls that must make sense to someone. The colourful end of the spectrum, the heavy artillery, are the elaborate murals that spring up on abandoned, unloved walls almost overnight, bringing life to demolition sites, gloomy underpasses and the façades of derelict buildings. The Rambla del Raval, the curving road behind the zoo, the labyrinth of underpasses at Plaça Lesseps, and even the low wall of the car park behind the Boqueria all have good examples. In between there is a rich and fertile seam of slogans and statements that combine good-natured nihilism and optimistic humour, spiced with a pinch of politics. These are the graffiti snipers, long-range but accurate.

In a way, this type of graffiti in Barcelona is a combination of two great Catalan traditions, art and anarchy. Whether it's bombing the opera house or building the Pedrera, from time to time, the normally staid Catalans throw up someone to challenge the status quo. Graffiti is the current lingua franca of that challenge, an expression of

the ideologues in their midst. Much of it comes from the Okupa movement (from *ocupar* – to occupy), the scruffy army of squatters who articulate and embody the extreme end of alternative, left-wing politics, embracing Catalan independence and anti-globalisation, and any other anti-establishment cause with a fight to fight.

Frequent public demonstrations are often announced on walls, usually with the desperately vague 'today, 5pm', and usually followed subsequently by demands for the release of those arrested. In 2000 the military held their annual parade in Barcelona, for the first time since Franco died, occasioning the prescient '27th May – trouble'. More general political observations include 'Why can money travel freely across borders and people not?' and 'Tourist, you are the terrorist' (in English, unusually). 'More colour, fewer nazis' and 'More condoms, fewer sermons' share a grammar, if not an ideology. The ultimate expression of anarchic nihilism comes with 'The street belongs to everyone. Burn your bit!', while 'Anarchy! – or whatever you want' is probably the most generous call to revolution imaginable.

One clue as to the origin of these messages lies in the spelling. C or Qu are written as K. It's not a sign of illiteracy but a form of self-identification. When a house is taken over as a squat, the inhabitants usually hang banners made from old sheets over the balconies, announcing their presence with the word 'Okupas', often with the anarchist's circled A, and an elongated,

This vaguely medievalist palace was built in 1886-8 as a residence for Gaudí's patron Eusebi Güell. It was Gaudí's first major commission for Güell, and one of the first buildings in which he revealed the originality of his ideas. Once past the fortress-like façade, one finds an interior in impeccable condition, with lavish wooden ceilings, dozens of snake-eye stone pillars and original furniture. The roof terrace is a garden of decorated chimneys, each one different from the other.

Palau Güell is very popular and queues are often long for the guided tours, so try to get there early; mornings are better than afternoons.

Sant Pau del Camp

C/Sant Pau 101 (93 441 00 01). Metro Paral.lel/20, 36, 57, 64, 91 bus. **Open** 11.30am-1pm, 6-7.30pm Mon, Wed-Sun; 11.30am-12.30pm Tue. **Admission** free. **Map** p340 C6.

slanted, arrow-tipped N, also circled. So in the examples above, street is *kalle* not *calle*, burn is *kema*, not *quema*, and trouble is *kanya*, not *canya*.

Ironically, the custom of daubing sheets with slogans has been adopted by any group of residents with a complaint to make to the city council, usually to complain about excess noise from late-night bars or buskers. Rather than write letters to the council, they try to embarrass the mayor by turning entire façades into fluttering criticisms. And usually it works. The anarchist's proud proclamation has been subverted by bourgeois whining.

In the Born they have gone a stage further, by getting the banners professionally printed and including a web address. Soon they'll be commissioning designers to spray paint their own front doors. It looks like the revolution might be a while in coming, after all.

Barcelona's oldest surviving church was built as part of a monastery in the 12th century, when the surrounding Raval was just open fields. The Romanesque structure has none of the towering grandeur of the cathedral or Santa Maria del Mar: it is a squat, hulking building, rounded in on itself to give a sense of intimacy and protection to worshippers. On either side of the portal are columns made from seventh- and eighth-century buildings.

Sant Pere, La Ribera & Born

Back on the east side of the Rambla, the Barri Gòtic is now effectively limited on its eastern flank by the long, straight **Via Laietana**. This is a 20th-century addition, cut through the old city in 1907. The *barris* to the right of it on the map were contained, like the Barri Gòtic, within the second, 13th-century city wall, and include some of the most fascinating parts of the medieval city.

Below the Ronda Sant Pere lies the district of Sant Pere, originally centred around the monastery of **Sant Pere de les Puelles**, which still stands, if greatly altered, in Plaça de Sant Pere. This was Barcelona's main centre of textile production for centuries, and to this day streets like Sant Pere Més Baix and Sant Pere Més Alt contain many textile wholesalers and retailers. The area may be medieval in origin, but its finest monument is one of the most extraordinary works of *Modernisme*, the **Palau de la Música Catalana**, facing C/Sant Pere Més Alt. Less noticed on the same street is a curious feature, the **Passatge de les Manufactures**, a narrow 19th-century arcade between C/ Sant Pere Més Alt and C/Ortigosa.

Like other parts of the old city Sant Pere looks very run-down in places, but as elsewhere is undergoing dramatic renovation, with the gradual opening up of a continuation of the Avda Francesc Cambó, which will eventually swing round to meet up with C/Allada Vermell, a wide street formed when a block was demolished in 1994. The district's market, **Mercat de Santa Caterina** – one of Barcelona's oldest – is being completely rebuilt, and remains of the medieval Santa Caterina convent will be shown behind glass at one end. In the meantime its stallholders have been relocated along Passeig Lluís Companys, by the park. Another convent worth visiting nearby is the **Convent de Sant Agustí**, now a civic centre, on C/Comerç. The entrance contains a magical 'light sculpture' by James Turrell, commissioned by the Ajuntament in the 1980s and best seen after dark. As with the Raval, the district's neglected state is an obvious explanation of why it has become home to many recent immigrants, the most prominent

The day is Mare. Have a coffee. Unwind. This is a place to take in the sea and enjoy shopping in a relaxed, informal atmosphere for everything you can buy. And everything you can eat. And everything you can look at.

SHOPS   GAMES

MAREMAGNUM ®

RESTAURANTS   CINEMAS   DRINKS

The night is Magnum. Have a drink. This is a place where you can ponder which film you are going to see. And what you will eat for dinner. And choose which music you will dance to.

Central park

The word 'park' is a term used loosely round these parts. It can all too often mean a traffic island turned exhibition space, or a scrubby patch of land with a see-saw where dogs and kids do what they do best with unpleasant consequences. All shortsighted urban planning is forgiven, however, with a visit to the verdant, fun-filled landscape of the **Parc de la Ciutadella**. Barcelona's most historic park, the Ciutadella occupies the site of the loathed 18th-century citadel. It was created for the 1888 Exhibition and just outside it is the **Arc de Triomf**, which formed the main entrance to the Exhibition. Although formally laid out, the park is large enough to provide a wonderfully relaxing oasis within the confines of busy thoroughfares such as Passeig Picasso and Passeig Pujades. If La Rambla is the main artery of the city, Ciutadella is very definitely its lung.

Surprisingly extensive, it also contains a host of attractions: the **Museu d'Art Modern**, sharing the surviving buildings of the Citadel with the Catalan parliament, the **Museu de Geologia** and **Museu de Zoologia**, housed in Domènech's 'Castell dels Tres Dragons'. In the middle of the park there is a **lake** with boats for hire (€2 per person, per half hour). Beside the lake is the **Cascade**, an ornamental fountain on which the young Gaudí worked as assistant to Josep Fontseré, the architect of the park.The **Zoo** (*see p222*), at least part of which is due to move to the Diagonal-Mar area by 2004, currently takes up over half the park's space. Not to be missed are Fontseré's **Umbracle** (literally, 'shade house'), built in the 1880s with a cast-iron structure reminiscent of his Mercat del Born on C/Comerç and beautifully restored to provide a mysterious pocket of tropical forest in the city, and the elegant **Hivernacle** (winter garden), with a fine café (*see p177*).

Dotted around the park is a fascinating array of statuary ranging from the magical (the deers who leap in a homage to Walt Disney outside the zoo), to the military (a grand statue of General Prim, the man who ordered the destruction of the hated citadel sits near the south entrance), and the moving (an imposing iron ring commemorating Catalan victims of Nazi concentration camps).

Parc de la Ciutadella
Passeig Picasso (no phone). Metro Arc de Triomf or Barceloneta/14, 39, 40, 41, 42, 51, 100, 141 bus. **Open** *Apr-Sept* 8am-9pm daily. *Oct-Mar* 8am-8pm daily. **Map** p341 E6.

of whom are black Latin Americans from the Dominican Republic – you can often hear salsa or merengue wafting out across medieval alleys.

The name of the area below Sant Pere, La Ribera (the waterfront), recalls the time before permanent quays were built, when the shoreline reached much further inland. One of the most engaging districts of the old city, it has, though, fallen victim to two historic acts of urban vandalism. The first took place after the 1714 siege, when the victors razed one whole corner of the Ribera in order to construct the fortress of the Ciutadella, now the **Parc de la Ciutadella** (*see p93* **Central park**). The second occurred when the Via Laietana was struck through the *barri* in the 1900s, in line with the contemporary theory of 'ventilating' insanitary city districts by driving wide avenues through them.

In Barcelona's Golden Age, from the 12th century onwards, La Ribera was both the favourite residential area of the city's merchant elite and the principal centre of commerce and trade. The **Plaça de l'Angel**, now a rather nondescript space on Via Laietana by Jaume I Metro station, is all that remains of the Plaça del Blat, the 'wheat square', where all grain brought into the city was traded. If the Palau Reial, Generalitat and Ajuntament were the 'official' centre of the medieval city, this was its commercial and popular heart, where virtually everybody had to come at least once a day.

The main street of La Ribera is still **C/Montcada**, one of the unmissable parts of old Barcelona. It is lined with an extraordinary succession of medieval palaces, the greatest of which house a variety of museums, including as the **Museu Tèxtil**, the **Museu Barbier-Mueller** of pre-Columbian art and, above all, the **Museu Picasso** – one of Barcelona's most visited museums. The surrounding streets were once filled with workshops supplying anything the merchant owners might need (*see p94* **Walk 2: La Ribera**).

Walk 2: La Ribera

Duration: 45 minutes
Map: Walk marked in **green** on p342-3.
Centuries of Barcelona life, work and wealth are reflected in the medieval streets of La Ribera. This walk begins, like that around the Roman city (*see p8* **Do as the Romans did**), on Plaça Sant Jaume. From there, walk down **C/Llibreteria**, as important in the Middle Ages as it had been as the Roman Cardus, and still the main north road. Cross **Plaça de l'Angel**, site of the Plaça del Blat, the grain market. The continuation of the Roman road across Via Laietana is **C/Bòria**, a name that probably means 'outskirts' or 'suburbs', since it was outside the original city.

C/Bòria continues into the extraordinarily evocative **Plaça de la Llana**, old centre of wool (*llana*) trading in the city, now an animated meeting place for the Dominican community. Alleys to the left were associated with food trades: **C/Mercaders** ('traders', probably in grain), **C/Oli** ('olive oil') just off it, and **C/Semoleres**, where semolina was made. To the right on Bòria is **C/Pou de la Cadena** ('well with a chain'), a reminder that water was essential for textile working.

After Plaça de la Llana the Roman road's name becomes **C/Corders** ('ropemakers'), and then **C/Carders** ('carders', or combers of wool). Where the name changes there is a tiny square, Placeta Marcús, with a smaller

Romanesque chapel, the **Capella d'en Marcús**, built in the early 12th century to give shelter to travellers who arrived after the city gates had closed for the night. Bernat Marcús, who paid for it, is also said to have organised the first postal service in Europe, and it was from here that his riders set off north. The chapel is rarely open (and then only for worship).

Carry on a little way along C/Carders to **Plaça Sant Agustí Vell**, different parts of which date from many periods, from the Middle Ages to the 19th century: just off it, on **C/Basses de Sant Pere** as it leads away to the left, there is an intact 14th-century house. Retrace your steps down C/Carders, to turn left into **C/Blanqueria** ('bleaching'). Here wool was washed before being spun. At **C/Assaonadors** ('tanners'), turn right. At the end of this street, behind the Marcús chapel, is a statue of John the Baptist, patron saint of the tanners' guild.

Here you are at the top of **C/Montcada**. In La Ribera's Golden Age this beautiful street was the broadest thoroughfare in the district, and its busiest. Its merchant residences conform to a typical style of Mediterranean urban palace – elegant entrance patios with the main rooms on the first floor – and are closely packed together. Most have features from several periods.

On the corner of C/Montcada and C/Assaonadors is the small chapel, the **Capella d'en Marcús**, built in the 12th century, when it was surrounded by fields and gardens. Close by was the main route through the district, along C/Corders and C/Carders. C/Princesa is a much more recent addition, created in the 1850s. From C/Carders, C/Montcada leads across C/Princesa to the centre of the Ribera, the **Passeig del Born**. 'Born' originally meant 'joust' or 'list', and in the Middle Ages and for many centuries thereafter this was the centre for the city's festivals, processions, tournaments, carnivals and the burning of heretics by the Inquisition. At one end of the square is the old **Born market**, a magnificent 1870s wrought-iron structure that used to be Barcelona's main wholesale food market. It closed in the 1970s, when the market was transferred to the other side of Montjuïc. Current plans are that it should house a library and arts centre, due to be finished in 2004.

At the other end of the Passeig from the market stands the greatest of all Catalan Gothic buildings, the magnificent church of **Santa Maria del Mar**. On one side of it a square was opened in 1989 on the site where it is believed the last defenders of the city were executed after the fall of Barcelona to the Spanish army in 1714. Called the **Fossar de les Moreres**, the 'Mulberry Graveyard', the square is inscribed with emphatic patriotic poetry, and nationalist demonstrations converge here every year on Catalan National Day, 11 September. The square is seen as a monument in itself and the recent addition of a tall structure curving over the C/Santa Maria and holding an 'eternal flame' to commemorate the victims has been badly received, not least by the original architect of the square, Carme Fiol.

The closure of the Born market led initially to a certain decline in this area, but it has survived as the home of an old-established community, and thanks to its inherent attractions for

Today this is one of Barcelona's great museum centres. The first palace you reach after crossing C/Princesa is the **Palau Berenguer d'Aguilar**, home of the **Museu Picasso**, which has also taken over four more palaces. Opposite is one of the finest and largest palaces, the **Palau dels Marquesos de Lió**, now the **Museu Tèxtil**, with a fine café; nearby is another great Montcada feature, **El Xampanyet** cava bar (*see p179*). A relative newcomer is the bar in the 17th-century **Palau Dalmases** (*pictured*).

To the right is C/**Sombrerers**, where hat makers worked; opposite it is Barcelona's narrowest street, C/**Mosques** ('flies'), not

even wide enough for an adult to lie across. It has since been closed off because too many people were pissing in it at night. Montcada ends at **Passeig del Born**, a hub of the city's trades for 400 years.

Turn left, and on the left is C/**Flassaders** ('blanket makers'), and to the right C/**Rec**, the irrigation canal. Go down Rec to turn right into C/**Esparteria**, where *espart* (hemp) was woven. Turnings off it include C/**Calders**, where smelting furnaces would have been found, and C/**Formatgeria**, where one would have gone for cheese. After that is C/**Vidrieria**, where glass was stored and sold.

Esparteria runs into C/Ases, which crosses C/**Malcuinat** ('badly cooked'), so there must have been evil smells nearby. Turn left into C/**Espaseria** ('sword-making') to emerge out of ancient alleys on to the open space of Pla del Palau. Turn right, and then right again into C/**Canvis Vells** ('old exchange'). A tiny street to the left, C/**Panses**, has an archway above it, with a stone sculpture of a face over the second floor. This face, called a *carabassa*, indicated the existence of a legalised brothel.

At the end of Canvis Vells you come to **Plaça Santa Maria** and La Ribera's superb parish church, **Santa Maria del Mar**: on the left-hand side is C/**Abaixadors** ('unloaders'), where porters would unload goods, and from the square C/**Argenteria** ('silverware') leads back to the Plaça de l'Angel.

Las Meninas (1957), from the **Museu Picasso.** *See p97.*

tourism and nightlife. As a nightlife haunt the Born tends to go in and out of fashion, with booms and slumps every few years; it certainly started the millennium on a roll, and the once quiet Passeig and its bars are still packed with wandering crowds on weekend nights. The area has no shortage of good bars and restaurants, and with the rumoured arrival of Nike on C/Rec and Giorgio Armani in the Plaça de les Olles, it seems that the Born's current fashionable status may be more than a passing fad. Since the 1980s it has also been a hub of the city's alternative arts scene. Around C/Banys Vells, parallel to Montcada, there is now an interesting selection of independent textile and craft workshops, set up by young designers (*see p196* **Born to shop**).

From the Born and Santa Maria, tiny streets lead through centuries-old arches and the little **Plaça de les Olles** to the harbourside avenue and another symbol of La Ribera, the **Llotja** (Exchange). Its outer shell is neo-classical, added in the 18th century, but its core is a superb 1380s Gothic hall, which, until the exchange moved to the Passeig de Gràcia in 1994, was the oldest continuously functioning stock exchange in Europe. It once housed the Consolat del Mar, the 'Consulate of the Sea', established to arbitrate in commercial disputes throughout the Mediterranean, and since then has accommodated a customs post and a school of fine arts, at which Picasso studied. Unfortunately, it can (usually) only be visited if you attend a function organised through its owner, the Chamber of Commerce (*see p309*).

Museu d'Art Modern

Edifici del Parlament, Parc de la Ciutadella (93 319 57 28/www.mnac.es). Metro Ciutadella/ 14, 39, 40, 41, 42, 51, 100, 141 bus. **Open** 10am-7pm Tue-Sat; 10am-2.30pm Sun. **Guided tours** noon Sat, Sun. **Admission** €3; €2.10 concessions; free under-7s. **Discounts** Articket, BC. **Credit** (shop only) V. **Map** p341 E6.
Sharing one of the 18th-century citadel buildings in the Parc de la Ciutadella with the Catalan parliament, this museum is not a 'museum of modern art' as understood elsewhere. Its theme is not 20th-century art, but Catalan art from the mid 19th century to the 1930s. It is therefore the main showcase for the great burst of creativity – including design – associated with *Modernisme*. Administratively part of the MNAC, it is destined to move to the Palau Nacional when the upper floors of the Montjuïc museum are completed in 2003.

The galleries begin with the Romantic painter Marià Fortuny, whose liking for oriental exoticism and ostentatious detail led to his *Odalisque* (1861). After the realism of the Olot school, there is some impressionist-influenced work by Ramon Casas and Santiago Rusiñol, the main *Modernista* painters. Casas' beloved image painted for the Els Quatre Gats café (*see p172*), of himself and the café's owner Pere Romeu riding a tandem, gives a vivid sense of the vibrant spirit of the close of the 19th century. *Modernisme* refused to discriminate between fine and decorative arts, and a major attraction is the superb selection of furniture and decorative objects by the likes of Gaudí, Puig i Cadafalch and talented furniture maker Gaspar Homar, Josep Llimona and the neo-classicist Josep Clarà represent figurative sculpture. Painters include Isidre Nonell (who influenced Picasso's Blue Period), Joaquim Mir and Josep de Togores. The collection trickles off at the end with just two paintings by Dalí and work by two avant-garde sculptors from the 1930s, Julio González and Pau Gargallo.

Museu Barbier-Mueller d'Art Precolombí

C/Montcada 14 (93 319 76 03). Metro Jaume I/17, 19, 40, 45 bus. **Open** 10am-6pm Tue-Sat; 10am-3pm Sun. **Admission** €3; €1.50 concessions. *Combined admission with Museu Tèxtil* €3.50; €2 concessions. Free under-16s. Free 1st Sun of the mth. **Discounts** BC. **Credit** (shop only) AmEx, MC, V. **Map** p343 C3.
Though Columbus' famed voyage took place in 1492, this museum demonstrates how the 'pre-Columbian' era extended well beyond that date, as the subjugation of indigenous cultures by the *conquistadores* lasted for decades. In 1996 the Barbier-Mueller museum in Geneva agreed to show pieces in Barcelona from its top-flight collection of New World art, on a rotating basis. To house them, the city renovated a floor of this medieval palace next to the Textile Museum; a rather expensive agreement as Barcelona city hall must pay to keep the deal alive (it has been renewed until late 2003).
The lighting is dark and overly theatrical (a cliché of 'tribal art' presentation), but the collection is impressive, highlighted by extraordinary pieces from Mexico (whose government is now claiming certain pieces were taken illegitimately), Central America, the Andes and the lower Amazon. Some exhibits date to the second millennium BC, and there are gold and silver objects from Peru and Bolivia. The Barbier-Mueller co-ordinates projects with other museums with connections to the Americas, such as the Museu Marítim and the Museu de la Xocolata.

Museu de Geologia

Passeig Picasso, Parc de la Ciutadella (93 319 68 95). Metro Arc de Triomf/14, 39, 40, 41, 42, 51, 141 bus. **Open** 10am-2pm Tue, Wed, Fri-Sun; 10am-6.30pm Thur. **Guided tours** by appointment (93 319 69 12). **Admission** €3; €1.50 concessions; free under-16s. Free 1st Sun of the mth. **Discounts** BC. **No credit cards. Map** p341 E6.

The Geologia is Barcelona's oldest museum, opened in 1882 to house the private holdings of founder Francesc Martorell, and was once known as the Museu Martorell. In one wing there is a rather dry display of minerals, painstakingly classified, alongside explanations of geological phenomena found in Catalonia. One of the better features looks at mineral colour under ultraviolet light. More interesting is the other wing, with a selection from the museum's collection of more than 300,000 fossils, including imprints of flora and fauna (even dinosaurs) and fossilised bones from many geological periods. Curiously enough, many were found on Montjuïc or inside caves on the site of the Parc Güell.

Museu Picasso

C/Montcada 15-23 (93 319 63 10/www.museu picasso.bcn.es). Metro Jaume I/17, 19, 40, 45 bus. **Open** 10am-8pm Tue-Sat; 10am-3pm Sun. **Admission** *Museum only* €5; €2.50 concessions. *Temporary exhibitions* €7.80; €4.50 concessions. Free under-12s. Free (museum only) 1st Sun of the mth. **Discounts** BC. **Credit** (shop only) AmEx, MC, V. **Map** p343 C3.
When his father José Ruiz Blasco was hired to teach at Barcelona's art school in 1895, 13-year-old Pablo Ruiz Picasso diligently whipped off a few drawings for the school's entrance exam and began his studies. By the time of his definitive move to Paris in 1904 he had already painted his greatest Blue Period works, and was on his way to becoming the most acclaimed artist of the century. Barcelona's Picasso Museum is testimony to these vital formative years, spent in the company of Catalonia's fin-de-siècle avant-garde.
The museum arose out of a donation to the city by Picasso's secretary and life-long friend Jaume Sabartès (seen in a Blue Period painting from 1901). It graces a tight row of medieval courtyard-palaces, appropriately just five minutes away from the old art school building, La Llotja. The main entrance is at the elegant Palau Berenguer d'Aguilar, though you can also get tickets a few metres down the street if the queue gets too long. Since opening in 1963, it has expanded to incorporate adjacent mansions: the later but also impressive Palaus Meca and Castellet, the baroque Casa Mauri and the early Gothic Casa Finestres. A courtyard behind them hosts the café. When restoration is completed in 2003 the plan is to show as much as possible of the more than 3,000 paintings, drawings and other work, as well as temporary shows (in mid 2002, *Paris-Barcelona* will look at the cultural relations between the two cities from the late 19th century to the 1937 Paris World Fair, where *Guernica* was first shown).
Two things stand out in the museum. The seamless presentation of Picasso's development from 1890 to 1904, from deft pre-adolescent portraits to sketchy landscapes to intense innovations in blue, is unbeatable. Then, in a flash, one bounds to a gallery of mature cubist paintings from 1917, and completes the hopscotch with a jump to oils from the late 1950s, including the complete series of studies

based on Velázquez' famous *Las Meninas*. This acrobatic leap could leave the visitor itching for more. The culmination of Picasso's early genius in *Les Demoiselles d'Avignon* (1907) and the first cubist paintings from the time (many of them done in Catalonia), as well as his collage and sculpture, are completely absent.

Museu Tèxtil i d'Indumentària

C/Montcada 12 (93 319 76 03/93 310 45 16). Metro Jaume I/17, 19, 40, 45 bus. **Open** 10am-6pm Tue-Sat; 10am-3pm Sun. **Guided tours** by appointment (93 280 50 20). **Admission** €3.50; €2 concessions. *Combined admission with Museu Barbier-Mueller* €3; €1.50 concessions. Free under-16s. Free 1st Sun of the mth. **Discounts** BC. **Credit** (shop only) AmEx, MC, V. **Map** p343 C3.
Through the handsome medieval courtyard of this C/Montcada palace, right across from the Picasso Museum, visitors come to the elegant displays of the Textile and Clothing museum. The collection occupies two adjacent buildings, the Palau Nadal and Palau dels Marquesos de Lló; the latter retains some of its 13th-century wooden ceilings. Items include medieval Hispano-Arab textiles, liturgical vestments and the city's lace and embroidery collection. The real highlight are the historic fashions – from baroque to 20th-century – that collector Manuel Rocamora donated in the 1960s, one of the finest collections of their type anywhere. Recent important donations include one from Spanish designer Cristóbal Balenciaga, famous for the 1958 'baby doll' dress and pill box hat. There's also an excellent shop and a very popular café (*see p178*).

Museu de Zoologia

Passeig Picasso, Parc de la Ciutadella (93 319 69 12). Metro Arc de Triomf/14, 39, 40, 41, 42, 51, 141 bus. **Open** 10am-2pm Tue, Wed, Fri-Sun; 10am-6pm Thur. **Admission** €3; €1.50 concessions; free under-16s. Free 1st Sun of the mth. **Discounts** BC. **No credit cards. Map** p341 E6.
Another of the city's older museums, the Zoology Museum occupies the much-loved 'Castell dels Tres Dragons', built by Domènech i Montaner as the café-restaurant for the 1888 Exhibition. The separation between structure and glass façade predates the curtain walls of the modern movement. Downstairs is the Whale Room (with a whale skeleton), which is also where temporary shows are organised; in 2002 there will be an exhibition on the Balearic Islands before human settlement. The upper floor has a big collection of dissected and preserved animals, displayed systematically according to group and species. A very thorough guidebook is available in English.

Palau de la Mùsica Catalana

C/Sant Francesc de Paula 2 (93 295 72 00/ www.palaumusica.org). Metro Urquinaona/ 17, 19, 40, 45 bus. **Open** *Box office* 10am-9pm daily. **Guided tours** 10am-3.30pm daily. **Admission** €5; €4 concessions. **Credit** (groups only, minimum 25) MC, V. **Map** p342 B-C2.

Possibly the most dazzling work of *Modernisme* in the city, Domènech i Montaner's Palace of Catalan Music was built in 1905-8. The façade, with its bare brick, busts and mosaic friezes representing Catalan musical traditions alongside great composers, is impressive enough, but it is surpassed by the building's staggering interior. Decoration erupts everywhere: the ceiling centrepiece is of multicoloured stained glass; 18 half-mosaic, half-relief figures representing the musical muses appear out of the back of the stage; and on one side, massive Wagnerian carved horses ride out to accompany a bust of Beethoven. The old Palau has been bursting under the pressure of the musical activity going on inside it, and an extension and renovation programme by Oscar Tusquets in the 1980s is being followed by yet more alterations by the same architect.
The best way to see the Palau is to go to a concert (*see p240*), but you can also visit it on a guided tour. Tours are available in English, Catalan or Spanish, last 50min and leave every 30min or so. They begin with a 20min video, which can make the remaining tour a bit rushed, and parts of the building (such as the exterior decoration) are not touched upon.

Sala Montcada

C/Montcada 14 (93 310 06 99). Metro Jaume I/ 17, 19, 40, 45 bus. **Open** 11am-3pm, 4-8pm Tue-Sat; 11am-3pm Sun. **Admission** free. **Map** p343 C3.
The Fundació La Caixa runs one of Barcelona's finest spaces for more daring contemporary art. Each year a different curator develops a mixed programme of Spanish and international artists; for 2002, Chus Martínez presents *Lowest Common Denominator*, a cycle dealing with the architecture of the art space, including the video work of Barcelonan Oriol Font, Berlin-based team Elmgreen and Dragset, and Frankfurt artist Tobias Rehberger.

Santa Maria del Mar

Plaça de Santa Maria (93 310 23 90). Metro Jaume I/17, 19, 40, 45 bus. **Open** 9am-1.30pm, 4.30-8pm daily. **Admission** free. **Map** p343 C3.
The city's finest and most popular church has twice narrowly escaped demolition; once in 1716 when a huge area of La Ribera was razed to make way for the citadel, and then again in 1936 when an anti-clerical mob set it ablaze. It's perhaps thanks to them that its superb features can be appreciated – without the wooden baroque images that clutter so many Spanish churches, the simplicity of its lines can emerge. Built remarkably quickly for a medieval building, between 1329 and 1384, it has an unusual unity of style. Inside, two rows of slim, perfectly proportioned columns soar up to fan vaults, creating a wonderful atmosphere of space and peace. There's also superb stained glass, particularly the great 15th-century rose window above the main door. The curiously incongruous modern window at the other end was a 1997 addition, belatedly celebrating the Olympics. To fully savour the building's extraordinary grace and strength, try to see a concert there, or catch choir practice.

Ports & Shoreline

Oh, we do like to be beside the seaside.

Port Vell

At the foot of the Rambla, Columbus – **Colom** in Catalan, as the monument is called – points out to sea from atop his column, confusingly enough towards Italy. To his right are the 14th-century shipyards, now the site of the **Museu Marítim**, and from near the foot of the column you can cross the harbour on the **Golondrinas** boat trips. These are features that have been in place for years. However, had you taken the lift to the viewing point at Columbus's feet in, say, 1980, you would have seen the harbour beneath you thronged with cargo ships waiting to load or unload. Today, they have disappeared, and the scene has changed utterly. Commercial traffic has moved away to container terminals outside the main port, in the Zona Franca. Simultaneously, Barcelona's inner harbour, rechristened the **Port Vell** or Old Port, has undergone an extraordinary overhaul to turn it into a waterside leisure area – so much so that 20 years on a visitor simply would not recognise it. In just a few years since the mid 1990s, the former dockside has become one of Barcelona's foremost party zones.

If you make your way through the traffic of the Passeig de Colom to the waterfront, you will come to the **Rambla de Mar**, a swivel-section wooden footbridge (which opens to let boats enter and leave) that leads to the **Moll d'Espanya** quay. The quay is dominated by the **Maremàgnum** complex, a trademark work by architects Helio Piñón and Albert Viaplana. As much an entertainment as a shopping centre (*see p184*), it contains dozens of shops and restaurants as well as clubs and bars, and on weekend evenings is packed with young crowds. Further along the same quay there's also an eight-screen cinema, the giant-format **IMAX** (*see p227*) and Barcelona's **Aquàrium** (*see p221*), one of the best of its kind in the world.

When you've had enough of Maremàgnum, recross the footbridge and turn right to the **Moll de la Fusta** (wood quay) – where wood used to be unloaded hundreds of years ago – which was the first part of the port to be redeveloped. When it was inaugurated in 1987 it contained a string of pavement bars and restaurants, later closed by the council after the riotous late-night scene caused too many complaints. Among the restaurants was

Gambrinus, topped by a giant fibre-glass lobster by designer Javier Mariscal – which became a symbol of 1980s, pre-Olympic Barcelona. Today, Gambrinus is still shut, though the lobster remains, but there are tentative moves to allow a few vigorously vetted restaurants back in, and to open a new tourist information office. The cobblestones, meanwhile, are being ripped up and replaced with nice, sensible, easy-to-clean asphalt.

Impossible to miss at the north end of the Moll de la Fusta, by the border of La Ribera, is the impressive 14-metre (46-foot) high mosaic sculpture *Barcelona Head*, by Roy Lichtenstein. To the right of this is the marina – with some very luxurious yachts – and a line of waterside restaurants. The *tinglados*, the huge dock storage sheds that once dominated **Passeig Joan de Borbó**, have nearly all been pulled down to open up an entirely new, positively gracious harbourside promenade on this side of Barceloneta. One exception is the **Palau de Mar**, a converted warehouse that now hosts a clutch of restaurants and the **Museu d'Història de Catalunya**. Set into the pavement around here, you will see the names of all the winds of the Catalan coast, by sculptor Lothar Baumgarten. The only remaining commercial section is a small area for fishermen.

Reading palms on **Barceloneta** beach.

If you continue walking beyond here you can go through the Barceloneta district to the Port Olímpic and the city's beaches.

Returning to Columbus's feet, if, instead of walking across to Maremàgnum or along the Moll de la Fusta, you head to the right, looking out to sea, you will come to the **Moll de Barcelona**. This is a working quay, the departure point for ferries to the Balearics (*see p303*). At the end of the quay is the **World Trade Center** (WTC), which opened in 1999. Resembling a vast docked oceanliner, the WTC has 130,000 square metres (400,000 square feet) of floor space containing offices, an exhibition hall, a conference centre and shops. On either side are cruise terminals, which will round off Barcelona's already hugely successful drive to become the dominant cruise port of the Mediterranean. The landward side of the complex is taken up with an enormous five-star hotel, due to open in spring 2002.

South of Montjuïc, work is under way on extending the Zona Franca industrial area to create a new 'Logistics Park' with optimum port, road, rail and air links. To facilitate this plan, the port has been divided in two, with the strictly commercial zone to be located south of the WTC, while cruise ships and pleasure craft will have their own new harbour entry across from the WTC. The terrible storms in late 2001, however, severely damaged the breakwater being built to protect the new entrance, and this may now not open until 2003.

A rather more successful part of this grand design is the immense drawbridge opened in 2000, the **Porta d'Europa**, the widest bridge of its type in the world (one metre or so more than Rotterdam's), which connects the old breakwater with the land. The objective of all this is to consolidate Barcelona as the foremost freight port and distribution centre in the western Mediterranean, ahead of eternal rivals Marseilles and Genoa. The strategy is evidently working, as multinationals have stampeded to fill the office space of the WTC.

Catamaran Orsom

Moll de Espanya, Maremàgnum (93 225 82 60/ www.barcelona-orsom.com). Metro Drassanes or Barceloneta/14, 17, 19, 36, 40, 45, 57, 59, 64 bus. **Maremàgnum to Port Olímpic** (approx 1hr 30min) *June-Sept* 3 daily. *Oct-May* 2 daily. **Tickets** €5-€12; free under-4s. **Credit** MC, V. **Map** p340 D7. For a different view of Barcelona, take a ride out to sea in a catamaran. The trip takes you past the breakwater, at which point the engine is turned off and the sail hoisted for a peaceful float along the coast to the Port Olímpic and back. The catamarans have room for 100 passengers, and are also available for private charters. All sailings are subject to weather conditions.

Colom

Plaça Portal de la Pau (93 302 52 24). Metro Drassanes/14, 20, 36, 38, 57, 59, 64, 91, 157 bus. **Open** *June-late Sept* 9am-8.30pm daily. *Late Sept-Mar* 10am-1.30pm, 3.30-6.30pm Mon-Fri; 10am-6.30pm Sat, Sun. *Apr, May* 10am-1.30pm, 3.30-7.30pm Mon-Fri; 10am-7.30pm Sat, Sun. **Admission** €1.80; €1.20 concessions; free under-4s. **Discounts** BC, BT. **No credit cards. Map** p343 A4.
Take a lift 60m (197ft) to the top of the Columbus column, which was built for the 1888 Exhibition, for a panoramic view of the Old City and the port from within the crown at the explorer's feet. The lift only holds four people and the attendant at any one time, so there's often quite a queue.

Las Golondrinas

Moll de Drassanes (93 442 31 06/www.las golondrinas.com). Metro Drasannes/14, 36, 38, 57, 59, 64, 157 bus. **Drassanes to breakwater & return** (35min) *July-late Sept* every 35-45min 11am-8pm daily. *Late Sept-June* (no stop at the breakwater) hourly 11.45am-5pm Mon-Fri; every 35min (phone to check times) Sat, Sun. **Tickets** €3.30, €1.70 concessions; free under-4s. **Drassanes to Port Olímpic & return** (1½hrs) *July-Sept* 11.30pm, 1.30pm, 4.30pm, 6.30pm, 8.30pm daily. *Apr-June* 11.30am, 1.30pm, 4.30pm Mon-Fri; 11.30pm, 1.30pm, 4.30pm, 6.30pm Sat, Sun. *Oct-Mar* 11.30am, 1.30pm Mon-Fri; 11.30am, 1.30pm, 4.30pm Sat, Sun. **Tickets** €8.10; €3.60-€5.90 concessions; free under-4s. *Both* **Discounts** BC, BT. **Credit** MC, V. **Map** p340 C7.
The double-decker 'Swallow Boats' take you around the harbour to the end of the breakwater, where you can take in the sea air, go fishing or come straight back. More substantial, sea-going boats run on a longer trip round to the Port Olímpic.

Transbordador Aeri

Miramar, Parc de Montjuïc to Torre de Jaume I, Port Vell to Torre de Sant Sebastià, Barceloneta (93 441 48 20). World Trade Center: Metro Drassanes/ 20, 36, 57, 64, 157, N0, N6 bus. **Open** *Mid June-mid Sept* 11am-8pm daily. *Mid Sept-mid Oct, ar-mid June* 10.45am-7pm daily. *Mid Oct-Feb* 10.30am-5.30pm daily. **Tickets** €7.20 single; €8.40 return. **No credit cards. Map** p340 C-D7.
The 1929 cable car rattles across the harbour from Miramar on Montjuïc to Barceloneta (and back), with a stop in the middle by the World Trade Center. Views of Barceloneta and the port are spectacular.

Barceloneta

The triangular district known as Barceloneta ('Little Barcelona'), the part of the city between the harbour and the sea, was the product of an early example of authoritarian town planning. When after 1714 a large section of La Ribera was razed to make way for the new citadel, the people displaced lived for many years in makeshift shelters on the beach, until in the 1750s the authorities decided to rehouse them in line with a plan drawn up by a Flemish

The best Things to do

On Monday
Stroll round the MACBA (*see p89*); most other museums and art galleries are closed today. See a movie: it's cheap night at most cinemas. Theatres, on the other hand, are generally dark on Mondays.

On Tuesday
Tuck into the seafood you couldn't get yesterday when the fish restaurants were closed, then enjoy cheap night at the theatre.

On Wednesday
It's the museums that are discounted today (perhaps you're beginning to see a pattern here), as are the remaining cinemas.

On Thursday
All back to full price. Console yourself with paella, on the *menú del dia* of many restaurants (though slopped out of a communal pan rather than made at your behest). There's also an antiques market in front of the cathedral (*see p207*).

On Friday
An artisan-produced food market specialising in cheese, honey, chocolate, olives and herbs takes place on alternate Fridays and Saturdays in the Plaça del Pi (*see p207*). Work off the calories off with some folk dancing (9-11pm) in the Plaça del Rei (*see p76*).

On Saturday
Wander through the art market in the Plaça Sant Josep Oriol (*see p207 –* though it's mostly pretty tacky stuff) and the handicrafts market at the foot of La Rambla (*see p79*). Saturday afternoon is *sardana* time in Plaça Sant Jaume (*see p84*).

On Sunday
Markets aplenty: Saturday's art market continues, there are coins and stamps in Plaça Reial, badges and pins beneath Arc de Triomf, and second-hand books, videos, computer games and even pornography at Mercat Sant Antoni (for all, *see p208*). Purify your soul with more *sardana* dancing, in front of the cathedral in the morning (*see p77*), and in Plaça Sant Jaume in the evening.

Sightseeing

Oarstruck at the **Museu Marítim**.

army engineer, Prosper Verboom. The new district was built on land reclaimed from the sea. The street plan of Barceloneta, with its long narrow blocks, reveals its military origins. In the 19th century this became the dockers' and fishermen's district, and a massive road and rail barrier was built that cut off Barceloneta from the rest of the city until the transformations of the 1990s. This barrier helped the area retain a distinctive atmosphere and identity; the local *festa major* (*see p218*) in September is a riot of colour.

Barceloneta has also traditionally been the city's gateway to the beach. Until not so long ago this was of interest only to a few devotees of sunbathing rather than seabathing. Some may cavil at the water quality even today, but since the comprehensive reconstruction of the city's beaches it has become far cleaner and more pleasant. Consequently, Barceloneta has become still more thronged on summer weekends, as crowds make their way through its streets for a meal or a swim.

Away from the beach and the city, at its 'tip', Barceloneta leads into **Passeig de l'Escullera**, the road along the breakwater that is eventually to be truncated by the new harbour entry for pleasure craft. Plans for this area, by the often-controversial Ricard Bofill, involve the creation of yet more leisure area on reclaimed land and, most spectacularly, the building of an 88-metre (290-foot) high, sail-shaped hotel. Originally, it was to be 150 metres (490 feet) high, until public outcry tamed the project somewhat. The stretch of beach running up to it is to be extended in length and width, and a new *rambla* for pedestrians and cyclists to be added.

A famous feature of Barceloneta was that it used to be possible to combine the district's two pleasures in the traditional paella and seafood restaurants that lined the beach. These basic *chiringuitos* were closed down by city edict in 1991. On the stretch of beach where they used to run stands *Homage to Barceloneta*, Rebecca Horn's wonderful structure of rusted cubes. For Barceloneta, the city's massive reworking of the old port – and the transformation of Passeig

Joan de Borbó from dockyard service road to waterside promenade – has in effect meant a complete re-orientation of the area through 180°, from looking out to sea to overlooking the port. Some former *chiringuito* owners have therefore gradually been encouraged to reopen, alongside smart all-new restaurants, on the new harbourside *passeig* and in the **Palau de Mar**, while other dock buildings have been torn down to open up a view of the harbour and Montjuïc that most Barceloneta residents had been unaware of all their lives.

Museu d'Història de Catalunya

Plaça Pau Vila 3 (93 225 47 00/www.cultura.gencat. es/museus/mhc). Metro Barceloneta/17, 39, 45, 47, 57, 59, 64, 157 bus. **Open** 10am-7pm Tue, Thur-Sat; 10am-8pm Wed; 10am-2.30pm Sun. **Admission** €3; €2.10 concessions; free under-7s. **Guided tours** noon Sun. **Discounts** BC, BT. **Credit** (shop only) MC, V. **Map** p343 C4.

Run by the Generalitat, this museum aims to explain Catalan history from start to finish. It's not a museum in the sense of a collection of treasured objects, but rather offers an overview from prehistory to the present, with visually dynamic displays taking the viewer through thematically organised sections. A multitude of materials is used to keep you entertained – texts, photographs, real objects, reproductions, videos, animated models and re-creations of domestic scenes. There are also hands-on exhibits, such as a waterwheel and wearable armour.

After the exhibitions were criticised for ignoring certain Catalan realities – such as the massive immigration from the rest of Spain since the 1930s – new director Jaume Sobrequés, a socialist historian, has decided to redo the entire second half, covering the past 200 years; it will be revamped starting in late 2002, meaning some parts may be closed. Large temporary exhibitions deal with just about everything imaginable, from the history of political parties to seemingly unrelated shows on the father of Andalucian nationalism, Blas Infante (in April 2002). A major exhibition on the Jewish presence in Catalonian history will finally open, after many delays, from April to late June 2002. The library upstairs has English material, and English tours are available for groups. The top-floor restaurant has an unbeatable view and good food. There is also an imaginative gift shop.

Museu Marítim

Avda de les Drassanes (93 342 99 29/www.diba.es/ mmaritim). Metro Drassanes/14, 20, 36, 38, 57, 59, 64, 91, 157 bus. **Open** 10am-7pm daily. **Admission** €5.50; €2.70 concessions; free under-7s. **Discounts** BC, BT. **Credit** MC, V. **Map** p343 A4.

The giant *drassanes* or medieval shipyards that house this museum are among the finest examples of civil Gothic architecture in the world. Since a 1990s face-lift, the impressively refined arches watch over one of the city's most attractive and most visited collections. The highlight is the full-scale reproduction of the Royal Galley, the flagship of Don Juan de Austria at the battle of Lepanto against the Turks in 1571. This battle and the subsequent history of Barcelona's port are presented in 'The Great Adventure of the Sea', a series of unashamedly audience-pleasing historical simulations, with headphone commentaries (also in English). Visitors are caught in a storm on a 19th-century trade ship, take a steamer to Buenos Aires and go underwater in the *Ictineo*, the prototype submarine of Catalan inventor Narcís Monturiol. The museum also has pleasure boats, fishing craft, figureheads, explanations of boat-building techniques and a section on map-making and navigation, plus a collection of paintings and drawings that show how the port of Barcelona has changed. Admission also gets you on board the historical *Santa Eulàlia* sailing ship docked nearby at the Moll de la Fusta. There's plenty of space for temporary shows, though restoration work means visitors could find small parts of the collection altered.

Vila Olímpica

In 1986, Barcelona was elected Olympic City for 1992 and the whole population seemed to pour into the streets to celebrate. Then the job began of preparing to build what would soon be called the city's newest *barri*, the Olympic Village, most ambitious of all the 1992 projects. It was a local cliché to say that Barcelona had turned its back to the sea, with barriers of railways, factories and dirty industrial roads that since the 1850s had cut its citizens off from their abandoned, refuse-strewn beaches. Now the plan was to open out.

Not since Cerdà or Gaudí has anyone had such an impact on the face of Barcelona as the architects Oriol Bohigas, Josep Martorell, long-time English resident David Mackay and Albert Puigdomènech, who were entrusted with the overall design of the all-new district, to be built on reclaimed industrial land. Constructed in just two years, it was initially named Nova Icària to recall the utopian socialist community that briefly existed in the area in the last century, but the name has never stuck. As well as a range of services, some 2,000 apartments were built, which it was hoped would provide low-cost housing once the athletes had vacated them after the Games. However, economic realities have since dictated otherwise.

Those who have paid the relatively high prices for flats in the village have at their disposal an impressive range of new leisure areas and seafront parks. Taken as a whole, the project is spectacular, even by Barcelona's standards. By far the most successful part of the Vila is the **Port Olímpic**, the leisure marina (with 743 mooring spaces) built from nothing since 1988, now lined with bars and restaurants packed with crowds of all ages every weekend night of the year. By day, it is also the place to hire sailing boats. Further inland, Ildefons Cerdà's original concept for the Eixample was taken as an inspiration, with semi-open blocks built around services and garden areas. Some sections, such as the skyscraper **Hotel Arts** (*see p59*), missed the deadline of July 1992 and were not opened until a good while later.

The final effect is of a rather cold, un-Mediterranean suburb, although the waterway parallel to C/Moscou and the red brick of **Plaça Tirant lo Blanc** soften the harshness. The glass and stone gateway buildings to the *barri* create a forbidding impression; there are few corner shops or cafés, and the spiky metal pergolas on Avda Icària look like a grim parody of trees. Even the jokey sculpture in Parc de Carles I, *David i Goliat*, leaves one with the feeling that this is a world in which the Goliaths usually slay the Davids. However, a touch of humour can be found in the same park, in the enormous six-metre (20-foot) sculpture of the lower half of a human body. Created by Basque artist Eduardo Úrculo, it has inevitably become known as *el culo de Úrculo*, Úrculo's arse. The Vila's open spaces are colonised by cyclists and rollerbladers at weekends.

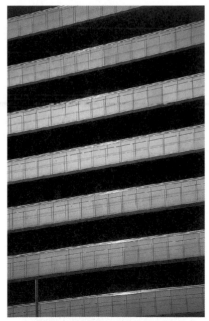

Torre Mapfre in the **Vila Olímpica**.

Montjuïc

Up, up and away from the crowds.

The huge, sprawling mass of Montjuïc, rising over the city from beside the port, is one of Barcelona's most loved features. The hill is a world of its own, encompassing a number of quite different areas. Hardly anyone lives there, but it is a delightful place for a stroll. From all over the hill you get wonderful views: they're particularly spectacular by the **Palau Nacional** and at **Miramar**, overlooking the harbour.

According to one legend of the origins of Barcelona, the city was founded by Hercules and populated by the crew of the ninth ship (*barca nona*) that went with him on his labours, after which Hercules sat on Montjuïc to admire his creation. But Montjuïc also has other associations. The **Castell de Montjuïc**, built in the 17th century, became a symbol of the suppression of Catalan liberties after 1714. As a prison and torture centre for rebels and radicals – or those deemed as such – it inspired fear and loathing for two centuries. The castle was finally handed over to the city by the army in 1960, but still houses the **Museu Militar**.

The military refused to allow much building on the mountain until well into the 20th century, and it was not until the run-up to the 1929 Exhibition that Montjuïc was landscaped. Today Montjuïc has been earmarked for some big changes, especially on its still semi-wild, mysterious southern flank. The old funfair has been closed down, perhaps because it was a bit vulgar and shabby for the planners, and work on a five-star hotel at Miramar has begun.

Despite all the activity on the mountain, its proximity to the city centre and the fun means of transport to get up there – the **Funicular**, **Telefèric** and **Tren Montjuïc** – it's surprisingly easy to find peaceful, shaded places among the many park areas. Below the castle, on the steep flank nearest the port, are the **Jardins Mossèn Costa i Llobera**, which abound in exotic plants, including a Mexican cactus popularly known as *el seient de la sogra*, 'mother-in-law's seat'. Not far above, on the Montjuïc road, Avda Miramar, are the **Jardins del Mirador**, from where there is a spectacular view over the harbour. Carry on along this road away from the sea and you will reach the **Jardins Cinto Verdaguer**, with a beautiful pond, flowers and more views; a little further on are the municipal swimming pool, spectacularly

rebuilt for the 1992 Olympic diving events, and the **Fundació Miró**. Continue uphill to reach the **Anella Olímpica** (Olympic Ring), a compact hub of buildings in contrasting styles.

The **Estadi Olímpic** – home to the city's 'second' football team, Espanyol – although entirely new, was built within the façade of an existing 1929 stadium by a design team led by Federico Correa and Alfonso Milà. Next to it is the most original and attractive of the Olympic facilities, Arata Isozaki's **Palau Sant Jordi** indoor hall, with a vast metal roof built on the ground and raised into place by hydraulic jacks. It now regularly serves as a venue for concerts and other events; in 2002 it will host the European MTV awards. In the *plaça* in front locals gather on Sundays for family walks and picnics, next to Santiago Calatrava's remarkable, bow-like communications tower. Further along is Barcelona's best swimming pool, the **Bernat Picornell** (*see p269*) – predating the Games, but rebuilt for them, and at the foot of the hill by Plaça d'Espanya is another sports hall, the **Palau dels Esports**, built in the 1960s but rebuilt for 1992.

If you turn right from the Fundació Joan Miró and head downhill you will come upon a veritable orgy of monumentalist and *Noucentista* architecture from 1929, which now

Font Màgica. *See p106*

contains the area's other main cultural centres. There are museums (the **MNAC**, the **Museu d'Arqueologia**, the **Museu Etnològic**), and the **Ciutat del Teatre** complex (*see p272*). Also on Montjuïc is the **Teatre Grec**, home of the **Festival del Grec** (*see p217*). Further down are the ineffable **Poble Espanyol** and the **Pavelló Barcelona** (aka **Pavelló Mies van der Rohe**). Across the road from the Mies Pavilion, Puig i Cadafalch's *Modernista* factory, the **Casaramona**, has been converted into a new home for the **Fundació La Caixa's** cultural centre. As you approach **Plaça d'Espanya**, Carles Buigas' water-and-light spectacular, the **Font Màgica**, is a breathtakingly tacky but unmissable end to a memorable walk, and next to Plaça d'Espanya are the trade fair buildings (the **Fira**). On the north side of the *plaça* is the disused and overgrown bullring, **Les Arenes**.

Font Màgica de Montjuïc

Plaça d'Espanya (93 291 40 42/www.bcn.es/fonts).
Metro Espanya/bus all routes to Plaça d'Espanya.
Fountain *May-Sept* 8pm-midnight Thur-Sun; music every 30min 9.30pm-midnight. *Mar, Apr, Oct-early Jan* 7-9pm Fri, Sat; music every 30min 7-9pm. **Map** p339 A5.
Fabulously kitsch and a must-see for anyone with a sense of humour, the 1929 'magic fountain' swells and dances to various hits ranging from Whitney Houston to the 1812 Overture, showing off its kaleidoscope of pastel colours, while searchlights play in a giant fan pattern over the palace dome.

Fundació la Caixa

CaixaForum, Avda Marquès de Comillas 6-8 (93 423 88 06/www.fundacio.lacaixa.es). Metro Plaça Espanya/13, 50 bus. **Open** 11am-8pm Tue-Sat; 11am-3pm Sun. Closed Aug. **Admission** free. **Credit** (shop only) AmEx, DC, MC, V. **Map** p339 A5.
Spain's largest savings bank, La Caixa, has a very high-profile cultural foundation with an excellent collection of international contemporary art and a Spain-wide exhibitions programme which also touches on ethnology and archaeology. The main cultural centre in Barcelona has just moved to this, the renovated Casaramona textile mill near Plaça d'Espanya, though the former centre at the Casa Macaya in the Eixample, a magnificent *Modernista* residence also by Puig i Cadafalch, will house shows until mid 2002. The much larger Casaramona is now called CaixaForum: its exterior is distinguished by creative brickwork, with the new entrance plaza designed by Arata Isozaki. The massive interior floor space will allow for part of the permanent collection, including installations by Joseph Beuys and Richard Serra, to be viewed at all times.

Temporary shows in 2002 include a spring impressionist exhibition from L'Orangerie collection, as well as 'Richard Avedon: In the American West' (late April to August). Around the same time, there will be another exhibition on the work of Mies van der Rohe, whose 1929 German Pavilion replica is just across the street. The CaixaForum also houses Barcelona's best documentary centre for video and media art (the Mediateca – *see p314*), and has an excellent bookshop.
Branch: Centre Cultural de la Fundació la Caixa, Passeig de Sant Joan 108, Eixample (93 476 86 00).

Plaça d'Espanya.

Fundació Joan Miró

*Parc de Montjuïc (93 329 19 08/www.bcn.fjmiro.es).
Metro Paral.lel, then Funicular de Montjuïc/61 bus.*
Open *July-Sept* 10am-8pm Tue, Wed, Fri, Sat; 10am-
9.30pm Thur; 10am-2.30pm Sun. *Oct-June* 10am-7pm
Tue, Wed, Fri, Sat; 10am-9.30pm Thur; 10am-2.30pm
Sun. **Guided tours** 12.30pm Sat, Sun. **Admission**
All exhibitions €7.50; €3 concessions. *Permanent
exhibitions* €4; €2 concessions. Free under-14s.
Discounts Articket, BC, BT. **Credit** (shop only)
MC, V. **Map** p339 B6.

Conceived by Miró in his final years, the foundation
celebrated its 25th anniversary in 2001 with the
opening of the Sala K, designed to show 23 first-class
Miró paintings from Japanese collector Kazumasa
Katsuta, and a downstairs gallery housing works by
other 20th-century masters such as Moore, Léger,
Balthus, Ernst and Oldenburg. Like all expansions
to the building, the new wing is inspired by the original architecture of Miró's friend Josep Lluís Sert:
white walls, rustic tile floors and an elegant system
of roof arches make this one of the world's great
museum buildings. The foundation houses a collection of more than 225 paintings, 150 sculptures and
all Miró's graphic work, plus some 5,000 drawings.

The permanent collection, highlighting Miró's
trademark use of primary colours and simplified
organic forms symbolising stars, the moon, birds
and women, occupies the second half of the exhibition space. It begins with a large tapestry created
with Josep Royo (similar to a piece lost in the New
York WTC terrorist attack), then, on the way to the
sculpture gallery, is Alexander Calder's reconstructed *Mercury Fountain*. In other works, Miró is
shown as a cubist (*Street in Pedralbes*, 1917), naïve
(*Portrait of a Young Girl*, 1919) or surrealist (*Man
and Woman in Front of a Pile of Excrement*, 1935),
while the Sala Pilar Juncosa features early depictions
of Montroig, where Miró summered, and other
mature works. Large, simpler, black-outlined paintings are from the final period, while more sculpture
is found on the roof terrace with its wonderful view.

In 2002 temporary shows include a spring exhibition on contemporary conceptions of space (with
work by Boltanski, Kabakov, Tony Cragg and
Günther Forg), and a summer show coinciding with
the 'International Year of Gaudí', based on Miró's
1979 series *Homage to Gaudí*. The Espai 13 in the
basement features young contemporary artists. The
Foundation hosts other activities, especially contemporary music, and has a fine research library.

Funicular de Montjuïc

*Metro Paral.lel to Avda Miramar (93 443 08 59/
www.tmd.net). Metro Paral.lel/20, 36, 57, 64, 91,
157 bus.* **Open** *June-Oct* 11am-10pm daily. *Nov-Apr*
10.45am-8pm Sat, Sun. *May* 10.45am-8pm daily.
Tickets €1.70 single; €2.50 return. **Discounts** BT.
No credit cards. Map p339-40 B-C6.

Mostly underground, so not much sightseeing, but
the cog-wheeled train brings you out well placed for
the Fundació Joan Miró and Miramar. It connects
with the Telefèric (cable car).

They've cut the bull at **Les Arenes**.
See p106.

See p106.

Sightseeing

Galeria Olímpica

*Estadi Olímpic, Parc de Montjuïc (93 426 06 60/
www.fundaciobarcelonaolimpica.es). Metro Espanya/
bus all routes to Plaça d'Espanya.* **Open** *Apr-Sept*
10am-2pm, 4-7pm Mon-Fri. *Oct-Mar* 10am-1pm,
4-6pm Mon-Fri. **Admission** €2.70. **Discounts**
BC, BT. **Credit** AmEx, MC, V. **Map** p339 A6.

This space commemorating the 1992 Olympics is a
hotchpotch of imagery and paraphernalia from the
Games – including the costumes from the opening
ceremony and the full array of marketing items featuring the ubiquitous mascot Cobi – illuminating its
spirit while offering little attraction for true sports
fans. Special attention is paid to Spanish medal winners. A spectacular video projection beneath the stadium is only shown to groups, though if you happen
to coincide with a screening they may invite you in.

Museu d'Arqueologia de Catalunya

*Passeig de Santa Madrona 39-41(93 423 21 49/
93 423 56 01/www.mac.es). Metro Poble Sec/
55 bus.* **Open** 9.30am-7pm Tue-Sat; 10am-2.30pm
Sun. **Admission** €2.40; €1.80 concessions; free
under-16s. **Discounts** BC. **Credit** (shop only)
MC, V. **Map** p339 B6.

With its art deco interiors, the Palace of Decorative
Arts, built for the 1929 Exhibition on Montjuïc, holds
one of the city's finest scientific museums. It is associated with a number of archaeological sites and
museums all over Catalonia (notably Tarragona,
Empúries and Ullastret), and is a good starting point
for related outings. Its artefacts come mostly from
digs all over Mediterranean Spain, starting with the
Palaeolithic period and moving on through subsequent eras, with relics of Greek, Punic, Roman and
Visigoth colonisers, up to the early Middle Ages.
There are objects related to early metallurgy, along
with models of Neolithic and Iron Age burial sites.

Fundació Joan Miró. *See p107.*

A few galleries are dedicated to the Majorcan Talaiotic cave culture, and there is a very good display on the Iberians, the pre-Hellenic, pre-Roman inhabitants of south-eastern Spain, whose level of decorative sophistication has been re-evaluated in recent years. Lovely terracotta goddesses and some beautiful jewellery taken from a dig on Ibiza recall the Carthaginian presence in the Balearics, and a large gallery is dedicated to the Greek remains at Empúries. Roman work includes original floor mosaics, and a reconstructed Pompeian palace room. There are also monumental Greek and Roman pieces, including a sarcophagus showing the rape of Persephone and Roman funerary *steles*. An huge statue of a sexually charged Priapus cannot be viewed up close (perhaps to protect school groups).

Museu Etnològic

Passeig de Santa Madrona 16-22 (93 424 68 07/ www.museuetnologic.bcn.es). Metro Poble Sec/55 bus. **Open** 10am-7pm Tue, Thur; 10am-2pm Wed, Fri-Sun. **Admission** €3; €1.50 concessions; free under-12s. **Discounts** BC. **No credit cards**. **Map** p339 A6.

The Ethnology Museum is one of the few Barcelona museums actually built for its current use. Massive collections from non-European cultures, totalling more than 30,000 pieces, are shown on a rotating basis, with emphasis increasingly given to contemporary cultures. A permanent Japan Space has a temporary show on Japanese food into mid 2002; other shows slated for 2002 include an in-depth look at the current cultural mosaic in Barcelona, and another of contemporary carved saints made in the Spanish colonial tradition (opening in spring).

Museu Militar

Castell de Montjuïc, Parc de Montjuïc (93 329 86 13). Metro Paral.lel, then Funicular and Telefèric de Montjuïc. **Open** *July-Sept* 9.30am-8pm Tue-Sun. *Oct-June* 9.30am-7pm Tue-Fri; 9.30am-8pm Sat, Sun. **Admission** €2.40; €1 concessions. **Discounts** BC. **No credit cards**. **Map** p339 B7.

The Military Museum has been under fire since the gift shop was found to be selling objects with Franco-era and Nazi symbolism; it was already controversial for the portrait gallery of repressive generals and Franco's equestrian statue (the only representation of the dictator left in Barcelona). The museum occupies the 18th-century fortress overlooking the city on the top of Montjuïc. Used to bombard rather than protect Barcelona in past conflicts, and as a prison and place of execution after the Civil War – a monument in the moat to Catalan President Lluís Companys recalls his death here in 1940 – the castle has strong repressive associations. However, its selection of historic weapons is quite special: armour, swords and lances; muskets (beautiful Moroccan *moukhala*), rifles and pistols; and menacing crossbows. Other highlights include 23,000 lead soldiers representing a Spanish division of the 1920s, and, oddly, a display of Jewish tombstones from the mountain's desecrated medieval cemetery, the only direct reminder of death in the building.

MNAC (Museu Nacional d'Art de Catalunya)

Palau Nacional, Parc de Montjuïc (93 622 03 60/ www.mnac.es). Metro Espanya/bus all routes to Plaça d'Espanya, then escalator. **Open** 10am-7pm Tue-Sat; 10am-2.30pm Sun. **Admission** €5.50; permanent exhibitions only €4.50; temporary exhibitions only €3; €2.10-€3.80 concessions; free under-7s. *Romanesque & Gothic collections* free 1st Thur of the mth. **Discounts** Articket, BC, BT. **Credit** (shop only) V. **Map** p339 A6.

Looking down from a regal perch on Montjuïc, the Palau Nacional looks like the baroque palace of some absolute monarch, although it was actually built as a 'temporary pavilion' for the 1929 Exhibition. The undisputed star is the Romanesque collection. Small churches and monasteries were founded in Catalonia in the 10th century, serving as beacons for beleaguered pilgrims and monks. Inside, primitive depictions of the Pantocrator (Christ in Majesty), the Virgin, biblical stories and the sufferings of the saints served to instruct doubting villagers in the basics of the faith. In the first decades of the 20th century, some art historians realised that scores of solitary churches in the Pyrenees were falling into ruin, and with them the extraordinary Romanesque mural paintings and sculptures that adorned their interiors. Entire chunks of buildings were 'saved' by private collectors to be set up elsewhere, but in Catalonia the laborious task was begun of removing murals intact from church apses.

The result is a series of images of extraordinary and timeless power. The display comprises 21 sections in loose chronological order, with the murals set into freestanding wood supports or reconstructed church interiors. One highlight is the tremendous Crist de Taüll, from the 12th-century church of Sant Climent de Taüll. The massive figure of the Pantocrator holds a book with the words *Ego Sum Lux Mundi*, 'I am the Light of the World'. Another treasure, from the church of Santa Maria de Taüll (in the same village as Sant Climent), has an apse of the Epiphany and Three Kings and a wall of the Last Judgement, packed with images of purgatory. Original 'graffiti' scratchings – probably by monks, of animals, crosses and labyrinths – have been preserved on some columns, and there are also some carvings and sculptures.

The Gothic collection is also excellent. Visitors can follow the evolution of Catalan Gothic painting, including altarpieces on wood panels and alabaster sculptures pulled from parish churches in Barcelona. Highlights are the works of the indisputable Catalan masters of the Golden Age, Bernat Martorell and the tremendously subtle Jaume Huguet. The international mix of works from the 15th to the 18th centuries in the Renaissance and baroque collections includes a few non-Spanish masters (Tintoretto, Rubens, De la Tour) mixed in with national figures (Zurbarán and Goya).

High-quality temporary shows are presented in the basement: in 2002 these include a summer show on Gaudí's talented collaborator Josep Maria Jujol, and *Modernista* posters and industrial design. Another show will deal with Catalan experiences in Nazi concentration camps. Restoration continues on the upper floors, where the Museu d'Art Modern, currently in the Ciutadella park, will eventually be

housed. The museum has good English labelling and a helpful English guidebook. The restaurant is the best dining option in the immediate area.

Pavelló Barcelona (Pavelló Mies van der Rohe)

Avda Marqués de Comillas (93 423 40 16/ www.miesbcn.com). Metro Espanya/bus all routes to Plaça d'Espanya. **Open** 10am-8pm daily. **Admission** €3.40; €1.50 concessions; free under-18s. **Credit** (shop only) MC, V. **Map** p339 A5.

The German Pavilion for the 1929 Exhibition, by Ludwig Mies van der Rohe, was also home to the 'Barcelona chair', copied in millions of office waiting rooms across the world. The pavilion was a founding monument of modern rationalist architecture, with a revolutionary use of stone, glass and space. It was demolished after the Exhibition, but a replica was built on the same site in 1986. Purists may think of it as a synthetic inferior of the original pavilion, but the elegance and simplicity of the design are still a striking demonstration of what rationalist architecture could do before it was reduced to production-line clichés.

Poble Espanyol

Avda Marqués de Comillas (93 325 78 66/ www.poble-espanyol.com). Metro Espanya/bus all routes to Plaça d'Espanya. **Open** 9am-8pm Mon; 9am-2am Tue-Thur; 9am-4am Fri, Sat; 9am-midnight Sun. **Admission** €7; €4.40 concessions; €3.60 7-12s; family ticket €12; free under-7s. **Discount** BC, BT. **Credit** AmEx, MC, V. **Map** p339 A5.

As part of the preparations for the 1929 Exhibition, someone had the bright idea of building, in one enclosed area, examples of traditional architecture from every region in Spain. The result was the Poble Espanyol, or 'Spanish village'. Inside it, a Castilian square leads to an Andalucian church, then to village houses from Aragon, and so on. There are

Religious art from the **MNAC**. *See p108.*

numerous bars and restaurants (including vegetarian), and 60-plus shops. Many are workshops in which craftspeople make and sell Spanish folk artefacts, such as ceramics, embroidery, fans, metalwork and candles. Some of the work is quite attractive, some tacky, and prices are generally high. Outside, street performers recreate bits of Catalan and Spanish folklore; there are special children's shows, and the 'Barcelona Experience', an audiovisual history presentation (available in English).

The Poble has an unmistakeable tourist-trap air, but it does have its fun side, and many of its buildings and squares are genuinely attractive. It also tries hard to promote itself as a nightspot, with karaoke bars, Cuban dinner-and-dance restaurants, discos and a flamenco show, and dance bands and music groups perform regularly in the main square. The grand entrance houses the bar that was once the pinnacle of Barcelona design-bardom, Torres de Avila (see p257), and one of the city's most popular clubs, La Terrrazza (or Discothèque, in its winter incarnation), is located at the back (see p256).

Telefèric de Montjuïc

Estació Funicular, Avda Miramar (93 443 08 59/ www.tmd.net). Metro Paral.lel, then Funicular de Montjüic/20, 36, 57, 64 bus. **Open** *June-mid Sept* 11.15am-9pm daily. *Mid Sept-Oct, Apr, May* 11am-7.15pm daily. *Nov-Mar* 11am-7.15pm Sat, Sun. **Tickets** €3.20 single; €4.50 return; €3.50 child return. **Discounts** BT. **No credit cards. Map** p339 B6.

Tree enterprise

There are 149,466 trees in Barcelona; if you don't believe it, count them yourself. The absurdly exact figure, courtesy of the parks and gardens department, makes one wonder if e'er a bough doth break without his master gardener knowing. For a city whose most famous park – Parc Güell – is renowned more for its mosaics than for its flora, the figure seems surprisingly high, especially since it does not include the Aleppo pines and holm oaks growing wildly on the hills above town.

King among the varieties lining the city's boulevards – with no fewer than 58,475 registered – is the London plane, a tall-growing, broad-leafed species originally imported from the Balkans, and easily trained to form a high canopy over the street (seen most prominently along the Rambla and Passeig de Gràcia). Its drawback is that it is disease-prone, giving it a muddy brown autumnal effect from late August until the final stubborn leaves drop just before spring. It is being replaced by varieties such as the European hackberry and Siberian elm, with beauties like the gnarly-trunked umbra tree preserved for grassy transitional spaces, such as at the foot of the Rambla.

Barcelona is experimenting with new trees in curious ways. Each neighbourhood of the Eixample, for example, has a distinguishing species for every intersection. Thus the cream-flowered Japanese pagoda tree has been chosen for the area around Sant Antoni market, the Judas tree (aka the 'tree of love') and the magnolia for the areas on the right- and left-hand sides of Passeig de Gràcia respectively, while the delicate lavender flowers of the Chinaberry grace the area around the Sagrada Família.

Quite a different story is told along the boulevards near the port and coastline, where palm trees meet strictly ornamental considerations. Stately palms are not native to Europe; only the low-lying European fan palm is local. Tall palms appeared in Catalonia in the 19th century when those returning with new-found fortunes from the Americas planted single palms in the gardens around their stately homes, still known as *cases indianes* (literally 'Indies houses'). Now the long lines of Canary Islands date palms and California fan palms lining the beach give the Barcelona summer scene that desired *Baywatch* feel, Pamela Anderson notwithstanding. The palm fruit is also the reason for a thriving population of feral parrots – said to be the descendants of a 1980s zoo escape – seen, and especially heard, along Diagonal and in the Parc de la Ciutadella.

The parks and gardens authorities tend five themed gardens in the city, including a rose garden at the Parc de Cervantes on the upper end of Diagonal. The other four are on Montjuïc. The **Jardí Botànic** (Botanical Garden), just next to the Olympic Stadium, probably needs a few years before its plantings from the Mediterranean and other comparable regions – western California, central Chile, South Africa and southern Australia – fill out, but with its dramatic landscaping and panoramic views, it's a peaceful place to wander. The Jardí Botànic is listed as a city museum, as its pavilions feature historical collections, such as the FX de Bolòs herb garden from the 18th and 19th centuries.

One of the lovelier gardens is the **Jardí Mossèn Costa i Llobera**, dedicated to cacti

The Montjuïc cable cars run between the funicular station and the castle at the top. Vertigo sufferers might not enjoy the trip, but there are superb views over Montjuïc and the port.

Tren Montjüic

Plaça d'Espanya (information Transporte Ciutat Comtal 93 415 60 20). Metro Espanya/bus all routes to Plaça d'Espanya. **Open** *Mid Apr-mid Sept* 11am-10pm daily. Closed mid Sept-mid Apr. **Frequency** every 30min. **Tickets** €1.80 single; €1.50 concessions. *All-day* €3; €2.40 concessions. **Discounts** BT. **No credit cards. Map** p339 A-B5. Not a train but an open trolley pulled by a truck, which goes up Montjuïc to Miramar, passing all the hilltop sights.

and other exotic species. The microclimate on the port side of Montjuïc sustains more than 800 species, including a 200-year-old Backeberg cactus native to the high Andes, its long white hairs punctuated by orange spines.

Wherever a tree is missing from the pavement, a small plaque is placed reading: 'The tree from this space will be replanted in the next planting campaign, during this species' period of growth dormancy.' And then there'll be 149,467.

Jardí Botanic

Doctor Font i Quer (93 426 49 35). Metro Espanya/bus all routes to Plaça d'Espanya. **Open** *Apr-June, Sept, Oct* 10am-5pm daily. *Nov-Mar, July, Aug* 10am-3pm daily. **Admission** €3; €1.50 concessions; free under-16s. Free last Sat of the mth. **No credit cards. Map** p339 A6-7.

Jardí Mossèn Costa i Llobera

Ctra de Miramar 1 (93 413 24 00/93 424 38 09). Metro Paral.lel or Drassanes/36, 57, 64, 91, 157 bus. **Open** 10am-sunset daily. **Admission** free. **Map** p339 B7.

Poble Sec & Paral.lel

The *barri* lining the side of the hill and ending at **Avda Paral.lel** is called **Poble Sec**. The name means 'dry village', fitting testimony to the fact that as late as 1894 the poor workers of the barri celebrated with dancing the installation of the area's first street fountain, which still stands in C/Margarit. By 1914, some 5,000 people lived in shanty towns up where the district meets Montjuïc. During the riots of the Setmana Tràgica in 1909, more religious buildings were destroyed here than in any other part of Barcelona.

The name Avda Paral.lel derives from the fact that it coincides exactly with 41° 44' latitude north, one of Ildefons Cerdà's more eccentric conceits. The avenue was the prime centre of Barcelona nightlife – often called its 'Montmartre' – in the first half of the 20th century, and was full of theatres, nightclubs and music halls. A statue on the corner with C/Nou de la Rambla commemorates Raquel Meller, a legendary star of the street who went on to equal celebrity around the world. She stands outside Barcelona's notorious modern live-porn venue, the Bagdad. Apart from this, most of its cabarets have disappeared, although there are still theatres and cinemas along the Paral.lel. A real end of an era came in 1997 when El Molino, most celebrated of the avenue's traditional, ultra-vulgar old music halls, suddenly shut up shop.

On the stretch of the Paral.lel opposite the city walls three tall chimneys stand amid modern office blocks. They are all that remain of the Anglo-Canadian-owned power station known locally as *La Canadença* ('The Canadian'), centre of the city's largest general strike, in 1919. Beside the chimneys an open space has been created – the **Parc de les Tres Xemeneies**, now popular with rollerbladers.

Today, Poble Sec is a friendly, working-class area of quiet, relaxed streets and squares. It has plenty of cheap bars, some more eccentric bars and several reasonable restaurants. Towards the Paral.lel are some distinguished *Modernista* buildings, which local legend has maintained were built for *artistas* from the cabarets by rich sugar-daddies. At C/Tapioles 12 is a beautiful, extremely narrow wooden *Modernista* door with typically writhing ironwork, while at C/Elkano 4 is **La Casa de les Rajoles**, which has a strange white mosaic façade that gives an impression of weightlessness. Poble Sec is also one of the most characterful access points to Montjuïc, and as you penetrate further into the densely populated *barri* the streets grow steeper, some becoming narrow lanes of steps that eventually provide a superb view of the city.

Sightseeing

Passeig de Gràcia, 107
08008 Barcelona
Tel. 34 93 238 40 00
Fax 34 93 238 40 10
www.gencat.es/probert

l'ànima
de la muntanya

Catalan Tourism
Information Centre

Sortida / Arribada

Opening times
Monday to Saturday
from 10 h to 19 h.

Sundays & Holidays
from 10 a 14.30 h.

Palau Robert

How to get to us
Underground lines
3 & 5 Diagonal Station

Railway
Ferrocarrils
de la Generalitat,
Provença Station

Bus
6, 7, 15, 16, 17,
22, 24, 28, 33, 34,
68 i T1

gaudí 2
Any Internacional G...
Barcelona, Catalu...

Generalitat de Catalunya
Government of Catalonia

les mil cares del foc

The Eixample

World-class architecture and seriously good shopping.

From the shadowy narrow streets of the once-walled Old City, the **Plaça Catalunya**, festooned with 1920s statues and fountains, acts as a grand portal to the uniquely laid-out Eixample. The Plaça Catalunya is an obvious city focal point and many trains and buses stop here. The side dominated by the monolithic façade of **El Corte Inglés** (*see p184*) is where the open-topped tourist buses (*see p72* **On the buses**) start and where the underground city tourist office (*see p320*) is – identified by large red signs with a white 'i' on them. Across the *plaça* from the Old City is where the **Passeig de Gràcia**, a smart shopping boulevard and treasure-trove of *Modernista* buildings, begins.

A fateful decision was taken in the 1850s when, after Barcelona was finally given permission to expand beyond its medieval walls, the plan chosen (by Madrid) was the regular grid of Ildefons Cerdà. Opinion in Barcelona was much more favourable to the fan-shaped design of the municipal architect Antoni Rovira i Trias, a reproduction of which can be seen at the foot of a sculpture of the man in Plaça Rovira i Trias, in Gràcia.

With time, though, the 'Extension' (Eixample in Catalan, Ensanche in Spanish) has become as much – if not more – of a distinctive feature of Barcelona as the medieval city. With its love of straight lines, parallels, diagonals and meridians, Cerdà's plan is a monumental example of 19th-century rationalism. The more utopian features of the plan, however – building on only two sides of each block, height limits of just two or three storeys, and gardens in the middle of the blocks – were quickly discarded. Today, most of the interior courtyards are car parks, workshops or shopping centres. The garden around the **Torre de les Aigües** water tower at C/Llúria 56 is one of the few courtyards where one can get a glimpse of how attractive Cerdà's plan could have been.

The building of the Eixample coincided with – and vitally encouraged – the great flowering of *Modernisme*, the distinctive Catalan variant of art nouveau. The equal weight *Modernistes* gave to decorative and fine arts is reflected in countless shopfronts, hallways and small gems of panelling or stained glass.

The Eixample is the economic and commercial core of Barcelona, with banks and insurance companies, fashion shops and arcades, any number of restaurants, good cinemas and the city's best art galleries and bookshops, as well as its world famous architecture. However, the fabric is beginning to show its age, to the extent that people have been killed in the past ten years by crumbling pieces of façades falling into the streets. More than 3,000 buildings have undergone face-lifts, but just under a tenth of all the façades in the Eixample still require urgent repairs. Traffic, which has become more and more dominant in the long one-way streets, is a major source of problems. The city council has set up a Pro-Eixample project to revitalise the area, one aim of which is to re-humanise its streets by recovering the inner courtyard of each block for communal use.

Casa Macaya. *See p116.*

▶ For more information on the major *Modernista* architects and buildings, *see* chapter **Modernisme**.

When the Eixample was first built and until the 1920s the rail line to Sarrià went above ground up C/Balmes, effectively cutting the district in two. Ever since then, the grid has been regarded as having two halves. The Dreta ('right') contains the most distinguished *Modernista* architecture, the main museums and shopping avenues. The Esquerra ('left') was built slightly later, and contains some great markets. Together they have formed the centre of Catalan middle-class life for most of the past 100 years, and to some extent, despite migration to quieter areas out of town, still do.

The Dreta

The great avenue of the **Passeig de Gràcia** is the centre of the district. It is famous for its architectural masterpieces, built as elegant residences, such as Gaudí's **La Pedrera** (also known as the **Casa Milà**) and the **Mansana**

de la Discòrdia, with buildings by Gaudí, Puig i Cadafalch and Domènech i Montaner. This and the parallel **Rambla Catalunya** are fashionable shopping streets, while shopping for art has traditionally been concentrated close by in C/Consell de Cent between Balmes and Rambla Catalunya, and nearby is one of the most impressive of the city's art spaces, the **Fundació Antoni Tàpies**.

As well as the most renowned *Modernista* buildings, the streets around Passeig de Gràcia are full of other extraordinary examples of work from that period, in the shape of whole buildings or just in small details. The section of the Eixample between C/Muntaner and C/Roger de Flor has been labelled the **Quadrat d'Or** or 'Golden Square' of *Modernisme*, and plaques have been placed on 150 protected buildings. Particularly of note are the hallway and exuberant decoration of **Casa Comalat**, designed by Salvador Valeri in 1906 (Avda

Walk 3: *Modernisme*

Duration: 1 hour 30 minutes
Map: Walk shown in **blue** on p336-7, p340-1. The grander (or more outrageous) *Modernista* buildings are easy to find, but one of the most striking things about the style is the way it appears at so many points in the city's fabric, often in unexpected places. This route covers a selection of lesser-known *Modernista* creations. The buildings are nearly all private, but it's often possible to look in the entrances; most also require repair work, however, so there's always a risk they may be under scaffolding.

The walk begins at Plaça Urquinaona. From there, go along C/Ausiàs Marc. At No.20 is **Casa Manuel Felip**, designed by a little-known architect, Telmo Fernández, in 1901, with tall graceful galleries to the left and right that connect the first and second floors. At No.31 is the **Farmàcia Nordbeck** (1905), with a rich dark wood exterior. *Modernisme* and pharmacies were peculiarly closely associated in the Eixample.

At the next corner, with C/Girona, is **Casa Antoni Roger** (1890), at Nos.33-5, by one of the more prominent (and bombastic) *Modernista* architects, Enric Sagnier. On the next block, at Nos.42-6, is **Casa Antonia Burés** (1906), a truly extraordinary building by another forgotten architect, Juli Batllevell. Two magnificent stone columns in the shape of trees seem to be holding up the building, anticipating the same motif in the Parc Güell.

Turn left at C/Bailen, then left again into C/Casp, and walk back two and a half blocks. At No.48 is Gaudí's **Casa Calvet** (1900), which now contains an excellent restaurant of the same name (*see p157*). The symmetrical façade seems very un-Gaudí-like, but the interlacing wrought-iron strips around the gallery – with mushroom motifs – and immense iron door-knockers betray the master's touch. Just after the next block, at C/Casp 22, is **Casa Llorenç Camprubí** (1901). The long, narrow windows in the first-floor gallery and neo-Gothic windows give a superb impression of verticality.

Turn back and left up C/Pau Claris, past **Laie Libreria Café** and bookshop (*see p181*). On the next corner, at Gran Via 650, is another extravagant *Modernista* pharmacy, **Farmàcia Vilardell** (1914). From there, walk along Gran Via three blocks, cross over and

Mansana de la Discordia. *See p117.*

turn left into C/Girona. **Casa Jacinta Ruiz**, designed by Ramon Viñolas in 1909, is at No.54. Glassed-in *galeries* characterise most *Modernista* houses, but here the spectacular four-storey gallery takes up the entire façade, and is almost modern rather than *Modernista* in the cleanness of its lines. The wrought iron of the balconies is also especially delicate.

Another block up, at C/Girona 73, on the corner of C/Consell de Cent, is **Forn Serrat**, also known as **Forn Vidal**. This bakery looks a little run-down; outside, though, it has curving woodwork framing a picture of a girl holding bales of wheat and ears of corn – a classic example of the *Modernista* tendency to round off work with a grand flourish.

At C/Girona 86, in the next block, is **Casa Isabel Pomar** (1906), an almost bizarrely narrow building by Joan Rubió i Bellver. Its neo-Gothic roof and pinnacle, like a church in the sky, may have been an architect's joke. Cross C/Aragó, and continue to C/València. Turn right to the next corner (C/Bailen) and the marvellous **Casa Manuel Llopis** (1902), No.339, by Antoni Gallissà and Gaudí's collaborator Josep Maria Jujol. It has angular galleries running almost the whole height of the building, together with very elaborate thin brickwork and lovely inlaid tilework.

If you retrace your steps along C/València and then continue for another two blocks, at the corner with C/Roger de Llúria you will come upon a veritable explosion of *Modernista* architecture. At No.312 is **Casa Villanueva** (1909), with thin graceful columns, elaborate glass galleries and a needle-topped tower. Opposite, at No.285, **Casa Jaume Forn** (1909) has beautiful stained glass and a magnificent carved door. Also on this crossing is **Queviures Murrià** grocery (*see p203*), with its tiled advertising posters, created from designs by Ramon Casas, still in place, and down the street at C/Roger de Llúria 74 is one more pharmacy, **Farmàcia Argelaguet** (1904), which has fine stained glass and floral decoration on the walls.

At the next junction uphill, C/Roger de Llúria-C/Mallorca, there are two major buildings by Domènech i Montaner. To the left, at C/Mallorca 278, is the **Palau Montaner** (1893), built for his own family and now government offices. At No.291 is **Casa Thomas** (1905), now, fittingly, home to the **BD** design company and shop (*see p190*). Much less known is the elegant **Casa Dolors Xiró** (1913), at C/Mallorca 302, by Josep Barenys. Turn left on Girona and left again on to Avda Diagonal. After a block you will come to Puig i Cadafalch's neo-Gothic fantasy house, the **Casa Terrades** (also called Casa de les Punxes), on your right, and his **Palau Baró de Quadras** on your left. A couple of blocks after that is the splendid **Casa Comalat** by Salvador Valeri (1911).

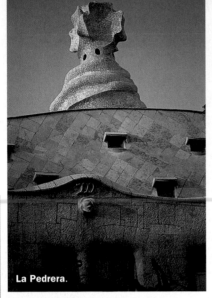

La Pedrera.

columns and parabolic arches, with no supporting walls, and supposedly without a single straight line or right-angled corner, this curving, globular apartment block contrasts strikingly with the angularity of much of the Eixample. Its revolutionary features were not appreciated by the Milà family – who paid for it – nor by contemporary opinion, which christened it La Pedrera ('the Stone Quarry') as a joke.

Run by Fundació Caixa de Catalunya as a cultural centre, the building features three complementary exhibition spaces. Access to the free art gallery is via the spectacular main entrance and staircase. The space itself is an excellent example of a Gaudí interior: fabulous plaster ceiling reliefs recall the building's marine-life themes, while heavy stone columns punctuate the open spaces. The gallery habitually programmes exhibits of top-tier international 20th-century art: sculptor Anthony Caro is the focus of a show in autumn 2002. An exhibition of Gaudí furniture and object design (June-Sept 2002) coincides with the 'International Year of Gaudí'.

The *pis de La Pedrera* ('the Pedrera flat') on the fourth floor is a finely tuned reconstruction of a *Modernista* flat interior (with only the floorplan by Gaudí) from the first decades of the 20th century. Notable is the bedroom suite by famed furniture designer Gaspar Homar, along with paintings by Modest Urgell and Ramon Casas, and the detailed recreation of the kitchen and other service areas. An adjacent space focuses on everyday life in Barcelona during the same period. The Espai Gaudí on the top floor occupies a space once partially open to dry residents' washing, but now appropriately enclosed. Beneath Gaudí's inspiring sequence of flat brick, Gothic-style arches, the Espai offers Barcelona's best systematic overview of the architect's œuvre. Drawings, photos, models and audiovisual displays give a brief yet clear idea of each of the master's important buildings, with special emphasis on La Pedrera itself. Above is the building's marvellous roof terrace with its extraordinary semi-abstract sculptures (actually ventilation shafts and chimneys). On summer nights the roof becomes La Pedrera de Nit (*see p259*), an unbeatably atmospheric terrace bar.

Diagonal 442-C/Còrsega 316). On Avda Diagonal are two characteristic buildings by Puig i Cadafalch, the **Palau Baró de Quadras** (No.373), and the **Casa Terrades** (No.416-20), an extraordinary neo-Gothic fantasy with pointed towers that gained it the alternative name of **Casa de les Punxes** ('House of Spikes'). Not far away – in the block on the corner of C/València and C/Bruc – is a market by Rovira i Trias, the **Mercat de la Concepció** with lovely tilework on its roof. It is possible to buy flowers 24 hours a day, although the flower stalls are now inside the building rather than on the street.

The outer Eixample above the Diagonal is a mainly residential area, for the most part built after 1910, but with some striking *Modernista* buildings such as Puig i Cadafalch's 1901 **Casa Macaya**, now a cultural centre of the **Fundació La Caixa**. The area is dominated, though, by the towering mass of the **Sagrada Família**. Not far away is another great *Modernista* project, Domènech i Montaner's **Hospital de Sant Pau**.

Espai Gaudí – La Pedrera

Passeig de Gràcia 92-C/Provença 261-5 (93 484 59 95/www.caixacat.es/fundcat.html). Metro Diagonal/ 7, 16, 17, 22, 24, 28 bus. **Open** *Mid June-mid Sept* 10am-8pm Mon-Thur, Sun; 10am-8pm, 9pm-1am Fri, Sat. *Mid Sept-mid June* 10am-8pm daily. **Admission** €6; €3 concessions (July-Sept house, concert, 1 drink €9). **Guided tours** (English) 11am, 5.30pm Mon-Fri. **Discounts** Articket, BC, BT, RM. **Credit** MC, V. **Map** p336 D4.
The last non-religious building Gaudí worked on represents his most radical departure from a recognisably *Modernista* style. Built entirely with

Fundació Antoni Tàpies

C/Aragó 255 (93 487 03 15/museu@ftapies.com). Metro Passeig de Gràcia/7, 16, 17, 22, 24, 28 bus. **Open** 10am-8pm Tue-Sun. **Admission** €4.50; €2.10 concessions; free under-16s. **Discounts** Articket, BC, RM. **Credit** MC, V. **Map** p336 D4.
Antoni Tàpies is Catalonia's best-known living painter, and his foundation in the Eixample is worth a visit, if not for obvious reasons. Rather than create a shrine to himself, Tàpies had the sense to approve a line of programming not overtly related to his style. The idiosyncratic three-floor gallery takes up a renovated early *Modernista* industrial building from the 1880s by Domènech i Montaner. A selection of Tàpies' own work is often shown on the upper floor, and sometimes throughout the entire

space. The winding tube sculpture on the roof, entitled *Núvol i Cadira* ('Cloud and Chair'), reflects Tàpies' fascination with eastern mysticism, and the library contains a fine collection of material on oriental art. Exhibitions in 2002 include one dedicated to Danish modernist Asger Jorn, followed by 'Contemporary Arab Representations' curated by Catherine David.

Fundació Francisco Godia

C/Valencia 284 pral (93 272 31 80/www.fundacion fgodia.org). Metro Passeig de Gràcia/7, 16, 17, 20, 22, 24, 28, 43, 44 bus. **Open** 10am-8pm Mon, Wed-Sun. **Admission** €4.50; €2.50 concessions; free under-5s. *Combined ticket with Museu Egipci* €8.50; €6.50 concessions. **Discounts** BC. **Credit** (shop only) MC, V. **Map** p336 D4.

Francisco Godia united two apparently incongruous passions: he was a Formula I racing car driver (for Maserati) and an avid art collector. This cosy private museum indicates his principal art interests:

medieval religious art, historic Spanish ceramics and modern painting. Medieval standouts include Alejo de Vahía's *Pietà* sculptural group. The modern collection has works by Joan Miró, Julio González and sculptor Manolo Hugúe, to whom a temporary show will be dedicated in late 2002. Other shows in 2002 include an exhibition of traditional Cambodian art, and one over the summer dedicated to Gaudí's artist friends. The collection continues to expand through purchases, many of contemporary artists. The Godia and the Museu Egipci, located next door, share a joint entry ticket.

La Mansana de la Discordia

Passeig de Gràcia 35-45 (93 488 01 39). Metro Passeig de Gràcia/bus all routes to Passeig de Gràcia. **Map** p336 D4.

The 'Block of Discord', on Passeig de Gràcia between Carrers Consell de Cent and Aragó, is so called because on it, almost alongside each other, stand buildings by the three greatest figures of

Hospital corners

A stone's throw from the crowds at the Sagrada Família is the blissfully camcorder-free haven of the Hospital de la Santa Creu i Sant Pau, Domènech i Montaner's wonderful 'garden city'; a match for its better-known religious neighbour for anyone interested in architecture. *Modernisme*'s greatest civic work, the hospital comprises 17 'pavilions', each with its own exuberant collection of sculpture, murals and mosaics and all connected by subterranean tunnels. Begun in 1901 as a long-overdue replacement for the old hospital in the Raval, it was not finished until 1930, by the architect's son.

The *Modernistes*, and Domènech in particular, were great believers in the therapeutic power of art and architecture, and painstaking effort was put into the slightest detail. The pavilions are all different, and the motifs and mosaics followed no set pattern. To create a atmosphere yet more distinct from the streets around the hospital, Domènech set the building at 45° from the rest of Cerdà's grid (of which he was emphatically not a fan).

As a place to nurse the sick, it really is wonderful – though not, alas, for much longer: Domènech's design is considered unsuitable for modern medicine, and work has begun on an ugly set of buildings at the furthest end of the grounds from the current entrance. The old pavilions will be used for research, but it is hoped that the public will still be free to wander through the courtyards and gardens.

Hospital de la Santa Creu i Sant Pau

C/Sant Antoni María Claret 167 (93 291 90 00). Metro Hospital de Sant Pau/15, 19, 20, 35, 45, 47, 50, 51, 92, N1, N4 bus. **Map** p337 F4.

Sightseeing

Sagrada Família.

Catalan *Modernista* architecture, all constructed between 1900 and 1907 in wildly clashing styles. At No.35, on the corner of C/Consell de Cent, is Domènech's Casa Lleó Morera, a classic *Modernista* building of exuberantly convoluted, decorative forms. Three doors up, at No.41, is Puig's Gothic-influenced Casa Amatller, and next to that Gaudí's Casa Batlló, rising like a giant fish out of the pavement. From March to September 2002, the Casa Batlló will be open to the public as part of the International Year of Gaudí. The Casa Lleó Morera is now a Centre del Modernisme, with a small exhibition on the style, and is the hub of the Ruta del Modernisme tour (*see p71*). Visitors to the centre also get to see the first floor of the building, which has a superb interior and fabulous stained glass.

Museu Egipci de Barcelona

C/Valencia 284 (93 488 01 88/www.fundclos.com). Metro Passeig de Gràcia/7, 16, 17, 20, 22, 24, 28, 43, 44 bus. **Open** 10am-8pm Mon-Sat; 10am-2pm Sun. **Admission** *Museum* €5.50; €4.20 concessions; free under-5s. *Guided tours* €11.50; €10 concessions. *Combined ticket with Fundació Godia* €8.50; €6.50 concessions. **Guided tours** (by appointment) 11am, 5pm Sat; 9.30pm Fri. **Discounts** BC. **Credit** MC, V. **Map** p336 D4.

Jordi Clos was still a teenager when his fascination for Ancient Egypt was sparked. Now a successful hotelier, Clos pours his passion and free time into Barcelona's Egyptian Museum. Run by Clos's prestigious archaeological foundation, reputable enough to do official digs in Egypt and run university programmes, the museum is the ideal showcase for a well-chosen collection that includes religious statuary, mummies, jewellery and elements from everyday life spanning over 3,000 years of Nile-drenched culture. The oldest objects include predynastic ceramics (3,500 BC), while some of the outstanding pieces are the friezes from the Tomb of Iny (Fifth or Sixth Dynasty), a *stele* representing Cleopatra VII, and the little mummy of the Girl of Kemet, from the Ptolemaic period. Dramatic re-creations of burial settings and impressive X-rays of mummified animals enhance the display. In 2002, 'The Golden Mummy' exhibition will include examples of wrapped former Nile-dwellers to complement a key piece in the museum collection. The gift shop is a mine of related books, games and trinkets.

Museu del Temple Expiatori de la Sagrada Família

C/Mallorca 401 (93 207 30 31/www.sagrada familia.org). Metro Sagrada Família/ 10, 19, 33, 34, 43, 44, 50, 51, 101 bus. **Open** *May-Sept* 9am-8pm daily. *Oct-Apr* 9am-6pm daily. **Admission** €6; €4 concessions; free under-10s. *Lift to spires* €1.50. **Discounts** BC, BT, RM. **Credit** (shop only) MC, V. **Map** p337 F4.

It is a supreme irony that what has become the emblematic symbol of the city and Gaudí's masterpiece (or monsterpiece, depending on your point of view) was neither begun nor finished by the great man. The project was initiated in 1882 by another architect, Francisco del Villar, and Gaudí's involvement did not begin until 1891. He did, however, transform the design completely and dedicate over 40 years of his life to the building – the last 18 years exclusively – often sleeping on site. Only the crypt, the apse and the four towers of the Façade of the Nativity, along C/Marina, were completed in his lifetime. Every element in the decoration, much of it carved from life, was conceived by Gaudí as having a precise symbolic meaning, and he was deeply opposed to the idea of anyone appreciating the building outside its religious context. An essential part of a visit to the Sagrada Família is to climb the towers beyond the level reached by the lift; this gives an extraordinary sensation of walking out into space. Descent via the spiral staircase, however, is not recommended for those suffering from vertigo.

The museum in the crypt contains models and a history of the project and other information on Gaudí. The Sagrada Família foundation is working hard to renew the display. Apart from the generous selection of early drawings and photographs, one can look in on the artisans in a workshop where plaster casts are prepared, with a plaster scale model of the temple nearby. The original casts for the sculptural work on the façade by Joan Matamala and Josep Maria Subirachs, along with alabaster and stone bits pulled off the building for reasons of erosion or damage, fill display cases like dinosaur fossils in a paleontology exhibition. Another curious piece is the catenary model for the Colònia Güell, an imaginative way of calculating structurally effective arches. Displays on related themes are often set up in other spaces of the church.

Gaudí himself is buried beneath the nave of the basilica, and steps towards his canonisation have been taken by Catalan bishops. Work on the temple was resumed in 1952 by some of Gaudí's assistants, who drew up plans based on some of his sketches and on what they remembered of the great man's ideas (he never used detailed plans). The work has accelerated considerably since the 1980s. Subirachs has completed the new towers of the Façade of the Passion along C/Sardenya – with sculptures that horrify many Gaudí admirers – and is now sculpting the apostles on the cathedral's bronze entrance.

The second sculptor working on the building is Japanese, Etsuro Sotoo, who seems to be adhering more faithfully to Gaudí's intentions, with six flowing, modest musicians at the rear of the temple. Among the next sections due for completion are the vaults of the main nave, which would for the first time give the Sagrada Família a substantial roof, but (as is often the case) work has been nowhere near advanced enough to meet the ambitious schedule. Work has also begun on the construction of four massive columns made of porphyry – the hardest stone in existence – to support the great dome, which will make the Sagrada Família once again the tallest building in Barcelona. No one is prepared to hazard a guess as to when it will be finished.

Parc de l'Estació del Nord

C/Nàpols (no phone). Metro Arc de Triomf/ 40, 42, 54, 141 bus. **Open** 10am-sunset daily. **Map** p341 E-F5-6.
A striking park behind the bus station; an open, grassy crescent with very few trees or benches, just flat ceramic forms in turquoise and cobalt, swooping and curving through the park – a landscape sculpture by Beverly Pepper.

The Esquerra

This side of the Eixample quickly became the new area for some activities of the city that the middle classes did not want to see on their doorsteps. A huge slaughterhouse was built in the extreme left of the area, knocked down and replaced by the **Parc Joan Miró** in 1979. The functional **Hospital Clínic** was sited on two blocks between C/Còrsega and C/Provença, and further out still on C/Entença is the city's 1905 **Modelo** prison, the relocation of which outside the city is currently under way. There are two great markets, the **Ninot**, by the hospital, and the **Mercat de Sant Antoni**, on the edge of the Raval, which is taken over by a great second-hand book market every Sunday morning. This is also an area for academic institutions, from the vast **Escola Industrial** on C/Comte d'Urgell to the original **Universitat** central building on Plaça Universitat, constructed in 1842.

Modernista architecture does extend over into the Esquerra (as the Quadrat d'Or concept recognises), with such superb examples as the **Casa Societat Torres Germans** (C/Paris 180-2) from 1905. The district also has Barcelona's biggest concentration of gay nightlife in the streets around the crossing of C/Consell de Cent and C/Muntaner – the area known as the 'Gaixample'. Beyond the hospital the outer Eixample has no great sights, but leads up to Plaça Francesc Macià, developed since the 1960s as the centre of the new business district, and the main crossroads of affluent Barcelona. Beyond the office blocks of the *plaça* lie the fashionable business, shopping and residential areas of the Zona Alta.

Parc Joan Miró
(Parc de l'Escorxador)

C/Tarragona (no phone). Metro Tarragona or Espanya/bus all routes to Plaça d'Espanya. **Open** 10am-sunset daily. **Map** p339 B4-5.
The Miró park, built on the site of a huge slaughterhouse (*escorxador*) mainly comprises stubby palmera trees, around half of which have been uprooted as work continues on an underground reservoir. It is still worth a visit, however, for Miró's huge phallic sculpture *Dona i Ocell* ('Woman and Bird') rising out of a shallow pool.

Gràcia & Other Districts

You want more parks, more museums, more art and more fun? You got it.

Gràcia

After the rigid monotony of the Eixample, the meandering streets of Gràcia have a welcome human scale. Before Cerdà's grid was built on the open fields, Gràcia was a thriving town out on its own, connected to Barcelona by a country lane, the **Passeig de Gràcia**. It wasn't until 1897, amid howls of protest, that the town was annexed to the city but the legacy of this separateness still remains and older *graciencs* are still protective of their identity.

Little more than a village in 1820, with about 2,500 inhabitants, Gràcia had become the ninth-largest city in Spain at the time of the annexation. It was also known as a radical centre of Catalanism, republicanism, anarchism and, to a certain extent, feminism. Place names

such as **Mercat de la Llibertat**, **Plaça de la Revolució** and **C/Fraternitat** tell their own story. Political activism is still strong within the *barri*, and dozens of properties have been taken over by the Okupas – a squatters' movement with an arsenal of axes to grind from anti-globalisation to the tyranny of television.

As you enter the district from the Eixample, the change in atmosphere is striking. Some streets consist of simple two-storey buildings, and a series of attractive small squares provide space to pause and talk. The most important of these are **Plaça Rius i Taulet**, site of the pre-1897 town hall and a magnificent clock tower designed by Rovira i Trias; **Plaça de la Virreina**, with its village-like church; **Plaça del Sol**; and the peaceful **Plaça Rovira i Trias**, with an appealing bronze statue of this underrated architect himself – he sits on a bench with his back to an Okupa house, with his unused vision for the Eixample laid out at his feet. **Plaça del Diamant** has a rather ugly sculpture to commemorate the novel written by Mercè Rodoreda and named after the square, as well as a Civil War air-raid shelter, recently discovered, which should eventually become a peace museum. Gràcia also acquired a new square in 1993, not elegant but unpretentious and designed for children: the **Plaça John Lennon**.

Gràcia contains one of Gaudí's earliest and most fascinating works, the **Casa Vicens** of 1883-8, hidden away in C/Carolines. As a private residence it is not open to visitors, but the geometrically tiled exterior with its Indian and oriental influences is impressive enough. Of course, the most visited place in the whole district is Gaudí's **Parc Güell**, on the Tibidabo side of the area above Plaça Lesseps, across the busy Travessera de Dalt. *Modernisme* is also represented by Domènech's **Casa Fuster** (1908-11) at C/Gran de Gràcia 2-4, and above all by the work of Francesc Berenguer, one of Gaudí's assistants, who designed the **Mercat de la Llibertat** and the old town hall in **Plaça Rius i Taulet**.

Gràcia's independent attitude is also reflected in a strong attachment to traditions such as its *festa major*, the biggest in Barcelona, which for a few days in August makes the *barri* a centre for the whole city (*see p217*). The district contains many small factories and workshops,

Parc de l'Espanya Industrial.
See p122.

and has a sizeable Catalan-speaking gypsy community. It's also home to a large number of students and a substantial creative colony of artists, actors, musicians, photographers and designers, all of whom can be seen hanging out in the many café terraces.

Coffee in Plaça del Sol is a relaxing alternative to busier places in the centre of the city, though the area is at its best after dark. The **Café del Sol** itself is an old favourite but the streets further down are full of other cafés. Gràcia had its turn as the city's most in-vogue area for night-time wandering in the 1980s, when many bars opened; since then it's settled into a comfortable position at neither the top nor the bottom of the fashion league, but remaining enduringly popular.

The educated nature of local residents is seen in the number of cultural venues in the district, such as the **Centre Artesà Tradicionarius** (CAT, *see p245*) for folk music and dance, theatres such as the innovative **Sala Beckett** (*see p273*), and two of the most enterprising cinemas in Barcelona, the **Verdi** and **Verdi Park** (*see p227*). The district is also home to the **Gràcia Territori Sonor** experimental music collective (*see p241*), which performs at Sónar and other festivals.

Parc Güell

C/d'Olot (Casa-Museu Gaudí 93 219 38 11). Metro Lesseps/24, 25, bus. **Open** 10am-sunset daily. **Admission** *Museum* €3. **Discounts** RM. **Credit** (shop only) MC, V. **Map** p337 E2.
In 1900 Gaudí's patron Eusebi Güell commissioned him to oversee the design of a garden city development on a hill on the edge of the city, which he envisaged would become a fashionable residential area. Gaudí was to design the basic structure and main public areas; the houses were to be designed by other architects. However, the wealthy families of the time did not appreciate Gaudí's wilder ideas, scarcely any plots were sold, and eventually the estate was taken over by the city as a park. Its most complete part is the entrance, with its Disneylandish gatehouses and the mosaic dragon that's become another of the city's favourite symbols. The park has a wonderfully playful quality, with its twisted pathways and avenues of columns intertwined with the natural structure of the hillside. At the centre is the great esplanade, with an undulating bench covered in *trencadís* (broken mosaic) – much of it not the work of Gaudí but of his overshadowed but talented assistant Josep Maria Jujol. Gaudí lived for several years in one of the two houses built on the site (not designed by himself); it is now the Casa-Museu Gaudí. The park stretches well beyond the area designed by Gaudí, into the wooded hillside. Guided tours are available, sometimes in English. The best way to get to the park is on bus 24; if you go via Lesseps metro, be prepared for a steep uphill walk.

Plaça de la Concòrdia. *See p122.*

Sants & Les Corts

Traditional Sants is a welcome breather from the hectic and over-packaged parts of Barcelona. There's not much to see, but there's a strong sense of community lacking in, say, the Barri Gòtic. Real people live and work here; the bars are more functional than fancy and the shops tend to be family run establishments specialising in things like slippers or housecoats.

Centred around an old Roman road called for centuries Camí d'Espanya, 'the road to Spain' – now **C/Creu Coberta-C/Sants** – this *barri*'s origins lay in its proximity to the city's walls. In the days when Barcelona's gates shut at 9pm every night, hostels, inns and smithies grew up around the city to cater for latecomers. During the 19th century, it became a major industrial centre, the site for giant textile factories such as Joan Güell's Vapor Vell, the Muntades brothers' L'Espanya Industrial and Can Batlló. Few of the people who admire Gaudí's work in the Casa Batlló, the Palau Güell or Parc Güell give much attention to the fact that it was these factories and the workers in them that produced the wealth necessary to support such projects. Sants was also a centre of labour militancy, and in 1855 the first ever general strike in Catalonia broke out there. Practically all Sants' industrial centres have

Nou Camp.

now disappeared. Thanks to the strength of a local neighbourhood campaign, the huge **Espanya Industrial** site became a futuristic park in 1985; and after a 20-year struggle by residents, El Vapor Vell opened again in 2000 as one of the city's biggest libraries.

The **Estació de Sants**, alongside the Espanya Industrial, also dominates the *barri*. In front of it is the ferociously modern **Plaça dels Països Catalans**, created by Helio Piñón and Albert Viaplana in 1983 on a site where, they claimed, nothing could be planted because of the amount of industrial detritus in the soil. It's an open, concreted space, with shelter provided not by trees but steel ramps and canopies; the kind of architecture you either find totally hostile or consider to have great monumental strength.

On the other side of the station are the more appealing squares of **Sants** and **Peiró**. In the latter The first-ever Catalan film, *Baralla en un café* ('brawl in a café') was shot in the latter, in 1898. Near the Plaça de Sants is a complex called **Les Cotxeres**, an old tram depot now converted into a multifunctional community and arts centre. From there, C/Creu Coberta runs to Plaça d'Espanya, where C/Tarragona, to the left, sharply marks the end of Sants and the beginning of the Eixample. This street has been changed totally by pre- and post-Olympic projects, with high-rise office towers that have led it to be dubbed – perhaps in hope – the 'Wall Street' of Barcelona.

Without a love of the beautiful game, it takes some perseverance to find any grace in Les Corts. It's even harder to discern the origins

of its name, 'the farmsheds', amid the row upon row of functional apartment blocks. However, **Plaça del Carme** and **Plaça de la Concòrdia**, remnants of the old village of Les Corts, annexed to Barcelona in 1867, still evoke the atmosphere of another era. For most Barcelona residents, though, Les Corts is synonymous with **Fútbol Club Barcelona**, whose massive sports complex takes up a great deal of the district's space. Curiously, at night the surrounding area becomes the haunt of prostitutes, transvestites and cruising drivers.

Nou Camp – FC Barcelona

Avda Arístides Maillol, access 7 & 9 (93 496 36 00/ www.fcbarcelona.com). Metro Maria Cristina or Collblanc/15, 52, 53, 54, 56, 57, 75 bus. **Open** *Museum* 10am-6.30pm Mon-Sat, 10am-2pm Sun. **Admission** *Museum* €3.80; €2.30 concessions. *Guided tour* €8.50; €5.80 concessions. **Discounts** BC, BT. **No credit cards. Map** p335 A3.
The largest football stadium in Europe, and a shrine to Barcelona FC. First built in 1954, the Nou Camp has since been extended to accommodate all the club's 100,000-plus members. It also contains the club museum (*see p132* **Collectors' items**); visitors to the museum also get to tour the stadium. For getting tickets for a game, *see p264*.

Parc de l'Espanya Industrial

Passeig de Antoni (no phone). Metro Sants-Estació/ bus all routes to Sants-Estació. **Open** 10am-sunset daily. **Map** p339 A4.
The Espanya Industrial, by Basque architect Luis Peña Ganchegui, is the most postmodern of Barcelona's new parks. Ten watchtowers look out over the boating lake; at night, lit up, they create the impression that some strange warship has managed to dock by Sants train station. Despite its periodic falls into disrepair, when the lake dries up to a muddy puddle and the place needs a good rake, this is one of the 1980s parks most liked by the public. Boats can (occasionally) be hired on the lake, and kids play on Andrés Nagel's *Gran Drac de Sant Jordi* dragon sculpture. Another sculpture is Anthony Caro's *Rapsòdia en alt*.

Tibidabo & Collserola

During his temptation of Christ, the Devil took him to a high mountain, with all the world below, and offered to give him everything in return for a little divine adoration. To name the peak towering over Barcelona after the words spoken (*tibi dabo* is Latin for 'To thee I will give') may seem an example of typical Catalan boastfulness, but the view from the top on a clear day is truly magnificent. The city is laid out as though in miniature, with familiar towers and roads easily discernible, all framed by Montjuïc and a vibrant blue sea. On those days when the traffic smog blots out the details, it's not quite as good, but at least the air is fresh. Tibidabo is, in fact, just one peak of the huge Collserola mountain range that dominates the landward side of the city.

Getting there, by the evocative Tramvia Blau (Blue Tram) and then the **Funicular de Tibidabo**, is part of the fun. The square between the tram and the funicular is one of the best places in the city for an al fresco drink or meal and at the very top of the funicular is a great **funfair** (*see p222*). For a limitless view, ascend the giant needle of Norman Foster's **Torre de Collserola**. Next to the funfair is a church, built in an extravagantly bombastic style and completed in 1940 to 'atone' for Barcelona's revolutionary role in the Spanish Civil War. It is not well loved by locals.

To the left of the church, on the other side of the ridge, are stunning views over the Vallès to the north, while down the hillside are tracks into the 6,550 hectares (16,000 acres) of the **Parc de Collserola**. The park is most easily reached by FGC train on the Terrassa-Sabadell line from Plaça Catalunya, getting off at Baixador de Vallvidrera station. A ten-minute walk from the station up into the woods along Carretera de l'Església will take you to the **Museu Verdaguer** (*see p132* **Collectors' items**) and the park's information centre (93 280 35 52, open 9.30am-3pm daily) where maps can be bought. This very helpful centre also has an exhibition area and a bar. There are seven suggested itineraries, ranging from an easy 20-minute walk to an excursion to the Serra d'en Cardona of two hours plus. It's also possible to cycle along the Carretera de las Aïgues, a 9.5-kilometre (six-mile) long path through the woods.

The great thing, however, is to explore for yourself, because the Collserola is a wonderful natural reserve, with the trees providing delicious shade on a hot day. Walking is easy, as the paths and climbs are well maintained. Holm oak and pines predominate, squirrels and rabbits are everywhere, and the scents and colours of herbs and wild flowers are exhilarating. For bird-watchers there is scarcely a better place in Catalonia.

One easy itinerary is the two-kilometre (1.2-mile) walk from the information centre to the quiet hilltop town of Vallvidrera, stopping on the way at the Font de la Budellera, a spring and picnic site. In Vallvidrera's main *plaça* there are a couple of bar-restaurants, while through town, at the end of a track, is **Ideal** restaurant (93 406 90 29), sister to the one on La Rambla. It has decent pizzas and great views over the pine forest. The Torre de Collserola is just a short walk away; or a ride down the funicular – with another

panoramic view – will take you to Peu del Funicular station, from where FGC trains run back to Plaça Catalunya.

Funicular de Tibidabo

Plaça Doctor Andreu to Plaça Tibidabo (93 211 79 42). FGC Av Tibidabo/17, 22, 58, 73, N8 bus, then Tramvia Blau. **Open** *Mid June-mid Sept* 10.45am-10.30pm Mon-Thur, Sun; 11.45am-1.15am Fri, Sat. *Mid Sept-mid June* 10.45am-7.15pm Sat, Sun. **Tickets** single €2; return €3. **No credit cards**. The funicular that takes you from the end of the tramline to the very top of the mountain is art deco-esque, like much of the funfair. Each train has two halves, one pointing down and one up, and from the 'down' end you get a panoramic view of the city.

Torre de Collserola

Ctra de Vallvidrera al Tibidabo (93 406 93 54/ www.torredecollserola.es). FCG Peu Funicular, then funicular. **Open** *July-Sept* 11am-2.30pm, 3.30-8pm Wed-Fri; 11am-8pm Sat, Sun. *May, June, Oct* 11am-2.30pm, 3.30-7pm Wed-Fri; 11am-7pm Sat, Sun. *Nov-Apr* 11am-2.30pm, 3.30-6pm Wed-Fri; 11am-6pm Sat, Sun. **Admission** €4.20; €3.60 concessions; free under-7s. **Credit** V.

Norman Foster's 288m (945ft) high communications tower, built in 1992 to take TV signals to the world, stands atop Collserola like some mutant insect poised to swoop on the city. A glass lift takes you to an observation deck 115m (378ft) up, which means you are 560m (1,838ft) above sea level. On a decent day, there 's a staggering eagle's-eye view of Barcelona, and a couple of times a year, you can see Mallorca. At other times, you might just see an endless haze.

Vallvidrera station.

Monestir de Pedralbes.
See p127.

Zona Alta

Before the massive regeneration of the waterfront in the run-up to the Olympics, it was very often said that Barcelona had turned its back on the sea. Those with enough money have always had a tendency to escape from the noise and the smog and the crush down below, and to flock to the **Zona Alta** (literally 'upper zone', or simply 'uptown'). This is the name given collectively to a series of *barris*, including **Sant Gervasi**, **Sarrià**, **Pedralbes** and **Putxet**, that fan out across the area above the Diagonal and to the left of Gràcia on the map. The air is more refined, as are the airs.

There are few major sights other than the remarkable **Museu Monestir de Pedralbes**, now home to a selection of religious paintings from the **Col.lecció Thyssen**, including Fra Angelico's spectacular *Madonna of Humility*. The centre of Sarrià and the streets of old Pedralbes around the monastery still retain an appreciable flavour of what were quite sleepy country towns until well into the 20th century.

The Zona Alta has dotted around it several interesting works by Gaudí. From wealthy Pedralbes a walk down Avda de Pedralbes leads to his wonderful gatehouse and gates, the **Pavellons de la Finca Güell** at No.15, with a bizarre wrought-iron dragon. In the garden of the **Palau Reial de Pedralbes** on Avda Diagonal, a former Güell residence, there is a delightful Gaudí fountain, and back on the other side of the Zona Alta off the Plaça Bonanova, near Tibidabo FGC station, is the remarkable Gothic-influenced **Torre Figueres**, or **Bellesguard**. Further into town near Putxet is one of Gaudí's larger but more sober designs, the **Col.legi de les Teresianes** (C/Ganduxer 85-105), from 1888-9.

The Palau de Pedralbes also contains two interesting museums, the **Museu de Ceràmica** and **Museu de les Arts Decoratives**. Around its outskirts, stretching out on either side of the Diagonal, is the bleakly functional **Zona Universitària**, chosen as the area for the expansion of Barcelona's main university in the 1950s. On the very fringes of the city, at the very end of the Diagonal, is the pretty **Parc de Cervantes** with a magnificent rose garden and a striking sculpture, *Dos Rombs* (Two Rhomboids), by Andreu Alfaro.

From the park, a turn back along the Diagonal toward Plaça Maria Cristina and Plaça Francesc Macià will take you to Barcelona's main business and, increasingly, shopping district. Despite the size of some of the buildings, especially the lumbering **L'Illa** mall (*see p184*), demand for office space around this area has outstripped supply. The

Fra Angelico's *Madonna of Humility*.

Ajuntament's relentless urban improvement programme aims to satisfy this demand by the extension of the Diagonal to the sea and the regeneration of the area around it.

Close to Plaça Francesc Macià is the small, popular **Turó Parc**, laid out in a semi-formal style, with plaques of poetry set among the bronze statuary to inspire contemplation. To the right of it on the map is Sant Gervasi, an area that had its moment of glory as the most fashionable night-time meeting point in early 1990s Barcelona. The **Jardins de la Tamarita,** at the foot of Avda Tibidabo, is a tranquil and verdant dog-free oasis with a pleasant children's playground, and nearby is where the **Tramvia Blau** starts its clanking journey up the hill, past the **Museu de la Ciència**, to the Funicular de Tibidabo. Further north, above the Parc Güell, is the extraordinary **Parc de la Creueta del Coll**, an old quarry that has been turned into a swimming pool.

Barcelona
Bus Turístic

gaudí 2'**002** Barcelona
Any Internacional Gaudí

To see, experience, and enjoy the most charming capital of the Mediterranean.

The Bus Turístic gives you two routes – with 27 stops – for the price of one, to visit the most emblematic sites of Barcelona. You can do the whole journey passing from one route to the other as often as you like, as both coincide at three points: Pl. de Catalunya, Pg. de Gràcia - La Pedrera, and Pl. de Francesc Macià.

Northern Route
Red

Southern Route
Blue

The ticket allows you to get on and off the bus as many times as you like. You will also receive a fantastic pass with considerable discounts, valid for a whole year, that you can make use of in the city's most interesting places.

ⓘ 010

www.barcelonaturisme.com

www.tmb.net

Col.lecció Thyssen-Bornemisza – Museu Monestir de Pedralbes

Baixada del Monestir 9 (93 280 14 34/www.museo thyssen.org). FGC Reina Elisenda/22, 63, 64, 75, 78 bus. **Open** 10am-2pm Tue-Sun. **Admission** *Monastery* €3; €1.80 concessions. *Col.lecció Thyssen* €5; €3 concessions. Free under-12s. Free 1st Sun of the mth. **Discounts** BC, BT. **Credit** (shop only) AmEx, DC, MC, V. **Map** p335 A1.

Founded in 1326 by Queen Elisenda, wife of Jaume II of Aragon, this wonderfully preserved convent is still home to the 'Poor Clares', whose nuns have no choice but to mould their contemplation to the pulse of visitors. A tour of the building provides a fascinating glimpse of life in a medieval convent: visitors can see the pharmacy, the kitchens and the huge refectory with its vaulted ceiling. The main attraction, though, is the convent itself and, above all, its magnificent, entirely intact, three-storey Gothic cloister. To one side is the tiny chapel of Sant Miquel, covered with striking murals from 1343 by Ferrer Bassa, a Catalan painter who was a student of Giotto. While most of Baron Hans-Heinrich von Thyssen-Bornemisza's remarkable art collection, acquired for Spain in 1993, is in his namesake museum in Madrid, the 90 works here harmonise with the setting, with religious images such as the Virgin predominant.

Occupying a former dormitory on one side of the 14th-century cloister, the collection specialises in Italian painting from the 13th to the 17th centuries – an important influence in Catalonia – and European baroque works. There is one true masterpiece: Fra Angelico's *Madonna of Humility* (c1430s). Notable paintings include a small *Nativity* (c1325) by Taddeo Gaddi, a subtle *Madonna and Child* (1545) by Titian, and a Zurbaran crucifixion. Other highlights are the portraits of saints by Lucas Cranach the Elder and Tiepolo's *Way to Golgotha* (c1728). The Velázquez portrait of Queen Maria Anna of Austria (1655-7) is magnificent. In 2002 there is temporary show on the Epiphany in medieval art. Catalan early music master Jordi Savall performs and programmes other concerts in the convent's spaces in the spring.

Museu de Ceràmica & Museu de les Arts Decoratives

Palau Reial de Pedralbes, Avda Diagonal 686 (Ceràmica 93 280 16 21/Arts Decoratives 93 280 50 24). Metro Palau Reial/7, 33, 67, 68, 74, 75 bus. **Open** 10am-6pm Tue-Sat; 10am-3pm Sun. **Guided tours** by appointment. **Admission** *Both museums* €3.70; €1.80 concessions. *1 museum* €2.50; €1.50 concessions. Free under-16s. **Discounts** BC, BT. **No credit cards. Map** p335 A2.

The Palau Reial on the Diagonal was originally built as a residence for the family of Gaudí's patron Eusebi Güell, and in one corner of the gardens is a famous iron gate designed by Gaudí. It became a royal palace and was greatly expanded in the 1920s, when it was given to King Alfonso XIII. It now houses two separate museums, both accessible on the same ticket; a project to create an applied arts

---

Top ten   Views

Cable car
An exhilarating ride from Montjuïc to Barceloneta. *See p101.*

Colom
A matchless view up La Rambla and out to sea from Columbus' feet. *See p101.*

Hotel Arts
Go for a duplex right at the top *(see p59)*. What do you mean, you can't afford it?

Parc Güell
A deceptively steep climb to the top, but worth the effort. *See p121.*

Museu d'Història de Catalunya
Watch the goings-on in the port from the terrace of the rooftop café. *See p102.*

El Corte Inglés
Up on the seventh floor is another café with a fantastic view. *See p184.*

Tibidabo
They say you can see Mallorca on a clear day. A very clear day. *See p122.*

Open-top buses
Get a head above the rest. *See p72.*

Sagrada Família
The reward for all those steps is a dizzying view from the spires. *See p118.*

Mirablau
Grab an ice-cold beer and enjoy one of the finest views of the city. *See p182.*

---

museum near Plaça de les Glòries for 2004 will mean the collections will have a new home in a few years. The Ceramics Museum has an exceptionally fine Spanish ceramics collection stretching back several centuries, expertly organised by sharply varying regional and historical styles. Especially beautiful are the medieval dishes, mostly for everyday use, such as those from Manises near Valencia. Catalan holdings feature two popular tile murals from the 18th century: *La Xocolatada* depicts chocolate-drinking at a garden party, while the other presents a chaotic baroque bullfight. Upstairs, the selection of 20th-century Spanish work is slated for renewal in late 2002, meaning possible closures; highlights are the refined simplicity of Catalan master Josep Llorens Artigas and pieces by Picasso and Miró. Excellent temporary exhibitions of contemporary ceramics are also mounted.

Sightseeing

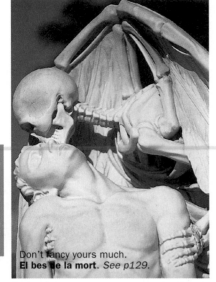

Don't fancy yours much.
El bes de la mort. *See p129.*

The Decorative Arts Museum occupies the other wing of the building. The palace's original painted walls provide a warm setting for furniture and decorative objects from the Middle Ages on, with styles from Gothic to romanticism, Catalan *Modernisme*, art deco and the present. Quality is high, although only a small portion of the first-class collections of decorative clocks, Catalan glasswork (comparable to the Venetian style) and other artefacts is shown at any one time. Visitors can also look down into the palace's sumptuously decorated oval throne room. There are also changing temporary shows usually dedicated to 20th-century Catalan industrial design.

Museu de la Ciència

C/Teodor Roviralta 55 (93 212 60 50/ www.fundacio.lacaixa.es). FGC Av Tibidabo, then Tramvia Blau/ 17, 22, 73, 85, 158 bus. **Open** 10am-8pm Tue-Sun. **Admission** €3; €2.50 concessions; free under-7s. Free 1st Sun of the mth. *Additional exhibitions* €2.50. **Discounts** BC. **Credit** MC, V.

Aimed especially at school groups and children, the science museum is designed to teach basic scientific principles in the most engaging way possible. The quality of the displays assures there's plenty to interest visitors of all ages, although some of the museum's hands-on exhibits, highly innovative when it opened in the 1980s, look a little 'mechanical' and dated now that many state-of-the-art museums are digitalised. The permanent section explains optical phenomena, quirks of perception, mechanical principles, meteorology, the solar system – there's a planetarium – and many other topics. The Clik dels Nens section is for small children. The museum will double in size when a new section is completed in 2003, so at the

end of 2002 some displays will be moved to La Caixa's former cultural centre at the Palau Macaya, on Passeig de Sant Joan. *See also p224.*

Parc de la Creueta del Coll

C/Mare de Déu del Coll (no phone). Metro Penitents/ 19, 25, 28, 87 bus. **Open** *May-Aug* 10am-9pm daily. *Apr, Sept* 10am-8pm daily. *Mar, Oct* 10am-7pm daily. *Nov-Feb* 10am-6pm daily. **Admission** free.

An impressive park created from an old quarry by Josep Martorell and David Mackay in 1987. It has a large lake with an artificial beach and modern sculpture: an Ellsworth Kelly and a monumental piece by Eduardo Chillida, *In Praise of Water*, hanging from cables. In 1998 one snapped and the massive block came crashing down, injuring three people. It has been restored, but people tend to give it a wide berth.

Tramvia Blau

Avda Tibidabo to Plaça Doctor Andreu (93 318 70 74). FGC Avda Tibidabo/17, 22, 58, 73, N8 bus. **Open** *July-mid Sept* 10am-8pm daily. *June, last 2wks Sept* 10am-8pm Sat, Sun. *Oct-May* 10am-6pm Sat, Sun. *Easter week* 10am-6pm daily. **Frequency** 30min Mon-Fri; 15min Sat, Sun. **Tickets** single €1.90; return €2.70; mth €19. **No credit cards**.

The Blue Trams, beautiful old machines in service since 1902, clank up Avda Tibidabo between the FGC station and Plaça Doctor Andreu. Once there, you can take in the view, have a meal or a drink, or catch the funicular to the funfair. In months when the tram only operates at weekends, a bus service runs instead during the week.

Poblenou, Clot & La Sagrera

These three districts, north of the Old City along the coast, once formed part of one large independent municipality, Sant Martí de Provençals. Originally a farming and fishing community, it was, like Sants, one of the areas chosen by manufacturers as they sought to expand, and became the great centre of heavy industry in Barcelona, disputing with Sabadell the title of 'La Manchester Catalana'. This brought the usual problems – child labour, disease, overcrowding, noise, smells, smoke – and the usual responses: co-operatives, unions, strikes and other conflicts. In 1897 it was absorbed into Barcelona, and split into three districts, Poblenou, Clot and La Sagrera.

Poblenou contained the greater part of Sant Martí's industry, and so continued to be a centre of radicalism and conflict. Then, in the 1960s, the *barri* began to change character as factories folded, moved to the Zona Franca or got out of the city altogether. The departure of the most historic, Can Girona, in 1992, marked the end of an epoch. Today Poblenou has become a laboratory for post-industrial experiments. Old factories are now schools, civic centres, workshops and open spaces. In the early 1990s many artists moved in, drawn by more working space and lower rents compared with the Old City. For a while Poblenou gained a reputation as a new centre for contemporary artistic activity, but more recently many artists have moved out again, as the cheap old buildings they occupied have been replaced by new blocks of flats.

One section of the *barri* is the Vila Olímpica; once a hive of dirty industry, it is now one of the gateways to the beach. In the middle of the district there are still parts of the old Poblenou, and even earlier Sant Martí: the lovely **Rambla del Poblenou** compares favourably with the more famous one in the city centre, and the area around **Plaça Prim** has kept its village atmosphere. And Poblenou still has Barcelona's oldest, most atmospheric cemetery (looking odd amid recent developments): the **Cementiri de l'Est**, with the extraordinary sculpture *El bes de la mort* ('Kiss of Death') to remind us of the brevity of human existence.

Nearby is **Plaça de les Glòries**, centrepiece of plans to upgrade this incorrigibly shabby area. According to Ildefons Cerdà's dream for the Eixample, the centre of the city should have been at Plaça de les Glòries and his rigid blocks should have continued north of the city along the coast almost as far as the Besòs river. What with one thing and another (unrest, civil war, dictatorship), these plans never materialised, and now the *plaça* is a suffocating traffic hub, and the area north of it stands as a monument to the stagnation of the Franco years.

Just to the north of Glòries, the walls of the old RENFE engine sheds have been incorporated into the **Parc del Clot**. In **Plaça de Valentí Almirall**, just beyond this park, lie the old town hall of Sant Martí and a 17th-century building that used to be the Hospital de Sant Joan de Malta, somewhat at odds with the buildings that have mushroomed around them.

Further north, up C/Sagrera, the entrance to a former giant truck factory now leads to the charming **Parc de la Pegaso**. The area also has a fine piece of recent architecture, the supremely elegant **Pont de Calatrava** bridge – designed by Santiago Calatrava – which links it to Poblenou via C/Bac de Roda. This is about the only new construction in the city to be known by the name of its architect. The nearby Sagrera train station is due to be extensively enlarged to accommodate a new high-speed line between Madrid and France.

Diagonal-Mar

The most monumental changes, however, are only now gathering momentum in the area on the north side of Poblenou along the coast towards the Besòs river; this is the part of Barcelona that has become Diagonal-Mar, the latest focus of attention of the city planners. The name is emblazoned everywhere, on buses, hoardings and in magazines, in an attempt to thrust it into the city's consciousness and ensure its successful completion. The starting point of the scheme, carried out in 1999, has been the extension all the way to the sea of **Avda Diagonal**, which – contrary to the Cerdà plan – used to fizzle out just east of Glòries. There are ambitious plans for skyscrapers, a new marina, a new business district, snappily called '22@', new beaches and a new site for at least the marine part of Barcelona's zoo, removing it from its cramped location in the Parc de la Ciutadella.

As in 1929 and 1992, though, Barcelona hopes to underpin its infrastructural schemes with an attention-grabbing international event, the highly controversial Fòrum Universal de les Cultures, scheduled for 2004. This was actually conceived entirely in Barcelona (and with Barcelona's own ends in mind), and how much interest (and so money) it will generate internationally is an open question. If it all comes to fruition, this will be one more area of Barcelona changed out of all recognition.

Got a light?
Oldenburg's **Matches**. *See p131.*

Guinardó, Horta & Vall d'Hebron

The opening of the Túnel de la Rovira in 1987 brought these hilly areas north of Gràcia in from the city's margins. Traditionally, the rich and poor have lived in parallel worlds; the former in large detached dwellings in the valleys and the latter perched on the hillsides. However, massive urbanisation since the 1920s and the proliferation of rather joyless apartment blocks have moderated the contrast between the haves and the have nots.

Joined to Gràcia by the long Avda Mare de Déu de Montserrat, **Guinardó** largely consists of two big parks. One, the **Parc de les Aigües**, contains a fun sculpture of a buried submarine by Josep Maria Riera, and Barcelona's most eccentrically beautiful municipal district headquarters, the **Casa de les Altures**, a neo-Arabic fantasy from 1890. The other, **Parc del Guinardó**, is one of the city's older parks, opened in 1920. Escalators have been installed in some of the district's steeper streets to save residents' legs.

Incorporated into Barcelona in 1904, the aptly named **Horta**, 'market garden', has retained many rural features, including some very well-preserved *masies,* traditional farmhouses. The medieval **Can Cortada**, in C/Campoamor, shows at a glance that these houses also served as fortresses, while **Can Mariner** in C/d'Horta is said to date back to 1050. Another houses a great restaurant, **Can Travi Nou** (*see p166*). Horta's abundant water supply once made it the laundry room of respectable Barcelona, with a whole community of *bugaderes* or washerwomen – as the open-air stone tanks along the lovely C/Aiguafreda attest.

The **Vall d'Hebron**, just above Horta along the Ronda de Dalt ring road on the flanks of Collserola, was one of the city's four main venues for Olympic events, and so has inherited centres for tennis, archery and cycling, at the **Velòdrom**. Around the sports venues are very striking examples of street sculpture, such as Claes Oldenburg's spectacular *Matches*, near the tennis centre, and Joan Brossa's *Visual Poem*, by the Velòdrom. There is also a reconstruction of the **Pavelló de la República** from 1937. One of the area's most distinctive assets is much older: the delightful, semi-concealed **Parc del Laberint** from 1791 – testimony to this hillside's much earlier role as a site for aristocratic country residences. For most locals, though, the Vall d'Hebron means above all the **Ciutat Sanitària**, the largest hospital in the city and the place where many first saw the light of day.

Parc del Laberint

C/Germans Desvalls, Passeig Vall d'Hebron (no phone). Metro Montbau/27, 60, 73, 76, 85, 173 bus. **Open** 10am-sunset daily. **Admission** €2; €1 concessions Mon, Tue, Thur-Sat; free under-6s, over-65s. Free Wed, Sun.

One of the city's most atmospheric (and leafiest) parks is also the most out of the way, in Vall d'Hebron. Originally the grounds of a mansion (long demolished), it is densely wooded with pines, and in the centre is an 18th-century formal garden with a deliberately picturesque fantasy element, including a romantic stream and waterfall. The maze that gives the park its name has often proved a match for cynics who thought it was only for children.

Pavelló de la República

Avda Cardenal Vidal y Barraquer (93 428 54 57). Metro Montbau/10, 27, 60, 73, 76, 85, 173 bus. **Open** 9am-8pm Mon-Fri. **Admission** free.

The Spanish Republic's pavilion for the 1937 Paris Exhibition, designed by Josep Lluís Sert, was where Picasso's *Guernica* was first exhibited, and is an emblematic work of rationalist architecture. It was demolished after the exhibition, but in 1992, following the re-creation of that other flagship building, Mies van der Rohe's Pavelló Barcelona, the controversial decision was taken to create a facsimile of Sert's building, even though it had no direct connection with Barcelona. Austerely functionalist, it forms a curious pair with Oldenburg's *Matches* across the street. It houses a research library, but visitors can explore most of the building.

Parc del Laberint: amazing.

Collectors' items

The city has many low-brow museums where the gathered pleasures of everyday life take precedence over high art or pure science. The rambling brood of private, small collections, hidden away in the oddest of places, includes those dedicated to food (chocolate), transport (horse-drawn hearses and carriages) and personal grooming (perfume, shoes and hairdressing). Future projects include a motorcycle museum in a renovated Poblenou factory, while the ambitious applied arts museum (projected for 2004 in the Plaça de les Glòries) may help to reverse the sometimes frustrating dispersion of quality pieces from the craft and design worlds.

Colección Privada de Peluquería Raffel Pagès

Rambla de Catalunya 99, Eixample (93 215 14 69/www.raffelpages.com/museo.html). Metro Diagonal/7, 16, 17, 20, 31, 43, 44, 67, 68 bus. **Open** *9am-1.30pm, 4-6.30pm Mon-Thur.* **Admission** *€4; €2 concessions.* **Credit** *MC, V.* **Map** *p336 D4.*

One of Barcelona's hairstyling dynasties manages this selection from a collection of more than 3,000 pieces related to the profession. Begun by Raffel Pagès' father in the 1940s, it offers a concise view into the culture of haircutting, with electric hair dryers up to 100 years old, combs, shaving kits and curlers – some going back over 200 years.

Museu d'Autòmates del Tibidabo

Parc d'Atraccions del Tibidabo, Zona Alta (93 211 79 42). FGC Av Tibidabo/17, 22, 73, 85 bus, then Tramvia Blau and Funicular de Tibidabo. **Open** *Mid June-mid Sept noon-10pm Mon-Thur, Sun; noon-1am Fri, Sat. Mid Sept-mid June noon-7pm Sat, Sun.* **Admission** €7 (includes six funfair rides). **Credit** MC, V.

This collection of electrified toys from the early 20th century, inside the Tibidabo funfair (*see p222*), contains some of the finest examples of coin-operated fairground machines in the world. Entertaining scenarios include the depiction of hell (El Infierno) – to the sound of roaring flames repentant maidens slide slowly into the pit, prodded by naked devils – and the saucy La Monyos (1913), named after a famed eccentric who cruised the Rambla: she claps her hands, shakes her shoulders and winks, pigtails flying. Unfortunately, you have to buy a (pricey) ticket for the funfair to enter.

Museu del Calçat (Shoe Museum)

Plaça Sant Felip Neri 5, Barri Gòtic (93 301 45 33). Metro Jaume I/17, 19, 40, 45 bus. **Open** 11am-2pm Tue-Sun. **Admission** €2; €1.50 concessions; free under-7s. **No credit cards. Map** p343 B3.

Run by a shoemakers' guild founded in 1203, this tiny museum reviews the cobbler's craft through originals and reproductions from Roman times to the present day. Stand-outs include embroidered satin dress shoes from the 19th century, and the enormous shoe made from the mould for the Columbus statue at the foot of the Ramblas. Shoes worn by the famous include pairs donated by the first Catalan to climb Everest, whose boots took local shoemaking to new heights.

Museu de Carrosses Fúnebres

C/Sancho de Avila 2, Eixample (93 484 17 20). Metro Marina/6, 10, 40, 42, 141 bus. **Open** 9am-1pm, 4-7pm Mon-Fri; 9am-1pm Sat, Sun (weekends call to confirm). **Admission** free. **Map** p341 F5.

Adjacent to the municipal Sancho de Avila funerary services, a dull basement holds a handsome collection of historic funeral carriages. Ask at the desk and they'll take you down to view some 20 horse-drawn carriages and a few motorised vehicles, which were used in Barcelona from the 18th century up to the 1970s. Carriages vary from ornate white hearses for children and 'single people' (presumably virgins) to a windowless black-velour mourning carriage that carried the unfortunate 'second wife' (mistress).

Museu de l'Eròtica

La Rambla 96 bis (93 318 98 65/www. erotica-museum.com). Metro Liceu/14, 38, 59, N6, N9 bus. **Open** *June-Sept 10am-midnight daily. Oct-May 11am-9pm daily.* **Admission** €7.20; €6 concessions. **Discounts** BT. **Credit** AmEx, MC, V. **Map** p343 A3.

This private museum's shabby display diminishes some genuine rarities of erotica, including Japanese drawings, 19th-century engravings by German Peter Fendi and compelling photos of brothels in Barcelona's Barrio Chino in the decadent 1930s. Other curiosities include S&M apparatus and simulated erotic telephone lines, but until things are sharpened up, the Eròtica is something of an embarrassment in a city with true connoisseurship for the bawdy.

Sightseeing

Museu FC Barcelona

*Nou Camp, Avda Arístides Maillol, access 9,
Les Corts (93 496 36 00/93 496 36 08).
Metro Maria Cristina or Collblanc/15, 52,
53, 54, 56, 57, 75 bus.* **Open** 10am-6.30pm
Mon-Sat; 10am-2pm Sun. **Admission** €3.80;
€2.30 concessions. *Guided tour* €8.50; €5.80
concessions. **Discounts** BC, BT. **No credit
cards**. **Map** p335 A3.
The museum at Barça's stadium, Nou Camp,
contains a vast collection of paraphernalia
that has accumulated since Swiss immigrant
Johan Gamper founded Barça in 1899. The
shiniest silver in the trophy case belongs to
the European Cup Winners' Cups of 1979,
1982, 1989 and 1997, and the club's
greatest treasure, the 1992 European Cup,
won at Wembley. Appropriately enough, the
museum bought Wembley memorabilia at
auction – goalposts, the royal box, historic
lighting fixtures – for a future re-creation of
the glorious moment. An old photo reveals the
origin of Barça fans' nickname, *culés* (from
culs, or 'bums'): spectators used to sit on the
high perimeter wall surrounding the old field,
their overhanging backsides offering a
singular view to those outside. The extensive
display has been magnificently enhanced by
Pablo Ornaque's first-class collection of world
soccer souvenirs, including sculptures,
posters, magazines, uniforms, boots and
balls, often shown in historical re-creations.
Visitors can also take a guided tour around
the stadium locker rooms, out through the
tunnels and on to the pitch – where they can
sit on the players' benches – and into the
presidential box. If you don't take a tour, you
can still step out into the stands for a view of
the cavernous stadium (capacity 115,000).
See also p264.

Museu del Perfum

*Passeig de Gràcia 39, Eixample (93 215 72
38/www.perfum-museum.com). Metro Passeig
de Gràcia/7, 16, 17, 22, 24, 28 bus.* **Open**
10.30am-1.30pm, 4.30-8pm Mon-Fri; 11am-
1.30pm Sat. **Admission** free. **Map** p336 D4.
Thousands of people walk past the Regia
perfumery (*see p205*) every day without
realising that the 'Museu del Perfum' sign is
not a gimmick. In a back room are hundreds
of scent bottles (*pictured*), dating from predynastic Egypt to the present. When owner
Ramon Planas moved his shop here in 1960,
he began gathering what is now one of the
world's finest collections. Many flasks trace
the period before perfumes were labelled,
including Egyptian, Greek and Roman
examples. The rest are shown by brands
(Guerlain, Dior, 4711), as well as limited-
edition bottles, such as a Dalí creation for
Schiaparelli, and a prized art nouveau flask
by René Lalique for the Coty Cyclamen brand.

Museu Verdaguer

*Vil.la Joana, Carretera de les Planes,
Vallvidrera (93 204 78 05/93 315 11 11).
By train FGC from Plaça Catalunya to Baixador
de Vallvidrera.* **Open** By appointment Tue-Fri;
10am-2pm Sat, Sun. **Admission** free.
Priest Jacint Verdaguer (1845-1902) was the
foremost poet of the 19th-century Catalan
Renaixença. Verdaguer spent his last weeks
in this bourgeois summer home up on
Collserola, now a shrine to his life and work.
Original furnishings, the old kitchen and a
small chapel give a clear image of life 100
years ago.

Museu de la Xocolata

*Antic Convent de Sant Agustí, Plaça Pons i
Clerch, La Ribera (93 268 78 78). Metro
Jaume I/17, 19, 39, 40, 45, 51 bus.* **Open**
10am-7pm Mon, Wed-Sat; 10am-3pm Sun.
Admission €3.50; €3 concessions; free under-
7s. **No credit cards**. **Map** p343 C3.
A museum-quality review of one of the world's
great temptations. It includes explanations of
chocolate's New World origins, its use in
medicine and as an aphrodisiac, and its
arrival in Europe, as well as many Catalan
Easter '*monos*' – huge, elaborate chocolate
sculptures for Holy Week that far outdo our
rudimentary bunnies. The museum shop is –
needless to say – mouth-watering.

Sant Andreu & Nou Barris

On the way out of Barcelona along the Meridiana, which like the Paral.lel derives its name from solar co-ordinates, Sant Andreu is to the right, and Nou Barris to the left.

Sant Andreu was another of the industrial and working-class hubs of the city. Much altered in the 1960s, it has seen some recent renovations: on Passeig Torres i Bages, at Nos.91-105, Josep Lluís Sert's **Casa Bloc**, a rationalist block of flats that was one of the main contributions to Barcelona of the brief republican era, has been restored, and, just off the Meridiana, a lovely wine press has been installed in Plaça d'en Xandrí. Two recent shopping areas are **La Maquinista** (*see p184*), built on the grounds of a long-defunct train station, and Heron City, which also has a multi-screen cinema.

Nou Barris (nine neighbourhoods) has a different make-up. In the 1950s, when the flow of migration into the city was at its height, ramshackle settlements were built here, followed by tower blocks. The price is now being paid, as flats scarcely 40 years old have fallen into ruins and are being demolished. Services of all kinds are deficient and although the city has now provided parks, sculptures and services – the **Can Dragó** sports complex has the biggest public swimming pool in Barcelona, and a **Parc Central** was completed in 1999 – overall these areas represent very much the 'other side' of the new Barcelona.

The Outer Limits

From the viewpoint of a bird, it might seem that the whole of the sprawling conurbation below would be the city of Barcelona. Not so; even though there are no visible city limits, Barcelona's boundaries lie, very approximately, along the Besòs river to the north and on the far side of Montjuïc to the south. Beyond these lie a ring of smaller cities, which until the 20th century were still rural, but since the 1920s have increasingly acquired industrial estates and large migrant populations from the rest of Spain. In many cases they have practically become dormitory towns for Barcelona.

Due north of the city and spanning both banks of the Besòs river, **Sant Adrià del Besòs** is famous for two things. The first is the district of **La Mina**, notorious as a hotbed of crime and poverty, although it is hoped it will benefit from the Fòrum 2004 to be staged nearby. The second is the **Feria de Abril** (*see p213*) – which is now held in the Diagonal-Mar development zone (and will be for the next few years). North of Sant Adrià, **Badalona**

is famous for its basketball team, **Joventut Badalona**, which has won the European Basketball Cup, something its rival FC Barcelona has never managed. It also has its own traditions, with a great *festa major* in May, climaxing with the *cremada del dimoni*, when a huge devil is burned on the beach.

Beyond the district of Sants and completely integrated into Barcelona's transport network, **L'Hospitalet de Llobregat** nevertheless asserts its identity with 'L'H' stickers on cars, and by having street signs pointing to 'Barcelona' even though the invisible boundary is only a few blocks away. With a large Andalucian-born population (most street signs are in Spanish rather than Catalan), it is Catalonia's main centre for flamenco; among the many *peñas* (clubs) are **Tertulia Flamenca** (C/Calderon de la Barca 12, 93 437 20 44), which also runs guitar classes. Equally, L'Hospitalet has plenty of bars and restaurants with good Andalucian specialities – try **Andalucía Chiquita** (Avda Isabel la Catòlica 89, 93 438 12 67), or sit out on the one of terraces running along around C/Luarca.

Tecla Sala Centre Cultural

Avda Josep Tarradellas 44, Hospitalet de Llobregat (93 338 57 71). Metro La Torrassa/bus L12 from Plaça Maria Cristina. **Open** 11am-2pm, 5-8pm Tue-Sat; 11am-2pm Sun. **Admission** free.
Barcelona's magnetism tends to condemn all suburban museums to anonymity, even when shows are top-notch. Tecla Sala is an attractive converted factory with exhibitions of international contemporary art. For 2002, director (and prestigious Barcelona critic) Victoria Comalia is presenting an exhibition of Spanish conceptual art from the Tous Collection (until the end of April), while a show of Dora Maar's photography and her connection with Picasso will be on from May to mid July.

Tecla Sala: *Oikonomos* by Francesc Torres.

Eat, Drink, Shop

Restaurants

If pre-packaged paella is your thing, read no further.

Eat, Drink, Shop

Barcelona has never been a more popular tourist destination than now, and this reflects strongly in most people's first culinary glimpse of the city: the restaurants packed along the La Rambla with their wipe-clean photographs of fried eggs and bacon, jugs of diluted sangria, and waiters hustling for trade in broken English. Even though this has become an undeniable part of what's on offer, you can do much better if you gather up the courage to go for something a little off the beaten track.

Barcelona has over 3,600 registered eateries, as well as more award-winning chefs and more innovative cuisine than anywhere else in Spain, including Madrid. This abundance of choice makes the Catalan capital unusually accessible for eating out on any kind of budget, and one of the greatest pleasures of the city is wandering the streets to see what's on offer: there'll be everything from traditional Catalan cuisine to flashy fusion dishes, vegetarian buffets, designer curries and delicious specialities from other regions in Spain. But if you insist on the straight and narrow of the tourist drag, then be warned: you have nothing to fear but food itself.

WHERE

Restaurants are scattered throughout the city, but some zones stand out for certain kinds of food and ambience. The neighbourhoods of the Born and La Ribera are where the new designer hotspots are cropping up, while most of the more prestigious places (including a few Michelin-starred establishments) are to be found in the Eixample and the Zona Alta. The best place for traditional seafood is in the old fishing district of Barceloneta, although the character of the beachfront restaurants becomes increasingly modern as you move towards the Port Olímpic. Most of the more traditional Catalan restaurants are concentrated in the Barri Gòtic, the Raval and Gràcia, and these areas are also home to the greatest range of regional and ethnic cooking in the city.

WHEN

Catalans eat late: lunch starts around 2pm and goes on until about 3.30 or 4pm, and dinner is served from 9pm until about 11.30pm or midnight (although tourist-oriented restaurants may serve as early as 8pm or even stay open all day). Reserving a table in mid- to upper-range restaurants is always a good idea (especially for

groups of more than four), and the same goes for any restaurant on Friday and Saturday night. Most restaurants close on Sunday evenings and those that do not fill up quickly. Many also close for holidays, including about a week off over Easter, two or three weeks in August or early September, and often the first week in January. Annual closures of more than two weeks are listed where possible, but it's always a good idea to call ahead in holiday periods just to be sure.

PRICES, TIPS AND SERVICE

By law, menus must declare if the seven per cent IVA (VAT) is included in prices or not, and also if there is a cover charge (for sneaky, law-dodging reasons, this may often be expressed as a charge for bread). You needn't automatically chip in a 12 per cent tip, but it is quite common to leave a euro or so as a token of your appreciation for good service. Waiters in Spain earn a salary, so although they're friendly enough, they don't tend to bow and scrape the way waiters relying exclusively on tips do.

In budget to mid-range establishments, it's worth noting that you are usually expected to use the same cutlery for the first and second courses, so don't be surprised if the waiter plonks your knife and fork back down before carrying off your plate. It's also not unusual for waiters to bring out dishes as they are ready, so you may get your main course while someone else at your table is still on their starter, or even find two courses put in front of you at once.

MENÚ DEL DÍA

All but the swanky restaurants are required by law to serve an economical fixed-price *menú* (not to be confused with the menu, which is *la carta*) at lunchtime – usually consisting of a starter, main course, dessert, bread and a fairly prosaic half-bottle of vino. The idea is to provide a cheaper meal than you would have if you ate the same items à la carte, and while it can be a real bargain, it is not by any means a taster menu or a showcase for the chef's greatest hits. The *menú del día* (also sometimes called the *menú turístico*, as it was originally designed to attract tourists in the 1960s) tends to repeat the same basic and universally acceptable dishes day in, day out – which may mean nothing more than a salad, followed by fried chicken and chips, with a yoghurt or piece of fruit for dessert. There are, of course, exceptions to this; we have highlighted those that are better than average.

Barri Gòtic

Agut
C/Gignàs 16 (93 315 17 09). Metro Jaume I/17, 40, 45 bus. **Open** 1.30-5pm, 9pm-midnight Tue-Sat; 1.30-5pm Sun. Closed Aug. **Average** €8.40-€16.10. **Set lunch** €9 Tue-Fri. **Credit** MC, V. **Map** p343 B4.
A staid meeting place for well-heeled Catalans of a certain age, Agut is known for its fresh pasta and huge, tender steaks, but the fish dishes can also be excellent. Food is imaginatively presented, and even the set lunch is prefaced with *amuse-bouches*. The pudding list also throws up some surprises, not least of which is a glorious mascarpone ice-cream in a lemon and ginger 'soup'.

Amaya
La Rambla 20-24 (93 302 61 38/www.amaya.com-actiu.es). Metro Liceu/14, 38, 59, 91, N9, N12 bus. **Open** 1-5pm, 8.30pm-midnight daily. **Main courses** €5.50-€7.80. **Set lunch** €6.60 Mon-Fri. **Credit** AmEx, DC, MC, V. **Map** p343 A4.
Formerly the domain of actors, writers, opera singers and politicians, but now a respected lunch venue for office workers and the odd tourist. The menu comprises mainly Basque specialities, with plenty of *merluza* (hake) and *bacalao* (cod), but there are dishes from all over the country. The deeper you go, the smarter it gets; the fruit machines and tobacco fumes of the entrance segue into a womb-like haven of peach tones and table linen a couple of rooms in.

Cafè de l'Acadèmia
C/Lledó 1 (93 319 82 53/93 315 00 26). Metro Jaume I/17, 19, 40, 45, N8 bus. **Open** 9am-noon, 1.30-4pm, 8.45pm-11.30 Mon-Fri. Closed 2wks Aug. **Main courses** €7.40-€12.50. **Set lunch** €7.20 €9.60 Mon-Fri. **Credit** AmEx, MC, V. **Map** p343 B3.
On everybody's list of favourite Barcelona restaurants, the Acadèmia still turns out superb Catalan dishes at reasonable prices, from *pintado rostit* (roast guinea fowl) with a tiny tarte tatin to risotto with duck foie gras and grapes. At lunchtime, the stone-walled dining room and terrace on the medieval Plaça Sant Just throng with politicians from the nearby Generalitat, and at night they play host to everyone else, so it makes sense to book ahead.

Can Culleretes
C/Quintana 5 (93 317 30 22). Metro Liceu/14, 18, 38, 59 bus. **Open** 1.30-4pm, 9-11pm Tue-Sat; 1.30-4pm Sun. Closed 3wks July. **Main courses** €6-€15.50. **Set lunch** €14. **Gourmet menu** €22. **Credit** MC, V. **Map** p343 A3.
Founded in 1786, Can Culleretes is still filling its warren of dining rooms with merry punters. Traditional dishes, such as roast *lechón* (suckling pig) and *cuixa d'oca amb pomes* (goose leg with apples), and a three-course menu of daisy-fresh

Can Culleretes.

seafood, are served with friendly efficiency. Prices are unbeatable, particularly for the wine; unfortunately, all Barcelona is aware of this, so you may need to reserve.

Cervantes
C/Cervantes 7 (93 317 33 84). Metro Jaume I/14, 18, 38, 59, N6, N9 bus. **Open** *Bar* 7am-8pm Mon-Fri. *Restaurant* 1-4pm Mon-Fri. Closed Aug. **Set lunch** €7.80. **No credit cards. Map** p343 B3.
Sturdy Catalan fare, which might involve a lentil dish or *habitas con jamón* (baby broad beans with ham) to start, followed by a stew, is the order of the day at this bustling lunch restaurant. Small tables, and plenty of them, can make your neighbours' elbows a frustrating feature of the meal.

El Gran Café
C/Avinyó 9 (93 318 79 86). Metro Liceu/14, 38, 59, 91, N9, N12 bus. **Open** 1-4.30pm, 8pm-12.30am Mon-Sat. **Main courses** €6.60-€11.80. **Set lunch** €9.30. **Credit** AmEx, DC, MC, V. **Map** p343 B3.
Everything in this fading but still elegant brasserie is geared towards making the foreigner happy – bread comes with butter; waiters come with aprons;

dinner comes with a pianist and, rather touchingly, vegetables come with salad. Ignore the bids for the tourist dollar on the menu (roast beef), and head for the wafer-thin carpaccios or the *magret de pato* (duck), both of which are delicious. Old-fashioned service and levels of comfort conspire to make this the sort of place your mother would love.

Mastroqué

C/Codols 29 (93 301 79 42). Metro Drassanes/14, 36, 57, 59, 64, 157, N6, N12 bus. **Open** 9-11.30pm Mon, Sat; 1.30-3.30pm, 9-11.30pm Tue-Fri. Closed most Aug. **Main courses** €5.80-€9. **Set lunch** €9. **Credit** MC, V. **Map** p343 B4.
Burnt yellow walls and mellow lighting give this restaurant – which is surprisingly spacious, despite its narrow entrance – an intimate feel. Mastroqué offers a small but interesting selection of regional dishes from France and Spain, served as *media raciones* (in other words, you can have two). Duck in all its forms is the speciality, but unusual dishes such as *morcilla con mermelada de cebolla* (black pudding with onion marmalade) also feature. At lunchtime, there is only a set menu with limited options, but all are well chosen.

Mercè Vins

C/Amargós 1 (93 302 60 56). Metro Urquinaona/ 17, 19, 40, 45, N8 bus. **Open** 8am-5pm Mon-Thur; 8am-5pm, 9pm-midnight Fri; 9am-noon, 8pm-midnight Sat. **Set lunch** €7.80 Mon-Thur. **Credit** V. **Map** p342 B2.
This tiny split-level restaurant has no à la carte menu, but its set menu (lunchtime only) features a better choice than usual, with interesting Catalan dishes, such as stuffed aubergines or *llom amb ametlles i prunes* (pork with almonds and prunes). Alternatively, there are *llesques* throughout the day (*see p168* **Bites to eat**).

Mesón Jesús

C/Cecs de la Boquería 4 (93 317 46 98). Metro Liceu/14, 38, 59, 91, N9, N12 bus. **Open** 1-4pm, 8-11pm Mon-Fri. Closed Aug-early Sept. **Main courses** €4.30-€14.20. **Set lunch** €7.80. **Set dinner** €10.80. **Credit** MC, V. **Map** p343 A3.
Gingham tablecloths, oak barrels, beaming waiters and traditional Spanish cooking make for a satisfyingly authentic experience in the heart of the Barri Gòtic labyrinth. Tourists are looked after with multilingual menus, but there's no shortage of munching locals, drawn in by a good-value lunch menu containing the odd surprise – such as a tasty courgette stuffed with pork and tomato.

Oolong

C/Gignàs 25 (93 315 12 59). Metro Jaume I/17, 40, 45 bus. **Open** noon-4pm, 8pm-midnight Mon-Sat; 1-4pm, 8pm-midnight Sun. Closed early Sept. **Main courses** €6-€9. **Set lunch** €7.50 Mon-Fri. **No credit cards. Map** p343 B4.
The one problem with Oolong is its immense popularity among the global hipsters roaming the Barri Gòtic; it can be hard to get a table and you may feel

Oolong. Like it says.

rushed once you're there. The food is innovative and vaguely oriental, with aromatic salads (oranges with caramelised almonds and a rose petal vinaigrette, anyone?) and delicious chicken dishes, but the funky music and beautiful people propping up the bar are really what the place is all about.

Pla

C/Bellafila 5 (93 412 65 52). Metro Jaume I/17, 19, 40, 45 bus. **Open** 9pm-2.30am Mon-Thur, Sun; 9pm-midnight Fri, Sat. **Main courses** €8.70-€12.30. **Credit** MC, V. **Map** p343 B3.
A dramatic, split-level space painted in deep colours with modern artworks and low lighting. The menu is a modish mix of oriental and Mediterranean dishes; Thai fish curry is well executed, as is duck confit with grapes and the chicken pancake. The salads and carpaccios can also be fantastic, and the puds round things off with panache. Try the lemon ice-cream, dotted with fresh raspberries and lethally doused in vodka, or the pear tatin with a hot chocolate sauce. Daily specials don't appear on the menu, but waiters will make a valiant attempt to explain in English, should you require it.

Polenta

C/Ample 51 (93 268 14 29). Metro Jaume I/17, 19, 40, 45 bus. **Open** 1pm-midnight Mon, Wed-Fri; 1pm-1am Sat, Sun. **Main courses** €5.30-€8.10. **Set lunch** €9 Mon, Wed-Fri. **Credit** AmEx, MC, V. **Map** p343 B4.
Polenta specialises in an unlikely fusion of Mediterranean and Japanese influences to form light and healthy dishes. Yakitori chicken and leek sticks, or the leafy salad with tofu and dabs of salty pink polenta, are served (all day) to a suitably international, suitably modern soundtrack. For dessert, try the optimistically named Aphrodisiac, comprising ice-cream, chocolate and candied ginger.

The **Pla** to be. *See p139.*

La Poste

C/Gignàs 23 (93 315 15 04). Metro Jaume I/17, 19, 40, 45, N8 bus. **Open** 1-4.30pm, 8-11.30pm Mon-Fri; 1-4.30pm Sat, Sun. Closed late Aug-early Sept. **Main courses** €5.40-€16.90. **Set menu** €6 Mon; €7.20 Sat; €7.80 Sun. **No credit cards. Map** p343 B4.
Home to what has to be the best value lunch menu in town, La Poste draws in a varied crowd, from postal workers from the nearby Correus to smartly dressed Catalan ladies who lunch. The dining area is oddly sterile and enjoys more air-conditioning than is called for, but no one's complaining when faced with an entire tortilla as a starter.

Les Quinze Nits

Plaça Reial 6 (93 317 30 75). Metro Liceu/14, 38, 59, 91, N9, N12. **Open** 1-3.45pm, 8.30-11.30pm daily. **Main courses** €4.40-€8.40. **Set lunch** €6.60 Mon-Fri; €7.20 Sat, Sun. **Credit** AmEx, DC, MC, V. **Map** p343 A3.
Opinions are sharply divided on this innovative chain of elegant, bustling restaurants, but to cavil at the occasionally variable quality of the main courses is to overlook the rock-bottom prices, incongruous in such a setting. Few other places can offer sophisticated menus of modern Catalan dishes in this price range, as the queues testify. For a shorter wait, head to one of the branches listed below.
Branches: **La Fonda** C/Escudellers 10, Barri Gòtic (93 301 75 15); **La Dolça Herminia** C/Magdalenes 27, Eixample (93 317 06 76); **Hostal de Rita** C/Aragó 279, Eixample (93 487 23 76); **L'Hostalet de la Mamasita** Avda Sarriá 10, Zona Alta (93 323 16 35).

El Salón

C/Hostal d'en Sol 6-8 (93 315 21 59/www.elsalon. net). Metro Jaume I/17, 19, 40, 45, N8 bus. **Open** 2-5pm, 8.30pm-midnight Mon-Sat. Closed 2wks Aug. **Main courses** €8.40-€11.10. **Credit** AmEx, MC, V. **Map** p343 B4.
The cuisine – such as starters of mushroom carpaccio with figs, or lentils with squid and raita; mains of roast rabbit in a creamy saffron sauce, or satay lamb and chicken with coconut rice – defies all attempts at labelling. The common traits of all dishes are that they are rich and that they are good. The restaurant itself is relaxed and informal, with

baroque touches giving the mismatched furniture and high-ceilinged room a bohemian air. There's also a handful of tables outside.

Slokai

C/Palau 5 (93 317 90 94). Metro Jaume I/17, 19, 40, 45 bus. **Open** 1.30-4pm, 9pm-midnight Mon-Fri; 9pm-midnight Sat. **Main courses** €7.20-€12. **Set lunch** €7.20. **Credit** MC, V. **Map** p343 B3.
A hip little spot filled with colourful artworks and beautiful youth, serving somewhat self-consciously trendy dishes such as kangaroo and ostrich. Portion sizes err on the side of cautious, but the set lunch is good value, with a buffet of interesting salads to start, followed by risotto, pasta or a meat dish.

Taxidermista

Plaça Reial 8 (93 412 45 36). Metro Liceu/14, 38, 59, 91, N9, N12 bus. **Open** noon-2am Tue-Sun. *Meals served* 1.30-4pm, 8.30-12.30pm. **Main courses** €11-€16.10. **Set lunch** €7.80. **Credit** AmEx, DC, MC, V. **Map** p343 A3.
As its name implies, this was once a shop for stuffed animals, but Taxidermista's owners have resisted the lure of stags' heads and turned it into an elegant restaurant, where shafts of sunlight fall on to a black and white tiled floor. You'll find high-quality dishes with a French influence, such as *rèmol* (turbot) with cider sauce and apple purée, and *poularde* stuffed with *espinacs a la catalana* and served with leek crisps. Outside, an ample terrace looks over the Plaça Reial, where tapas are served all day.

International

Machiroku

C/Moles 21 (93 412 60 82). Metro Urquinaona/ 17, 19, 40, 45 bus. **Open** 1.30-3.30pm, 8.30-11.30pm Mon-Fri; 8.30-11.30pm Sat. **Main courses** €6.60-€8.90. **Set lunch** €7.20-€7.80 Mon-Fri. **No credit cards.**
A few steps from the culinary wasteland of Plaça de Catalunya, Machiroku provides an oasis of Japanese calm. Service is charming and friendly and the three different lunchtime menus offer incredible value for money. These include a seaweed and sesame salad, miso soup and generous portions of sushi, sashimi or nigiri zushi, although there are plenty of other dishes to choose from if you go à la carte.

Peimong

C/Templaris 6-10 (93 318 28 73). Metro Jaume I/ 17, 19, 40, 45, N8 bus. **Open** 1-4.30pm, 8pm-midnight Tue-Sun. **Main courses** €6-€9. **Credit** MC, V. **Map** p343 B3.
Not, perhaps, the fanciest-looking restaurant around (think Peruvian gimcracks and strip lighting) or, indeed, the fanciest-looking food, but it sure tastes like the real thing. Try the ceviche for an explosion of lime and coriander or the spicy corn tamales. Service is particularly warm and friendly, there are two types of Peruvian beer and even – for the very nostalgic or the hypoglycaemic – Inca Kola.

Top Cat: Ferran Adrià

What Willy Wonka was to chocolate, Ferran Adrià is to Catalan cuisine. His fantastical, playful creations fuse science with poetry to create a culinary voyage, taking the diner on a journey by mouthfuls. If that sounds far-fetched, how about a bed of algae foam supporting three tiny heaps; one containing an explosive combination of Thai flavours, the next Japanese and, finally, a spoonful of Mexico? Or how about a 'Kellogg's paella', where featherlight, toasted grains of rice infused with prawn and squid flavours are served in a plastic sachet, to be ripped open and the contents poured into the mouth? Then there is the ravioli, where the pasta is actually a gossamer-thin sheet of squid, filled with coconut milk. Tortilla is deconstructed and served as three mounds of foam; one potato, one egg and one onion. Even the most reviled of British food is given a twist, with a paper cone full of tiny battered fish, and an exuberant take on the ice-cream wafer sandwich; here, the wafers are crunchy and cheese-flavoured and the ice-cream is parmesan.

Adrià started working at El Bulli restaurant outside Barcelona at the tender age of 22, and within a few months had become head chef. Now, 17 years later, he is one of the world's finest cooks – with three Michelin stars under his belt – and almost certainly the world's most inventive. Gourmet pilgrims travel from around the world to the remote culinary mecca of El Bulli, several kilometres

from Roses, up an almost inaccessible dirt track. It is rumoured that only a third of the staff in the kitchens of El Bulli is paid, and still there are chefs lining up to work with him.

Some of the most coveted positions are in Adrià's workshop in the Barri Gòtic, where he spends half the year (when the restaurant is closed) inventing new fantasies in foam and leafing through his vast library, looking for more dishes to deconstruct. He and his team of alchemists play around with texture, temperature and, above all, smell, creating aerosols evoking the mustiness of a forest, or the salty air and seaweed of the coast.

It has to be said that this wizardry does not come cheap. The 30 or so heavenly treats that comprise the *menú degustacion* at El Bulli (and having come this far, why settle for anything less?) costs over €125, not including wine. This is the price you pay for the kind of genius that makes something delicious from an aubergine ravioli filled with yoghurt foam and flavoured with a melted Fisherman's Friend.

El Bulli

Cala Montjoi (972 15 04 57/www.elbulli.com). By car A7 or N11 north (7km/4.5 miles from Roses)/by train RENFE from Sants or Passeig de Gràcia to Figueres, then bus to Roses, then taxi. Open Apr-June 8-10pm Wed-Sun. June-Sept 8-10pm daily. Closed Oct-Mar. **Main courses** €22-€84.30. **Gourmet menu** €126.30. **Credit** AmEx, DC, MC, V.

Eat, Drink, Shop

GRUPO TRAGALUZ

NEGRO

Cosmopolitan cuisine.
DJ and drinks until 02 am.
Diagonal 640 08017 Barcelona
Telephone: 93 405 94 44

Finalist FAD 2000 award.

EL JAPONES

Young and dynamic atmosphere.
Passatge de la Concepció 2
08008 Barcelona
Telephone: 93 487 25 92

Finalist FAD 2000 award.

AGUA

Rice dishes, fish dishes and tapas.
Passeig Marítim 30
08003 Barcelona
Telephone: 93 225 12 72

Paseo de Gracia, 60
Tel.: 93 487 76 72
www.grupotragaluz.com

Creative cuisine.
Passatge de la Concepció 5
08008 Barcelona
Telephone: 93 487 06 21
93 487 01 96

Finalist FAD 1991 award.

TRAGALUZ

Garden restaurant.
Fresh mediterranean cuisine.
Milanesat, 19 08017 Barcelona
Telephone: 93 203 06 58

ACONTRALUZ

Restaurant. Private rooms.
Banquet´s saloon.
Provença 286 / 288
08008 Barcelona
Telephone: 93 272 08 45

2001 Saloni award.

PRINCIPAL

The maverick veggie option with hallucinogenic graffiti on the walls, thumping eurotrance and scatty waitresses fresh off their Erasmus schemes. The soup, served with wholewheat breads, changes daily, and there is a thali plate of roast vegetables, sauces, and pulses. As the name suggests, they specialise in freshly squeezed juices, shakes and smoothies.

Juicy Jones.

Raval

El Cafetí
C/Hospital 99 (93 329 24 19/www.elcafeti.com). Metro Liceu/14, 38, 59, N9, N12 bus. **Open** 1.30-3.30pm, 9-11.30pm Tue-Sat; 1.30-3.30pm Sun. Closed 3wks Aug. **Main courses** €7.70-€12.90. **Set lunch** €7.20 Tue-Sat. **Credit** AmEx, DC, MC, V. **Map** p340 C6.
Tucked away in a Raval alley, this seductively cosy restaurant evokes the sitting room of an elegant but slightly batty old lady, and is said to be a favourite of London mayor Ken Livingstone. Specialities include paellas, *mar i muntanya* dishes, duck and occasionally venison. A room upstairs can be booked for large groups.

Ca l'Estevet
C/Valldonzella 46 (93 302 41 86). Metro Universitat/ bus all routes to Plaça Universitat. **Open** 1.30-4pm, 8.30-11pm Mon-Sat. Closed 2wks Aug. **Main courses** €5.70-€13.20. **Set lunch** €7.20 Mon-Fri. **Credit** AmEx, DC, MC, V. **Map** p342 A1.

La Verònica
C/Avinyó 25 (93 412 11 22). Metro Liceu/14, 38, 59, 91, N9, N12 bus. **Open** 7.30pm-1.30am Tue-Fri; 1pm-1.30am Sat, Sun. **Main courses** €5.30-€8.30. **Credit** MC, V. **Map** p343 B3.
A colourful, elegantly constructed space with food to match: thin, crispy pizzas and designer salads. During the summer, tourists fill the outside tables on Plaça George Orwell, but late nights and winter months draw a hip, mainly gay, local crowd, to munch on such delights as carrot and parsnip shavings doused in ginger vinaigrette.

Vegetarian

Govinda
Plaça Vila de Madrid 4-5 (93 318 77 29). Metro Catalunya/bus all routes to Plaça Catalunya. **Open** 1-4pm, 8.30-11.45pm Tue-Sat; 1-4pm Mon, Sun. **Main courses** €6-€8.40. **Set menu** €11.90 Fri pm-Sun. **Credit** AmEx, DC, MC, V. **Map** p342 B2.
Barcelona's only vegetarian Indian restaurant, serves the odd Spanish item such as gazpacho alongside uthapam bread, coconut puddings and excellent curried vegetables. Note that there is no alcohol or coffee and smoking is permitted only in the evening.

Juicy Jones
C/Cardenal Casañas 7 (93 302 43 30). Metro Liceu/ 14, 38, 59, 91, N9, bus. **Open** 9am-midnight daily. **Set lunch** €7.50. **No credit cards. Map** p343 A3.

Oooh, saucy!

There are four basic sauces that form the foundation of many Catalan dishes, and are so ubiquitous that they are almost never explained, or even mentioned, on menus.

All i oli tells it like it is, with just two ingredients: *all* (raw garlic) crushed up in a pestle and mortar with *oli* (olive oil) to form a mayonnaise-like mixture. The result is as eye-watering as it is mouth-watering (and you won't smell that great, either), but it's worth it for the explosive combinations with seafood dishes such as *fideuà* or roast meat, especially rabbit. A relative of *romesco* (*see p148* **Know your onions**), *picada* is a mash of nuts, garlic, parsley, bread, chicken liver and little *bicho* chilli peppers, which is often used to enrich and thicken dishes. *Sofregit* is a quintessentially Mediterranean base of tomato, garlic and onion slowly sautéed in olive oil until it's soft and sticky, while *samfaina*, a mix of onion, garlic, aubergine and red and green peppers (similar to ratatouille), often accompanies grilled meat and fish.

Back in the '60s, Estevet was the place for writers, artists and politicians to hang out and chat – witness the signed photos and artistic doodlings around the walls – and little has changed since. The menu features the same dishes of *filet de Café Paris*, served in a buttery, herby sauce with wild mushrooms, and succulent *cabrito* (kid) that it always did. At times, the food is secondary to the atmosphere; starters can be spartan and desserts tend towards the pre-packaged, but this remains a fabulously welcoming, relaxed place to spend an evening with friends.

Ca l'Isidre

C/Les Flors 12 (93 441 11 39/93 442 57 20). Metro Paral.lel/20, 64, 91, N0, N6 bus. **Open** 1.30-4pm, 8.30-11.30pm Mon-Sat. Closed 2wks Aug. **Main courses** €10.50-€40.90. **Credit** AmEx, DC, MC, V. **Map** p340 C6.
Traditional Catalan cuisine bolstered with the freshest ingredients that La Boqueria has to offer. The steak tartare is renowned, and the dishes with duck's liver are also superb. Excellent desserts are provided by Isidre's daughter, master *pastissera* Núria Gironès, and the wine list is encyclopaedic. The picture-lined dining room (the collection includes a couple of original Dalis, or so they say) is small, and booking is essential.

Can Lluís

C/Cera 49 (93 441 11 87). Metro Sant Antoni or Paral.lel/20, 24, 64, 91, N6 bus. **Open** 1.30-4pm, 8.30-11.30pm Mon-Sat. **Main courses** €5.40-€19. **Set lunch** €6.30 Mon-Fri. **Gourmet menu** €20.60. **Credit** AmEx, DC, MC, V. **Map** p340 C6.
This restaurant has the same menu as its sister, Els Ocellets (just a minute's walk away on the other side of the Ronda), and is equally popular, but it's got bags more atmosphere. Try the spicy *romescado* salad with anchovies or the hearty *estofat* (stew). Bookings are only taken for groups, so get there early to avoid having to wait.
Branch: **Els Ocellets** Ronda Sant Pau 55, Barri Gòtic (93 441 10 46).

La Casa de la Rioja

C/Peu de la Creu 8-10 (93 443 33 63). Metro Catalunya/bus all routes to Plaça Catalunya. **Open** 1-4pm, 8.30-11pm Mon-Sat; 1-4pm Sun. **Main courses** €5.60-€6.30. **Set lunch** €7.70 Mon-Fri. **Set dinner** €10.30 Mon-Fri; €12.50 Sat, Sun. **Credit** MC, V. **Map** p340 C5.
Just as it begins to seem that all set menus comprise a saucer of sopping iceberg, a lozenge of fried pork and a yoghurt washed down with a goblet of paintstripper, this far-flung outpost of the Rioja region opens to show 'em how it's done. For the price of a bottle of wine, you might get a crab and salmon salad followed by a hearty stew; both delicious, but eclipsed by ambrosial desserts such as homemade chocolate and pistachio ice-cream, or an inspired Roquefort cheesecake – *and* a bottle of wine. Enthusiastic staff and a stylish paint job make eating here a delight.

Casa Leopoldo

C/Sant Rafael 24 (93 441 69 42). Metro Liceu/14, 38, 59, 91, N9, N12 bus. **Open** 1.30-4pm, 9-11pm Tue-Sat; 1.30-4pm Sun. **Main courses** €9.70-€21.40. **Set dinner** €39.20 Tue-Fri. **Credit** AmEx, DC, MC, V. **Map** p340 C6.
This friendly family restaurant opened in the 1930s, and time seems to have stood still ever since. Bullfighting paraphernalia, wooden fittings and *azulejos* (tiles) give plenty of old-style charm, and traditional food is still the order of the day with generous and excellent seafood, steaks and homey stews. It seems the only thing to have moved with the times is the bill, which can actually become almost futuristic if you order the fish of the day.

El Convent

C/Jerusalem 3 (93 317 10 52). Metro Liceu/14, 38, 59, N9, N12 bus. **Open** 1-4pm, 8pm-midnight Mon-Sat. **Main courses** €6.50-€14.80. **Set lunch** €7.20. **Credit** AmEx, DC, MC, V. **Map** p342 A2.
A convivial place, with handsome antique fittings and enjoyable food. The menu is traditional Catalan, with some interesting game dishes: *estofado de jabalí* (wild boar stew) and *solomillo de ciervo* (venison steak). Be prepared to take a seat and wait, particularly at lunchtime.

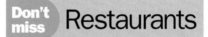

Don't miss Restaurants

The Old City
Cafè de l'Acadèmia (see p137); **El Cafetí** (*pictured, see p144*), **Passadis del Pep** (see p149); **Pla** (see p139); **El Salón** (see p140).

Eixample
Casa Calvet (see p157); El Racó d'en Baltà (see p157); **Tragaluz** (see p159).

Gràcia and other districts
Gaig (see p166); **Laurak** (see p162); **Neichel** (see p166); **La Parra** (see p165); **Els Pescadors** (see p166).

Eat, Drink, Shop

Grape expectations

People used to think of Spanish wines as nothing more than cheap plonk, and as for Catalan wines, well, nobody thought about those at all. These days, however, Catalonia has a number of wines that are attracting international attention. Restaurant wine lists are usually heavy on local producers, so look out for the eight wine regions (called *denominación de origen* or DO) in Catalonia: Allela and Empordà in the north-east, Costers del Segre in the north-west; and Penedès, Tarragona, Priorat, Terra Alta and Conca de Barberá to the south of Barcelona.

Despite a gradual move to lighter red wines and whites, heavy reds are still the overwhelming favourites in Spain. If you like them deep, strong and powerful, then you can't do better than Priorat, currently the hottest red wine region in Spain. Limited production means prices can be high; a top label such as Alvaro Palacios' L'Ermita will set you back a staggering €160, although much cheaper versions can be found from Onix and Scala Dei. Another star label is Raïmat from the Costers del Segre region, whose rich red Cabernet Sauvignons and Merlots come highly recommended, especially for drinking with heavy meat dishes.

Penedès is the largest wine region and produces everything from young fruity whites to crisp rosés and reds. Reliable names are Miguel Torres, Albet i Noya (one of the few organic producers in Catalonia) and the charismatic Jean Leon – an ex-Los Angeles restaurateur, and allegedly one of the last people to see Marilyn Monroe alive.

Also from the Penedès region is cava, a sparkling wine that is made by the same method as French champagne and includes local grape varieties as well as the traditional Chardonnay. It's generally cheaper than champagne and many Catalans routinely drink cava throughout a meal, and especially like a bit of bubbly with dessert. As well as the big names (Freixenet, Cordoniu), look out for smaller boutique labels such as Llopart, Huguet and Masia Freixe (another organic producer).

As for Spanish wines, Rioja is by far the most famous, although quality has become somewhat variable in recent years. Rising stars are the regions of Navarra and especially the Ribera del Duero, where labels such as Marques de Griñon have become very popular.

When deciphering wine lists it helps to remember that *vino joven* is wine made for immediate drinking, while *vino de crianza* must have been stored for a minimum period: one year for whites and rosés, two years for reds. A *reserva* requires a year's additional storage on top of that, and *gran reserva* is a title permitted only for particularly outstanding vintages that must have spent at least two years in storage and three in the bottle. Prices rise accordingly.

Elisabets

*C/Elisabets 2-4 (93 317 58 26). Metro Catalunya/
bus all routes to Plaça Catalunya.* **Open** 7.30am-
11pm Mon-Thur, Sat, Sun; 7.30am-3am Fri. Closed
3wks Aug. **Set lunch** €6.60. **Set dinner** €9-€12.
No credit cards. Map p342 A2.

An unpretentious but friendly place to have lunch
among the denizens of the Raval and those on their
way back from the MACBA. *Menús* of traditional
Catalan dishes are decent value, and a jumble of old
radios and other eccentric touches make this a
preferable option to most of the cheapies hereabouts.

La Gardunya

*C/Jerusalem 18 (93 302 43 23). Metro Liceu/14,
38, 59, 91, N9, N12 bus.* **Open** 1-4pm, 8pm-1am
Mon-Sat. **Main courses** €6.30-€25.60. **Set
lunch** €8.80 Mon-Fri. **Set dinner** €10.90 Mon-
Fri. **Credit** AmEx, DC, MC, V. **Map** p342 A2.

A tall, thin, glass and steel building, funkily decorated, with a mosaic of stone and sand in the floor
and a colourful spiral staircase leading up to a mez-
zanine. Grab a table there to get a view into La
Boqueria market, and watch your *sardinas* or *man-
itas de cabrito* (kid's trotters) being haggled over.

La Llotja

*Museu Marítim, Avda Drassanes (93 302 64 02).
Metro Drassanes/14, 38, 59, N9, N12 bus.* **Open**
2-3.45pm Mon-Thur, Sun; 2-3.45pm, 9-11.30pm Fri,
Sat. **Main courses** €10.90-€16. **Set lunch** €7.80.
Credit MC, V. **Map** p343 A4.

The tables at La Llotja are dwarfed beneath the lofty
arches of the magnificent 14th-century *drassanes*
(shipyard), also home to the Museu Marítim. The
menu is a short but good selection of Catalan food
that might include rabbit, roast beef or duck and a
couple of French-influenced dishes, such as *lluç*
(hake) *en papillotte amb gorgonzola*. The restaurant
is entered from the garden beside the museum
entrance, and is not very obvious from the street.

Mama Café

*C/Doctor Dou 10 (93 301 29 40). Metro Catalunya/
bus all routes to Plaça Catalunya.* **Open** 1-5pm Mon;
1pm-1am Tue-Sat. **Main courses** €4.20-€12. **Set
lunch** €7.10. **Credit** DC, MC, V. **Map** p342 A2.

This cheerful, brightly painted warehouse space
matches hallucinogenic projections with breakbeats
and rare groove as a backdrop to its interesting cuisine. Vegetarians can choose from luxurious pastas
and salads (try fig with wild mushrooms, parmesan
and rocket), although there are also great burgers
and fresh fish. Friendly service and a sumptuously
rich chocolate cake make this a spot to remember.

Mesón David

*C/Carretas 63 (93 441 59 34). Metro Paral.lel/20,
36, 57, 64, 91, 157, N0, N6 bus.* **Open** 1-4pm, 8pm-
midnight Mon, Tue, Thur-Sun. Closed Aug. **Main
courses** €2.40-€10.80. **Set lunch** €5.70 Mon, Tue,
Thur, Fri. **Credit** AmEx, MC, V. **Map** p340 C6.

Ordering here can be a bit of a lottery, but favourites
such as *pulpo gallego* (Galician-style octopus), *trucha*

navarra (trout stuffed with *jamón serrano* and
cheese) or *lechazo* (a sticky, roasted pork knuckle)
are safe bets – and at these absurdly low prices, you
can't go too far wrong. Be sure to tip your waiter
when you pay at the cash register – he/she will toss
the money into a large metal pot behind the counter
and ring the bell above the till, at which point everyone in the restaurant stops eating and cheers.

Pla dels Àngels

*C/Ferlandina 23 (93 329 40 47). Metro Universitat/
bus all routes to Plaça Universitat.* **Open** 1.30-4pm
Mon; 1.30-4pm, 9pm-11.30pm Tue-Thur; 1.30-4pm,
9pm-midnight Fri, Sat. **Main courses** €3.20-€5.80.
Credit DC, MC, V. **Map** p340 C5.

In keeping with its position smack in front of the
MACBA, Pla dels Àngels is artistically and colourfully decorated, and buzzes with animated conversation. A short menu comprises imaginative
salads, great spaghetti and gnocchi dishes, carpaccios of duck, salmon or octopus and a few meat
dishes (try chicken with tiger nut sauce). Prices are
admirably reasonable for what is often excellent
cooking. Restaurants from the same stable include
Coses de Menjar (*see p149*).

Punjab Restaurante

*C/Joaquín Costa 1B (93 443 38 99). Metro Liceu/
14, 38, 59, 91, N9, N12 bus.* **Open** 11am-midnight
daily. **Main courses** €4.20-€7.20. **Set lunch** €3.60.
Set dinner €4.80. **No credit cards. Map** p340 C5.

Absurdly cheap and gloriously, unintentionally
kitsch (those tablecloths are the real thing). The
Punjab offers salad, curry with rice and naan and a
pudding for an unbeatable €3.60. Anyone prepared
to go the extra euro is rewarded with a wider choice
involving tandooris, birianis and couscous. A recent
Latin liaison in the kitchen has added an incongruous list of South American dishes.

International

Fil Manila

*C/Ramelleres 3 (93 318 64 87). Metro Catalunya/
bus all routes to Plaça Catalunya.* **Open** noon-4pm,
8-11.30pm Mon, Wed-Sun. **Main courses** €3.60-
€11.60. **Set menu** €8.40 Mon, Wed-Fri. **No
credit cards. Map** p342 A2.

A staggering menu (more than 100 dishes) is made
only slightly easier to digest by being divided into
sections: grilled, barbecue, sizzling, rice and noodle
dishes, and so on. Fil Manila was until recently the
city's only Filipino restaurant, and is still the best,
with a great selection of dishes, such as sautéed jack-
fruit with shrimp and coconut milk, and meat and
fish cooked on sizzling stone platters. At teatime
(4-8pm), there are lighter *merienda* dishes on offer.

Shalimar

*C/Carme 71 (93 329 34 96). Metro Liceu/14, 38,
59, 91, N9, N12 bus.* **Open** 1-4pm, 8-11.30pm Mon,
Wed-Sun; 8-11.30pm Tue. **Main courses** €5.90-
€7.80. **Credit** MC, V. **Map** p340 C6.

Eat, Drink, Shop

Homesick Brits (and, indeed, Pakistanis) will feel right at home here, in one of the best places in town for tandoori dishes, birianis and a fiery vindaloo. There are several types of naan, lassi and a good 'tandoori mix' plate, which serves two.

Silenus

C/Angels 8 (93 302 26 80). Metro Liceu/14, 38, 59, 91, N9, N12 bus. **Open** 1.30-4pm, 8.30-11.45pm Mon-Sat. **Main courses** €11.50-€17.20. **Set lunch** €10.80-€12 Mon-Fri. **Credit** DC, MC, V. **Map** p342 A2.

At its best, Silenus offers a stunning selection of artistically presented dishes, mainly modern Catalan but drawing heavily on the current vogue for all things Japanese. Simple classics are given a twist; *crema verde de guisantes* (pea soup) is served with lime ice-cream and pancetta; salt-cod dishes are joined on the menu by kangaroo. It's a pity that the attention paid to aesthetic considerations – the place is run by two artists and is an elegant venue for regular art exhibitions – doesn't always extend to the service, which can be infuriatingly relaxed.

Vegetarian

L'Hortet

C/Pintor Fortuny 32 (93 317 61 89). Metro Liceu/14, 38, 59, N9, N12 bus. **Open** 1.15-4pm, 8.30-11pm Mon-Wed; 8.30-11pm Thur-Sun. **Set lunch** €7.50 Mon-Fri; €9.50 Sat, Sun. **Set dinner** €9.50 Mon-Sat. **Credit** MC, V. **Map** p342 A2.

This popular vegetarian restaurant serves an excellent salad buffet for one of the first-course options, as well as soups, stews and a good range of daily-changing pastas. They also have a pizza oven and offer a fixed selection of veggie pizzas along with freshly squeezed juices.

Sant Pere, La Ribera & Born

Bar Mundial

Plaça Sant Agustí Vell 1 (93 319 90 56). Metro Arc de Triomf/39, 40, 41, 42, 51, 141 bus. **Open** *Bar* 9am-11.30pm Mon-Sat; 9am-5pm Sun. *Restaurant* 1-3.30pm, 7.30-11pm Mon-Sat. Closed last 2wks Aug. **Main courses** €4.80-€12. **No credit cards. Map** p342 C2.

A welcome antidote to many of the fussy, touristy, seafood restaurants hereabouts, this is a no-nonsense place run by three generations of a very welcoming family. Be warned that some of the fare on offer is tinned or frozen, but the *parrillada* (€24 for two), a towering heap of langoustines, prawns, clams, razor clams, octopus and more, is a fantastic bargain.

Café de la Ribera

Plaça de les Olles 6 (93 319 50 72). Metro Barceloneta/14, 17, 40, 45, 51 bus. **Open** 11am-1am Mon-Thur; 11am-2am Fri, Sat. *Meals served* 1-4pm, 8pm-midnight Mon-Sat. **Main courses** €4.50-€7.80. **Set lunch** €8.70 Mon-Fri. **Set dinner** €9.60. **Credit** DC, MC, V. **Map** p343 C4.

Not as popular as it was, but still a peaceful place to sit out on a traffic-free square and watch the world walk by. Dishes include peppers filled with cod, and superb stuffed aubergines. The set lunch changes daily, and salads and pizzas are available all day.

Cal Pep

Plaça de les Olles 8 (93 310 79 61). Metro Barceloneta/14, 17, 40, 45, 51 bus. **Open** 8pm-midnight Mon; 1.15-4.15pm, 8pm-midnight Tue-Sat. Closed Aug. **Main courses** €6.10-€12.60. **Credit** AmEx, DC, MC, V. **Map** p343 C4.

Pep once left this great bar-restaurant to run the wonderful Passadis del Pep (*see p149*), but came back, missing the banter. Most people choose to eat

Know your onions

If you're in Catalonia between late January and early May, you'll probably get a chance to try *calçots* – a long, sweet spring onion grown principally in the area around Valls, a few miles north of Tarragona. *Calçots* are more than just overgrown onions, though – they have been the subject for many a sentimental ode or folksong, and they're a great excuse for a big rowdy get-together. Known as *calçotadas*, these occasions rival medieval feasts for messy displays of unbridled gluttony (many careful Catalans take the precaution of covering up in bibs before the gorging begins), and usually consist of barbecued *botifarra* sausages, chops, steaks and prodigious quantities of cava or red wine to accompany the star of the show: the huge

stacks of charred black *calçots*. You eat them by peeling off the burnt outer layer, draping the soft flesh through a bowl of *romesco* sauce (made of pounded garlic, nuts, black *nyora* chilli peppers, tomatoes and bread, with a good slug of *aguardiente*) and then, throwing your head back like a baby bird, you neck the *calçot* from below, as if it were a worm. After a few of these, you should be liberally smeared with sauce and soot; dignity is not an option.

In town, you can try them at **La Parra** (*see p165*) or, if you want a more communal experience, keep an eye out in the newspapers for the many neighbourhood *calçotadas*, held outside in local squares. Anyone can join the feasting for a small fee.

at the bar, but there's a brick-lined restaurant at the back decorated with a boar's head and antique cash registers. The fish and seafood dishes can be exceptional, and it pays to get here early.

La Cocotte
Passeig del Born 16 (93 319 17 34). Metro Jaume I/ 17, 19, 40, 45 bus. **Open** 1.30-4pm, 9pm-midnight Mon-Sat; 1.30-4pm Sun. **Main courses** €4.50-€7.80. **Set lunch** €5.70 Mon-Fri. **No credit cards**. **Map** p343 C3.
To style a restaurant around a 1950s casserole dish (*cocotte*) seems an odd conceit, but it works rather well. Old *Good Housekeeping* ads vie for wall space with post-war tiling and Campbell's soup cans. The menu, unintentionally or not, harks forward a couple of decades to '70s exotica – chilli con carne, spring rolls, lasagne and moussaka; too postmodern for many tastes, but pretty good for these prices.

Coses de Menjar
Pla de Palau 5 (93 310 60 01). Metro Jaume I/17, 19, 40, 45 bus. **Open** 1.30-4pm, 9-11.30pm Mon-Thur; 1.30-4pm, 9pm-midnight Fri, Sat. **Main courses** €10.20-€15.10. **Credit** MC, V. **Map** p343 C4.
Yet another hit from the Parellada dining dynasty (others include Pla dels Àngels – *see p147*), launched by daughter Ada. The décor is comfortable and luxurious, but livened up by Ada's trademark taste for quirkiness with wine glass chandeliers, menus glued to wine bottles and napkin rings made from bent forks. Thoughtful and immaculately presented Mediterranean cooking – red mullet with almond sauce and fresh figs; pumpkin salad with soft cheese and cherries – plus a 300-strong wine list make it worth visiting, especially for lunch when the prices drop dramatically.
Branch: **Semproniana** C/Roselló 148, Eixample (93 453 18 20).

El Pebre Blau.

La Flauta Magica
C/Banys Vells 18 (93 268 46 94). Metro Jaume I/17, 19, 40, 45 bus. **Open** 8.30-11.30pm Mon-Thur, Sun; 8.30pm-midnight Fri, Sat. **Main courses** €8.20-€12.10. **Credit** DC, MC, V. **Map** p343 C3.
A hip hangout for New Age rich kids, with funky purple and orange walls, Astor Piazzolla on the stereo and a menu featuring inventive vegetarian dishes or organic meat. The food looks divine (on the menu as well as the plate), but the sauces for pasta and meat can be cloying; banana leaf tamales or sushi are a safer bet. A €1 cover charge includes wholemeal bread and tapenade.

Passadís del Pep
Pla del Palau 2 (93 310 10 21). Metro Barceloneta/ 14, 36, 57, 59, 157 bus. **Open** 1.30-3.30pm, 9-11.30pm Mon-Sat. Closed 3wks Aug. **Gourmet menu** €64.50. **Credit** AmEx, DC, MC, V. **Map** p343 C4.
A nightmare to find – go up the long corridor next to the Caixa bank on the corner – but once inside it's a blast of colour and activity and surprisingly lively for such an upmarket restaurant. There's no written menu, but the charming waiters will guide you through the first-course buffet and the day's specials, usually excellent seafood and rice dishes, including some outstanding paellas or a lobster *fideuà*. Wine is changed with every course and included in the price. For a cheaper option, try its nearby sister restaurant, Cal Pep (*see p148*).

El Pebre Blau
C/Banys Vells 21 (93 319 13 08). Metro Jaume I/ 17, 19, 40, 45, N8 bus. **Open** 8pm-midnight daily. **Main courses** €7.70-€16.30. **Credit** MC, V. **Map** p343 C3.
The Catalan Gothic arches of these old stables are given a subtle, intimate look with soft lighting and a cascade of colourful lightshades. A French-Moroccan menu includes excellent lamb tajine and inventive meat dishes, such as duck mole with plantains. Puds are also delicious; try the goat's cheese in a tuile basket with ginger marmalade. Service is,

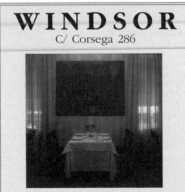

seemingly without exception, young, attentive and charming, and Edith Piaf provides the final touch. **Branch: L'Ou Com Balla** C/Banys Vells 20, Born (93 310 53 78).

Peps Bufet

C/Grunyi 5 (93 310 07 09). Metro Jaume I/17, 19, 40, 45, N8 bus. **Open** 8.30pm-1am Tue-Sat. **Dinner buffet** €16.80. **Credit** MC, V. **Map** p343 C3.
A buffet of good-quality, seriously Catalan dishes in a 17th-century merchant's house. Anna and Xavier are extremely friendly and ready to explain any of the dishes, including young rabbit in rosemary sauce, pig's trotters and *empedrat* (salt cod salad), but there's very little for strict vegetarians. House wine is a must-try Priorat at a fraction of the normal price, and the desserts are a memorable selection of chocolate mousses, eggy custards and fruit salads.

Pla de la Garsa

C/Assaonadors 13 (93 315 24 13). Metro Jaume I/ 17, 19, 40, 45, N8 bus. **Open** 8pm-1am daily. **Main courses** €4.80-€12. **Set lunch** €11.90 Mon-Fri. **Credit** AmEx, MC, V. **Map** p342 C2.
A 16th-century dairy converted into an elegant restaurant, with marble-topped tables and a wrought-iron spiral staircase leading up to another secluded dining room. The strong suits here are cheeses, pâtés and cold meats, as well as salmon or tuna carpaccio and some excellent duck dishes. Be sure to leave room for the various 'taster dishes' of the dessert menu.

Restaurant L'Econòmic

Plaça Sant Agustí Vell 13 (93 319 64 94). Metro Arc de Triomf/39, 40, 41, 42, 51 bus. **Open** 12.30-4.30pm Mon-Fri. Closed Aug. **Main courses** €3.40-€7.10. **Set lunch** €7.20. **No credit cards**. Map p342 C2.
A deep, narrow restaurant lined with Andalucian tiles and oil paintings. It's always packed, but there are chairs on the pretty *plaça* outside for anyone waiting for a table. The set lunch offers old faves such as *escudella* (stew), followed by veal escalope or roast rabbit, and an unusually good range of puddings, including a dreamy lemon mousse.

Rodrigo

C/Argenteria 67 (93 310 30 20). Metro Jaume I/17, 19, 40, 45 bus. **Open** 8am-5pm, 8.30pm-1am Mon, Wed-Sun; 8am-5pm Tue. Closed Aug. **Main courses** €4.50-€13.30. **Set lunch** €7.20 Mon-Sat; €9.30 Sun. **Set dinner** €9.30. **Credit** MC, V. **Map** p343 C3.
A bargain institution, famous for bocadillos, towering club sandwiches and vermouth. There are also full meals at lunchtime, featuring all the usual Catalan suspects. Things can get a little chaotic among the jumble of marble-topped tables, and this is emphatically not a place for an intimate meal *à deux* or anyone with a headache.

Salero

C/Rec 60 (93 319 80 22). Metro Barceloneta/14, 39, 51 bus. **Open** 8.45am-noon Mon-Fri; 9pm-midnight Mon-Wed; 9pm-1am Thur-Sat. **Main courses** €8.20-€15.10. **Credit** AmEx, MC, V. **Map** p343 C3.

It's **Peps Bufet**, but he's willing to share.

A stylish, candlelit space with a preponderance of English accents. The dishes come from all corners of the globe – mee goreng, kangaroo steak, lamb with rosemary – and are impressively presented, but there are occasional triumphs of style over substance. Cheesecake with marmalade may look and sound interesting, but it tastes like, well, cheesecake with marmalade. The music and atmosphere are cool and relaxed, however, and apart from the €1.25 cover charge, prices are unfashionably low.

Senyor Parellada

C/Argenteria 37 (93 310 50 94). Metro Jaume I/17, 19, 40, 45, N8 bus. **Open** 1-3.45pm, 8.30-11.45pm Mon-Sat. **Main courses** €4.50-€11.40. **Credit** AmEx, DC, MC, V. **Map** p343 B3.
Senyor Parellada reopened in autumn 2001 with a ritzier look and a new menu. The desperately old-fashioned concept of starters and main courses has been replaced with a system of various medium-sized *platillos*, which will arrive in stages (sound familiar?) and will comprise tasty Catalan favourites (plus ça change…). Try the seafood, or the ferociously good *xai a les dotze cabeces d'all* (lamb with 12 heads of garlic). Prices appear to have dropped a bit and, thankfully, the long-suffering, old-school waiters are still with us.

Sikkim

Plaça Comercial 1 (93 268 43 13). Metro Jaume I/17, 19, 40, 45 bus. **Open** 9pm-1am Mon-Sat. **Main courses** €8.40-€14.20. **Credit** MC, V. **Map** p343 C3.
Bordello lighting, wafting red chiffon and a generous scattering of bric-a-brac from India give this restaurant a cosy, intimate feel. Despite the Eastern decor, the food is mainly Mediterranean in style, mixing local ingredients with the occasional piece of exotica, such as shark or crocodile meat. Try the

Eat, Drink, Shop

Sikkim. *See p151.*

red mullet in shiitake oil with braised sweet potato, seared tuna with three-onion jam and lemon cream or a vegetarian risotto of nuts and wild mushrooms.

International

Bunga Raya
C/Assaonadors 7 (93 319 31 69). Metro Jaume I/ 17, 19, 39, 40, 45, 51, N8 bus. **Open** 8pm-midnight Tue-Sun. **Main courses** €4-€5. **Set dinner** €12 Tue-Fri. **No credit cards. Map** p343 C3.
A tiny restaurant with Malaysian tourist posters on the bamboo-lined walls, and often a Malaysian video providing the soundtrack. The great value set dinner involves beef rendang, chicken curry, lamb satay, squid and various pickles, sambal and coconut, as well as a beer and a dessert. An incredibly friendly and relaxed place.

Habana Vieja
C/Banys Vells 2 (93 268 25 04). Metro Jaume I/17, 19, 40, 45, N8 bus. **Open** 10am-4pm, 8pm-midnight Mon-Thur, Sun; 8pm-1am Fri, Sat. **Main courses** €9.60-€12. **Credit** AmEx, DC, MC, V. **Map** p343 C3.
A funky and convivial Cuban restaurant with turquoise paintwork and, naturally, a great soundtrack. Like it says, this is a taste of old Havana; *ropa vieja* (shredded beef) or *moros y cristianos* (rice and beans) are served with all the trimmings (want a fried banana on that?) and washed down with copious Mojitos. Simple, satisfying desserts include *pudín de coco* (soft slices of cornmeal-based cake topped with syrup-sweetened coconut).

Al Passatore
Pla del Palau 8 (93 319 78 51). Metro Barceloneta/ 14, 36, 57, 59, 157 bus. **Open** 1pm-1am daily. **Main courses** €5.40-€9.60. **Set lunch** €6.60 Mon-Fri. **Credit** MC, V. **Map** p343 C4.
There's a good range of pasta dishes and a decent-value set lunch, but the fabulous pizzas, piping hot from the wood-fired oven, are the real reason to come here. The restaurant's enormous popularity means that service gets a bit pushed, and there is usually a queue. Get there earlier to grab one of the outside tables on the square.

Branches: **Al Passatore** Moll de Gregal 25, Vila Olímpica (93 225 00 47); **Montello** Via Laietana 42 (93 310 35 26).

Taira
C/Comerç 7 (93 310 24 97). Metro Arc de Triomf/ 39, 40, 41, 42, 51, 141 bus. **Open** 1-4pm, 9pm-12.30am Tue-Sun. **Main courses** €7.70-€16.10. **Credit** AmEx, DC, MC, V. **Map** p343 C3.
About as authentically Japanese as *botifarra*, Taira is not for purists, but it's popular enough to make booking essential. Backed by '90s design temple Otto Zutz nightclub, Taira has a similarly stylish look, which draws a painfully hip crowd to munch on specialities such as *tamagoyaki*, a Japanese tortilla rolled up and flambéed in *dashi* (a sweet and aromatic type of saké), tempuras, soups and a variety of sushi.

Vegetarian

Comme Bio
Via Laietana 28 (93 319 89 68/www.commebio.es). Metro Jaume I/17, 19, 40, 45, N8 bus. **Open** 1-4pm, 8.30-11pm Mon-Fri, Sun; 1-4pm, 8.30-midnight Sat. **Main courses** €6-€9.30. **Set lunch** €7.80 Mon-Fri; €8.40 Sat, Sun. **Set dinner** €9.30. **Credit** AmEx, DC, MC, V. **Map** p343 B3.
The Comme Bio chain has become a lifesaver for vegetarians all over Spain, and this stylish branch always has queues at lunchtime for the downstairs all-you-can-eat bargain buffet of soups, salads and pastas. Upstairs, there's partial waiter service and a

Pigging out

In a country where the average inhabitant eats more than 36 whole pigs in a lifetime, the business of pork is taken very seriously. It is said that every part of the animal is eaten 'except the squeal' – a phrase borne out in the trotters, snouts, intestines, ears and cheeks that frequently grace restaurant menus.

Besides these, and all the usual chops and ribs, you'll find a host of other ingenious ways to consume pork. A rather gruesome sight to the uninitiated is the rack of black pigs' legs dangling overhead in more traditional restaurants (the little white cups underneath are to stop any melting fat dripping on to your head), but once sliced by an expert hand, these yield dark and delicious cured ham. This *jamón* (*pernil* in Catalan) is often served as a starter with honeydew melon, or as part of a selection of meats and cheeses. Most of these hams are *jamón serrano* (mountain

choice of slightly more complex dishes, such as wild mushroom ragout or spinach and ricotta pancakes, plus a well-stocked organic food shop.
Branches: Gran Via de les Corts Catalanes 603, Eixample (93 301 03 76); **Biocenter** C/Pintor Fortuny 25, Raval (93 301 45 83).

Port Vell & Barceloneta

Can Majó

C/Almirall Aixada 23 (93 221 54 55/93 221 58 18). Metro Barceloneta/17, 39, 45, 57,59, 64, 157, N8 bus. **Open** 1-4pm, 8-11.30pm Tue-Sat; 1-4pm Sun. **Main courses** €7.10-€18.70. **Credit** AmEx, DC, MC, V. **Map** p340 D7.
Barceloneta is so flooded with seafood restaurants that sometimes it seems impossible to choose, but Can Majó consistently stands out from the crowd in its quality of service and cooking. Try grilled razor clams as an appetiser before a bubbling cauldron of fish stew with anisette. or a show-stopping seafood platter. There's a pretty beach terrace, but the constant attentions of rose and hanky sellers can be rather distracting.

Can Maño

C/Baluard 12 (93 319 30 82). Metro Barceloneta/17, 39, 45, 57, 59, 64 bus. **Open** 8am-11am, noon-4pm, 8-10.30pm Mon-Fri; 8am-4pm Sat. **Main courses** €2.10-€4.80. **No credit cards. Map** p341 E7.
Enjoy big, steaming plates of freshly caught seafood in a restaurant that's always rowdy and packed to the gills with locals. The friendly waiters reel off the daily specials at lightning speed, but the best thing to choose is nearly always the soft, creamy *sepia* (cuttlefish) cooked in garlic and parsley. There are chips with everything, and a big doorstep of watermelon for dessert.

Can Ramonet

C/Maquinista 17 (93 319 30 64). Metro Barceloneta/17, 39, 45, 57, 59, 64, 157, N8 bus. **Open** 10am-4pm Mon-Sat. Closed 2wks Jan, 2wks Aug. **Main courses** €8.40-€14.80. **Credit** AmEx, DC, MC, V. **Map** p341 E7.
This quaint, rose-coloured restaurant is an old favourite among uptown yuppies visiting downtown Barceloneta, usually for a good Sunday paella in the sunshine with all the family. Spectacular displays of fresh seafood show what's on offer that day, and you can either have a full menu or just sit around the giant wooden barrels to nibble some traditional seafood tapas.

Ruccula

World Trade Centre, Moll de Barcelona (93 508 82 68). Metro Drassanes/20, 36, 57, 64, 157, N0, N6 bus. **Open** 1-4pm, 8.30-11.45pm daily. **Main courses** €9-€19.30. **Set lunch** €16.10 Mon-Fri. **Credit** AmEx, DC, MC, V. **Map** p340 C7.
Ruccula's location in the ultra-modern World Trade Centre allows privileged views over the port, not to mention the besuited dotcommers eating inside. The atmosphere suffers a little from the sterility of a business setting, and the dark brown and grey decor doesn't help, but fortunately the food itself is all

ham); for a more expensive treat, try *jamón ibérico* from black Iberian pigs or empty your wallet completely for *jamón ibérico de bellota* from Iberian pigs fed on nothing but acorns.

Another mysterious sight for visitors are shallow earthenware pots filled with lard. Underneath, lying in suspended animation, is *lomo en manteca*, the most meltingly soft chunks of pork imaginable. Don't worry, most of the fat is scraped off before serving.

The mind-boggling array of *embotits* (processed cold meats and sausages) are enjoyed sliced up as a snack or to add flavour to salads, soups, stews and just about anything. A good way to try them is to order an *amanida catalana*, salad with sliced sausages and meat, or a selection on a wooden board. One of the most versatile types is *xoriço* (chorizo), a rusty-red cured sausage dyed with red pepper; a great cooking sausage, it crops up in everything from soups to stuffings and stews. In

spreadable form it's known as *sobrassada*, a Mallorcan speciality that often finds its way into pastries and sauces. The garlicky, dry-cured *fuet* is long and thin (its name means 'whip' in Catalan), while its cousin, *morcilla*, is a kind of black pudding. But the Catalan sausage par excellence will probably always be the *botifarra*, which can be mixed with egg (*botifarra blanca*) or blood (*botifarra negre*) and is invariably eaten with haricot beans.

Eat, Drink, Shop

warmth and vitality, with a mix of Japanese, French and Catalan food from chef Joan Piqué. There's live music in the evenings.

Salamanca

C/Almirante Cervera 34 (93 221 50 33). Metro Barceloneta/14, 17, 40, 45, 51 bus. **Open** 8.30am-1am daily. **Main courses** €9.60-€17.60. **Set lunch** €7.80. **Credit** AmEx, DC, MC, V. **Map** p341 E7.
A stone's throw from the beach, Salamanca is a chaotic boiler-room of a place, full of the hiss of frying fish. The house specialities are *jamón*, huge seafood platters and meat grills, devoured by a mix of locals and foreigners at the scrubbed wooden tables. It's also one of the few places to provide a scaled-down children's menu. If there's no room, just nip over the road to the identical Salamanca II.

Set Portes

Passeig d'Isabell II 14 (93 319 30 33/93 319 29 50/ www.7puertas.com). Metro Barceloneta/36, 57, 59, 64, 157, N0, N6 bus. **Open** 1pm-1am daily. **Main courses** €8-€22.20. **Credit** AmEx, DC, MC, V. **Map** p343 C4.
Founded in 1836, the gigantic 'Seven Doors' has reached the status of an institution. It is, without doubt, Barcelona's most famous temple to the paella, and there is always a queue of hungry pilgrims outside at lunchtime and in the evening. Despite its popularity, Set Portes has managed to maintain the quality of its seafood and rice dishes, although the vastness of the place can be offputting – as can the house pianist playing 'Three Times a Lady' on the baby grand. The waiters and maître d' are fabulously accommodating and the most stubborn of non-linguists will be coaxed through the menu.

International

dZI

Passeig de Joan de Borbó 76 (93 221 21 82). Metro Barceloneta/17, 39, 64 bus. **Open** 1-4pm, 8pm-midnight daily. **Main courses** €5.50-€18.10. **Set lunch** €8.10 Mon-Wed. **Credit** AmEx, MC, V. **Map** p343 C4.
dZI's healthy pan-Asian cuisine offers a change from all the seafood on the way down to the beach. Service is unerringly polite, and dishes have little in common with the MSG-laden salt licks that pass for food in some of the cheaper Asian restaurants in Barcelona. Try the chicken with black mushrooms, water chestnuts and rice baked in a banana leaf, the green curry soup or the spicy tiger prawns while enjoying the view of the port from the shady terrace.

Vila Olímpica – Port Olímpic

Agua

Passeig Marítim de la Barceloneta 30 (93 225 12 72). Metro Barceloneta/45, 57, 59, 157, N8 bus. **Open** 1.30-4pm, 8.30-midnight Mon-Thur, Sun; 1.30-4pm, 8.30pm-1am Fri, Sat. **Main courses** €6.10-€14.80. **Credit** AmEx, MC, V. **Map** p341 F7.

Another hit restaurant from the Tragaluz group, this one sits at the very edge of the beach, with unobstructed views from the terrace. The stylish decor has a clean, marine feel without falling into kitschy lobster pots and decorative fishing nets, with squidgy sofas and newspapers to amuse you while you wait. The crowd is generally young and informal. House specialities include *arroz al carbón*, fresh fish and seafood tapas, but the steaks and carpaccios can also be good. Booking is essential for Sunday lunchtime.

Newport Room

Hotel Arts, C/Marina 19-21 (93 221 10 00). Metro Ciutadella-Vila Olímpica/10, 36, 45, 57, 59, 71, 92, 157 bus. **Open** 7pm-11.30pm daily. **Main courses** €29-€35.40. **Gourmet menu** €90-€115.50. **Credit** MC, V. **Map** p341 F7.
The newly refurbished star restaurant of the monumental Hotel Arts (*see p59*), with unrivalled views of the sea and Frank Gehry's wonderful bronze fish sculpture, The knowledgeable but unstuffy service complements the internationally influenced, gourmet cuisine, which must be only a hair away from earning American chef Toni Bombaci his first Michelin star. Try generous shavings of white truffles and pasta, duck breast with tissue-thin bacon and date paste, or leek soup over creamy foie gras ice-cream. All the ingredients are superlatively fresh and often locally produced, while the wine selection is everything you would hope for in a restaurant of this quality.

El Rebujito de Moncho's

C/Marina 16 (93 221 38 83). Metro Ciutadella-Vila Olímpica/10, 36, 45, 57, 59, 71, 92, 157 bus. **Open** noon-midnight daily. **Main courses** €4.80-€15. **Lunch buffet** €9.60 Mon-Fri; €10 Sat, Sun. **Credit** AmEx, MC, V. **Map** p341 F7.
Not the most atmospheric of restaurants, but certainly the most affordable on this strip, with a well-priced all-you-can-eat buffet. The food includes pasta, paella, chicken and a couple of fish dishes, with plenty of salads. To get away from the coach parties – or at least have something else to look at – sit out on the terrace and watch the boats chinking together in the harbour.

Xiringuitó Escribà

Litoral Mar 42 (Platja Bogatell) (93 221 07 29). Metro Ciutadella-Vila Olímpica/36, N6, N8 bus. **Open** 11am-5pm, 9-11.30pm Tue-Thur, Sun; 9-11.30pm Fri, Sat. *Tapas served* 11am-5pm Tue-Sun. *Meals served* 1-4.30pm Tue-Thur; 1-4.30pm, 9-11pm Fri-Sun. **Main courses** €11.40-€25.30. **Credit** MC, V. **Map** p341 F7.
Service in this family-run restaurant is so attentive and informal that they'll even provide blankets if you want to sit outside in winter, or towels if you're still wet from a dip in the sea. The brief but well-chosen menu offers specialities such as tuna carpaccio, sardines with mint and an excellent selection of paellas, including *arròs negre* or Valencian-style with rabbit and snails. Leave some room for dessert as

the Escribàs are one of Barcelona's great pastry-making dynasties and their melt-in-the-mouth tarts provide a very happy ending to every meal.

Poble Sec

La Bodegueta
C/Blai 47 (93 442 08 46). Metro Poble Sec/20, 57, 64, 157, N16 bus. **Open** 1.30-4pm, 8.30pm-midnight Tue-Sun. Closed 2wks Aug. **Main courses** €5.80-€13.10. **Credit** MC, V. **Map** p323 B6.
Another wonderful old *bodega*-turned-restaurant, with oak barrels of wine, sherry and anis piled high. Hunks of *pa amb tomàquet* (*see p160* **What's cooking?**) accompanied by plates of anchovies, tuna, smoked salmon, *jamón iberico* and Cabrales cheese are the main event here, but there are also great *a la brasa* dishes: entrecôte, rabbit, pork and lamb cutlets.

Elche
C/Vila i Vila 71 (93 441 30 89). Metro Paral.lel/ 20, 36, 57, 64, 91, 157, N0, N6 bus. **Open** 12.45-4.30pm, 8pm-midnight Mon-Fri; 1pm-12.30am Sat, Sun. **Main courses** €8-€17.30. **Credit** AmEx, MC, V. **Map** p340 C6.
Originally run by two brothers (one now runs the sister restaurant in Maremàgnum) who still make use of their mother's recipes, Elche specialises in all types of paellas and *fideuàs*. The starters (which can be had in half-portions) are delectable; try the peppers stuffed with cream of monkfish. The split-level restaurant is slightly lacking in character, however, and the piped music doesn't really help.
Branch: **L'Elche al Moll** Maremàgnum, Moll d'Espanya, Port Vell (93 225 81 17).

La Tomaquera
C/Margarit 58 (no phone). Metro Paral.lel/20, 36, 57, 64, N6, N9 bus. **Open** 1.30-4.30pm, 8.30-11.30pm Tue-Sat. Closed Aug. **Main courses** €5.70-€13.40. **No credit cards. Map** p339 B6.
From the moment you enter the world of red gingham and bright lights that is La Tomaquera, staff will bark instructions at you, many of which are reproduced on the walls. There are no bookings, there is only house wine, there is only *a la brasa* meat – and if you don't like it, you can go elsewhere. Barcelonans obviously do like it, for they come in droves to tuck into huge portions of perfectly cooked meat served with weapons-grade *all i oli*.

Eixample

El Asador de Burgos
C/Bruc 118 (93 207 31 60). Metro Verdaguer/20, 39, 43, 44, 45, 47, N6, N7 bus. **Open** 1-4pm, 9-11pm Mon-Sat. Closed Aug. **Main courses** €14.50-€32.10. **Credit** AmEx, DC, MC, V. **Map** p337 D4.
From deepest Castilla, this roasting house is of one of the big boys in the steak stakes, serving every type of traditional Spanish meat dish with almost no vegetable relief whatsoever. Portions are on the hefty side and the whole roast suckling pigs and

Can Ramonet. *See p153.*

Flintstones-sized steaks kick sand in the face of ordinary entrecôtes. Before you come a-running, note that booking is essential as some dishes must be put in to roast more than three hours in advance.

Casa Calvet
C/Casp 48 (93 412 40 12). Metro Urquinaona/ 41, 47, 55, 62, 141, N4, N8 bus. **Open** 1-3.30pm, 8.30-11pm Mon-Sat. **Main courses** €16.80-€25.80. **Gourmet menu** €45.20. **Credit** AmEx, DC, MC, V. **Map** p342 B-C1.
Casa Calvet has one of Gaudí's less characteristic exteriors, but the swirling woodwork and stained glass inside offer more familiar theme – and a gorgeous setting for this quality restaurant. Well-heeled diners enjoy old fashioned service, a comprehensive wine list and modernised Catalan cuisine, such as duck confit with lentil and curry vinaigrette, prawns on spinach with cava sauce, or pine nut tart with foamed *crema catalana* for dessert.

Jaume de Provença
C/Provença 88 (93 430 00 29). Metro Entença/41, 43, 44, N7 bus. **Open** 1-4pm, 9-11.30pm Tue-Sat; 1-4pm Sun. Closed Aug. **Main courses** €10.30-€29. **Gourmet menu** €54.80. **Credit** AmEx, DC, MC, V. **Map** p339 B4.
A little off the beaten track, this tranquil restaurant is worth going out of your way for: Jaume's restrained and subtle hand turns out some of the most prestigious cooking in town, although it's not

a fashionable joint. Classic dishes, such as the truffle cannelloni and rack of tender suckling pig, blend with an occasional surprise such as sole stuffed with spider crab. One of the best wine selections in town rounds off the treat.

El Racó d'en Baltà
C/Aribau 125 (93 453 10 44). FCG Provença/54, 58, 64, 66, 67, 68 bus. **Open** 1-4pm, 9-11pm Tue-Sat. **Set lunch** €7.80 Tue-Fri. **Credit** MC, V. **Map** p336 C4.
This two-floor restaurant with a bar next door offers modern Catalan cuisine in original, vibrant surroundings. The best seats are in the airy upstairs room, where you can enjoy spring lamb in a reduction of brandy and honey, or a herbed goat's cheese salad, followed by a delicious banana bavarois trickled with golden syrup. The decor is a bizarre mix of '50s memorabilia (menus are presented on old record sleeves) and artist Steve Forster's sculptures incorporating spray-painted Marigolds and bathplugs. The clientele is generally young and up for it, and the service very friendly and informal.

Sar Gan Tan A
C/Enric Granados 34 (93 451 45 03). Metro Liceu/ 14, 38, 59, N9, N12 bus. **Open** 1-3.45pm, 9-11.45pm daily. **Main courses** €4.80-€10.50. **Set lunch** €7.20 Mon-Fri. **Credit** MC, V. **Map** p336 C4.
Entering Sar Gan Tan A is a bit like fighting your way through an overgrown jungle: tendrils, leaves

Eat, Drink, Shop

International rescue

If London could be said to offer the world on a plate, then Barcelona offers it on a cocktail stick: the city's international food scene is pretty marginal, but it can at least offer a small taste of everything. The closest to a Little Italy or Chinatown is probably the Raval area, predictably dubbed Ravalistan for its high number of Pakistani inhabitants and restaurants. These curry houses are usually good value for money and a favourite among British ex-pats who can't wean themselves off vindaloo, along with growing numbers of local converts who, just a decade ago, wouldn't have known a popadom from a pork chop.

While French and Italian restaurants have always been popular, it is oriental cooking that has experienced the biggest boom in recent years. There's westernised MSG glop by the shovel-load, of course, but also a number of decent places to try more authentic food, including Thai (**Thai Gardens** – *see p160*), Malaysian (**Bunga Raya** – *see p152*) and even Filipino (**Fil Manila** – *see p147*). Japanese sushi restaurants are the latest trend (**SoNaMu** – *see p164*; **Taira** – *see p152*;

Machiroku – *see p140*), and have become so popular that even the giant Tragaluz group has an entire branch devoted to Japanese food.

Gràcia is gaining fame for its Middle Eastern restaurants (**Mesopotamia** – *see p164*; **Habibi** – *see p164*), and there are many falafel houses and exotic tea rooms clustered around C/Torrent de l'Olla and C/Verdi. Mexican food is also a perennial favourite; although much of it is second-rate Tex-Mex, there are places offering authentic village cooking, notably **Cantina Machito** (*see p163*). Other Latin American exotica include Peruvian at **Peimong** (*see p140*) and Cuban at **Habana Vieja** (*see p152*).

Not wanting to be left behind, many Catalan restaurants have absorbed international influences in the form of the dreaded F-word. Yup, that's right: 'fusion'. Bizarre offerings such as Thai pizzas, frankfurter paella and curried pigeon have all reared their improbable heads, and plenty of places think nothing of jumbling French, Mexican and Greek dishes on the same menu. What's next, one wonders. Toad-in-the-hole masala?

Come to Samoa and discover the freshest Mediterranean cuisine and our extraordinary specialities livened up by live piano music. Enjoy the most exclusive terrace with a privileged view of "La Pedrera".

En Samoa podrá descubrir una fresca cocina mediterránea y unas tentadoras sugerencias amenizados por la noche con piano. Disfrute de la más selecta terraza con privilegiadas vistas a "La Pedrera".

SAMOA

BAR ☆ RESTAURANT ☆ PIZZERIA

Pg. De Gràcia, 101   Tel. 93 218 47 82   08008 BARCELONA

and bushes sprout from every surface. The fixed menu is excellent value, with modern Catalan favourites such as leek tart, seafood vol-au-vents and brochette of tiger prawn and salmon. There's also an appropriately leafy range of salads and some imaginative desserts.

Seltz

C/Rossellò 154 (93 453 38 42). Metro Hospital Clínic/ 14, 31, 58, 59, 63, 64 bus. **Open** 1.30-4pm, 9pm-midnight Mon-Fri; 9pm-midnight Sat. **Set lunch** €13 Mon-Fri. **Gourmet menu** €21.30. **Credit** AmEx, MC, V. **Map** p336 C4.
Instead of a traditional menu, the blindingly modern Seltz has a huge range of small, innovative taster dishes (*platitos*, €1.40-€5.20), such as lobster with black squid lasagne or aubergine tartlets with cream of sesame: you won't find any tortilla or meatballs here. It's great for people who want to try a bit of everything, and if you're vegetarian or don't like seafood, then call in advance and Seltz will happily prepare some dishes to suit you; if you're lucky, they'll even throw in their trademark vermouth and seltzer aperitif.

Tragaluz

Passatge de la Concepció 5 (93 487 01 96/ www.grupotragaluz.com). Metro Diagonal/7, 16, 17, 22, 24, 28, N4 bus. **Open** 1.30-4pm, 8.30pm-midnight Mon-Wed, Sun; 1.30-4pm, 8.30pm-1am Thur-Sat. **Main courses** €12.20-€20.60. **Set lunch** €19.30 Mon-Fri. **Gourmet menu** €48.30. **Credit** AmEx, DC, MC, V. **Map** p336 D4.
The first thing anyone will tell you about Tragaluz is that its glorious, light-filled interior was designed by '80s wunderkind Javier Mariscal; in fact, he only designed the menus. The next thing they'll wax lyrical about is the food, and here they're not wrong. How about a delicious warm duck salad to start, or a creamy cauliflower soup with lychee granita and *jamón iberico*, followed by tender, flaky sea bass with an onion millefeuille and tomato marmalade? Puddings are spectacularly good; try apricot and strawberry soup with iced yoghurt and Szechuan pepper. Downstairs, Tragarrapid serves lighter meals all day, and the group also runs a Japanese restaurant across the street.
Branches: Negro Avda Diagonal 640, Eixample (93 405 94 44); **El Japonés** Passatge de la Concepció 2, Eixample (93 487 25 92); **Acontraluz** C/Milanesat 19, Zona Alta (93 203 06 58).

Windsor

C/Còrsega 286 (93 415 84 83/www.restaurant windsor.com). Metro Diagonal/54, 66, 67 bus. **Open** 1-4pm, 8.30-11pm Mon-Fri; 8.30-11pm Sat. **Main courses** €14.10-€21.20. **Gourmet menu** €38.70-€58. **Credit** AmEx, DC, MC, V. **Map** p336 D4.
Through a majestic doorway and at the end of a long red carpet, Windsor is a restaurant impersonating an English stately home, complete with satin wallpaper, courtyard and chandeliers. Don't bother looking for roast beef and spotted dick, however – expert chef Ignasi Colomer serves up a creative

Seltz: overwhelming underlighting.

Mediterranean menu, including rice with young pigeon and wild mushrooms, shoulder of milk-fed goat and superlative desserts.

International

Conducta Ejemplar – El Rodizio

C/Consell de Cent 403 (93 265 51 12). Metro Girona/6, 19, 47, 50, 51, 55, N1, N4 bus. **Open** 1-4pm, 8.30pm-midnight Mon-Thur; 1-4pm, 8.30pm-1am Fri, Sat; 1-4pm Sun. **Lunch buffet** €7.20 Mon-Fri; €10.20 Sat. **Dinner buffet** €10.20. **Credit** MC, V. **Map** p337 E5.
Vegetarians steer clear: this is a large, modern and efficiently run *rodizio*, or Brazilian meat buffet, where you can eat until the cows run out. That chargrilled smell seems to push appetites to new frontiers and customers devour improbable amounts of roast meat, sausage, steak, veal, chicken, marinated pork chop, salad, rice and pasta.

Le Relais de Venise

C/Pau Claris 142 (93 467 21 62). Metro Passeig de Gràcia/22, 24, 28, 39, 45, N6 bus. **Open** 1.30-4pm, 8.30pm-12.30am Mon-Sat; 1.30-4pm, 8.30pm-midnight Sun. **Main courses** €13.90-€19.30. **Credit** DC, MC, V. **Map** p342 B1.
This smart restaurant is French down to its manicured fingertips. Even the waitresses are kitted out in frilly black and white outfits – although any garter-twanging Benny Hill antics would not be

welcome: Relais de Venise is a sober place where voices are subdued and mobile phones must be switched off. Although there's a large range of succulent crêpes, tarts and gateaux, an oddity is that they only serve one main course – almost always an impeccably dressed steak.

Thai Gardens

C/Diputació 2737 (93 487 98 98). Metro Universitat/ bus all routes to Plaça Universitat. **Open** 1.30-4pm, 8.30pm-midnight daily. **Main courses** €11-€31. **Set lunch** €11.90 Mon-Fri. **Gourmet menu** €25.10. **Credit** MC, V. **Map** p340 D5.

With its waterfalls, orchid overkill and cocktail umbrellas, it's hard to decide whether Thai Gardens is cheesy or exotic, but either way the food is absolutely exquisite. Unless you're very tall, sit at one of the low bamboo tables while you munch phom pha lobster tails in rice paste, beef strips in red Thai curry, or a 'Golden Bang' of rice paste crêpes stuffed with spicy pork. Or try a bit of everything with one of the excellent taster menus. The Opium Café next door serves Thai takeaway.

Vegetarian

Arco Iris

C/Roger de Flor 216 (93 458 22 83). Metro Verdaguer/19, 33, 34, 46, 44, 50, 51 bus. **Set lunch** €7.70. **No credit cards. Map** p337 E4.

The noticeboard in this minty green corner joint is feathered with flyers for rebirthing and crystal healing, but if that's no great temptation, then just keep your eyes on the menu. The lunchtime deal offers not two but three imaginative savoury courses – such as pumpkin soup or tofu chow mein, with many vegan dishes – and the unusually wide choice of desserts includes homemade pies and cheesecakes.

L'Atzavara

C/Muntaner 109 (93 454 59 25). Metro Diagonal or Hospital Clínic/20, 43, 44, 54, 58, 64, 66, N3, N7 bus. **Open** 1-4pm Mon-Sat. **Main courses** €5.40-€7.80. **Set lunch** €7.20-€8.40 Mon-Fri. **Credit** MC, V. **Map** p336 C4.

Very popular at lunchtime, the menu at this friendly restaurant changes daily and offers excellent value

What's cooking?

It's very telling that the single most emblematic dish of Catalonia is also the simplest: *pa amb tomàquet* is merely toasted country bread rubbed with a ripe tomato and drizzled with olive oil, but the passions it arouses are nothing short of miraculous. With the same perversity with which the rest of Spain ignores it, Catalans serve their beloved tomato bread with almost everything and, just like the rest of the region's traditional classics, it's stout, hearty and about as far as you can get from nouvelle cuisine. As a rule of thumb, if it's fussy and can be consumed in under five mouthfuls, it's not Catalan.

Probably the most striking feature of traditional Catalan cooking lies in the combinations of apparently disparate ingredients, a tendency that reaches a climax in the ancient dish of *niu* (nest) which unites swordfish, cod tripe and wildfowl. Seafood is commonly combined with meat (known as *mar i muntanya*, the Catalan version of surf 'n' turf, with chicken or pork alongside prawns and crayfish) or with game (the poetic *mar i cel*, sea and sky). Another quirky mix is that of savoury with sweet, such as duck with pear, or partridge with grapes; a habit that also extends to vegetable dishes such as *espinacs a la catalana* (spinach with garlic, pine nuts and raisins). Other non-meat favourites are *escalivada* (onions, red peppers and aubergine roasted and peeled)

and the huge range of funghi, such as *ceps* (porcini), truffles and the orange-gilled *rovellons* that appear every autumn.

You'll find huge stewy *cassoles* cooked in earthenware pots, which are sometimes divided into three courses (first the broth, then the vegetables and, finally, the meat or fish). And, of course, there's the great sweep of rice dishes that are related to the famous Valencian paella, but with a distinctive Catalan flavour of their own: *arròs negre* (black rice darkened with squid ink), *arròs de conill i salsitxes* (rice with rabbit and sausage) and *fideuà*, which is made with noodles rather than rice. (These all feature in the pre-prepared Paellador! range that is plied in restaurants up and down La Rambla, but it goes without saying that this denatured gunk is about as authentically Catalan as a Big Mac.)

As in the rest of Spain, meat and fish figure prominently; salt cod, rabbit and duck are particular regional favourites, but pork in any form is the leader of the pack (*see p152* **Pigging out**). The chubby *botifarra* sausage cooked over an open fire with *mongetes* (haricot beans) is, for many, the quintessential Catalan meal.

After such heavy food, it's not surprising that desserts tend to keep a low profile: there's usually just a few simple choices, such as *crema catalana* (think crème brûlée) and *flam* (think crème caramel) or even just for money, with three savoury courses of vegetarian classics, such as tofu burgers and mushroom stroganoff, and a range of soups and consommés. They mark 'light' dishes and will remove any sauces or potatoes if you wish, although no one should miss the wonderful home-baked cakes. Check the noticeboard to see if there's still a woman offering macrobiotic cucumber massages.

Gràcia

Botafumeiro

C/Gran de Gràcia 81 (93 218 42 30/ www.botafumeiro.es). Metro Fontana/22, 24, 28, N4 bus. **Open** 1pm-1am daily. Closed 3wks Aug. **Main courses** €11.40-€29.20. **Credit** AmEx, MC, V. **Map** p336 D3.
A Barcelona classic and the best known of the 18-strong Moncho Neira restaurant dynasty, this is still one of the most popular places in town for sparkling fresh (if frighteningly priced) fish and seafood. Despite space for almost 300 diners, it's always

packed, so be warned that only a miracle or a famous face will get you seated without a booking. Once inside, the decor is reassuringly grand and squadrons of white-jacketed staff cater to your every need, but, unfortunately, the sheer size of the operation precludes any real warmth.

Caliu 2

C/Francisco Giner 21 (93 217 06 05). Metro Diagonal/22, 24, 28, 39, N4 bus. **Open** 1-4pm, 8.30-11pm Mon-Thur; 8.30pm-midnight Fri, Sat. **Main courses** €5.10-€7.80. **Set lunch** €6 Mon-Fri. **Credit** MC, V. **Map** p336 D3.
Food on the nearby Balearic Islands is quite distinct from the mainland, and Caliu 2's sunny back garden is a great place to try an assortment of Mallorcan dishes. *Sobrassada* is a kind of spreadable, spicy red sausage meat and *tumbet* is a ratatouille-style dish, while for dessert there are *ensaimadas* the size of dustbin lids, their pastry spirals dusted lightly with sugar. These and other delicacies are for sale, along with Menorcan cheeses and handmade goods from the Balearic Islands.

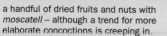

a handful of dried fruits and nuts with *moscatell* – although a trend for more elaborate concoctions is creeping in.

Words and phrases below are given in Catalan, Spanish and English respectively.

Essential terminology

una cullera	*una cuchara*	a spoon
una forquilla	*un tenedor*	a fork
un ganivet	*un cuchillo*	a knife
un tovalló	*una servilleta*	a napkin
una ampolla de	*una botella de*	a bottle of
una altra	*otra*	another (one)
més	*más*	more
pa	*pan*	bread
oli d'oliva	*aceite de oliva*	olive oil
sal i pebre	*sal y pimienta*	salt and pepper
amanida	*en salada*	salad
truita	*tortilla*	omelette

(note: **truita** can also mean trout)

la nota	*la cuenta*	the bill
un cendrer	*un cenicero*	an ashtray
vinagre	*vinagre*	vinegar

vi negre/ rosat/ blanc	*vino tinto/ rosado/blanco*	red/rosé/ white wine
bon profit	*aproveche*	Enjoy your meal
sóc vegetarià/ ana	*soy vegetariano/a*	I'm a vegetarian
sóc diabètic/a	*soy diabético/a*	I'm a diabetic

Cooking terms

a la brasa	*a la brasa*	charcoal-grilled
a la graella/ planxa	*a la plancha*	grilled on a hot metal plate
a la romana	*a la romana*	fried in batter
al forn	*al horno*	baked
al vapor	*al vapor*	steamed
fregit	*frito*	fried
rostit	*asado*	roast
ben fet	*bien hecho*	well done
a punt	*medio hecho*	medium
poc fet	*poco hecho*	rare

Catalan specialities

amanida catalana/*ensalada catalana* mixed salad with a selection of cold meats
arròs negre/*arroz negro* 'black rice', seafood rice cooked in squid ink
bacallà a la llauna/*bacalao 'a la llauna'* salt cod baked in garlic, tomato, paprika and wine
botifarra/*butifarra* Catalan sausage: variants include *botifarra negre* (blood sausage) and *blanca* (mixed with egg)

▶

El Glop

C/Montmany 46 (93 213 70 58). Metro Joanic/39, 55, N6 bus. **Open** 1-4pm, 8pm-1am Tue-Sun. **Main courses** €4.20-€19.50. **Set lunch** €6.90 Tue-Fri. **Credit** MC, V. **Map** p337 E3.

This long-running Gràcia institution is housed in a rambling building with low beams upstairs and a kind of indoor patio with a retractable roof downstairs. The specialities are traditional chargrilled meat (try the succulent *filete de ternera*) washed down with fiercesome Priorat reds drunk from a *porró*, and snails cooked *a la llauna*. The *suquet de rape* (monkfish stew) arrives sizzling in a terracotta dish and is enough for two.

Branches: El Nou Glop C/Montmany 49, torre, Gràcia (93 219 70 59); **El Glop de la Rambla** Rambla Catalunya 65, Eixample (93 487 00 97).

Jean-Luc Figueras

C/Santa Teresa 10 (93 415 28 77). Metro Diagonal/ 6, 15, 22, 24, 28, 33, bus. **Open** 1.30-3.30pm, 8.30-11.30pm Mon-Fri; 8.30-11.30pm Sat. Closed 2wks Aug. **Main courses** €24.80-€35.50. **Gourmet menu** €67.60. **Credit** AmEx, DC, MC, V. **Map** p336 D4.

Now Michelin-starred, Jean-Luc Figueras's eponymous restaurant is simply one of the most outstanding in Barcelona. It is housed in a 19th-century palace on a quiet back street and exquisitely fitted out in silky creams and yellows, with tables that are masterpieces of sumptuous refinement. Jean-Luc serves creative Catalan cuisine with a subtle French accent. Specialities include a creamy pistachio soup with ginger and lobster ravioli, and red mullet with crab apple and port. The petits fours are legendary (try the wild baby strawberries in chocolate) and the desserts superlative.

Laurak

C/La Granada del Penedès 14-16 (93 218 71 65). FCG Gràcia/16, 17, 22, 24, 27, 28, 31, 32 N4 bus. **Open** 1-4pm, 9-11.30pm Mon-Sat. Closed Aug. **Main courses** €18.40-€21.80. **Set lunch** €15.10 Mon-Fri. **Gourmet menu** €43.50. **Credit** AmEx, DC, MC, V. **Map** p336 D3.

A sleek, ocean-liner-style cocktail bar opens out to a spacious and quiet dining room given warmth by red table linen, soft lighting and attentive service.

▶ ## What's cooking? (continued)

botifarra amb mongetes/*butifarra con judías* sausage with haricot beans

calçots a specially sweet variety of large spring onion (scallion), available only from November to spring, and eaten char-grilled, with *romesco* sauce

~~**carn d'olla** traditional Christmas dish of~~ various meats stewed with *escudella*, then served separately

conill amb cargols/*conejo con caracoles* rabbit with snails

crema catalana custard dessert with burnt sugar topping, similar to crème brûlée

escalivada/*escalibada* grilled and peeled peppers, onions and aubergine

escudella winter stew of meat and vegetables

espinacs a la catalana/*espinacas a la catalana* spinach quick-fried in olive oil with garlic, raisins and pine kernels

esqueixada summer salad of marinated salt cod with onions, olives and tomato

fideuà/*fideuá* paella made with noodles

pa amb tomàquet/*pan con tomate* bread prepared with tomato, oil and salt

peus de porc/*pies de cerdo* pig's trotters

romesco a spicy sauce from the coast south of Barcelona, made with crushed almonds and hazelnuts, tomatoes, oil and a special type of red pepper (*nyora*)

sarsuela/*zarzuela* fish and seafood stew

sípia amb mandonguilles/*sepia con albóndigas* cuttlefish with meatballs

suquet de peix/*suquet de pescado* fish and potato soup

torrades/*tostadas* toasted *pa amb tomàquet*

xató salad containing tuna, anchovies and cod, with a romesco-type sauce

Carn i aviram/Carne y aves/ Meat & poultry

ànec	*pato*	duck
bou	*buey*	beef
cabrit	*cabrito*	kid
conill	*conejo*	rabbit
embotits	*embotidos*	cold cuts
faisà	*faisán*	pheasant
fetge	*higado*	liver
llebre	*liebre*	hare
llengua	*lengua*	tongue
llom	*lomo*	loin of pork
ous	*huevos*	eggs
perdiu	*perdiz*	partridge
pernil (serrà)	*jamón serrano*	dry-cured ham
pernil dolç	*jamón york*	cooked ham
pollastre	*pollo*	chicken
porc	*cerdo*	pork
porc senglar	*jabalí*	wild boar
ronyons	*riñones*	kidneys
vedella	*ternera*	veal
xai/be	*cordero*	lamb

Peix i marisc/Pescado y mariscos/ Fish & seafood

anxoves	*anchoas*	anchovies

Its deservedly renowned menu includes Basque specialities such as black pudding from Besain, Idiazábal cheese, and imaginatively crafted combinations such as duck foie gras with toffee-glazed slices of banana, or red mullet with a sesame crust and black olive vinaigrette. The puddings are also supremely luxurious; try the pistachio biscuit with praline mousse and chocolate *crocante*. The *menú de degustación* is really excellent value – make sure to wash it down with a bottle of white Txakoli.

Octubre

C/Julián Romea 18 (93 218 25 18). FCG Gràcia/16, 24, 27, 31, 32 bus. **Open** 1.30-3.30pm, 9-11pm Mon-Fri; 9-11pm Sat. Closed Aug. **Main courses** €7.80-€11.60. **Credit** AmEx, DC, MC, V. **Map** p336 D3.
This intimate restaurant is the perfect spot for a romantic tête-à-tête over sensual, lovingly cooked food. The wine list is well priced and perfectly complements the Catalan dishes on offer, such as veal stacked with melting foie gras, stuffed artichoke hearts, and a sumptuous chocolate soufflé cake. The menu changes according to what's in season.

Roig Robí

C/Sèneca 20 (93 218 92 22). Metro Diagonal/6, 7, 15, 16, 17, 22, 24, 28, 33 bus. **Open** 1.30-4pm, 9-11.30pm Mon-Fri; 9-11.30pm Sat. Closed 2wks Aug. **Main courses** €11.60-€19.60. **Gourmet menu** €48.30. Credit AmEx, DC, MC, V. **Map** p336 D3.
Famous for her superlative rice dishes or cod dishes such as *bacallà al pil-pil*, self-taught chef Mercè Navarro has made 'Red Ruby' a favourite among local writers, politicians and artists, including Antoni Tàpies, who designed the menu. It's a small, simply decorated space, where booking is highly recommended, especially if you want to sit in the gorgeous garden terrace at the back.

International

Cantina Machito

C/Torrijos 47 (93 217 34 14). Metro Joanic/39, 55 bus. **Open** 1-5pm, 7pm-2am daily. **Main courses** €6.30-€13. **Credit** MC, V. **Map** p337 E3.
By far the most authentic Mexican restaurant in Barcelona, the family-run Cantina Machito serves

bacallà	bacalao	salt cod
besuc	besugo	sea bream
calamarsos	calamares	squid
cloïsses	almejas	clams
cranc	cangrejo	crab
escamarlans	cigalas	crayfish
escopinyes	berberechos	cockles
gambes	gambas	prawns
llagosta	langosta	spiny lobster
llagostins	langostinos	langoustines
llenguado	lenguado	sole
llobarro	lubina	sea bass
lluç	merluza	hake
musclos	mejillones	mussels
pop	pulpo	octopus
rap	rape	monkfish
salmó	salmón	salmon
sardines	sardinas	sardines
sípia	sepia	cuttlefish
tonyina	atún	tuna
truita	trucha	trout
(note: **truita** can also mean an omelette)		

Verdures/Legumbres/Vegetables

all	ajo	garlic
alvocat	aguacate	avocado
bolets	setas	wild mushrooms
ceba	cebolla	onion
cigrons	garbanzos	chick peas
col	col	cabbage
enciam	lechuga	lettuce

endivies	endivias	chicory
espinacs	espinacas	spinach
mongetes blanques	judías blancas	haricot beans
mongetes verdes	judías verdes	French beans
pastanagues	zanahorias	carrots
patates	patatas	potatoes
pebrots	pimientos	peppers
pèsols	guisantes	peas
tomàquets	tomates	tomatoes
xampinyons	champiñones	mushrooms

Postres/Postres/Desserts

flam	flan	crème caramel
formatge	queso	cheese
gelat	helado	ice-cream
mel i mató	miel y mató	curd cheese with honey
pastís	pastel	cake
tarta	tarta	tart

Fruïta/Fruta/Fruit

figues	higos	figs
maduixes	fresas	strawberries
pera	pera	pear
plàtan	plátano	banana
poma	manzana	apple
préssec	melocotón	peach
raïm	uvas	grapes
taronja	naranja	orange

For a juicy steak
Agut (see p137), El Asador de Burgos (see p156) and Le Relais de Venise (see p159).

For crustacea
Bar Mundial (see p148), Cal Pep (see p148), Can Maño (see p153) and Casa Leopoldo (see p145).

For wicked puddings
Ca l'Isidre (see p145), Tragaluz (see p159) and Xiringuitó Escribà (see p155).

To take your parents
El Gran Café (see p137), Set Portes (see p155) and Jaume de Provença (see p157).

For mellow grooves
Oolong (see p139), Pla (see p139) and Polenta (see p139).

For budget bites
Can Culleretes (see p137), Mesón David (see p147) and Pla dels Àngels (see p147).

For a menú del día
Bunga Raya (see p152), La Poste (see p140), La Casa de la Rioja (see p145) and Nostromo (see p171).

For a bit of glam
Taira (see p152), Newport Room (see p155) and Seltz (see p159).

For tranquil terraces
Cafè de l'Acadèmia (see p137), Café de la Ribera (see p148) and Els Pescadors (see p166).

For leafy gardens
La Buena Tierra (see p165), Roig Robí (see p163), La Balsa (see p166) and Can Travi Nou (see p166).

classics such as *mole poblano* (shredded turkey breast smothered in a chilli mole sauce) and tender lamb *al pastor*, all accompanied by beans, salsas and salads. For dessert, the lime and tequila mousse is to die for. The family also holds celebrations on Mexican national holidays, when you can try the likes of *pan de muertos* ('bread of the dead') or rare tequilas.

Habibi
C/Gran de Gràcia 7 (93 217 95 45). Metro Diagonal/ 22, 24, 28 bus. **Open** 1pm-1am Mon-Fri; 2-4.30pm, 8pm-2am Sat. **Main courses** €4.20-€7.30. **Set lunch** €5.70 Mon-Wed, Fri; €7.20 Thur. **Credit** AmEx, DC, MC, V. **Map** p336 D3.

Habibi ('my darling' in Arabic) is a refuge of calm from the noisy Gràcia traffic, with winding plants and trickling waterfalls. Welcoming owner Hassan is one of few people organic meats and vegetables. As well as classic shawarmas and falafels, there are more elaborate dishes such as *kube halabi* (spiced lamb in a sealed semolina pancake with fruits and nuts) or *matabal* aubergine dip. The wide and inventive range of vegetarian dishes includes stuffed vine leaves, couscous salads and *urugi* burgers with houmous.

Mesopotamia
C/Verdi 65 (93 237 15 63). Metro Fontana/22, 24, 28 bus. **Open** 8.30pm-midnight Mon-Sat. **Main courses** €5.50-€8. **Gourmet menu** €18. **Credit** MC, V. **Map** p336 D3.

The terracotta and adobe decor gives a *Temple of Doom* effect to Barcelona's only Iraqi restaurant, and you almost expect Indiana Jones to come bursting out from behind the wonderful ziggurat friezes. Owner Pius has done an equally excellent job on the menu, which is based on Arab 'staff of life' foods, such as yoghurt and rice. Best value is the enormous taster menu, which includes quality Lebanese wines, a variety of dips for your *riqaq* bread – such as *tamr wa laban* (toffee-sweet date sauce with onion, cumin and walnuts) – aromatic roast meats, sticky *baqlawa* and Arabic teas.

SoNaMu
Passatge Josep Llovera 11 (93 209 65 83). FCG Gràcia/27, 32, 58, 64, N8 bus. **Open** 1.30-3.30pm, 8.30-11.30pm Mon-Sat. **Main courses** €5.70-€15. **Set lunch** from €8.10 Mon-Sat. **Credit** DC, MC, V. **Map** p336 C3.

SoNaMu offers Korean and Japanese specialities of consistently good quality. The *dolsot* is a searingly hot stone bowl filled with rice, meat and vegetables; there are also different kinds of sushi and a selection of Korean-style barbecued meat. If you want a quick, healthy lunch, try one of the bento boxes: each contains four or five treats, such as steamed *gyoza* dumplings, a stack of vegetable and prawn tempura, sushi, sashimi, wasabi, and seaweed and noodle salad.

Specchio Magico
C/Luis Antúnez 3 (93 415 33 71). Metro Diagonal/ 22, 24, 28, N4 bus. **Open** 2-4pm; 9-11pm Mon-Sat; 2-4pm Sun. **Main courses** €9.70-€19. **Credit** AmEx, DC, MC, V. **Map** p336 D3.

The wall-to-wall wood panelling covered in postcards and framed letters may make Specchio Magico look a little like a rumpus room at a Moose Lodge, but the warm and friendly service more than make up for it. There are no pizzas, but the four Italian chef/owners serve top-quality pasta dishes, from *rigatoni alla putanesca* to *sedanini* with truffles and foie gras, in gigantic portions. There's also a solid selection of Italian and Spanish wines, plus excellent meat dishes and traditional desserts, such as homemade panna cotta and tiramisu.

Eat, Drink, Shop

Vegetarian

La Buena Tierra

*C/Encarnació 56 (93 219 82 13). Metro Joanic/
39, 55, N6 bus.* **Open** 1-4pm, 8pm-midnight Mon-
Sat. Closed 2wks July-Aug. **Main courses** €4.40-
€12.70. **Set lunch** €6.60 Mon-Fri. **Credit** MC, V.
Map p337 E3.

A pretty vegetarian restaurant that occupies an old
townhouse and pocket-handkerchief-sized garden,
and serves subtler, more imaginative dishes than
most other veggie places. Specialities of their seasonal menu include cannelloni with porcini and delicate girgola mushrooms, fruity soups, and a range
of vol au vents with fillings such as asparagus and
artichoke hearts.
Branch: La Llar de Foc C/Ramón y Cajal 13,
Gràcia (93 284 10 25).

L'Illa de Gràcia

*C/Sant Doménech 19 (93 238 02 29). Metro
Diagonal/22, 24, 28, N4, N6 bus.* **Open** 1-4pm,
9pm-midnight Tue-Fri; 2-4pm, 9pm-midnight Sat,
Sun. Closed late Aug. **Main courses** €3.20-€5.
Set lunch €5.40 Mon-Fri. **Credit** DC, MC, V.
Map p336 D3.

The sleek, minimalist decor, dark wooden slab
tables and exposed brick walls make L'Illa de Gràcia
one of the few vegetarian restaurants in Barcelona
to make any concession to style or ambience. The
extensive menu features no less than 14 different salads as well as dishes such as pan-fried tofu with
alfalfa and wild rice, plus several filled crêpes, homemade cakes or fruit puddings – all of which are
excellent value for money.

Sants

La Opalina

*C/Riego 25 (93 421 84 74). Metro Plaça de Sants or
Sants Estació/30, 56, 57, 157, N2, N7, N14 bus.*
Open 1-4pm, 9pm-midnight Mon-Sat. **Main
courses** €4.40-€9.30. **Set lunch** €6.60-€10.80.
No credit cards. Map p339 A4.

Five minutes' walk from the Sants train station, this
low-ceilinged, brightly coloured restaurant is an
agreeable place to grab a cheap bite before your train
leaves. The lunch menu is good value and might feature *llenguado* (sole) with an almond sauce, or spare
ribs with *all i oli*. There's also a slightly pricier set
menu with an emphasis on inventive cod dishes.

La Parra

*C/Joanot Martorell 3 (93 332 51 34). Metro
Hostafrancs/30, 56, 57, 157, 53N, N2, N14 bus.*
Open 8.30pm-12.30am Tue-Fri; 2-4.30pm, 8.30pm-
midnight Sat; 2-4.30pm Sun. Closed usually Aug.
Main courses €7.70-€18. **Credit** MC, V. **Map**
p339 A4.

This 19th-century coaching inn now houses one of
the city's best restaurants for Catalan *a la brasa*
cooking. Boulders of meat, still spitting from the
fierce wood-fired grill, are served on slabs of wood
and accompanied by ferociously strong *all i oli*.
Lamb (actually mutton, and none the worse for it) is
served alongside goat, horse, beef and rabbit, but
the tastiest dish might just be the succulent *galtes*
(pig's cheeks). The cosy and traditionally decorated
interior is the perfect place to be on a cold winter's
night, while in summer the eponymous vine (*parra*)
provides cool shade on the peaceful terrace.

Eat, Drink, Shop

Els Pescadors. *See p166.*

Peixerot

C/Tarragona 177 (93 424 69 69). Metro Sants Estació/27, 30, 109, 215, N0, N7 bus. **Open** Jan-July, Sept-Dec 1-4pm, 8.30-11pm Mon-Sat; 1-4pm Sun. Aug 1-4pm, 8.30-11pm Mon-Fri; 1-4pm Sat. **Main courses** €12.20-€21.30. **Credit** AmEx, DC, MC, V. **Map** p339 A-B4.

An excellent, smartish seafood restaurant with a loyal following among local business people. The speciality here is paella, and there's also a great arròs a la marinera (rice in a fish broth with seafood), arròs negre (paella made with squid ink), fresh fish and other classic dishes of the Catalan coast. The service is immaculate and the wine list is more than adequate.

Tibidabo & Zona Alta

La Balsa

C/Infanta Isabel 4 (93 211 50 48). FCG Av Tibidabo/22, 58, 73, 75, 85 bus. **Open** 9-11.30pm Mon; 2-3.30pm, 9-11.30pm Tue-Sat. **Main courses** €10.30-€20.60. **Credit** AmEx, MC, V.

Go through the forged iron gate in the form of a giant spider, and you'll arrive in one of the loveliest restaurant gardens in Barcelona. Filled with lush plantlife and wicker furniture, Oscar Tusquets' stunning design won a top architecture award in 1979, and is still the perfect place to spend a hot summer evening. The Mediterranean-inspired dishes are good value, especially the angler fish Orly, the stews and the all-you-can-eat buffet, which is served only in August.

Neichel

C/Beltrán i Rózpide 16 bis (93 203 84 08/ www.relaischateaux.fr/neichel.com). Metro Maria Cristina/7, 33, 63, 67, 68, 78, N12 bus. **Open** 1-3.30pm, 8.30-11.30pm Tue-Sat. Closed Aug. **Main courses** €13.90-€33.10. **Gourmet menu** €56; €63. **Credit** AmEx, DC, MC, V.

Now with its second Michelin star, Jean-Luis Neichel's restaurant has long been recognised as one of the very finest in the city. The elegance and simplicity of the award-winning decor contrast with the extravagantly baroque menu, which favours complex combinations such as those involved in a risotto made with black truffles, porcini mushrooms, parmesan, farmhouse duck and wild rice. The gourmet menus are matched with superlative wines, desserts and cheeses, and provide a memorably opulent dining experience.

La Venta

Plaça Doctor Andreu 1 (93 212 64 55). FCG Av Tibidabo, then Tramvia Blau/17, 22, 58, 73, 75, 85, 101 bus, then Tramvia Blau. **Open** 1.30-3.15pm, 9-11.15pm Mon-Sat. **Main courses** €11.10-€17.70. **Credit** AmEx, DC, MC, V.

Ask to be seated on the terrace, and you'll get the best of La Venta: incredible panoramic views and a warm mountain breeze. Inside, the airy conservatory maintains the outdoor feel, while the curious

mozarabic decor adds colour. La Venta attracts a very fashionable, upper-class clientele, who come to see and be seen, but also to enjoy friendly, professional service and competently cooked, imaginative dishes, such as the house speciality of sea urchin au gratin.

Poblenou

Els Pescadors

Plaça Prim 1 (93 225 20 18). Metro Poblenou/41 bus. **Open** 1-3.45pm, 8pm-midnight daily. **Main courses** €9.50-€27.70. **Credit** AmEx, DC, MC, V.

A very attractive restaurant in a small square in the old village of Poblenou, back from the beach area, with tables outside on a beautiful terrace in summer. Inside, there are two dining rooms in contrasting styles: the first room is in traditional Barcelona café style, with a tiled floor and marble tables; further in, the decor is more plush and more intimate. It specialises in refined Catalan fish and seafood dishes, and the oven-cooked fish specials, using the pick of the same day's catch from ports on the coast, are superb. There are also frequently interesting vegetarian options.

Horta

Can Travi Nou

C/Jorge Manrique (93 428 03 01). Metro Horta/ 10, 45, 102 bus. **Open** 1.30-4pm, 8.30pm-midnight Mon-Sat; 1.30-4pm Sun. **Main courses** €6.60-€31.30. **Credit** AmEx, DC, MC, V.

In summer, diners sit on a vast covered terrace surrounded by dense vegetation, seemingly a million miles from the bustle of the city. In winter, the action (and tables) move inside the huge, beautiful, old farmhouse, perched on a hill above the former village of Horta. The food is traditional Catalan, with speciality mar i muntanya dishes, such as sípia amb mandonguilles and cueta de rap amb all torrat (monkfish tail with toasted garlic). Can Travi is difficult to reach by public transport – best to take a cab – but very worth finding.

Gaig

Passeig Maragall 402 (93 429 10 17). Metro Horta/ 19, 45, N4 bus. **Open** 1.30-4pm, 9-11pm Tue-Sat; 1.30-4pm Sun. Closed 3wks Aug. **Main courses** €15.80-€30.10. **Credit** AmEx, DC, MC, V.

A bit of a trek from the centre, but undoubtedly worth the effort. Over 100 years old and still one of the most consistently highly rated restaurants in Barcelona, Gaig's elegant decor and quiet terrace provide a perfect backdrop for Carles Gaig's spectacular cooking. His light touch breathes new life into old Catalan favourites, such as the house speciality, arrós de colomí i ceps (young pigeon with rice and porcini mushrooms) and a superlative crema catalana. The 400-strong wine list and a helpful sommelier to guide you through make the drink a pleasure to match the food.

Cafés & Bars

Bustling *bodegas*, cosy cafés, tasty tapas and much more. Salut!

The streets of Barcelona are lined with places for residents and tourists alike to share a drink, chat or just watch the world go by. Some are meeting points around which neighbourhood life turns, others are old *bodegas* with an ageing clientele sampling wine from the barrel; there are outdoor cafés on sunny squares and designer spots geared to a more cosmopolitan clientele. Without paying a few of them a visit, you won't really get to know what Barcelona is all about.

Tapas in Barcelona are generally not as varied as in some parts of Spain, but great examples can be found, and most bars offer food of some kind. Be advised that some of the bars listed do serve a set lunch menu and that if you try to occupy one of their tables during the lunch hours, you will probably be asked to leave. Be aware that taking a seat on an outside table will probably push up prices, and drinks are often more expensive at night – though at what time they go up and by how much is seldom, if ever, established. The difference in cost is unlikely to be more than a euro. With regard to tips, five per cent is considered courteous, although not expected.

Opening hours will vary (many close earlier or later at night, according to trade), and those listed should be taken as guidelines rather than fixed hours. For bars more clearly oriented to night-time socialising, *see chapter* **Nightlife**.

Barri Gòtic

L'Antiquari
C/Vequer 13 (93 310 04 35). Metro Jaume I/17, 19, 40, 45, N8 bus. **Open** *mid Sept-May* 5pm-2am daily. *June-mid Sept* 10am-2.30am daily. **No credit cards.** **Map** p343 B3.
This old bar has choice seating smack in the middle of the wonderful Plaça del Rei. Inside, dark wood and low lighting create a warm, comfortable atmosphere, while mostly out-of-date music (often '80s rock) plays. Downstairs, a tiny, stone-walled basement is a nice spot for a private drink.

Arc Café
C/Carabassa 19 (93 302 52 04). Metro Jaume I/17, 19, 40, 45 bus. **Open** 10am-2am Mon-Thur, Sun; 10am-3am Fri, Sat. **Credit** AmEx, DC, MC, V. **Map** p343 B4.
Tucked into a charming, crooked sidestreet, this popular café is unpretentious and welcoming. Modern, tasteful and soothing in design, it has a

double-height main room and, upstairs, an entire wall painted like the inside of a giant red onion. Breakfast is good – muesli with yoghurt, fresh juice or pastries – but the Mediterranean lunch and dinner menu is unexceptional.

The Bagel Shop
C/Canuda 25 (93 302 41 61). Metro Catalunya/ bus all routes to Plaça Catalunya. **Open** 9.30am-9.30pm Mon-Sat; 11am-4pm Sun. **No credit cards.** **Map** p342 B2.
The name says it all – almost. Aside from an ample selection of bagels with mouth-watering combinations of toppings (pesto with melted cheddar and mushrooms, for example), they serve wonderful cakes and cookies, and, in the morning, pancakes with maple syrup. On Sundays, you can enjoy a 'North American-style' breakfast; the owner is Canadian, so knows a thing or two about bacon 'n' eggs and French toast. It's too bad about the cramped quarters and slow service, however.

Bar Celta
C/Mercè 16 (93 315 00 06). Metro Drassanes/ 14, 36, 57, 59, 64, 157, N6 bus. **Open** noon-midnight Mon-Sat. **Credit** MC, V. **Map** p343 B4.
This tapas bar is not pretty with its bright lights and outdated '60s decor, but it is friendly and fun. Huge trays laden predominantly with seafood tapas line the bar, where patrons wade ankle-deep in balled-up napkins. Particularly good are the *rabas* (deep-fried chunks of squid) and *pimientos del padron* (small, mostly mild, green peppers).

Bilbao-Berria
Plaça Nova 3 (93 317 0124). Metro Jaume I/ 17, 19, 40, 45 bus. **Open** 9am-midnight daily. **Credit** AmEx, MC, V. **Map** p342 B2.
One of the many Basque bars that seem to sprout up around the city every month. Choose from the dozens of quality *pintxos* lining the counter, or order a *cazuelito* – a small earthenware dish – of one of the delicacies (usually seafood) on display at the end of the bar. There are tables outside and an excellent restaurant downstairs.

Bliss
Plaça Sant Just 4 (93 268 10 22). Metro Jaume I/ 17, 19, 40, 45 bus. **Open** 10am-11.30pm Mon-Fri; 1.30pm-midnight Sat. **Credit** MC, V. **Map** p343 B3.
Bliss offers delicious homemade brownies and cakes (including lemon, ginger and walnut), fresh juice and exquisite quiches. You can enjoy them in a sitting-room area with couches and armchairs (and a clearly visible section of Roman wall) or the fresh and cool, high-ceilinged main room or, in

Eat, Drink, Shop

Bites to eat

SPANISH TAPAS

The Spanish *tapa* (meaning 'lid') was originally a saucer that innkeepers garnished with tit-bits from the kitchen, and placed on top of the drink offered to coachmen when they stopped at inns on their journeys. The tradition took hold and tapas are now prepared in a thousand different combinations, including whole mushrooms fried in white wine and garlic (*champiñones al ajillo*), prawns and garlic (*gambas al ajillo*), mussels in a tomato and onion sauce (*mejillones a la marinera*), cuttlefish fried in batter (*chocos*), steamed clams with garlic and parsley (*almejas al vapor*), octopus (*pulpo*) and little green peppers (*pimientos del padrón*), which are great to share on a plate between friends since they constitute a kind of culinary Russian roulette – not all are hot, but one or two have a vicious bite.

Although tapas bars are not nearly as popular in Catalonia as they are in the rest of Spain, there are some excellent exceptions. Try the **Cervecería Catalana** (*see p180*); **La Estrella de Plata** (*see p178*), for very good but expensive tapas; and restaurant **Cal Pep** (*see p148*).

Barcelona does, however, have hundreds of tiny, brightly lit snack and sandwich bars that serve food in smaller portions (*raciones*), but which don't necessarily qualify as tapas bars, and cater for the workers. They offer some of the typical, less elaborate and cheaper Spanish dishes, such as *tortilla* (omelette), *patatas bravas* (fried potatoes in a spicy red sauce and/or garlic mayonnaise), snails (*caracoles*) in a delicious onion sauce, skewered meat (*pinchos morunos*), which,

though in name owe something to the Moorish legacy, are usually made of pork. Ham is a staple of the Spanish diet and you'll often see legs of it hanging in bars or propped up on a carving block next to the cash register.

Jamon de York, or *jamon dulce,* is just boiled ham, but cured ham is what locals call 'real ham' or *jamon de verdad*, and there are many kinds, varying greatly in quality and price: *del pais, serrano, de bellota* or *jabugo* are the most common, the latter two being the most prized. *Bellota* means acorn, and this meat is obtained from pigs fed on acorns.

CATALAN LLESQUES

Catalonia does have its own style of snack food equivalent to tapas. Specialities include *escalivada* (roasted aubergines, peppers and onions peeled and served cold with olive oil), *esqueixada* (cod salad) and an assortment of cold meats, pâtés and cheeses almost invariably accompanied by *pa amb tomàquet* (bread with tomato), a tradition hailing from leaner years when old stale bread was made softer by smearing tomato on to it. Now, fresh garlic is also rubbed on, with olive oil drizzled on top. Also distinctly Catalan are *llesques*, which are large slices of toasted bread, prepared as above, but with a variety of toppings such as anchovies, *escalivada*, tuna, cheese or pâté.

BASQUE PINTXOS

Perhaps even more popular in Barcelona than tapas bars and Catalan *llesquerias* are Basque bars. They are usually quite open, rustic, wood and stone affairs with stools and standing space around the bar. While most of these bars do serve full meals, they are known more for their *pintxos*, small pieces of bread topped with some ingenious culinary combination. They are too numerous to mention, but they will include cheese, anchovies, pâté de Roquefort, cured ham, eel, black pudding (*morcilla*), croquettes (they usually contain chicken), dates wrapped in bacon, small roast red peppers filled with tuna, quail eggs, spicy peppers and, naturally, *tortilla*.

Each *pintxo* is impaled by a toothpick, which you should keep on your plate, so that the barman knows how many you had. It's worth noting that the trays of *pintxos* are generally brought out at certain hours, often midday and 7pm.

spring and summer, outside in a quiet, centuries-old square. A great selection of teas and international publications make this a perfect spot to unwind.

Boadas

C/Tallers 1 (93 318 95 92). Metro Catalunya/ bus all routes to Plaça Catalunya. **Open** noon-2am Mon-Thur; noon-3am Fri, Sat. **No credit cards. Map** p342 A2.

This tiny cocktail bar is difficult to spot, but it doesn't need a neon sign – locals know where it is. While the crowds and heat rage just outside on La Rambla, inside, this 1930s institution is cool and relaxing with black-jacketed and professional barman. The daytime clientele are usually well dressed and elderly, while the night-time patrons are a more varied bunch, creating a livelier atmosphere.

El Bosc de les Fades

Passatge de la Banca (93 317 26 49). Metro Drassanes/14, 36, 38, 59, N9, N12 bus. **Open** 10.30am-1am Mon-Thur, Sun; 10.30am-2am Fri, Sat. **No credit cards. Map** p343 A4.

The name means 'Fairies' Forest' and that is precisely what they have tried to create in this darkened bar next to the Museu de Cera at the bottom of the Rambla. Sit under a huge fake tree and listen to the crickets chirp, or sip your overpriced wine while perched on a rock near a babbling brook.

Buenas Migas

C/Baixada Santa Clara 2, off Plaça del Rei (93 412 16 86/93 318 37 08). Metro Jaume I/17, 19, 40, 45 bus. **Open** 11am-9pm daily. **Credit** AmEx, MC, V. **Map** p343 B3.

Space is limited in this homey café, with the only seats lined up along the windows that overlook the ancient stone streets behind the cathedral. The speciality is a light focaccia bread with a variety of toppings, although the sweet treats (pear and cream cake or apple crumble) are pretty special as well. The similar branch in the Raval has tables outside. **Branch:** Plaça Bonsuccés 6, Raval (93 319 13 80).

Café La Cereria

C/Baixada Sant Miquel 3-5 (93 301 85 10). Metro Liceu/14, 38, 59, 91, N9, N12 bus. **Open** 9.30am-10pm Mon-Sat. **No credit cards. Map** p343 B3.

This friendly and fresh café, run as a co-operative, is always crowded, but the waiters – many of them co-owners – do their utmost to cope. Vegetarian relief is supplied in the form of creative and healthy sandwiches, and there are milkshakes, fresh juices, a long list of herbal teas and *maté*.

Cafè d'Estiu

Museu Frederic Marès, Plaça Sant Iu 5 (93 310 30 14). Metro Jaume I/17, 19, 40, 45, N8 bus. **Open** *Apr-Sept* 10am-10pm Tue-Sun. Closed Oct-Mar. **Map** p343 B3.

Nobody seems to be especially hurried in this Gothic courtyard, with a fish pond made of stone and a number of old citrus trees. On offer at the outdoor café is a standard selection of coffee, tea, drinks and some light pastries. It's a wonderfully peaceful place to enjoy a quiet drink, but only in summer, as its name – Summer Cafe – indicates.

Café de l'Opera

La Rambla 74 (93 317 75 85/93 302 41 80). Metro Liceu/14, 38, 59, N9, N12 bus. **Open** 8am-2.15am Mon-Thur, Sun; 8am-3am Fri, Sat. **No credit cards. Map** p343 A3.

Opened around 1890 as a place for Barcelona's elite to see and be seen after the opera at the Liceu across the street, this is now everyman's café, with locals, a large gay contingent and foreigners of every stripe all rubbing elbows. There are standard tapas, good desserts, a long list of brandies and a good selection of foreign and national beers. Two comfortable upstairs salons (recently refurbished) open in the evening to accommodate the growing crowds.

Café Zurich

Plaça Catalunya 1 (93 317 91 53). Metro Catalunya/ bus all routes to Plaça Catalunya. **Open** *June-end Oct* 8am-1am Mon-Fri; 10am-1am Sun. *End Oct-May* 8am-11pm Mon-Fri, Sun; 8am-midnight Sat. **No credit cards. Map** p342 B1.

Generations of Barcelonans and travellers have whiled away afternoons on this sunny, sprawling terrace, although the original much-loved bar was torn down in 1997 to make way for the El Triangle shopping centre. The new Zurich was decorated with generic, old-style fittings (the stopped clock is the only piece saved from the wreckage), which, unsurprisingly, misses the mark somewhat. Still, it has regained its status as a meeting spot for locals, backpackers and other urban wanderers.

Escribà

La Rambla 83 (93 301 60 27). Metro Liceu/ 14, 38, 59, N9, N12 bus. **Open** 8.30am-9pm daily. **Credit** (over €9) MC, V. **Map** p343 A3.

If you think this lovely *Modernista* façade with its colourful mosaic tiles is a treat in itself, just wait until you sample some of the homemade chocolates and pastries waiting inside. They also sell local *moscatell* in cute, decorative bottles and have a handful of tables outside in the shade of a narrow street.

Glaciar

Plaça Reial 3 (93 302 11 63). Metro Liceu/ 14, 38, 59, N9, N12 bus. **Open** 4pm-2.15am Mon-Sat; 8am-2.15am Sun. **No credit cards. Map** p343 A3.

High ceilings, old dark wood and warm lighting provide the sort of ambience that never really goes out of style. This is the one outdoor terrace cafés of the many in Plaça Reial that resists the vagaries of fashion, and where locals and resident foreigners still congregate to people-watch and meet friends.

La Granja

C/Banys Nous 4 (93 302 69 75). Metro Liceu/ 14, 38, 59, 91, N9, N12 bus. **Open** 9.30am-2pm, 5-9.30pm Mon-Sat; 5.30-9.30pm Sun. **Closed** 3wks end Aug/Sept. **No credit cards. Map** p343 B3.

Eat, Drink, Shop

Try the breakfast at the **Mesón del Café**. Not just the oranges get squeezed.

This homey, antique-filled café is representative of the many changes that the Barri Gòtic has undergone over the centuries: the uneven floors and walls change from wood to tile to stone – and there's even a section of Roman wall in the back. Try the *mini suizo* if the standard heaped mug of thick, steaming chocolate and cream (an ordinary *suizo*) is too much.

Leticia

C/Còdols 21 (93 302 00 74). Metro Drassanes/14, 36, 57, 59, 64, 157, N6 bus. **Open** 7pm-3am Mon, Wed-Sun. **Credit** MC, V. **Map** p343 A4.
Located on one of the medieval city's narrowest streets, Leticia is cool and relaxed, with comfy chairs and a sofa on which to chat, play chess and chill out to drum 'n' bass, rare soul, flamenco and jazz. There's an excellent range of salads, homemade *bocadillos*, cakes and vegetarian dishes. Cocktails and quality teas are also available.

Margarita Blue

C/Josep Anselm Clavé 6 (93 317 71 76). Metro Drassanes/14, 18, 38, 59, N6, N9 bus. **Open** 11am-2am Mon-Wed; 11am-3am Thur, Fri; 7pm-3am Sat; 7pm-2am Sun. **Credit** MC, V. **Map** p343 A4.
It must be the hot tunes that keep the punters coming, because the quality of what they are asking you to believe is Mexican food seems to have been sacrificed in the name of expediency, and the so-called Margaritas (yes, they're blue) come from a slush-puppy machine. Still, this is a colourful and stylish bar/restaurant, which is always filled to capacity with a young (and especially foreign), party-going crowd. Rita Blue – another massively

popular branch of the Blue empire – has a more varied menu, similarly hip decor, a terrace in a pleasant square and a subterranean party area.
Branches: El Taco de Margarita Plaça Duc de Mediniceli 1, Barri Gòtic (93 318 63 21); **Rita Blue** Plaça Sant Agustí 3, Raval (93 412 34 38).

Mesón del Café

C/Llibreteria 16 (93 315 07 54). Metro Jaume I/17, 19, 40, 45, N8 bus. **Open** 7am-9.30pm Mon-Sat. **No credit cards. Map** p327 B3.
This charming little (and we mean little) bar just off the Plaça de Sant Jaume looks something like a miniature Swiss chalet. Start your day with toast and jam and a steaming cup of very good coffee at one of its chunky wooden tables.

Nostromo

C/Ripoll 16 (93 412 24 55). Metro Urquinaona or Jaume I/17, 19, 40, 45, N8 bus. **Open** 2pm-2.30am Mon-Thur; 2pm-3am Fri; 8pm-3am Sat. **Credit** MC, V. **Map** p342 B2.
Named after the Conrad novel and run by a retired sailor, this is a relaxed haven for landlubbers and mariners alike. Chess sets are available, and shelves of mostly Spanish-language books on the sea and exotic lands are distributed about the bar. There's an excellent lunch menu, and dinners are cooked to order (by advance reservation only).

La Palma

C/Palma de Sant Just 7 (93 315 06 56). Metro Jaume I/17, 19, 40, 45, N8 bus. **Open** 8am-3.30pm, 7-10pm Mon-Thur; 8am-3.30pm, 7-11pm Fri, Sat. **No credit cards. Map** p327 B3.

The assorted paintings on the walls in this family-run bar are the originals by a group of artists – called the Internos – who frequented the place in the 1950s. Don't expect to tap dance on the tables here – the regulars come for a quiet glass of wine, poured from one of the many barrels lining the walls, and the easy familiarity that has reigned for nearly 70 years.

Pilé 43

C/Aglà 4 (93 317 39 02). Metro Liceu/14, 38, 59, N9, N12 bus. **Open** 1.30-4.30pm, 7pm-2am Mon-Thur; 1.30-4.30pm, 7pm-3am Fri, Sat. **Credit** MC, V. **Map** p327 A3.
People don't generally drink while shopping, because of the obvious deleterious effects it can have on one's bank account. Beware, then, this combination bar/furniture shop, where almost everything – from the chair you're sitting on to the glass you're drinking your cocktail from – is a 1960s or '70s collectible and for sale. Food is also available.

El Portalón

C/Banys Nous 20 (93 302 11 87). Metro Liceu/ 14, 38, 59, N9, N12 bus. **Open** 9am-midnight Mon-Sat. Closed Aug. **No credit cards. Map** p327 B3.
While the rest of the Barri Gòtic is busy modernising and prettifying, this *bodega* remains untouched. As a result, it has a faded, run-down feel as well as the still discernible rustic charm of old. Created in the 1860s from the stables of a centuries-old palace, it's been offering bargain food and wine ever since to the regulars, who sit chatting at wooden booths under massive clusters of garlic.

Els Quatre Gats

C/Montsió 3 bis (93 302 41 40). Metro Catalunya/ bus all routes to Plaça Catalunya. **Open** 9am-2am Mon-Sat; 5pm-2am Sun. Closed 3wks Aug. **Credit** AmEx, DC, MC, V. **Map** p342 B2.
Not so much an institution as a monument. In 1897, Pere Romeu opened this café in a *Modernista* building by Puig i Cadafalch, and for a few years it was the great meeting point of bohemian Barcelona. Major artists of the day such as Rusiñol and Casas painted pictures for it, and the menu cover was Picasso's first paid commission. It closed in 1903, and was used as a textile warehouse until it was restored and reopened in the 1980s, with reproductions by contemporary artists of the original paintings. It's now more smart than bohemian, but it's an attractive place for a coffee and some good, though pricey, tapas. In the room at the back, where Pere Romeu once presented avant-garde performances, there is a restaurant, with a good set-lunch menu.

Schilling

C/Ferran 23 (93 317 67 87). Metro Liceu/14, 38, 59, N9, N12 bus. **Open** 10am-1.30am Mon-Sat; noon- 2.30am Sun. **Credit** V. **Map** p327 A3.
Spacious and utterly elegant – with a particularly large gay clientele – this bar/café provides front-row seats for watching the ebb and flow of humanity on the bustling street outside. Schilling enjoyed a brief stint as 'the place to be' when it opened a few years ago, but the beautiful people have since grown restless and sashayed away. Still, it is comfortable and popular, despite the famously slow service.

Sit on that chair, quick, before someone buys it: **Pilé 43**.

Fancy a drink?

YOU LIKE COFFEE, I LIKE TEA

If you're the kind of person who needs a coffee to get you going in the morning, you've come to the right place: Spanish coffee is very strong and generally very good. The three basic types are *café solo* (*cafè sol* in Catalan), a small strong black coffee; *cortado/tallat*, the same but with a little milk; and *café con leche/cafè amb llet*, a white coffee, but with more milk and less water than in northern Europe or America. Then there's *café americano* (a tall black coffee diluted with more water), and spiked coffee: a *carajillo*, which is a short, black coffee with a liberal dash of brandy. If you want another type of liqueur, you have to specify, such as *carajillo de ron* (rum) or *carajillo de whisky*. A *trifásico* is a *carajillo* with a bit of milk. Decaffeinated coffee (*descafeinado*) is widely available, but ask for it *de máquina* if you don't want a sachet of Nescafé with hot milk.

Tea is not common and is not usually worth asking for, unless the bar clearly mentions it as one of their specialities. If you want a tea with milk, then ask for a little cold milk on the side (*leche fría aparte*) otherwise anything could happen; a glass of hot milk and a teabag is not unheard of. Herbal teas, such as chamomile (*manzanilla*), lime flower tea (*tila*) and mint (*menta*), are generally easier to find.

Many bars offer freshly squeezed orange juice (quaintly served with a sachet of sugar for the really sweet of tooth), while *horchata* (tiger nut milk) makes a unique and refreshing drink in summer. Still water is *agua sin gas* and sparkling is *agua con gas*, not to be confused with *gaseosa*, which is a kind of lemonade used for adding to cheap red wine at meals or making shandy (*clara*) – though, in Barcelona, shandy will usually be made with bitter lemon.

WINE AFTER BEER

The most common brand of beer in Catalonia is Damm, with Estrella – a good standard lager – the most popular variety. Damm also produces a stronger lager (Voll Damm) and a dark one (Bock Damm). For draught beer,

ask for it *de barril/a pressió*. A *caña* is around half a (UK) pint, a *quinto* smaller still. Occasionally, you will find *jarras*, which are more like a pint.

Among the wines, Rioja is well known, but in the north of Spain there are many excellent wines from other regions, such as the Penedès in Catalonia, Navarra or El Duero. Most of the wine is red (*tinto/negre*), but Galicia produces a good, slightly sparkling white wine (*vino turbio*). The Basques have a similar, clearer wine called Txakolí and, of course, Catalonia has its marvellous selection of cavas, of which *brut nature* is top of the range. *See also p146* **Grape expectations**.

ABSENTA AND FRIENDS

Of Spanish liquors and spirits, the most famous are the full-bodied, dark brandies, such as Torres 5 or 10, which have been aged five or ten years respectively. Mascaró, Magno and Carlos III are also good. Note that measures are enormous. Anís is popular, as is a range of very strong firewaters, including *orujo* and absinthe (*absenta*). Galician *orujo* is like French *eau de vie* or Italian *grappa*. It is distilled from what is left after wine grapes have been pressed and is a good digestive.

Absinthe, which was popular with artists such as Van Gogh in the 19th century, is worthy of some explanation. It can have as many as 27 psycho-active ingredients including aniseed, liquorice and wormwood. This last is the one that sets it apart from other drinks and is the reason for absinthe being illegal in many countries. Admittedly, the potency of this medicinal herb is nowadays much lessened, as it is now prepared from the leaves and not the root, but its effect is still unique and can be quite devastating. It is usually served with a sugar lump, some water and a spoon, the idea being to rest the sugar on the spoon and dissolve it gradually by pouring the water over it and into the glass. It can be ordered in many bars – including **Leticia** (*pictured – see p171*), **Bar Ra** (*see p175*) and **Bar Pastís** (*see p175*) – but has become associated in the minds of many with **Marsella** (*see p177*).

Eat, Drink, Shop

Les Tapes

*Plaça Regomir 4 (93 302 48 40). Metro Jaume I/
17, 19, 40, 45, N8 bus.* **Open** 9am-11pm Mon-Sat.
Closed Aug. **No credit cards. Map** p327 B3.
The sign 'We cheat drunks and tourists' above the
bar shouldn't worry you, for this small bar is especially welcoming to English-speaking tourists (nor,
it seems, are they averse to drunks). There's UK
football on the TV and a shelf of English books to
browse through or swap – take one, leave one. It can
get cramped and muggy in the summer, but not
enough to dampen the friendly atmosphere.

Taverna Basca Irati

*C/Cardenal Casañas 17 (93 302 30 84). Metro
Liceu/ 14, 38, 59, N9, N12 bus.* **Open** noon-
midnight Tue-Sat; noon-4.30pm Sun. Closed 3wks
Aug, 2wks Christmas. **Credit** AmEx, MC, V.
Map p327 A3.
Forget dignity: grab a friend's sleeve for support,
thrust your arm through the mass of people gathered at the bar, sniffing and pawing the plates on
display, and take one of everything you see, then
wash it down with a glass of wine or beer. Loud conversation is also welcomed (indeed, necessary) at
this Basque-style bar, where the fare is *pintxos* at the
front or a full menu in the restaurant at the back.

Travel Bar

*C/Boqueria 27 (93 342 52 52/www.barcelonatravel
bar.com). Metro Liceu/14, 38, 59, N9, N12 bus.*
Open 9am-2am Mon-Thur, Sun; 9am-3am Fri, Sat.
No credit cards. Map p342 A3.
The ideal place for fun-seeking travellers to hook up
to the Internet (€1 for 15 minutes) or to hook up with
friends. The ever-helpful staff organise pub crawls,
city tours (bicycle and walking) and weekend trips.
The decor consists of slightly garish murals, and
there are a few tables outside.

Venus Delicatessen

*C/Avinyó 25 (93 301 15 85). Metro Liceu/14, 38,
59, N9, N12 bus.* **Open** noon-midnight Mon-Sat.
Closed 2wks Nov. **No credit cards. Map** p327 B3.
This little café has a relaxed feel, with regularly
changing displays of art on the walls, and plenty of
newspapers and magazines. Light meals and salads
are served from noon to midnight uninterrupted.
Likewise, cool tunes play at all hours, attracting a
young-spirited, international clientele.

Xocoa

*C/Bot 4 (93 318 89 91). Metro Liceu/14, 38, 59, N9,
N12 bus.* **Open** 10am-10pm Mon-Sat. **Credit** MC, V.
Map p342 A2.
Sit at a low bar in retro, half egg-shaped chairs and
watch the chefs prepare your crêpes. This spacious
and modern café serves innovative meals and
dessert samplers delivered in cutesy little glasses.
The nearby branch on Petritxol, which serves more
chocolate and less food, is more straightforward.
Branches: C/Petritxol 11, Barri Gòtic (93 301 11 97);
C/Roger de Llúria 87, Eixample (93 487 24 99);
C/Ramon i Cajal 106, Gràcia (93 213 04 00).

Raval

Bar Fortuny

*C/Pintor Fortuny 31 (93 317 98 92). Metro
Catalunya/bus all routes to Plaça Catalunya.*
Open 10am-12.30am Tue-Sun. Closed 1wk Aug.
No credit cards. Map p342 A2.
The design elements here include white walls with
colourfully painted pop-art circles, a playful mural
of Bacchus-inspired dancing bottles, and some retro
lamps. The end result is a bar that is as laid-back as
its faithful regulars, who might spend hours here
playing chess or chatting over a healthy meal.
Popular with gay women.

Bar Kasparo

*Plaça Vicenç Martorell 4 (93 302 20 72/
www.kasparo.com). Metro Catalunya/bus
all routes to Plaça Catalunya.* **Open** *Summer*
9am-midnight daily. *Winter* 9am-10pm daily.
Closed Jan. **No credit cards. Map** p342 A2.
Located under the high arcade of this sunny, traffic-
free *plaça*, there are few places this peaceful in the
heart of the Old City. The bar is friendly, Australian-
run and serves a mean chicken salad. Almost all the
seating is outside, so it's ideal in spring and summer.

Bar Mendizábal

*C/Junta de Comerç 2 (no phone). Metro Liceu/
14, 38, 59, N9, N12 bus.* **Open** 8am-midnight
daily. **No credit cards. Map** p327 A3.
This is a tiny place – no more than a colourful little bar and an awning; you stand on the pavement
or sit in the scenic square just across the street to
be served. For most of the last century, it was a
popular workers' hangout. Recently reopened, it
still draws local workers, while also attracting a new
generation of culturally savvy patrons, who come to
enjoy the fresh juices, milkshakes, inventive sandwiches and what are probably the best tortillas in
town, made by the owner's grandmother.

Bar Pastís

*C/Santa Mònica 4 (93 318 79 80). Metro Drassanes/
14, 38, 59, 91, N12 bus.* **Open** 7.30pm-2.30am Mon-
Thur, Sun; 7.30pm-3.30am Fri, Sat. **Credit** AmEx,
MC, V. **Map** p327 A4.
A larger-than-life papier-mâché woman, grinning
drunkenly and clutching a drink in one hand and a
cigarette in the other, is suspended from the ceiling
of this very quirky little bar. It was opened in the
1940s by Quimet and Carme, a Catalan couple who'd
lived in Marseilles, and the pictures around the walls
were painted by Quimet himself, apparently always
when drunk. The current management is upholding
tradition by continuing to play exclusively French
music and serving pastís and absinthe.

Bar Ra

*Plaça de la Gardunya 3 (93 423 18 78). Metro
Liceu/14, 38, 59, N9, N12 bus.* **Open** 1.30-4pm,
9pm-midnight Mon-Sat. **Credit** AmEx, DC, MC, V.
Map p342 A2.

Eat, Drink, Shop

A better name couldn't have been chosen for this happening bar in the square behind the Boqueria market. Ra was the sun god, and sun is what this large terrace receives year-round (large, colourful umbrellas provide shade in summer). Foreigners craving something more than the standard croissant for breakfast will be delighted by the bacon, eggs, toast, juice, muesli, yoghurt and oatmeal on offer. Lunch and dinner ranges from Mexican to Thai to West Indian fare, served to the beat of drum 'n' bass, ambient, jazz or whatever suits the prevailing mood.

Bar 68/The Kitchen BCN

C/Sant Pau 68 (93 441 31 15). Metro Paral.lel/20, 24, 57, 64, 91, 157, N0, N6 bus. **Open** *Bar* 8pm-2am Tue-Thur; 8pm-3am Fri, Sat. *Restaurant* 9pm-midnight Tue-Sat. **No credit cards. Map** p340 C6.
The charm of this candelit place comes from its stripped-down style, and its emulation of a clandestine after-hours bar. A row of glowing orange lamps made from recycled water bottles hangs over the bar, there are slide projections on the wall and a DJ plays mellow modern music. They also serve dinner (perhaps the reason the bar has two names).

Casa Almirall

C/Joaquín Costa 33 (no phone). Metro Universitat/bus all routes to Plaça Universitat. **Open** 7pm-2.30am Mon-Thur; 7pm-3am Fri, Sat. **No credit cards. Map** p340 C5.

Opened in 1860, the Almirall is the oldest continuously functioning bar in the city. It still has its elegant early (and charmingly unkempt) *Modernista* woodwork. Iron beams supporting the original wooden crossbeams are the result of city-enforced renovations; the big soft sofas have been allowed to stay.

La Confitería

C/Sant Pau 128 (93 443 04 58). Metro Paral.lel/20, 57, 64, 91,157, N6 bus. **Open** 6pm-3am Mon-Sat; 6pm-2am Sun. **No credit cards. Map** p340 C6.
A friendly hangout, charmingly done up with old chandeliers, *Modernista* wood panelling and murals of rural scenes dating from the 1920s. It's a popular bar attracting a wide cross-section of people.

Granja M Viader

C/Xuclà 4-6 (93 318 34 86). Metro Liceu or Catalunya/14, 38, 59, 91, N9, N12 bus. **Open** 5-8.45pm Mon; 9am-1.45pm, 5-8.45pm Tue-Sat. Closed 1wk Aug. **Credit** MC, V. **Map** p342 A2.
The council-awarded pavement plaque outside commemorates this establishment's 130-plus years of service as a *granja* (literally, farm): a café that specialises in dairy products and such things as *suizos* (thick hot chocolate topped with whipped cream). You can sample *mel i mató* (curd cheese with honey) at one of the marble-topped tables, while sitting with the mainly elderly locals, or take away some local honey, cheese, meat or chocolate.

Café culture

Feeling neglected or disdained by your waitress? Don't take it personally, she's not against you because you are a tourist; she's just doing her job well. In Spain, a professional waiter or waitress is quick and efficient, but not necessarily personable, and there simply isn't anything to compare with Anglo-Saxon verbal acrobatics – all that hi-how-are-you-today-what-would-you-like waste of words and time. A typical greeting is '¿Que quiéres?' (What do you want?), '¿Que?' or even just a raised eyebrow. You're free to answer by simply saying what you want: '*Una cerveza*', or '*Una copa de vino, por favor.*'

Equally liberating is the practice of tossing your napkin on to the floor. Why this is acceptable is a mystery, but might have something to do with the fact that a 'napkin' is often nothing more than a tiny slip of non-absorbent tissue paper, necessitating the use of over 20 just to get through a small plate of *patatas bravas*. It's probably safe to assume that if you're in the kind of bar that uses 'napkins', you're in the kind of bar where napkins can be balled up and thrown on to the floor – along with cigarettes.

Not everyone is indifferent to this habit ('Once the floor is full, please use the ashtrays,' reads a sign at the Black Horse Pub), so it's not always a good idea to do as the locals do.

The tiny, brightly lit bars that abound in Barcelona are surprising to visitors, not only for their sheer number, but for their complete lack of aesthetic considerations. Fluorescent tube lighting and a cold metal bar is the norm. So, if you're looking for a traditional tapas bar, don't be disappointed if you're directed to a place that seems to look more like an office than a place for a friendly beer – you're probably in a bar that is just as traditional as a rustic, old *bodega*.

Be warned that the bill almost never magically appears on your table: when you are ready to leave, you will have to hunt down the waiter and let him know you would like the bill ('*la cuenta, por favor*'). Again, this is an example of professional service. A visitor may feel forgotten, but the message behind this civilised custom is, 'stay as long as you wish'. In some outdoor cafés, you may be asked to pay when your drink arrives, but this is the exception rather than the rule.

Bar Hivernacle: no stone-throwing.

Horiginal

C/Ferlandina 29 (93 443 39 98). Metro Sant Antoni/20, 24, 38, 41, 55, 64, 141 bus. **Open** 8.30pm-2.30am Mon-Thur; 8.30pm-3am Fri, Sat. **Credit** MC, V. **Map** p340 C5.

A colourful new café by the MACBA, Horiginal is warm and relaxed, with shelves of poetry (all for sale), monthly art exhibitions, an excellent mix of music (jazz, flamenco and more) and clients ranging from laid-back locals to book-reading travellers. The tables outside offer a great view of the museum and the square, and there's a good Mediterranean menu at lunchtime. On Thursday and Friday nights at 10pm, poetry readings and small concerts are held.

Hooka Lounge

C/Cera 23 (93 443 04 34). Metro Sant Antoni/20, 24, 57, 64, 91, 157, N0, N6 bus. **Open** 5pm-3am daily. **No credit cards**. **Map** p340 C6.

In true caterpillar-on-a-mushroom fashion, you can sample hookah pipes filled with apple-flavoured tobacco (or your own smokable mix), while chilling out to ambient, drum 'n' bass, house, dub, trance or bossa beat, spun by a different DJ every night. This bar doesn't share owners with New York's Hooka Lounge, but does on occasion enjoy the company of some of the same DJs. The back room serves dinner.

Iposa Bar

C/Floristes de la Rambla 14 (93 318 60 86/ www.bariposa.com). Metro Liceu/14, 38, 59, N9, N12 bus. **Open** 1pm-3am Mon-Sat. **Credit** MC, V. **Map** p342 A2.

Iposa is fresh, cool and colourful. Art photos are projected on to a huge burlap screen on a back wall, and the house DJ might play anything from Cuban rhythms to ambient and house. Excellent meals are served at both lunch and dinner, along with yummy homemade tapas. There are also tables outside on a pleasant, leafy square.

London Bar

C/Nou de la Rambla 34 (93 318 52 61). Metro Liceu/14, 38, 59, N9, N12 bus. **Open** 7.30pm-4.30am Tue-Thur, Sun; 7pm-5am Fri, Sat. Closed 2wks end Aug. **Credit** MC, V. **Map** p327 A3.

The London Bar hasn't changed its extravagant look (nothing like an English pub) since it was

opened in 1910. It's popular among young resident ex-pats and a mixed bunch of party-going Barcelonans. There are regular live gigs, for which there's no entrance fee, but note that drink prices do go up accordingly.

Marsella

C/Sant Pau 65 (93 442 72 63). Metro Liceu/14, 38, 59, N9, N12 bus. **Open** 10pm-2am Mon-Thur; 10pm-3am Fri, Sat. **No credit cards**. **Map** p340 C6.

A well-loved bar that's been in the same family for five generations. It's said that Jean Genet, among other notorious artists and petty thieves, used to come here – attracted, no doubt, by the locally made absinthe, which is still stocked. Dusty, untapped 100-year-old bottles sit in tall glass cabinets, old mirrors line the walls, and assorted chandeliers loom over the cheerful, largely foreign crowd.

Muebles Navarro

C/Riera Alta 4-6 (no phone). Metro Sant Antoni/20, 24, 38, 64, N6 bus. **Open** 6pm-midnight Tue-Thur, Sun; 6pm-3am Fri, Sat. **No credit cards**. **Map** p340 C6.

There's more room in this café (a former furniture shop, as the name implies), than its owners know what to do with, so they've stuffed it with mismatched old chairs, sofas and dim lamps. The result is a funky space, with plenty of comfortable places to lean back and enjoy some of the best New York cheesecake this side of the Atlantic.

Sant Pere, La Ribera & Born

Bar Hivernacle

Parc de la Ciutadella (93 295 40 17). Metro Arc de Triomf/39, 40, 41, 42, 51, 141 bus. **Open** 10am-1am daily. **Credit** AmEx, DC, MC, V. **Map** p341 E6.

An elegant and luminous bar inside the beautiful iron-and-glass *hivernacle* (greenhouse) of the Parc de la Ciutadella, built in 1884. With three parts (one shaded room, one unshaded and a terrace), Bar Hivernacle hosts exhibitions and occasional jazz and classical concerts. As well as the plants around the bar, there's a fine display of tropical greenery in one of the rooms alongside.

The Black Horse Pub

Avda Allada Vermell 16 (93 268 33 38). Metro Jaume I/17, 19, 40, 45 bus. **Open** 11am-2.30am daily. **Credit** MC, V. **Map** p327 C3.

Three TVs and a satellite link-up in this welcoming English pub keep football junkies supplied with a steady fix of UK and Spanish league matches. There's also a pub quiz, in English and Spanish, on Sunday evenings.

Café del Born

Plaça Comercial 10 (93 268 32 72). Metro Jaume I/14, 39, 51 bus. **Open** 9am-1am Mon-Wed, Sun; 9am-3am Thur-Sat. **Credit** MC, V. **Map** p327 C3.

An airy café opposite the old Born market, with an interesting food selection (including great desserts), papers to read and the odd exhibition from local

Cafés & Bars

Eat, Drink, Shop

Born Market, with an interesting food selection.

Time Out Barcelona Guide **177**

artists. It's under new management and now has flamenco acts on Mondays, and jazz on Tuesdays. There are also tables outside.

La Estrella de Plata
Pla del Palau 9 (93 319 60 07). Metro Barceloneta/ 14, 36, 57, 59, 64, 157, N0, N6 bus. **Open** 1-4pm, 8pm-midnight Mon-Sat. **No credit cards.** **Map** p327 C4.
To meet increasing demand, this tapas bar has recently opened a new branch, just a few doors away at No.13. The narrow bar at No.9 used to be a hangout for workers from the port, but now caters mostly to a more genteel crowd. No.13 also has a few tables and a reservations-only back room. On offer at both are very good (and expensive) 'designer' tapas, such as foie gras simmered in port wine, along with an ample selection of seafood.

Euskal Extea
Placeta Montcada 1-3 (93 310 21 85). Metro Jaume I/ 17, 19, 40, 45, N8 bus. **Open** *Bar* 9am-11.30pm Tue-Sat; 12.45-3.30pm Sun. *Restaurant* 1-3.30pm, 9-11.30pm Tue-Sat. Closed Aug. **Credit** MC, V. **Map** p327 C3.
Catalonia may not be famous for tapas, but the Basque Country certainly is, and this bar has the best Basque tapas in Barcelona: a mouth-watering array of small *pintxos* (from chunks of tuna and pickles to deep-fried crab claws and complicated mixed tapas). They make a grand entrance at midday and at 7pm; get there early for the best selection, and be prepared to stand. There's also a full restaurant with a Basque menu.

La Idea
Plaça Comercial 2 (93 268 87 87/www.ideaborn. com). Metro Jaume I/14, 39, 51 bus. **Open** 8am-1am Mon-Thur; 8am-3am Fri; 10am-3am Sat; 10am-11pm Sun. **No credit cards.** **Map** p327 C3.
Spacious and with a comfortable, sitting-room feel, La Idea has a small, eclectic selection of books for sale, more than a dozen international newspapers and plenty of computers located downstairs (€1.20 per half-hour). In the main room, a massive floor-to-ceiling canvas bears the UN Universal Declaration of Human Rights, and the café often has exhibitions focusing on human rights issues.

Mudanzas
C/Vidrieria 15 (93 319 11 37). Metro Jaume I/ 17, 19, 40, 45 bus. **Open** 10am-2.30am daily. **Credit** MC, V. **Map** p327 C3.
Few of the many cafés and bars surrounding the increasingly trendy Born area manage to capture the relaxed ambience of this bar, with its chequered tiled floor and marble-topped tables. There's a rack of newspapers and magazines, many in English, and some tables outside.

El Nus
C/Mirallers 5 (93 319 53 55). Metro Jaume I/ 17, 19, 40, 45 bus. **Open** 7.30pm-2.30am Mon, Tue, Thur-Sun. **No credit cards.** **Map** p327 C3.

Coming round to **La Idea**?

White lace curtains, stone walls, dusty chandeliers, wood and the liberal use of red paint make this a charming place to enjoy a quiet drink, while low-key jazz plays in the background. The sage-looking gent pondering the crowd from a large black and white photo fixed to the ceiling is the bar's original owner.

Over the Game
C/Fusina 7 (93 268 10 80). Metro Jaume I/17, 19, 40, 45 bus. **Open** 9.30am-3am daily. **Credit** MC, V. **Map** p327 C3.
This Internet bar/café next to the Born market is in a category all its own. Orange lights peep out from beneath the glass surface of the computer tables, and electric blue accents overhead give everyone a bloodless, *Matrix*-chic look. Bulky grey tubes dangling from the ceiling like futuristic umbilical cords are connected to the dozens of computers, and music is pumped through the sound system day and night.

Palau Dalmases
C/Montcada 20 (93 310 06 73). Metro Jaume I/ 17, 19, 40, 45, N8 bus. **Open** 8pm-2am Tue-Sat; 6-10pm Sun. **Credit** MC, V. **Map** p327 C3.
An elderly gentleman greets customers at the door of this 17th-century residence, and ushers them through the courtyard to the 'Espai Barroc'. The walls are adorned with paintings, there is ornate furniture, and spectacular displays of flowers, fruit and aromatic herbs give it the look of an Italian still life. Suitably baroque music, occasionally live, plays in the background. It's deeply eccentric, decadent and a tad pretentious, but soothing to ear, nose and eye – and worth the elevated prices.

Têxtil Cafè
C/Montcada 12-14 (93 268 25 98). Metro Jaume I/ 17, 19, 40, 45, N8 bus. **Open** 10am-midnight Tue-Sun. **Credit** MC, V. **Map** p327 C3.
With tables in the tranquil courtyard of the 14th-century Palau dels Marquesos de Lió – now home to the Museu Têxtil and Museu Barbier-Mueller – this café is popular with visitors and locals, and is a great place to stop while sightseeing.

La Tinaja
C/Esparteria 9 (93 310 22 50). Metro Jaume I/ 14, 17, 39, 40, 45, 51, 100 bus. **Open** 6pm-2am Mon-Sat. **Credit** AmEx, DC, MC, V. **Map** p327 C4.
A rustic place with soft candlelight and high arched ceilings, this romantic locale was once the ground

floor (probably the stables) of a 17th-century palace. It serves a wide variety of Spanish wine, cheese and ham. No two tables are the same, and the ornately carved bar was made from panelled artwork found in the palace chapel.

La Vinya del Senyor

Plaça Santa Maria 5 (93 310 33 79). Metro Jaume I/ 17, 19, 40, 45, N8 bus. **Open** noon-1.30am Tue-Sat; noon-4pm Sun. **Credit** DC, MC, V. **Map** p327 C4.

An elegant little wine-taster's bar with an outdoor, front-row view of the glorious façade of Santa Maria del Mar. With a superb list of more than 300 wines and selected cavas, sherries and *moscatells*, changed every 15 days, the Iberian ham and French cheese come in very handy for their qualities of absorption.

El Xampanyet

C/Montcada 22 (93 319 70 03). Metro Jaume I/ 17, 19, 40, 45, N8 bus. **Open** noon-4pm, 6.30-11.30pm Tue-Sat; noon-4pm Sun. Closed Aug. **Credit** MC, V. **Map** p327 C3.

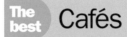

The best Cafés

For a shady patio

Cafè d'Estiu (*see p169*), **Bar Hivernacle** (*see p177*) and **Têxtil Cafè** (*see p178*).

For breakfast

The Bagel Shop (*see p167*), **Bar Ra** (*see p175*), **Escribà** (*see p169*) and **Les Tapes** (*see p175*).

For spit and sawdust

Bar Celta (*see p167*), **Can Paixano** (*see p179*), **Casa Quimet** (*see p181*) and **Bar Tomás** (*see p182*).

For coffee and a read

Bliss (*see p167*), **Laie Llibreria Cafè** (*see p181*) and **Nostromo** (*see p171*).

For chilling

Hooka Lounge (*see p177*), **Les Gens Que J'Aime** (*see p180*) and **Leticia** (*see p171*).

For surfing the net

La Idea (*see p178*), **Over the Game** (*see p178*) and **Travel Bar** (*see p175*).

For people-watching

Café Zurich (*see p169*), **Glaciar** (*see p169*), **Horiginal** (*see p177*) and **Schilling** (*see p172*).

For city-watching

Mirablau (*see p182*).

Run by the same family since the 1930s, this 'little champagne bar', is one of the eternal attractions on this ancient street. It's lined with coloured tiles, barrels and antique curios, and there are a few marble tables. El Xampanyet has three specialities: anchovies, fresh cider and 'champagne' (a pretty plain cava, if truth be told, but very refreshing), served by the glass or bottle.

Port Vell & Barceloneta

Can Paixano

C/Reina Cristina 7 (93 310 08 39). Metro Barceloneta/14, 36, 69, 51, 57, 59, 64, 157 bus. **Open** 9am-10.30pm Mon-Sat. **No credit cards.** **Map** p327 C4.

Do yourself a favour and leave your inhibitions at the door of Can Paixano. You'll need to master the art of elbowing and sidling at this standing-room only *bodega* – some of whose most ardent fans don't even know its real name, as it's known popularly as the 'champagne bar'. Indeed, the cava flows liberally at all hours, accompanied by dirt-cheap toasted *bocadillos*.

Jai-ca

C/Ginebra 13 (93 319 50 02). Metro Barceloneta/ 17, 39, 45, 57, 59, 67, 157, N8 bus. **Open** 10am-midnight daily. **Credit** MC, V. **Map** p341 E7.

The jumble of tables in the tight space inside this no-nonsense tapas bar spills out on to a pleasant, shaded terrace. Its location on the corner of two quiet streets, the fresh breeze wafting through, the informality and the permanently stopped clock all conspire to make for a laze-inducing atmosphere – a perfect pre- or post-beach stop off.

Luz de Gas – Port Vell

Opposite the Palau de Mar (93 209 77 11/ www.luzdegas.com). Metro Barceloneta or Jaume I/ 14, 36, 57, 59, 54, 157, N6 bus. **Open** Mar-Oct noon-3am Mon-Fri; 11am-3am Sun. Closed Nov-Feb. **Credit** AmEx, MC, V. **Map** p340 D7.

Run by the same people who run the Luz de Gas music hall (*see p244*), this floating bar is docked in the Port Vell alongside a promenade buzzing with strollers, cyclers and rollerbladers. Catch some sun over a cold drink on the upper deck, or rest in the shade on the lower. With nightfall, candles are brought out, wine is uncorked and the scene is bestowed with an air of romance.

El Vaso de Oro

C/Balboa 6 (93 319 30 98). Metro Barceloneta/ 17, 39, 45, 57, 59, 64, 157, N8 bus. **Open** 9am-midnight daily. Closed Sept. **No credit cards.** **Map** p341 E7.

So narrow that patrons find themselves having to go out one door and in at another just to get to the toilet, this bar has a wide selection of tapas and a jovial atmosphere (read 'loud'). No, they aren't German, they're just particularly fond of steins and will serve your draught beer in one of them.

Vila Olímpica – Port Olímpic

Port Olímpic has a line of bars with little to choose between them, if go-go dancers and the latest cheesy hits are your thing. However, there is one place worth singling out.

Café & Café
Moll del Mestral 30 (93 221 00 19). Metro Ciutadella-Vila Olímpica/36, 41, 71, 91, 100, N6, N8 bus. **Open** 3pm-3am Mon-Thur; 4pm-5am Fri, Sat; noon-3am Sun. **Credit** AmEx, DC, MC, V. **Map** p341 F7.
An oasis of calm on this noisy strip, this café-cum-cocktail bar has a mind-boggling range of coffees, often lethally combined with alcohol.

Poble Sec

Bar Primavera
C/Nou de la Rambla 192 (93 329 30 62). Metro Paral.lel/20, 36, 57, 64, 157, N6 bus. **Open** May-Oct 8am-10pm Tue-Sun. *Nov-Apr* 8am-5pm Tue-Sun. **No credit cards**. **Map** p339 B6.
Halfway up Montjuïc, this peaceful outdoor bar/café feels well away from the urban activity bubbling below. The bar is a humble affair, with tables in a leafy garden and grapevines providing shade. Rudimentary *bocadillos* and snacks are available.

Cervecería Jazz
C/Margarit 43 (93 443 32 59). Metro Paral.lel/20, 57, 64, 157, N0, N16 bus. **Open** 7pm-3am Mon-Sat. **No credit cards**. **Map** p339 B6.
German and Belgian beers, a long wooden bar and a rustic-meets-baroque interior make this one of the area's more original bars. The earthenware jug on the bar holds olives and pickles, and very good sandwiches are served. The music (mixed jazz, mainly) is never so loud as to inhibit conversation.

Quimet i Quimet
C/Poeta Cabanyes 25 (93 442 31 42). Metro Paral.lel/20, 57, 64, 157, N0, N16 bus. **Open** 7pm-3am Mon-Sat. **No credit cards**. **Map** p339 B6.
The most is made of limited space in this popular *bodega*: shelves reaching the ceiling are stocked to overflowing with wine, beer, liqueur and cava, ranging from bargain-basement to the stuff of a connoisseur's dreams. There are only three tables and nowhere to sit, and it can get overwhelmingly crowded thanks to a good selection of tapas.

Eixample

La Barcelonina de Vins i Esperits
C/Valencia 304 (93 215 70 83). Metro Passeig de Gràcia/22, 24, 28, 43, 44, N6, N7 bus. **Open** 6pm-2am Mon-Fri; 7.30pm-2am Fri, Sat. **Credit** MC, V. **Map** p337 E4.
A wine- and champagne-lover's heaven. To the left is a wall displaying the many varieties of wine available. To the right is a bar, where you will be served

Can Paixano: cava and crowds. *See p179.*

post-haste. Straight ahead, tables and, yet more important as the night wears on, chairs. There is also a selection of assorted meats and cheeses.

La Bodegueta
Rambla de Catalunya 100 (93 215 48 94). Metro Diagonal/FGC Provença/7, 16, 17, 20, 31, 43, 44, 67, 68, N7 bus. **Open** 8am-2am Mon-Sat; 6.30pm-1am Sun. **No credit cards**. **Map** p336 D4.
Many of the elderly folk frequenting this little cellar bar have been coming here since their youth. A recent renovation has tidied it up a bit, while leaving the original rose petal tiles and old charm. It's especially crowded around lunch, with more suits and ties than overalls these days; just one more sign of the Eixample's upward march.

Cervecería Catalana
C/Mallorca 236 (93 216 0368). Metro Passeig de Gràcia/22, 24, 28, N4, N6 bus. **Open** 7.30pm-1.30am Mon-Fri; 9pm-1.30am Sat, Sun. **Credit** AmEx, DC, MC, V. **Map** p336 D4.
A professional, slightly upmarket treatment of the traditional tapas bar – perfect for those looking for the tapas experience but who aren't sure they're really ready for sawdust on the floor. They offer a fantastic selection of tapas at mid-range prices.

Les Gens Que J'Aime
C/Valencia 286 (93 215 68 79). Metro Passeig de Gràcia/22, 24, 28, N4, N6 bus. **Open** 7pm-3am Mon-Sat; 7pm-2.30am Sun. **No credit cards**. **Map** p336 D4.
Ageing, red velvet sofas and antique lamps casting the dimmest light possible make the patrons look mysterious and bohemian – an optical illusion only, for this beautiful bar's location means its clientele

are largely middle-class locals. Still, it's a great place for a quiet drink and, in keeping with the bohemian theme, a tarot card reader holds court.

La Gran Bodega

C/Valencia 193 (93 453 10 53). Metro Universitat or Passeig de Gràcia/20, 43, 44, 54, 58, 63, 64, 66, 67, 68, N3, N7, N8 bus. **Open** 11am-1am Tue-Sun. **Credit** MC, V. **Map** p336 C4.

'If the sea were wine, we should all be sailors,' proclaims one of the many colourful tiles lining this tapas bar. The walls are also filled with weathered photos of the original owner with sundry famous personalities (Muhammed Ali and Sean Connery, among others). This is a fun first stop for students and office workers before a night out.

Jabugo

C/Enric Granados 6 (93 451 19 28). Metro Universitat/bus all routes to Plaça Universitat. **Open** 8.30am-1.30am Mon-Thur; 8.30am-2am Fri, Sat. **Credit** AmEx, DC, MC, V. **Map** p336 C4.

This little bar specialises in ham and is named after a particularly prized variety from acorn-fed pigs. There are outdoor tables where you can enjoy a cold beer over a plate of, well, ham from one of the legs above the bar. Ham consumption, however, is not obligatory and vegetarians will not be penalised.

Laie Libreria Cafè

C/Pau Claris 85 (93 302 73 10). Metro Urquinaona/ 22, 28, 39, 41, 45, 55, 141, N1, N2, N4, N8 bus. **Open** *Café* 9am-1am Mon-Fri; 10am-1am Sat. *Bookshop* 10.30am-9pm Mon-Sat. **Credit** AmEx, DC, MC, V. **Map** p342 B1.

Bookshop-cafés are a godsend for bookworms, for there's nothing like buying a book and sitting down to read it right away. This one is a gem, with its rich tones, old tiles and great cakes and coffee. There are tables on a covered patio, and live jazz some nights.

Stinger

C/Còrsega 338 (93 217 71 87). Metro Diagonal/ 6, 15, 22, 24, 28, 33, 34, N4 bus. **Open** 6.30pm-3am Mon-Thur; 6.30pm-3.30am Fri, Sat. **Credit** MC, V. **Map** p336 D4.

Jai-ca: tapas and a terrace. *See p179.*

This cocktail bar treads a line somewhere between romantic and serious. In the downstairs area only, presided over by a huge oval-shaped lamp with leaf-like iron edges and a hundred amber eyes, salads and *torrades* (large slabs of toast with various toppings) are served along with the fabulous cocktails.

Valor Chocolatería

Rambla Catalunya 46 (93 487 62 46). Metro Passeig de Gràcia/7, 16, 17, 22, 24, 28 bus. **Open** 8.30am-12.30pm, 4.30-11pm Mon-Fri; 9am-1am Sat, Sun. **No credit cards. Map** p336 D4.

This spacious, cheerful café is designed to resemble an old ice-cream parlour: mission accomplished. There is an ample terrace and, naturally, a selection of homemade chocolate to take away in little boxes

Gràcia

Adarra

C/Torrent de l'Olla 148 (93 218 9237). Metro Fontana/22, 24, 28, 39, N4 bus. **Open** 6pm-12.30am Mon-Thur; 6pm-1.30am Fri-Sun. **Credit** MC, V. **Map** p336 D3.

Chunky wooden tables and stools and a bar heavy with platters of bite-size delicacies on tiny slices of bread mean you're in a Basque bar. Aside from the vast array of *pintxos*, they also prepare some mouth-watering *cazuelitos* (small earthenware dishes filled with anything from clams to cod to freshwater crayfish, all prepared with traditional sauces). Yum.

Bodega Manolo

C/Torrent de les Flors 101 (93 284 43 77). Metro Joanic/39, 55, N6 bus. **Open** 12.30-4.30pm, 8pm-12.30am Tue-Sat; 12.30am-4.30pm Sun. Closed Aug. **No credit cards. Map** p337 E3.

Don't be alarmed. The dusty paint curlicues hanging from the ceiling could only be classified as unhygienic if one actually fell into your foie gras with port and apple. The atmosphere, classifiable as grim if you're peeking in from the street, is actually friendly and comfortable once inside, and those old barrels lining the walls really are filled with wine. Dinner is served 9-11.30pm Thur-Sat.

Casa Quimet

Rambla de Prat 9 (93 217 53 27). Metro Fontana/ 22, 24, 28, N4 bus. **Open** 6.30pm-2am Tue-Sun. Closed Feb, Aug. **No credit cards. Map** p336 D3.

Known locally as the 'guitar bar', Casa Quimet has more than 200 guitars lining the walls and ceiling; you're welcome to grab one and join in the noisy jamming session. From the myriad faded black-and-white photographs to the somewhat gloomy greenness of this down-and-out bar, there is not a single polished element here, so come as you are. It's open on Mondays if it's a public holiday.

Flash Flash

C/La Granada del Penedès 25 (93 237 09 90). FGC Gràcia/16, 17, 22, 24, 27, 28, 31, 32 N4 bus. **Open** 1pm-1.30am daily. **Credit** AmEx, DC, MC, V. **Map** p336 D3.

Make some friends at **Virreina Bar**.

Flash back to the swinging '60s with white leatherette banquettes, walls lined with monochrome life-size photos of a frolicking, Twiggyesque model and a kitsch fest on the stereo. Opened in 1970, this bar was a design sensation in its day and the owners never saw the need to change with the times. Decades passed and – what do you know! – it's suddenly hip again. They call it a *tortilleria*, and they mean it, with more than 50 variations on the theme, including a handful of dessert tortillas.

Gasterea

C/Verdi 39 (93 237 23 43). Metro Fontana/ 22, 24, 28, 39, N4 bus. **Open** 7.30pm-1am Mon, Tue, Thur, Sun; noon-3am Fri, Sat. **No credit cards. Map** p337 D3.
This looks like any one of a dozen other friendly bars in the area. But second glance reveals above-average *pintxos* and even homemade chocolate truffles, properly tooth-picked. Unlike other hands-on Basque bars, they will serve the goods for you. Don't lose your coaster – the bill is tabulated on the back.

Salambó

C/Torrijos 51 (93 218 69 66). Metro Joanic/39 bus. **Open** noon-2.30am daily. **Credit** V. **Map** p337 E3.
This elegant two-storey café opened in 1992, but deliberately echoes the large literary cafés of the 1930s, with plenty of seating, billiard tables and an unusual selection of fragrant teas, sandwiches and salads. It's extremely popular, especially with the crowds from the Verdi cinemas.

Sol Soler

Plaça del Sol 21 (93 217 44 40). Metro Fontana/ 22, 24, 28, N4 bus. **Open** *May-Sept* noon-2am Mon-Thur, Sun; noon-3am Fri, Sat. *Oct-Apr* 4pm-2am Mon-Wed; 3pm-2am Thur; 2pm-3am Fri; noon-3am Sat; noon-2am Sun. **No credit cards. Map** p336 D3.

Whimsical old *Modernista* tiles, wood-lined walls and intimate lighting are just part of the appeal of this bar in Plaça del Sol, one of Gràcia's most lively squares. There is also an inventive selection of non-traditional tapas: tabouleh, guacamole or feta and tomato salads, for example.

Sureny

Plaça Revolució 17 (93 213 75 56). Metro Joanic/ 39, 55, N6 bus. **Open** 8pm-1.30am Tue-Sun. **No credit cards. Map** p336-7 D3.
It's not just the cosiness, but the list of addictive tapas that sets Sureny apart from the rest. The cod-based *esqueixada* topped with an olive and caper purée is exquisite. Also, this might be the only place in town that serves the simple dessert to which Catalan country grandmothers treat their grand-children: bread with cinnamon, sugar and red wine.

Virreina Bar

Plaça de la Virreina 1 (93 237 98 80). Metro Fontana/21, 39, N4 bus. **Open** 10am-2.30am Mon-Sat; 10am-midnight Sun. **No credit cards. Map** p337 E3.
In a human-sized Gràcia square is this friendly meeting place, which serves imported beers as well as good *bocadillos* and sandwiches.

Zona Alta

Bar Tomás

C/Major de Sarriá 49 (93 203 10 77). FGC Sarriá/ 22, 33, 64, 66, 75 bus. **Open** 7.45am-10pm Mon, Tue, Thur-Sun. **No credit cards. Map** p335 B1.
This is a typical neighbourhood, sawdust-on-the-floor bar, where the TV is always on and fluorescent tube lighting makes everyone look like crap. But the one thing that keeps those in the know (and this seems to be just about everyone) coming back are the famed *patatas bravas*. A heaped little plate will cost little more than a euro, and you can also get them to go. Be advised: they take the garlic part of the *all i oli* equation very seriously.

Gimlet

C/Santaló 46 (93 201 53 06). FGC Muntaner/ 14, 27, 32 bus. **Open** 7pm-3am daily. **Credit** MC, V. **Map** p336 C3.
With its black bar, red stools and predominance of straight lines, there's something very '80s about this friendly bar. Despite this, it's never really gone out of style for those looking for a well-mixed cocktail.

Mirablau

Plaça Doctor Andreu (93 418 58 79). FGC Av Tibidabo/17, 22, 58, 73, 75, 85, 101 bus, then Tramvia Blau. **Open** 11am-4.30am Mon-Thur, Sun; 11am-5am Fri, Sat. **Credit** MC, V.
By day or night, the best views of the city are to be had from this bar at the end of the tramline to Tibidabo. There is a cool garden terrace outside, while, inside, a row of stools lined up along the floor-to-ceiling windows provides a privileged vantage point of Barcelona below and, beyond, the sea.

Shops & Services

Barcelona's wide range of shops – from retail giants to family-run speciality shops – makes it hard to leave the city empty-handed.

Thanks to local talent and a flood of tourists willing to part with their hard-earned euros, Barcelona has become a shopping mecca. New shops are rising like *magdalenas*, and the city's quirky, old-world boutiques and markets are struggling to survive alongside glitzy new shopping malls and chainstores. Barcelona's shops are concentrated in the Eixample and the Old City, particularly Barri Gòtic and La Ribera and the Born. Whether on the hunt for local delicacies or the season's coolest shoes, shoppers will discover that these areas have a distinct personality. Home design and stylish, smart fashions are the buzz in the Eixample, where stores line Rambla de Catalunya and Passeig de Gràcia (dubbed 'Fifth Avenue' by locals). Top designers and big-name brands are also crowded along Diagonal. But for one-of-a-kind purchases, no destination beats the Old City, whose narrow streets are dotted with antique shops,

unusual boutiques, artisan workshops and the latest street fashions. Barcelona has some delightful, ancient shops; those that are over 60 years old and that preserve their architectural heritage have special brass pavement plaques awarded by the Ajuntament.

Note that if you're paying by credit card, you will usually have to show photographic ID, such as a passport or driving licence.

OPENING HOURS

Sunday and holiday opening hours have traditionally been closely regulated. However, new legislation passed in June 2001 somewhat liberalised opening times. Small shops (under 300 square metres/1,076 square feet in size) that are not part of a chain can now open throughout the day, seven days a week. 'Large spaces' – big stores and malls – are allowed to stay open for a total of 90 hours a week from Monday to Saturday, and on eight Sundays a year,

Fans of colourful kitsch will feel at home at **D Barcelona**. *See p189.*

Eat, Drink, Shop

including all four Sundays prior to Christmas (special conditions apply to Maremàgnum, which is open every day). Most smaller shops close for lunch on weekdays, and a diminishing number only open in the morning on Saturdays.

SALES AND TAX REFUNDS

Sales usually run from the second week in January to the end of February, and during July and August. The rate of sales tax (IVA) depends on the type of product: it's currently seven per cent on food, 16 per cent on most other items. Return policies vary from shop to shop. Ask before you buy.

In many shops, non-EU residents can request a Tax-Free Cheque on purchases over €90, which can be cashed at Customs when leaving Spain to reclaim tax. Participating shops have a 'Tax-Free Shopping' sticker on their doors.

GETTING AROUND

A special shopping bus service called TombBus (93 415 60 20 – a spooky-sounding name that actually means 'round-trip bus') runs regularly between Plaça de Catalunya (in front of Banc d'Espanya or El Corte Inglés) and Plaça Pius XII on Diagonal. The blue buses make 28 stops along the way, and a single ticket costs €1.15. Buses operate from 7.30am to 9.30pm on weekdays, and from 9.30am to 9.30pm on Saturdays. They run every six minutes, except during lunch (2.45pm-4pm) when they run every ten minutes.

One-stop shopping

Barcelona Glòries

Avda Diagonal 208, Eixample (93 486 04 04). Metro Glòries/7, 56, 60, 92 bus. **Open** *Shops* 10am-10pm Mon-Sat.
This huge, drive-in shopping centre with more than 200 shops is located by the Plaça de les Glòries, near Els Encants. It's built around an open-air *plaça* with bars, restaurants and a multiplex cinema.

Bulevard Rosa

Passeig de Gràcia 55, Eixample (93 309 06 50/ www.bulevardrosa.com). Metro Passeig de Gràcia/ 7, 16, 17, 22, 24, 28 bus. **Open** 10.30am-8.30pm Mon-Sat. **Credit** AmEx, DC, MC, V. **Map** p336 D4.
This arcade opened in the 1980s amid the *galeria* boom and is still one of the most popular places for browsing for men's and women's fashions. Among the 120 shops are some of Barcelona's most innovative designers of clothing, shoes and jewellery.

El Corte Inglés

Plaça Catalunya 14, Eixample (93 306 38 00/ www.elcorteingles.es). Metro Plaça Catalunya/ bus all routes to Plaça Catalunya. **Open** 10am-10pm Mon-Sat. **Credit** AmEx, DC, MC, V. **Map** p342 B1.

El Corte Inglés, founded in 1940, simply dominates retailing in Spain, and has recently expanded further by moving into competitor Marks & Spencer's store, which shut down in December 2001. As the country's only true department store, El Corte Inglés must appeal to all fashion tastes and cater to all needs, from key cutting and beauty treatments to shoe repair. To prove its motto *'hay de todo'* ('there's everything'), it even sells insurance and has its own travel agency. The Plaça Catalunya branch has nine floors of merchandise, plus a supermarket in the basement and a rooftop café with a splendid view. The Portal de l'Àngel branch is a leisure megastore specialising in music, electronics, books and sporting goods. If there is anything that you can't find in the main stores (and you have a car), the company also has two giant Hipercor hypermarkets.
Branches: El Corte Inglés Avda Diagonal 471-473, Eixample (93 419 20 20); Avda Diagonal 617-619, Eixample (93 366 71 00); Portal de l'Àngel 19, Barri Gòtic (93 306 38 00); **Hipercor** Avda Meridiana 350-356, Sant Andreu (93 346 38 11); C/Salvador Dali 15-19, Cornella de Llobregat, Outer Limits (93 475 90 00).

L'Illa

Avda Diagonal 545-557, Eixample (93 444 00 00/ www.lilla.com). Metro Maria Cristina/6, 7, 30, 33, 34, 66, 67, 68, 78 bus. **Open** 10am-9.30pm Mon-Sat. *Supermarkets* 9.30am-9.30pm Mon-Sat. **Map** p343 B3.
Thanks to its prime location in the fashionable business area on the upper Diagonal, L'Illa attracts a more upmarket clientele than its counterparts on the city's fringes. It has trendier fashion shops, a Caprabo supermarket, a Decathlon sports shop and a FNAC.

La Maquinista

Passeig de Potosí 2, Sant Andreu (902 24 88 42). Metro Sant Andreu or Torras i Bages/11, 12, 35, 40, 42, 62, 73, 96, 173 bus. **Open** 10am-10pm Mon-Sat.
Built to breathe life into the Sant Andreu district, La Maquinista is Catalonia's largest and newest mall. The three levels of this open-air complex house 225 shops, ranging from top-rung designers (Adolfo Domínguez, Purificación García) to ready-to-wear fashions (Benetton, H&M). There's also a cinema, a bowling alley and a Carrefour hypermarket.

Maremàgnum

Moll d'Espanya, Port Vell (93 225 81 00/ www.maremagnum.es). Metro Drassanes/14, 19, 36, 38, 40, 57, 59, 64, 157 bus. **Open** 11am-11pm daily. **Map** p340 D7.
An all-round leisure complex, with restaurants, games, cinemas and nightclubs as well as shops. It's unique because of its port setting, because it was designed by two of the leading architects of the new Barcelona, Viaplana and Piñón, and because you get to it via a bridge linking it with the Rambla. For those who find normal malls claustrophobic, it's a delight, and the giant mirror-wall above the main entrance creates spectacular visual effects. Its shops, though, are mostly better for fun and souvenir shopping than for buying clothes or other things that you really want.

El Triangle

C/Pelai 39, Eixample (93 318 01 08/www.triangle.es).
Metro Catalunya/bus all routes to Plaça Catalunya.
Open 10am-10pm Mon-Sat. **Credit** MC, V.
Map p342 A1.
Dominating one side of Plaça Catalunya, the bunker-like Triangle houses a FNAC, Habitat and many small, trendy fashion shops, including Camper for shoes. But the most spectacular store is the Sephora cosmetic and perfume mega-space. For the nostalgic, El Triangle has a version of the emblematic Café Zurich in one corner (*see p169*).

Antiques

The streets around C/Palla, in the Barri Gòtic, are crowded with small, idiosyncratic antique shops. Antiques are also found around C/Consell de Cent in the Eixample, and there are some less expensive shops around C/Dos de Maig near Els Encants flea market (*see p208*). On Thursdays, an antiques market is held in front of the cathedral (*see p207*) and dealers set up stands at the Port Vell (*see p208*) at weekends.

L'Arca de l'Àvia

C/Banys Nous 20, Raval (93 302 15 98). Metro Liceu/14, 38, 59, 91 bus. **Open** 10.30am-2pm, 5-8pm Mon-Fri; 11am-2pm Sat. **Credit** MC, V. **Map** p343 B3.
The beautifully displayed antique cottons, linens and silks are not cheap, but the Spanish shawls, patchwork quilts, dresses and antique beaded bags are lovely to behold. Popular with brides looking for something special.

Bulevard dels Antiquaris

Passeig de Gràcia 55, Eixample (93 215 44 99). Metro Passeig de Gràcia/7, 16, 17, 22, 24, 28 bus. **Open** *Sept-May* 9.30am-1.30pm, 4.30-8.30pm Mon-Sat. *June-Sept* 10am-1.30pm, 4.30-8.30pm Mon-Fri. **Credit** AmEx, MC, V. **Map** p336 D4.
Beside the main Bulevard Rosa fashion mall (*see p184*), this arcade houses 73 shops selling antiques, from fine paintings to religious artefacts and estate jewellery. In Turn of the Century, you'll find miniature musical instruments from the 1930s and dolls' furniture; Trik-Trak specialises in old tin toys.

Gothsland Galeria d'Art

C/Consell de Cent 331, Eixample (93 488 19 22). Metro Passeig de Gràcia/7, 16, 17, 22, 24, 28, 63, 67, 68 bus. **Open** 10am-1.30pm, 4.30-8.30pm Mon-Sat. **Credit** AmEx, DC, MC, V. **Map** p340 D4-5.
A near-unique specialist in original Catalan *Modernista* art, furniture and decoration. Delights include a spectacular selection of fine furniture (including some pieces by Gaspar Homar), polychrome terracotta sculptures by Casanovas, Pau Gargallo and Lambert Escaler, alabaster by Cipriani, *Modernista* vases and mirrors and 19th-century paintings. It also hosts exhibitions of painting and other work from the era.

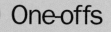

One-offs

Angel Batle
Rare books, maps, prints and nautical charts. *See p187.*

Bagués
Modernista jewellery in a building designed by Puig i Cadafalch. *See p197.*

Caelum
Artisan food products, made by Spanish monks. *See p203.*

Colmado Quilez
A fantastic food emporium with delicacies from all over the world. *See p203.*

Escribà
Exquisite pastries in a *Modernista* shop. *See p201.*

Herboristeria del Rei
A stunning, historical space stocked with herbs. *See p204.*

El Ingenio
Costumes for Carnaval, including *capgrosses*. *See p188.*

Rafael Teja
One-of-a-kind, handprinted silk scarves (*pictured*) in the textile district. *See p200.*

El Rei de la Magia
A magician's training ground. *See p209.*

Regia
A venerable perfumery, with a wonderful perfume museum in the back. *See p205.*

Eat, Drink, Shop

Urbana

C/Sèneca 13, Eixample (93 237 36 44). Metro
Diagonal/6, 7, 15, 16, 17, 33, 34 bus. **Open**
Jan-July, Sept-Dec 10am-2pm, 4.30-8pm Mon-Fri.
Aug 10am-2pm, 4.30-8pm Mon-Fri; 10am-2pm Sat.
Credit MC, V. **Map** p336 D3.
Urbana salvages architectural parts from demoli-
tions and restores them to their original splendour.
The Còrsega store is devoted to fireplaces, mirrors
and hardware, while the Sèneca location concen-
trates on furniture and doors. You might find a
marble fireplace, a *Modernista* door frame or chairs
from a demolished theatre.
Branch: C/Còrsega 258, Eixample (93 218 70 36).

Bookshops

A wide selection of books on Barcelona can
be found at the city information centre in the
Palau de la Virreina on the Rambla, as well
as at the city's main tourist office on Plaça
Catalunya. The Generalitat's Palau Robert on
Passeig de Gràcia has a selection of books on
both Barcelona and Catalonia. For all, *see p320.*
Laie Libreria Café (*see p181*) has an
imaginative arts-based stock.

Casa del Llibre

C/Passeig de Gràcia 62, Eixample (93 272 34 80/
www.casadellibro.com). Metro Passeig de Gràcia/
22, 24, 28 bus. **Open** 9.30am-9.30pm Mon-Sat.
Credit AmEx, DC, MC, V. **Map** p336 D4.
Opened in 2001, the 'House of the Book' belongs to
a Spanish chain whose website stocks more than
500,000 titles. The Barcelona shop has an extensive
collection of books on law and art and design. Also
worth browsing is the section devoted to English-
language bestsellers and literature.

FNAC

El Triangle, Plaça Catalunya 4, Eixample (93 344
18 00/www.fnac.es). Metro Plaça Catalunya/bus all
routes to Plaça Catalunya. **Open** 10am-10pm Mon-
Sat. **Credit** AmEx, MC, V. **Map** p342 A1.
This French-owned megastore chain has spread
ripples throughout the bookselling world in Spain
with its huge stocks of titles (with French and
English sections) in modern displays at discount
prices. As well as books, it has CDs, videos, cameras,
games and other software, a very international
newsstand and a concert ticket desk (*see p210*).
Branch: L'Illa, Avda Diagonal 549, Eixample
(93 444 59 00).

Llibreria Francesa

Passeig de Gràcia 91, Eixample (93 215 14 17).
Metro Diagonal/7, 16, 17, 22, 24, 28 bus. **Open**
9.30am-2.30pm, 4-8.30pm Mon-Fri; 9.30am-2pm,
5-8.30pm Sat. Closed Sat afternoon June-mid Sept.
Credit AmEx, MC, V. **Map** p336 D4.
A long-established bookshop offering Catalan,
Spanish, French and English books, as well as a very
good selection of foreign press.

Specialist

Angel Batle

C/Palla 23, Barri Gòtic (93 301 58 84). Metro Liceu/
14, 38, 59, 91 bus. **Open** 9am-1.30pm, 4-7.30pm
Mon-Fri; 9am-1.30pm Sat. **No credit cards.**
Map p342 B2.
Despite the dusty window display of old paper-
backs, this is a venerable antiquarian bookshop,
specialising in books on art, history and literature
from the 17th to the 20th centuries. There's also an
enormous collection of 19th-century prints – both
originals and copies – priced from €12.

Altaïr

Gran Via de les Corts Catalanes 616, Eixample
(93 342 71 71/www.altair.es). Metro Universitat/
bus all routes to Plaça Universitat. **Open** 10am-2pm,
4.30-8.30pm Mon-Sat. **Credit** AmEx, MC, V.
Map p336 D4.
After 22 years in the business, this travel bookshop
recently moved its 50,000 titles to this new location
on Gran Via. Altaïr has guidebooks and maps of
Catalonia, Spain and the rest of the world, as well as
books about anthropology, photography and world
music. Many titles are in English.

BCN Books

C/Roger de Lluria 118, Eixample (93 476 33 43).
Metro Passeig de Gràcia/7, 16, 17, 22, 24, 28 bus.
Open 9am-2pm, 4-8pm Mon-Fri; 10am-2pm Sat.
Credit AmEx, MC, V. **Map** p340 D4.
Everything is here at this English-language book-
shop, from computer manuals and teaching mate-
rials to the latest bestsellers. There is also a large
selection of dictionaries and reference books.

Come In

C/Provença 203, Eixample (93 453 12 04). Metro
Hospital Clínic/FGC Provença/7, 16, 17, 31, 38, 63,
67, 68 bus. **Open** 10am-2pm, 4.30-8pm Mon-Sat.
Closed Aug. **Credit** MC, V. **Map** p336 C4.
Barcelona's largest English bookshop has teaching
books and general material, from Milton to Shirley
MacLaine. Check the noticeboard if you're looking
for Spanish, Catalan or private English classes.

Llibreria Quera

C/Petritxol 2, Barri Gòtic (93 318 07 43/
www.llibreriaquera.com). Metro Liceu/14, 38, 59, 91
bus. **Open** 9.30am-1.30pm, 4.30-8pm Mon-Fri; 10am-
1.30pm, 5-8pm Sat. **Credit** MC, V. **Map** p342 A2.
If you're planning trips to the Catalan countryside
and the Pyrenees, this is the ideal place to find good
walking maps for every part of the country. Staff
also have information on mountaineering and all
kinds of outward-bound adventures.

Norma Comics

Passeig de Sant Joan 9, Eixample (93 244 8420/
www. normacomics.com). Metro Arc de Triomf/
19, 39, 40, 41, 42, 51, 55, 141 bus. **Open** 10.30am-
2pm, 5-8.30pm Mon-Sat. **Credit** AmEx, MC, V.
Map p341 E5.

Eat, Drink, Shop

Stylish bookshop-cum-gallery **Ras**.

The largest comics shop in Barcelona: one floor is dedicated to European and US comics, another to Japanese manga, and there are special sections for *Star Wars*, model kits and the like.

Pròleg
C/Dagueria 13, Barri Gòtic (93 319 24 25/ www.mallorcaweb.net/proleg). Metro Jaume I/ 17, 19, 40, 45 bus. **Open** *Sept-July* 5-8pm Mon; 10am-2pm, 5-8pm Tue-Fri; 11am-2pm, 5-8pm Sat. *Aug* 5-8.30pm Mon-Fri. **Credit** MC, V. **Map** p343 B3.
Barcelona's only feminist bookshop, Pròleg also organises writing workshops, exhibitions, poetry readings and discussions on literature and cinema.

Ras
C/Doctor Dou 10, Raval (93 412 71 99/ www.actar.es). Metro Catalunya/bus all routes to Plaça Catalunya. **Open** 1-9pm Tue-Sat. Closed 2wks Aug. **Credit** AmEx, DC, MC, V. **Map** p342 A2.
Ras combines a gallery, exhibiting young designers' creations, with a highly stylish bookshop, specialising in recent publications on architecture, design and photography.

Children

Clothes

Children's clothes tend to be expensive in Spain. Some adult chains, such as **Zara** (*see p195*), also have imaginative and reasonably priced children's lines. Madrid designer Agatha Ruiz de la Prada sells her playful fashions for girls at **El Corte Inglés** (*see p184*).

Du Pareil au Même
Rambla Catalunya 95, Eixample (93 487 14 49/ www.dpam.com). Metro Passeig de Gràcia/22, 24, 28 bus. **Open** *Jan-July, Sept-Dec* 10.30am-8.30pm Mon-Sat. *Aug* 10.30am-2.30pm, 5-8.30pm Mon-Sat. **Credit** AmEx, MC, V. **Map** p336 D4.
New outfits arrive twice a week at this colourful shop that is great for cheerful and cheap basics for youngsters aged zero to 14. The garments are surprisingly durable, and sizes tend to run small.

Mullor Infants
Rambla Catalunya 102, Eixample (93 215 12 02). Metro Diagonal/22, 24, 28 bus. **Open** 10am-2pm, 4.15-8.15pm Mon-Sat. **Credit** AmEx, MC, V. **Map** p336 D4.
The Mullor family shop sells clothes fit for a prince. All the essentials for the newborn are made by hand in the adjacent workshop, including smocked dresses and over-the-top christening gowns.

Prénatal
Gran Via de les Corts Catalanes 611, Eixample (93 302 05 25/www.prenatal.es). Metro Passeig de Gràcia/7, 16, 17, 22, 24, 28, 50, 54, 56, 67, 68 bus. **Open** 10am-8.30pm Mon-Sat. **Credit** AmEx, DC, MC, V. **Map** p340 D5.
This French-owned chain has everything: good quality pushchairs, cots, feeding bottles, toys, plus clothes for the pregnant mum and for kids aged up to eight. Branches include a large, central one in Galeries Maldà on C/Portaferrissa in the Barri Gòtic. **Branches**: throughout the city.

Toys

Drap
C/del Pi 14, Barri Gòtic (93 318 14 87/ www.ample24.com/drap). Metro Liceu/14, 38, 59, 91 bus. **Open** 9.30am-1.30pm, 4.30-8.30pm Mon-Fri; 10am-1.30pm, 5-8.30pm Sat. **Credit** AmEx, DC, MC, V. **Map** p342 B2.
The name means rag (as in dolls), and Drap sells everything related to dolls' houses, much of it handmade. You can buy a chair for €12 or an empty house (made to your own spec) for around €300.

El Ingenio
C/Rauric 6, Barri Gòtic (93 317 71 38). Metro Liceu/ 14, 38, 59, 91 bus. **Open** 10am-1.30pm, 4.15-8pm Mon-Fri; 10am-2pm, 5-8.30pm Sat. **Credit** MC, V. **Map** p343 A3.

El Ingenio lives up to its name with an ingenious range of cardboard, feather and papier-mâché masks, puppets, tricks and party accessories. The shop does booming business at Carnaval time, for which there are fancy dress outfits and traditional *capgrosses* (big heads). Stick-on Dalí moustaches cost €1 each, and can be twisted into shape.

Joguines Foyé

C/Banys Nous 13, Raval (93 302 03 89). Metro Liceu/14, 38, 59, 91 bus. **Open** 10am-2pm, 4.30-8pm Mon-Fri; 10am-2pm, 5-8.30pm Sat. **Credit** AmEx, MC, V. **Map** p343 B3.

As well as all the usual novelties, Joguines Foyé also stocks a wonderful collection of tin toys made from original moulds, English and German music boxes, porcelain dolls, furniture for dolls' houses and more oddities. Unusual PVC dolls from eastern Europe are also available.

Joguines Monforte

Plaça Sant Josep Oriol 3, Barri Gòtic (93 318 22 85). Metro Liceu/14, 38, 59, 91 bus. **Open** 9.30am-1.30pm, 4-8pm Mon-Sat. **Credit** AmEx, MC, V. **Map** p343 A3.

Wooden croquet and bowling sets are the speciality of this traditional toy shop, one of the oldest in Barcelona. A wide selection of kites, Spanish dolls and board games will also tempt the little ones.

Cleaning & repair

You'll also find a good range of services, including shoe repair, dry-cleaning, custom tailoring and alterations, at **El Corte Inglés** department store (*see p184*).

5 a Sec

L'Illa, Avda Diagonal 545-557, Eixample (93 444 00 34). Metro Maria Cristina/6, 7, 33, 34, 63, 66, 67, 68, 78 bus. **Open** 9.30am-9.30pm Mon-Sat. **Credit** MC, V. **Map** p343 B3.

This efficient dry-cleaner has several branches throughout the city.

Jaimar

C/Numància 91-93, Sants (93 322 78 04). Metro Sants Estació/30, 43, 78 bus. **Open** 9.30am-1.30pm, 5-8pm Mon-Fri; 11am-1.30pm Sat. **No credit cards**. **Map** p343 B3.

This place near the Sants Estació will repair or alter virtually any piece of clothing.

Mr Minit

Barcelona Glòries, Avda Diagonal 208, Eixample (93 486 03 52). Metro Glòries/7, 56, 60, 92 bus. **Open** 10am-10pm Mon-Sat. **Credit** V.

On-the-spot shoe repairs (heels €4.50) and key cutting (from €1.35) at many points around town.

Tintorería Pep i Pak

C/Amargós 10, Barri Gòtic (93 318 31 47/93 301 36 87). Metro Urquinaona/17, 19, 40, 45 bus. **Open** 9am-9pm Mon-Sat. **No credit cards**. **Map** p342 B2.

This shop will pick up clothes, clean, iron and deliver them within 24 hours. Their policy with regard to bulk laundry is: in by 10am, out by 8pm.

Crafts & gifts

Art Escudellers

C/Escudellers 23-25, Barri Gòtic (93 412 68 01/ www.escudellers-art.com). Metro Drassanes/14, 38, 59, 91 bus. **Open** 11am-11pm Mon-Sun. **Credit** AmEx, DC, MC, V. **Map** p343 A-B3.

This large shop sells artisan products from all over Spain, including ceramics, blown glass and jewellery, which they can ship worldwide. Downstairs, there is an extensive selection of Spanish wines and some olive oils, as well as a small bar where you can sample typical tapas, such as *jamón serrano* and Manchego cheese.

D Barcelona

Avda Diagonal 367, Eixample (93 216 03 46/ www.d-barcelona.com). Metro Diagonal/6, 15, 33, 34 bus. **Open** 10.30am-2pm, 4.30-9pm Mon-Sat. **Credit** AmEx, DC, MC, V. **Map** p336 D4.

Don't miss — Gift shops

Don't forget that museums also have excellent gift shops. The following are particularly good.

Espai Gaudí – La Pedrera

Gaudí-inspired gifts from dragon pencil-holders to La Pedrera mouse mats, plus the best postcards in the city. See p116.

Fundació Joan Miró

Gloriously colourful calendars, puzzles, bags, dominoes and more, as well as an impressive contemporary art library. See p107.

MACBA

Great kids' drawing and painting kits, Kandinsky dominoes, everything Alessi has ever made and a superb selection of art books. See p89.

Museu Tèxtil i de la Indumentària

Handmade buttons in every conceivable shape, colourful jewellery, handpainted scarves and groovy threads from local designers. See p98.

Museu de la Xocolata

You guessed it: chocolate. Look out for the pearls of exquisite Valrhona chocolate in little tins. See p133.

This gift shop is a temple to all things kitsch; you'll find imaginative watches, jewellery and gadgets. At the back of the store, the work of a young artist is showcased each month, among the home accessories and fun shower curtains.

Dos i Una

C/Rosselló 275, Eixample (93 217 70 32). Metro Diagonal/7, 16, 17, 22, 24, 28 bus. **Open** 10.30am-2pm, 4.30-8.30pm Mon-Sat. **Credit** AmEx, DC, MC, V. **Map** p336 D4.

The first ever design shop in Barcelona (established 1977), and an early patron of Mariscal, Dos i Una has grown up into a high-class gift shop, selling designer crockery, lamps, postcards, earrings and T-shirts.

Inicial G

C/Balmes 458, Zona Alta (93 418 56 18). FCG Avda Tibidabo/17 bus. **Open** 10am-2pm, 5-8.30pm Mon-Sat. **Credit** AmEx, DC, MC, V.

On your way up to Tibidabo? Before you board the tram, head down Balmes to this designer boutique, with its imaginative and enticing window displays. Here you'll find gifts galore – from silk scarves and Antonio Miró desk accessories to photo boxes and cow-printed dustpans – at prices to suit all budgets.

1748

Placeta Montcada 2, Born (93 319 54 13). Metro Jaume I/17, 19, 40, 45 bus. **Open** 10am-8pm Mon-Sat; 10am-3pm Sun. **Credit** MC, V. **Map** p343 C3.

Carmen Albarran's shop is overflowing with ceramics from Catalonia's ceramic capital, La Bisbal, on the Costa Brava. The selection includes fired Mediterranean green, blue and yellow dish sets, plus floral sangria pitchers and olive trays from other parts of Spain.

2 Bis

C/Bisbe 2 bis, Barri Gòtic (93 315 09 54). Metro Jaume I/17, 19, 40, 45 bus. **Open** 10am-8.30pm Mon-Sat. **Credit** AmEx, DC, MC, V. **Map** p343 B3.

Quirky objects for everyone: toys for kids and adults, tin planes, life-size Tintin characters, and lots of other items in wood, paper and papier-mâché.

Design & household

BD Ediciones de Diseño

Casa Thomas, C/Mallorca 291, Eixample (93 458 69 09/www.bdbarcelona.com). Metro Passeig de Gràcia/ 20, 39, 43, 44, 45, 47 bus. **Open** 10am-2pm, 4-8pm Mon-Fri; 10am-2pm, 4.30-8pm Sat. Closed 3wks Aug. **Credit** AmEx, DC, MC, V. **Map** p336 D4.

Located in a magnificent *Modernista* house built by Domènech i Montaner in 1895, BD is an institution of the Barcelona design world. The shop is best known for its reproductions of classic designs by giants like Gaudí, Dalí and Josef Hoffmann. This is the place to buy Gaudí's curvaceous Calvet arm-chair or his Batlló bench. The stunning art nouveau space also showcases works by contemporary designers, such as Ricard Bofill, Mariscal and the shop's co-founder Oscar Tusquets.

Dom

Passeig de Gràcia 76, Eixample, (93 487 11 81/ www.id-dom.com). Metro Passeig de Gràcia/20, 22, 24, 28, 43, 44 bus. **Open** 10.30am-8.30pm Mon-Fri; 10.30am-9pm Sat. **Credit** DC, MC, V. **Map** p336 D4.

Shop under a disco ball for funky furniture, gift items and knick-knacks for the home. Gigantic lava lamps, plastic blow-up armchairs and fluorescent flower vases are among the wide selection of mer-chandise. A stall in one sells fresh tropical flowers. **Branch**: C/Avinyó 7, Barri Gòtic (93 342 55 91).

Eric Artesania

C/Sant Antoni dels Sombrerers 7, Barri Gòtic (93 310 20 24/www.eric-artesania.com). Metro Jaume I/17, 19, 40, 45 bus. **Open** 11am-2pm, 5-9pm Tue-Sat. **No credit cards. Map** p343 C3.

Tucked away in a tiny street off C/Sombrerers is this treasure trove of Moroccan and Indian furniture. Lampshades in all sizes and colours are the special-ity, along with mosaic-topped tables and chests of drawers painted with intricate Moorish designs.

Gemma Povo

C/Banys Nous 5-7, Raval (93 301 34 76/www. gemmapovo.com). Metro Liceu/14, 39, 59, 91 bus. **Open** 10am-1.30pm, 4.30-8pm Mon-Sat. Closed 2wks Aug. **Credit** AmEx, DC, MC, V. **Map** p343 B3.

A family-run, artisan shop specialising in beautiful wrought-iron lamps and bedsteads, all designed by the owner. She also sells Mallorcan glass vases, and rustic tables. Well worth a browse.

Gotham

C/Cervantes 7, Barri Gòtic (93 412 46 47). Metro Jaume I/17, 40, 45 bus. **Open** 10.30-2pm, 5-8.30pm Mon-Sat. **Credit** DC, MC, V. **Map** p343 B3.

On a corner of Plaça Sant Miquel, behind the Ajuntament, this hip, off-the-wall shop has a highly original exterior. Most of its great range of furniture is from the 1930s and '40s, while accessories – lamps, vases, glassware – hail from the '50s or '60s. There are also many completely new, up-to-the-minute items. The owners are interior designers, and will undertake restorations.

Ici et Là

Plaça Santa Maria del Mar 2, La Ribera (93 268 11 67/www.icietla.com). Metro Jaume I/17, 19, 40, 45 bus. **Open** 4.30-8.30pm Mon; 10.30am-8.30pm Tue-Sat. **Credit** AmEx, MC, V. **Map** p343 C3-4.

The brainchild of three women – two French and one Spanish – who believe that original furniture and accessories shouldn't be limited to the well-heeled. Wacky ethnic objects and striking contem-porary creations are sourced from Barcelona, Europe and around the world, and sold at prices that are deliberately reasonable.

Matarile

Passeig del Born 24, La Ribera (93 315 02 20). Metro Jaume I/14, 39, 51 bus. **Open** 5-8.30pm Mon, Sat; 10.30am-2pm, 5-8.30pm Tue-Fri. **Credit** MC, V. **Map** p343 C3.

Second best

There was a time when vintage culture simply did not exist in Barcelona. People threw away old clothing and coated used furniture with lacquer, so that it looked shiny and new. In recent times, however, Barcelonans have discovered the joys of second-hand goods, and a network of shops is growing in response to the city's new appreciation for retro.

In May 2001, two young Catalans opened **Seneca 8**, an antique shop jam-packed with odds and ends from the last 150 years. The owners sell by commission and salvage goods from estate sales and the flea market, **Els Encants** (*see p208*). Depending on when you visit, you might find some 1960s sunglasses, a theatre chair from Madrid's Teatro Real or musical items ranging from second-hand pianos to an old jukebox. The second floor displays furniture from the 1950s, '60s and '70s: two-seater sofas, armchairs and sidetables.

On the fashion front, **Lailo** (*pictured*) is prime hunting ground for vintage clothing. This spacious emporium is packed with historical garments: 1950s cocktail dresses in organdie and silk, leather jackets galore and wonderful costumes from local theatres and opera houses. The medieval jewelled gowns and *bandoleras* from the Liceu's production of *Carmen* can be hired, while up a narrow, winding staircase is an assortment of wedding gowns and military jackets. Lailo is more than just a vintage shop: it's a clothing museum.

Lailo, like several of the city's second-hand clothing shops, is in C/Riera Baixa in the Raval. This fashionable street hosts a *mercat alternatiu* or 'alternative street market' of fashion, vintage clothing and other items every Saturday from May to September and in December, and on the first Saturday of every other month from October to April.

Smack in the middle of the Riera Baixa scene is the groovy clothing shop **Recicla Recicla**. Run by sisters Laura and Fran (who also own the popular bar Pilé 43 – *see p172*), 'Recycle Recycle' stocks mainly clothing from the 1950s to the '70s, with the odd hat from the '20s or even a current suit from Armani thrown in. Plastic and leather furniture and lamps from the '60s and '70s decorate the shop, and all items are for sale.

Finally, if it's vintage gems you're after, head to **Novecento** on Passeig de Gràcia and drool over shop windows chock-full of antique jewellery. Novecento deals in

bijouterie from all eras, including Victorian, art deco, retro '40s and *belle époque*. The knowledgeable owners specialise in pieces from the turn of the 20th century, when Barcelona jewellery-making was at its height, but they also stock second-hand modern designs, as well as a few antiques such as art nouveau crystal vases.

Lailo
C/Riera Baixa 20, Raval (93 441 37 49).
Metro Sant Antoni/20, 24, 38, 64 bus.
Open 10.30am-2pm, 5-8.30pm Mon-Sat.
Credit MC, V. **Map** p340 C6.

Novecento
Passeig de Gràcia 75, Eixample (93
215 11 83). Metro Passeig de Gràcia/
22, 24, 28 bus. **Open** 10am-2pm, 4.30-
8pm Mon-Sat. **Credit** AmEx, MC, V.
Map p336 D4.

Recicla Recicla
Riera Baixa 13, Raval (93 443 18 15).
Metro Sant Antoni/20, 24, 38, 64 bus.
Open 11am-2pm, 5-9pm Mon-Sat.
No credit cards. **Map** p340 C6.

Seneca 8
C/Sèneca 8, Gràcia (93 218 44 17).
Metro Diagonal/7, 16, 17, 22, 24, 28 bus.
Open 10.30am-2pm, 5-8pm Mon-Fri. Closed
Aug. **No credit cards**. **Map** p336 D3.

Eat, Drink, Shop

timeout.com

The online guide to the world's greatest cities

Visit **Vinçon** for top tables.

Owners Mauricio and Maya sell lamps and lighting, including their own designs made of handmade papers, wild grasses and polished woods. For a more kitsch, '50s mood, they've come out with Day-glo fixtures and lamps.

Pilma

Avda Diagonal 403, Eixample, (93 416 13 99/ www.pilma.com). Metro Diagonal/6, 15, 33, 34 bus. **Open** 10am-2pm, 4.30-8.30pm Mon-Sat. Closed 2wks Aug. **Credit** AmEx, DC, MC, V. **Map** p336 D4.
What started as a small cabinetmaker's workshop in the 1930s has transformed into a pillar of BCN design. Ramps connect the store's four levels, with sections devoted to furniture, lighting, gifts and kitchen/bathroom products. Even if you're not in the market for furnishings, this is a great place to keep up with cutting-edge design.

Vinçon

Passeig de Gràcia 96, Eixample (93 215 60 50/ www.vincon.com). Metro Diagonal/7, 16, 17, 22, 24, 28 bus. **Open** 10am-2pm, 4.30-8.30pm Mon-Sat. **Credit** AmEx, MC, V. **Map** p336 D4.
Barcelona's renowned design palace is a shrine to 20th-century European design, featuring everything for the home from contemporary furniture to corkscrews. While most of the products in the lighting, kitchen, bathroom and fabric departments are affordable, the furnishings on the upper level can be expensive. Each December, Vinçon hosts Hipermerc'art, an 'art supermarket' where astute buyers can pick up originals by young artists for as little as €55. As part of its steady corporate expansion, Vinçon has opened a shop around the corner called TincÇon, Catalan for 'I'm sleepy'. Dedicated to the bedroom, this offshoot is a good source for plain cotton PJs and Sybilla's linens embroidered with red roses or green iguanas
Branch: TincÇon Rosselló 246, Eixample (93 215 60 50).

Fashion

Most street-fashion shops are around C/Portaferrissa, off La Rambla, and other streets thereabouts. C/Avinyó is also worth a look to find work by young local designers. In the past couple of years, C/Riera Baixa in the Raval has also become a centre for second-hand shops, innovative boutiques, tattoos and piercings. It's also worth checking out **Els Encants** market (*see p208*), for old and new objects, and some vintage clothes stalls.

Bad Habits

C/Valencia 261, Eixample (93 487 22 59). Metro Passeig de Gràcia/20, 22, 24, 28, 43, 44 bus. **Open** 10.30am-2.30pm, 4.30-8.30pm Mon-Sat. **Credit** AmEx, DC, MC, V. **Map** p336 D4.
You might miss the low entrance to Bad Habits (the name of the label, too), where Mireya Ruiz sells her avant-garde yet wearable fashions. Many pieces are limited editions – buy now or miss out.

Four Elements

C/Duc de la Victòria 5, Barri Gòtic (93 412 61 66). Metro Liceu/14, 38, 59, 91 bus. **Open** 10.30am-8.30pm Mon-Sat. **Credit** MC, V. **Map** p342 B2.
A tasteful selection of pieces by the likes of Block 60, Sabotage, Acupuncture, and Amaya Arzuaga makes this shop the perfect place to get your club and urbanwear. Cool Japanese-style outfits and jewellery by the popular Locking Shocking guarantee success in Barcelona's club scene.

Custo Barcelona. *See p195.*

Mango

Passeig de Gràcia 65, Eixample (93 215 75 30/
www.mango.es/www.mangoshop.com). Metro
Passeig de Gràcia/7, 16, 17, 22, 24, 28 bus.
Open 10.15am-8.30pm Mon-Fri; 10.15am-9pm
Sat. **Credit** AmEx, DC, MC, V. **Map** p336 D4.
Mango is undoubtedly enjoying ripe times. In just
18 years, the Barcelona-based company has built a
chain of roughly 600 shops around the world.
Mango puts out four collections a year, making it
a bit less trend-driven than its rival Zara. It is the
more expensive of the two, but the clothes tend to
be more durable in terms of both fashion and quality. This is also a great place to pick up handbags,
belts and shoes.

Massimo Dutti

El Triangle, C/Pelai 39, Eixample (93 412 28 28/
www.massimodutti.com). Metro Catalunya/bus all
routes to Plaça Catalunya. **Open** 10am-10pm Mon-
Sat. **Credit** MC, V. **Map** p342 A1.
What started as a shirt business has turned into a
fashion success, with 13 shops in Barcelona alone.
There's a whole range of basic, modern men and
womenswear, including lingerie. The prices are a bit
higher than the other chains, but the quality is
arguably better.

El Mercadillo

C/Portaferrissa 17, Barri Gòtic (93 301 89 13).
Metro Liceu/14, 38, 59, 91 bus. **Open** 11am-9pm
Mon-Sat. **Credit** MC, V. **Map** p342 B2.
Neon lights and a life-size fibreglass camel mean
it's hard to miss the entrance to El Mercadillo,
Barcelona's grunge fashion arcade. Patience is necessary for discovering the trousers, heavy boots or
garish tops you like in the crammed shelves. You
can find colourful shirts by Replay and discounts

on classics such as Levi 501s. The wonderful bar
at the back opens to an old patio with tables, chairs
and a particularly lurid mural.

On Land

C/Princesa 25, La Ribera (93 310 02 11/www.on-
land.com). Metro Jaume I/17, 19, 40, 45 bus. **Open**
5-8.30pm Mon; 11am-2pm, 5-8.30pm Tue-Sat. Closed
1wk Aug. **Credit** AmEx, MC, V. **Map** p343 C3.
The Italian owners of this groovy red shop design
their own casual collection for men and women.
They also sell women's brands such as Celia Vega
and Giménez & Zuazo, and some stylish menswear
from up-and-coming young designer Josep Abril.
Branch: C/Valencia 273, Eixample (93 215 56 25).

So_da

C/Avinyó 24, Barri Gòtic (93 412 27 76/93 342 45
29). Metro Liceu/14, 38, 59, 91 bus. **Open** 11am-
2.30pm, 4.30pm-9pm Mon-Sat. *Bar* 9pm-2am daily.
Credit MC, V. **Map** p343 B3.
This minimalist space is both bar and fashion shop.
File through a small but choice selection of men's
and women's clothes by Energy, Miss Sixty and Levi's
Red before heading to the bar at the back, where a
DJ cranks out tunes for a hip and pretty crowd.

Tactic

C/Enric Granados 11, Eixample (93 451 03 87).
Metro Plaça Universitat/bus all routes to Plaça
Universitat. **Open** 10.45am-2.30pm, 5-8.15pm
Tue-Sat. **Credit** AmEx, MC, V. **Map** p336 C4.
This laid-back shop just behind the central university provides fashion for surfers and skaters, from
the likes of Quiksilver, Ripcurl, Volcom and many
others. They also specialise in snowboarding,
windsurfing and kitesurfing, and have an array of
clothing and accessories, for both adults and kids.

Tribu

C/Avinyó 12, Barri Gòtic (93 318 65 10/
www.dresslab.com). Metro Jaume I/17, 19,
40, 45 bus. **Open** 11am-2.30pm, 4.30-8.30pm
Mon-Sat. **Credit** AmEx, MC, V. **Map** p343 B3.
Tribu is a maze of rooms where urbanites can
browse through alternative unisex designs by E-
Play, Marithé & François Girbaud, D&G and Diesel.
The back room is a shrine to shoes, and the walls
are decked each month with new work by young,
mainly unknown artists.

Zara

C/Pelai 58, Eixample (93 301 09 78). Metro
Catalunya/bus all routes to Plaça Catalunya.
Open 10am-9pm Mon-Sat. **Credit** AmEx, DC,
MC, V. **Map** p342 A1.
Zara is a fashion empire based in Galicia, with
some 500 shops in 30 countries. The secret of its
success is a simple, functional formula of reasonable prices, intelligent copies of top designs and an
unbelievable capacity to react to changes in consumer taste, enabling them to draw in a clientele
running from the very trendy to those just looking
for good, wearable clothes.
Branches: throughout the city.

Designer

Adolfo Domínguez

Passeig de Gràcia 32, Eixample (93 487 41 70/
www.lineau.com). Metro Passeig de Gràcia/7, 16,
17, 22, 24, 28 bus. **Open** 10am-8.30pm Mon-Sat.
Credit AmEx, DC, MC, V. **Map** p340 D5.
One of the foremost names in Spanish fashion,
Galician Adolfo Domínguez deserves his reputation
as a designer of well made, timeless clothes for men
and women, usually in stylishly austere colours.
Branches: Avda Diagonal 490, Gràcia (93 416 17
16); Avda Pau Casals 5, Zona Alta (93 414 11 77);
La Maquinista, C/Ciutat d'Asunción, Sant Andreu
(93 360 8753); Passeig de Gràcia 89, Eixample
(93 215 13 39).

Antonio Miró

C/Consell de Cent 349, Eixample (93 487 06 70/
www.antoniomiro.es). Metro Passeig de Gràcia/
22, 24, 28 bus. **Open** *Jan, Mar-July, Sept-Dec*
10am-8.30pm Mon-Sat. *Feb, Aug* 11am-2pm,
5-8pm Tue-Sat. **Credit** AmEx, DC, MC, V.
Map p336 D5.
Barcelona's beloved style-setter Toni Miró designs
wearable clothing with an urban flair. Miró began
his career as a tailor and, though he designs both
men's and women's fashions, is best known for his
men's suits, which are well constructed and made
out of irresistible materials. Miró fashions are also
sold at Groc (*see below*).

Armand Basi

Passeig de Gràcia 49, Eixample (93 215 14 21/
www.armandbasi.com). Metro Passeig de Gràcia/
7, 16, 17, 22, 24, 28 bus. **Open** 10am-8.30pm
Mon-Sat. **Credit** AmEx, DC, MC, V. **Map** p336 D4.

The pleasant flagship shop of this ultra-hip Spanish
designer is suitably in the centre of things, and is
the only place in town where you can find everything in his men's and women's collections, from soft
leather jackets to more timeless suits, classic knits,
evening dresses and a wide variety of accessories.

Custo Barcelona

Plaça de les Olles 7, La Ribera (93 268 78 93/
www.custo-barcelona.com). Metro Jaume I/17, 19,
40, 45 bus. **Open** 10am-10pm Mon-Sat; 1-9pm Sun.
Credit AmEx, DC, MC, V. **Map** p343 C4.
After conquering the fashion world with his psy-
chedelic T-shirts, designer Custodio Dalmau
returned to Barcelona to open this, his first boutique, in the heart of the Born. Green tiles and funk
music set off his wildly creative tops for men and
women, including sweaters, long-sleeved T-shirts
and tank tops. Be warned; you may end up parting
with €80 for a T-shirt.

David Valls

C/València 235, Eixample (93 487 12 85). Metro
Passeig de Gràcia/7, 16, 17, 20, 43, 44, 63, 67, 68
bus. **Open** 10am-2pm, 4.30-8.30pm Mon-Sat. Closed
2wks Aug. **Credit** AmEx, DC, MC, V. **Map** p336 D4.
David Valls produces original upmarket knitwear
for new bohemians, using the latest technology to
create unique textures and fabrics. His shop has an
extensive collection of body-hugging jumpers for
women and stylish yet classic sweaters for men.

Giménez y Zuazo

C/Elisabets 20, Raval (93 412 33 81). Metro
Catalunya/bus all routes to Plaça Catalunya.
Open 10.30am-2pm, 5-8.30pm Mon-Sat. **Credit**
MC, V. **Map** p342 A2.
This duo won a national competition for young
Spanish designers back in 1984. Fabric is the essen-
tial starting point of their garments: their designs
mix and play with different textures, using clean
cuts and surprising, original details. They also
create unisex pieces.

Groc

Rambla Catalunya 100, Eixample (93 215 01 80).
Metro Diagonal/FGC Provença/7, 16, 17, 20, 22,
24, 28, 43, 44 bus. **Open** 10am-2pm, 4.30-8.30pm
Mon-Sat. **Credit** AmEx, DC, MC, V. **Map** p336 D4.
Groc is the place to find men's and women's cloth-
ing by one of the most admired of current Catalan
designers, Antonio Miró (*see also above*). Shoes by
Miró and jewellery by Chelo Sastre also feature.
Branch: C/Muntaner 385, Zona Alta (93 202 30 77/
93 202 00 01).

Jean-Pierre Bua

Avda Diagonal 469, Eixample (93 439 71 00/
www.jeanpierrebua.com). Bus 6, 7, 15, 33, 34.
Open 10am-2pm, 4.30-8.30pm Mon-Sat. **Credit**
AmEx, DC, MC, V. **Map** p336 C3.
The first, and for many years, the only Barcelona
shop to sell avant-garde international designer
fashion. Enjoy exclusive selections from Dries van

Born to shop

The neighbourhood known as the Born, to the east of the Via Liaietana, inside La Ribera, has in recent years transformed from shabby to chic. Ten years ago, architects brought the 'loft' concept to the area by turning some of the rundown buildings into spacious apartments and shops. The idea took off and today the Born is a designer destination, and home to stylish boutiques such as **Custo Barcelona** (*see p195*) and **On Land** (*see p194*).

In particular, the Born is known for its textiles. It was the centre of Barcelona's weaving and textile trades for centuries, and over the past few years city authorities have attempted to revive this tradition by encouraging young designers to move into the area's old workshops. Craftsmen have set up shops throughout the labyrinth of medieval streets (which are best explored with a map). Some weave by hand; others design clothes, home accessories, lace, hats or handbags.

Workshop-browsing is one of the best ways to appreciate the Born's charm. On the second Saturday of every month, there's a free guided **Itinerari Tèxtil** (Textile Itinerary) tour, beginning at the district office in Plaça Bonsuccés 3, over in the Raval, and ending at the Museu Tèxtil on C/Montcada. If you prefer to browse on your own, a free leaflet with a map and workshop addresses is available from the museum or from the tourist office at Palau de la Virreina (*see p321*).

While the tour spans the entire Old City, the largest concentration of workshops is in La Ribera. The Moroccan owner of **Otman** (*see p200*) sews simple, comfortable clothing out of natural Moroccan fabrics, while close by, at **Cocon** (C/Cotoners 8; 93 319 11 79), the Japanese owners stock Japanese textiles and specialise in calligraphy and handmade lamps.

Next door at **Luna** (C/Cotoners 10; 93 310 44 31), young designer Cristina Pella Franco creates fresh, colourful fashions out of the bolts of fabric hanging at the back. Attractive shop **Nu** (C/Vigatans 2; 93 310 34 70) sells two brands of handwoven knitwear, and at **Fet amb Love** (*see p199*), two sisters make handbags out of such materials as jute, raw silk and linen. Down the street, at **Rafael Teja** (*see p200*), there is a wide selection of lovely scarves, made in the adjacent workshop.

For more information, call 93 310 41 09 or visit www.itineraritextil.com. To take part in the Textile Itinerary tour, call Biblioteca Bonnemaison (93 268 01 07).

Luna: if the hat fits...

Noten, Sybilla and personal friend Jean-Paul Gaultier: this is also the place to head if you're looking for stylish and modern bridalwear. Luis and Adolfo make everyone welcome, and it's worth checking for special sales.

Josep Font

C/Provença 304, Eixample (93 487 21 10/ www.josepfont.com). Metro Diagonal/22, 24, 28, 100, 101 bus. **Open** 10am-8.30pm Mon-Sat. **Credit** AmEx, MC, V. **Map** p336 D4.
This promising young designer has swept the board of Spain's fashion awards with his gorgeous and imaginative clothes. Clients flock to his new boutique to appreciate his handsewn garments, which often feature classic Spanish embroidery, and border on haute couture.

Noténom

C/Pau Claris 159, Eixample (93 487 60 84). Metro Passeig de Gràcia/22, 24, 28, 39, 43, 44, 45 bus. **Open** 4.30-8.30pm Mon; 10.30am-2pm, 4.30-8.30pm Tue-Fri; 11am-2pm, 5-8.30pm Sat. **Credit** AmEx, DC, MC, V. **Map** p336 D4.
Noténom ('It has no name') is a focal point for all the newest trends and lines, selected from around the world – including labels such as Exté, Comme des Garçons, Maurizio Pecoraso and D2. The two-level shops sells clothes for both sexes, and men in particular can find daring pieces that are difficult to locate anywhere else in town. There is also a selection of fashion jewellery and accessories.

Designer bargains

Contribuciones

C/Riera de Sant Miquel 30, Gràcia (93 218 71 40). Metro Diagonal/6, 7, 15, 16, 17, 22, 24, 28, 33, 34 bus. **Open** 11am-2pm, 5-9pm Mon-Sat. **Credit** AmEx, DC, MC, V. **Map** p336 D3.
Labels – usually Spanish and Italian ones, such as Dolce & Gabbana – vary according to what's available. The beauty of this spacious fashion shop is that everything is sold at half-price.

Factory Store

Passeig de Gràcia 81, Eixample (93 215 03 80). Metro Passeig de Gràcia/22, 24, 28 bus. **Open** 10.30am-8.30pm Mon-Sat. **Credit** MC, V. **Map** p336 D4.
For chic Italian threads at up to 50% off the retail price, head down to this basement shop. New merchandise for men and women rolls in each season from names such as Trussardi, Gianfranco Ferré, Versace and Moschino.

Stockland

C/Comtal 22, Barri Gòtic (93 318 03 31). Metro Urquinaona/17, 19, 40, 45 bus. **Open** 10am-8.30pm Mon-Sat. **Credit** AmEx, DC, MC, V. **Map** p342 B2.
Originally known as Preu Bo ('good price'), this outlet for designer clothes, with friendly staff, is still living up to its former name, with up to 65% off end-of-lines by various designers, including Roberto

Verinno, Jordi Cuesta, Purificación García, Joaquim Verdú, María Encarnación and C'est Comme Ça. **Branches:** C/Balmes 308, Zona Alta (93 414 44 57); C/Craywinckel 5, Zona Alta (93 418 81 74).

Fashion accessories

Dress & costume hire

To buy an outfit for Carnaval, try **Lailo** (*see p191* **Second best**) or **El Ingenio** (*see p188*).

Casa Peris

C/Junta de Comerç 20, Raval (93 301 27 48). Metro Liceu/14, 38, 59, 91 bus. **Open** 9am-2pm, 3.30-6.30pm Mon-Fri. **No credit cards. Map** p343 A3.
A old family firm that has supplied the Liceu and Madrid operas and stocks close to a million theatrical costumes. A walk through the large warehouse reveals a Don Giovanni opera outfit and many film costumes, as well as military uniforms. Men's formal wear can be hired for €85.

Jewellery

Bagués

Passeig de Gràcia 41, Eixample (93 216 01 73). Metro Passeig de Gràcia/20, 22, 24, 28, 43, 44 bus. **Open** 10am-8.30pm Mon-Sat. **Credit** AmEx, DC, MC, V. **Map** p336 D4.
Founded in 1839, this jeweller and watchmaker has a privileged location: Puig i Cadafalch's Casa Amatller. Bagués is especially known for its art nouveau jewellery, one line of which combines enamels and precious gems to depict the figure of a woman fused with nature. In 2001, the jeweller presented a collection inspired by mosaics. **Branch:** C/Rambla de les Flors 105, Barri Gòtic (93 481 70 50).

Forvm Ferlandina

C/Ferlandina 31, Raval (93 441 80 18/www. forvmjoies.com). Metro Universitat/24, 41, 55, 64, 91, 141 bus. **Open** 10.30am-2pm, 5-8.30pm Tue-Fri; 11am-2pm Sat. **Credit** AmEx, MC, V. **Map** p340 C5.
Near the MACBA, this space features all styles of contemporary jewellery. It has exclusively designed pieces in materials from precious stones to plastic; there are also exhibitions by leading jewellery artists. For further information, check the frequently updated website.

Hipótesis

C/Provença 237, Eixample (93 215 02 98). FGC Provença/7, 16, 17, 20, 22, 24, 28, 43, 44 bus. **Open** 10am-1.30pm, 5-8.30pm Mon, Sat; 10am-8.30pm Tue-Fri. **Credit** AmEx, DC, MC, V. **Map** p336 D4.
A wonderful place to find contemporary European jewellery made of innovative materials. The unique pieces range from wool bracelets to paper necklaces and are usually limited editions. The shop also holds occasional exhibitions of glass and ceramics.

Eat, Drink, Shop

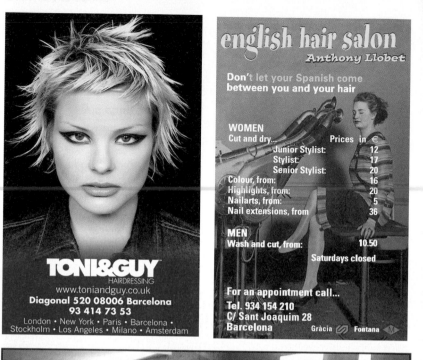

Joaquín Berao

C/Rosselló 277, Eixample (93 218 61 87/
www.joaquinberao.com). Metro Diagonal/7,
16, 17, 22, 24, 28 bus. **Open** 10.15am-2pm,
5-8.30pm Mon-Sat. Closed Sat afternoon Aug.
Credit AmEx, DC, MC, V. **Map** p336 D4.
This Madrid-based designer sells his stunning –
and expensive – gold, diamond and silver designs
at this boutique, which won architectural awards
when it opened in 1984.

San-Do

C/Cardenal Casañas 5, Barri Gòtic (93 302 64 33).
Metro Liceu/14, 38, 59, 91 bus. **Open** 4.30-8pm
Mon; 10.30am-1.30pm, 4.30-8pm Tue-Sat. **Credit**
AmEx, DC, MC,V. **Map** p343 A3.
Perhaps the smallest shop in Barcelona, with a
broad range of jewellery styles, from traditional
pieces in gold to original designs in silver, some by
the owner himself or his son Albert. Small silver
boxes for collectors are also available.

Leather & luggage

Calpa

C/Ferran 53, Barri Gòtic (93 318 40 30). Metro
Liceu/14, 38, 59, 91 bus. **Open** 9.30am-2pm,
4.30-8pm Mon-Fri; 10am-2pm, 5-8.30pm Sat.
Credit AmEx, DC, MC, V. **Map** p343 B3.
You'll find bags for every taste, from €18 carry-alls
to beautifully finished leather cases for €300.
Branch: C/Pi 5, Barri Gòtic (93 412 58 22).

Casa Antich SCP

C/Consolat del Mar 27-31, La Ribera (93 310 43 91/
www.casaantich.com). Metro Jaume I/17, 19, 40, 45
bus. **Open** 9am-8pm Mon-Fri; 9.30am-8.30pm Sat.
Credit AmEx, MC, V. **Map** p343 B4.
This part of the Ribera has dealt in luggage for centuries, and family-owned Casa Antich is one of a
clutch of shops that keeps up the tradition, with a
vast range of bags, briefcases, suitcases and enormous metal trunks at reasonable prices. In 2001, it
opened a new space next door with the latest
designs from Mandarina Duck, Samsonite and
Rimowa. And if they haven't got what you want,
they'll make it for you.

Loewe

Passeig de Gràcia 35, Eixample (93 216 04 00).
Metro Passeig de Gràcia/7, 16, 17, 22, 24, 28 bus.
Open 10am-8.30pm Mon-Sat. **Credit** AmEx, DC,
MC, V. **Map** p340 D5.
The celebrated leather company Loewe has its main
Barcelona shop in the Casa Morera in the 'Mansana
de la Discòrdia'. Inside, there are high-priced bags,
suitcases, scarves and other accessories of superb
quality. Architectural purists tend to boycott the
shop since the firm altered Domènech i Montaner's
original *Modernista* façade by replacing part of it
with glass windows.
Branches: Avda Diagonal 570, Eixample (93 200
09 20); Avda Diagonal 606, Eixample (93 240 51 04).

Lingerie & underwear

Ciutad

Avda Portal de l'Àngel 14, Barri Gòtic (93 317
04 33). Metro Catalunya/bus all routes to Plaça
Catalunya. **Open** 10am-8.30pm Mon-Fri; 10.30am-
9pm Sat. **Credit** AmEx, DC, MC, V. **Map** p342 B2.
This charming shop opened in 1892, and sells
some of the prettiest women's underwear you can
find. The sign at the door says 'manufacturers of
combs and articles for the dressing-table', and its
collection of combs is indeed something to behold.
Opening times might vary in August.

Isla Margarita

Bulevard Rosa, Passeig de Gràcia 55-57, Eixample
(93 487 14 34/www.bulevardrosa.com). Metro
Passeig de Gràcia/7, 16, 17, 22, 24, 28 bus.
Open 10.30am-8.30pm Mon-Sat. **Credit** AmEx,
DC, MC, V. **Map** p336 D4.
The racks of this small boutique tucked in a corner of Bulevard Rosa display playful, comfortable
lingerie by TCN, Petit Bateau and Grafiti. In the
summer, swimwear takes over. To alleviate the
agony of bikini shopping, they allow you to mix
and match tops and bottoms.

Janina

Rambla Catalunya 94, Eixample (93 215 04 21).
Metro Diagonal/FGC Provença/22, 24, 28 bus.
Open 10am-8.30pm Mon-Sat. **Credit** AmEx, DC,
MC, V. **Map** p336 D4.
A well-established shop that sells its own exclusive
silk and satin underwear, nightwear and robes, as
well as stockings by Risk and La Perla. A large selec-
tion of swimsuits and bikinis is also available.
Branch: Avda Pau Casal 8, Sarría (93 202 06 93).

Scarves & textiles

Although there are textile shops and workshops
all over the Old City, the largest concentration
is in La Ribera. For information about browsing
the workshops or taking a tour of the official
'Textile Itinerary', *see p196* **Born to shop**.

Almazul

C/Amargós 15, Barri Gòtic (93 412 20 45/93 430
01 21). Metro Urquinaona/17, 19, 40, 45 bus.
Open 10am-2pm, 4.30-8.30pm Mon-Fri, 10am-2pm,
5-8.30pm Sat. **Credit** MC, V. **Map** p342 B2.
Violeta and Ana, the friendly owners of this shop
near Portal de l'Àngel, sell everything from scarves
to tablecloths and rugs, all handmade from beautiful natural fibres and dyes.

Fet amb Love

Passeig del Born 2, La Ribera, (93 319 66 42).
Metro Jaume I/ 17, 19, 40, 45 bus. **Open**
10am-2pm, 4.30-8.30pm Mon-Sat. **Credit** MC, V.
Map p343 C3.
Two sisters, Ana and Eva, have a small workshop
at the back of this tiny shop, making practical hand-

Eat, Drink, Shop

bags out of materials such as jute, raw silk and linen. The bags cost between €9-€42. There is also a small selection of beaded jewellery.

Otman
C/Banys Vells 21 bis, La Ribera (93 319 29 34). Metro Jaume I/17, 19, 40, 45 bus. **Open** 11am-2pm, 5-9pm Mon-Sat. **Credit** V. **Map** p343 C3.
This shop's Moroccan owner, Otman, designs and sells simple, comfortable clothing made out of natural fabrics imported from Morocco, including linen, cotton and wool.

Rafael Teja
C/Santa Maria 18, La Ribera (93 310 27 85). Metro Jaume I/17, 19, 40, 45 bus. **Open** 10am-2pm, 4.30-8.30pm daily. **Credit** AmEx, MC, V. **Map** p343 C3.
In his shop by Santa Maria del Mar, Rafael Teja offers a wide selection of scarves, including beautiful handprinted silk foulards, from €12-€270. The new branch in the Eixample is stunning.
Branch: Conde de Salvatierra 10, Eixample (93 237 70 59).

Shoes

Each year, Spain produces more than 200 million pairs of shoes. To see the latest styles, head to Portal de l'Àngel or C/Pelai, where there's a great selection of shoe shops. For traditional Catalan footwear, try on *espardenyes* (also called *alpargatas*), a type of espadrille with ribbons attached.

Camper
El Triangle, C/Pelai 13-37, Eixample (93 302 41 24/www.camper.es). Metro Plaça Catalunya/ bus all routes to Plaça Catalunya. **Open** 10am-10pm Mon-Sat. **Credit** AmEx, DC, MC, V. **Map** p342 A1.
Camper's *pelota* bowling shoes have been wildly fashionable around the world for the past couple of years, and are showing no signs of slowing. Buy them here, where they are considerably less expensive. There are seven branches in Barcelona – this one is the most central.

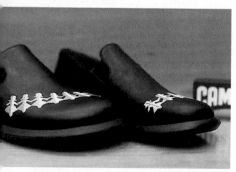

Camper: inspiration for body and sole.

Cristina Castañer
C/Valencia 274, Eixample (93 487 21 62). Metro Passeig de Gràcia/20, 22, 24, 28, 43, 44 bus. **Open** 10.30am-8.30pm Mon-Sat. **Credit** AmEx, DC, MC, V. **Map** p336 D4.
The Castañer family helped make espadrilles chic in the 1980s, when the company designed rope-soled shoes for designers such as Donna Karan and Jean-Paul Gaultier. Castañer still introduces a zippy line of espadrilles and sandals each summer, but they have also branched into selling stylish leather shoes for women.

La Manual Alpargatera
C/Avinyó 7, Barri Gòtic (93 301 01 72). Metro Liceu/14, 38, 59, 91 bus. **Open** *Jan-Sept, Dec* 9.30am-1.30pm, 4.30-8pm Mon-Sat. *Oct, Nov* 9.30am-1.30pm, 4.30-8pm Mon-Fri; 10am-1.30pm Sat. **Credit** AmEx, DC, MC, V. **Map** p343 B3.
This shop and workshop in the Old City sells the city's best selection of traditional espadrilles at reasonable prices. They have dozens of styles, including the traditional Tabarner model (€19), which Catalans wear to dance the *sardana*. If you can't find a pair that fits, they will custom-make them.

Muxart
C/Rosselló 230, Eixample (93 488 10 64/ www.muxart.com). Metro Diagonal/7, 16, 17, 22, 24, 28 bus. **Open** 10am-2pm, 4.30-8.30pm Mon-Fri; 10am-2pm, 5-8.30pm Sat. **Credit** AmEx, MC, V. **Map** p336 D4.
Barcelona shoe designer Hermenegildo Muxart is famous for his works of art for the feet. Shoe lovers of both sexes swoon at the sight of his original, high-quality designs, ranging from printed cowboy boots to strappy sandals, bags and accessories.
Branch: Rambla Catalunya 47, Eixample (93 467 74 23).

Noel Barcelona
C/Pelai 46, Eixample (93 317 86 38). Metro Plaça Catalunya/bus all routes to Plaça Catalunya. **Open** 10am-9pm Mon-Sat. **Credit** MC, V. **Map** p342 A1.
All kinds of shoes, from practically unwearable 30cm (12in) platform boots in garish colours to the trendiest sneakers. Noel Barcelona's footwear is undoubtedly not for the shy.
Branch: **Noel Fun** C/Santa Anna 37, Barri Gòtic (93 412 68 80).

Royalty
Portal de l'Àngel 36, Barri Gòtic (93 317 16 32/ www.royalty.es). Metro Catalunya/bus all routes to Plaça Catalunya. **Open** 10am-8.30pm Mon-Fri; 10am-9pm Sat. **Credit** AmEx, DC, MC, V. **Map** p342 B2.
This shoe gallery has its finger on the pulse of the shoe world. On display are the latest designs for men and women from major Spanish brands such as Ras, Camper, Pedro García and Superga, and from international names such as Clarks, Mephisto and Timberland.
Branch: C/Calvet 23, Zona Alta (93 209 51 32).

Espadrilles in every size and colour at **La Manual Alpargatera.** *See p200.*

Flowers

Florists and plant shops can be found all over Barcelona, but tend to specialise in rather fussy arrangements rather than simple bunches of flowers. Many of them offer the Interflora delivery service. As well as the flower stalls on the Rambla, there are stalls at the **Mercat de la Concepció**, on the corner of C/València and C/Bruc (map p337 E4), which are open all night.

Flors Navarro

C/Valencia 320, Eixample (93 457 40 99/ www.florsnavarro.com). Metro Verdaguer/ 43, 44 bus. **Open** 24hrs daily. **Credit** AmEx, MC, V. **Map** p336 D4.
A flower and plant paradise with all types of freshly cut blossoms, arrangements, plants and planters. Open 24 hours, Navarro has a delivery service and runs a stall (7am-10pm) at Mercat de la Concepció.

Food & drink

Chocolate, cakes & bread

Cacao Sampaka

C/Consell de Cent 292, Eixample, (93 272 08 33/ www.cacaosampaka.com). Metro Passeig de Gràcia/ 20, 22, 24, 28, 54, 58, 63, 64, 66, 67, 68 bus. **Open** 9am-8.30pm Mon-Sat. **Credit** AmEx, DC, MC, V. **Map** p336 D5.
A visit here might lead to chocolate addiction. Cacao Sampaka makes its own chocolate using artisan methods. Bon-bon collections come in stylish packages and they sell over 100 types of chocolate bars, as well as chocolate sauces and ice-creams.

Escribà

Gran Via de les Corts Catalanes 546, Eixample (93 454 75 35). Metro Urgell/9, 14, 20, 38, 50, 56, 59 bus. **Open** 8am-9pm daily. **Credit** MC, V. **Map** p340 C5.
Antoni Escribà – many times champion *pastisser* of Barcelona – is a local celebrity. His pastries are edible sculptures and he is particularly well known for his elaborate, custom-made cakes. The Rambla branch is in the Antigua Casa Figueras, which has a beautiful mosaic façade, while down by the Port Olímpic, the family runs a popular restaurant, Xiringuito Escribà (*see p155*).
Branch: La Rambla 83, Barri Gòtic (93 301 60 27).

Forn de Pa Sant Jordi

C/Llibreteria 8, Barri Gòtic (93 310 40 16). Metro Jaume I/17, 19, 40, 45 bus. **Open** 7am-9pm Mon-Sat; 8am-2pm Sun. **No credit cards**. **Map** p342 B3.
There's nearly always a queue outside the Sant Jordi bread shop – testimony to the delicious cakes on sale inside. The bread is good, and the *xuxos/chuchos* (cream doughnuts) are extremely tasty.

Pastisseria Maurí

Rambla Catalunya 102, Eixample (93 215 10 20). Metro Diagonal/FGC Provença/7, 16, 17, 22, 24, 28 bus. **Open** *Sept-June* 8am-9pm Mon-Sat; 9am-3pm, 5-9pm Sun. *July, Aug* 8am-9pm Mon-Sat; 9am-3pm Sun. **Credit** MC, V. **Map** p336 D4.
This shop opened in 1885 as a grocery specialising in cakes, and the elaborate painted ceiling dates from that time. Enjoy delicate sandwiches or cakes in the tea room, or take away a ready-to-eat meal (at a price) from what remains of the grocery store.
Branch: Rambla Catalunya 103, Eixample (93 215 81 46).

Designer genes

Barcelona has the highest concentration of designers in Spain. They spread their talent over a number of fields, from fashion to interiors to graphics. In terms of international recognition and export figures, however, the city's most successful design area is furniture. Barcelona *mobles* have been turning heads since *Modernista* times, and the quest for innovative furnishings continues. Contemporary Catalan furniture is above all curvaceous and playful, with exceptional standards of workmanship. Many designs respond to the strong artistic and architectural foundation laid by *Modernista* architects such as Gaudí, Domènech i Montaner and Puig i Cadafalch (for more info, *see chapter* **Modernisme**). The influence of Catalonia's art nouveau is evident in contemporary pieces – such as the Banco Catalano designed by Òscar Tusquets and Lluís Clotet. This steel bench, characterised by the bends in its back, sits in parks throughout the city and was inspired by a Gaudí bench in Parc Güell. Another Catalan classic is Jorge Pensi's Toledo chair, which introduced curves to cast aluminium in the late 1980s. Toledo chairs now grace the outdoor terraces of cafés all over Europe.

For an overview of Catalan design, stroll through the design showroom **BD Ediciones** (*see p190*). BD's objective is twofold: it produces and markets contemporary furniture and also reproduces historic designs by greats such as Gaudí, Dalí and Hoffmann. Founded in 1972 by young architects and design professionals, BD occupies two floors of Casa Thomas, the refurbished Domènech i Montaner building on C/Mallorca. This is the place to contemplate Dalí's hot pink sofa Vis-à-Vis de Gala, alongside contemporary classics such as Antoni de Moragas's spectacular Vague Stelle chandelier, a sculpture of halogen tubes that you'll find illuminating theatres, restaurants and foyers around the city.

Another mandatory visit is **Pilma** (*see p193*), an extensive design store with four levels and sections devoted to every area of the home (*pictured*). The design shrine **Vinçon** (*see p193*) is also worth a browse. Cutting-edge furniture can be found on the second floor, in the former apartment of the great *Modernista* artist Santiago Rusiñol.

While some designers display their products in the city's swankier stores, many others are still toiling away in the background. In recent years, furniture designers from all over the world have set up studios in Barcelona. Take Miguel Ángel González, for example, a 37-year-old actor-designer-electrician, who dreams up extraordinary, one-of-a-kind lamps in his Raval home and workshop (**Lamparas González**; 93 317 10 46). González makes the lamps out of recycled materials that he gathers on the street. His innovations often combine 1950s machine parts with random metal objects such as colanders or cocktail shakers, and while they are constructed out of old parts, they are decidedly futuristic, and – like most Catalan furniture design – one step ahead of their time.

Colmados/general food stores

Colmado Afro-Latino

Via Laietana 15, La Ribera (93 268 27 43). Metro Jaume I/17, 19, 40, 45 bus. **Open** 9am-9pm Mon-Sat; 10am-9pm Sun. **Credit** MC, V. **Map** p343 B3.

An impressive selection of food and drink from Latin America, Africa and further afield. Whether you're looking for *maté* from Argentina, *cachaça* from Brazil, Cameroonian palm wine, Peruvian beer or authentic, imported soy sauce, you'll find what you're after here – at eminently reasonable prices.

Colmado Quilez

Rambla Catalunya 63, Eixample (93 215 23 56/ www.lafuente.es). Metro Passeig de Gracia/7, 16, 17, 22, 24, 28 bus. **Open** 9am-2pm, 4.30-8.30pm Mon-Sat. Closed Sat afternoon Jan-Sept. **Credit** MC, V. **Map** p336 D4.

One of the monuments of the Eixample. The windows and walls of this fabulous emporium are lined with delicacies from all over the world. There's olive oil, sweets and a huge variety of hams and cheeses, plus every type of alcohol imaginable: dozens of beers, sake, a wall of whiskies, and cava from more than 55 bodegas – one, Cava La Fuente, is sold exclusively in this shop. The store's coffee brand, Café Quilez, is imported from Colombia, and ground for you on the premises.

Queviures Murrià

C/Roger de Llúria 85, Eixample (93 215 57 89). Metro Passeig de Gràcia/20, 39, 43, 44, 45, 47 bus. **Open** 9am-2pm, 5-9pm Mon-Sat. **Credit** MC, V. **Map** p336 D4.

This magnificent *Modernista* shop, photographed time and again for its original 1900s tiled decoration by Ramon Casas, and still run by the Murrià family, is not only an architectural attraction. Its wonderful food includes a superb range of individually sourced farmhouse cheeses, and more than 300 wines, including its own-label Cava Murrià.

Food specialities

Caelum

C/Palla 8, Barri Gòtic (93 392 69 93). Metro Liceu/ 14, 38, 59, 91 bus. **Open** noon-8.30pm Mon-Sat. **Credit** MC, V. **Map** p342 B2.

This lovely shop offers 'delicacies and other temptations from monasteries'. The owners search Spain for the best artisan products made by monks, including marzipan, *yemas* (a sweet made of egg yolks), truffles, chocolates and wines. The downstairs area, formerly the site of a 15th-century Jewish bath, now contains a Zen-like café.

Cafés El Magnífico

C/Argenteria 64, La Ribera (93 319 60 81/ www.cafeselmagnifico.com). Metro Jaume I/ 17, 19, 40, 45 bus. **Open** 8.30am-1.30pm, 4-8pm Mon-Fri; 9am-2pm Sat. Closed 3wks Aug. **Credit** AmEx, MC, V. **Map** p343 C3.

Cacao Sampaka: for chocoholics. *See p201.*

Since 1919, the Sans family has imported, prepared and blended coffees from around the world. Prices vary from €10/kg for a simple blend to €78/kg for the especially smooth Jamaican coffee. They also stock more than 300 cases of tea, including blends from Taiwan, Nepal, India, Sri Lanka, China, Japan and Sikkim. There's a great collection of antique tea and coffee cups.

Branch: Sans & Colonials C/Argentería 59, La Ribera (93 319 60 81).

Casa del Bacalao

C/Comtal 8, Barri Gòtic (93 301 65 39). Metro Urquinaona/17, 19, 40, 45 bus. **Open** 9am-2.30pm, 5-8.30pm Mon-Sat. **Credit** AmEx, MC, V. **Map** p342 B2.

Beware the overwhelming fishy odour when you walk through the door; the 'house of cod' sells nothing else – salted and dried, with no chemical additives. Salt-cod features in many Catalan and Spanish dishes, which require different parts of the fish: the cheek (*mejilla*) for *bacalao* with *salsa verde*; broken-up pieces (€17/kg) for *esqueixada*, and small *kokotxes* for Basque *bacalao al pil-pil*. Travellers, note: staff can now vacuum-pack your choice piece to take home – don't, though, forget to de-salt it overnight before cooking it.

Casa Gispert

C/Sombrerers 23, La Ribera (93 319 75 35/www. casagispert.com). Metro Jaume I/17, 19, 40, 45 bus. **Open** *Jan-July, Sept-Dec* 9am-1.30pm, 4-7.30pm Tue-Fri; 10am-2pm, 5-8pm Sat. *Aug* 10am-2pm, 5-8pm Tue-Fri. **Credit** DC, MC, V. **Map** p343 C3.

Founded in the 1850s, Casa Gispert is a wholesale outlet famous for top-quality nuts, dried fruit and coffee. All are roasted on site in the magnificent original wood-burning stove; you can delve into enormous baskets of almonds and hazelnuts, still warm from the oven. There are special packs for certain recipes, such as *romesco* sauce, or seasonal goodies, such as *coca de Sant Joan* in June or *panellets* at Hallowe'en (for both, *see p220* **Sacred tart**). The packaging is also wonderful, and this is a great place to buy delicious presents.

Eat, Drink, Shop

Formatgeria La Seu

C/Daguería 16, Barri Gòtic (93 412 65 48). Metro
Jaume I/17, 19, 40, 45 bus. **Open** 10pm-3pm,
5-8pm Tue-Sat. **No credit cards. Map** p343 B3.
Katherine McLaughlin of Scotland sells a fine range
of *denominación origen* Spanish cheese from this
quaint shop, located near Plaça Sant Jaume in
Barcelona's first buttermaking factory. La Seu
offers monthly cheese courses (taught in Spanish),
and on Saturdays you can sample three cheeses
with a taste of wine for €1.50.

La Italiana

C/Bon Succes 12, Raval (93 318 20 42). Metro
Catalunya/bus all routes to Plaça Catalunya.
Open 9am-2pm, 5-8pm Mon-Fri, 9am-2pm Sat.
Closed Aug. **Credit** MC, V. **Map** p342 A2.
The Rivali family of Genova opened this Italian
emporium in 1904. Their speciality is fresh pasta,
but they also carry wonderful ingredients for *la
dolce vita*, including grappas, Italian wines, cheeses
and prepared foods.

La Pineda

C/Pi 16, Barri Gòtic (93 302 43 93). Metro Liceu/
14, 38, 59, 91 bus. **Open** 9am-3pm, 5-10pm Mon-
Sat; 11am-3pm, 7-10pm Sun. **Credit** AmEx, DC,
MC, V. **Map** p342 B2.
La Pineda has specialised in *jamón serrano* since
1930, together with other fine cold meats and a
wide range of cheeses and wines. The shop – a
charming Barri Gòtic survivor – also functions as
a local *bodega*, with a few humble tables and stools
where you can snack on these delicacies, washed
down with a good Rioja.

Tot Formatge 2

Passeig del Born 13, La Ribera (93 319 53 75).
Metro Liceu/14, 38, 59, 91 bus. **Open** 7.30am-
1.15pm, 4.30-7.30pm Mon-Fri; 9am-1.15pm Sat.
No credit cards. Map p343 C3.
Probably the most comprehensive cheese specialist
in Barcelona, with cheeses from all over Catalonia
and Spain, France, Italy and many other parts of
Europe. The goat's cheeses from Extremadura are
excellent; if you prefer something milder, try the
Catalan *mató* (curd cheese).

Health & herbs

Herbolari Ferran

Plaça Reial 18, Barri Gòtic (93 304 20 05). Metro
Liceu/14, 38, 59, 91 bus. **Open** 9.30am-2pm,
4.30-8pm Mon-Sat. **Credit** MC, V. **Map** p343 A3.
Herbolari Ferran has been serving a faithful public
since the 1940s. Its large basement area comprises
an old-fashioned herb shop, a modern self-service
shop, a coffee/teashop, a bookshop and an exhibition area, providing an all-round healthstore service.

Herboristeria del Rei

C/Vidre 1, Barri Gòtic (93 318 05 12). Metro
Liceu/14, 38, 59, 91 bus. **Open** 10am-2pm,
5-8pm Mon-Sat. **Credit** MC, V. **Map** p343 A3.

This unique shop was founded in 1818 by Josep Vilà,
as La Lineana, after the great botanist Linnaeus. It
was decorated by the theatre designer Francesc
Soler i Rovirosa and the interior is ornate: a grand
balcony winds around the shop at second-floor level,
while the walls below are lined with hundreds of
tiny specimen drawers all individually worked in
marquetry or decorated with miniature water-
colours. In 1858, the shop became official herbalist
to Queen Isabel II, and changed its name to
Herboristeria del Rei; it went back to La Lineana in
the two republican periods. These name changes
are still visible in the gold lettering on the door.

Macrobiòtic Zen

C/Muntaner 12, Eixample (93 454 60 23). Metro
Universitat/bus all routes to Plaça Universitat.
Open 9am-2pm, 5-8pm Mon-Fri. Closed 2wks Aug.
Credit MC, V. **Map** p340 C5.
This shop specialises in vegetarian, macrobiotic and
ecological food products, including fresh vegetables,
soy-based desserts and tofu. There's a self-service
canteen at the back of the shop.

Wine

Craft shop **Art Escudellers** (*see p189*) has
a good selection of wines in its cellar. For
information on local wines, *see p146* **Grape
expectations**.

El Celler de Gélida

C/Vallespir 65, Sants (93 339 26 41/www.
mestres-celler.com). Metro Plaça del Centre or
Sants Estació/ bus all routes to Estació de Sants.
Open 9am-2pm, 5-8.30pm Mon-Fri; 9.30am-2.30pm,
5-8.30pm Sat. Closed Aug; Sat afternoon July-Sept.
Credit MC, V. **Map** p335 A4.
A little way off the beaten track in Sants, this cellar
dates from 1895 and has more than 3,200 labels,
including an unbeatable selection of Catalan wines.
The knowledgeable staff advise many restaurants
on their wine lists.

Lafuente

C/Johann Sebastian Bach 20, Zona Alta (93
339 26 41). FGC Bonanova/14 bus. **Open**
9am-2pm, 4.30-8.30pm Mon-Sat. **Credit** MC, V.
Map p336 C2.
This smart wine store in the Zona Alta has a huge
selection of wines, *caves* and spirits, including a good
choice of non-Spanish wines.
Branch: C/Ferran 20, Barri Gòtic (93 412 29 49).

Vila Viniteca

C/Agullers 7-9, La Ribera (93 310 19 56/
www.vilaviniteca.es). Metro Jaume 1/17,
19, 45 bus. **Open** 8.30am-2.30pm, 4.30-
8.30pm Mon-Sat. **Credit** AmEx, DC, MC, V.
Map p343 B4.
Joaquim Vila took over the shop from his grand-
father, who opened it in 1932. It offers a wide range
of wine and cava. The excellent grocery store next
door is owned by the same family.

Hair & beauty

Beauty treatments

Instituto Francis
Ronda de Sant Pere 18, La Ribera (93 317 78 08).
Metro Catalunya/bus all routes to Plaça Catalunya.
Open 9.30am-8pm Mon-Fri; 9.30am-4pm Sat.
Credit DC, MC, V. **Map** p342 B1.
Eight floors dedicated to making you look and feel
great; from make-up and makeovers on the first floor
up through hairdressing, waxing, facials, slimming
and massages. Not cheap, but a real treat.

Masajes a 1000
C/Mallorca 233, Eixample (93 215 85 85).
Metro Diagonal/FGC Provença/7, 16, 17, 22,
24, 28 bus. **Open** 7am-1am daily. **Credit** AmEx,
V. **Map** p336 D4.
This beauty centre offers everything from inexpensive, professional massages (from ten minutes
for €6 to an hour at €33) to pedicures, manicures
and peelings. They also do a 'siesta' massage – a
short massage after which you can have a nap. The
perfect solution to a hard day's shopping.

Cosmetics & perfumes

Perfumería Prat
La Rambla 68 (93 317 71 39). Metro Liceu/14, 38,
59, 91 bus. **Open** 10am-2pm, 4-8.30pm Mon-Sat.
Credit AmEx, DC, MC, V. **Map** p343 A3.
This beautiful perfumery, which until 1997 occupied
part of the Liceu building, has been transported
pillar by pillar to a new site across the Rambla.
This undertaking was justified by its history: it was
the first *perfumería* established in Spain, by Renaud
Germain in 1847. It still thrives today, with a fine
selection of perfumes and cosmetics.

Regia
Passeig de Gràcia 39, Eixample (93 216 01 21/
www.perfum-museum.com). Metro Passeig de Gràcia/
7, 16, 17, 22, 24, 28 bus. **Open** 10am-8.30pm Mon-
Fri; 10.30am-2pm, 5-8.30pm Sat. **Credit** AmEx, DC,
MC, V. **Map** p336 D4.
Regia has been serving a very select Barcelona clientele in its main shop and beauty salon on Passeig de
Gràcia since 1928. It stocks more than 60 types of
scent, plus all the best beauty potions. For those
interested in olfactory nostalgia, it also contains the
remarkable Museu del Perfum, tucked away at the
back of the shop.

Sephora
El Triangle, C/Pelai 13-39, Eixample (93 306 39 00).
Metro Catalunya/bus all routes to Plaça Catalunya.
Open 10am-10pm Mon-Sat. **Credit** AmEx, DC, MC,
V. **Map** p342 A1.
Truly the most sophisticated of perfumeries, this
French mega-shop has taken Barcelona by storm.
The 'perfume street', with a striking red, black and
white colour scheme, occupies almost 2,500sq m

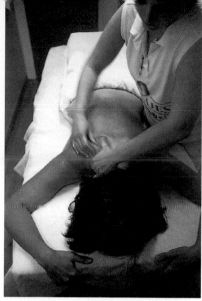

Lie back and relax at **Masajes a 1000**.

(26,800sq ft) of space in what was once a dingy
underground arcade; all the huge stock is on display,
and you are invited to try out each and every one, if
your sense of smell can stand it. Shoppers can consult the 'perfume stock market' wall panel for fluc-
tuating prices of perfumes in capitals around the
world, browse through a perfume and fashion
library, or log on to the free Internet service.
Branch: La Maquinista, C/Ciutat d'Asunción,
Sant Andreu (93 360 87 21).

Hairdressers

Anthony Llobet
C/Sant Joaquim 28, Gràcia (93 415 42 10/mobile
639 931 555). Metro Fontana/22, 24, 28 bus.
Open 10am-8pm Mon-Fri. Closed Aug. **Credit** MC,
V. **Map** p336 D3.
If you don't trust your Spanish , this is the place for
you. Anthony and his team all speak English and are
very competent hairdressers. Prices are reasonable.

Clear
C/Pi 11, pral 10, Barri Gòtic (93 317 08 22/
www.clear-bcn.com). Metro Liceu/14, 38, 59, 91 bus.
Open 10am-8pm Mon-Sat. **Credit** AmEx, MC, V.
Map p342 B2.
Welcome to the place where the stylish go for min-
imalist cuts, crazy extensions and makeovers. The
salon's all-white futuristic decor is worth a look.

Llongueras
C/Balmes 162, Eixample (93 218 61 50/
www.llongueras.com). Metro Diagonal/FGC
Provença/7, 16, 17, 31, 67, 68 bus. **Open**
Jan-June, Sept-Dec 9.30am-6.30pm Mon-Sat.
July, Aug 9.30am-6.30pm Mon-Fri; 9.30am-2pm
Sat. **Credit** AmEx, DC, MC, V. **Map** p336 D4.

This is the best known hairdressing chain in Spain, with more than a dozen branches in the city, including three in major branches of El Corte Inglés. It's also expensive, but the C/Balmes salon's hairdressing school offers cheaper cuts.
Branches: throughout the city.

Peluquería Vicente
C/Tallers 11, Raval (no phone). Metro Catalunya/ bus all routes to Plaça Catalunya. **Open** 9am-1pm, 4-8pm Mon-Fri; 9am-1pm Sat. **No credit cards.** **Map** p342 A1.

Gentlemen: for a no-nonsense haircut and one of the closest shaves in the world, try out this small traditional barber's shop.

Markets

If you love markets, this is the city for you. From coins to clothes, books to bric-a-brac, flowers to furniture, there's something for all tastes (for details, call 010 for the council information line). For details of Barcelona's food markets, *see below* **On the market**.

On the market

Markets are central to the life of Barcelona residents – whether coins, stamps or clothes – and every *barri* has its own food market, 40 in total. **La Boqueria** (*see below*) is deservedly the most famous, but there are others worth visiting. **Mercat Sant Antoni**, near the Paral.lel, has a clothes market around the edge and food stalls in the middle, while **Mercat de la Llibertat** in Gràcia has a more villagey atmosphere. In the Eixample, **Mercat del Ninot** at the junction of C/Mallorca and C/Casanova offers everything you could think of, and **Mercat de la Concepció** on the corner of C/València and C/Bruc is famous for flowers.

Markets open early (8am or before) and most close by about 2pm or 3pm. Monday is not a good day to go, as stocks are low and there is no fresh fish.

WHAT TO BUY

Look out for the many Spanish cheeses with a *denominación de origen*; try pungent *cabrales* from Asturias, dry *mahón* from Menorca, or the delicious *garrotxa*, a Catalan cheese made from goat's milk, not to mention the many delicious *manchegos*. *Seco* is strong and dry; for a milder version, try *semi* or *tierno*.

The other favourite ingredient of the Spanish diet is, of course, dry-cured ham, *jamón serrano* (*pernil serrà* in Catalan). The very best comes from south-west Spain, but it's found everywhere, and is one thing that unites Catalans with the rest of the country. The quality of *jamón* varies a good deal, and you can expect to pay up to €90 per kilo for the best, entirely traditionally cured ham. The biggest distinction is between *jamón del país* (generic *serrano*) and *jamón iberico* or *pata negra* (black foot), from the native Iberian breed of black pig, kept free-range and fed on acorns. The best, and most expensive, *pata*

negra comes from Jabugo in Andalucia. As well as *jamón*, stalls offer many other cold meats, such as chorizo, *salchicón*, Catalan *botifarra* and spicy Mallorcan *sobrassada*.

La Boqueria (Mercat de Sant Josep)
La Rambla 91, Barri Gòtic (93 318 25 84). Metro Liceu/bus 14, 38, 59, 91. **Open** 8am-8.30pm Mon-Sat. **Map** p342 A2.
The Boqueria is one of the greatest food markets in the world, and is looking better than ever. A new roof allows more light in, making it easier to appreciate the orderliness of its structure: fruit and vegetables around the edge, separate meat and chicken stalls, and fish and seafood in the centre, arranged in a circle.

Enter through the main gates, set back from the Rambla, amid great colourful heaps of dried and fresh fruits and nuts. Don't buy here though: the stalls by the entrance are more expensive than those further inside. They do, however, offer delights such as *palmitos* (palm roots), *higos chumbos* (Indian figs) or *caña dulce* (sugar cane sticks). The stall to the right of the entrance specialises in fresh herbs, tropical fruit and African food. It's one of the few places selling fresh coriander, tarragon, ginger and okra throughout the year.

Admire the glistening meat and fish stalls, kept firmly in order by ladies in spotless white overalls, or continue to Llorenç Petras's stall at the back, with its staggering display of wild mushrooms (*bolets* in Catalan, *setas* in Spanish). Mushroom hunting is big business in Catalonia, and entire families take to the hills in the autumn in the pursuit of highly valued, sweet *rovellons*, tasty *llenegues*, nutty *girgoles* or the small earthy *moixernon*. If you plan on trying this yourself, best to come here first and take a few tips from the master.

Eat, Drink, Shop

Antiques Market

Avda de la Catedral 6, Barri Gòtic (93 302 70 45).
Metro Jaume I/17, 19, 40, 45 bus. **Open** *Jan-July,*
Sept-Dec 10am-9pm Thur. Closed Aug. **No credit**
cards. **Map** p342 B2.
This bustling antiques market – open only on
Thursdays – is located in front of the cathedral.
Vendors display pocket watches, antique lace,
decanters and a random assortment of jewellery
among the bric-a-brac. Prices are high, so come prepared to bargain. Before Christmas, the market
transfers to the Portal de l'Àngel.

Art Market

Plaça Sant Josep Oriol, Barri Gòtic (no phone).
Metro Liceu/14, 38, 59 bus. **Open** 11am-
8.30pm Sat; 10am-3pm Sun. **No credit cards**.
Map p343 A3.
Every weekend, an art market of variable quality is
held in Plaça Sant Josep Oriol. Paintings range from
the typical rendering of La Rambla to nudes, still
lifes and even abstract art. On the first and third
weekend of every month, merchants set up a food
fair in the adjacent Plaça del Pi, to sell their artisan
food products, including honey and cheese.

Eat, Drink, Shop

Book & Coin Market

Mercat de Sant Antoni, C/Comte d'Urgell 1,
Eixample (93 423 42 87). Metro Sant Antoni/
20, 24, 38, 64, 91 bus. **Open** 9am-2pm (approx)
Sun. **No credit cards. Map** p340 C5.

This second-hand book and coin market is something of an institution in Barcelona. It takes place
in Mercat de Sant Antoni, a wonderful iron building dating from 1876. At around 9am on Sunday
mornings, crowds gather to rummage through
boxes of dusty tomes, old magazines and video
games, and whole collections of old coins. If claus-
trophobia sets in, sit at one of the nearby bars to
watch the bargain-hunters pass by.

Brocanters del Port Vell

Moll de les Drassanes, Port Vell (no phone). Metro
Drassanes/14, 36, 38, 57, 59, 64, 100, 157 bus.
Open 11am-9pm Sat, Sun. **No credit cards.**
Map p343 A4.

This bric-a-brac and antiques market is held in a
prime position on the seafront between the monument to Columbus and the Maremàgnum bridge
(the Rambla del Mar). The only antiques market
held on Sundays, it's popular with locals on the
lookout for china, coins, collectors' records, costume
jewellery, mantillas and old lace, toys, pocket
watches, fountain pens and even military gear.
Show up around 11am for the best selection. Prices
are more reasonable than at the Barri Gòtic market.

Els Encants

C/Dos de Maig 186, Plaça de la Glòries, Eixample
(93 246 30 30). Metro Glòries/62, 92 bus. **Open**
8.30am-6pm (auctions 9am-5pm) Mon, Wed, Fri, Sat.
No credit cards. Map p341 F5.

Els Encants (also known as the Mercat de Bellcaire)
remains the most authentic of flea markets – from
its fringes, where old men lay out battered shoes
and toys on cloths spread on the ground, to the centre, where you'll find real and fake antiques, tools,
paint, second-hand clothes, new textiles and loads
of fascinating junk. If possible, avoid Saturdays,
when it's very crowded – and watch out for short-
changing and pickpockets. The market is officially
open in the afternoons, but many stalls pack up at
midday; for the best stuff, get there around 8am and
be prepared to haggle.

Stamp & Coin Market

Plaça Reial 1, Barri Gòtic. Metro Liceu/14, 38, 59
bus. **Open** 9am-2.30pm (approx) Sun. **No credit**
cards. Map p343 A3.

Stamp collecting (*filatelia*) and coin collecting
(*numismàtica*) are taken seriously in Barcelona,
where there are various clubs and societies devoted
to the trades, and dozens of dealers. This somewhat
incongruous gathering for enthusiasts was first held
in 1890 and blends surprisingly well with the
somewhat shady goings-on in the Plaça Reial.
Having inspected the coins, stamps and rocks, take
an aperitif in the sun and watch the experts pore
over each other's collections.

Music

Large mainstream music shops can also be
found in the huge Portal de l'Àngel branch of
El Corte Inglés (*see p184*) and the **FNAC**
(*see p187*). C/Tallers, C/Bonsuccés and C/Riera
Baixa in the Raval are dotted with speciality
shops catering to all tastes and formats.

La Casa

Plaça Vicenç Martorell 4, Raval (93 412 33 05).
Metro Catalunya/bus all routes to Plaça Catalunya.
Open 11am-2pm, 5-9pm Mon-Sat. **Credit** MC, V.
Map p342 A1-2.

Probably the most respected record shop in the
dance music scene. Its owners are mines of information on dance music across the board. There's a
decent vinyl selection.

New Phono

C/Ample 37, Barri Gòtic (93 315 13 61/www.
newphono.es). Metro Jaume I/14, 17, 19, 36, 40,
45, 57, 59, 64, 157 bus. **Open** 9.30am-2pm, 4.30-
8pm Mon-Wed, Fri; 9.30am-8pm Thur; 9.30am-2pm
Sat. **Credit** AmEx, DC, MC, V. **Map** p343 B4.

Founded in 1834, this is one of the oldest shops in
Spain, and specialises in the manufacture, sale and
repair of musical instruments. The wide selection
of guitars includes some fine ones by Ramirez.

Discos Castelló

C/Tallers 3, Raval (93 318 20 41/www.discos
castello.es). Metro Catalunya/bus all routes to Plaça
Catalunya. **Open** 10am-2pm, 4.30-8.30pm Mon-Sat.
Credit AmEx, DC, MC, V. **Map** p342 A2.

A chain of small shops, each with a different emphasis. This one specialises in classical; the branch in Nou
de la Rambla is good for ethnic music and flamenco.
Branches: C/Tallers 7, Raval (93 302 59 46);
C/Tallers 9, Raval (93 412 72 85); C/Tallers 79,
Raval (93 301 35 75); C/Nou de la Rambla 15, Raval
(93 302 42 36); C/Creu Coberta 73, Sants (93 424 57
96); La Maquinista, C/Ciutat d'Asunción, Sant
Andreu (93 360 80 78).

Edison's

C/Riera Baixa 9-10, Raval (93 441 96 74/
www.discos-edisons.com). Metro Liceu/20, 64,
91 bus. **Open** 10am-2pm, 4.30-8.30pm Mon-Sat.
Credit AmEx, DC, MC, V. **Map** p340 C6.

Edison's buys and sells unlisted vinyl LPs, singles,
and CDs from the 1950s to the '90s, of all persua-
sions. One part of the shop is dedicated to dance and
pop; the other to second-hand vinyl.

Etnomusic

C/Bonsuccés 6, Raval (93 301 18 84/www.etno
music.com). Metro Catalunya/bus all routes to
Plaça Catalunya. **Open** 5-8pm Mon; 11am-2pm,
5-8pm Tue-Sat. **Credit** MC, V. **Map** p342 A2.

This ethnic music shop in the Raval has music from
all over the planet, although most foreign visitors
seem to be hunting for rare flamenco. Staff know
their business and are extremely helpful.

Opticians

Arense

Ronda Sant Pere 16, Eixample (93 301 82 90).
Metro Catalunya/bus all routes to Plaça Catalunya.
Open 10am-9pm Mon-Sat. **Credit** AmEx, DC, MC,
V. **Map** p342 B1.
This full-service optician occupies a gorgeous
Modernista space, built in 1874 as the art supply
store Casa Teixidor. They sell big-name brands at
reasonable prices and an optometrist works in the
back behind a stained glass window. The down-
stairs lab turns specs around within two days.

Grand Optical

*El Triangle, Plaça Catalunya 4, Eixample (93 304
16 40). Metro Catalunya/bus all routes to Plaça
Catalunya.* **Open** 10am-10pm Mon-Sat. **Credit**
AmEx, MC, V. **Map** p342 A1.
English-speaking staff at Grand Optical offer eye-
tests and can provide new glasses within two hours,
or one hour if you have your prescription. Lens
prices begin at about €27.

Photography

Arpi Foto Video

*La Rambla 38-40 (93 301 74 04). Metro Drassanes
or Liceu/14, 38, 59, 91 bus.* **Open** 9am-2pm,
4-8pm Mon-Sat. **Credit** AmEx, DC, MC, V.
Map p343 A3.
This giant specialist camera store has a wide range
of professional-standard cameras and accessories
and a good basic repair department. Service has
improved, but can still be snail-like at times – but
the staff do know what they're doing. Stock ranges
from happy-snappers to studio Hasselblads.

Fotoprix

*C/Pelai 6, Raval (93 318 20 36). Metro Universitat/
bus all routes to Plaça Universitat.* **Open**
9.30am-2pm, 4.30-8.30pm Mon-Sat. **Credit** V.
Map p342 A1.
Fotoprix has more than 100 branches in the city,
offering one-hour film developing. A standard set of
36 colour prints costs €10.40.

Speciality shops

Traditionally, shops in Barcelona specialised
in a certain trade. The result is a wide range of
quirky, often historic, speciality shops unlike
anywhere else.

Almacenes del Pilar

*C/Boqueria 43, Barri Gòtic (93 317 79 84). Metro
Liceu/14, 38, 59, 91 bus.* **Open** 10am-2pm, 4.30-8pm
Mon-Sat. Closed 2wks Aug. **Credit** AmEx, MC, V.
Map p343 A3.
This quaint shop stocks *mantones de Manila*
(fringed and embroidered silk shawls), mantillas and
materials used for traditional costumes in all regions
of Spain. There's also a good selection of fans.

Aureliano Monge

*C/Boters 2, Barri Gòtic (93 317 94 35). Metro
Liceu/14, 38, 59, 91 bus.* **Open** 9am-1.30pm, 4-8pm
Mon-Sat. **Credit** AmEx, DC, MC, V. **Map** p342 B2.
Even if old stamps and coins are not your thing,
this *Modernista* shop is worth a look through the
window. Designed in 1904 by Calonge, a disciple
of Gaudí, it has dark mahogany walls and four
seats that beat classification.

Cereria Subirà

Baixada de Llibreteria 7, Barri Gòtic (93 315 26 06).
Metro Jaume I/17, 19, 40, 45 bus. **Open** 9am-
1.30pm, 4-7.30pm Mon-Fri; 9am-1.30pm Sat.
Credit AmEx, MC, V. **Map** p343 B3.
Opened in 1761 as a ladies' fashion store, this has
been a candle shop for many decades. It's worth a
visit for the original decor alone, with steps swirling
down from the gallery, and two black maidens
holding torch-like lights at the foot of the stairs.

Condom Globe

*Maremàgnum, Moll d'Espanya, Port Vell (93 665
10 42/www.condomglobe.com). Metro Drassanes/
14, 19, 36, 38, 40, 57, 59, 64, 157 bus.* **Open**
11am-11pm daily. **No credit cards**. **Map** p340 D7.
This kiosk in Maremàgnum sells more than 100
types of condoms from around the world. There's
Durex from the UK, Control from Italy and other
brands from Germany, Sweden and Denmark. You'll
also find gag gifts, such as breast-shaped pasta.

Flora Albaicín

*C/Canuda 3, Barri Gòtic (93 302 10 35). Metro
Catalunya/bus all routes to Plaça Catalunya.* **Open**
10.30am-1pm, 5-8pm Mon-Sat. **Credit** AmEx, MC, V.
Map p342 A-B2.
This tiny shop piles high flamenco skirts, sevillana
dresses, shoes, combs, shawls and everything you
need to dance except talent. They also make outfits
to measure and stock men's riding boots.

El Rei de la Magia

*C/Princesa 11, La Ribera (93 319 39 20/
www.elreidelamagia.com). Metro Liceu/14, 38,
59, 91 bus.* **Open** 10am-2pm, 5-8pm Mon-Fri;
10am-2pm Sat. **Credit** AmEx, MC, V. **Map** p343 B3.
Founded in 1881, this shop is many a magician's
training ground. Walls are covered with auto-
graphed photos of magicians. There are no set prices
and you don't go there to buy a specific item, but
rather to develop an idea or concept that might
require the use of a special chair, box or mechanism,
made for the purpose. Ritual is perhaps the key to
describing the way things happen here.

Sombrereria Obach

*C/Call 2, Barri Gòtic (93 318 40 94). Metro Liceu/
14, 38, 59, 91 bus.* **Open** 9.30am-1.30pm, 4-8pm
Mon-Fri; 9.30am-1.45pm, 4.30-8pm Sat. Closed Sat
afternoons Aug. **Credit** MC, V. **Map** p343 B3.
Here you'll find hats of all varieties, from nylon
pom-poms and top-quality felt berets to formal
headgear for men and women.

Eat, Drink, Shop

Sport

La Botiga del Barça

Maremàgnum, Moll d'Espanya, Port Vell (93 225 80 45). Metro Drassanes/14, 19, 36, 38, 40, 57, 59, 64, 157 bus. **Open** 11am-11pm daily. **Credit** AmEx, DC, MC, V. **Map** p340 D7.

If you feel a visit to Barcelona would be incomplete without acquiring some FC Barcelona paraphernalia, look no further. The Botiga del Barça has every permutation of Barça merchandise imaginable, from scarves, towels and hats, through (of course) shirts, to an appalling range of claret-and-blue clocks. Barça being a club that fancies itself, there are also 'classy' items such as champagne glasses. **Branches**: Gran Via de les Corts Catalanes 418, Eixample (93 423 59 41); Museu del FC Barcelona, Nou Camp (93 496 36 00).

Decathlon

C/Canuda 20, Barri Gòtic (93 342 61 61/ www.decathlon.es). Metro Catalunya/bus all routes to Plaça Catalunya. **Open** 10am-9pm Mon-Fri; 10am-9.30pm Sat. **Credit** DC, MC, V. **Map** p342 B2.

This well-stocked international sporting goods shop, just off La Rambla, has attire and equipment for every sport, from scuba diving to cycling. They also have a trustworthy repair department for bicycles. **Branch**: L'Illa, Avda Diagonal 549, Eixample (93 444 01 54).

Ticket agents

Tickets for many concerts and events are sold through savings banks (*caixas*). The best places to get advance tickets are often the venues themselves; concert tickets for smaller venues may be sold in record shops; look out for details on posters. The bullring has its own ticket office, and football tickets can also be bought from the clubs (for both, *see chapter* **Sport**).

FNAC

El Triangle, Plaça Catalunya 4, Rambla (93 344 18 00). Metro Catalunya/bus all routes to Plaça Catalunya. **Open** 10am-10pm Mon-Sat. **Credit** AmEx, DC, MC, V. **Map** p342 A1.

FNAC has an efficient ticket desk to compete with the *caixas*. Mainly good for rock/pop concerts.

Servi-Caixa – La Caixa

902 33 22 11/www.servicaixa.com. **Credit** MC, V.
Next to the cash machines in branches of the biggest savings bank of all, the Caixa de Pensions (better known just as La Caixa), you'll find a machine called a Servi-Caixa. With a Caixa account or a credit card, you can use this to get T10 and T-50/30 travel cards, local information and tickets to a great many attractions and events, including Universal Studios Port Aventura, Barça football games, the Teatre Nacional and the Liceu, 24 hours a day. You can also order tickets by phone (many of the staff speak some English) or through their website.

Tel-entrada – Caixa Catalunya

902 10 12 12/www.telentrada.com. Central desk: Plaça Catalunya, La Rambla (no phone). Metro Catalunya/bus all routes to Plaça Catalunya. **Open** 9am-9pm Mon-Sat. **Credit** MC, V. **Map** p342 B1.

Tel-entrada sells tickets for many theatres over the counter at all its branches. You can also book tickets by phone with a credit card (many of the staff speak reasonable English); you must collect the tickets at the venue itself. You can phone from outside Spain (on 34 93 479 99 20), or buy tickets on the Internet. Also, you can get tickets for half-price by buying them (cash only) within three hours of a performance at the Tel-entrada desk at Plaça Catalunya.

Tobacco & cigars

L'Estanc de Laietana

Via Laietana 4, La Ribera (93 310 10 34). Metro Jaume I/17, 19, 40, 45 bus. **Open** 9am-2pm, 4-8pm Mon-Fri; 10am-2pm Sat. **Credit** (gifts only, not cigarettes) AmEx, MC, V. **Map** p343 B4.

The busiest and most famous of the tobacco shops in Barcelona, run with zest and enthusiasm by Sr Porta. More than 100 brands of cigarettes and 100 types of rolling tobacco are on sale; he also has a humidor at sea level in his underground cellar to store his exceptional range of fine cigars.

Gimeno

Passeig de Gràcia 101, Eixample (93 237 20 78/ www.gimeno101.com). Metro Diagonal/7, 16, 17, 22, 24, 28 bus. **Open** 10am-2pm, 4-8.30pm Mon-Sat. **Credit** AmEx, DC, MC, V. **Map** p336 D4.

Gimeno has anything and everything to do with smoking, with hundreds of pipes and lighters, plus an interesting collection of ornate walking sticks.

Travel services

Travel agents have become more competitive, and it pays to shop around to find good deals.

Halcón Viajes

C/Aribau 34, Eixample (93 454 59 95/902 30 06 00/www.halcon-viajes.es). Metro Universitat/ bus all routes to Plaça Universitat. **Open** 9.30am-1.30pm, 4.30-8pm Mon-Fri; 10am-1.30pm Sat. **Credit** AmEx, DC, MC, V. **Map** p340 C5.

This chain travel agency is part of a group that also owns the airline Air Europa, and so often has exclusive bargain deals on its Spanish domestic and European flights. It also has a hotel booking service, and good deals on car rental.

Nouvelles Frontières

C/Balmes 8, Eixample (93 304 32 33/reservations 902 21 21 20/www.nouvelles-frontieres.es). Metro Universitat or Plaça Catalunya/bus all routes to Plaça Catalunya. **Open** 9.30am-8pm Mon-Fri; 10am-6pm Sat. **Credit** AmEx, DC, MC, V. **Map** p340 D5.

A no-nonsense agency with very competitive prices. **Branch**: C/Pallars 73, Eixample (93 485 79 00).

Arts &
Entertainment

By Season

Cracking Catalan carnivals, castles, cakes and Christmas crappers. Crikey.

Whatever the season, there is always plenty to do in Barcelona. The city lends itself to outdoor activity, and the Catalans pride themselves on their sense of community and tradition, turning out in force for all events, whether cultural, sporting, political or even religious. With an excellent climate, an attractive urban landscape as a backdrop, and plenty of energy and enthusiasm on tap, in Barcelona you are never more than a few days away from some festival, fair or feast day.

For a crash-course in Catalan traditions, you can't beat the local celebrations (*festes majores*) held in each area of the city. The main one in Barcelona is the **Mercè** in September (*see p216* **Mercè mission**), though there are smaller, very popular versions in Gràcia, Sants, Barceloneta and most local districts, most of which involve a individual blend of concerts, street parties, human castles, parades of giants and fatheads, and the pyromaniac pandemonium of the *correfoc*.

Festivals of music, cinema, dance and anything else that can be watched, performed, eaten, swapped, sold, sweated over or otherwise enjoyed are plentiful. The main ones include the **Grec** festival of music, theatre and dance (*see p217*), the **Sónar** electronic music festival and the **Festa de la Diversitat** (for both, *see p214*), which celebrates the city's cultural and ethnic diversity. And for the more athletically inclined, there are several sporting events open to public participation, including the marathon (*see p266*), a couple of fun runs, a mass skate-in and a chilly swim across the port on Christmas Day. The main events are listed below.

INFORMATION
The best places for finding out what's going on are the tourist offices or the city's cultural information office in the Palau de la Virreina (*see p321*). Another good source is the city's information phone line on 010 as well as its website at www.bcn.es – go to the cultural

The boys in the hoods celebrate **Setmana Santa** in their own special way. *See p213.*

Arts & Entertainment

agenda section. Unless we've listed a separate information source, try these. The daily papers also carry details, especially in their Friday or Saturday supplements. Events listed below that include public holidays are marked *.

Spring

Festes de Sant Medir de Gràcia

Gràcia to Sant Cugat and back, usually via Plaça Lesseps, Avda República Argentina & Carretera de l'Arrabassada. Starting point: Metro Fontana/ 22, 24, 28 bus. **Date** 3 Mar. **Map** p336 D2-3.

If you happen to have packed your horse, you can taste the full joys of this charming local celebration, but if you haven't, there are sweet consolations. Following a tradition that goes back to 1830, a troupe of decorated horses, some pulling carts, gathers around the Plaça Rius i Taulet in the morning to ride up the winding Arrabassada road into the Collserola hills above Barcelona, ending at the Sant Medir Hermitage, where mass is celebrated, *sardanas* danced and *butifarras* (Catalan sausages) barbecued. (Alternatively, it's about an hour's pleasant walk through the woods from Sant Cugat – about 25 minutes from Plaça Catalunya by FGC train.) At the same time, small processions of horse-drawn carts drive around Gràcia and other areas, notably Sarrià and Sants, throwing sweets to the cheering crowds and leaving behind a fragrant trail of discarded wrappers, manure and grannies scrabbling to fill their shopping bags with a year's supply of sickly boiled sweets.

Setmana Santa* (Holy Week)

Date 24 Mar-1 Apr 2002.

Holy Week in Barcelona is a lot more low key than in the south, no doubt because of the Catalans' more sober character. Nevertheless, the blessing of the palms on Palm Sunday is an exuberant spectacle: natural palm fronds, some up to 2m (6½ft) long, are bleached and woven into intricate designs and sold at stands on La Rambla, in front of the cathedral and outside all local churches. Once blessed, the palms are often placed on balconies, where they remain for the next 12 months. On Good Friday, a series of small processions and blessings take place in front of the cathedral, starting with the Via Crucis in the morning, the blessing of the Christ of Lepanto in the afternoon, and a procession that sets out from the church of Sant Agustí in C/Hospital at around 5pm and arrives at the cathedral a couple of hours later.

Sant Jordi

La Rambla, and all over Barcelona. **Date** 23 Apr.

St George becomes Sant Jordi in Catalonia, where he is the patron saint and can be seen everywhere, immortalised in statues and paintings slaying his dragon – or, in some cases, a large and not-very-impressive-looking lizard. Jordi is also the most traditional name for Catalan men. Sant Jordi's day is the day you declare your feelings for your beloved – a kind of Valentine's Day without the grubby-fingered anonymity. Traditionally, men gave women a rose, and women reciprocated with a book. In these enlightened times, either gift is suitable for either sex, as it is nowadays widely accepted that women can read, and there's nothing suspect about men who like flowers. Publishers wheel out their bestselling authors for marathon sessions of book-signing and flesh-pressing. The focus of activity is around the Rambla, Rambla de Catalunya and Passeig de Gràcia, which can become almost impassable from mid-morning on. Traditionally, this is also the day of the year when the public go to the Palau de la Generalitat to see the palace's own dazzling displays of red roses.

Feria de Abril

Diagonal-Mar, Sant Adrià del Besòs. Metro Besòs-Mar, then special buses. **Information** Federación de Entidades Culturales Andaluces en Cataluña (93 488 02 95). **Date** 26 Apr-6 May 2002.

If you can't make it to Seville for the original of the ten-day Andalucian fiesta, this satellite version is a good substitute, when Barcelona's Andalucian population shows the locals how to really party. Decorated tents offer food, drink and music, and there is plenty of opportunity to practise your *sevillanas* and flamenco, or just watch the experts. The traditional way to arrive is by horse and carriage, elaborately decorated with flowers, and there are riding exhibitions during the day. Alternatively, a special bus service runs to the venue, which is by the beach, a few kilometres from the Port Olímpic.

Festival de Música Antiga

CaixaForum, Avda Marquès de Comillas 6-8, Montjuïc (902 22 30 40/www.fundacio.lacaixa.es). Metro Plaça de Espanya/13, 50 bus. **Date** 17 Apr-15 May 2002. **Map** p339 A5.

This early music festival is the highpoint in Fundació la Caixa's admirable series of cultural events. Performers come from all over Europe and have included Thomas Zehetmair, Christophe Coin, Rinaldo Alessandrini, Andreas Staier and Musica Antiqua Köln. The accompanying fringe festival offers young performers the chance to practise and perform alongside more established musicians. You can get tickets in advance from Servi-Caixa and www.serviticket.com.

Dia del Treball* (May Day)

Date 1 May.

On May Day committed unionists join marches, organised by the main trade unions, along Passeig de Gràcia down to Plaça Sant Jaume – although in these apolitical times, for most workers it's just a day off to enjoy the arrival of spring.

Saló International del Còmic

Estació de França, Avda Marquès de l'Argentera 6, Barceloneta. Metro Barceloneta/14, 39, 40, 51 bus. **Information** Ficòmic (93 301 23 69/ www.ficomic.com). **Date** 9-12 May 2002. **Map** p341 E6.

Comics are big business in Spain, and the Barcelona comics fair is one of the largest in Europe. As well as publishers' stands and comics marts, events include celebrity autograph sessions, conferences, workshops and activities for kids. A smaller *manga* fair is held in L'Hospitalet in October.

Sant Ponç

C/Hospital, Raval. Metro Liceu/14, 38, 59, 91 bus. **Date** 11 May. **Map** p342-3 A2-3.
Barcelona's many herbalists attest to the lengthy tradition of homeopathic remedies in Catalonia. In celebration of Sant Ponç, the patron saint of bee-keepers and herbalists, C/Hospital becomes a charming outdoor market for the day, full of fresh herbs, home-produced honey, natural infusions and candied fruit, most of it straight off the farmer's cart.

Festa de la Diversitat

Montjuïc. Metro Espanya/bus all routes to Plaça Espanya. **Information** SOS Racisme (93 301 05 97/ www.sosracisme.org). **Date** May or June 2002. **Map** p343 A-B4.
Although this festival has temporarily moved from its harbour-front home to the less picturesque trade-fair centre at the foot of Montjuïc, and along Avda Reina Maria Cristina, it is still a bright and breezy celebration of the city's cultural and ethnic diversity, attracting more than 50,000 visitors to its three days of concerts, conferences, music and cookery workshops and kids' activities. Local immigrant organisations set up stalls with food, clothes, jew-ellery and information. Profits help sustain SOS Racisme in its vigilant fight against racism in Barcelona and throughout Spain.

Festa de la Bicicleta

Information Servei d'Informació Esportiva (93 402 30 00). **Date** one Sun in May.
With a growing network of cycle lanes and several miles of cycle-friendly footpaths along the beach-front, the bicycle is rapidly growing in popularity, both for transport and leisure. Sympathetic voices in the Ajuntament have helped, not least those of the current and previous mayors, Pasqual Maragall and Joan Clos, both regularly seen pedalling from one mayoral meeting to another (though the former was taken to court by a private individual for cycling on the pavement). This event is a relaxed, family affair, attracting around 40,000 participants for a 16km (10-mile) ride around the city centre, starting at C/Aragó and ending at Plaça de les Glories, where there are bike-related activities, stands and enter-tainment. Bike hire is available.

Barcelona Poesia

All over Barcelona. **Information** Institut de Cultura (93 301 77 75/www.bcn.es/icub). **Date** 10-16 May 2002.
The *Jocs Florals* (Flowery Games) were poetry con-tests started by King Joan I in 1393. Having died out in the mid-15th century, they were resuscitated in 1859 and have been held ever since, with prizes awarded for the three best poems. The *Jocs* were recently combined with the annual International Poetry Festival and expanded to a week of poetry, with thematic readings as well as a poetic walk through Barcelona. While most poems are in Catalan and Spanish, the International Festival, held on the final day, features works in half a dozen other languages. Schools also hold their own mini-versions of the *Jocs*.

Summer

Sónar

Information Sónar (93 442 29 72/www.sonar.es). **Date** 13-15 June 2002.
Sónar – the International Festival of Advanced Music and Multimedia Art – is a voracious monster threatening to grow out of control. Its three days of neurone-threatening overload feature the latest developments in electronica of one form or another. The festival has many faces. Sónarnight is the most primordial and unrestrained part of the festival, with techno, hardcore and more esoteric outpourings from dusk till dawn and beyond. Sónarday is a com-bined warm-up and chill-out for the coming/previous night, based at the CCCB, with DJ sessions, exhi-bitions of electronic and Internet art, a record fair and a cutting-edge hardware showcase. For the cognoscenti, Sónarday is the more interesting. Sónarnight has moved from its idyllic, beachside venue to a soulless and virtually inaccessible con-crete bunker/trade fair centre miles from civilisation. As a metaphor for modern society it is unbeatable. As a musical experience it has its flaws. Tickets for the full weekend cost around €90.

Marató de l'Espectacle

Mercat de les Flors, C/Lleida 59, Poble Sec. Metro Poble Sec or Espanya/bus all routes to Plaça Espanya. **Information** Associació Marató de l'Espectacle (93 268 18 68/www.marato.com). **Date** 7-8 June 2002. **Map** p339 B6.
An anarchic, action-packed explosion of theatre, dance, performance and circus skills takes place late into the night over the two consecutive evenings of this performance marathon. With more than 80 acts, mostly based in Spain but with a few groups from the rest of Europe and beyond, there's certainly no time to get bored, as the maximum time allotted to each act is ten minutes. Audience and performers mingle together, drifting from space to space or to the bar, or to admire the art installations in the foyer. While there are inevitable fluctuations in quality, the marathon is an interesting mosaic of talent, and helps make up for the lack of alternative performance in the Festival del Grec (*see p217*) a few weeks later.

L'Ou com Balla

Ateneu Barcelonès, C/Canuda 6; Casa de l'Ardiaca, C/Santa Llúcia 1; Cathedral cloisters; Museu Frederic Marès; all in Barri Gòtic. Metro Jaume I or Liceu/ 17, 19, 40, 45 bus. **Information** Institut de Cultura (93 301 77 75/www.bcn.es/icub). **Date** 2-9 June 2002. **Map** p343 B3.

Castles in Spain

You're a skinny five-year-old being shouted at by a man with a clipboard to climb a rickety structure ten metres (33 feet) high that's about to come tumbling down around you, and you daren't refuse because whole crowds of strangers are staring at you, willing you upwards. A Victorian factory? A Brazilian goldmine? Grounds for calling in social services? Or one of Catalonia's most charming and egalitarian traditions?

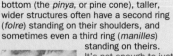

These are the human castles (*castells*), currently enjoying a renaissance. Though the traditional heartland of *castellers* lies in the province of Tarragona, other more recent groups, including those in Barcelona and its dormitory towns, are increasingly giving the old hands a run for their money.

Contests usually take place on Sundays, between April and October, and usually feature three or more groups (*colles*), who take turns to attempt three towers of different types, each aiming to trump the others. Eight levels are considered average, nine are where it's at, and ten have only been achieved a handful of times. Castles are described in people per level and number of levels, so a *tres de nou* (a three by nine) has three people per level and nine levels (except for the penultimate level, which has one or two small kids forming a base for the even smaller kid, the *anxaneta*, at the top).

As well as a large ground crew at the bottom (the *pinya*, or pine cone), taller, wider structures often have a second ring (*folre*) standing on their shoulders, and sometimes even a third ring (*manilles*) standing on theirs. It's not enough to just get the tower up, however. It only counts if is disassembled properly, too.

With over 100 people needed for some towers, *colles* accommodate people of both sexes and all shapes and sizes. In fact, they are a wonderful metaphor for a utopian society, with everyone working together towards a common, non-competitive goal. Unlike other team sports, everyone is equal and essential.

More importantly, in many small towns *castells* are playing an important role in the integration of recent immigrants. The small kids that climb to the top are increasingly non-Catalan, and with any luck, as they grow and take their places further down the tower, their participation will help engender good relationships with the people scrabbling up their backs, standing on their shoulders and sticking their toes in their ears.

As well as competing all around Catalonia, *castells* are a regular feature of the *festa major* of most areas, and can be seen at the Mercè. National and local press have details, as does the information service 010.

Before the 19th century, Corpus Christi was one of the most important celebrations in the year; since then it has lost a lot of its significance. The tradition of L'Ou com Balla ('the egg that dances') continues: a hollowed-out egg is placed on the spout of a small fountain, where it spins and bobs, supported by the jet of water. Fountains are garlanded with spectacular flower displays, and a funnel-like structure guides the egg back on to the water spout whenever it falls off. L'Ou com Balla can also be seen in the cathedral during Easter week.

Festa de la Música

All over Barcelona. **Information** Institut de Cultura (93 301 77 75/www.bcn.es/icub). **Date** 21 June 2002.

With so much music in Barcelona all year round, International Music Day may seem almost superfluous, especially since official support for it is minimal. Although hundreds of musicians take to the streets, it sometimes seems as if quality is playing second fiddle to quantity. Nevertheless, with every square, park, museum and cultural centre in the city

Mercè mission

Every Catalan town has a *festa major*, but naturally Barcelona's is bigger than most. It is called the Mercè, after one of the patron saints of the city, Our Lady of Mercy, who stamped out a plague of locusts in 1637 and was rewarded with city celebrations 250 years later. The Mercè is an extravaganza of music, colour, excitement and fun – held on 24-29 September 2002 – and whether you're a life-long Barcelonan, a temporary resident or just passing through, it really does have something for everyone.

For a crash course in Catalan folk culture, there are traditional celebrations rooted in Barcelona's medieval past, from the castles (*castells – see p215* **Castles in Spain**) to giants (*gegants*) and fatheads (*capgrossos*). The giants (*pictured*) are sober, sedate figures three or four metres (ten to 13 feet) tall, usually modelled on historical figures like Jaume I, or on animals. The fatheads are more caricatured, more irreverent and more mobile, and caper madly around the crowd while the giants plod on demurely.

The Mercè also has elaborate firework displays, on the beach and in Plaça Espanya, but the real red-hot action takes place during the *correfoc* (literally 'fire-run'). A parade of dragons terrorises the city, breathing fire and filling the streets with smoke, accompanied by drummers and impish devils with tridents spouting showers of sparks, which they use to chase off anyone who gets too close. Catalan youths stand in front of the dragons shouting '*no passareu!*' ('You're not coming

through!') or calling up to the balconies for water when the fireworks fizzle out and are being replaced. It's anarchic, exciting and not for the faint-hearted. Wear old clothes made of natural fibres, a hat and even a scarf

involved, and all genres of music on show, it makes for a pleasant enough day, and there are usually a handful of decent concerts worth rooting out.

Sant Joan*

All over Barcelona. **Date** night of 23 June.

One could argue that Catalans are a nation of pyromaniacs – witness the *correfoc* – and there's no better evidence for this than the night of 23 June, the *verbena* (eve) of Sant Joan, strictly speaking the feast of Saint John the Baptist. This is *la nit del foc*, the 'night of fire', throughout Catalonia and the Balearics, marking the summer solstice (to which St John's is the nearest saint's day). Clearly pagan in origin, it's the wildest night of the year. Nowadays, the huge bonfires that used to burn at every road junction in the city have been banned, but they still fill the *ramblas* of towns up and down the coast, and even in the city there are still one or two 'private initiatives'.

For a week before Sant Joan, the June air is ripped apart by explosions, as every schoolkid in town spends his or her pocket money on terrifying bangers. Come the night itself, the city sounds like a virtual war zone, with impromptu firework displays exploding from balconies and squares. There are big displays on Tibidabo, Montjuïc and, especially, by the beach, with live bands – these are good to head for, as well as smaller events in squares across the city, and countless house and terrace parties. It's obligatory to consume *coca de Sant Joan*, a shallow, bread-like cake decorated with very sweet candied fruit, and as much cava as you can manage (sold from stalls along the Rambla). The best thing to do is keep going all night, and a traditional way to end Sant Joan is to head for the beach at dawn, to watch the sunrise. The following day, 24 June, is a public holiday, and nothing moves before mid-afternoon.

to protect your face. For the fire-wary, there's a dry run the preceding night, though it's not half as enjoyable.

The other main element of the Mercè is music, from folk to pop to rock to Mediterranean *mestizo* and more. Lou Reed played in front of the cathedral a couple of years ago, and in 2001, Manu Chao packed out Plaça Catalunya. Concerts are free. At the same time, the BAM festival offers an alternative (in both senses) musical menu (also free, apart from concerts at the Estació de Franca). For a more traditional knees-up, there are *sardanas*, with different bands (*coblas*) playing on different days in front of the cathedral, in Plaça Sant Jaume and in the Plaça de la Mercè.

There's also street theatre, free admission to certain museums, open visits to various public buildings, a photography competition, conferences, debates and an air show at the beach. And not actually part of the Mercè, but timed to coincide with it, is a festival of short films and a showcase of Catalan wine, cheese and *embutidos* (cold meats and sausages). If you still have any energy after all this, you can run a half-marathon or swim across the port.

You'll find information on the Mercè activities in a small booklet available from tourist offices (*see p320*) and information points, and also on the Ajuntament's website at www.bcn.es.

Classics als Parcs
Information Parcs i Jardins (93 413 24 00/ www.bcn.es/parcsijardins). **Date** 8am-3pm Mon-Fri June-July.
On balmy evenings in early summer, what could be more pleasant than listening to classical music in some of the city's most attractive parks? There is a wide-ranging programme for small ensembles and soloists, and usually two or three concerts to choose from each week, in venues including Gaudí's Parc Güell, and the Ciutadella and Laberint parks.

Festival del Grec
Information Institut de Cultura (93 301 77 75/ www.bcn.es/icub). **Date** 25 or 26 June-31 July 2002.
The Grec, which celebrated its 25th anniversary in 2001, is Barcelona's main performing arts festival, with an emphasis on theatre and music, plus some dance. It takes its name from the wonderful mock-Greek, open-air theatre on Montjuïc, where many

of the main shows are staged against a natural backdrop of an old quarry, complete with hanging greenery and hard seats (cushions are for hire).

With 75 shows and 275,000 tickets, the festival has slimmed down in recent years, aiming for a more intense, but also more mainstream, experience. Alternative performance is almost non-existent, although a new initiative at the CCCB is attempting to remedy this. Most of the theatre is in Catalan or Spanish, with a smattering of work in other, mainly European, languages. Dance is mostly contemporary and is similarly weighted to home-grown talent. Music is particularly strong on flamenco and jazz. Tickets generally cost €12-€24 and can be bought from the special booth in Plaça Catalunya, from the Palau de la Virreina (*see p321*) or by credit card from Tel-entrada (*see p210*).

Dies de Dansa
Information Associació Marató de l'Espectacle (93 268 18 68/www.marato.com). **Date** 19-21 July 2002.
Three days of dance performance in various venues, day and night, featuring both local and international dance companies. Some shows are free, particularly those held outdoors. The most spectacular of the venues are Parc Güell and the terrace of the Miró Foundation, but there also dynamic performances in and around the MACBA and CCCB.

Festa Major de Gràcia
All over Gràcia. Metro Fontana/22, 24, 28, N4 bus. **Information** Festa Major de Gràcia (93 459 30 80/ www.festamajordegracia.org). **Date** 15-22 or 24 Aug 2002. **Map** p336-7 D-E2-3.
Of all the local celebrations around the city, the *festa major* in Gràcia is one of the most idiosyncratic and, after the Mercè (*see p216* **Mercè mission**), the most popular. Around 40 of the maze-like streets in the district take part in the best-dressed street competition, disguising themselves as desert islands, dream landscapes or spaceships. Each street also lays on its own entertainment, which usually includes an open-air meal for all the residents, live music and DJs. A victim of its own success – especially as it's August and there's not a lot else to do at night – the streets are usually packed, though the atmosphere is resolutely friendly, and the music can be good (though it can also be diabolical). Bigger concerts and events are centred on Plaça Rius i Taulet, Plaça de la Revolució, Plaça del Sol and Plaça de la Virreina. The festival opens with *gegants* and *castells* in Plaça Rius i Taulet, and climaxes on the last night with a *correfoc* and more fireworks.

Festa Major de Sants
All over Sants. Metro Plaça de Sants or Sants Estació/ bus all routes to Estació de Sants. **Information** Federació Festa Major de Sants (93 490 62 14). **Date** 24 Aug-1 Sept 2002. **Map** p339 A4.
No sooner has Gràcia taken down its decorations then it is the turn of the district of Sants, though its *festa major* is less well known and more traditional. Major events, such as the *correfoc*, are held in the

Parc de l'Espanya Industrial; others are centred on Plaça del Centre, C/Sant Antoni, Plaça de la Farga and Plaça Joan Peiro, behind Sants station.

Autumn

Diada National de Catalunya*

All over Barcelona. **Date** 11 Sept.

It is curious that the Catalan National Day celebrates a crushing national defeat in 1714, when, after a 13-month siege, Barcelona fell to the Castilian/French army in the War of the Spanish Succession, a disaster that led to the loss of all Catalan institutions for 200 years. In 1977, the first year the day could be celebrated openly after the dictatorship, over a million people took to the streets. It's now lost some of its vigour, but is still a day for national reaffirmation, with the Catalan flag displayed on buses and balconies. Catalan separatist groups hold a march, which usually attracts the attention of Spanish nationalists (including skinheads and neo-Nazis) and the riot police, and can sometimes degenerate into street skirmishing between the three groups.

Festa Major de la Barceloneta

All over Barceloneta. Metro Barceloneta/17, 36, 39, 40, 45, 57, 59, 64, 157, N6, N8 bus. **Information** Associació Vecinos de la Barceloneta (93 221 72 44). **Date** 22-30 Sept 2002. **Map** p343 C4.

The proximity of the port and the beach make these local celebrations even more picturesque than most. All the usual ingredients are packed into Barceloneta's tight grid of narrow streets, including *castells, gegants* and a *correfoc*. Celebrations are led by the piratical, cannon-firing caricature of a supposedly French general, General Bum Bum (Boom Boom, possibly named after Prosper Verboom, the French army engineer who designed the *barri*), in a tradition said to date from 1881. At night, there's dancing on the beach, and some people take to boats to eat, drink and watch the fireworks from the sea.

Mostra de Vins i Caves de Catalunya

Maremàgnum, Moll d'Espanya, Port Vell. Metro Drassanes/14, 19, 36, 38, 40, 57, 59, 64, 157 bus. **Information** INCAVI (93 487 67 38). **Date** 20-24 Sept 2002. **Map** p340 D7.

The Penedès region, Catalonia's most important wine- and cava-producing area and home to cava labels such as Freixenet and Codorniu, is less than an hour from Barcelona. For four days (coinciding with the date of Mercè), the Catalan Institute of Wine and Cava brings together around 50 of the province's wine producers, along with makers of other Catalan specialities, including cheese, *embotits* (charcuterie) and anchovies.

Festival International de Jazz de Barcelona

Information The Project (93 481 70 40/ www.the-project.net). **Date** Nov-Dec.

Barcelona has a strong jazz tradition and this is the key event in the jazz-lover's annual calendar, attracting a handful of major and less major international names. Though 'festival' is perhaps overstating the case, there are around a dozen concerts at the Palau de la Música, Luz de Gas, Sala Apolo and L'Auditori. Get advance tickets from Tel-entrada (*see p210*).

Festival de Jazz de Ciutat Vella

All over the Old City. **Information** Zingaria Produccions (93 310 07 55). **Date** mid Nov-mid Dec.

Inevitably more low key than the international festival with which it overlaps, the Festival de Jazz de Ciutat Vella features dozens of concerts (most of which are free) in bars and other small venues. All kinds of jazz feature, from trad jazz to bossa nova, by local and some international groups.

Festa de Patines del Corte

El Corte Inglés, Plaça Catalunya 14, Eixample (93 306 38 00/www.elcorteingles.es). Metro Plaça Catalunya/bus all routes to Plaça Catalunya. **Date** 6 Oct 2002. **Map** p342 B1.

This rollerblading day outside El Corte Inglés has hair-raising exhibitions of stunts, including hockey, half-pipes and, for the truly insane, an 11m (36ft) jumping ramp. An 8km (5-mile) circuit around the city starts and finishes in Plaça Catalunya, passing through Plaça Espanya, Paral.lel, Passeig de Colon, Parc de la Ciutadella and Arc de Triomf. There are also sprint races, slaloms and obstacle courses. You can join in many of the events, but you should sign up at El Corte Inglés in advance. The store also organises a fun-run in the spring.

Festival de Músique del Món

CaixaForum, Avda Marquès de Comillas 6-8, Montjuïc (902 22 30 40/www.fundacio.lacaixa.es). Metro Plaça de Espanya/13, 50 bus. **Date** 1-31 Oct 2002. **Map** p339 A5.

This is a genuinely mixed festival, with authentic indigenous music from all corners of the globe. The 14 or so concerts are particularly strong on Asian music of various latitudes, but also include major contributions from eastern Europe and north and sub-Saharan Africa. The festival is organised by La Caixa's cultural foundation, which also runs the Festival of Ancient Music in May (*see p213*), and an impressive range of educational family concerts throughout the year.

Tots Sants* (All Saints' Day)

All over Barcelona. **Date** 1 Nov.

All Saints' Day is traditionally devoted to the dead; entire families trek to the graves their departed relatives, causing traffic jams around, and sometimes actually inside, the city's cemeteries. While for the recently bereaved it is often an emotional visit, for many it is more an unquestioned duty. Visitors come armed with fresh flowers, dustpans and brushes and even window-cleaner, to make the grave tidy for another year. Outsiders are not particularly welcome, so discretion and sensitivity are vital. The day is known colloquially as the Castanyada, and it is

Holy shit!

Christmas in Catalonia: saints, shopping and... shit. Yes, there's something inescapably scatological about the Catalan Christmas.Take the nativity scene. Here are the usual figurines: Mary, Joseph, Baby Jesus, a few shaggy shepherds, a donkey or two and, crouching round the back of the stable with his trousers round his ankles, the figure of the *caganer* or 'shitter', complete with a couple of graphic turds steaming on the ground behind him. The Angel of the Lord comes down, Glory shines around and inevitably some people are going to experience a certain looseness of the bowels, what with all that blinding light, celestial choirs and attendant special effects and everything. The alternative theory is that the *caganer* emphasises the normality of the situation into which the Son of God was born. People were just innocently going about their business: tending their flocks, winnowing their grain, taking a dump... Needless to say the *caganer* is everyone's favourite figurine. There is a *caganer* collector's club and new figures are brought out every year, including caricatures of celebrities, politicians and football players, complete with Barça colours.

The other outburst of scatology at Christmas comes with the presents. No beaming Santa in red coat and cotton-wool beard here. Presents traditionally come from two sources, the Three Kings and the Shit Log. The Kings pass by on Twelfth Night (6 January), after a time lag sure to drive children hysterical and parents to distraction, and giving the brats no time to destroy their new toys before they're back to school and getting them nicked by the class bully. In some families, the Kings leave a kiss on the child's cheek, pink in the case of Melchior and Gaspar, and black if it's Balthasar, though perhaps this quaint custom will soon fall prey to political correctness.

Good children get presents, of course, but naughty children get a lump of coal – if they're lucky it's edible coal, made of sugar. Alternatively, you guessed it, they get an edible turd. Freud would have had a field day. The scatology doesn't stop here, though. They also get presents from the Caga Tió (Shit Log). The child hits the smiley-faced log with a stick a nd recites a poem. There are several variations, but the gist is, 'log, log, shit me a present'. The kid then runs into the next room and back, by which time, lo, the log has done just that.

You can buy, or just admire, shit logs and *caganer*s at the Santa Llúcia market, where you can also buy Christmas trees, decorations and the other, tighter-bowelled, nativity figurines. To see the shitter in situ, there is a nativity scene inside the cathedral and other churches. For something more dramatic a life-sized scene is usually set up in Plaça Sant Jaume, complete with real bushes and palm trees, and featuring life-like human models. But minus the *caganer*, alas.

Fira de Santa Llúcia

Pla de la Seu & Avda de la Catedral.
Metro Jaume I/17, 19, 40, 45 bus.
Dates 1-22 Dec. **Map** p335 B2-3.

customary to eat *castanyas* (roast chestnuts), *moniatos* (sweet potatoes) and *panellets*, small sweet cakes made from almonds and pine nuts, washed down with sweet dessert wines.

Fira del Disc de Col.leccionista

Fira de Barcelona, Avda Reina Maria Cristina 1, Montjuïc. Metro Espanya/bus all routes to Plaça d'Espanya. **Information** Catalunya Radio (93 306 92 00/www.catradio.com). **Date** 8-10 Nov 2002. **Map** p339 A4.
Curiously, Barcelona hosts the largest second-hand record fair in Europe: a vast array of vinyl LPs, 45s, tapes and CDs, ending in an auction of rock memorabilia that draws buyers from around the world. Admission costs around €6.

Winter

Cap d'Any (New Year's Eve)

All over Barcelona. **Date** 31 Dec & 1 Jan*.
As on Sant Joan (*see p216*), discos and bars charge outrageous admission for New Year parties; the mass public celebrations around the city are cheaper. Plaça Catalunya is generally a good place to start, and further afield, Sitges often has parties on the beach. Wherever you are at midnight – well announced on TV – you'll be expected to start stuffing 12 grapes into your mouth, one for every chime of the bell, without stopping until the New Year has been fully rung in. Otherwise, it's bad luck. Many taxi drivers take the night off, so it can be hard to get around.

Cavalcada dels Reis

Route *Kings usually arrive at Moll de la Fusta, then parade up La Rambla to Plaça Sant Jaume, then continue on Passeig de Gràcia; the detailed route changes each year.* **Information** Centre d'Informació de la Virreina & 010. **Date** 5 Jan. **Map** p342-3 A-B1-4.

Times being what they are, you don't have to trek down to the harbour to watch the Three Kings arrive by boat, since it is all televised live. If you have kids you probably won't get off so lightly. The kings are driven around town in an open carriage, throwing sweets. (Don't tell the kids, but there are usually three teams of kings working different beats; it's a big city for three travel-weary kings. Routes are published in the newspapers.) There is also a toy market in Gran Via. *See also p219* **Holy shit!**

Festa dels Tres Tombs

Sant Antoni. Metro Sant Antoni/20, 24, 38, 64, N6 bus. **Date** 17 Jan. **Map** p339-40 B-C5.

Sant Antoni Abat is patron saint of domestic animals and muleteers. A procession of horsemen, in tailcoats and top hats, commemorates his day by riding three times (*tres tombs*, three turns) around a route from Ronda Sant Antoni, through Plaça Universitat and Plaça Catalunya, down the Rambla and along Nou de la Rambla. This coincides with the week-long *festa major* of the *barri* of Sant Antoni.

Carnestoltes (Carnival)

All over Barcelona. **Date** 7-13 Feb 2002.

Though you have to go to Sitges for a more carnivalesque (or, at least, more outrageous) Carnival, there are still plenty of celebrations in Barcelona. The origins of Carnival are in a once-traditional outburst of eating, drinking and fornicating prior to the privations of Lent; King Carnestoltes – the masked personification of the carnival spirit – also used to criticise the authorities and reveal scandals, a tradition that, unfortunately, has died out.

The opening of the ten-day event is a procession of figures in stunning outfits, from Brazilian dancers to the usual Catalan monsters, led by Don Carnal and el Rei Carnestoltes, amid a confusion of confetti, blunderbuss salvos and fireworks. Other events include dancing in Plaça Catalunya, concerts, and a Gran Botifarrada Popular on the Rambla, when sausage is handed out. There are also children's fancy dress carnivals, and Carnival is a big celebration in the city's markets, where even the traders don costumes. The end of Carnival on Ash Wednesday is marked by the Enterrament de la Sardina (the burial of the sardine), on Montjuïc or in Barceloneta, when a humble fish – symbol, perhaps, of the penis – is buried to emphasise that even frugal fare will not be consumed for 40 days (and fornication, presumably, is out of the question).

Sacred tart

'To every day a saint, to every saint a cake', as the popular refrain nearly runs. Catalans love cakes; no less than 20 saints' days have a cake associated with them, and bakeries are very popular. Not that Catalan pastries are much to write home about. They are more like turkey at Christmas: solid, traditional and reliable. Edible, they are. Ambrosia, they ain't.

The most popular cake, *coca*, is eaten especially at Sant Joan, Sant Pere and New Year, swilled down with plenty of cava. They are big and flat and designed for sharing. Of the two main types, one is more brittle, with a texture like pastry, and is covered in sugar, almonds and sometimes *llardons* (don't ask – not for vegetarians). The other is chewier, and covered in candied fruit or sweet cream. *Tortell de marzapan* is similar, but round and filled with marzipan, and eaten for Sant Antoni and the Día dels Reis, when it comes with a surprise inside and a paper crown for whoever bites into it.

On All Saints' Day, there are *panellets*: rich, stodgy balls of marzipan goo coated with pine nuts. And at Easter, children get a *mono*, an elaborate and scrumptious construction of chocolate, which might be egg-shaped but is more likely to come in the form of ducks, rabbits, Hansel and Gretel cottages, Mickey Mice and all things nice. Santa Llucía, patron saint of dressmakers, is honoured in December with a rather dull, cream-filled sponge in the shape of a pair of scissors.

So why are Catalan pastries so different to the flamboyant marvels of their near neighbours, the French? Blame it on the pigs. Whereas the French long ago realised the marvels of butter, the Spanish are still up to their elbows in pig fat. Consider the croissant – here you are less likely to breakfast on the light, melting mouthful of your dreams than on a rude awakening of acrid pastry. But then the French don't usually eat their pastries with champagne.

Children

Fireworks, film, football and all the fun of the fair.

What's not to love? Gingerbread houses, fire-breathing dragons, living statues, medieval castles, an entire museum filled with life-size chocolate cartoon characters – all in a day's fun in Barcelona. Then there's the attention lavished upon the little treasures by everyone who meets them. Your children will be considered public property; you can expect them to be scooped out of pushchairs, tossed in the air, dandled on knees and passed around like wedding photos. They will be ice-breakers, ambassadors and talking points.

So far, so Mediterranean. Unlike their small southern European neighbours, however, little Catalans are taught to behave like little Catalans, and a dim view is taken of kids running riot in restaurants or staying up until all hours. This attitude brings with it a lack of child-specific concessions and facilities: public transport is free only for children under four, and few metro stations are easily negotiable

for those with pushchairs. It's impossible to find baby-changing facilities except in shopping centres – **La Maquinista** (*see p184*) has one, and also a breastfeeding room. Your best bet for changing nappies in the centre of town is **El Corte Inglés** (*see p184*). Barcelona restaurants rarely offer children's menus, though many will provide small portions on request, and only a handful have non-smoking areas. Try to adapt to the local timetable: most restaurants don't serve lunch before 2pm or dinner before 8pm. While few hotels offer special services, some of the more upmarket establishments do have family suites and a childminding service, and many cheaper places will be happy to contact babysitters for you.

The city's beaches are reasonably clean and have plenty of lifeguards, showers, play areas and ice-cream kiosks, but the beaches further out of town, in **Casteldefells** or **Sitges** (*see p277*), have shallower waters. Unfortunately, none has many public toilets or babychanging facilities.

Attractions

Outside Barcelona lies a raft of attractions – water parks, theme parks and beaches – but in the city itself kids' stuff can seem a little thin on the ground. The best fun to be had in Barcelona lies in getting around it. The drama of narrow medieval streets opening on to wide sunny squares is not lost on children, and they love La Rambla with its street performers, living statues and rows of caged birds. The forms of transport are unbeatable; the cable car to Montjuïc, the tram to Tibidabo, the open-topped buses, the swallow boats (*golondrinas*) and the catamaran are all surefire hits (for all, *see section* **Sightseeing**). Poble Espanyol is also popular with kids, who enjoy watching the glass-blowers and jewellery-makers.

L'Aquàrium de Barcelona

Moll d'Espanya, Port Vell (93 221 74 74/ www.aquariumbcn.com). Metro Barceloneta/14, 19, 36, 40, 57, 59, 64, 157, N6 bus. **Open** *July, Aug* 9.30am-11pm daily. *Sept-June* 9.30am-9pm Mon-Fri; 9.30am-9.30pm Sat, Sun. **Admission** €10; €6 concessions; free under-4s. **Advance tickets** Tel-entrada & Caixa de Catalunya. **Discounts** BC, BT. **Credit** MC, V. **Map** p340 D7.

The real highlight here is the Oceanari, an 80m (260ft) underwater glass tunnel, where you find yourself surrounded by sharks, eels and all kinds of prehistoric-looking creatures. There are also 20 themed tanks (a coral reef, the Ebre Delta and so on), but this area can become impossibly crowded if your visit coincides with that of a coach party. Upstairs, there are touchy-feely activites for young children, including 'touch the starfish' and 'stroke the skate', and small tanks containing tiny but fascinating species; don't miss the delicate sea dragons.

Màgic BCN

Passeig Lluís Companys 10, La Ribera (93 300 29 93). Metro Arc de Triomf/19, 39, 40, 41, 42, 51, 55, 141 bus. **Open** *Information 9.30am-2pm Tue-Fri. Shows 12.15pm, 1.15pm, 5.15pm, 6.15pm, 7.15pm Sat, Sun.* **Admission** *€5.30; €4.30 concessions.* **Credit** MC, V. **Map** p341 E6.

This is a trainspotter's delight: four superbly crafted train sets run through landscapes from various parts of the world. More than 40 miniature trains reproduce almost every type of locomotive from the past 150 years. The audience sits on a moving platform in a darkened auditorium, taking about 40 minutes to reach the end of the line.

Parc d'Atraccions del Tibidabo

Plaça del Tibidabo, Tibidabo (93 211 79 42). FGC Av Tibidabo/17, 22, 58, 73, 85 bus, then Tramvia Blau and Funicular to park. **Open** *Mid June-mid Sept noon-10pm Mon-Thur, Sun; noon-1am Fri, Sat. Mid Sept-mid June noon-7pm Sat, Sun.* **Admission** *Six rides €7. Unlimited rides €17; €4 children under 1m 10cm tall.* **Discounts** BC, BT. **Credit** MC, V.

A truly vertigo-inducing combination of fairground rides and a spectacular mountain-top view. All the old favourites (bumper cars, big wheel, ghost train) are here, and it's worth trying Aero Magic; a short-lived but breathtaking ride on a train that skirts the mountain suspended beneath a rail. Children also enjoy the Museu d'Automates, a wonderful collection of old fairground machines, and the puppet shows that take place on the hour.

Zoo de Barcelona

Parc de la Ciutadella, La Ribera (93 225 67 80/ www.zoobarcelona.com). Metro Barceloneta or Ciutadella-Vila Olímpica/14, 39, 40, 41, 42, 51, 141 bus. **Open** *Mar-Sept 10am-7pm daily. Oct-Feb*

Monkey business

In September 2001 a nation held its breath as one of its most loved and revered citizens was treated for a malignant tumour. A month later, they were hanging out the bunting and baking an almighty fruitcake to celebrate both his birthday and his return to health. Schoolkids around the world rejoiced, his fans posted congratulatory emails in dozens of languages, and even the Brixton massive paid tribute in the shape of a *Basement Jaxx* album cover.

Citizen Snowflake remained impassive throughout. After 33 years living in a cage, he's not much given to emotional outburst. Copito de Nieve (also known as Snowflake, or Floquet de Neu to Catalans) is an albino gorilla, possibly the only albino gorilla in the world. He was brought to Barcelona as a tiny orphan in 1966 and, after living for a couple of years with his captor, internationally respected primate expert Jordi Sabater Pi, moved to Barcelona Zoo. In the ensuing years, he has become a symbol of the city and his scowling visage has graced

many a postcard and key fob. His apologists are quick to explain that the frowning and gurning are a result of his condition, which carries with it poor eyesight and extreme sensitivity to sunlight.

Copito is knocking on a bit in gorilla terms, and Barcelona city council and the zoo are understandably concerned about what will

happen to business when he moves up to the swinging tyre in the sky. Attempts to breed another in his image have failed; he's sired almost 30 babies, all of them as swarthy as their mothers, and a debate is now raging over whether or not to attempt cloning.

The director of the zoo thinks it would be unethical, and a shallowly disguised dry run at human cloning. The mayor's office, meanwhile, is anxious to reassure the public that it has plenty of other animals lined up to act as city mascot – but it seems unlikely somehow that a vegetarian hyena or a three-humped camel could ever conquer quite as many hearts.

10am-5pm daily. **Admission** €10; €5-€6.60 concessions. **Discounts** BC, BT. **Credit** MC, V. **Map** p341 E6.

A surprisingly large zoo hidden away at one end of the Ciutadella park. The big cats, elephants and gorillas are in depressingly small enclosures, but the sea-lions look delighted to be there, as do most of the chimps. There are pony rides (€2.25), regular shows at the Dolphinarium, a corner where kids can stroke the usual farmyard friends, and a picnic area. And don't miss Copito de Nieve, the only albino gorilla in captivity (*see p222* **Monkey business**).

Babysitting & childcare

These agencies employ qualified childminders, and can supply an English-speaker if necessary. Supervised daycare centres offer parents the chance of a few child-free hours.

Cangur Serveis

C/Aragó 227 pral, Eixample (93 488 26 01). Metro Passeig de Gràcia/7, 16, 17, 22, 24, 28 bus. **Open** *Sept-June* 9am-6pm Mon-Fri. *July, Aug* 9am-2pm Mon-Fri. **No credit cards. Map** p336 D4.

Babysitting charges begin at €7.50 per hour, whether for a few hours or all night.

Cinc Serveis

C/Pelai 50, 3º 1ª, Eixample (93 412 56 76/ 24hr mobile 639 36 11 11). Metro Catalunya/ bus all routes to Plaça Catalunya. **Open** 9.30am-1.30pm, 4.30-8.30pm Mon-Fri. **No credit cards. Map** p342 A1.

After 9pm the basic babysitting rate at Cinc Serveis is €7.80 per hour, plus the cost of the sitter's taxi home. Day and longer-term rates are cheaper.

Happy Parc

C/Comtes de Bell.lloc 74-78, Sants (93 490 08 35/ www.happyparc.com). Metro Sants Estació/bus all routes to Estació de Sants. **Open** 5-9pm Mon-Fri; 11am-9pm Sat, Sun. **Rates** €3.70 per hr daily; €1 each subsequent 15mins. **No credit cards. Map** p343 A3.

A huge indoor fun park and drop-in daycare centre for kids aged two to 12.

Branch: C/Pau Claris 97, Eixample (93 317 86 60).

Entertainment

It's almost inevitable that a visit to Barcelona will overlap with some festival or other. Small kids will adore the fancy dress parades of **Carnestoltes** (Carnival) in February, while teenagers will enjoy the fireworks and late-night beach parties of **Sant Joan** in June. The various *festes majores* later in the year are great fun, and the scatological details of a Barcelona **Christmas** bring a gleeful grin to any child's face. For details, *see chapter* **By Season**.

The **Palau de la Virreina** (*see p321*) has information on cultural activities for kids. Plays

and puppet shows are shown all over the city, but theatres with consistent programming for children are the **Jove Teatre Regina** (C/Sèneca 22; 93 218 15 12/www.jtregina.com), the **Nou Tantarantana** (C/Flors 22; 93 441 70 22/www.teatral.net/tantarantana) and the **Teatre Poliorama** (*see p273*). The **Poble Espanyol** (*see p109*), the **Fundació Joan Miró** (*see p107*) and the **Pati Llimona** (*see p8*) present puppet or theatre shows for kids on Sunday mornings.

L'Auditori (*see p239*) has a cycle of Concerts en Família from December to June, where the kids can meet the musicians and play with the instruments before and after the performance. Every three months, the Ajuntament presents a programme of special entertainment for children aged three and up, called Espectacles Infantils + a prop (roughly, 'Children's performances closer to you'). Events include concerts and marionette and magic shows that usually take place in neighbourhood civic centres. Check with the venues about a performance's suitability for non-Catalan or Spanish speakers.

The **Verdi** cinema shows children's films undubbed, and the **Filmoteca** shows original language children's films on Sundays at 5pm. On a rainy day, a good but pricey standby can be the **IMAX** 3-D cinema, but films are only shown in Spanish and Catalan. For all, *see chapter* **Film**.

Museums

Many museums have workshops or events for children throughout the year, and many also take part in the Estiu als Museus ('Summer in the Museums') programme in July and August, providing fun, educational activities for kids.

The children's exhibitions at the **Museu de Zoologia** (*see p98*) in the Parc de la Ciutadella will delight budding zoologists, while the **Museu Marítim** (*see p102*) has life-size models of boats and cabins, an oared galley and an audio-visual exhibit on life at sea. The **Museu de la Xocolata** (*see p133*) has a great collection of chocolate sculptures of cartoon figures, famous buildings and even a Madonna and Child. Look hard and you'll see tiny teethmarks here and there. There's also a workshop where children can make their own chocolate figures. The biggest hit with kids, though, is often the Barça football museum, **Museu del FC Barcelona** (*see p133*).

Museu de Cera

Passatge de la Banca 7, Barri Gòtic (93 317 26 49/ www.museoceracbn.com). Metro Drassanes/ 14, 38, 59, 91 bus. **Open** *July-Sept* 10am-10pm daily. *Oct-May* 10am-1.30pm, 4-7.30pm Mon-Fri;

11am-2pm, 4.30-8.30pm Sat, Sun. **Admission** €7;
€4 concessions; free under-4s. **No credit cards**.
Map p343 A4.
The Wax Museum is an entertaining place, if only
for its shortcomings: Che Guevara has the newspaper open at the share prices; Diana looks alarm-
ingly like Lady Thatcher and is eclipsed by a radiant
Camilla Parker-Bowles; Alice and Snow White look
like fishwives; and Jacko has been restored to the
colour God intended. Madame Tussaud's it ain't, but
it makes for a mildly diverting afternoon, particularly if combined with a trip to its achingly kitsch
café, El Bosc de les Fades (*see p169*).

Museu de la Ciència

*C/Teodor Roviralta 55, Tibidabo (93 212 60 50/
www.fundacio.lacaixa.es). FGC Av Tibidabo, then
Tramvia Blau/17, 22, 73, 85, 158 bus.* **Open** 10am-
8pm Tue-Sun. **Admission** €3; €1-€2 concessions;
free under-7s. **Discounts** BC. **Credit** MC, V.
Leave your under-eights in the care of multilingual
monitors in the inventive, hands-on Clik dels Nens
workshop, and on your return the kids will explain
the scientific principles behind the wind tunnel, see-
saw, bubble-blowers and 'communication tubes'.
Children over ten enjoy the planetarium, while the
'sound telescope' outside the museum entrance is
fascinating for kids of all ages.

Parks & playgrounds

Many of the parks in the city centre turn out
to be nothing more than concrete squares with
a token see-saw, with the exception of the
wonderful **Ciutadella** (*see p98* **Central park**).
The bright ceramic sculptures in **Parc Güell**
(*see p121*) appeal to kids, and, further away,
Parc del Laberint (*see p131*) is named after
its fantastic maze, and also has picnic areas.
For a real day out, head for the huge **Parc de
Collserola** (*see p123*) behind Tibidabo, which
is dotted with pine forests and picnic spots. It
can be difficult to find dog-free parks where
little ones can gambol freely, but an exception is
the lovely, hidden **Jardins de La Tamarita**
next to the stop for the Tramvia Blau. For a
clean, central playground in an (almost) traffic-
free square, try the **Plaça Vicenç Martorell**
(map p342 A1-2).

Parc del Castell de l'Oreneta

*Camí de Can Caralleu & Passatge Blada, Zona
Alta (93 413 24 80/www.bcn.es/parcsijardins).
By car Ronda de Dalt exit 9/by bus 30, 60, 66, 94.*
Open *May-Aug* 10am-9pm daily. *Apr, Sept*
10am-8pm daily. *Mar, Oct* 10am-7pm daily.
Nov-Feb 10am-6pm daily.
At the foot of the Collserola hills is this sprawling
park, with picnic areas, pony rides for three- to 12-
year-olds on Saturdays and Sundays (10am-2pm,
€4.50) and playgrounds. On Sundays, you can hop
aboard the miniature steam train (11am-2pm, €1.20).

Out of town

Universal Studios Port Aventura (*see
p284*), one of Europe's biggest and best theme
parks, is near Tarragona. As well as the two
waterparks mentioned below, Catalonia has five
others: **Aqua Brava** (in Roses), **Aquadiver**
(Platja d'Aro) and **Water World** (Lloret de
Mar) along the Costa Brava, **Marineland** in
Palafolls and **Aqua Park** near Port Aventura.

Aqualeón Safari

*Finca les Basses, Albinyana, Outer Limits (977 68
76 56/www.aspro-ocio.com). By car A2, then A7
south or N340 to El Vendrell, then right to Albinyana
(65km/40 miles).* **Open** *Mid June-mid Sept* 10am-
6pm daily. Closed mid Sept-mid June. **Admission**
€15; €11 concessions; €10.50 3-12s; free under-3s.
Credit AmEx, DC, MC, V.
An exhausting water-cum-safari park, with 600
animals including tigers, elephants, kangaroos,
parrots and birds of prey, as well as giant water
slides, fun pools and wave machines.

Catalunya en Miniatura

*Can Balasch de Baix, Torrelles de Llobregat, Outer
Limits (93 689 09 60/www.catalunyaenminiatura.
com). By car N11 south to Sant Vicens dels Horts,
then left to Torrelles de Llobregat (10km/6 miles)/
by bus Oliveras from Plaça Espanya.* **Open** *Aug*
10am-8pm Tue-Sat. *May-July, Sept-Oct* 10am-7pm
Tue-Sat. *Nov-Apr* 10am-6pm Tue-Sat. **Admission**
€8.50; €5-€6 concessions. **Credit** MC, V.
Welcome, as the name says, to Catalonia in miniature. You'll find Lilliputian models of Catalan towns
and monuments, Montserrat, the Sagrada Familia
and so on, with a miniature train to take you round
it all. On Wednesdays at 1pm during the school
term, clowns put on a show.

Isla de Fantasia

*Finca Mas Brassó, Vilassar de Dalt, Outer Limits
(93 751 45 53/www.illafantasia.com). By car N11
north to Premià de Mar, then left (24km/15 miles).*
Open *June-mid Sept* 10am-7pm Mon-Fri, Sun; 10am-
7pm, 9pm-4am Sat. Closed mid Sept-May. **Admission**
€12; €7 2-10s; free under-2s. **Credit** MC, V.
Dozens of pools with water slides requiring various
levels of daring, foam baths and adventure playgrounds. On Saturday evenings year round, it
becomes a disco (11pm-7am; admission €6-€9).

El Parc de les Aus

*Carretera de Canbrils, Vilassar de Mar, Outer Limits
(93 750 17 65/www.elparcdelesaus.com). By car N11
north to Vilassar de Mar, then left to park (24km/
15 miles)/by train RENFE from Sants or Plaça
Catalunya to Vilassar de Mar, then taxi.* **Open** *July,
Aug* 10am-9pm Tue-Sun. *Sept-Feb* 10am-5.30pm Tue-
Sun. *Mar-June* 10am-8pm Tue-Sun. **Admission** €9;
€5.70 3-12s; free under-3s. **Credit** AmEx, DC, MC, V.
A colourful park full of peacocks, parrots, toucans
and 300 other species of birds and animals, as well
as a farmyard corner, trampolines and a mini train.

Film

Every sort of cinema for every sort of movie. Especially the dubbed sort.

Almodóvar's *Todo Sobre Mi Madre*.

Catalan cinema achieved an historic first in 2001, when a Catalan-language production, *Pau i el seu germà* by Marc Recha, was shown in competition at the Cannes Film Festival. It's unlikely that anyone is going to get up and boast to the world that the Catalans are coming, but there are a handful of Catalan film-makers producing interesting work alongside their more prolific Spanish colleagues.

The Spanish film industry is vibrant and healthy, producing around 250 features a year. Pedro Almodóvar is the name most people associate with contemporary Spanish film – now more than ever after the international success of *Todo Sobre Mi Madre* (*All About My Mother*, 1999), much of which was shot in Barcelona – but another generation of film-makers is snapping at his heels. Three Spanish directors whose films are most likely to achieve a wider audience are Julio Medem, Álex de la Iglesia and, of course, Alejandro Amenábar.

Medem specialises in ethereal, poetic films that dabble lightly in magical realism, producing an enigmatic body of work that just manages to avoid being precious or whimsical. Álex de la Iglesia, in contrast, has a dark and frenzied comic-book imagination, bathed in black

humour with a surrealistic edge. In 2001, the biggest winner at the box office was Alejandro Amenábar with his third film – and his first in English – *The Others*, starring Nicole Kidman. In just three films (following *Tesis* and *Abre los Ojos*), Amenábar has gone from low-budget wunderkind to international star through the unusual expedient of making simple but intelligent psychological thrillers that grip the viewer by the lapels and don't let go.

Making films in English is catching on in Catalonia, too. Ventura Pons, a kind of Catalan Woody Allen – at least in work rate if not in humour – has just completed his first film in English. Catalan ad director Isabel Coixet's well-received second film, *Things I Never Told You*, was filmed in Seattle, and after a less successful digression with a Spanish period adventure piece, *A Los Que Aman*, her fourth film, *My Life Without Me*, is also set in the US, and due out in late 2002/early 2003. Meanwhile, Barcelona film production company Filmax has set up a production wing to make English-language horror/fantasy films in the Catalan capital, although their first three offerings, *Faust*, *Arachnid* and *Dagon*, have met with little enthusiasm.

Two other major Catalan directors, Bigas Luna and Marc Recha, have yet to succumb to the temptations of English. Recha is resolutely Catalan in milieu and language and his two films so far have been minimalist, hyper-realist, post-Dogme slices of village life. Slow and uneventful, they have a certain charm, though Recha is more of an academic (anti-)stylist than a storyteller. The opposite is true of the most commercial Catalan director, Bigas Luna. From an arty, polemical background, Bigas Luna (Bigas and Luna are his two surnames – no one uses his first name) has mellowed, now producing expansive, allegorical narratives that indulge his love of storytelling.

He is probably best known in Britain for his trilogy *Jamón Jamón*, *Huevos de Oro* (*Golden Balls*) and *La teta y la luna* (*The Tit and the Moon*), all sensual, symbol-rich attempts to untangle the Spanish psyche. These were followed by the charming but slight *La Camarera del Titanic*, a fiction about fiction, while his two latest films – *Son de Mar* and, before that, *Volavérunt*, a widely panned historical re-creation of Goya's supposed love affair with the Duchess of Alba – have been somewhat disappointing.

SEEING FILMS

Film-going is very much part of life in Barcelona, and the city has no shortage of cinemas, from monumental, old-fashioned pleasure palaces and charming single-screen venues to spanking new multiscreens that serve up popcorn and pap in equal, industrial quantities. In addition to Spanish films, there are plenty of South American imports, lots of commercial and independent films from the rest of Europe and the US, and an increasing interest in Asian film. Hollywood blockbusters continue to dominate box-office figures, accounting for all but one or two of the top 25 films in any given year. Nevertheless, there are usually one or two prints of foreign films available, even for the most banal, commercial movies. Foreign films are usually dubbed, but they can also be seen in their original language with Spanish subtitles at the cinemas listed below.

Newspapers carry full details of screenings, as does the weekly *Guía del Ocio*. Subtitled films are marked VO for *versió original* or, in some cases, VOSE (*versió original subtitulado en espanyol*). Some of the larger cinemas open at 11am, though most open at around 4pm. Early-evening screenings start between 7.30pm and 8.30pm, and later screenings between 10.15pm and 10.45pm. On Fridays and Saturdays, many cinemas also have a late-night session starting around 1am. All cinemas have a cheap night

The **Rex**: king of cinemas. *See p227.*

(*dia del espectador*), which is usually Monday, though sometimes Wednesday. Increasingly, you can buy tickets over the Internet or via Servi-Caixa (*see p210*). Weekend evenings can be very crowded, especially for recent releases, so turn up early.

Original-language cinemas

Casablanca

Passeig de Gràcia 115, Eixample (93 218 43 45). Metro Diagonal/22, 24, 28, N4 bus. **Tickets** €3.90 Mon; €5.30 Tue-Fri; €5.10 Sat, Sun. **No credit cards. Map** p336 D4.

The Casablanca is a two-screen art cinema featuring non-mainstream US and European films for long runs. It's also currently unchallenged as the most uncomfortable cinema in the city.

Icària Yelmo Cineplex

C/Salvador Espriu 61, Vila Olímpica (93 221 75 85/ www.yelmocineplex.es). Metro Ciutadella-Vila Olímpica/41, 71, 92, 36, N6, N8 bus. **Tickets** €3.90 Mon, before 2.30pm Tue-Sun; €5.30 after 2.30pm Tue-Sun, late shows. **No credit cards. Map** p341 F7.

This is an ugly cinema in an ugly shopping mall behind the Olympic Port, though it does have 15 screens. It shows mostly commercial US and English films, all subtitled.

Maldà

C/Pi 5, Barri Gòtic (93 317 85 29). Metro Liceu/ 14, 38, 59, N9, N12 bus. **Tickets** €3.90 Mon; €4.80 Tue-Fri; €5.10 Sat, Sun. **No credit cards. Map** p342 B2.

A pokey old dive of a cinema housed in an 18th-century palace now fallen on hard times, the Maldà is nevertheless a much-loved institution. It shows a weekly double bill of recent second-run features, often with some kind of thematic link. The entrance is up a staircase just inside the Galerías Maldà, up from the Plaça del Pi.

Méliès Cinemes

C/Villaroel 102, Eixample (93 451 00 51). Metro Urgell/14, 20, 38, 59, N12 bus. **Tickets** €3 Mon; €4.20 Tue-Sun. **No credit cards. Map** p340 C5.
This small, two-screen cinema was opened in 1997 by an idealistic film fan to show popular classics and accessible old art-house films. The programme changes regularly and features up to eight films on any one day. In summer, there are weekly cycles of films linked by director, actors or subject matter.

Renoir-Les Corts

C/Eugeni d'Ors 12 , Les Corts (93 490 55 10). Metro Les Corts/15, 43, 59, 70, 72, N3 bus. **Tickets** €3.90 Mon; €5.30 Tue-Fri; €5.40 Sat, Sun. **No credit cards. Map** p319 A3.
Not far from Les Corts metro, this six-screen cinema shows both Spanish and European films in their original language. The cinema is comfortable enough, but it's in the middle of nowhere, and is a slog to get back from, especially midweek, when the metro shuts at 11pm.

Rex

Gran Via de les Corts Catalanes 463, Eixample (93 423 10 60). Metro Rocafort/9, 50, 56, N1, N2, N13, N14, N15 bus. **Tickets** €5.30 Mon, Tue, Thur; €4.20 Wed; €5.40 Fri-Sun. **No credit cards. Map** p339 B5.
One of the nicest cinemas in Barcelona, the single-screen Rex shows both Spanish and foreign films. Its big, red box of an auditorium, complete with original but tasteful '70s decor and traditional, plush red seats, make for a charming cinematic experience.

Verdi

C/Verdi 32, Gràcia (93 238 79 90/93 238 78 00). Metro Fontana/22, 24, 28, N4 bus. **Tickets** €3.90 Mon; €5.40 Tue-Sun. **No credit cards. Map** p336 D3.
The Verdi has long been a champion of independent film-making from all over the world, and a pioneer in showing Asian cinema in Barcelona. With five screens at the main cinema, and a further four at the Verdi Park on the next drag over, the narrow streets are often packed with waiting cinema-goers (don't mistake the ticket queue with the entrance queue). On the back of the cinema's success, C/Verdi has become a lively street full of fast food in the form of pizzas, Basque tapas and falafel bars.
Branch: Verdi Park C/Torrijos 49, Gràcia (93 238 79 90).

Specialist cinemas

Cine Ambigú

Sala Apolo, C/Nou de la Rambla 113, Paral.lel (93 441 40 01/www.retinas.org). Metro Paral.lel/ 20, 36, 57, 64, 91, 157, N0, N6 bus. **Shows** 8.30pm, 10.30pm Tue. **Tickets** €3.60 or €5 (incl 1 drink). **No credit cards. Map** p340 C6.
This old-time music hall doubles up as a techno venue, and triples up on Tuesdays as a cinema, screening, for one night only, movies that rarely

make it out of their country of origin. The films are shown in their original language (which may or may not have subtitles in another foreign language on the print) and subtitled electronically in Spanish.

Filmoteca de la Generalitat de Catalunya

Cinema Aquitania, Avda Sarrià 31-33, Eixample (93 410 75 90/www.cultura.gencat.es/filmo). Metro Hospital Clínic/27, 32, 63, 66, 68 bus. **Closed** Aug. **Tickets** €2.70; €2 concessions; €33 block ticket for 20 films; €66 block ticket for 100 films. **Credit** (block tickets only) MC, V. **Map** p336 C3.
A worthy but rather dry institution, the Catalan government-funded Filmoteca shows overlapping, short cycles of films, grouped by theme, country, style or director, and subtitled in Catalan. The programme changes daily, with most films appearing two or three times in the space of a couple of weeks. Sessions start at 5pm, 7.30pm and 10pm, except when the preceding film is longer than average. Latecomers are not admitted. Neither is popcorn. A fortnightly information sheet contains full programme details and other notes, and kids' films are shown on Sundays at 5pm. The Filmoteca also has a reasonable library of books, videos and magazines at the bottom of the Ramblas, in the same block as the Centre d'Art Santa Monica.

IMAX Port Vell

Moll d'Espanya, Port Vell (902 33 22 11). Metro Barceloneta or Drassanes/14, 36, 57, 59, 64, 157 bus. **Tickets** €7-€10. **Discount** BT. **Credit** MC, V. **Map** p340 D7.
A white monolith squatting at one end of the port's Maremagnum complex, and offering a choice of mega-formats, including 3-D and towering OMNI-MAX. The problem is that there are few decent films made for these screens, so programmes rarely stray from a repetitive round of nature films and uninspiring documentaries.

Festivals

There are a number of short annual film festivals – with themes including Asian, Jewish, African, women, and gay and lesbian. See the *Guía del Ocio* or check www.bcn.es for details.

Festival Internacional de Cinema de Catalunya, Sitges

93 419 36 35/93 419 06 61/fax 93 439 73 80/ www.sitges.com/cinema/. **Advance tickets** from Tel-entrada. **Date** 1st half of Oct.
The ten-day Sitges Film Festival offers the unique and slightly disturbing combination of a quaint seaside town filled with gore, horror and sci-fi. Though the organisers dropped 'fantasy' from the title a few years ago to flirt with mainstream cinema, they have recently returned to genre cinema in all its gory glory. In 2001, the main prize went to French period fantasy thriller *Vidocq*, and there was a particularly strong presence from Asian film-makers.

Galleries

Amid a conservative commercial scene, alternative arts flourish.

Barcelona's vibrant art scene is more an amalgam of isolated energies than anything that can be grasped or enjoyed as a coherent, tangible whole. Though recent mega-shows of locally based artists, such as You Are Here, in 2001, have tried to alter this by throwing those free-roaming atoms that are the city's artists into collision, Barcelona creators remain loath to hang out together, tending to labour in solitude until opening night (preferably theirs) lures them from the cave. A lack of collective energy and engaged dialogue explains why those yearning for more (whether scene or sales) make a beeline for New York or Berlin. Artists who are successful internationally – including granddaddy Antoni Tàpies, the senior generation of Antoni Muntadas, Francesc Torres and Susana Solano, or the younger crop led by Eulàlia Valldosera, Antoni Abad and Montserrat Soto – make it on their own, with little help from local dealers or curators.

Barcelona was a minor hotspot of the early 20th-century avant-garde, with Picasso, Miró and Dali the most luminous figures. The creative spirit that fostered them was all but paralysed after the Civil War and the advent of dictatorship. Eventually, the art world scraped back: the 1950s saw the emergence of strong abstract painting, whileconceptualism found its local expression in the '70s. Following the city's triumphant reawakening in the 1980s and '90s, the Barcelona art world threw tremendous energy into self-promotion, based mainly on building expensive galleries where contemporary artists, including Barcelona's own, could be shown.

As a result, a new generation of artists has come to share the benefits of globalised culture, participating in biennials and museum shows worldwide, but the verve of Barcelona art-making has had little effect on local art finances. Amid the city's overall economic buoyancy, a dead-weight art market has cut in on dealers' room for manoeuvre; even the most prestigious private galleries have lost their reputation as trendsetters, often descending into caprice, conservatism and, at times, plain bad taste. The local annual art fair New Art in December (93 310 54 43/www.artbarcelona.es/htm/newart.htm), is a piddling affair that only reinforces Madrid's ARCO as the premium Spanish gallery encounter. In 2002, galleries and museums alike will participate in the Primavera Fotogràfica (Photography Spring), a huge, weakly defined biannual project featuring all kinds of photography.

If anything, the slack has been picked up by public institutions and private foundations, which together make up a formidable phalanx on the contemporary art front. Innovative enough to usurp the role normally reserved for alternative spaces (the MACBA even pays for activities by political artists close to anti-globalisation circles), they have nevertheless given the city art scene a rather bureaucratic façade, cutting in on artists' self-initiative.

There is no definitive guide to galleries and artistic activities. Listings appear in the weekly *Guia de Ocio* and some newspapers, but are rarely comprehensive. The simplest plan is to go to a gallery district and do the rounds. Almost all galleries are closed on Sundays and Mondays and only a few are open in August. Exhibition openings typically take place around 8pm midweek, and all are welcome.

Commercial galleries

The Barri Gòtic and the Eixample's C/Consell de Cent are Barcelona's longest established gallery districts, but in recent years new clusters of contemporary spaces have developed in the Born and around the MACBA in the Raval.

Barri Gòtic

Galeria Segovia Isaacs (C/Palla 8; 93 302 29 80) is also of interest.

Antonio de Barnola
C/Palau 4 (93 412 22 14). Metro Liceu or Jaume I/ 14, 38, 59, 91 bus. **Open** 5-9pm Tue-Fri; noon-2pm, 5-9pm Sat. Closed Aug. **No credit cards.** **Map** p342 B3.
This handsome space presents impeccable shows of Spanish contemporary artists. Regulars include national photography prizewinner Humberto Rivas and Madrid painter José Manuel Ballester, who applies his disturbing realism to modern architecture, one of Barnola's favoured themes.

Artur Ramon
C/Palla 10, 23 & 25 (93 302 59 70). Metro Liceu/ 14, 38, 59, 91 bus. **Open** *Oct-June* 10am-1.30pm, 5-8pm Tue-Sat. *July, Sept* 10am-1.30pm, 5-8pm Tue-Fri. Closed Aug. **No credit cards.** **Map** p342-3 B2-3.

Sala Parés.

The best of the local dynasties dealing in historic art and objects, the Artur Ramon family has now opened a gallery for contemporary work (at C/Palla 10 – his fourth space on the same street). The finest shows, however, are the exhibitions of historical Spanish and European art and craft, along with thematic shows pulled from private collections – from Piranesi engravings to Spanish glasswork – sharply presented at No.23.

Sala Parés
C/Petritxol 5 (93 318 70 08/www.salapares.com). Metro Liceu/14, 38, 59 bus. **Open** *Oct-May* 10.30am-2pm, 4.30-8.30pm Mon-Sat, 11.30am-2pm Sun. *June-Sept* 10.30am-2pm, 4.30-8.30pm Mon-Sat. Closed 3wks Aug. **Credit** AmEx, MC, V. **Map** p342 A2.
The Sala Parés opened in 1840 and has long been a symbol for the Catalan bourgeoisie, who still make up the majority of its rather staid clientele. A hundred years ago it promoted the Catalan avant-garde, and it was here that Picasso had his first one-man show. Now the spacious renovated gallery specialises in figurative and historical painting. Just a step away at No.8, the associated Galeria Trama offers contemporary work.
Branches: Galeria Trama C/Petritxol 8, Barri Gòtic (93 317 48 77);**Galeria 18** C/Jacinto Benavente 18, Barri Gòtic (93 241 14 95); **Edicions Margall** Rambla Catalunya 116, Eixample (93 415 96 92).

Raval

Other galleries worth a look are **Galeria Ferran Cano** (Plaça dels Àngels 4; 93 310 15 48), **Cotthem Gallery** (C/Doctor Dou 15;

93 270 16 69), with an interest in American post-pop, and nearby **Alter Ego** (C/Doctor Dou 11; 93 302 36 98).

Galeria dels Àngels
C/Àngels 16 (93 412 54 54/www.artbarcelona.com). Metro Catalunya/bus all routes to Plaça Catalunya. **Open** noon-2pm, 5-8.30pm Tue-Sat. Closed Aug. **No credit cards. Map** p342 A2.
This somewhat awkward space is used by collector Emilio Álvarez, who shows his preferred artists, including abstract painters Miquel Mont and Santi Moix (both exhibiting in 2002), and the photography-based work of Juan Urrios and Canadian Lynn Cohen. A nearby space (open only by appointment) is used for installations.

Galeria Claramunt
C/Ferlandina 27 (93 441 88 17/galeriaclaramunt @teleline.es). Metro Catalunya/bus all routes to Plaça Catalunya. **Open** 11am-2pm, 5-8.30pm Mon-Sat. **No credit cards. Map** p340 C5.
At her space directly facing the MACBA, Valencia-born Carmen Claramunt presents new contemporary work in all media, serving a largely foreign clientele. Artists include Barcelona-based Japanese artist Akané, and Catalans Joana Cera and Oriol Font, both showing in late 2002.

La Ribera & Born

Also try **Tristan Barberà** (C/Fusina 11; 93 319 46 69) for limited-edition prints, and **Galeria 44** (C/Flassaders 44; 93 310 01 82), a gallery that works with many cutting-edge Barcelona artists.

Galeria Berini

Plaça Comercial 3 (93 310 54 43/www.berini.com).
Metro Jaume I/14, 39, 51 bus. **Open** *Sept-June*
10.30am-2pm, 5-8.30pm Tue-Sat. *July* 10.30am-2pm,
5-8.30pm Tue-Fri. Closed Aug. **Credit** MC, V.
Map p343 C3.

Toni Berini has moved away from presenting
painting and now specialises in photography and
new media. The clever visual 'falsifications' of
Catalan photographer Pere Formiguera are set for
spring 2002, while a summer group show has the
'magical object' as its theme.

Galeria Maeght

C/Montcada 25 (93 310 42 45/www.maeght.com).
Metro Jaume I/17, 19, 40, 45 bus. **Open** 10am-
2pm, 4-8pm Tue-Sat. **Credit** AmEx, DC, MC, V.
Map p343 C3.

The Paris-based Maeght gallery opened this handsome space in the 1970s. Occupying a Renaissance
palace near the Picasso museum, with a lovely
courtyard and staircase, it shows established
Spanish and European painters and sculptors.
Despite its prestigious name, the Maeght struggles
for relevance in the Barcelona scene.

Metrònom

C/Fusina 9 (93 268 42 98). Metro Jaume I/39, 51
bus. **Open** 10am-2pm, 4.30-8.30pm Tue-Sat. Closed
Aug. **Map** p336 C3.

Run by collector Rafael Tous, this was Barcelona's
most lively art space in the 1980s. After a brief hiatus,
it has won back some of its original impetus, focusing on photography and multimedia installations.
Metrònom has a video programme and organises an
annual festival of contemporary music in January
beneath its gorgeous *belle époque* glass ceiling. Work
is not for sale. *See also p242.*

Eixample

Galeria Carles Taché

C/Consell de Cent 290 (93 487 88 36/www.carles
tache.com). Metro Passeig de Gràcia/7, 16, 17, 63,
67, 68 bus. **Open** *Sept-June* 10am-2pm, 4-8.30pm
Tue-Sat. *July* 10am-2pm, 4-8.30pm Tue-Fri. Closed
Aug. **No credit cards. Map** p340 D5.

Carles Taché represents some of the most established senior Spanish painters, such as Arroyo,
Broto and Campano. Blue-chip internationals such
as Sean Scully and Jannis Kounellis can also be
seen, along with Catalan sculptor Jordi Colomer and
the clever pop of Carlos Pazos.

Galeria Estrany-de la Mota

Passatge Mercader 18 (93 215 70 51/www.estrany
delamota.com). FGC Provença/7, 16, 17, 20, 31, 43,
44, 67, 68 bus. **Open** *Sept-June* 10.30am-1.30pm,
4.30-8.30pm Tue-Sat. *July* 10.30am-1.30pm, 4.30-
8.30pm Mon-Fri. Closed Aug. **No credit cards.**
Map p336 D4.

This iron-columned basement gallery works well for
Antoni Estrany's selection of neo-conceptualists,

among them the intelligent photo-montages of
Montserrat Soto and the rather pretentious Pep Agut.
International artists represented include Thomas
Ruff (showing in early 2002), Jean-Marc Bustamante
and Douglas Gordon.

Galeria Joan Prats

Rambla Catalunya 54 (93 216 02 84/www.galeria
joanprats.com). Metro Passeig de Gràcia/7, 16,
17, 22, 24, 28, 63, 67, 68 bus. **Open** *Sept-June*
10.30am-1.30pm, 5-8.30pm Tue-Fri. Closed Aug. **Credit**
AmEx, V. **Map** p340 D4-5.

This gallery was born out of the 1920s friendship
between Joan Prats, son of a fashionable hatmaker,
and artist Joan Miró. Nowadays, the only remnant
of the original business is the name and the headgear motifs on the shopfront; the Prats' Miró collection is now in the Fundació Miró. Along with a crop
of senior Catalan painters, 'La Prats' represents
high-profile emerging artist Eulàlia Valldosera, the
quirkiness of Catalan Perejaume (showing in early
2002) and Evru, as well as British photographer
Hannah Collins. The nearby branch on C/Balmes
has limited-edition prints.
Branch: Joan Prats-Artgràfic C/Balmes 54
(93 488 13 98).

Galeria Metropolitana
de Barcelona

Rambla Catalunya 50, pral 1ª (93 487 40 42/
www.galeria-metropolitana.com). Metro Passeig
de Gràcia/22, 24, 28 bus. **Open** 11am-1.30pm,
5-8.30pm Mon-Sat. Closed Aug. **No credit cards.**
Map p336 D4.

Long based in Gràcia, in 2001 Pere Soldevila moved
to the Eixample with his fresh combination of projects by film-makers (such as Bigas Luna), web art
initiatives and Spain-based photographers and
painters. Vanessa Pey and Roberto Delgado will be
featured during the 2002 Primavera Fotogràfica.

Kowasa Gallery

C/Mallorca 235 (93 487 35 88/www.kowasa.com/
gallery). FGC Provença/7, 16, 17, 20, 31, 43, 44,
67, 68 bus. **Open** 11am-2pm, 5-8.30pm Tue-Sat.
Credit AmEx, MC, V. **Map** p336 D4.

This photography gallery is located above the excellent specialised bookshop of the same name. Its two
spaces are used for Spanish and international work
from artists such as Martí Llorens, Ramon David
and the famed Civil War chronicler Agustí Centelles.
The gallery has holdings by hundreds of photographers, among them Nadar, Cartier-Bresson, Josef
Sudek and Madrid's much admired Ouka Lele.

Gràcia & Zona Alta

Galeria Alejandro Sales

C/Julián Romea 16 (93 415 20 54/www.alejandro
sales.com). FGC Gràcia/16, 17, 22, 24, 27, 28, 31,
32 bus. **Open** *Sept-June* 11am-2pm, 5-8.30pm Tue-
Sat. *July, Sept* 11am-2pm, 5-8.30pm Tue-Fri. Closed
Aug. **No credit cards. Map** p336 D3.

Alejandro Sales is one of the city's most successful young dealers. As well as hosting impeccable shows by international blue-chip artists, he represents Barcelona sculptor Sergi Aguilar (showing in spring 2002) and painter Eduard Arbós (with a show in late summer 2002). Work by young creators is shown in Blackspace, a smaller side gallery.

Galeria H₂0

C/Verdi 152 (93 415 18 01). Metro Lesseps/22, 24, 25, 28, 31, 32, 39, 74 bus. **Open** 11am-1pm, 5.30-8pm Tue-Fri; 11am-1pm Sat. Closed Aug. **No credit cards. Map** p337 E2.
Architect Joaquim Ruiz Millet and writer Ana Planella publish books and run a gallery out of this charming Gràcia home, with a cosy back garden. H₂O shows international design and architecture, photography and contemporary art. The visual poetry of Sean Mackaoui will be seen in March 2002, with photographers Juan de la Cruz Megías and Clemente Padín showing in the summer.

The fringe scene

Present-day art activism in Barcelona is typified by a distinctly iconoclastic Catalan style. Some initiatives imitate 1970s models (art parties, performance cabaret, open studios), while others are aligned with anti-globalisation currents. Many galleries are run by collectives and work as mini-cultural centres, while other groups are nomadic. Initiatives worth checking out are the spacious gallery at **Centre Civic Can Felipa** (C/Pallars 277; 93 266 44 41), the artists collective **La Xina Art** (C/Doctor Dou, baixos; 93 301 67 03), the **22A** group of artists, critics and musicians (93 44 184 81), which generates projects throughout the city, and the multi-disciplinary free-for-all of **Centro Cultural La Santa** (C/Àngels; 93 342 59 46). An artist open studio project in the Old City is held in early June, with an information point at the FAD (Convent dels Àngels, Plaça dels Àngels 5-6; www.digiteca.com/tallersoberts).

Established centres complementing the fringe are **Metrònom** (*see p230*), the Fundació la Caixa's **Mediateca** (*see p314*), and the **CCCB** (C/Montalegre 5; 93 306 41 00), which hosts the **Sònar** music festival (*see p214*), and other film, video and new media events. The alternative scene also blends into the Barcelona's nightlife frontier, where many of the city's loose ends eventually meet. For more on all this, and more venues, *see p256* **Alternative medicine**.

If you're looking for somewhere to stay and study art, there are no residential art centres for visitors in Barcelona itself. The nearest and best is **Can Serrat**, a converted farmhouse near Montserrat (93 771 00 37/93 771 03 29/ www.canserrat.org).

Beat it to up-tempo **Metrònom**. *See p230.*

Box 23

C/Ample 23 entl, Barri Gòtic (93 302 38 82). Metro Drassanes/14, 36, 57, 59, 64, 157 bus. **Open** 5-8.30pm Wed-Sat. Closed Aug. **No credit cards. Map** p343 B4.
Brazilian Edgar Dávila started this gallery with the idea of challenging the conventional exhibition space – as its curtain-lined walls attest. Shows tend to involve mostly foreigners (such as Louise Sudell from the UK), with installations, reflections on ephemeral architecture, and audiovisual work predominating. The ongoing, live-in 'Box Hotel' project will continue in 2002.

Hangar

Passatge del Marqués de Santa Isabel 40, Poblenou (tel/fax 93 308 40 41/www.hangar.org). Metro Poblenou/40, 42 bus. **Open** *Information* 9am-2pm Mon-Fri. Closed Aug. **No credit cards.**
Besides being a multi-disciplinary production centre with studios and facilities for the production of video and Internet art, Hangar has added workshops, video screenings and debates that are open to the public, while offering a regular 'showroom' of residents' work. Run by the Catalan Visual Artists Association, Hangar also spearheads an open studio project for Poblenou artists in June. Those interested in visiting should call first.

Arts & Entertainment

Gay & Lesbian

A small scene, but a perfectly formed one.

Sun-washed Barcelona is a mecca for gays. In fact, there are too many bars, dance clubs, gymnasiums, restaurants, shops and services that cater specifically to the gay market to mention here, and the average tourist doesn't stay long enough in the city to make the most of the abundance it has to offer the queer visitor. And 20 minutes away is the beautiful beach town and gay magnet of Sitges.

Barcelona's gay and lesbian community is a substantial force, both economically and politically. One area of the Eixample – roughly in the blocks around the junction of C/Muntaner and C/Consell de Cent (map p340 C5) – has acquired such a concentration of gay venues that it has become known as the *Gaixample*, and is well on the way to becoming the Soho or West Hollywood of Barcelona. So it's not surprising that Barcelona is one of the few Spanish cities to recognise significant rights of gay domestic partners.

Be adventurous, keep an open mind and remember that some of the best places to hang out in are not strictly gay. Barcelona's nightlife brings many different types of people together and the gay scene, sometimes called *el ambiente*, literally, 'atmosphere', is quite gender- and persuasion-mixed. The biggest concentration of gay places is in the Eixample, but there are others scattered round and about. Don't worry about dress codes: you can wear just about anything or almost nothing.

Seasonal gay highlights include Sitges' **Carnival** in February and the **International Lesbian & Gay Film Festival** (www. festivalbarcelona.com) in mid October.

A gay Barcelona map and other information are available in sex shops Sestienda (*see p235*) and Zeus (*see p236*). There are also several free gay rags, such as *Shangay*, *gcn-gaycelona*, *Lambda* and *Shanguide*, which have updated listings and details of current events. Sleek local magazine *Nois* (www.revistanois.com) has a great map of gay-owned/friendly places throughout Catalonia. For information on gay organisations, *see p310*.

Cafés & bars

Although **Café de l'Opera** (*see p169*) and **Schilling** (*see p172*) are not gay per se, they are regularly frequented by gays and lesbians.

Acido Oxido

C/Joaquín Costa 61, Raval (93 412 09 39). *Metro Universitat/24, 41, 55, 64, 91, 141, N6 bus.* **Open** 10pm-2.30am daily, plus 4-10.30am Fri-Sun. **Admission** €6. **No credit cards**. **Map** p340 C5.
A dusky, oblong, industrial-style venue (men only) with a panoramic view of the main floor from the urinals. The place to go after a night at Metro (*see p234*), Acido Oxido is at its most pulsating around 7-8am. The darkroom gets quite risqué as dawn approaches.

Café de la Calle

C/Vic 11, Eixample (93 218 38 63/www.cafedelacalle. es.fm). *Metro Diagonal/16, 17, 22, 24, 28, N6, N9 bus.* **Open** 6pm-3am Tue-Sun. **No credit cards**. **Map** p336 D3.
Want to get away from the hustle and bustle for an intimate conversation with someone special or to chat in a small group? This is a well-lit, cosy and orderly environment with pleasant music and good sandwiches. Women like it just as much as men.

Café Dietrich

C/Consell de Cent 255, Eixample (93 451 77 07). *Metro Universitat/bus all routes to Plaça Universitat.* **Open** 10.30pm-3am Mon-Thur, Sun; 10.30pm-3.30am Fri, Sat. **No credit cards**. **Map** p340 C5.
A very popular venue. The elegant baroque entrance is a runway that leads to a small dancefloor. The DJ plays funky house music, and there are short drag shows. It attracts a youthful, good-looking and hungry crowd, most of whom are reserving themselves for the action in the late-night dance clubs.

Caligula

C/Consell de Cent 257, Eixample (93 451 48 92). *Metro Universitat/14, 54, 58, 64, 66, N3 bus.* **Open** 8pm-3am daily. **No credit cards**. **Map** p340 C5.
The lushly overdone candlelit environment makes Caligula a worthwhile stop when there is no room to move in the ever-popular Café Dietrich, located practically next door. Recently, more lesbians have begun to frequent the place, and are made welcome.

The Eagle

Passeig de Sant Joan 152, Eixample (93 207 58 56/ www.eaglespain.com). *Metro Verdaguer/15, 55 bus.* **Open** 10pm-2.30am Mon-Thur, Sun; 10pm-3am Fri, Sat. **No credit cards**. **Map** p341 E4.
The Eagle is a bit on the rough side, with a mostly moustached and bearded clientele, and subdued lighting. The dress code stipulates jeans and leather, especially on Fridays. Club nights Underwear Party and Hard Sex Night (usually monthly) draw a substantial crowd, but don't be surprised to find almost naked gents strutting their stuff at all times.

Look, my mum made it, OK? **The Eagle.** *See p232.*

Ironic Café

C/Consell de Cent 242 bis, Eixample (627 92 98 53).
Metro Universitat/14, 54, 58, 59, 64, 66, N3 bus.
Open 6pm-3am daily. **No credit cards.**
Map p340 C5.
You can't miss the Ironic Café's huge, welcoming
wooden doors on your way to Zeltas Club (*see below*).
The interior maintains the warm wood motif while
celebrating minimalism, with two long, ornate,
antique wooden bars and wrought-iron furnishings
from the turn of the 20th century. There's a happy
hour with free canapes on Thursdays (7-10pm).

Medusa

C/Casanova 75, Eixample (93 454 53 63/
www.medusacafe.com). Metro Urgell/9, 50,
54, 56, 58, 64, 66, N1, N2, N3 bus.
11pm-3am Mon-Thur, Sun; 11pm-3.30am Fri, Sat.
No credit cards. Map p340 C5.
Medusa started the minimalist trend in bar decor
and is still at the vanguard. It has sofas, comfy
chairs and coffee tables for chatting or taking the
load off. The punters tend to trendy and may be a
little uptight, but you have to admit they're pretty.

New Chaps

Avda Diagonal 365, Eixample (93 215 53 65).
Metro Diagonal or Verdaguer/6, 15, 33, 34, N4,
N6 bus. **Open** 9pm-3am Mon-Sat; 7pm-3am Sun.
No credit cards. Map p336 D4.
New Chaps is the city's western bar and attracts the
mature and manly. Regular theme nights draw a full
house, as does the sleazy downstairs darkroom.
Sunday evenings are also popular. The atmosphere
is friendly and unpretentious.

Ouí Café

C/Consell de Cent 247, Eixample (no phone).
Metro Universitat/14, 54, 58, 59, 64, 66, N3 bus.
Open 5pm-2am Mon-Thur, Sun; 5pm-3am Fri, Sat.
No credit cards. Map p340 C5.
An oasis of intimacy located near several other popular bars, Ouí Café is a pleasant, stylish place
attracting a diverse crowd. Come here to chat and
down the first cocktail of the night. There's also gay
soft-porn for those in a more contemplative mood.

Punto BCN

C/Muntaner 63-65, Eixample (93 453 61 23/
93 451 91 52). Metro Universitat/14, 54, 58,
59, 64, 66, N3 bus. **Open** 6pm-2am Mon-Thur,
Sun; 6pm-2.30am Fri, Sat. **No credit cards.**
Map p340 C5.
Punto BCN opens early, and is the city's after-work
and pre-dinner gay bar for a varied crowd. Plenty of
seating upstairs offers a view of the entrance and
the main bar, and regularly changing exhibitions by
local artists. The Wednesday evening happy hour
is the starting gate to the weekend.

Zeltas Club

C/Casanova 75, Eixample (93 454 19 02). Metro
Urgell/9, 50, 54, 56, 58, 64, 66, N1, N2, N3 bus.
Open 11pm-3am Wed-Sat. **No credit cards.**
Map p340 C5.
A large and very welcoming bar in the Gaixample,
Zeltas draws a very friendly crowd, and has almost
surpassed the once-supreme Medusa (*see above*) in
popularity. Drinks are more expensive than else-
where, but the funky house sounds create a great
environment for some really serious cruising.

Arts & Entertainment

Clubs

Clubs with a established gay following include **La Concha** (*see p251*), **La Terrrazza** (*see p256*), **Bar Six** (*see p258*) and **Discothèque** (*see p251*).

Arena Classic

C/Diputació 233, Eixample (93 487 83 42/ www.arenadisco.com). Metro Passeig de Gracia or Universitat/N1, N2 bus. **Open** 12.30am-5am Fri, Sat. **Admission** (incl beer or soft drink) €5 Fri; (incl any drink) €9 Sat. **No credit cards. Map** p340 D5.
In the tradition of a classic gay disco, Arena Classic offers *petarda* (hot and popping tunes) and sounds from the 1960s and '70s. As the night goes on, a contagious singalong mood develops. Arrive as early as possible to avoid a block-long queue.

Arena Madre

C/Balmes 32, Eixample (93 487 83 42/ www.arenadisco.com). Metro Passeig de Gracia or Universitat/7, 16, 17, N1, N2 bus. **Open** 12.30am-5am Tue-Sat; 7pm-5am Sun. **Admission** (incl beer or soft drink) €5 Tue-Fri, Sun; (incl any drink) €9 Sat. **No credit cards. Map** p340 D5.
Large and cavernous, like Metro (*see below*), Arena Madre has a spacious dancefloor, good lighting and special effects, and pounding house and garage sounds. It attracts a younger crowd than Arena Classic, which is practically next door.

Arena VIP

Gran Via de les Corts Catalanes 593, Eixample (93 487 83 42/www.arenadisco.com). Metro Universitat/bus all routes to Plaça Universitat. **Open** 12.30am-5am Fri, Sat. **Admission** (incl beer or soft drink) €5 Fri; (incl any drink) €9 Sat. **No credit cards. Map** p340 D5.
Arena VIP draws a very mixed gay, lesbian and straight crowd, hopping to great new and not-so-new dance music. Its two floors offer different music (classic disco upstairs, contemporary house, garage and trance downstairs) until about 4am, when the whole place begins to rock to the same rhythms.

Martins

Passeig de Gràcia 130, Gràcia (93 218 71 67). Metro Diagonal/22, 24, 28, N4, N6 bus. **Open** midnight-5am daily. **Admission** (incl 1 drink) €7.80. **Credit** MC, V. **Map** p336 D3-4.
Martins has experienced a comeback as a very late-night venue, and both New Chaps (*see p233*) and the Eagle (*see p232*) empty into here when they close, especially on their co-operative theme nights. Three floors provide plenty of room to roam about, and the ample darkroom has many a story to tell. It's not as frenetic as in the other discos, so you can take it all in before making a move.

Metro

C/Sepúlveda 185, Eixample (93 323 52 27). Metro Universitat/24, 41, 55, 64, 91, 141, N6 bus. **Open** midnight-5am Mon-Thur, Sun; midnight-6am Fri, Sat. **Admission** (incl 1 drink) €9. **Credit** MC, V. **Map** p340 C5.
Metro works hard to keep its finger on the pulse of BCN gay nightlife, and very successful it is too. It gets packed at the weekend, while regular midweek party nights include the popular Foam Party. The backroom can be an entertaining, thrashing labyrinth – but take care with valuables.

Salvation

Ronda Sant Pere 19-21, Eixample (93 318 06 86/ www.matineegroup.com). Metro Urquinaona/16, 17, 18, 19, 40, 45 bus. **Open** midnight-5am Fri, Sat, 6pm-5am Sun. **Admission** €11. **No credit cards. Map** p340 D5.
Two large dancefloors, decent music and a handsome, muscular, barebacked clientele. On Sunday night, the club becomes La Madame, with a fun-loving gay/straight mix. Other events include an after-hours weekend party at Souvenir in Viladecans (admission includes coach transport from Salvation or Plaça Espanya) and a Sunday evening 'T-Dance session' at Illusion (*see p260*).

Restaurants

La Veronica (*C/Avinyó 30, Barri Gòtic; 93 412 11 22*) and **Venus Delicatessen** (*see p175*) also attract a large gay and lesbian clientele.

La Bodegueta de Muntaner

C/Muntaner 64, Eixample (93 451 51 04). Metro Universitat/14, 54, 58, 59, 64, 66, N3 bus. **Open** 9pm-midnight Tue-Sun. **Main courses** €4.30-€12. **Credit** MC, V. **Map** p340 C4.
This restaurant offers an enchanting, old-world atmosphere and an excellent Catalan/Mediterranean menu. Although it's open to all during the day, it becomes predominantly gay/lesbian in the evening. Asparagus au gratin and *escalopina* (beef fillet) with roquefort are sure bets. It's a good idea to book; ask for a table looking out on to the enclosed garden.

Café Miranda

C/Casanova 30, Eixample (93 453 52 49). Metro Universitat/bus all routes to Plaça Catalunya. **Open** 9pm-1am daily. **Main courses** €7.40-€18. **Credit** MC, V. **Map** p340 C5.
This was the first cabaret restaurant in Barcelona. The drag shows are highly professional (the same drag queens appear at Café Dietrich – *see p232*), and the food's not bad, either. Some say the Miranda has the most attractive waiters in town: you be the judge.

Castro

C/Casanova 85, Eixample (93 323 67 84). Metro Universitat/bus all routes to Plaça Catalunya. **Open** 1-4pm, 9pm-midnight Mon-Fri; 9pm-midnight Sat. **Main courses** €5.20-€8.60. **Set lunch** €7.30 Mon-Fri. **Credit** DC, MC, V. **Map** p336 C4.
The decor, a modern mix of industrial and elegant, keeps the eye entertained while you enjoy one of the best Mediterranean-style menus available in gay

Just say yes at the **Ouí Café**. *See p233.*

Barcelona. Try *pechuga de pavo con petalos de rosa* (turkey breast with rose petals) or the delicious salmon with sesame sauce. Book in advance.

Cubanito

C/Casanova 70, Eixample (93 454 31 88).
Metro Universitat/bus all routes to Plaça Catalunya.
Open 1-4.30pm, 8.30pm-midnight Mon-Thur, Sun;
9pm-1am Fri, Sat. **Main courses** €5-€12.20. **Set**
lunch €6.10 Mon-Fri. **Credit** MC, V. **Map** p336 C4.
The arches, low ceiling, old-fashioned wooden furnishings, paintings and colourful tablecloths are redolent of old Havana. You'll find Cuban dishes such as *ropa vieja* (shredded beef) and *picadillo a la habanera* (minced beef, olives and raisins), both served with rice and black beans, and also some good Mediterranean fare. The waiters are cute, too.

Roma

C/Alfons XII 39-41, Gràcia (93 201 35 13).
Metro Fontana/14, 16, 17, 24, 25, 30, 31, 58,
64 bus. **Open** 8.30am-1am Mon-Fri; 7pm-1am Sat.
Main courses €6.20-€15.10. **Set lunch** €7.50
Mon-Fri. **Set dinner** €21.10. **Credit** AmEx, MC, V.
Map p336 D3.
This long-time uptown survivor continues to serve more-than-decent Mediterranean food at reasonable prices. Try the grilled sea bream with wild asparagus and beetroot Parmentier sauce. Enjoy the congenial staff, warm setting and after-dinner cocktails at its busy bar.

Services

Accommodation

Hostal Qué Tal

C/Mallorca 290, Eixample (93 459 23 66). Metro
Passeig de Gràcia or Verdaguer/6, 15, 33, 34, 45,
N4, N6 bus. **Rates** single €33.10; double €49.40-
€63.30. **No credit cards. Map** p336 D4.
The 'How Are You' *hostal* is exceptionally clean, with an attractive, simple decor and fantastically

helpful staff. It's also close to everything, so you won't get lost on the way back home. Book well in advance as it's extremely popular.
Hotel services *Multilingual staff.*

Hotel California

C/Rauric 14, Barri Gòtic (93 317 77 66/fax 93 317
54 74). Metro Liceu/14, 18, 38, 59, N6, N9 bus.
Rates single €45.20; double €72.30. **Credit** AmEx,
DC, MC, V. **Map** p343 A3.
The very comfortable California is centrally located in the heart of the Old City, and has long been a landmark hotel for gay and lesbian visitors. All 31 rooms have en suite bathrooms; there's no bar, but breakfast is available. Book ahead.
Hotel services *Air-conditioning. Laundry.*
Multilingual staff. Safe. Room services Room
service (24hrs). Telephone. TV.

Saunas

There are at least eight gay saunas in Barcelona, all with showers, bar, porno lounge and cubicles. You get a locker, towel and shower sandals, and everything is charged to your locker/key number.

Sauna Casanova

C/Casanova 57, Eixample (93 323 78 60).
Metro Urgell/9, 45, 56, 58, 64, 66, N1, N2,
N3 bus. **Open** 24hrs daily. **Admission** €10.80
Mon, Wed, Fri-Sun; €8.50 Tue, Thur. **Credit** MC,
V. **Map** p340 C5.
By far the most popular sauna, and one of the cleanest. It attracts a young, pretty, muscled crowd that is inclined to do a few kilometres in the corridors before making the final decision on who's to be the lucky fellow. It gets busy just after midnight most nights, and on Tuesdays and Thursdays it's packed.

Sauna Condal

C/Espolsa Sacs 1, Barri Gòtic (93 301 96 80)
Metro Urquinaona/16, 17, 18, 19, 40, 45
bus and all night buses to Plaça Catalunya.
Open 11am-5am Mon-Thur, 11am Fri-5am
Sun. **Admission** €8.50 Mon, Wed; €10.80
Tue, Thur-Sun. **Credit** MC, V. **Map** p342 B2.
This is the oldest sauna in town – with two spacious floors and hardworking staff – and is also very popular. It's frequented by all kinds of gay men, who are pretty upfront about their reasons for being here.

Sex shops

Sestienda

C/Rauric 11, Barri Gòtic (93 318 86 76/
www.sestienda.com). Metro Liceu/14, 16, 38,
59, N6, N9 bus. **Open** 10am-8.30pm Mon-Sat.
Credit MC, V. **Map** p343 A3.
Nowadays sex shops abound in Barcelona, but this was one of the first. Staff are friendly and helpful, and there are backroom cabins for previewing the large video selection.

Arts & Entertainment

Zeus

C/Riera Alta 20, Raval (93 442 97 95). Metro Sant Antoni/24, 64 bus. **Open** 10am-9pm Mon-Sat. **Credit** V. **Map** p340 C5.

More spacious and modern-looking than Sestienda, but similarly well equipped. The clientele seems to lean towards the leather/bear/western type, and the viewing cabins get plenty of use.

Shops

Antinous Libreria Café

C/Josep Anselm Clavé 6, Barri Gòtic (93 301 90 70/ www.antinouslibros.com). Metro Drassanes/14, 18, 36, 38, 57, 59, 64 bus. **Open** 11am-2pm, 5-9pm Mon-Fri; noon-2pm, 5-9pm Sat. **Credit** AmEx, DC, MC, V. **Map** p343 A4.

Natural lighting and ample space make this bookshop a great place to browse and cruise, or to have some refreshment in the little café at the back. It stocks a wide range of gay and lesbian literature (books, magazines and newspapers) and has a bulletin board with details of upcoming cultural events.

Complices

C/Cervantes 2, Barri Gòtic (93 412 72 83/ http://personal1.iddeo.es/complices). Metro Jaume I/ 17, 19, 40, 45 bus. **Open** 10.30am-8.30pm Mon-Fri; noon-8.30pm Sat. **Credit** MC, V. **Map** p343 B3.

This was Barcelona's first gay bookshop, run by a largely female group. Its stock in English is limited, but there's a wide selection in Catalan and Spanish.

M69 attracts a mixed clientele.

M69

C/Muntaner 69, Eixample (93 453 62 69). Metro Universitat/14, 54, 58, 59, 64, 66, N3 bus. **Open** 10.30am-2pm, 5pm-8.30pm Mon-Sat. **Credit** MC, V. **Map** p343 B3.

M69 is a reference point for men's fine fashions, stocking the latest lines by a number of designers, including Paul Smith and Amaya Arzuaga. There's also music and books on design, sex, cooking and everything else the modern gay male might need.

Ovlas

Via Laietana 33, Barri Gòtic (93 268 76 91). Metro Jaume I/17, 19, 40, 45 bus. **Open** 10.30am-8.30pm Mon-Sat. **Credit** AmEx, MC, V. **Map** p343 B3.

This somewhat outlandish but undoubtedly trendy men's store reminds some of Frederick's of Hollywood in Los Angeles. Whatever you fancy here will catch eyes, whether it be from their outerwear department or their extensive underwear section. Prices are a little on the high side. There's also a café-bar serving cocktails, coffee and pastries.

Zona Eleven

C/Muntaner 61, Eixample (93 453 71 45). Metro Universitat/14, 54, 58, 59, 64, 66, N3 bus. **Open** 10.30am-2pm, 5pm-8.30pm Mon-Sat. **Credit** Amex, DC, MC, V. **Map** p343 B3.

Zona Eleven – which has two shops in the Eixample – is aimed at the more adventurous dresser, somewhere between M69 and Ovlas. Prices aren't cheap, but they're not exorbitant.

Branch: C/Diputació 188, Eixample (93 451 45 70).

Lesbian Barcelona

The lesbian scene isn't very prominent in Barcelona (though Girona and Figueres are increasingly becoming fun places to be for lesbian nightlife), but you'll find women in many places frequented by gay men. Gay women's idea of social life is less tied to the bar scene: instead, there are regular events and parties organised by a whole variety of collectives and groups: **Complices** (*see above*) – as much a gay women's as a gay men's bookshop – and **Ca La Dona** (*see p322*) are good places to get information. Of other gay venues, **Café de la Calle** and **Caligula** (for both, *see p232*) are almost as popular with lesbians as with gay men.

Films on lesbian themes are shown at the Women's Film Festival in June.

Bahia

C/Sèneca 12, Gràcia (no phone). Metro Diagonal/ 6, 7, 15, 22, 24, 27, 28, 33, 34, N4, N6 bus. **Open** 10pm-3am daily, plus 6-9am Fri, Sat. **No credit cards**. **Map** p336 D3.

A pleasant, laid-back Gothic bar with a friendly atmosphere and good music. It's especially popular as a place to go with a group of friends.

Aire

C/Valencia 236, Eixample (no phone/
www.arenadisco.com). Metro Passeig de Gràcia/
7, 16, 17, 54, 58, 64, 66, N3 bus. **Open** 10pm-
3am Tue-Sun. **No credit cards. Map** p336 C4.
A stylish airy bar, with colourful decor and a
youthful feel. There are plenty of intimate tables
and a small dancefloor. It's popular with young gay
men, who are welcomed – except on Sundays, when
there are women-only festivities and shows. A
must for the lesbian tourist.

La Rosa

C/Brusi 39, Zona Alta (93 414 61 66). FGC Sant
Gervasi/16, 17, 27, 58, 64, 127, N8 bus. **Open**
11pm-3am Fri, Sat. **Credit** MC, V. **Map** p336 C2.
La Rosa is a little on the tacky side, but this veteran
bar with an intimate, small-town atmosphere still
draws a crowd of mature women at weekends.

La Singular

C/Francisco Giner 50, Gràcia (93 237 50 98). Metro
Diagonal/22, 24, 28, N4, N6 bus. **Open** 1-4pm,
8pm-midnight Mon-Fri; 1-4pm, 8pm-1am Sat. Closed
end Aug-end Sept. **Main courses** €7.20-€12.20.
Set lunch €7.20. **Credit** MC, V. **Map** p336 D3.
The women who run this Mediterranean restaurant
truly believe in customer satisfaction; you'll find
good tapas and home-cooked meals at very economical prices. The menu changes daily, so take the
chef's recommendation on the best fare of the day.

Sitges

Sitges – 41 kilometres (25 miles) east along
the coast from Barcelona – is second only to
Ibiza as a gay beach destination, but has a
completely distinct feel. A good deal of its
old fishing village charm remains, but at night
it comes alive with song, dance and rowdy
camaraderie. Mutual tolerance is what makes
having a good time in Sitges possible for all
who visit it, whether or not they're gay. The
gay scene in Sitges is at its height from June
to September, when gay males from all over
the world converge there – although the most
emblematic event is probably Carnival in
February. For more on Sitges, including how
to get there, *see p277.*

Accommodation

Most of the numerous hotels and *pensions* in
Sitges welcome gay clients – but you should
book in advance. **La Masia Casanova**
(Passatge Casanova 8; 93 818 80 58) offers
luxury suites (double €90) with a pool, a bar
and lots of tranquillity. Book well in advance
for the minimum three-day stay. If you're at a
loss, Peter and Rico at **RAS** (607 14 94 51/fax
93 894 42 72/www.raservice.com) can help find
accommodation in both Sitges and Barcelona.

Hotel Liberty

C/Illa de Cuba 35 (93 811 08 72/fax 93 894 16 62/
www.hotel-liberty-sitges.com). **Rates** €96-€110.
Credit AmEx, MC, V.
The popular Hotel Liberty has recently undergone
a complete renovation. Its 14 charmingly decorated
rooms come with all mod cons, including en suite
bathrooms. They also have completely furnished
multi-room apartments. Rates include breakfast.
Hotel services *Air-conditioning. Bar. Garden.*
Room services *CD player. Minibar. Safe. TV.*

Hotel Romàntic

C/Sant Isidre 33 (93 894 83 75/fax 93 894 81 67).
Rates single €70; double €82.90. **Credit** MC, V.
One of Sitges' most popular gay-friendly hotels, the
Romàntic is a beautifully restored 19th-century
house with a palm-filled patio. **La Renaixença**
(C/Illa de Cuba 7; 93 894 81 67/fax 93 894 81 67),
which is under the same management, is not quite
as architecturally or historically distinctive, but also
offers attractive gardens and reasonable prices.
Room services *Telephone.*

Bars

Crowds move around, and venues change hands
and names from season to season, so it's best to
refer to the free gay map for orientation.
 The year-round pub **Bar 7** (C/Nou 7) makes
an interesting stop early in the evening, and the
two-floored **Mediterraneo** (C/Sant Bonaventura
6) is still an international happening spot; an
appearance here is obligatory before going on
to Trailer. The **B Side Bar** (C/San Gaudenci 7)
is new, popular and very friendly; with a
spacious darkroom. Go to **Parrot's Pub** (Plaça
de l'Industria) for a cool drink on the streetside
terrace after a hard day at the beach. **Organic**
(C/Bonaire 15) is a very popular all-gay disco,
but the perennial favourite is **Trailer** (C/Angel
Vidal 36); the only bar in town to charge
admission, but everybody ends up here all the
same. It draws international DJs and the scene
is hot and heavy until closing time at 5am.

Restaurants

The garden settings at **Flamboyant** (C/Pau
Barrabeitg 16, 93 894 58 11, set dinner €15)
and **Ma Maison** (C/ Bonnaire 28, 93 894 60 54,
main course €10.50) are attractive, and the
more traditional **Can Pagés** (C/Sant Pere 24-26,
93 894 11 95, closed Mon, set lunch €7.20,
set dinner €13.30) is also a good bet. For
something lighter, **Sucre Salé** (C/Sant Pau 39,
93 894 23 02) serves great crêpes (€5.40-€7.20).
Eterna (C/Bonnaire 26, 93 894 80 36, closed
lunch Mon-Fri, closed Sun, set meals €9-€15)
serves a traditional Mediterranean-style menu
and has a lovely garden.

Arts & Entertainment

Music

A conducted tour of the sounds of the city.

Classical & Opera

Barcelona breathes music. There must be something in the air or the architecture. You can't walk through its Gothic streets without stumbling across a classical guitarist, a haunting flautist or a Conservatory-trained string quartet. Whether you're after symphonies, synthesisers or *sardanas*, there is always something on offer, with concerts almost every day of the year. And now, after several years with a distinct lack of venues, Barcelona has the musical infrastructure to meet audience demands. In 1999, L'Auditori, the new, hi-tech, municipal concert hall, opened its doors and the Liceu opera house, which burned down in 1994, sprang triumphantly from the ashes. Meanwhile, the *Modernista* masterpiece, the Palau de la Música, has continued to make up for its acoustical shortcomings with its architectural brilliance. What's more, both the Auditori and the Palau de la Música are in the process of adding medium-sized chamber halls.

Palau de la Música. *See p240.*

On the whole, Catalan audiences know what they like, like what they know, and like to let the orchestra know when they like it. Not so much undiscerning as easy to please, they prefer their composers to be mostly male, preferably Germanic and entirely dead, and this is generally what they get. There is, however, also support for Spanish and Catalan composers. Xavier Montsalvatge and Frederic Mompou are two of the more highly considered representatives of the old guard, while, of the current generation, Albert Guinovart, Joan Guinjoan and Salvador Brotons enjoy healthy reputations. Independent of the mainstream, Carles Santos composes, stages and performs in his own idiosyncratic creations of manic, surreal works that blur the lines between opera, performance and theatre. Barcelona prides itself on its commitment to experimental and avant-garde of all types, and there is also a healthy contemporary music scene.

The main musical calendar mimics the school calendar, stretching from September to June – when the city orchestra, the OBC, offers weekly concerts at the Auditori, playing a repertoire of orchestral classics. The Auditori also hosts other concert cycles, as does the Palau. In summer, the focus of activity moves. Various public art galleries and museums – including the Museu Marítim, the Barbier-Mueller Museum and La Pedrera – hold small, outdoor evening concerts. There are also weekly concerts in several of the city's parks (*see p217* **Classics als Parcs**). The more serious musical activity, though, follows its audience and heads up the coast, to major international festivals in the towns of Perelada, Cadaqués and Toroella de Montgrí.

INFORMATION AND TICKETS

Apart from the venues themselves, the most thorough source of info is the monthly leaflet *Informatiu Musical*, published by Amics de la Música (93 268 01 22), which details concerts across all genres. You can pick up a copy at tourist offices (*see p320*), record shops or at the cultural information centre in the Palau de la Virreina (*see p321*), or at the Generalitat's bookshop almost opposite. The weekly entertainment guide *Guía del Ocio* has a music section, while both *El País* and *La Vanguardia* list forthcoming concerts in their classified ads sections, and usually publish details for each

L'Auditori.

day's more important concerts. Also check the Ajuntament's website at www.bcn.es. Tickets for most major venues can be bought by phone, or over the Internet from the venue itself (check venue listing), or from Tel-entrada or Servi-Caixa (for both, *see p210*).

Venues

L'Auditori

C/Lepant 150, Eixample (93 247 93 00/ www.auditori.com). Metro Marina/6, 7, 10, 56, 62, N2, N3 bus. **Open** *Information* 8am-3pm, 4-6pm Mon-Fri. *Box office* noon-9pm daily. *Performances* 8pm Mon-Thur; 9pm Fri; 7pm Sat; 11am Sun. **Tickets** varies. **Advance tickets** also from Tel-entrada. **Discounts** (OBC concerts) BC. **Credit** MC, V. **Map** p341 F5.

Since its inauguration in 1999, Rafael Moneo's state-of-the-art concert hall has had its share of teething problems, though these have been largely political rather than architectural or musical. Although the 400-seat Sala Polivalent is closed until 2004 while building work goes on, the 2,300-seat main auditorium, the Sala Simfónica, continues to provide a world-class venue. With its stark lines and wood-cladding, it manages to be both minimalist and warmly welcoming. This is more than can be said of the surrounding area, which is something of a cultural and social desert, despite the presence of the neo-classical temple of the Teatre Nacional across the road. Fortunately, the metro is nearby, and a special bus service runs back to civilisation (Plaça Catalunya) after concerts.

Gran Teatre del Liceu

La Rambla 51-59, Barri Gòtic (93 485 99 00/ information 93 485 99 13/www.liceubarcelona.com). Metro Liceu/14, 38, 51, 91, N9, N12 bus. **Open** *Information* 9am-2pm Mon-Fri. *Box office* 2-8.30pm Mon-Fri; 1hr before performance Sat, Sun. Closed 2wks Aug. **Tickets** €9-€129; €6.30-€90.30 (2hrs before performance) concessions. **Credit** AmEx, DC, MC, V. **Map** p343 A3.

Since it reopened in 1999, the Liceu has gone from strength to strength. The number of opera performances has risen from 112 in the 2001/01 season to 133 in 2001/02, and annual season-ticket sales have shot to a staggering 21,000, triple the number before fire destroyed the theatre in 1994. In fact, it is beginning to look as if the welder's spark that burned down the original Liceu was a blessing in disguise. Plans for expansion had already been afoot, and the spanking new 2,340-seat opera house is now three times its original size, and equipped with the latest technology. The auditorium has been recreated in all its red-velvet and gold-leaf glory, for that luxuriant, 19th-century opera feel. A large subterranean foyer used for talks, late-night recitals, children's puppet shows and other musical events.

One advantage is that the Liceu can now join up with its counterparts elsewhere in Europe to bring exciting and innovative co-productions to a city that was long used to duller, more complacent work. And in an attempt to make it accessible to a wider public, several productions feature a couple of reduced-priced nights sung by understudies, new singers at the beginning of their careers or well-known names now past their peak. The Liceu occasionally hosts other concerts by the likes of Björk and Jessye Norman. Tickets sell out early, so book as far in advance as possible (preferably months, not weeks).

Palau de la Música Catalana

C/Sant Francesc de Paula 2, Eixample (93 295 72 00/www.palaumusica.org). Metro Urquinaona/ 17, 19, 40, 45, N8 bus. **Open** *Box office* 10am-9pm Mon-Sat; 1hr before performance Sun. **Tickets** varies. **Advance tickets** also from Servi-Caixa & Caixa de Catalunya. **Credit** MC, V. **Map** p342 B-C2.

The Palau de la Música has never been an ideal concert hall acoustically, but visually it is unbeatable, arousing loyalty and affection from performers and concert-goers alike. Commissioned and paid for by the Orfeó Català in 1908, Domènech i Montaner's *Modernista* masterpiece has long been seen as the spiritual home of Catalan music. The effusive detail and florid decoration both complement and are complemented by music in performance, and while it is possible to visit on a guided tour, the experience is just not the same. Although it was conceived with very populist intentions, the narrow shape of the auditorium means most seats are rather far from the stage. Avoid the rear half of the upper circle (here called the second floor) if you possibly can. Current renovations, projected to finish in 2003, will add a subterranean 600-seat hall for chamber music and conferences, as well as a small plaza for outdoor concerts.

Churches & smaller venues

Various churches around Barcelona, particularly in the Old City, hold occasional concerts. The most beautiful is probably **Santa Maria del Mar** in La Ribera, whose tall, ghostly interior exemplifies the Gothic intertwining of music, light and spirituality. Concerts include everything from Renaissance music to gospel singers. At the main cathedral there is a free organ concert every month, usually, but not always, on the second Wednesday of the month. Other churches with regular concerts include **Santa Maria del Pi**, **Sant Felip Neri**, **Santa Anna** and the monastery in **Pedralbes**. In May, keep an eye out for the **Festival de Música Antiga** (*see p213*), when concerts of early music are held in different locations in the Old City.

Auditori Winterthur

Auditori de l'Illa, Avda Diagonal 547, Les Corts-Sants (93 290 10 90/www.winterthur.es). Metro Maria Cristina/6, 7, 33, 34, 63, 66, 67, 68, N12 bus. **Open** *Information* 8.30am-4.30pm Mon-Thur; 8am-2pm Fri. **Tickets & credit** varies according to production. **Map** p335 B3.

An intimate, modern venue in the unlikely surrounds of the L'Illa shopping centre, which hosts a dozen or so chamber concerts, including an annual Schubert cycle and a series of song recitals.

Orchestras & ensembles

La Capella Reial de Catalunya, Le Concert des Nations, Hespèrion XXI

Information 93 580 60 69.

Led by the indefatigable and inspirational early music specialist Jordi Savall, these three groups have the highest international reputation of Barcelona's musicians, playing around 300 concerts a year worldwide, as well as finding time to create a long list of prize-winning recordings. La Capella Reial specialises in Catalan, Spanish Renaissance and baroque music, vocal or instrumental. Le Concert des Nations is a period-instrument ensemble playing orchestral and symphonic work from 1600 to 1850, and Hespèrion XXI limits itself to music from before 1800.

Orfeó Català

Information 93 295 72 00/www.palaumusica.org.

The Orfeó Català had its origins in the patriotic and social movements at the end of the 19th century; it was one of over 150 choral groups that sprang up in Catalonia at that time. It was sufficiently successful to be able to commission the Palau de la Música, with which it is inseparably identified. Although no longer as pre-eminent as it once was, the Orfeó still stages around 25 performances a year, giving a cappella concerts as well as providing a choir for the OBC and other Catalan orchestras. The group is largely amateur, but includes a small professional nucleus, the Cor de Cambra del Palau de la Música, which gives some 50 performances a year.

Orquestra Simfònica de Barcelona i Nacional de Catalunya (OBC)

Information 93 247 93 00/www.obc.es.

The OBC is like a mid-league football team. It has a foreign manager/conductor, Lawrence Foster, a majority of local players bolstered by a handful of foreigners, and a faithful following which doesn't expect any great surprises. They get the work done, but aren't in line for promotion (or relegation) in the near future.

Concerts, which are held at the Auditori most weekends from October to May, are performed on Friday, then repeated on Saturday night and again on Sunday morning (minus formal dress). Under new management, the resolutely traditional repertoire has become even more traditional, though there are occasional programmes of cinema music, with guest appearances in the 2001/02 season by composer/ directors Maurice Jarre and Elmer Bernstein.

Orquestra Simfònica i Cor del Gran Teatre del Liceu

Information 93 485 99 13/www.liceubarcelona.com.

Since reopening in 1999, the Liceu has walked a tightrope between pleasing the reactionary and vociferous old guard while trying to follow more forward-looking currents in European opera. The last

Arts & Entertainment

Contemporary music

Avuimusics

Associacio Catalana de Compositors, Passeig Colom 6, space 4, Barri Gòtic (93 268 37 19/ www.accompositors.com). Metro Jaume I/14, 36, 57, 59, 64, 157, N6 bus. **Open** *Information* 9.30am-1.30pm Mon-Fri. *Box office* 30min before concert. **Tickets** €6; €3 concessions. **No credit cards**. **Map** p342 B4.

For lovers of written (rather than improvised) contemporary music, this increasingly successful series features 14 concerts from October to May. Run by the Association of Catalan Composers, about half the repertoire is by living Catalans and half by international 20th-century heavyweights. Concerts are held at the CCCB and the address above.

Festival de Músiques Contemporànies

Information 93 247 93 00/www.auditori.com.

This short autumn festival (usually held from October to December) offers the widest possible interpretation of the term contemporary music, exploring different developments on all musical fronts, from new flamenco to electronic to contemporary classical to jazz to experimental. Among the 2001 highlights were Dave Douglas, Duquende and John Duncan. Concerts are held in various venues, including the Auditori, CCCB and Metrònom.

Fundació Joan Miró

Parc de Montjuïc, Montjuïc (93 329 19 08/ www.bcn.fjmiro.es). Metro Paral.lel, then Funicular de Montjuïc/50 bus. **Open** *Box office* from 8pm Thur. *Performances* 9pm Thur. **Advance tickets** also from Tel-entrada. **Tickets** €7; €15 for 3 concerts; €27 for 7 concerts. **Credit** MC, V. **Map** p339 B6.

It may not be the world's best auditorium, but the brief series of concerts at the Fundació Miró that runs from the end of June to September features an interesting selection of improvised music by an array of international musicians. Several of the more light-hearted concerts are held on the roof terrace overlooking the city.

Gràcia Territori Sonor

Information 93 237 37 37/www.gracia-territori.com. This small collective organises various events throughout the year, covering music of all types and genres. Their main festival activity is the free LEM event, which is usually held from October to early December. (The meaning of the letters LEM changes from year to year. When they started, it was Ladrar a las Estrellas del Mar (Barking at the Starfish). In 2000, it stood for Logarithm Elastic Metabolic; in 2001 it was Languages, Species and Metaphors.) The music tends to be experimental, electronic and often improvised, and is performed mostly in bars and clubs in Gràcia, though some of the larger events are at L'Espai. The festival also presents poetry, sound installations, DJs and dance.

two seasons have included at least one polemical production, including a *Lohengrin* set in a school room and, in the year of Verdi's centenary, a version of *Un Ballo in Maschera* that included defecation, nudity and homosexual rape. Productions at the other extreme have been coma-inducingly traditional, including a Cecil B DeMille-style *Aida*, and a stultifying *Samson and Delilah*.

The 2001/02 season treads more of a middle ground. Interesting productions from abroad include Opera North's versions of Britten's *Gloriana* and Janáček's *Cunning Little Vixen* and a Royal Opera House *La Traviata*. Homegrown fare comes in the ample shape of *Henry VIII* by Saint-Saëns, featuring Catalan diva Montserrat Caballé (though not in the title role), a charming revival of last season's *The Magic Flute*, and Monteverdi's *Orfeo* – though be warned: the last time they put this on, they burned the place down.

The opera season runs from October to July. In addition to the dozen or so operas, there are recitals, concerts, lectures and two or three dance productions, both classical and contemporary, including, in 2002, Nacho Duato's Compañia Nacional de Danza.

Orquestra Simfònica del Vallès

Information 93 727 03 00/www.osvalles.com.

Though not quite at the level of the two main city orchestras, this country cousin from the nearby town of Sabadell performs regularly in Barcelona, particularly at the Palau de la Música, and is worth looking out for. Established in 1987, its reputation is largely due to its dynamic young conductor/composer Salvador Brotons, whose work it often performs, alongside stalwarts of the classical repertoire and some more modern work.

Metrònom

*C/Fusina 9 (93 268 42 98). Metro Jaume I/
39, 51 bus.* **Open** 10am-2pm, 4.30-8.30pm
Tue-Sat. Closed Aug. **Map** p336 C3.

Best known as an alternative art space (*see p230*),
Metrònom has increased its commitment to current
music in recent years. The high point is a hugely
successful international festival of contemporary
and experimental music in January, featuring everything from minimalist weirdos extracting sound
from credit cards and wire loops, to extreme noisist
types doing things to vinyl that would make your
average DJ break out in a cold sweat. A second,
shorter festival takes place in June.

Rock, Roots & Jazz

Barcelona likes to see itself as an avant-garde,
cosmopolitan city, and the consolidation of
several innovative musical initiatives of the
1990s has certainly helped it to live up to this
reputation. These initiatives include the BAM
festival (*see p216* **Mercè mission**) featuring
mostly alternative (and mostly free) rock
concerts in the old town's marvellous squares,
and **Sónar** (*see p214*), the internationally
renowned electronic music festival. One of
the latest schemes to bear fruit is the B-Parade,
Barcelona's answer to the Love Parade, which
debuted in September 2001. The success of
this lively techno procession, which attracted
some 50,000 fans, reflects the current
predominance of DJs and electronic dance
music, but good ol' rock 'n' roll, jazz, flamenco
and world music are never hard to find.

Local rock talent currently in the limelight
includes pop group Élena, funky retro
disco band Fundación Tony Manero and hip
hoppers 7N7C. Part-time Barcelona resident
Manu Chao and band Dusminguet are the
best-known representatives of *mestizo* rock,
while Lax 'n' Busto and Els Pets are popular
rock català groups.

Catalan folk music was politically charged
in the 1960s and '70s, but has now lost most
of its radical edge, even though some of its
original exponents – such as Lluís Llach and

Top Cat: Manu Chao

Multicultural, colourful, contrary and
controversial, Manu Chao may not have family
ties to Catalonia (he's French born with a
Galician father and Basque mother), but
he's become as emblematic of Barcelona's
spirit to today's generation as Gaudí was
to previous generations. Yet this chart-
conquering, ethno-rock musician is a recent
immigrant, settling here in 1999 after the
release of his massively successful album,
Clandestino. The record came about after
his group, French/Spanish anarcho-rockers
Mano Negra, disbanded, and Chao spent
five years on the road in South America,
Africa and Europe, where he played in the
streets, taped fellow buskers and local
musicians, discovered new sounds and
affirmed his political beliefs. But even a
traveller needs roots, so Chao planted his
in Barcelona. He says it was 'because after
30 years in Paris, an exciting city with a cold
heart, I wanted sun and warmth.'

The place Chao can most often be found
playing is Plaça George Orwell, the square
he sees as one big living room. He hangs
out in Bar Bahia or outside in the square,
strumming his guitar, playing football,
chatting with fans – and those who don't
know who he is. He says he's happy not to
be recognised: 'I like to rehearse in the
street. People say to me: "You play well,
you play like the real Manu Chao!" It's
important to be a nobody.'

When Chao's second solo album, *Próxima
Estacion: Esperanza*, was released and shot
to No.1 in Europe and Latin America in 2001,
it became clear he certainly isn't a nobody.
Its sales were probably helped by Chao's
increasing association with the anti-
globalisation movement, inspired by his
concerts for Subcomandante Marcos in
Mexico City and for the protesters in Genoa,
as well as the messages in his music.

In Barcelona, he's faced with the issues
that inform his music every day. Just before
Chao played in Plaça Catalunya in 2001 for
the Mercè festival, the Ajuntament evicted
immigrants who had set up camp there. An
ironic preparation for a gig by an artist whose
anthem 'Clandestino' is a lament for all
those human beings condemned as 'illegal'.

Despite this, it seems there's something
special going on between Manu and
Barcelona. For Manu, 'It's a very beautiful
city. I have many friends here. The relation
with my neighbours is very good. I'm just one
of them. I feel at ease here.' And for the city?
Well, some 90,000 people braved heatstroke
and floods of urine to see him play in Plaça
Catalunya. He's one of the family now.

Maria del Mar Bonet – still perform. A younger generation of folkies include Catalan-American Paul Fuster, who sings in English, and duo Silvia Comas and Lidia Pujol.

Barcelona's gypsy culture is represented by two well-established genres: flamenco and rumba catalana. Catalan flamenco might sound unlikely, but local artists Mayte Martín, Miguel Poveda and Duquende, the offspring of Andalucian migrants, are considered among the most accomplished voices in Spain. El Payo Malo and Ojos de Brujo are a lot less conventional, mixing flamenco with soul, R&B, funk, hip hop or reggae. Peret is the gypsy king of rumba, and local rumba band Estopa was one of the surprise top-of-the-chart acts in Spain in 2001.

Jazz has traditionally had a strong following in Barcelona, and local music schools keep churning out new talent. The city is home to competent jazz artists such as Carme Canela, Lluís Vidal and Horacio Fumero, and established festivals such as the **Festival Internacional de Jazz** (*see p218*).

The diverse music styles of Latin America and Africa are also very popular, and not just among the city's growing immigrant community. Cuban singer Lucrecia is based in Barcelona, as is Chab Samir, the urban-style *raï* group. Big-name world music concerts take place regularly, especially during the **Festival del Grec** (*see p217*) in summer.

Outdoor concerts in a Mediterranean city like Barcelona are common events, especially during summer festivals, and settings such as the Plaça del Rei, the main square of the Poble Espanyol, the Teatre Grec, the CCCB's Pati de les Dones, or Avinguda de la Catedral are hard to beat.

INFORMATION AND TICKETS

Unfortunately there is no comprehensive listings guide; your best bet is to get your hands on one or more of the following. The weekly *Guia del Ocio*, is available at any newsstand, while in bars and record shops you can pick up the monthly giveaways *Barcelona Metropolitan* (in English), *AB*, *Go Mag*, *Mondo Sonoro* and the very practical *Butxaca*. You can also obtain concert information at www.atiza.com. Local papers also publish entertainment supplements on Fridays; 'Tentaciones' in *El País* is the best one for music. The cultural information centre in the Palau de la Virreina (*see p321*) is another good source, and many of the record shops along C/Tallers, near Plaça Catalunya, display concert info on noticeboards and sell tickets. Books-and-everything superstore FNAC (*see p210*) sells tickets for many venues and festivals and often hosts free preview performances by musicians playing in the city. Finally, you can always ring 010.

Rock & pop

Pop and rock superstars often perform in one of the sports barns up in Montjuïc, either at the acoustically deprived **Palau d'Esports** or the preferable **Palau Sant Jordi** (for both, *see p263*). See also **Astin**, **KGB**, **Mond Club/Sala Cibeles**, **La Ruta de los Elefantes** and the **Sidecar Factory Club**, all in *chapter* **Nightlife**.

Bikini

C/Déu i Mata 105, Les Corts (93 322 08 00/ www.bikinibcn.com). Metro Les Corts/15, 30, 43, 59 bus. **Open** midnight-4.30am Tue-Thur; midnight-5.30am Fri, Sat. *Gigs* 9/10pm-11.30pm Thur. **Admission** midnight-1am (incl 2 drinks), 1am-4.30/5.30am (incl 1 drink) €9. *Gigs varies.* **Credit** AmEx, V. **Map** p335 B3.
Bikini has been a leading light of the Barcelona music scene for almost half a century, but you sense little history here. It was given a makeover a few

Gimme an R, gimme an... A? **Razzmatazz**. *See p245.*

years ago as part of the development of the L'Illa shopping centre, and its decor has that mall-like look. It's well designed, however, with metres of bar winding through the three spaces (main venue and two smaller ones), plus quiet chill-out areas. The smooth surroundings make a suitably adaptable background for the heterogeneous fans coming to watch the enormous variety of acts – from ex-Velvet Undergrounder John Cale to British indie-rock upstarts Muse, as well as Spanish sounds from rock to rumba. *See also p262.*

Garatge Club

C/Pallars 195, Poblenou (93 309 14 38). Metro Llacuna/40, 42, 92, N11 bus. **Open** 1-6am Fri, Sat. Closed 2wks Aug. **Admission** varies. **No credit cards.**

'Garage' is the place for hardcore, speedcore, black metal, nu-metal and old punk. This is where you go to see the kind of band that makes sexual gestures with bananas. If you like your metal softened by a few weeks in the charts, this is also the place to catch the sales-friendly likes of At the Drive-In.

Jazz Sí Club/Cafè

C/Requesens 2, Raval (93 329 00 20/www.taller demusics.com). Metro Sant Antoni/20, 24, 38, 41, 55, 64, N6 bus. **Open** 9am-11pm Mon-Fri; 6-11pm Sat, Sun. **Admission** €2.50-€4.20. **No credit cards. Map** p340 C5.

The Barcelona contemporary music school, which is situated opposite, runs this small, friendly bar (and a good café by day) as a space for students, teachers and music lovers to meet, practise, perform and listen. Each night is devoted to a different musical genre, with new and improvised work on Mondays, pop/ rock/blues jams on Tuesdays, jazz jams on Wednesdays, some of the city's best Cuban

son on Thursdays, flamenco on Fridays, and rock jams on Sundays. On Saturdays, invited groups perform just about anything.

Luz de Gas

C/Muntaner 246, Eixample (93 209 77 11/ www.luzdegas.com). Bus 6, 7, 15, 27, 32, 33, 34, 58, 64, N8. **Open** 11pm-4.30am Mon-Thur, Sun; 11pm-5.30am Fri, Sat. *Gigs* 12.30am daily. Closed Sun in Aug. **Admission** €15 Mon-Sat; €12 Sun (opera). **Credit** AmEx, DC, MC, V. **Map** p340 C3.

A dressed-up, grown-up crowd queues to get into this lovingly converted old music hall, garnished with chandeliers and classical friezes. They come to see classic MOR acts, such as Kool and the Gang, Level 42 and Simple Minds. In between the visits from foreign 'names', you'll find nightly residencies: blues on Mondays, Dixieland jazz on Tuesdays, cover bands on Wednesdays and Saturdays, soul on Thursdays, rock on Fridays and opera on Sundays.

Magic

Passeig Picasso 40, La Ribera (93 310 72 67). Metro Barceloneta/14, 39, 51 bus. **Open** 11pm-6am Thur; 11pm-7am Fri, Sat. **Admission** *Gigs* €15. *Disco* (incl 1 drink) €9. **No credit cards. Map** p341 E6.

With its black walls and decor of booze logos, Magic is a stalwart of the local punk/indie scene. Don't be surprised to see black eyelinered and stockinged vocalists draping themselves over the bar (and that's just the guys). This is a good place to pick up on trends in the alternative rock scene, such as instrumental post-rock (check out local exponents 12twelve). One Saturday a month, the Magic in the Air Club turns back time with a R&B band and, bizarrely, a Northern Soul disco. Sadly, sometimes there aren't just enough Wigan Pier veterans in town to conjure up much of an atmosphere.

Razzmatazz

*C/Almogávers 122, Poblenou (93 272 09 10/
93 320 82 00). Metro Marina/6, 40, 42, 141,
N6 bus.* **Open** *Gigs* start at 8.30-11.30pm Fri,
Sat. *Disco* 1-5am Fri, Sat. **Admission** *Gigs*
€15-€21. *Disco* (incl 1 drink) €9. **No credit
cards. Map** p341 F6.

In early 2000, Razzmatazz opened on the site of the
legendary venue Zeleste, and continues its tradition
of presenting quality music, mainly of an alternative rock and dance flavour. This is Barcelona's key
non-stadium venue, servicing a core constituency of
savvy, tuned-in, turned-on twentysomethings. The
industrial space has been starkly converted, making a feature of its air-con vents and raw concrete.
A nod to comfort comes from the ample toilet space,
and a gallery overlooking the main hall offers respite
from over-enthusiastic dancers. As well as hosting
established faves like Pulp and Orbital, Razz is
sharp at booking up-and-coming international acts,
such as Detroit's retro-rockers the White Stripes.

Sala Apolo/Nitsaclub

*C/Nou de la Rambla 113, Paral.lel (93 441 40 01/
www.nitsa.com). Metro Paral.lel/36, 57, 64, 91,
N6, N9 bus.* **Open** *Gigs* varies. *Disco* 12.30-6.30am
Fri, Sat. **Admission** (incl 1 drink) *Gigs & disco* €12.
No credit cards. Map p340 C6.

One of the oldest dance halls in Spain, the Apolo
opened in 1940 and its decor has changed little since
then. Red drapes, polished wood and globe lights are
the backdrop to occasional gigs by alternative rock
and leftfield dance acts. Previous treaders of Apolo's
boards include Britpop troupers Ocean Colour Scene
and wistful pop-rockers the Divine Comedy.

When this madly popular venue reaches critical
mass, you can try to find chilling space on the balcony level. At the weekend, Nitsaclub (*see p255*)
takes over and hordes of techno fiends polish the
boards even more with their sweat and hotstepping.

Flamenco

If you're not shy of mixing with the locals
and have your street wits about you, take a
trawl around the lower Raval, where you
may find impromptu performances in the
local bars. See also **L'Auditori** (*see p239*),
Jazz Sí Club/Cafè (*see p244*) and **Harlem
Jazz Club** (*see p246*).

Soniquete

*C/Milans 5, Barri Gòtic (mobile 639 382 354).
Metro Drassanes or Jaume I/14, 36, 57, 59,64,
N6 bus.* **Open** 9pm-3am Thur-Sun. **No credit
cards. Map** p343 B4.

Pass through a doorway framed by a glass case
packed with plastic flowers and 'enter into a paradise
of flamenco', as they say. A candlelit bar with bits
of kitsch and strings of fairy lights plays host to
homesick Andalucians strumming their fingers raw
on Thursday, Friday and Saturday nights. If you're
unlucky and no one shows up to play or sing, it's

still an atmospheric place for a beer. If Soniquete
catches on – it opened only in late 2001 – there are
plans to open it every night.

El Tablao de Carmen

*Behind Poble Espanyol, Avda Marquès de Comillas,
Montjuïc (93 325 68 95/www.tablaodecarmen.com).
Metro Espanya/13, 50, 61 bus.* **Open** 8pm-2am
Tue-Sun. *Flamenco show* 9.30pm, 11.30pm Tue-
Thur, Sun; 9.30pm, midnight Fri, Sat. **Admission**
Poble Espanyol €7; €5 concessions. *El Tablao de
Carmen* show & 1 drink €27; show & dinner €51.
Credit AmEx, DC, MC, V. **Map** p339 A5.

A rather sanitised version of the traditional flamenco
tablao, befitting its strange faux Andalucian surroundings in the Poble Espanyol (if you book for the
show in advance, you don't have to pay the Poble
Espanyol entrance fee). You'll find both established
stars and young new talent, displaying the various
styles of flamenco singing, dancing and music. It's
a good place for a thorough, professional introduction to flamenco. However, because each artist takes
it in turn to demonstrate his or her particular skill,
the show can lose momentum. The emphasis here is
on panache, rather than passion, so you might prefer
your flamenco with a bit more spit and less polish.
Bookings are recommended.

Los Tarantos

*Plaça Reial 17, Barri Gòtic (93 319 17 89/tablao
93 389 16 61/www.masimas.com). Metro Liceu/
14, 38, 59, 91, N9, N12 bus.* **Open** *Flamenco show*
10.30pm-midnight daily. *Disco* midnight-5am Mon-
Sat. **Admission** (incl 1 drink) *Flamenco show* €24;
€15.10 concessions. *Disco* €12. **Credit** MC, V. **Map**
p343 A3.

Neighbour and sister bar to Jamboree (*see p246*),
this long-established, respected flamenco *tablao* has
presented many top stars over the years. It caters
mainly to the tourist trade, but avoids the fripperies
of some coach-party venues. The modern, simple,
open space feels a bit like a school hall with its fold-
away wooden chairs, except that there's a bar and,
of course, as this is Barcelona, you have to smoke.

Folk & world

For Northern European/Celtic folk music
(of often dubious quality), try Barcelona's
ex-pat pubs. The **Quiet Man** (C/Marqués de
Barbera 11; 93 412 12 19) hosts occasional
performances, usually when it can grab top
performers who happen to be in town. See also
Jazz Sí Club/ Café (*see p244*), **Harlem Jazz
Club** and **Teatreneu** (for both, *see p246*).

CAT

*Trva de Sant Antoni 6-8, Gràcia (93 218 44 85/
www.tradicionarius.com). Metro Fontana/22, 24,
28, 39, N4 bus.* **Open** *Bar* 5pm-midnight daily.
Gigs about 10pm Fri. Closed mid July-end Aug.
Admission €6-€9. **No credit cards. Map** p336 D3.

Founded in 1993, the Centre Artesà Tradicionàrius
promotes traditional Catalan music and culture. It

hosts a number of music festivals, including the Festival Tradicionàrius, a showcase of folk music and dance held between January and April. Concerts, workshops and classes cover indigenous music from countries such as Greece, Ireland, Italy and France, and other parts of Spain. It's not all old stuff, however. The centre also takes part in the LEM festival of experimental music (*see p241* **Gràcia Territori Sonor**), which usually features more bleeps than bagpipes.

Jazz, soul, blues & funk

In summer, two of the most pleasant places for jazz and a drink are **La Pedrera de Nit** (*see p259*) and **Bar Hivernacle** (*see p177*) in the Parc de la Ciutadella. The **Pipa Club** (*see p247*) in the Plaça Reial holds an autumn jazz festival in the Scotch Bar at the Hotel Ritz.

La Boîte

Avda Diagonal 477, Eixample (93 319 17 89/ www.masimas.com). Bus 6, 7, 15, 27, 32, 33, 34, 63, 67, 68, N12. **Open** *Gigs* midnight-1.30am Mon-Sat. *Disco* 1.30-5am Mon-Sat. **Admission** *Gigs* €9. *Disco* (incl 1 drink) €15. **No credit cards. Map** p336 C3.
Barcelona's serious live music scene is somewhat dominated by the Mas siblings (*see p248* **Top Cats: Los Mas i Mas**). They took over La Boîte more than ten years ago, when it was, in their own words, a 'tacky jet-set' kind of place. Now it's a credible venue attracting up-and-coming stars (like 'the new Dylan', Willie Nile) and old troupers like the Supremes. You could hear anything from hip hop to South American *cantautores* here, but the emphasis is on jazz, blues and funk, mostly from Spanish artists.

La Cova del Drac

C/Vallmajor 33, Zona Alta (93 319 17 89). FGC Muntaner/14, 58, 64, N8 bus. **Open** *Gigs* 11pm-12.30am Tue-Sat. *Disco* 12.30-5am Tue-Sat. **Admission** *Gigs* €6 Tue-Thur; €9 Fri, Sat. *Disco* (incl 1 drink) €12. **No credit cards. Map** p336 C2.
La Cova is one of those places that is name-dropped by artists who play there, thanks to its fantastic history as a seminal jazz venue. At its previous site on the celebrated 'Tuset Street' it was a refuge for bohemians and intellectuals during Franco's rule, but it was also the only major jazz venue in town, attracting big American stars. It moved to its present location in 1990 and, after a few bad years at the end of the '90s, was bought and refurbished by the ubiquitous Mas siblings. Following the Mas recipe of quality and accessibility with a dash of sophistication, La Cova is now a 'jazzoteca' hosting two sets of jazz followed by DJs playing house and funk until 5am, all aimed at the beautiful (though not necessarily young) people of the city.

Harlem Jazz Club

C/Comtessa de Sobradiel 8, Barri Gòtic (93 310 07 55). Metro Jaume I/17, 19, 40, 45, N8 bus. **Open** 8pm-4am Tue-Thur, Sun; 8pm-5am Fri, Sat.

Gigs 10.30pm, midnight Tue-Thur, Sun; 11.30pm, 1am Fri, Sat. Closed some wks Aug. **Admission** 1-drink minimum Tue-Thur; €5 Fri-Sun. **No credit cards. Map** p343 B3.
Squeeze past the narrow bar and the room opens up (slightly) to accommodate a small, low stage and a laid-back crowd sitting cross-legged on the floor. Jazz and blues often make way for world music, particularly Afro-Caribbean sounds, as well as rock and flamenco-fusion.

Jamboree

Plaça Reial 17, Barri Gòtic (93 301 75 64/ www.masimas.com). Metro Liceu/14, 38, 59, N9, N12 bus. **Open** 10.30pm-5am daily. *Gigs* 11pm-12.30am daily. **Admission** (incl 1 drink) €12. **No credit cards. Map** p343 A3.
This long-established jazz 'cave' is one of the principal jazz clubs in Barcelona, if not all Europe. A cosy, stone-vaulted cavern (with eggbox-enhanced acoustics), it's another part of the Mas siblings' empire. Old greats like Chet Baker have played here, and today's stars – such as guitar guru Larry Coryell and Buena Vista's Jimmy Jenks – maintain its heady reputation. Or how about a jazz vs hip hop sound-off, or poetry jams? All part of Jamboree's extensive repertoire. *See also p248.*

Teatreneu

C/Terol 26-28, Gràcia (93 285 79 00). Metro Fontana or Joanic/22, 24, 28, 39, N4, N6 bus. **Open** *Gigs* 9-11pm Tue-Thur; 10pm-midnight Fri, Sat; 6-8pm Sun. **Admission** €11-€21. **Credit** MC, V. **Map** p336 D3.
On a site where Gràcia's weavers used to meet, the Teatreneu complex combines a music venue with a restaurant and bar-cum-theatre. Concerts usually feature jazz and world music, complementing the flavour of the fringe theatre productions. One jazz group, the Ignasi Terraza Trio, even held a season of concerts here in the dark.

Latin

Many of the venues in this section host performances of a Latin variety, but see also **Bar Pastis**, **Domèstic**, **La Paloma** and **La Pedrera de Nit**, all in *chapter* **Nightlife**.

Antilla Barcelona

C/Aragó 141, Eixample (93 451 21 51/www.antilla salsa.com). Metro Hospital Clínic/43, 44, N7 bus. **Open** 11pm-4am Mon-Thur, Sun; 11pm-5am Fri, Sat. **Admission** (incl 1 drink) €9. **Map** p336 C4.
This salsa/Latin club got itself in the Guinness Book of Records in 1994 with a record 24-hour rumba. This may have been the inspiration for the club's motto: 'Salsa and pleasure until the dawn'. The club also publishes a magazine and holds exhibitions and courses on all things Latino. Wednesdays and Thursdays are the main nights for invited artists, when you can get down among a hot and happy crowd to merengue, salsa and more, or take a break at the bar decorated with totally tropical taste.

Nightlife

Once the sun has gone down behind the hills, Barcelona makes a spectacular backdrop for all shades of nightlife.

While Barcelona basks in its international reputation as a glittering nightlife capital, there's still plenty of impetus in the evolution of its diverse nocturnal scenes. By turns it can be glamorous, sleazy, adrenalin-filled, laid-back, shabby and chic: it's also compact, with an eminently strollable centre, and most other places within easy taxi range.

Starting at the seafront, Maremàgnum and Port Olímpic are lined with dockside bars and nightclubs and swarm with tourists in summer. The labyrinthine backstreets of the Barri Gòtic are always pulsating with life, especially around C/Escudellers and the Plaça Reial, where many near-perfect little late-night bars are tucked into the murky alleyways. Across La Rambla, through the Raval and spilling over Paral.lel into Poble Sec, you'll find underground, alternative spaces, some long-established drinking dens with exceedingly chequered histories, and La Paloma and Sala Apolo, two emblematic city clubs in venues rich with vintage atmosphere.

Up in the elegant gridwork of the Eixample, tourists are less in evidence, and classy designer bars are spread throughout the district. Broadly, altitude corresponds to class, with the well-heeled crowds heading high, up to the Zona Alta and even Tibidabo; two of the city's most spectacular clubs are located on the slopes of Montjuïc. Gràcia and the Born possess a special, self-contained feel of their own, with their nightlife centred around bars and bar terraces in Gràcia's squares and around the Passeig del Born (neither have many all-night clubs).

In general, in a city that goes out late and stays out late, barlife and nightlife overlap – several places featured in the Cafés & Bars chapter could easily have appeared here. Some establishments describe themselves as *bares musicales*, which can mean anything from a fixed music policy to DJs and a dancefloor. But distinctions get blurred: in some cases, it's hard to tell whether a place is primarily a bar, a restaurant or a club. As a consequence of so many late-night dancing options, nightclubs that charge admission don't really get into full swing until at least 2am. Check your ticket for the words *con consumición*: this means you can exchange it

for a drink at the bar – which is worth knowing, as there's a steep increase in prices once you're inside. This may be why locals are noticeably inclined to pace their drinking – this and the fact that many of them will be staying out well into the next day and have no desire to peak early and flake out.

Club culture exploded in Barcelona in the 1990s, finding two main channels of expression: on the one hand, transgressive, omnisexual, Ibiza-style circus spectaculars, and on the other, a more pared-down, musically pioneering scene whose annual highpoint is the Sónar festival (*see p214*). Sónar has been instrumental in attracting major artists, and the attention of the international club community, to the city. Some notable adoptive residents are Glaswegian DJ and producer Funk d'Void, and Icelandic dance collective Gus Gus. Meanwhile, Barcelona DJs such as the omnipresent Sideral have gained a high level of recognition, and native techno DJs such as Oscar Mulero and Àngel Molina can pack large venues.

INFORMATION

New clubs open (and close) all the time, but to stay informed of changes and the programmes at established clubs, look no further than the obligatory smorgasbord of flyers on display in any fashionable clothes or record shop, or in the bars themselves. The free (Spanish-language) magazines *punto H*, *aB* and *go BCN* are exhaustive documents of the creative synergy between art, fashion, design and music that is played out on the city's club scene.

Barri Gòtic

Barcelona Pipa Club
Plaça Reial 3, pral (93 302 47 32/ www.bpipaclub. com). Metro Liceu/14, 38, 59, N9, N12 bus. **Open** 11pm-3am daily. **No credit cards.** **Map** p343 A3.
Pipa as in pipe: this is a private pipe-smokers' club, as the rough-cut pipe bowls, chillums, tobacco ads and smoker's paraphernalia on display will confirm. But after the dottle's dried, it's also one of the city's best late-night bars; the wood-panelled Sherlock Holmes-style saloon and ex-jazz lounge fill up until, after 1am, it's standing room only. To get in, ring the buzzer next to the sign of the pipe: if there's no answer, it may be that there's just no room.

Café Royale

C/Nou de Zurbano 3 (93 412 14 33). Metro Liceu or Drassanes/14, 38, 59, N9, N12 bus. **Open** 6pm-2.30am Mon-Thur; 6pm-3am Fri, Sat; 7pm-2.30am Sun. **No credit cards. Map** p343 A3.

With its pleasantly scuffed look, mellow orange-velvet curtains and bottomless sofas, this place looks like a fabulous '70s *Vogue*-style lounge club. Early in the week you may find space to relax and listen to the dog-eared library of bossa nova and Latin jazz shelved behind the DJ's cabinet. At weekends, however, it's packed to squeaking point with a high-sheen, high-maintenance fashion crowd. For an alley off the Plaça Reial, the glamour quotient is way off the scale: it's where Almodóvar threw his end-of-filming party for *All About My Mother*.

Dot

C/Nou de Sant Francesc 7 (93 302 70 26/www. dotlightclub.com). Metro Drassanes/14, 38, 91, N9, N12 bus. **Open** 10pm-2.30am Mon-Thur, Sun; 10pm-3am Fri, Sat. **No credit cards. Map** p343 A4.

Dot has a sharp scarlet front bar and a tiny backroom dancefloor, connected by what looks like a decommissioned teleport unit. There's different music every night, including phat beatz, space funk, phuture soul and lounge. It's held in great affection by a heterogeneous crowd, and for a cramped but good-natured boogie with your eyes glued to the Godzilla/Betty Page/Jackie Chan movie on the back wall, it's hard to beat. One question – what is Mr Spock doing behind the bar? Yours to find out.

Fonfone

C/Escudellers 24 (93 317 14 24/www.fonfone.com). Metro Drassanes/14, 38, 59, 91, N9, N12 bus. **Open** 10pm-2.30am Mon-Thur, Sun; 10pm-3am Fri, Sat. **Credit** MC, V. **Map** p343 A3.

A deep dark bar barely lit by the multicoloured radioactive glow of its Lego-like brick decorations, Fonfone seems to draw a steady throughput of people in search of any up-tempo beats, from drum 'n' bass to house, to spark the evening off. Just across the street you can catch some of the same DJs at the new (and still slightly musty) club Technique.

Jamboree

Plaça Reial 17 (93 301 75 64/www.masimas.com). Metro Liceu/14, 38, 59, N9, N12 bus. **Open** 10.30pm-5.30am daily. *Gigs* 11pm-12.30am daily. **Admission** (incl 1 drink) €12. **No credit cards. Map** p343 A3.

A jazz cellar with a distinguished history (*see below* **Top Cats: Los Mas i Mas**), Jamboree's cavernous brick walls reverberate to soul, funk and R&B when it turns into a nightclub after the evening's gig. The crowd is a mix of tourists and locals glad to have lit on black grooves in this predominantly house city. Punters can also head upstairs, where flamenco venue Los Tarantos (*see p245*) serves as a lounge bar/chill-out zone, on a Latin tip. *See also p246.*

Karma

Plaça Reial 10 (93 302 56 80). Metro Liceu/14, 38, 59, N9, N12 bus. **Open** midnight-4am Tue, Wed, Sun; midnight-5am Thur-Sat. **Admission** (incl 1 drink) €7. **No credit cards. Map** p343 A3.

Top Cats: Los Mas i Mas

Barcelona residents sometimes see a wry irony in the city's reputation for nightlife, certainly those who remember the dull years that preceded its transformation. When the Mas siblings – sisters Marta and Ana and brother Joan – opened the Mas i Mas bar 15 years ago, it was one of a wave of new bars whose groundbreaking design and style expressed the city's newfound confidence in itself. Since then, the family's restless energy has been a vital component in the regeneration of Barcelona's nightlife, overseeing the reopening of some of the city's most emblematic venues.

In 1990, they took over a basement club just off Plaça Francesc Macià that until then had been a tacky executive lounge bar. Music had always been a passion, especially for Joan, and they established La Boîte (*see p258*) as a venue offering blues and jazz concerts seven nights a week. For much of the audience, live music was a totally new experience; at that time, the only real

competition was the rock venue Zeleste (now Razzmatazz) and, not surprisingly, La Boîte was an enormous success.

So much so that in 1992, the family were offered the chance to run Jamboree (*see p248*), a jazz cellar on Plaça Reial that was struggling to regain the legendary stature it had won hosting Memphis Slim, Chet Baker, Dexter Gordon and other greats of jazz's golden age. The lively scene at La Boîte spilled over to the new Jamboree, and it saw a renaissance that is still going strong, with appearances from contemporary international stars such as Wynton Marsalis and the Lou Bennett Trio.

Jamboree was one of the haunts of Barcelona's so-called 'gauche divine' – the loosely defined social movement that opposed the 'divine right' of the dictatorship, bringing together left-leaning architects, designers, photographers, writers and the whole swinging bohemian world of Barcelona during the 1960s and '70s, whose antics were a

Its age measurable only in donkey's years, this unredeemed cellar club (with its unmissable entrance among the arcades of Plaça Reial), attracts a huge queue of people willing to pay to get in. Chart pop from the '80s and '90s pounds the eardrums of unfussy locals and a high proportion of tourists enjoying themselves in a perverse so-bad-it's-good way.

La Macarena

C/Nou de Sant Francesc 5 (no phone). Metro Liceu/ 14, 38, 59, N9, N12 bus. **Open** 11pm-4am Mon-Sat. **No credit cards**. **Map** p343 A4.

Once a cosy little flamenco joint, the only remnants of its former existence are the strutting silhouettes on the sign high up on the wall outside, and the Virgin of Seville (La Macarena) behind glass above the exit. The rest has been mercilessly stripped down and built up again, with chunky, steel-framed expanses of bare plaster with a warm, suede-like texture. A soundproof electro beatbox, it's been packed to the gills since it reopened in October 2001.

Malpaso

C/Rauric 20 (93 412 60 05). Metro Liceu/14, 38, 59, N9, N12 bus. **Open** 10pm-3am daily. **No credit cards**. **Map** p343 A3.

You don't have to be a feng shui expert to work out that with an entrance on the two dingiest backstreets in town, and few bar stools, Malpaso is the kind of place where you meet up, drink up and move on. But, with the right DJ behind the bar and the right random crowd, this little lime-green corner bar can generate an upbeat atmosphere worth staying for.

Shanghai

C/Aglà 9 (no phone). Metro Liceu or Drassanes/ 14, 38, 59, N9, N12 bus. **Open** 7pm-2am Mon-Thur, Sun; 7pm-3am Fri, Sat. **No credit cards**. **Map** p343 A3.

A saucy little mock-oriental drinking hole off C/Escudellers that mixes down-at-heel glamour with laid-back eccentricity. From the tasselled light fittings to the shattered corner of the huge mirror, it's scruffily beguiling, although the cocktails can take forever to appear.

Sidecar Factory Club

Plaça Reial 7 (93 302 15 86). Metro Liceu/ 14, 38, 59, N9, N12 bus. **Open** 8pm-2.30am Tue-Thur; 8pm-3am Fri, Sat. *Gigs* 10.30pm Tue, Thur-Sat. *Cinema* 10.30pm Wed. Closed Aug. **Admission** (incl 1 drink) €4. **No credit cards**. **Map** p343 A3.

A well-established indie/rock disco and venue with an upstairs terrace that overlooks the Plaça Reial. It's popular with students: if guitar pop is what strums your heartstrings, you can bounce around on the long basement dancefloor to your heart's content, amid a friendly crowd. In the week, there are occasional B-movie specials and theatre performances, with Thursday nights given over to 'Soul Food', featuring Manu Chao-style *mestizo* sounds.

So_da

C/Avinyó 24 (no phone). Metro Liceu/14, 38, 59, N9, N12 bus. **Open** 9pm-2.30am daily. **No credit cards**. **Map** p343 B3.

glittering beacon of cultural resistance to the stifling orthodoxy of Franco's last decade. The connection with those heady, rebellious days was further cemented when the family reopened La Cova del Drac (*see p246*) in November 2001 with a concert by Charlie Watts' jazz 'tentet'. In its original location, La Cova was a meeting place for the creators of *la nova cançó*, the Catalan-language song-writing movement that focused

catalanista opposition to centralist authority – it's said to be where Generalitat president Jordi Pujol met his wife.

Nor is the Mas family's interest confined to jazz and blues. Upstairs from Jamboree they run the flamenco venue Los Tarantos (*see p245*), and in 1996 they opened the tiny techno club Moog (*see p252*). Despite its size, Moog, under the direction of DJs Loe and Omar, has established its own special character, booking the most innovative European DJs and performers, and playing an important role in the growth of Barcelona's electronic clubbing scene.

The siblings are still very hands on: Marta, the organised one, looks after the office, and either Ana or Joan is out and about every night, checking that their different concerns are running smoothly. From blues at La Boîte and jazz at La Cova del Drac to late night R&B at Jamboree and drum 'n' bass at Moog, they've made a unique contribution to Barcelona's nocturnal scene.

Once the high-fashion wares are safely locked up in the great white wardrobes near the entrance, and the tubular curtains of the changing room are twisted up out of the way, a spruce clothes shop becomes a surprisingly scruffy and comfortable bar. There are decks on a trestle table in the corner; it can be lively or laid-back, depending on the DJ.

Raval

Aurora

C/Aurora 7 (93 442 30 44). Metro Paral.lel/14, 20, 24, 38, 59, 64, 91, N6, N9, N12 bus. **Open** 8pm-3am daily, plus 6am-noon Fri, Sat. **Admission** €3 6am-noon Fri, Sat. **No credit cards. Map** p340 C6.
Since the Rambla del Raval opened up, it's been easier to find this idiosyncratic little bar, but style-wise it's still way off the beaten track, with murals and fittings that have been following their own weird course of evolution for years. The many arty/creative/unkempt regulars can make for a cliquey feel, but it's basically friendly, with seats in the cosy loft space upstairs.

Benidorm

C/Joaquin Costa 39 (93 317 80 52). Metro Universitat/bus all routes to Plaça Universitat. **Open** 7pm-2am Mon-Thur, Sun; 7pm-2.30am Fri, Sat. **No credit cards. Map** p340 C5.
A sunken sitting room behind a glass front, flock wallpaper, charity-shop souvenirs and granny-chic: this could be a 22nd-century antiquarian's confused reconstruction of the way we used to live. With pop/electronic DJs and a mix of foreigners and home-turf dudes, the smoky atmosphere is usually buzzing; you may even find a seat in the small back lounge.

La Concha

C/Guàrdia 14 (93 302 41 18). Metro Drassanes/14, 38, 59, 91, N9, N12 bus. **Open** 4pm-3am daily. *Gigs* midnight-2am Fri, Sun. **No credit cards. Map** p343 A3.
The sequins, slingbacks, pathos and paunches of the Raval's surviving drag cabaret scene live on down the street in transvestite bar El Cangrejo, but occasionally make an appearance here, amid the myriad faces – from '60s sex kitten to kohl-eyed diva – of Spanish screen and drag icon Sara Montiel, which fill the walls from ceiling to floor. The cobwebs have been dusted off and the wilted flowers replaced to attract a gay-friendly but very mixed new crowd. There's even dancing on the chequered tiles to rai, flamenco and live bands at the weekend.

Enfants

C/Guàrdia 3 (93 412 00 48). Metro Drassanes/14, 38, 59, 91, N9, N12 bus. **Open** midnight-5am Thur-Sat. **Admission** (incl 1 drink) €5 Thur; €6 Fri; €9 Sat. **No credit cards. Map** p343 A3.
Although the management is working hard to make the most of Enfants' central location, with heavy flyer distribution on La Rambla and a rapid succession of different house/techno-oriented nights, the premises are something of a let-down: a single room with a Christmas cake icing ceiling in dire need of redecoration.

Kentucky

C/Arc del Teatre 11 (93 318 28 78). Metro Drassanes/14, 38, 59, N9, N12 bus. **Open** 10pm-3am Tue-Thur; 10pm-4.30am Fri, Sat. Closed Aug. **No credit cards. Map** p343 A4.
Duck under the shutter after the official closing time, and enter Barcelona's most notorious end-of-night

Arts & Entertainment

La Concha: for divas only.

dive. The portraits of battlecruisers and ripped-off US Navy insignia are mementos of its history as a red-light bar in the 1960s, and if you fight your way in under the pink neon arch, past the jukebox to the dingy scrum at the far end, you'll find that it starts seedy and gets seedier the deeper you go. Early on you'll find only locals; later, it's jam-packed with a random mix of survivors and, despite the slurred voices and noise, it's generally an amicable mix.

Moog

C/Arc del Teatre 3 (93 301 72 82/www.masimas. com). Metro Drassanes/14, 38, 59, N9, N12 bus. **Open** 11.30pm-5am daily. **Admission** (incl 1 drink) €12. **No credit cards. Map** p343 A4.

Through the uniquely aromatic arches off La Rambla, Moog is a nightly classic, a compact club that roams the electronic wavebands. Closely associated with

Barcelona record label Minifunk, it features frequent international guests exploring drum 'n' bass, techno and electro. The even smaller upstairs dancefloor is open for the Vilarosa nights (Wed-Sat): 1970s and '80s disco with its tongue firmly in its cheek.

La Paloma/Bongo Lounge

C/Tigre 27 (93 301 68 97). Metro Universitat/ bus all routes to Plaça Universitat. **Open** *La Paloma* 6-9.30pm Thur, Sun; 11.30pm-5am Fri, Sat. *Bongo Lounge* midnight-5am Thur. **Admission** *Bongo Lounge* (incl 1 drink) €6-€8. **No credit cards. Map** p340 C5.

An enormous 1903 dancehall in the heart of the Raval, La Paloma is a stunning venue, with a luridly glitzy ceiling. From the balcony you can watch dignified older couples execute dignified cha-chas on the polished dancefloor until midnight. Then it's

Afters thoughts

If you're still phased by the idea of stepping out for a pre-club drink at 1am, you'll never get your head round this: going to bed *early on Friday night*, getting up around 6am on Saturday, dressing yourself up to the nines, and striding fresh-faced and clear-eyed through the groggy after-hours crowd in a club that's just opened its doors. Plenty of Barcelona residents swear it's the best way to start the weekend.

That said, for most, *los afters* are what sorts the pussycats from the tigers when ordinary clubs close; a floating world where a few long-standing independent operators – notably Fritz and Matinee group – flit between short-term occupations of different premises, and only flyers distributed outside clubs will keep you right up to the minute. As you might imagine, the 24-hour *afters* scene has a distinctly gay/mixed character, and drag queens and other weird night fauna flourish.

Below are some of the more stable propositions, and one dawn hostelry for those who want a drink but can manage without a pounding techno soundtrack. If you have a car, you could also head to one of the most popular out-of-town *afters*: Souvenir (C/Noi de la Sucre 75), a warehouse on the motorway to Viladecans. It's ugly on the outside, beautiful on the inside, very gay, very house, very expensive.

Chez Popof

C/Aroles 5, Barri Gòtic (93 318 42 26). Metro Liceu/14, 38, 59, N9, N12 bus. **Open** noon-4am Wed-Sun. **No credit cards. Map** p343 A3.

Presumably at some stage this bar was what it looks like: a rustically appointed cava emporium with a gruffly appealing Catalan charm. For as long as anyone can remember, though, its sole selling point has been the fact that its wooden doors are just ajar when everywhere else is closed: at 4am it's a haze of smoke and broken resolutions, supervised by unsmiling waiters of the old school.

Heart

C/Moianès 16-18, Sants (93 422 48 28). Metro Hostafrancs/91, N1, N15 bus. **Open** 5am-2pm Mon, Fri-Sun. **Admission** €12. **No credit cards. Map** p339 A5.

Bright red, dripping with sweat and crammed with lost souls, Heart sometimes looks like a stage set for a scene in hell, except for the fact that the populace is shimmying without a regret in the world to hard house laid down by DJ Oskar Babyface.

Morning 88

C/Balmes 88, Eixample (no phone). Metro Passeig de Gràcia/7, 16, 17, 20, 43, 44, 63, 67, 68 bus. **Open** 6am-noon Sat, Sun. **Admission** €12. **Credit** MC, V. **Map** p336 D4.

Opening when most breakfast chefs are turning their griddles on to warm up, Morning 88 is tucked into the pavement just before Balmes reaches Diagonal. If you're looking for a soft come-down, perhaps a neck-rub and an alka seltzer, head for home – on Sundays mornings, DJ Oscar Egoista forcibly reanimates a club crowd for whom the truth just hasn't sunk in.

I'm in the **Moog** for dancin'. See p252.

changeover time: the screens come out, the projections come on, a young, hyperactive crowd floods in and the club segues into the freestyle frenzy of Bongo Lounge. Anything goes – hip hop, Brazilian jazz, straight house, funk, rappers, musicians, dancers – and on some nights it works better than others, but the basic success of Professor Angel Dust's Thursday night has become the envy of promoters all over town.

Rita Blue

Plaça Sant Agustí 3 (93 412 34 38/www. margarita blue.com). Metro Liceu/14, 38, 59, N9, N12 bus. **Open** noon-2am Mon-Wed, Sun; noon-3am Thur-Sat. **Credit** AmEx, DC, MC, V. **Map** p343 A3.
The food is affordable Mexican, although you may find yourself whacking on more chilli, but the place to cradle a luminous blue Margarita is downstairs in El Sotano, the restaurant's cellar, where there are plenty of chairs to slump in and room to dance to full-belly-friendly deep house grooves. Occasionally, there are Latin bands or live jazz.

La Ruta de los Elefantes

C/Hospital 48 (93 301 16 81). Metro Liceu/ 14, 38, 59, N9, N12 bus. **Open** 8.30pm-2.30am Mon-Thur; 8.30pm-3am Fri, Sat. **No credit cards.** **Map** p342 A2.
Behind the wrought-ironwork of the arabesque double doors, La Ruta is a self-regulating enclave for a raggle-taggle mix of travellers, students and street characters, plus the odd off-duty living statue in silver paint. Indeterminately ethnic and definitely alternative, djembes and didgeridoos with an earthy Latin flavour get the dreadlocks frugging at the back on live music nights. You can cool off with homemade ice-cream on the way out.

Salsitas/Club 22

C/Nou de la Rambla 22 (93 318 08 40). Metro Liceu/14, 38, 59, N9, N12 bus. **Open** 11pm-3am Wed-Sat. **Credit** MC, V. **Map** p343 A3.
As white and tropical as the inside of a Bounty Bar, it is perhaps despite and not because of the pillars made over as coconut palms that Salsitas (the bar-restaurant) and Club 22 (the club after midnight) have been riding a tsunami of popularity for so long. The crowd is tanned, toned and trendy. DJs Bass and Sideral keep the dancefloor swinging, with nu-jazz and cocktail house in the second room.

Sant Pere, La Ribera & Born

Astin Bar Club

C/Abaixadors 9 (93 442 96 69/www.nitsa.com/astin). Metro Jaume I/17, 19, 40, 45 bus. **Open** 11pm-3am Thur-Sat. **Admission** (incl 1 drink) €3 Fri, Sat. **No credit cards.** **Map** p343 B3.
Shake the letters out of the box and build your own nightlife empire: Nitsa at Apolo (*see p255*), Nasti in Madrid, and Astin, which has a reputation for esoteric, intense rock and a wilfully obscure record selection from resident DJ Coco and his regulars. The hard-edged decor is as uncompromising as the music; if you want to lounge in comfort, you'll just have to wait for Satin to open – it can't be long.

Bass Bar

C/Assaonadors 25 (no phone). Metro Jaume I/17, 19, 40, 45, N8 bus. **Open** 8pm-3am Mon-Fri; 9.30pm-3am Sat, Sun. **No credit cards.** **Map** p343 C3.
A couple of battered sofas, a pile of free music rags, and a handful of locals working on their dreadlocks jostle for space in this small offbeat bar. Exhibitions of local artists and collectives adorn the walls, and the music covers everything from Spanish ska to world drumming to Latin.

Magic/Magic in the Air Club

Passeig Picasso 40 (93 310 72 67). Metro Barceloneta/14, 39, 51 bus. **Open** 11pm-6am Thur; 11pm-7am Fri, Sat. **Admission** *Gigs* €15. *Disco* (incl 1 drink) €9. **No credit cards.** **Map** p341 E6.
There's magic in the air – but there's not much air in Magic, an awkward basement club whose big pull is the music: blistering Northern Soul, rare grooves and raucous funk for a crowd of ex- and aspirant mods.

Miramelindo

Passeig del Born 15 (93 310 37 27). Metro Jaume I/17, 19, 40, 45, N8 bus. **Open** 8pm-2.30am Mon-Thur; 8pm-3am Fri, Sat; 7pm-2.30am Sun. **No credit cards.** **Map** p343 C3.
A Born classic, so well established it can almost dispense with signs outside. Inside, it glows with the mellow sheen of surfaces on which care is unstintingly lavished every day: from the spotless mirror to the tiled corner where grave-faced cocktail waiters in long aprons prepare Mojitos, all bespeaks class. No wonder it's Michael Douglas's favourite bar when he's in town. This is a great choice for a smooth late-

Arts & Entertainment

night drink; if none of the wicker seats is free, you could try the smaller bars immediately next door: Tripode, Berimbau or Copetin.

República

Estació de França, Avda Marquès de l'Argentera 6 (93 300 50 50). Metro Barceloneta/14, 36, 39, 51, 57, 59, 64, N0, N6 bus. **Open** 1.30-8am Fri, Sat. **Admission** (incl 1 drink) €10. **No credit cards.** **Map** p343 C4.

Once known (and notorious) as Fellini, and more recently as Woman Caballero, this subterranean club has discarded its previous incarnations and updated the decor of the hulking concrete pillars that support the station above it. The space is the same – two dancefloors and a semi-private bar for the select few – but the music is now hard house, and it's tinged with a fetish theme, from the trussed-up *Bizarre* dolls on the posters to occasional live stage shows. The crowd is dressed for the dancefloor rather than the dungeon: gay/mixed and up for good time.

Suborn

C/Ribera 18 (93 310 11 10). Metro Barceloneta/ 14, 39, 51 bus. **Open** 8.30pm-3am Tue-Sun. **Credit** MC, V. **Map** p343 C4.

With tables under the arches looking on to the Ciutadella park, this bar-restaurant metamorphoses into a small club at some unspecified point in the evening, and the raised metal dancefloor fills up to the beats of hectic techno and house. It's friendly, uninhibited and somewhat cramped. The café/club vibe that works so well here has been taken upscale by the unfortunately named s:pic on the same street – with what success is yet to be seen.

Port Vell & Port Olímpic

Around the right-angled quayside of the Port Olímpic, you'll find dance bars interspersed with seafood restaurants, fast-food outlets, ice-cream parlours, coffee shops and mock-Irish pubs; with video screens, glittery lights and go-go girls and boys in abundance, there's little to choose between them. Across the road there are a row of clubs on the Passeig Marítim, with entrances upstairs on the promenade and terraces downstairs that face the end of the beach: **Baja Beach Club**, with the pumped-up atmosphere of an 18-30 pool party, and **El Cel**, offering hedonistic house, are the most lively.

Maremàgnum

Moll d'Espanya. Metro Drassanes/14, 36, 56, 57, 64, 157, N6 bus. **Map** p341 D7.

Built out over the marina, this artificial island of restaurants, shops and bars is reached by a series of wooden walkways that continue the terrestrial Rambla. At sea level, facing inland, you'll find a strip of merengue bars, complete with pumping sound systems and cruising clientele assessing the dance troupes through the glass fronts of the bars. On the top level, bizarrely arranged around the AstroTurf

of a rooftop miniature golf course, are two enormous discos, Starwinds and Nayandei, as well as a couple of big franchise pub-style bars.

Montjuïc & Poble Sec

Sala Apolo/Nitsaclub

C/Nou de la Rambla 113 (93 441 40 01/ www.nitsa.com). Metro Paral.lel/36, 57, 64, 91, N6, N9 bus. **Open** *Gigs* varies. *Disco* 12.30-6.30am Fri, Sat. **Admission** (incl 1 drink) €12. **No credit cards.** **Map** p340 C6.

In full fling, with twisted electronica bouncing off the walls and sweat dripping off the timbers, Nitsa is one of the most reliably messy nights out in Barcelona. Clubbers who first went eight years ago might complain about the 'kids' who fill it these days, but it's got the sharpest dance music in the city, from Dave Clarke to Kitty-Yo via Basement Jaxx. Housed in a one-time theatre and sometime art cinema, the dancefloor is overlooked by a wooden balcony bar. Upstairs, two much smaller rooms serve as chill-outs, although if the local DJs bring many of their friends, it can be hard to squeeze in, let alone chill.

Barcelona de Noche

Avda Paral.lel 106 (93 441 10 07). Metro Paral.lel/ 14, 38, 59, N9, N12 bus. **Open** midnight-6am Fri, Sat. **Admission** (incl 1 drink) €9. **No credit cards.** **Map** p340 C6.

A venue that's seen its fair share of new ventures gets a new name and turns house at the weekends. DJs Javier Navines and Sideral had the circular dancefloor packed at its reopening in late 2001, but it's yet to be seen if the new incarnation will take.

Barcelona Rouge

C/Poeta Cabanyes 21 (93 442 49 85). Metro Paral.lel/20, 57, 64, 157, N16 bus. **Open** 11pm-4am Tue-Sat. **Credit** MC, V. **Map** p339 B6.

Maybe it's the buzzer in the cherub-encrusted doorway that gives this place its clandestine feel; inside it's an offbeat, cocktail-sipping chill-out, with intimate table-and-chairs set-ups along the passage way, and fuddled oil paintings, enigmatic murals and battered soft furnishings in the main bar. The music wriggles its way from leftfield to laid-back.

Discothèque

Poble Espanyol, Avda Marquès de Comillas (93 423 12 85/www.nightsungroup.com). Metro Espanya/ 13, 50 bus. **Open** *19 Oct-11 May* 1-6am Fri, Sat. Closed 12 May-18 Oct. **Admission** (incl 1 drink) €15. **No credit cards.** **Map** p339 A4.

Discothèque, the winter flagship of promoters Nightsun (*see also p256* La Terrrazza), is housed in a replica of the palace of the Marquès de Peñaflor in Seville. With queues that provide the longest-legged drag demi-divinity a strut-past opportunity of reasonable duration, and collaborations with Decadance and Ibizan superclub Pacha, it has few rivals as the apotheosis of glam clubbing in BCN. The podia and

Arts & Entertainment

dancefloor swarm with several rare nocturnal species, competing to get into the more exclusive second space Flamingos, restyled as a louche 1950s lounge.

Downbeat

C/Elkano 67 (93 441 24 31). Metro Poble Sec/ 57, 157, N0 bus. **Open** 11pm-3.30am Thur-Sat. **No credit cards. Map** p339 B6.

Reggae has a broad appeal for many different Barcelona subcultures, from dreadlocked crusties to sharp scooter kids who come to it via ska, and promoters such as Abdenegus Reggae Shack bring the great names of the genre to the city on a regular basis. Downbeat is a new proposition: a reggae café that books DJs and MCs for its tiled backroom dancefloor.

Japan

Avda Paral.lel 37 (93 442 44 28). Metro Paral.lel/ 20, 36, 57, 64, 157, N6 bus. **Open** 1-5am Thur-Sun. **Admission** €7 Thur; €9 (incl 1 drink) Sat. **No credit cards. Map** p340 C6.

Bright red, and sticking out on to Paral.lel like a sore elbow, Japan styles itself a loft club and has picked up a strong following over the past year. Inside, it seems to fold over on itself, the upstairs level connected by multiple staircases to the downstairs bar and the dancefloor with its wall-mounted DJ cabin. Currently, there's house on its eponymous Saturday night, techno at Future Sound on Fridays, and hip hop, soul and funk at Skyfunk on Thursdays.

La Terrrazza

Poble Espanyol, Avda Marquès de Comillas (93 423 12 85/www.nightsungroup.com). Metro Espanya/13, 50 bus. **Open** 18 May-12 Oct midnight-6am Thur-Sun. Closed 13 Oct-19 May. **Admission** (incl 1 drink) €18. **No credit cards. Map** p339 A4.

If you make it past the critical eye of the doorstaff, pick your way past the slightly creepy, not-quite-life-size replicas of Spanish squares and alleyways in the Poble Espanyol to the definitive summertime

Alternative medicine

Going out is big business in Barcelona, but if the idea of high-turnover commercial bars and clubs turn you off, or if you're just looking for something different, there are myriad interwoven alternative scenes, often friendly and open to outsiders, offering underground music, theatre, riotous parties and a different perspective on the city. Catalans are friendly to the idea of the social club, from chess clubs to football supporters' associations, and a little paperwork will get your *lokal*, or ground floor premises, a limited licence as a 'cultural association'; many of these are de facto bars and performance spaces.

On the other side of the legal/illegal divide are the squatters (*okupas*), some of whose high-profile squats and social centres are the sites of parties and fundraising shows, usually featuring punk bands or circus artists. Look out for posters and flyers and bear in mind that you're stepping out of the world of regulations and safety inspections.

Ateneu del Xino

C/Robador 25, Raval (no phone). Metro Liceu/ 14, 38, 59, N9, N12 bus. **Open** 9pm-3am Fri, Sat; 9-11.30pm Sun. Closed Aug. **No credit cards. Map** p340 C6.

Unpretentious and unkempt social centre for veteran anarchists, featuring some relaxed live music at weekends and a very friendly atmosphere. This is also somewhere you can pick up information about one-off parties or festivals at other squatted properties around town.

Colours Under Water

C/Sant Climent 11, Raval (no phone). Metro Sant Antoni/20, 24, 38, 64, 91, N6 bus. **Open** 6pm-1am Mon-Wed; 6pm-3am Thur-Sat; 6-11pm Sun. **No credit cards. Map** p340 C6.

The mixed-nationality collective that runs this cultural association have created a colourful and inviting space filled with imaginatively reclaimed materials. During the week they run yoga courses, while at the weekend it's an invitingly laid-back place to chill out on comfy sofas with random canine friends. Try the cinnamon tea in hand-thrown pots, or get more active at occasional late-night parties.

Conservas

C/Sant Pau 58, baixos, Raval (93 302 06 30). Metro Liceu or Paral.lel/14, 20, 38, 59, 64, 91 bus. **Admission** varies. **No credit cards. Map** p340 C6.

The ramshackle entrance under the Conservas sign opens on to a surprisingly well-designed theatre space – rehabilitated by performance artist Simone Levi – which functions as a medium-sized alternative venue. It hosts action installations, performances and off-the-wall theatre pieces with a touch of magic. Ring for information and reservations.

Heliogabal

C/Ramon y Cajal 80, Gràcia (no phone). Metro Joanic/39, 55, N6 bus. **Open** 10pm-2am Mon-Wed, Sun; 11pm-5am Thur-Sat. **No credit cards. Map** p337 E3.

Arts & Entertainment

haunt of your fashion-conscious Barcelona hedonist. The club is an open courtyard, with palm trees, a minimal folly of a building, restless go-gos above the DJ cabin, and more posers than podium space. The main terrace sways like a hi-gloss sea of toned flesh, pouts and designer accessories – big-lensed, off-tint shades, soft leather bondage cuffs, pink studded chokers (much more and you're over-dressed). Resident DJ Sergio Patricio mixes the playlist around house.

Tinta Roja

C/Creu dels Molers 17 (93 443 32 43). Metro Poble Sec/57, 157 bus. **Open** 5pm-1.30am Tue-Thur, Sun; 5pm-3am Fri, Sat. **Admission** €5 tango Sat. **No credit cards. Map** p339 B6.

Buenos Aires, anyone? You could well have time-warped into this small, smoky bar painted a rusty red and green and decorated with items recycled, rescued or bought at fleamarkets. The walls are full of yellowing photos of tango shows and old

Argentina, set off by dozens of 1960s and '70s-style dressing table mirrors and fairy lights. Deeper into the bar and you're pleasantly surprised by an avant-garde art exhibition that opens up to a theatre.

Torres de Avila

Entrance to Poble Espanyol, Avda Marquès de Comillas (93 424 93 09/www.torresdeavila.com). Metro Espanya/13, 50 bus. **Open** 12.30pm-7am Fri, Sat. **Admission** (incl 1 drink) €12. **Credit** MC, V. **Map** p339 A5.

The grand, mock-medieval gatehouse of the Poble Espanyol houses a bar/club that in its time generated excitement and disdain in equal measure: a temple to designer hedonism dreamed up in the late 1980s by Javier Mariscal (the illustrator behind Barcelona's Olympic mascot) and architect Alfredo Arribas. You move between the multiple levels of thumping revival house on hanging steel staircases or in the glass elevator, emerging on the roof terrace in summer for a neat city view.

The red and black shutter proclaiming 'Art Tot' is always down, so ring the buzzer to enter Heliogabal (*pictured*), a narrow little bar with a tiny back courtyard. It's arty and offbeat, and a young local crowd cram in after other bars close to hear live bands and other performances.

Mau Mau

C/Fontrodona 33 (676 72 22 44). Metro Paral.lel/20, 57, 64, 157, N6 bus. **Open** 11pm-2.30am Thur; 11pm-3.30am Fri, Sat; 6.30-11.30pm Sun. **Admission** €3.60. **No credit cards. Map** p340 C6.

Deep house and spot-on grooves at this semi-understated soundtrack at this semi-underground warehouse chill-out. Keep following Fontrodona up after it zigzags

across C/Blesa, and buzz for admission at the white door on the left-hand side. Mau Mau works as a members-only cultural association, so to enter you have to 'join'; unfortunately, this doesn't guarantee you a sofa to collapse into.

Merry Ant

C/Peu de la Creu 23, Raval (no phone). Metro Sant Antoni/20, 24, 38, 64, N6 bus. **Open** 8pm-2am Tue-Sun. **No credit cards. Map** p340 C5.

The bizarre and slightly unhinged work of a rebellious carpenter, the Merry Ant functions more as a bar than a cultural association. Local artist Toto sawed, hammered and glued a collection of found objects into a remarkable, Frankenstein-like vision of interior design. An easy-going artsy crowd unwinds amid soft red lighting.

FREE PARTIES

A combination of relatively tolerant official attitudes and truly spectacular rural locations have ensured that Barcelona has a thriving free party scene. French, British and local sound system crews scout inland sites and put on weekend-long parties throughout the summer; in the winter, the scene moves inside to derelict industrial buildings and squats. You'll find flyers all over town, usually with a mobile phone number to call on the night, but if you want to get really informed it's best to ask at Tazmaniac record shop on Plaça Vicenç Martorell.

Eixample

Antilla Barcelona

*C/Aragò 141-143 (93 451 21 51/www.antilla
salsa.com). Metro Hospital Clínic/43, 44, N7 bus.*
Open 10.30pm-4am Mon-Tue, Sun; 10.30pm-5am
Wed; 11pm-6am Fri, Sat. **Admission** (incl 1 drink)
€9. **No credit cards. Map** p336 C4.
Barcelona's best-known *salsoteca* shimmied into life
in 1993 and has been supplying mambo, merengue
and cha-cha ever since, to Catalans with a yen for
Caribbean rhythms and homesick Caribbean émigrés.
It even entered the *Guinness Book of Records* for the
longest ever *son* session in 1994. The hip-wriggling
live music has a real mix of nationalities and ages
dancing all night. While there is a mix of levels, you
need some moves under your belt: classes start at
10.30pm Monday to Thursday.

Bar Six

*C/Muntaner 6 (93 453 00 75). Metro Universitat/
bus all routes to Plaça Universitat.* **Open** 8.30pm-
3am Tue-Sat. Closed 2wks end Aug. **Credit** AmEx,
DC, MC, V. **Map** p340 C5.
Label fashion meets lava-lamp kitsch in the bar
paired with the restaurant next door, Cosmopolita.
A serious party crowd charge up on good-time
house and exotic shots before migrating en masse
to the night's main course.

La Boîte

*Avda Diagonal 477 (93 419 59 50/www.masimas.
com). Bus 6, 7, 15, 27, 32, 33, 34, 63, 67, N12.*
Open *Disco* 10pm-5am daily. *Gigs* varies.
Admission (incl 1 drink) *Disco* €15. *Gigs* €18.
No credit cards. Map p336 C3.

The entrance to this purpose-built music venue and
nightclub glows like a lighthouse cabin behind
uptown office blocks and car parks off the Plaça
Francesc Macià. You're then swallowed up into an
underground space with glittering pillars and sinuous lines. The DJ usually follows the concert with
highly danceable soul.

Bucaro

*C/Aribau 195 (93 209 65 62). FGC Provença/
54, 58, 64, 66, N3, N8 bus.* **Open** 10.30pm-3am
Mon-Sat. **Credit** V. **Map** p336 C3.
Bucaro means vase, and this Manhattan-style bar is
a casual arrangement of select blooms. To share air-
space with Spanish supermodels, visiting Hollywood
celebs and Barcelona's own A-list it may help if you
bring your own most recent magazine cover/*Vogue*
fashion shoot/forthcoming blockbuster movie, or at
the very least dress the part. Inside, it's plush but
relaxed, and the smart set goes on to dance at Luz
de Gas (*see p244*) after closing time.

City Hall/Fun is Back

*Rambla de Catalunya 2-4 (93 317 21 77).
Metro Catalunya/bus all routes to Plaça Catalunya.*
Open 1am-5am Thur-Sat. **Admission** (incl
1 drink) €9 Thur, Fri; €12 Sat. **No credit cards.**
Map p342 A1.
You get some idea of just how 'in' this club is as you
walk down the mirrored entrance corridor; in, and
further in, till you hit the open patios and steps sunk
deep into the heart of a super-central city block.
After 2am a dressed-up crowd mingles outside in the
candlelight. The downstairs dancefloor warms up
much later, with monthly residences from Funk
d'Void and their home DJs.

Summer in the city at **La Terrrazza**. *See p256.*

Chikita – Dificil de Matar

C/Gran Via de les Corts Catalanes 770 (93 232 43 45). Metro Monumental/6, 7, 10, 56, 62, N2, N3 bus. **Open** midnight-5.30am Fri, Sat. **Admission** (incl 1 drink) €9. **No credit cards.** Map p341 F5.
'Difficult to kill', indeed; this survivor among semi-legal after-hours clubs goes 'respectable', taking over a low-ceilinged, mirror-ball-spangled disco. Louche and glamorous, with outrageous drag acts and a mixed crowd, it opens at exactly one minute to midnight – just when good girls are tripping over their glass slippers to get home.

La Fira

C/Provença 171 (no phone). Metro Hospital Clínic/ 31, 38, 63, N3, N8 bus. **Open** 10pm-3am Mon-Thur; 10.30pm-4.30am Fri, Sat. **No credit cards.** Map p336 C4.
Decked out with furnishings from defunct Barcelona funfairs, La Fira is an ample bar space that also houses a serious collection (dodgem cars, one-armed bandits, table football, crazy mirrors, circus posters, merry-go-round horses) – although its popularity at weekends may preclude a closer view. Under the Big Top, large groups, class reunions and the odd hen night whoop it up to pop salsa and disco classics.

Fuse

C/Roger de Llúria 40 (93 301 74 99). Metro Passeig de Gràcia/7, 16, 22, 24, 28, 39, 45, 47, N4, N6 bus. **Open** midnight-3.30am Fri, Sat. **No credit cards.** Map p340 D5.
'A laboratory of the sensations' – that means they lay on the grub before carting off the tables, as at any parish hall disco – only the menu's fashionably globe-trotting and the changeover actually makes for a pleasurable anticipation as the crowd builds up in the shiny white entry bar. There's a surge into the spacious back room around 1am, where chunky house resounds off fat tapering pillars, and a fashionable, but not ridiculous crowd has room to breathe and really dance.

Lo-li-ta

Plaça Joan Llongueras (entrance from C/Beethoven) (93 272 09 10/www.lolita.net). Bus 6, 7, 33, 34, 63, 64, 67, 68, N12. **Open** 12.30-5.30am Fri, Sat. **Admission** (incl 1 drink) €11. **Credit** MC, V. Map p336 C3.
Home from home for various of the International DJ Gigolos and with DJ Hell as éminence grise, Lo-li-ta goes hammering down the catwalk of electronic decadence with such grim flair it's no wonder it often marches right off the end. After its first summer of such louche brilliance and sprawling accidents, it reopened in what was the original Nitsaclub in October 2001 with an inaugural night from Zombie Nation: former regulars noted that the ceiling downstairs was as low as ever, but that the one-time revolving dancefloor was not in working order. Next door, blue-lit chill-out bar Vlad, under the same management, opens late and books a strong mix of local and international DJs.

The towering **Torres de Avila**. See p257.

El Otro

C/Valencia 166, Eixample (no phone). Metro Universitat/37, 63, N7 bus. **Open** 10.30pm-3am Tue-Sat. **No credit cards.** Map p336 C4.
With swathes of coloured light spilling out in unexpected directions on to creamy walls, El Otro is a bar that's stylish without committing to any particular fashion. With resident DJs serving up a mixed menu of beats and tunes, frequent exhibitions and occasional concerts, it's a relaxed start to the night.

La Pedrera de Nit

C/Provença 261-265 (93 484 59 95). Metro Diagonal/7, 16, 17, 22, 24, 28 bus. **Open** July-Sept 9pm-midnight Fri, Sat. Closed Oct-June. **Admission** (incl 1 drink) €9. **Credit** MC, V. Map p336 D4.
In summer, the swerving, rolling roof terrace of Gaudí's visionary La Pedrera is open on Friday and Saturday evenings for drinks, live music and fine views of the city, but it's almost essential to book.

Risco

C/Balmes 49 (93 423 12 85/www.nightsungroup. com). Metro Hospital Clínic/54, 58, 64, 66 bus. **Open** 11pm-3am Wed-Sun. **Admission** (incl 1 drink) €9. **Credit** MC, V. Map p336 D4.
In a distinctly unglamorous entrance to a concrete car park, Risco's doorstaff exercise a 'looks alone' entrance policy. Inside, the low, sleek, purple-tinted space could be the set for a futuristic game show, with ranks of white seats for the jury. With sharp house on Thursdays and Saturdays, it's the 'official' pre-club bar for Discothèque (see p255) and La Terrrazza (see p256), and if you look hip enough, you can pick up entry passes – although Risco wants you to come back again on Sunday night for '80s-tinted house at Bloody Mary.

Latin fever at **Antilla Barcelona**. *See p258.*

Row Club

C/Rosselló 208 (93 215 65 91/www.rowclub.com).
Metro Diagonal/FGC Provença/7, 16, 17, 31, 67,
68 bus. **Open** 11.30pm-5.30am Thur-Sat. *Gigs* 1am.
Admission (incl 1 drink) €11-€18. **Credit** AmEx,
MC, V. **Map** p336 D4.

Designed as if for a high-concept Duran Duran video
in the mid '80s, complete with shimmering TV wall
and swinging pendulum, this extravagant bar space
has all the immortal poise of Limahl's feathered
mullet. Starting with drum 'n' bass on Thursday
night, Row now packs the venue throughout the
weekend with cutting-edge techno and house. The
promoter also runs Florida 135, the superclub in
the Montenegros desert, ensuring massive names
(Jeff Mills, Richie Hawtin).

Salsa Buenavista

C/Rosselló 217 (93 237 65 28/www.salsabuenavista.
com). Metro Diagonal/FGC Provença/7, 16, 17,
22, 24, 28, 31, 67, 68 bus. **Open** 11pm-3am
Wed, Thur; 11pm-5.30am Fri, Sat; 8pm-1am Sun.
Admission (incl 1 drink) €9 Sat, Sun. **No credit
cards. Map** p336 C4.

With pink walls, shimmering silver palm trees and
a glistening expanse of dancefloor, Buenavista
serves up salsa as we're told it should be served: a
young, extrovert crowd, lots of silk shirts, clinging
silver lamé skirts and even the odd pair of hotpants,
along with non-stop Caribbean rhythms. It's also
regarded as a very good place to learn, with lessons
after 10pm on weekdays.

Santécafé

C/Comte d'Urgell 171 (93 323 78 32). Metro
Hospital Clínic/14, 59, 63, N12 bus. **Open** 8am-
3am Mon-Fri; 5pm-3am Sat, Sun. **No credit
cards. Map** p336 C4.

Cool but sociable locals hang out until late in this
stylish night café with a clued-up music policy.
With low lighting, immaculate grooves from what
used to be called acid jazz to funky hip hop to deep
house, and plenty of tables, Santé is the kind of
place you can arrange to meet before going on somewhere else – and end up staying.

Zsa Zsa

C/Rosselló 156 (93 453 85 66). FGC Provença/
14, 54, 58, 59, 63, 64, 66, N3, N8 bus. **Open**
10pm-3am Mon-Sat. **Credit** V. **Map** p336 C4.

A chic bar patronised by designers, media people
and older types, who go to talk and sample a
sophisticated range of cocktails. An innovation of
designers Dani Freixes and Vicente Miranda is the
lighting, which changes continuously and subtly,
so the mirrored wall may appear completely black
and at other times ablaze with colour.

Gràcia

Gusto

C/Francisco Giner 24 (no phone). Metro Diagonal/
22, 24, 28, N4 bus. **Open** 11pm-2.30am Wed, Thur;
11pm-3am Fri, Sat. **No credit cards. Map** p336 D3.

A young crowd, a neat little front bar where the DJ
plays pre-club electronica, and a turquoise-lit back
room that feels weirdly outdoors, although, in fact,
it isn't: the sand-strewn floor makes it either an
indoor beach or a room-sized ashtray.

Illusion

C/Lepant 408 (93 347 36 00/www.matineegroup.
com). Metro Alfons X/10, 15, 20, 25, 45, 47, N4
bus. **Open** midnight-6am Fri, Sat; 7pm-midnight
Sun. **Admission** (incl 1 drink) €6 Fri; €9 Sat;
€7.80 Sun. **No credit cards. Map** p337 F3.

On Sunday evenings, the cafés along Lepant are full of hyped teenagers with tight tops and gelled hair getting clear the story of the weekend so far, before it enters its last mad paroxysm at Illusion. This is the Cathedral Sunday T-Dance Session: a gay/mixed maelstrom with drag performers urging on a thrill-hungry crowd.

KGB

C/Alegre de Dalt 55 (93 210 59 06). Metro Joanic/39, 55, N6 bus. **Open** *Gigs* 10pm-1am Fri, Sat. *Disco* 1am-5am Fri, Sat. **Admission** *Gigs* varies. *Disco* (incl 1 drink) €8.5; (incl 2 drinks) €9. **No credit cards. Map** p337 E3.
A constantly renewed section of glazed-eyed and predominantly male city youth have been battling it out at KGB for years. Sometimes the music policy (hard techno) and the grim security staff seem to bear out the totalitarian connotations of the name all too well, but the management makes periodic attempts to update the blueprint, booking bigger names such as local techno hero Àngel Molina. Handy tip: the high-level observation gantry is for spotting lost friends possibly injured by the beat, before they're trampled underfoot.

Mond Bar

C/Plaça del Sol (93 272 09 10). Metro Diagonal/22, 24, 28, 39 bus. **Open** 8.30pm-2.30am Mon-Thur, Sun; 8.30pm-3am Fri, Sat. **No credit cards. Map** p336 D3.
Over the little footbridge from the main square, this diminutive bar on the Plaça del Sol is Mond Club's little sister, and all week it runs youth-team try-outs for aspiring and usually very good local DJs. The ambience is cliquey and in-the-know, but hospitable, with the emphasis on the offbeat fashion move and the recondite but spot-on musical reference.

Mond Club

Sala Cibeles, C/Còrsega 363 (93 317 79 94/93 272 09 10/www.mondclub.com). Metro Diagonal/22, 24, 28, 39 bus. **Open** 12.30-5.30am Fri. **Admission** (incl 1 drink) €12. **No credit cards. Map** p336 D4.
A old-style dancehall becomes a coruscating electro-pop fantasy on Friday nights – with the emphasis firmly on the pop side of the formula. Mop-haired waifs in straggling mascara manage a distracted boogie to resident DJ Buenavista and Spanish freak-pop icon Alaska, while chinstrap-bearded adepts take notes when international guest stars like Mani or JJ Johansson bring in their favourite records. It's a hectic whirl for your networked Barcelona pop clubber; a spectacle of youthful enthusiasm for your travelled cynic – and good clean fun either way.

Otto Zutz

C/Lincoln 15 (93 238 07 22/www.ottozutz.com). FGC Gràcia/16, 17, 25, 27, 31, 32, N4 bus. **Open** 11pm-6am Tue-Sat. **Admission** (incl 1 drink) €15. **Credit** AmEx, DC, MC, V. **Map** p336 D3.
Otto Zutz has been around a while, and the absolute indifference with which the doorstaff usher in the desirables and charge the rest is understandable:

they've seen them all, from Prince in his heyday, through Bono (who flew in from Florence for a private party), to the Spice Girls in the days when they were five. Besides, it's not as if there's room to waste on people who haven't made an effort. The illusion of space on the downstairs dancefloor is due to that enormous mirror, the soul/funk floor is no bigger, and to get into the VIP room at the top you'll have to summon whatever reserves of inner glamour are left to you after getting in.

Sabor Cubano

C/Francisco Giner 32 (93 217 35 41). Metro Diagonal/22, 24, 28, 39, N4 bus. **Open** 10pm-3am Mon-Sat. **No credit cards. Map** p336 D3.
Underlit in electric blue, this bar is a meeting point with the seal of approval of Cuban residents, where you can sip some of the best Mojitos in town and even unleash some spontaneous salsa moves.

Terrasamba

C/La Perla 34 (93 218 82 60). Metro Fontana or Joanic/22, 24, 28, 39, N4, N6 bus. **Open** 7pm-3am Tue-Sun. **No credit cards. Map** p337 E3.
Named after the famous Brazilian band, this place is unmissable for all aspiring samba dancers. Shake your thing to the instructions of Toninho on Wednesdays, when you can get a free dance lesson for the price of a Caipirinha. An hour and a couple of Caipirinhas later, everyone is dancing samba and/or falling over. Terrasamba's compact size means it can get kind of stuffy, so dress to sweat.

The best Places for...

Latin dance
Serious salsa at **Antilla Barcelona** (*see p258*) or **Salsa Buenavista** (*see p260*). **Sabor Cubano** (*see p261*) has a more intimate vibe.

Dancehall style
Ballroom elegance – overrun by freestyle madness at **La Paloma** (*see p252*) or indie-pop peacocks at **Mond Club** (*see p261*).

Late-night 'n' louche
Chilling at **Barcelona Rouge** (*see p255*) or pouting at **La Concha** (*see p251*).

Catwalk clubbing
Dance in these heels? You must be joking... at **Café Royale** (*see p248*) or **Fun is Back** at **City Hall** (*see p258*).

Sweaty decadence
Tech-house with a fetish twist at **República** (*see p255*) and the twist with a tech-fetish at **Lo-li-ta** (*see p259*).

Tibidabo & Zona Alta

Atlantic Bar

C/Lluís Muntadas 2 (93 418 71 61). FGC Av Tibidabo/60 bus. **Open** 10.30pm-5am Thur-Sat. **Admission** (incl 1 drink) €8. **Credit** V.

On a wedge-shaped chunk of land and with its precipitous grey perimeter walls topped by fluttering banners, there's something of the ocean liner about this exclusive Tibidabo club. With a pool, mermaid murals and multiple decks, the impression continues once you're through the gate: this is a smooth, mansion-clubbing experience way up above the city.

Bikini

C/Déu i Mata 105 (93 322 08 00/www.bikinibcn. com). Metro Les Corts/15, 30, 43, 59 bus. **Open** midnight-4.30am Tue-Thur; midnight-5.30am Fri, Sat. **Admission** midnight-1am (incl 2 drinks), 1am-4.30/5.30am (incl 1 drink) €9. *Gigs varies.* **Credit** AmEx, V. **Map** p335 B3.

Bikini has been around in various incarnations since the 1950s; the present avatar is a three-room club. The main room is reputed to have the best concert sound system in Barcelona, and after the gig it gets to run through its paces with chart rock and pop; the Arutanga room plays salsa and Latin music, while the Dry room features a distinctly wet bar with plentiful seating. *See also p243.*

Mirabeye

Plaça Doctor Andreu (93 417 92 79). FGC Av Tibidabo, then Tramvia Blau/60 bus. **Open** noon-2.30am Mon-Thur, Sun; noon-3.30am Fri, Sat. **Credit** MC, V.

Perhaps it's the difficulty of getting up to the foot of the funicular without your own (preferably fast, expensive) private form of transport that makes this place so appealing to the jet set. Park the Porsche and join members of the different Barcelona FC teams in the lounge or the saloon. Later on, the crowd crosses to the late-night disco in Mirablau.

Partycular

Avda Tibidabo 61 (93 211 62 61/www.partycular. com). FGC Av Tibidabo/17, 22, 58, 73, 75, 85 bus. **Open** 7pm-3am Wed-Sun. **Credit** MC, V.

Across the road from Atlantic (*see above*) and attracting a similar clientele, this is a seriously high-class pleasure dome housed in a three-storey mansion on the way to Tibidabo. Blue-carpeted steps welcome a well-heeled crowd to the plush if conservatively appointed bar and restaurant. The gardens and terraces that spill downhill, dotted with bars and secluded areas, are ideal for a summer evening.

Universal

C/Marià Cubi 182 bis-184 (93 201 35 96). Bus 6, 7, 14, 15, 27, 32, 33, 34, 63, 67, 68. **Open** 11pm-4.30am Mon-Sat. **Credit** MC, V. **Map** p336 C3.

The production values of this well-established club on the corner of C/Marià Cubi and C/Santalo are unstinting, but the prices are steep. Multi-angled lights on clustered gantries set up a flattering,

cabaret-like semi-darkness on the ground floor, through which you can shimmy to the diagonal bar or try a disembodied boogie. Or float upstairs to the more laid-back first-floor bar, with its blue-velvet seats, gleaming grand piano, heavy curtains and chandeliers like anchors wrapped in tulle and fairy lights. The usual weekend crowd is moneyed but not oppressively cool; the music policy is mainstream.

Poblenou

Lokotron

C/Almogàvers 86-88 (no phone). Metro Marina/ 6, 40, 42, 141, N6 bus. **Open** 5pm-midnight Sun. **Admission** (incl 1 drink) €9; (incl 2 drinks) €12. **No credit cards. Map** p341 F5.

A dark warehouse teetering on the edge of the railway tracks, which vibrates to remorselessly looped techno for a Sunday night crowd in deep denial. You don't have to be loco to dig it, but it helps.

Razz Club

Razzmatazz, C/Almogàvers 122 (93 272 09 10/ 93 320 82 00). Metro Marina/6, 40, 42, 141, N6 bus. **Open** *Disco* 1-5am Fri, Sat. **Admission** *Disco* (incl 1 drink) €9. **No credit cards. Map** p341 F6.

C/Almogàvers runs the gauntlet between insomniac factories towards Poblenou. It's the last place you'd expect to find Razzmatazz (*see p245*), but, wham, there it is: a looming warehouse of a music venue. The hangar-like ground floor is an enormous black hole, which opens up after the gig as Razz Club, with DJ Amable on the decks. At the front of the building, looking over the acres of peeling concert posters on the other side of the street, the glass-fronted Pop Bar jives to indie and '60s pop, and on the top floor is Templebeat, playing gothic and industrial. On Sunday nights, the Royal Session of Sound fills the bottom floor with a Mad Max-meets-Las Vegas fancy dress techno party.

Outer Limits

Planet

Avda Industria 12, Sant Just Desvern (93 499 03 42/ www.elmirador.org). Bus 63. **Open** midnight-5.30am Fri, Sat. **Admission** (incl 1 drink) €9; (incl 2 drinks) €12. **Credit** (restaurant only) AmEx, MC, V.

In the suburb/town of Sant Just Desvern on the western edge of metropolitan Barcelona, Planet is a post-industrial, sci-fi fantasy housed in an ex-cement factory, with a crystal-ceilinged, flying saucer-like restaurant 30m (100ft) up the factory's chimney. Designed by Alfredo Arribas, architect of the Torres de Avila (*see p257*), it sits next door to Ricard Bofill's famous Walden Seven building. Music is techno/house, with a wide range of programming, including concerts by international groups, performances by bizarre circus artists and a bevy of very skilled go-go dancers. At the very top of the chimney, 100m (330ft) up, there's a viewing area from where you can gaze down on the city's twinkling lights. Wow.

Sport & Fitness

A rich inheritance of Olympics venues and not a lot to do in them.

Two overriding factors influence sport in the city: the world-renowned 'Barca' and the residual effects of hosting the 1992 Olympics. While Barcelona FC may be famous for its football team, the club also supports professional basketball, roller hockey and handball teams, and a semi-pro ice hockey team. More than 100,000 fanatical members mean there is little room for competition.

As a result of hosting the Olympic Games, the city's residents have been left with a vastly improved sporting infrastructure, with around 1,000 sports centres within the city.

Spectator sports

Tickets can often be purchased by credit card through Servi-Caixa or Tel-entrada (*see p210*).

Major sports venues

Montjuïc venues

Estadi Olímpic de Montjuïc *Passeig Olímpic 17-19, Montjuïc (93 426 20 89). Metro Espanya, then escalators, or Paral.lel, then Funicular de Montjuïc/50 bus.* **Map** p339 A6.
Palau Sant Jordi *Passeig Olímpic 5-7, Montjuïc (93 426 20 89). Metro Espanya, then escalators, or Paral.lel, then Funicular de Montjuïc/50 bus.* **Map** p339 A6.
Palau dels Esports *C/Joaquim Blume, Montjuïc (93 423 15 41). Metro Espanya or Poble Sec/55 bus.* **Map** p339 B5-6.
A legacy of the Olympics, these huge multi-purpose sports and concert venues have been largely underused ever since. However, the Estadi Olímpic has taken on a new life since it became home to the Espanyol football club (*see p264*) and the Barcelona Dragons American football team (*see below*).

Velòdrom d'Horta

Passeig Vall d'Hebron 185, Horta-Guinardó (93 427 91 42). Metro Montbau/27, 73 bus.
Open 4-8pm daily. Closed Aug. **Admission** free.
Another underused Olympics leftover, the Velòdrom incorporates centres for tennis, archery and cycling.

American football

Barcelona Dragons

Estadi Olímpic de Montjuïc, Passeig Olímpic 17-19, Montjuïc (93 425 49 49/www.dragons.es/ www.nfleurope.com). Metro Espanya, then escalators, or Paral.lel, then Funicular de Montjuïc/50 bus.

Ticket office from 2hrs before kick-off on match days. **Tickets** *Members* €29.10-€130.30. *Non-members* €8.10-€25.30 per game. **Advance tickets** Caixa de Catalunya or Servi-Caixa. **Credit** (advance tickets) MC, V. **Map** p339 A6.
The Barcelona Dragons continue to find new recruits for their fan base, with average attendance currently standing at 14,600. Runners-up in the 2001 World Bowl final, the Dragons have played in four of the past ten World Bowl finals and were finally rewarded for their persistence with a win in 1997. The promoters liven up the games with Americana razzle-dazzle, including cheerleaders. Most players are American, though there are a few locals in the squad. Games are held at 5pm on Saturdays, from April to June.

Basketball

The second most popular sport after soccer. The season runs from September to early June; most league games are played on Saturday and Sunday evenings.

Club Joventut Badalona

C/Ponent 143-161, Badalona, Outer Limits (93 460 20 40/www.penya.com). Metro Gorg/44 bus. **Ticket office** from 1hr before match. **Tickets** €15.10-€20.50. **No credit cards.**
Badalona's standard-bearers stand head to head with their wealthier neighbours, FC Barcelona, and unlike them, have actually won the European Basketball Cup. Games are officially held at 6pm on Sundays, but this can change according to the demands of TV coverage. Fans can be even more passionate than in Barcelona, in part because they are not distracted by other teams within the club.

FC Barcelona

*Palau Blaugrana, Avda Aristides Maillol, Les Corts
(93 496 36 75/www.fcbarcelona.com). Metro Maria
Cristina or Collblanc/15, 52, 53, 54, 56, 57, 75 bus.*
Ticket office 9.30am-1.30pm, 4.30-7.30pm; tickets
available from 1 day before match. **Tickets** €3.30-
€22.90. **No credit cards.**

Club members have access to all games, for all the
teams promoted by the club, for a nominal charge;
non-members pay standard ticket prices. The much
sought-after European League Trophy continues to
elude the team, but its popularity hasn't waned and
it's still advisable to book. League games are held
mainly on Saturdays at 7pm and on Sundays at
noon or 7pm; Cup and European games are at
8.30pm during the week, usually on Thursdays.
Tickets are also available from Servi-Caixa.

Bullfighting

Plaza de Toros Monumental

*Gran Via de les Corts Catalanes 749, Eixample
(93 245 58 04/93 215 95 70). Metro Monumental/
6, 7, 10, 56, 62 bus.* **Open** *Bullfights* (Apr-Sept)
5-7pm Sun. *Museum* 10.30am-2pm, 4-7pm daily.
Advance tickets also available from Servi-Caixa.
Admission *Bullfights* €18.10-€96.50; under-14s €5.
Museum €2.50. **No credit cards. Map** p341 F5.
Most Catalans have little interest in bullfighting and
the Monumental bullring (also known as the Plaça
de Braus, in Catalan) is the only still functioning
bullring in the city. It holds fights on Sundays in
season, and also has a small museum.

Football

The city's two first-division clubs are **FC
Barcelona** and **RCD Espanyol**. Such is
Barça's all-absorbing power that lower-division
teams tend to be reduced to semi-pro status
through lack of support, but there's fun to
be had watching the likes of Hospitalet or
Poblenou's Jupiter. The season runs from late
August to May. League games are traditionally
played at 5pm or 7pm on Sundays, but at least
one game a week is played at 8.30 or 9pm on
Saturdays. Canal Barça, the team's TV channel,
pumps out team news, interviews and official
releases – but not live games – and can seem
like overkill for even the most dedicated fan.

FC Barcelona

*Nou Camp, Avda Aristides Maillol, Les Corts
(93 496 36 00/www.fcbarcelona.com). Metro Maria
Cristina or Collblanc/15, 52, 53, 54, 56, 57, 75 bus.*
Ticket office 9.30am-1.30pm, 4.30-7.30pm Mon-Fri;
tickets available 1 week before each match. **Tickets**
€18.10-€90.40. **Advance tickets** (league games
only) Servi-Caixa. **No credit cards. Map** p335 A3.
Barça have introduced a scheme whereby members
can officially sell their reserved seats through the
Servi-Caixa machines. It is hoped that this will help

fill the giant stadium (capacity 115,000), which has
in the past been known to be half empty for less
important matches. There are also other options; a
week before each match, Barça puts around 4,000
tickets up for sale; phone the club to find out when
and queue an hour or two beforehand at the ticket
office at the intersection of Travessera de les Corts
and Avda Aristides Maillol. You can also try your
luck with the ticket touts, or just try asking at the
entrance gates if anyone has an extra ticket. There's
a range of ticket prices, but the cheaper *entrades
generals* areas are very high up. Barcelona also has
teams in the Spanish second division and at amateur level. The second-division Barça-B plays in the
Miniestadi, a 16,000-seat arena that is connected to
the main stadium. Tickets cost about €6-€12, and
games usually start at 5pm on Saturdays. If A and
B teams are both playing at home, a joint ticket
allows you to see both games. You can also watch a
training session (usually held at 10am) and visit the
club's popular museum.

RCD Espanyol

*Estadi Olímpic de Montjuïc, Passeig Olímpic 17-19,
Montjuïc (93 292 77 00/www.rcdespanyol.com).
Metro Espanya, then escalators or Paral.lel, then
Funicular de Montjuïc/50 bus.* **Ticket office**
10am-1.30pm, 5-8pm Fri; 10am-2pm Sat; 10am-
match time on match days. **Tickets** €18.10-€42.20.
No credit cards. Map p339 A6.
With 25,000 season ticket holders and a 60,000-seat
stadium, it is considerably easier to get a ticket for
an Espanyol game than it is to get into Nou Camp.
The spacious feel of this ex-Olympic athletics stadium can, however, make for a less than atmospheric experience. On match days, two hours before
kick-off, free buses transport ticket holders up
Montjuïc from a special stop at Plaça Espanya. To
buy a ticket, head to the ticket booth at the right-
hand side of the stadium entrance.

Ice hockey

FC Barcelona

*FC Barcelona Pista de Gel, Avda Aristides Maillol,
Les Corts (93 496 36 30/www.fcbarcelona.com).
Metro Maria Cristina or Collblanc/15, 52, 53, 54,
56, 57, 75 bus.* **Admission** (non-members) €4.
No credit cards.
Barça sponsors the only semi-pro ice hockey team
in town. The rink is open to the public on non-match
days (*see p268*). The season runs from October to
March; games are usually held on Saturdays (2pm
juniors, 9.15pm seniors).

Roller hockey

FC Barcelona

*Palau Blaugrana, Avda Aristides Maillol, Les Corts
(93 496 36 00). Metro Maria Cristina or Collblanc/
15, 52, 53, 54, 56 bus.* **Ticket office** 2hrs before
matches. **Tickets** prices vary. **No credit cards.**

On the ball

More than in any other European city, football is a part of Barcelona's lifeblood. Founded in 1899, FC Barcelona has come to embody the spirit of Catalan identity. Barcelona – or *el Barça* – is *més que un club*, 'more than a club', and is Catalonia's most prominent national symbol. This process started in the Franco years, when the Catalan language could not be publicly spoken anywhere except in the Nou Camp – it is difficult to arrest 100,000 people simultaneously – and the centralist regime, symbolised by arch enemy Real Madrid, could not be challenged except on the football field.

The club's role in public life has outlived the dictator, with every card-carrying Catalan having an opinion on events on the pitch, and acres of column inches devoted to goings-on at the club. It is no exaggeration to say that the big news story in Spain in 2000, surpassing the impact of that year's general election, was Luis Figo's sensational transfer from Barcelona to Real Madrid.

The fact remains, however, that the team has rarely fulfilled its potential. Despite the club's high international profile, for most of its history FC Barcelona has had plenty of big signings and massive support, but has won very few trophies. Some of the world's best players, including Cruyff, Maradona and Romário, have graced the Nou Camp, but *el Barça* has always been overshadowed by *los blancos* from the capital.

There was a brief period when this was not true. Ex-player Johan Cruyff was appointed manager in 1988, and within six years the team had won four consecutive league titles, the Spanish Cup and a European Cup, playing adventurous, attacking and occasionally breathtaking football. However, club president Josep Lluís Núñez got tired of the Dutchman's abrasiveness and his hogging of the limelight, and used the pretext of two trophyless seasons to sack Cruyff in May 1996.

Ever since, the club has been struggling to recover from the internal power struggle caused by Cruyff's dismissal. His successors failed to impress the Catalan public – Bobby Robson was seen as just too much of an old codger for perhaps the most high-pressure job in world football, and Dutchman Louis van Gaal came across as just plain rude. Neither

was helped by their close relationship with Núñez, and the failure of van Gaal's team to win anything at all in the 1999-2000 season, combined with Real Madrid's European Cup victory the same year, led to Núñez's resignation after 20 years as president.

Since then, new president Joan Gaspart has been trying to heal old wounds at boardroom level, while van Gaal's successors have been attempting to sort things out on the pitch. Although Gaspart has succeeded to some extent, the team again failed to win anything in 2000-2001, and still has something of a transitional look about it. New manager Carles Rexach – who as a player turned out more than 600 times for Barça and was Cruyff's sidekick during the team's glory years – was appointed in April 2001, and has based the side on a pragmatic approach and signings that have an eye to the future, such as Argentine teenager Javier Saviola and Brazilians Rochemback and Geovanni.

If you do go to a match, be prepared for one or two disappointments. Although the ground is majestic, it is often less than half full. On the occasions when it is rammed to the rafters – against Real Madrid or for important European matches – it will be prohibitively expensive. And don't expect Latin drums, firecrackers and people lighting bonfires in the stands. Here at Nou Camp, the typical punter is firmly middle-aged and middle-class.

Bearing all that in mind, it is worth going if Barça are playing at home. The team has some of the world's best players, including Rivaldo and Kluivert, and when they click, the football is at a technical level rarely seen elsewhere. If you can catch a game against Real Madrid, it may well be the definitive football experience.

Put your best foot forward at **La Foixarda**. *See p267.*

Roller hockey is wildly popular in Catalonia. It is similar to ice hockey, but tends to be slower and less aggressive. Matches are played at this arena from October to June; phone or see the press for times.

Other events

Barcelona Marathon

Information & entry forms *C/Jonqueres 16, 15°, La Ribera (93 268 01 14/www.redestb.es/marathon_ cat). Metro Urquinqona/17, 19, 40, 45 bus.* **Office** 5.30-8.30pm Mon-Fri. **Date** 16 or 24 March 2002. **Fee** €36.10. **No credit cards. Map** p342 B1.
Until 2001, dedicated runners had been punishing themselves every year along the miserable Olympic marathon course that started up the coast in Mataró, slogging their way through miles of bleak industrial wasteland and ending at the top of the only hill in town. No wonder the marathon attracted universal indifference. Finally the penny has dropped, and 2001 saw the inauguration of a new course that stays within the city limits and ends at the bottom of the hill instead of the top. Organisers are hoping the new route will attract 10,000 runners once word gets out. The city also holds two half-marathons, including the Cursa de la Mercè, during the Mercè (*see p216*).

Motor sports

Circuit de Catalunya, Carretera de Parets del Vallès a Granollers, Montmeló, Outer Limits (93 571 97 00/ www.circuitcat.com). By car C17 north to Parets del Vallès exit (20km/13 miles). **Times & tickets** vary according to competition; available from Servi-Caixa. **Credit** MC, V.
The Circuit de Catalunya is home to the Spanish Formula 1 Grand Prix, which in 2002 will run from 28-29 April, with a motorbike Grand Prix scheduled for 16-18 June. The track can also be used by the public, driving their own cars and bikes, on 12 weekends a year. To celebrate the circuit's tenth anniversary in 2002, there will be an exhibition of historical cars and bikes on 20 October.

Tennis

Reial Club de Tennis Barcelona-1899, C/Bosch i Gimpera 5-13, Les Corts (93 203 78 52/ www.rctb1899.es). Bus 63, 78. **Open** (members only except during competitions) 8am-10pm daily. **Ticket office** (during competitions) 9am-6pm daily. **Credit** AmEx, MC, V.
The Trofeig Comte de Godó, part of the men's ATP tour, is held at Barcelona's most prestigious tennis club during the last week of April. This highly rated ten-day international tournament is the only opportunity to get inside these members-only club grounds. Tickets, available through Servi-Caixa or the club, cost €19-€61.40; *bono* tickets (€147-€282) give you admission to all ten days .

Active sports/fitness

The Ajuntament runs an extensive network of *poliesportius* or sports centres. Some have basic gyms and indoor halls suitable for basketball and five-a-side football; others offer a lavish range of facilities including swimming pools and running tracks. Charges are low, and you don't have to be a resident to use them.

All of Barcelona's beaches have wheelchair ramps and most of the city's pools are fully equipped for disabled people (one exception is the ageing Piscina Municipal Folch i Torres – *see p269* – which is set to be replaced in 2003/4 by a new sports centre in the Raval). For a list of facilities with disabled access, check with the Servei d'Informació Esportiva.

Servei d'Informació Esportiva

Avda de l'Estadi 30-40, Montjuïc (information 93 402 30 00). Metro Espanya, then escalators, or Paral.lel, then Funicular de Montjuïc/50 bus. **Open** 25 Sept-23 June 8am-2.30pm, 4-6.15pm Mon-Thur; 8am-2.30pm Fri. *24 June-24 Sept* 8am-3pm Mon-Thur. **Map** p339 A6.

The Ajuntament's sports information service is located alongside the Piscina Bernat Picornell (see p269). It distributes leaflets listing district sports centres, or you can phone to find the nearest to you. Staff are helpful, but only some speak English.

Bowling

In all, there seven bowling alleys in Barcelona, with a new one in the **La Maquinista** shopping mall (see p184).

Bowling Pedralbes

Avda Dr Marañón 11, Les Corts (93 333 03 52). Metro Collblanc/7, 54, 67, 68, 74, 75 bus. **Open** 10am-1am daily (Aug open from 5pm only). **Rates** (per person per game) €2.30 until 5pm Mon-Fri; €3.30 from 5pm Mon-Thur, until 5pm Sat, Sun; €4.40 from 5pm Fri-Sun. **Credit** MC, V.
Not just 14 bowling lanes to choose from, but also snooker, pool and darts. Early afternoon is the best time, but if it's full (which it often is), leave your name at reception and they will page you at the bar when a lane becomes free. Shoe hire is included.

Climbing

There are a number of indoor climbing walls (*rocodrums*) associated with clubs in Barcelona, but they are often not very high. As a general rule, climbers should bring proof of national federation membership or climbing credentials.

Complex Esportiu La Verneda

C/Binefar 10-14, Sant Martí (93 305 49 59). Metro La Pau/43, 44 bus. **Open** 7am-10pm Mon-Fri; 7am-7pm Sat; 7am-2pm Sun. **Rates** (non-members) €4.80 per day; €30.10 per month. **No credit cards.**
This municipal centre has ten climbing walls of varying difficulties, up to 12m (39ft) high. Visitors can use the walls and ropes, but must show proof of membership of their national climbing federation. Courses are also available.

La Foixarda

Camí de la Foixarda, Parc de Montjuïc. Metro Espanya/9, 13, 38, 61, 65, 91 bus.
Individual climbers have quietly taken over a road in Montjuïc, where a vertical rock face has been graded and had bolts attached. Further along the road, a tunnel has had artificial hand and footholds attached throughout, with colourful stalactites for added effect. These popular areas are unsupervised and accessible to anyone for free, but be aware that, climbers or not, cars still use the tunnel.

Cycling

Although the council continues to expand existing cycle routes, there is still a long way to go before cyclists can be confident that they won't suddenly find themselves thrown into the maelstrom of regular motor traffic. Maps of established cycle routes

are available at tourist information centres (see p320), and you can hire bikes (see p307). The Collserola hills at the back of the city are a good area to explore. There are numerous trails for the seasoned biker, but if you want something a little more relaxing, the Carretera de les Aigües cuts a fairly flat route through the hills, with good views of the city.

Probike

C/Villarroel 184, Eixample (93 419 78 89). Metro Hospital Clínic/14, 59, 63 bus. **Open** 10am-2pm, 4.30-8.30pm Mon-Sat. Closed 2 wks Aug. **Credit** AmEx, DC, MC, V. **Map** p336 C4.
This extensive shop and repair centre specialises in mountain biking and also doubles as a club. There are organised activities most weekends, which are usually free (apart from transport costs). The club also maintains an archive of mountain bike routes; if you're interested in a particular area, they will photocopy the relevant sections for you.

Football

Barcelona International Football League

Information 93 218 67 31/649 261 328/ nicksimonsbcn@yahoo.co.uk.
For those wanting a more active footballing experience, there is the BIFL, created in 1991, with an 18-team league which runs from September till June. New arrivals looking for a team should contact BIFL president Nick Simons.

Golf

Spurred on by the popularity of home-grown talent such as Seve Ballestros and Sergio 'El Niño' Garcia, golf courses are on the increase, with at least seven new courses opening around Barcelona in recent years. Many require proof of a handicap to play, so check beforehand.

Club de Golf Sant Cugat

C/Villa, Sant Cugat del Vallès, Outer Limits (93 674 39 58). By car Túnel de Vallvidrera (C16) to Valldoreix/by train FGC from Plaça Catalunya to Sant Cugat. **Open** June-Oct 8.30am-9pm Tue-Sun. Nov-May 8.30am-5.30pm Tue-Sun. **Rates** (non-members) €45.20 Mon; €69.30 Tue-Fri; €132.50 Sat, Sun. **Credit** MC, V.
A young Seve Ballestros made his professional debut at this attractive and well equipped 18-hole course, which was first designed in 1919, making it one of the oldest in Spain. Visitors can hire clubs and trolleys, and green fees allow access to several other facilities, including the bar, restaurant and pool.

Parc Esportiu Can Drago

C/Rossello i Porcel 7-11, Nou Barris (93 276 04 80/ www.ubae.org). Metro Torras i Bages/35, 40, 62, 73, 96, 173 bus. **Open** 7am-11pm Mon-Fri; 9am-9pm Sat; 9am-2pm Sun. **Admission** (non-members) €5.40 per day; €34.90 per month. **Credit** MC, V.

Arts & Entertainment

The only municipal offering in town for golfers, this centre has a practice area with three putting greens. There are also two covered swimming pools, a gym and an indoor athletics area.

Gyms/fitness centres

Sport centres run by the city are cheaper and generally more user-friendly than private clubs. Phone the **Servei d'Informació Esportiva** (*see p266*) for centres with the right facilities.

Centres de Fitness DIR

C/Casp 34, Eixample (901 30 40 30/93 450 48 18/www.dirfitness.es). Metro Catalunya/bus all routes to Plaça Catalunya. **Open** 7am-11pm Mon-Fri; 9am-3pm Sat, Sun. **Rates** from €10.80; €25.30 for seven days. **No credit cards. Map** p342 B1.

With seven branches well spaced throughout the city and a further six on the drawing board, it is likely that there's a DIR fitness centre near you. They offer excellent facilities (weights, pools, saunas), as well as numerous classes (including aerobics, t'ai chi and yoga) and flexible rates for non-members. Call for information about the one nearest to you.

Europolis

Travessera de les Corts 252-254, Zona Alta (93 363 29 92). Metro Les Corts/15, 43, 59 bus. **Open** 7am-11pm Mon-Fri; 8am-8pm Sat; 9am-3pm Sun. **Rates** *Non-members* €7.80 per day. *Membership* €36.70 per month plus €62.70 joining fee. **Credit** MC, V.

This modern sports complex is located in Les Corts, a block from Diagonal. The fitness rooms have new machinery and there are 38 classes a day (spinning, aerobics, yoga etc). The 'thermal zone' includes saunas, vapour baths and two indoor pools. A one-day pass permits access to all sports facilities, but treatments at the health and beauty centre are extra. **Branch**: **Europolis** C/Sardenya 549-553, Gràcia (93 210 07 66).

Horse riding

Escola Municipal d'Hípica La Foixarda

Avda Montanyans 14-16, Montjuïc (93 426 10 66). Bus 50, 61E. **Open** 5-8pm Sat; 9am-2pm, 6-8pm Sun. **Rates** *(non-members)* Lesson €7.50; ten lessons €124; pony ride €3.60. **Credit** MC, V. **Map** p339 A5.

This municipal centre has three arenas for lessons, offers weekday and weekend courses and sells ten-lesson vouchers, which are valid for 12 months. A test (€11) is required to determine a rider's ability.

Hípica Sant Jordi

Carretera de Sant Llorenç Savall, Cànoves i Samalús (93 843 40 17). By car C58 or N150 to Sabadell, then B124 to Sant Llorenç Savall (42km/26 miles). **Rates** from €20 per 1½ hrs. **No credit cards**.

A child-friendly riding establishment in the hills near the Montseny, which offers varied programmes and excursions for both beginners and experienced riders. Call ahead to book and get directions to the centre. English is spoken.

Ice skating

FC Barcelona Pista de Gel

Avda Arístides Maillol, Les Corts (93 496 36 00/ www.fcbarcelona.com). Metro Maria Cristina or Collblanc/15, 52, 53, 54, 56, 57, 75 bus. **Open** 10am-2pm, 3.30-6pm Mon; 10am-2pm, 3.30-7.30pm Tue-Thur; 10am-2pm, 3.30-8pm Fri; 10am-2pm, 4.30-8.45pm Sat, Sun. Closed Aug. **Admission** (incl skates) €6.60 Mon-Fri; €7.80 Sat, Sun; gloves/socks €1.20. **No credit cards**.

The skating rink in the Barça complex is open to the public when it is not needed for ice hockey games. The rink is quite functional, and prices are low.

Skating Roger de Flor

C/Roger de Flor 168, Eixample (93 245 28 00/ www.skatingbcn.com). Metro Tetuan/6, 19, 50, 51, 54, 55, N1, N3, N4, N5 bus. **Open** 10.30am-1.30pm Tue-Sun; 5-10pm Wed; 5-9pm Thur; 5pm-midnight Fri; 4.30pm-midnight Sat; 4.30-10pm Sun. **Rates** (incl skates) €9. **No credit cards. Map** p341 E5.

This modern rink, with good bar and restaurant facilities, offers discounts to groups of ten or more if you arrange your visit at least one day in advance.

Jogging & running

Enjoyable places to jog are the seafront and Montjuïc: run up from Plaça d'Espanya, or start at the top. For a flat, dirt road and a great view of the city, jog along the Carretera de les Aigües at the top of Avda Tibidabo in the Collserola.

Sailing

Sailing facilities are concentrated in the Port Olímpic. *See also section* **Trips Out of Town**.

Base Nàutica de la Mar Bella

Avda Litoral, between Platja Bogatell & Platja de Mar Bella, Port Olímpic (93 221 04 32/ www.basenautica.net). Bus 36, 41. **Open** *June-Sept* 10am-8pm daily. *Oct-May* 10am-5pm daily. **Rates** membership €13.90 per year; boat hire & courses prices vary. **No credit cards**.

Base Nàutica de la Mar Bella, on the third beach north after the Port Olímpic, hires out several types of boats and windsurfing and snorkelling equipment. Sailing credentials are needed for equipment hire, otherwise you have to take a proficiency test (the cost of which is deductible from the hire cost if the test is passed). There are courses for beginners.

Centre Municipal de Vela

Moll del Gregal, Port Olímpic (93 225 79 40/ www.vela-barcelona.com/). Metro Ciutadella-Vila Olímpica/10, 36, 45, 59 bus. **Open** *Centre June-Sept* 9am-7.30pm daily. *Nov-May* 9am-7pm daily. *Office*

10am-7pm daily. **Rates** individual sessions from
€24.10 per hr; 17½-hour course €177.70; €90.40
children. **Credit** MC, V. **Map** p341 F7.
A relaxed sailing club offering courses at reasonable
prices, with a sea-christening session for complete
novices. Prices go down by 10% from in winter.

Squash

Squash 2000

C/Sant Antoni Maria Claret 64 66, Gràcia (93 160
22 02). Metro Joanic/15, 20, 45, 47 bus. **Open**
7.30am-11.30pm Mon-Fri; 9am-10pm Sat; 9am-3pm
Sun. **Rates** (non-members) from €9 per ½hr; €17.50
per hr. **Credit** AmEx, MC, V. **Map** p337 E3.
Squash 2000 has ten courts (book in advance), plus
a sauna, bar and restaurant.

Swimming

The Servei d'Informació Esportiva (*see p266*)
can provide a list of the city's 27 council-run
pools, and there is a complete list of public and
commercial pools, 180 in total, listed on the
council's website at www.bcn.es. The **Piscina
Municipal de Montjuïc** (Avda Miramar 31,
Montjuïc; 93 443 00 46/93 402 30 49) has two
outdoor pools and a three-storey diving board,
but is only open from June to September. It may
be closed for refurbishment in 2002, so phone to
check. Barcelona's beaches are clean and safe
for swimming and have lifeguards.

Leg it to the **Bernat Picornell** Olympic pool.

Club de Natació Atlètic Barceloneta

Plaça del Mar, Port Vell (93 221 00 10). Bus 17,
45, 57, 59, 64. **Open** 7am-11pm Mon-Sat; 8am-5pm
Sun. **Admission** (non-members) €6.60 per day.
No credit cards. Map p340 D7.
These municipal pools – one indoor and one outdoor
– are located at Banys de Sant Sebastià (Passeig Joan
de Borbó 93), where the Passeig meets the beach.
Other facilities include a bar and restaurant, a gym
and a massage/sauna area.

Piscina Bernat Picornell

Avda de l'Estadi 30-40, Montjuïc (93 423 40 41/
www.picornell.com). Metro Espanya, then escalators,
or Paral·lel, then Funicular de Montjuïc/50 bus.
Open June-Sept 7am-midnight Mon-Fri; 7am-
9pm Sat; 7.30am-8pm Sun. Oct-May 7am-
midnight Mon-Fri; 7am-9pm Sat; 7.30am-4pm
Sun. **Admission** Oct-May €8; €4.50 under-15s.
June-Sept €4.50; €3 under-15s. Free under-6s.
No credit cards. Map p339 A6.
Built in 1969, this pool was lavishly renovated for
the 1992 Olympics. There are two Olympic-size
pools, one indoor and the other outdoor (heated in
early spring). You can also tone up in a gym/
weights room. During the Grec festival (*see p217*),
the pool hosts a joint swimming/film session from
around 10.30pm, and there are also sessions for nud-
ists (9-11pm Sat, 4.15-6pm Sun).

Piscina Municipal Folch i Torres

C/Reina Amàlia 31, Raval (93 441 01 22). Metro
Paral·lel/20, 36, 57, 64, 91 bus. **Open** Sept-July
7am-9.30pm Mon-Fri; 8am-7.30pm Sat; 8.30am-
1.30pm Sun. Aug 7am-3pm Mon-Fri. **Admission**
(non-members) €5.40; €3 6-14s; €1.50 under-6s.
No credit cards. Map p340 C6.
This city complex on the edge of the Raval has three
covered pools and a sauna and weights room. There
is no wheelchair access. It is set to be replaced in
2003/04 by a new sports centre.

Tennis

Barcelona Tenís Olímpic

Passeig de la Vall d'Hebron 178-196, Vall d'Hebron
(93 427 65 00/bto@fctennis.org). Metro Montbau/10,
27, 60, 73, 76 bus. **Open** 8am-11pm Mon-Fri; 8am-
9pm Sat; 8am-7pm Sun. **Rates** (non-members) courts
€14.50 per hr; floodlights €4.20. **No credit cards.**
The city tennis centre, built for the Olympics, is
some way from the centre of town. It has 17 clay
courts, seven asphalt courts and four paddle courts.
Racquets can be hired and balls are for sale.

Centre de Tennis Montjuïc

C/Foixarda, Montjuïc (93 325 13 48). Bus 50.
Open 8am-11pm Mon-Fri; 8am-10 Sat, Sun.
Rates €111 per term (3mths). **No credit cards.**
A less-extensive option closer to the centre of town,
this place has six tennis courts and two open-air
swimming pools. You can buy tennis balls (€10 for
four) and they will lend you racquets.

Arts & Entertainment

Theatre & Dance

Adventures in the avant-garde.

The Catalan stage has its own distinct style, which is less dependent on plot or dialogue than on a festive blend of music, choreography, multimedia sleight-of-hand and extravagant production values. With little classical theatre or dance to fall back on, performing artists in Barcelona move freely between genres and registers, easily blending popular, low-culture traditions with distinctly avant-garde ideas.

In theatre, this crowd-pleasing approach often crosses language barriers – as, indeed, for economic reasons it must – drawing enthusiastic responses from critics and audiences around the world for groups as radically contrasting as La Fura dels Baus and La Cubana. Equally accessible for visitors are the many local variations on puppetry, circus, mime and vaudeville.

The vibrancy of this kind of theatre, added to Barcelonans' love for musicals and light comedy, has sparked a spectacular growth in attendances across the board. As a result, private programmers now surpass public ones in prestige and power, and they control the large theatres. With Catalan television actors serving as box-office draws, more and more venues are dedicated to unabashedly money-making shows, such as a recent Spanish-language adaptation of *The Full Monty*.

The winding queues outside the large commercial theatres at the weekend have their counterpoint in a network of modest independent spaces, where a dense, experimental text one week could easily be followed by a rollicking literary cabaret the next. Though these spaces receive some public funding, they remain poor cousins to massive projects such as the Generalitat-sponsored Teatre Nacional de Catalunya (TNC), opened in 1997, and the Ciutat del Teatre (Theatre City) on Montjuïc, a rival project unveiled by the Ajuntament in late 2001.

The Ciutat del Teatre brings together three buildings and seven stages around a common square: the innovative Mercat de les Flors space, the recently moved Teatre Lliure, and the new Institut del Teatre, the city's most prestigious training ground for the performing arts. A number of local theatre companies and musicians participate in the Ciutat del Teatre, taking up office space and enjoying booking privileges on its stages.

In dance, what most surprises is the dearth of classical or modern ballet, with no major schools, no local companies and no consistent programming anywhere. The voices crying in the wilderness for a Catalan national ballet have met with an official deaf ear; classical dance is not part of the otherwise ambitious dream to revitalise culture in Catalonia. Spanish-style dance has suffered a similar fate. Fans must wait for short annual appearances by major Spanish companies, such as Nacho Duato's Compañía Nacional de Danza (performing at the Liceu in February 2002), or the lively shows of flamenco artists Joaquín Cortés and Sara Bara. At the city's flamenco *tablaos*, performers are rarely first rate, although even middling flamenco can provide a memorable evening.

However, Barcelona excels in contemporary dance, a genre that blossomed only after Franco's body-queasy mentality was shed in the late 1970s. In 1981, an avant-garde school called La Fábrica was founded, attracting dancers and teachers from around the world. The school closed in the early '90s, though not before training artists such as Cesc Gelabert of Gelabert-Azzopardi, Ramón Oller of Metros, María Muñoz of Mal Pelo and Juan Carlos García of Lanònima Imperial, all of whom have found international acclaim for their work. This mid-career generation is slowly making room for a slew of younger dancers, whose work can be viewed in the cutting-edge evenings organised by La Porta. However, despite its virtues and vitality, contemporary dance is still a poor cousin to theatre.

SEASONS AND FESTIVALS

The main performing arts season runs from September to June, but the success of the **Festival del Grec** (*see p217*) has resulted in promoters presenting programmes in July and even August. The Grec festival is the best time to catch visiting theatre and dance companies, both Spanish and international. New theatre and dance are showcased at the amateur free-for-all **Marató de l'Espectacle** (*see p214*) and at the high-profile **Sitges Teatre Internacional** (www.sitges.com/teatre), both held in late May-early June. The annual **Dies de Dansa** (*see p217*) offers three days of national and international dance companies in various architecturally significant sites.

TICKETS AND TIMES

Main shows start late, around 9-10.30pm. Many theatres also have earlier (and cheaper) shows at 6-7pm, often on Wednesday and Saturday or Sunday. There are also late shows on weekend nights. Most theatres are closed on Mondays. Advance bookings are best made through the ticket sales operations of Servi-Caixa or Tel-entrada (*see p210*). Theatre box offices often take cash sales only.

The best places to find information are the *Guia del Ocio*, newspapers and, for Tel-entrada theatres, the *Guia del Teatre*, free at Caixa Catalunya branches.

Top Cats: La Fura dels Baus

La Fura dels Baus have come a long way since they clamped a mule to a gypsy caravan and dragged their scruffy antics around rural Catalonia like the Merry Pranksters meet Mad Max. That was more than 20 years ago, back in what La Fura calls their 'Prehistoric Stage'.

Since then, their direct and often frightening approach has found a rich repertoire in theatrical performance, audiovisual production and art direction for cinema and opera. It has also been put to the service of rather embarrassing ad campaigns for such major corporations as Mercedes-Benz. After La Fura's recent hobnobbing with the upper echelons of European cultural respectability – peaking with their appearance at the première of the movie *Fausto 5.0* at the 2001 Venice Film Festival – many hardcore fans are beginning to wonder if the animal has finally been tamed.

La Fura of the 21st century contrasts with their early reputation, based on classics such as *Suz-O-Suz* (1985), and *Tier Mon* (1988), where unsuspecting audiences were tossed like flotsam in a free-flowing storm of industrial noise, raw flesh and primitive ritual. In those days, the obnoxiously mono-gender La Fura spent most of their time hanging their naked, shaven (male) torsos off whatever scaffolding could be found. Anxiety abounded. Comparisons with post-punk counterparts Survival Research Laboratories and Einsturzende Neubaten were inevitable. The turning point came in 1992 with their monumental contribution to Barcelona's Olympic opening ceremony. It was then that the group realised that their fascination for the great myths of European civilisation and its discontents could find form in productions with a greater narrative content.

What better story, then, than the classic tale of Faust? La Fura has built a trilogy around the conscience-torn doctor and his struggle between reason and desire. Starting with a stage version, *Faust 3.0*, moving on to the art direction of Berlioz's opera *La Damnation de Faust*, and rounding things off with their new film *Fausto 5.0*, a gripping psycho-thriller set against the almost unrecognisable backdrop of a futuristic Barcelona.

In 2002, besides designing operas in Mannheim and Madrid, their new show *XXX* will come to the Teatre Lliure in July as part of the Grec festival. It's a Marquis de Sade-inspired porno cabaret, and will no doubt split audiences down the middle. Which is probably just what they hoped for.

Arts & Entertainment

The imposing **Teatre Nacional**.

Associació dels Professionals de Dansa de Catalunya

Via Laietana 52, entl 7, La Ribera (93 268 24 73/ www.dancespain.com). Metro Urquinaona/17, 19, 40, 45 bus. **Open** 10am-2pm Mon-Fri. **Map** p342 B2.
Acts as a clearing-house for the dance companies, with information on who is doing what at any time.

Major venues

Large central theatres such as the **Borràs** (Plaça Urquinaona 9; 93 412 15 82) or **Tivoli** (C/Casp 10-12; 93 412 20 63) are used for large-scale commercial productions, while the **Club Capitol** (La Rambla 138; 93 412 20 38) has been turned into a comedy hall after years as a cinema. The **Monumental** bullring (*see p264*) is used for mega-shows in the off-season. Ballet and modern classics occasionally appear at the **Liceu** opera house (*see p239*) and even the **Teatre Nacional**, while cultural centres such as the **CCCB** (C/Montalegre 5; 93 306 41 00) and art gallery **Metrònom** (*see p230*) are used for contemporary dance.

L'Espai

Travessera de Gràcia 63, Gràcia (93 414 31 33/ www.cultura.gencat.es/espai). FGC Gràcia/16, 17, 27, 31, 32, N4 bus. **Box office** 6.30-9.30pm Tue-Sat; 5-7pm Sun. **Advance tickets** also from Servi-Caixa. **Tickets** around €9-€12. **Credit** AmEx, DC, MC, V. **Map** p336 C3.
This Catalan government showcase for the performing arts combines dance shows (nearly always contemporary) with music. In 2002, watch for the dance cycle *En dansa* in the spring, and another dance programme in the autumn.

Institut del Teatre

Plaça Margarida Xirgú, Montjuïc (93 227 39 00/ www.diba.es/iteatre). Metro Espanya or Poble Sec/ 55 bus. **Box office** 2hrs before show Mon-Sat; 1hr before show Sun. **Advance tickets** also from Tel-entrada. **Tickets** €10.80-€12.60; €8.10-€9.50 concessions. Free student shows Mar, May, June. **No credit cards. Map** p339 B6.
Three stages in the spacious new premises of Barcelona's leading theatre and dance school offer intriguing (and inexpensive) shows. Student pro-

ductions and workshop projects with prestigious visiting directors are often staged. The expanded dance school also means more new choreography from student troupe IT Dansa. The fine collection of the Performing Arts Museum is also here.

Mercat de les Flors

Plaça Margarida Xirgu, C/Lleida 59, Montjuïc (93 426 18 75/www.mercatflors.com). Metro Espanya or Poble Sec/55 bus. **Box office** 1hr before show. **Advance tickets** also from Tel-entrada & Palau de la Virreina. **Tickets** €7.20-€18. No credit cards. **Map** p339 B6.
A huge converted flower market with two spaces, the Mercat has long been the favoured venue for flexible staging and multidisciplinary performances by the likes of La Fura dels Baus. As some of its public theatre functions are being usurped by the neighbouring Lliure, it has diversified, adding more dance (companies Búbulus in March and Senza Tempo in April 2002) and events such as experimental architecture festival Metàpolis and the Audiovisual & New Media Festival, both in the autumn.

Teatre Lliure

Plaça Margarida Xirgu, Montjuïc (93 289 27 70/ www.teatrelliure.com). Metro Espanya or Poble Sec/ 55 bus. **Box office** 11am-3pm, 4.30-9pm Mon-Fri; 4.30-9pm Sat; 4-6pm Sun. **Advance tickets** also from Tel-entrada. **Tickets** *Fabià Puigserver* €15 Tue, Wed; €20 Thur-Sun; €16 Thur-Sun concessions. *Espai Lliure* varies. **Credit** MC, V. **Map** p339 B6.
Barcelona's most reputable theatre company, since 1976 Teatre Lliure (literally the 'Free Theatre') has presented classic and contemporary drama by Catalan and international writers. The Lliure has finally settled into its new home in the overhauled Palace of Agriculture, built for the 1929 Universal Exposition. It will programme its own work and host other shows in the ultra-modern Fabià Puigserver space and the smaller Espai Lliure, with 2002 highlights including dancer Cesc Gelabert's *Preludis* in March and the summer Grec festival. It will also continue to programme in its intimate space in Gràcia (C/Montseny 47; 93 218 92 51). The Lliure also has a fine chamber orchestra.

Teatre Nacional de Catalunya (TNC)

Plaça de les Arts 1, Eixample (93 306 57 00/ www.tnc.es). Metro Glòries/7, 18, 56, 62, N3, N9 bus. **Box office** noon-3pm, 4-9pm Mon; noon-9pm Tue-Sat; noon-6pm Sun. **Advance tickets** also from Servi-Caixa. **Tickets** €15.60-€20; €11.70-€15 Thur. **Credit** MC, V. **Map** p341 F5.
Architect Ricard Bofill's Parthenon-like TNC is by far the most imposing theatre building in the city, standing alone on a grand lot near the Plaça de les Glòries. After a controversial opening in 1997 (the prestigious actor/director Josep Maria Flotats was sacked as the institution's head for political reasons), the TNC has settled into filling its technically superb halls with solid programming, from translated classics and Catalan and Spanish drama to all genres of

dance. In June 2002, besides Catalan versions of Shakespeare and Camus, Les Ballets de Monte-Carlo will present choreographer Jean-Christophe Maillot's lauded *Romeo and Juliet*.

Teatre Poliorama

La Rambla 115, Barri Gòtic (93 317 75 99/www.teatre poliorama.com). Metro Catalunya/bus all routes to Plaça Catalunya. **Box office** 5pm to start of show Tue-Sat. **Advance tickets** also from Servi-Caixa. **Tickets** varies. **Credit** MC, V. **Map** p342 A2.

This comfortable theatre was acquired by the Catalan government in 1984 to house the national company, but since the 1997 opening of the TNC, commercial producers tresX3 use it to present modern drama, often in translation.

Teatre Principal

La Rambla 27, Barri Gòtic (93 301 47 50). Metro Drassanes/14, 38, 59, 91, N9, N12 bus. **Box office** 4.30-8pm Tue-Sun. **Advance tickets** also from Servi-Caixa. **Tickets** €12-€24 Tue-Sun; €9.60-€19.50 Tue, Thur-Sun concessions; €6-€12 Wed concessions. **No credit cards. Map** p343 A3.

The Principal stands on the site of Barcelona's first theatre, the Teatre de la Santa Creu, opened in 1597 and rebuilt in the 1850s. Recently refurbished, it offers everything from music to opera and serious drama.

Sala Beckett

C/Alegre de Dalt 55 bis, Gràcia (93 284 53 12/ www.teatral.net/beckett). Metro Joanic/24, 25, 31, 32, 39, 55, 74, N6 bus. **Open** *Information office* 10am-2pm, 4-8pm Mon-Fri. *Box office* from 8pm Wed-Sat. **Tickets** €15; €11.30 concessions. **Credit** MC, V. **Map** p337 E3.

Founded by the Samuel Beckett-inspired Teatro Fronterizo group, whose guiding light, José Sanchis Sinisterra, is one of Spain's finest contemporary playwrights, this small Gràcia space offers challenging new theatre, including work developed out of playwriting workshops. La Porta habitually presents its dance evenings here.

Teatre Malic

C/Fusina 3, La Ribera (93 310 70 35). Metro Jaume I/ 39, 51 bus. **Open** *By phone* 10am-6pm daily. *Box office* 2hrs before performance. **Shows** 9pm Mon, Tue; 9pm, 11pm Wed-Sun. **Advance tickets** also from Tel-entrada. **Tickets** €12. **Credit** MC, V. **Map** p343 C3.

A tiny (60-seat) theatre in a Born basement, the Malic presents everything from mini-musicals to one-person diatribes. It has also hosted English-language productions of Steven Berkoff plays from local company Escapade.

Other venues

Other spaces include **Artenbrut** (C/Perill 9-1; 93 457 97 05), **Nou Tantarantana** (C/Flors 22; 93 441 70 22), **Espai Escènic Joan Brossa** (C/Allada Vermell 13; 93 310 13 64) and **Conservas** (C/Sant Pau 58; 92 302 06 30). In July 2002, Conservas will run its successful four-day In Motion festival, with theatre, dance and film showings and a mass outdoor dinner.

Theatre companies

Other companies to look for include the innovative **General Elèctrica**, the intelligent drag queen camp of the **Chanclettes** (whose *Gone With the Wig* was a hit at the 2001 Edinburgh Festival), and the **Compañia Nacional Clásica** for versions of the Spanish masters. *See also p272* **Teatre Lliure** and *p270* **Top Cats: La Fura dels Baus.**

Gelabert-Azzopardi company. *See p274.*

Els Comediants

For more than 30 years, this colourful street theatre troupe has enlivened scores of open-air festivals and soirées with its unique brand of mime, circus and Mediterranean folklore, all wrapped in vivid costumery. Accessible to international audiences young and old, thanks to their limited use of dialogue, Comediants also create works for traditional stages, such as *BI*, a spectacular collaboration with the Chinese National Acrobatics Company in 2001. Comediants claim to defend the child within us all, dishing up a naïve optimism that seasoned audiences might find a tad irritating.

La Cubana

Much loved for their offhand style and disarming humour, La Cubana has thrived on a dazzling mix of satire, camp music and audience participation. After *Cegada de Amor*, which blew audiences away at the 1997 Edinburgh Festival by mixing film and theatre conventions, in 2001 they came up with *Una Nit d'Òpera*, a light-hearted spoof designed to expose the behind-the-stage intrigues of an opera house. The show will be on tour in 2002.

Dagoll Dagom

Under the direction of Joan Lluís Bozzo, this group has fine-tuned Catalan musical theatre, coming up with stellar productions in the old-time Broadway vein. After a recent show exploiting Caribbean clichés in music and eroticism (*Cacao*), they will spend most of 2002 working on a TV comedy series.

Els Joglars

Joglars revolves around their founder and leader, Albert Boadella, a Dario Fo-type provocateur who was imprisoned under the Franco regime for his politics. Using sardonic humour as well as Catalan mime and dance skills, Boadella relies heavily on the comic genius of lead actor Ramon Fontserè. *Daaalí*, a thinking-person's portrait of the eccentric painter (played by a superb Fontserè), was performed at London's Barbican in autumn 2001. Joglars's spoofs of the powers that be can seem a bit repetitive.

Dance companies

Other groups worth looking out for include **Búbulus**, **Companyia Andrés Corchero/Rosa Muñoz**, **Nats Nus**, **Las Malqueridas**, **Transit** and the increasingly appreciated theatricality of **Sol Picó**.

Gelabert-Azzopardi Companyia de Dansa

Cesc Gelabert studied at the Cunningham School in New York. His intensely personal choreographic ideas get a boost from partner Lydia Azzopardi's wonderful understanding of staging and costume. Dance lovers should not miss his long-limbed intelligence in a new solo piece, *Preludis*, to be premiered at the Teatre Lliure in March 2002.

Lanònima Imperial Companyia de Dansa

Founder and choreographer Juan Carlos García spent time with Galotta in France and Cunningham in the US, and has developed a rich and sombre body-centred language, with roots in tradition. For 2002 he is preparing a version of *The Rite of Spring* with music by Igor Stravinsky and Gavin Bryars. For more information, visit www.lanonima.com.

Mal Pelo

Mal Pelo means 'bad hair', implying a rebellious spirit, and the group's work combines abstract dance with a strong storyline. Formed in 1989 by dancers Pep Ramis and María Muñoz, the group has performed across Europe and the US. Mal Pelo has just moved its headquarters to a beautiful farmhouse in Celrà, near Girona, which they also hope to use as a workshop and activities centre, open to outsiders (for more information, call 972 49 41 27).

Metros

Ramón Oller, an award-winning Catalan choreographer with a substantial theatre background, set up Metros in 1984. The company is still touring its 2000 piece *Pecado Pescado*, while a new small-scale work will tour throughout 2002. A larger production is being prepared for late in the year.

Mudances

Director Àngels Margarit has been gaining in stature as a choreographer throughout the past decade, producing highly structured, complex work that involves a creative use of video. In 2001, Mudances premiered *El Somriure* in Barcelona. The company also runs workshops. More info on their website: www.margarit-mudances.com.

La Porta

La Porta is not a company but a showcase for new choreography, seen more or less monthly at the Sala Beckett. Visiting foreign groups and established dancers from other local groups often perform. La Porta is working to set up an annual small-format festival, provisionally set for spring at the CCCB.

Dance schools & workshops

Barcelona has numerous centres where visitors can take short workshops or single classes. For all levels and styles, including ballet, jazz and ballroom, try **Escola de Ballet Eulàlia Blasi** (C/Ali Bei 113, baixos; 93 246 59 62/93 231 11 21/ebeb@inicia.es) or **Varium** (C/Jaume Piquet 7; 93 203 13 01). Two leading contemporary dance ensembles also offer classes and workshops that you can join for short periods or just a day: **Mudances** (93 430 87 63/mudances@margarit-mudances.com) and **Metros** (93 453 75 73/ramonoller@abaforum.es). Note that you'll need to book in advance for all classes.

Trips Out
of Town

Getting Started

Get your bearings before you get out of town.

Venturing beyond Barcelona's cosmopolitan confines, you'll find idyllic beaches, dramatic mountains and lush countryside all within easy reach of the city centre and serviced by an excellent transport system and road network. And if walking, swimming, skiing, wine-tasting or simply relaxing in picturesque village doesn't appeal to you, several regional cities combine historic splendour with a sophisticated lifestyle. While pockets of Catalonia haven't changed for centuries, other areas combine rustic charm with internationally renowned restaurants and elegant hotels.

The **Palau Robert** information centre (*see p321*) and local tourist offices have brochures (some in English) on the districts (*comarques*) into which Catalonia is divided, as well as topics ranging from *Modernisme* to water sports. Staying in the countryside is now easier with many *masies* (farmhouses) taking guests – a guide to them, *Residències – Casa de Pagès*, is available at tourist offices and bookshops; other Generalitat guides include *Hotels Catalunya* and *Catalunya Campings*.

The Generalitat also has an excellent website – www.gencat.es/probert – with particularly good information on walks, divided by area, time of year, type and length. For organised walks, try **Spain Step by Step** (93 302 76 29). For information on roads and public transport within Catalonia, visit the Generalitat thorough www.mobilitat.org.

By bus

Coach services around Catalonia are operated by some half a dozen private companies, concentrated mostly (but not entirely) at the **Estació d'Autobusos Barcelona-Nord**, C/Ali Bei 80 (*see p303*). General information is on 93 265 65 08, but each company has its own phoneline. The **Costa Brava** is better served by buses (with the **Sarfa** company) than trains.

By road

Driving in or out of Barcelona, you will come across the *rondes*, or ring roads. The **Ronda de Dalt** runs along the edge of Tibidabo, and the **Ronda Litoral** along the coast, meeting at either side of the city. They intersect with several motorways (*autopistes*): the C31

(heading up the coast); the C33/A7 (to Girona and France); the C58 (Sabadell, Manresa); the A2 (Lleida, Madrid), a continuation of Avda Diagonal which connects with the A7 south (Tarragona, Valencia); and the C32 to Sitges. All are toll roads. Where possible, we've given toll-free alternatives. The Túnel de Vallvidrera, the continuation of Via Augusta that leads out of Barcelona under Collserola to Sant Cugat and Terrassa, also has a high toll. For more on driving and car hire, *see p306*.

A WARNING
In July 2001, the Generalitat introduced a new system for naming roads according to the direction in which they run: roads beginning C1 run north–south; C2 run east–west; C3 run parallel to the coast. Thus the A16 and A19 have become the C32; the A18 the C16, and so on. Maps, guidebooks and even some road signs had been slow to update at the time of writing.

By train

RENFE trains are useful for the coast, **Girona**, the **Montseny** and the **Penedès**. All trains stop at **Barcelona-Sants** station. Tickets for local and suburban (*rodalies/cercanías*) services are sold at separate windows. In the city centre, some routes (the coast north, the **Montseny**, the **Penedès**) also stop at the **Plaça Catalunya**; others (the coast south, **Girona**), at **Passeig de Gràcia**. Regional trains include the *regulars*, stopping at every station; the *deltas*, stopping at nearly every station; and the *Catalunya Exprés*, stopping less often and costing more. Long-distance (*largo recorrido*) services also stop at main stations, but supplements are paid for high-speed services.

RENFE fare structures are complicated, but special deals are available and there are also *días azules* (blue days, usually midweek) when long-distance services are cheaper. For RENFE information, call 902 24 02 02 (English spoken), or visit its website – www.renfe.es – for prices, times and routes (partly in English).

Catalan Government Railways (**FGC**) serves some destinations from its two main stations in Barcelona: **Plaça d'Espanya**, for **Montserrat** and **Manresa**, and **Plaça Catalunya** for the line within Barcelona and trains to **Sant Cugat**, **Sabadell** and **Terrassa**. You can get FGC information on 93 205 15 15.

Short Trips

Coastal towns, mountain-top monasteries and natural delights await within an hour from the city.

Costa de Garraf

The first resort on the south coast is **Castelldefels**, home to wide, sandy beaches and a string of seafood restaurants. Just 20 kilometres (12 miles) from Barcelona, the town has always attracted big summer crowds and is now a busy year-round suburban residence. A few kilometres further south is the tiny village of **Garraf**, built on a small, pretty beach with a couple of relaxed beach bars. The nearby Celler de Garraf is a dazzling *Modernista* creation designed by Gaudí for the Güell family in 1895.

Sitges, one of Catalonia's best known and most picturesque resorts, lies just beyond the nature reserve of the Garraf mountains. The former fishing village became popular with artists and intellectuals in the 1890s when it was 'discovered' by *Modernista* artist/writer Santiago Rusiñol, whose entourage included the teenage Picasso. Since the 1960s, Sitges has also been a favourite holiday destination with the international gay community (*see p237*), who share the beaches and quaint alleyways with rich Barcelonans and visiting families. There are nine beaches along the seafront, and quieter, if snobbier, beaches at the (artificial) port of **Aiguadolç** – to get there, turn left out of the station. For nudist beaches, go to the seafront, turn right, and keep going (it's quite a walk).

Even when crowded, Sitges is charming, with a beautiful medieval heart, tiny streets of white-washed houses and a long promenade, the Passeig de la Ribera, snaking along the waterfront. Beautiful buildings cluster around the town's most visible monument, the 17th-century church of **Sant Bartomeu i Santa Tecla**, which has a spectacular view of the coast. Almost adjacent are the old market, the Ajuntament and the **Museu Cau Ferrat** (C/Fonollar, 93 894 03 64, admission €3-€5.40, closed Mon). Rusiñol's old home, it was bequeathed to the town as a ready-made museum full of paintings – including works by Rusiñol, El Greco and some early Picassos – archaeological finds, wrought-iron pieces and Modernista creations. Opposite is the spectacular, Gothic **Palau Mar i Cel** (Palace of the Sea and Sky), which houses an eclectic collection of medieval and baroque artwork, but, sadly, is not open to the public.

Sant Bartomeu i Santa Tecla church.

The **Museu Romàntic** in Casa Llopis, (C/Sant Gaudenci 1, 93 894 29 69, admission €3, closed Mon) portrays the lifestyle of an upper-class Sitges family through various displays of furniture, clocks and antique dolls. Sitges also hosts a string of events through the year, including the spectacularly over-the-top Carnestoltes (Carnival) in February, a theatre festival in June, and the Film Festival in October (*see p227*).

South from Sitges, **Vilanova i la Geltrú** is one of Catalonia's busiest ports and the harbour is always bustling with tiny fishing boats battling huge ships for space. There are some pleasant beaches and several museums, including the important **Biblioteca-Museu Balaguer** (Avda Victor Balaguer, 93 815 42 02, admission €1.80, closed Mon), which contains some El Grecos and many other artefacts. The town is also known for its Carnival, and its ultra-fresh seafood.

Amsterdam	Barcelona	Berlin	Boston	Brussels	Budapest
Buenos Aires	Chicago	Copenhagen	Dublin	Edinburgh	Florence
Havana	Hong Kong	Istanbul	Las Vegas	Lisbon	London
Los Angeles	Madrid	Miami	Moscow	Naples	New Orleans
New York	Paris	Prague	Rome	San Francisco	South of France
Sydney	Tokyo	Venice	Vienna	Washington, DC	

The **Time Out City Guides** spectrum

Available from all good bookshops and at www.timeout.com/shop

Where to stay & eat

In Castelldefels, there are several cheap seafront paella restaurants, or the more upmarket **Nàutic** (Passeig Marítim 374, 93 665 01 74, main courses €21.10). For a luxurious hotel, try the **Gran Hotel Don Jaime** (Avda del Hotel, 22, 93 665 13 00, rates €128-€192.60), which has indoor and outdoor pools and a garden.

In Sitges, the **Sitges** restaurant (C/Parellades 61, 93 894 34 93, closed Sun dinner, Mon, set lunch €8.40 Tue-Fri) and **La Salseta** (C/Sant Pau 35, 93 811 04 19, closed Sun dinner, Mon, set lunch €10.30 Tue-Fri) are both good value. **Vivero** (Passeig Balmins, 93 894 21 49, closed Tue mid Jan-early Apr, closed mid Dec-mid Jan, set lunch €15.50) has unbeatable water views to accompany your seafood, while **Al Fresco** (C/Pau Barrabeig 4, 93 894 06 00, mains €15.10) breaks the Catalan mould, offering excellent Mediterranean food with creative Asian touches. If you want to stay over in Sitges, the **Celimar** (Passeig de la Ribera 20, 93 811 01 70, rates €77-€124) is a comfortable seafront hotel; some rooms have balconies with views. **Hostal Maricel** (C/Tacó 13, 93 894 36 27, rates €38.60-€54) is a good budget option, as is the **Parellades** (C/Parellades 11, 93 894 08 01, rates €38, closed Oct-Mar). *See chapter* **Gay & Lesbian** for more accommodation options.

In Vilanova i la Geltrú, **Peixerot** (Passeig Marítim 56, 93 815 06 25, closed Sun dinner mid Sept-June, mains €33.10) gets the pick of the day's fish, and there's excellent grilled meat at **Can Pagès** (C/Sant Pere 24, 93 894 11 95, closed lunch Mon-Fri, set menu €12.70). For a pleasant place to stay, the **Hotel César** (C/Isaac Peral 4-8, 93 815 11 25, rates €70-€116) is set in a garden with a heated pool and spa, and is only a minute's walk from the beach. Rooms with sea views and terraces are more expensive, but worth it. The hotel also has a restaurant, **La Fitorra** (mains €23.80), serving Mediterranean food, with several fish dishes.

Water sports

Water sports – scuba diving, windsurfing, sailing and kayaking – are incredibly popular all along the coast, and there's no shortage of places to rent equipment or take lessons.

In Castelldefels, you can rent sea kayaks and all classes of catamaran from the **Catamaran Center** (Port Ginesta, local 324, 93 665 22 11), while windsurfing centre **Club Mar** in Sitges (Passeig Marítim, 93 894 09 05) has classes and a restaurant. **Windcat House** (Passeig Marítim 174, 977 69 30 72) in Calafell, south of Vilanova i la Geltrú, runs sailing courses. Alternatively, in Barcelona you can hire a yacht

with captain from **Jack London Charters** (C/Riera Alta 10, 93 442 08 69/678 60 42 40) for trips along the coast, to the Balearics or the Caribbean. Each is open all year.

Getting there

By car

C32 to Castelldefels, Garraf, Sitges (41km/25 miles) and Vilanova (extra tunnel toll between Garraf and Sitges), or C31 via a slow, winding drive around the Garraf mountains.

By train

RENFE trains leave approx every 20min from Sants or Passeig de Gràcia to Platja de Castelldefels (20min journey), Sitges (30min) and Vilanova (40min); not all stop at Castelldefels and Garraf. The last train back to Barcelona leaves Vilanova at 10.20pm and Sitges at 10.25pm, even on Saturday nights.

Tourist information

Oficina de Turisme de Castelldefels

Plaça de l'Església 1 (93 664 23 61). **Open** 8am-3pm Mon-Fri.

Oficina de Turisme de Sitges

C/Sínia Morera (93 894 42 51/www.sitges.org). **Open** *July-Sept* 9am-9pm daily.*Oct-June* 9am-2pm, 4-6.30pm Mon-Fri.
C/Fonollar (93 811 06 11/www.sitges.org). **Open** *July-Sept* 10am-1.30pm, 5-9pm daily. *Oct-June* 11am-2pm, 4-7pm Sat; 11-2pm Sun.

Oficina de Turisme de Vilanova i la Geltrú

C/Torre de Ribarroges (93 815 45 17). **Open** 10am-1.30pm, 5-8pm Tue-Fri; 10am-2pm, 5-8pm Sat; 10am-2pm Sun.

Costa del Maresme

Immediately north-east of Barcelona, the Maresme coast, or 'marshy coast', is an easy day trip. Of the string of small towns along the shoreline, both **Caldes d'Estrac** (also known as **Caldetes**) and **Sant Pol de Mar** have good beaches (some nudist), and plenty of tourists. The wealth of *Modernista* houses in Caldetes is the legacy of summer visitors who flocked to the hot-water springs at the turn of the 20th century. A newly restored park with fine views adds to the town's appeal. Sant Pol is a tranquil, mostly unspoilt, if yuppified fishing village. While railway tracks run close to the beach along much of this coast, some of Sant Pol's beaches are separated from roads and rail by rocky cliffs.

Between these two villages is the larger town of **Canet**, where the influential *Modernista* architect Domènech i Montaner lived. His

Trips Out of Town

former home is now a museum and the town boasts some of his finest work, including his remodelled castle of **Santa Florentina**, complete with the intact remains of the 13th-century entrance towers.

Where to stay & eat

In Caldes d'Estrac, the best mid-price restaurant is probably **Can Suñe** (C/Callao, 93 791 00 51, main courses €14, closed Mon, closed Mon-Wed Dec-May).There are also double rooms if you want to stay over (June-Sept only, €35.40). For lunch on the seafront, try the **Voramar** (Passeig de Musclera 10, 93 791 09 44, mains €12, closed Wed, closed Oct). In Sant Pol, **La Casa** (C/Riera, 13, 93 760 23 73, mains €9, closed Mon, Tue) is a funkily decorated restaurant with great *torrades*. Canet has the **Mitus** (C/Riera de la Torre 20, 93 794 29 03, rates €30-€45.20), a charming, family-run hostal. There are plenty of places to eat on the tree-lined Passeig del Maresme.

El Racó de Can Fabes

C/Sant Joan 6, Sant Celoni (93 867 28 51/ www.racocanfabes.com). By car A7 or C35 (60 km/37 miles)/by train RENFE to Sant Celoni. **Open** 1.30-3.30pm, 8.30-10.30pm Tue-Sat; 1.30-3.30pm Sun. Closed 1st 2wks Feb, last wk June, 1st wk July. **Main courses** €32.50-€65.50. **Gourmet menu** €89.90. **Credit** AmEx, DC, MC, V. If you want a real treat, head to this small, rustic place in Sant Celoni, at the foot of the Montseny mountains. It has a grand total of three Michelin stars, and charismatic chef Santi Santamaria has long been acclaimed as a leader among European chefs. Seasonal specialties include prawn ravioli with wild mushroom oil and hot and cold mackerel with cream of caviar. Desserts are superb and there's a fine range of cheeses. Expect a gourmet treat – but without the airs and graces usually associated with this class of restaurant.

Getting there

By car

NII to Caldes d'Estrac (36km/22 miles), Canet (42km/26 miles) and Sant Pol (48km/30 miles).

By train

RENFE trains leave every 30min from Sants or Plaça Catalunya for Caldes d'Estrac, Canet and Sant Pol. Journey takes approx 45min-1hr.

Inland – the Vallès

Just half an hour on a train will take you into relatively unspoilt countryside dotted with fine examples of *Modernista* architecture. The plain of the Vallès unfolds just behind the mountain of Tibidabo. A little further along from the road

and rail tunnels is **Les Planes**, a picnic area on the edge of **Collserola** park with cheap restaurants and a *merendero* – an area with tables and grills where people can bring food for barbecues. There's an attractive walk or cycle ride from Les Planes towards **El Papiol**, a town with a medieval castle, unusual rock formations – signposted **Les Escletxes** – and the remains of an Iberian settlement.

A little further north is **La Floresta**, a garden suburb located on a quiet, pine-covered hillside. It was once called 'La Floresta Pearson', after the Canadian engineer who brought mains electricity to Barcelona in 1911, and planned the village. In the 1970s it was Barcelona's hippy haven – 'Fat Freddy's Cat' cartoonist Gilbert Shelton even lived here for a while. La Floresta is a great place for an easy, short walk, with beautiful views.

Below Collserola stands **Sant Cugat**, a fast-growing town with a Romanesque monastery and, on the Arrabassada road back towards Barcelona, the **Casa Lluch**, a striking 1906 *Modernista* creation with superb tiling. The Vallès also contains two large towns, Sabadell and Terrassa, that were at the centre of Catalonia's industrial revolution. **Terrassa** – also known as the 'Catalan Manchester' (it once won a Japanese award as the world's ugliest city) – is a busy industrial town that has at its centre three unique Visigothic-Romanesque churches, **Santa Maria, Sant Miquel** and **Sant Pere**, parts of which date from the sixth century. The town also has a handful of stunning *Modernista* buildings, including the outlandish **Masía Freixa**, a unique building surrounded by Gaudiesque white arches and the **Aymerich i Amat** factory.

Where to eat

Sant Cugat has a very good grilled-meat restaurant, **Braseria La Bolera** (Rambla de Celler 43, 93 674 16 75, closed Sun dinner, mains €16.60). In Terrassa, **Casa Toni** (Ctra de Castellar 124, 93 786 47 08, closed Sat, set lunch €7.10-€10.30) offers a fine range of wines.

Getting there

By car

To Les Planes, La Floresta and Sant Cugat: A7 via Túnel de Vallvidrera (exit 8 off Ronda de Dalt, toll), or the winding but scenic Ctra de l'Arrabassada (exit 5 off Ronda de Dalt) for free. To El Papiol: A2, then B30 from Molins de Rei. To Terrassa: C58 or C16. Both are toll-free.

By train

FGC trains leave from Plaça Catalunya to Terrassa. Journey time is 15-25min.

Montserrat

Montserrat, or the 'saw-tooth mountain', forms a striking silhouette as it towers above gently rolling hills covered in vines. Distinct geologically from the terrain that surrounds it, the mountain's strange bulbous peaks make a dramatic setting for the spiritual heart of Catalonia. The monastery of Montserrat sits atop these spectacular mountains surrounded by hermitages and tiny chapels. It is accessible only by circuitous roads with breathtaking views or, more spectacularly still, by cable car.

Hermits came here as long ago as the fifth century and by 1025 one of the hermitages had been expanded to become a Benedictine monastery. The Moreneta or 'Black Virgin', a small wooden figure, was installed in the 12th century and countless legends have grown up around it; she is the patron saint of Catalonia and Montserrat is still the most common name for Catalan women. In the Middle Ages, the monastery became an important place of pilgrimage. It grew rich and powerful, its remote position helping to ensure its independence. In 1811 the French destroyed the monastery, killing the monks. By 1844 it has been rebuilt. During the Franco era, it became a bastion of non-violent Catalan nationalism.

Queues of people wait to touch the statue of the virgin inside the 16th-century basilica (8am-10.30am, noon-6.30pm), and pray for a miracle. The museum (8.30am-5.45pm) houses liturgical gold and silverware, archaeological finds, gifts presented to the virgin, works by Picasso, Caravaggio and El Greco, and an audiovisual display offers an interesting overview of the day-to-day life of the Montserrat monks.

The monastery itself (open 8am-8pm) is not particularly interesting, however, and the cafeterias and souvenir shops strike an ugly and commercial note. It's the walks and views around the mountain, a nature reserve ten kilometres (six miles) long, that are truly spectacular. As well as the cave where the virgin was discovered (a 20-minute walk from the monastery), there are 13 hermitages, the most accessible of them being **Sant Joan**, reached by funicular from the monastery or a 20-minute walk with superb views. The tourist office has details of longer walks including a circuit of all the hermitages and the (relatively easy) trek to the peak of Sant Jeroni, at 1,235 metres (4,053 feet). Climbing is also popular.

Where to stay & eat

Restaurants on Montserrat are expensive and unimpressive. The café at the top of the Funicular de Sant Joan is better, but only open

Montserrat: monks, mugs and mousemats.

in summer. Your best bet is a picnic. There are two hotels run by the monks: the recently renovated **Hotel Abat Cisneros** (93 877 77 01, double €40.70-€76.30), where you also eat, or the lower-category **Hotel-Residència Monestir** – due to reopen in March 2002 after renovation. The Hotel Abat Cisneros also has information about the campsite located beyond the Sant Joan funicular; look out for the sign.

Getting there

By bus

A Julià-Via bus leaves at 9am from Sants bus station; journey time is approx 80min. Julià-Via also run guided tours to Montserrat.

By car

Take the NII to exit km 59; or the A2 to the Martorell exit, then through Abrera and Monistrol (60km/37 miles). The road to the monastery is steep with sharp bends and is often crowded and very slow, especially on weekends, public holidays and holy days.

By train

FGC trains from Plaça d'Espanya every 2hrs daily from 8.30am to the Aeri de Montserrat (journey time approx 1hr); then a cable car (leaving every 15min) to the monastery. Last train leaves Aeride Montserrat at 7.30pm. Return fare (including cable car) is €11.40.

Tourist information

Oficina de Turisme de Montserrat

Plaça de la Creu, Montserrat (93 877 77 77/ www.abadiamontserrat.net). **Open** *Apr-Oct* 9am-7pm daily. *Nov-Mar* 9am-6pm daily.

Tarragona & the Costa Daurada

Head south for Roman ruins, ancient monasteries and vineyards.

Tarragona

The seaside city of Tarragona was once a mighty Roman metropolis, capital of over half the Iberian peninsula. It retains a spectacular collection of Roman buildings and ruins – the largest in Spain – including the waterfront amphitheatre, the original city walls, the circus and the vast aqueduct, and combines this historic wealth with an active cultural scene and some excellent restaurants. Tarragona was declared a World Heritage site by UNESCO in 2000, which may change the surprising fact that so few international visitors have Tarragona on their itinerary.

Walking along the **Passeig Arqueològic** (Avda Catalunya, entrance at Portal del Roser, 977 24 57 96) gives a good introduction to the ancient city; it follows the old Roman ramparts, built on earlier walls of massive stones, and commands a great view of Tarragona's hinterland and the sea. The walls support three impressive towers, two of which were rebuilt in medieval times. Inside the walls, in the **Plaça del Rei**, you will find the ancient **Pretori** (praetorium), now called **Castell del Rei** (977 24 19 52), which has been used as a palace and government office and is rumoured to have been the birthplace of Pontius Pilate. From here you can walk to the ruins of the **Circ Romans**, the first-century Roman circus. Excavations suggest that chariot races were once held here. The **Museu Nacional Arqueològic**, home to an important collection of Roman artefacts and some stunning mosaics, is nearby. Tickets for this also allow entry to the **Museu i Necròpolis Paleocristians**, located on the site of a cemetery where Tarragona's early Christians were buried. Thousands of graves have been uncovered and the museum displays some interesting if morbid finds, including beautifully decorated sarcophagi.

Back in the old town, the **Passeig de las Palmeres** leads from the Roman circus to the 'Balcó del Mediterrani' from where you can look down over the spectacular arena of the Roman **amphitheatre** (Parc del Miracle, 977 24 25 79), once the scene of gladiator fights,

and the 12th-century Romanesque church of **Santa María del Miracle**, set on the grandly named **Platja del Miracle**. The Passeig de las Palmeres also takes you to the bustling pedestrian street of the **Rambla Nova**, from where you can follow C/Canyelles to the **Fòrum** (C/Lleida, 977 24 25 01) to visit the remains of the juridical basilica and Roman houses. The narrow medieval streets of the beautiful Part Alta (High Part) – the name given to the old city – are well preserved and this is a good place to find small restaurants and tucked-away bars.

The majestic **Catedral de Santa María** was built on the site of a Roman temple to Jupiter, and is Catalonia's largest cathedral. The cloister, built in the 12th and 13th centuries, is glorious, and has some intriguing details including the famous 'Procession of the Rats' relief – a bizarre set of illustrations of rats at a cat's funeral. To see all parts of the cathedral and cloister, not to mention some wonderful religious art and archaelogical finds, you will need a ticket for the **Museu Diocesà** (Pla de la Seu, 977 23 86 85, closed Sun, admission €2.40).

The fishing harbour is a good place to wander, and, naturally, the best place for seafood restaurants. A half-hour walk to the north of the city brings you to the most spectacular of Tarragona's historic relics: the **Pont del Diable** (Devil's Bridge), a wonderfully preserved Roman aqueduct built in the first century.

You have to pay separate admission to the Passeig Arqueològic; the praetorium and circus; the amphiteatre; and the Fòrum. Each costs €1.80 (60¢ concessions, free under-16s), although entry is free to holders of **Port Aventura** tickets (see p284). Opening hours are the same for all: Easter-mid Oct 9am-9pm Tue-Sat; 9am-7pm Sun; mid Oct-Easter 9am-5pm Tue-Sat; 10am-3pm Sun.

Museu Nacional Arqueològic de Tarragona

Plaça del Rei 5 (977 23 62 09). **Open** *June-Sept* 10am-8pm Tue-Sat; 10am-2pm Sun. *Oct-May* 10am-1.30pm, 4-7pm Tue-Sat; 10am-2pm Sun.

Trips Out of Town

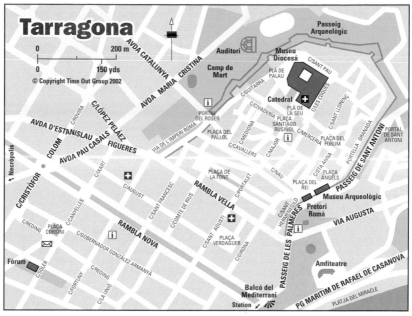

Tarragona

0   200 m

0   150 yds

© Copyright Time Out Group 2002

Admission (incl entrance to Museu i Necròpolis Paleocristians) €2.40; €1.20 concessions; free under-16s, over-65s. **No credit cards.**

Museu i Necròpolis Paleocristians

Avda Ramón y Cajal 80 (977 21 11 75).
Open *June-Sept* 10am-1pm, 4.30-8pm Tue-Sat; 10am-2pm Sun. *Oct-May* 10am-1.30pm, 3-5.30pm Tue-Sat; 10am-2pm Sun. **Admission** (incl entrance to Museu Nacional Arqueològic) €2.40, €1.20 concessions, free under-16s, over-65s. **No credit cards.**

Where to eat

In the centre of the old town, **Palau del Baró** (C/Santa Anna 3, 977 24 14 64, closed Sun, mains €12.50) serves excellent, traditional Catalan food in a series of elegant dining rooms furnished with antiques. Just below the cathedral is the great-value **La Cuca Fera** (Plaça Santiago Rusinyol 5, 977 24 20 07, closed Mon, closed Nov, set lunch €9.70); try the delicious *cazuela de romesco*.

Good seafood is to be found at **Cal Martí** (C/Sant Pere 12, 977 21 23 84, closed Sun dinner, Mon, closed Sept, mains €14.10) – they're particularly proud of their paella. **La Puda** (Moll Pescadors 25, 977 21 15 11, closed Sun dinner Oct-Mar, mains €15.40), opposite the site of the fish auctions, is another place to find truly fresh fish. Cheap, reliable Catalan

meals are available at the **Bufet el Tiberi** (C/Martí d'Ardenya 5, 977 23 54 03, closed Sun dinner, Mon, buffet €11).

Where to stay

The ambitious curved design of the **Imperial Tarraco** (Rambla Vella 2, 977 23 30 40, rates €112-€134.50) mirrors the Roman amphitheatre, which it overlooks. The hotel also has a swimming pool and restaurant. A good-value mid-range hotel, also with a pool, is the **Lauria** (Rambla Nova 20, 977 23 67 12, rates €57.80-€68.50). Both hotels give hefty discounts at weekends out of season. You'll find cheaper digs at the **Pensión Forum** (Plaça de la Font 37, 977 23 17 18, rates €30-€36) and the nearby **Pensión La Noria** (Plaça de la Font 53, 977 23 87 17, rates €27-€36). Other mid-range hotels include the **Astari** (Via Augusta 95, 977 23 69 00, rates €57), which has a pool with good views, and the central **Hotel Urbis** (C/Reding 20 bis, 977 24 01 16, rates €56.30-€87.80).

Getting there

By car

Take the A2, then A7 via Vilafranca (Tarragona 98km/60 miles); or the toll-free N340 (Molins de Rei exit from A2).

By train

RENFE from Sants or Passeig de Gràcia. Trains hourly from about 6am-9.30pm. Journey time to Tarragona is 1hr 6min.

Tourist information

Oficina de Turisme de Tarragona

C/Fortuny 4 (977 23 34 15). **Open** 9am-2pm, 4-6.30pm Mon-Fri; 9am-2pm Sat.

Costa Daurada

If you're looking for castles and sand, **Altafulla**, between Vilanova and Tarragona, has both, plus one of the best preserved medieval centres on the coast. The modern section is close to the seafront, where there are fine white sand beaches between rocky outcrops, and a picturesque seaside castle at nearby **Tamarit**. The old walled town – which is crowned by the imposing **Castell d'Altafulla** and floodlit at night – is a ten-minute stroll inland. Local folklore has it that the old town has been home to a coven of witches for centuries. Further south along the coast towards the rather unlovely resort of Salou is the popular **Port Aventura** theme park.

Universal Studios Port Aventura

977 77 90 90/www.portaventura.es. By car A2, then A7 to exit 35, or N340 (108km/67 miles). By train RENFE from Sants or Passeig de Gràcia to Port Aventura (1hr 15min). **Open** *Late June-mid Sept* 10am-9pm daily. *Mar-late June, mid Sept-late Oct* 10am-7pm daily. **Admission** *1 day* €30; €24 concessions. *2 consecutive days* €45.20; €33.10 concessions. *3 consecutive or alternate days* €60; €45.20 concessions. Free under-5s. *Night ticket* (mid June-mid Sept 7pm-midnight) €23; €16 concessions. **Credit** AmEx, DC, MC, V. Port Aventura is a vast theme park with undeniably spectacular rides. It is divided into five sections – the Wild West, China, Mexico, the Mediterranean and Polynesia – each built in an appropriate traditional style, complete with local plants and specialised restaurants (though it has to be said that food is not the park's strong suit). The massive Dragon Khan rollercoaster, with eight 360° loops and a speed of 60 miles/95km per hour has long been a stomach-churning favourite, while newer attractions include an eerie underwater journey on the Sea Odyssey submarine, dreamed up by the special effects wizards who created *Jurassic Park*. Video cameras and buggies can be hired, and there are facilities for the disabled.

Where to stay & eat

In Altafulla is the **Faristol** (C/Sant Martí 5, 977 65 00 77, closed Mon-Thur Oct-May, rates €57), a well-priced hotel, bar and restaurant

in an 18th-century house run by an Anglo-Catalan couple, with a pleasant outdoor terrace. The restaurant is particularly good (main courses €21.10).

A decent bed can be found at **Yola** (Via Augusta 50, 977 65 02 83, closed late Sept-Easter, rates €51-€78), a modern place with a new swimming pool. To rent rooms in the old town, ask at **El Corral** bar (977 65 04 86) or the Faristol.

Getting there

By car

Take the A2, then A7 via Vilafranca; or the toll-free N340 (Molins de Rei exit from A2).

By train

RENFE from Sants or Passeig de Gràcia to Altafulla (1hr 15min). Trains run hourly approx 6am-9.20pm.

Tourist information

Oficina de Turisme de Altafulla

Plaça dels Vents (977 65 07 52). **Open** *May-Oct* 10am-2pm Mon-Sat. Closed Nov-Apr.

The Royal Monasteries

Montblanc, 112 kilometres (70 miles) due west of Barcelona and inland from Tarragona and the Costa Daurada, is one of the most beautiful towns in western Catalonia. For some reason it is still almost unknown to foreign visitors, perhaps because it is relatively isolated,

Tamarit: now that's a proper sandcastle.

Romanesque church near Vilafranca del Penedès in the wine country.

although very easy to get to by train. Around it, roughly forming a triangle, are three exceptional Cistercian monasteries: **Poblet**, **Santes Creus** and **Vallbona de les Monges**.

In the Middle Ages, Montblanc was one of Catalonia's most powerful centres, with an important Jewish community, a past that is reflected in its **Carrer dels Jueus** (Jews' Street), the magnificent 13th-century town walls (two-thirds of which are still intact), the churches of **Santa Maria la Major**, **Sant Miquel** and **Sant Francesc**, the **Palau Reial** (royal palace) and the **Palau del Castlà** (chamberlain's palace).

The great monasteries of the region enjoyed a uniquely close relationship with the Catalan-Aragonese monarchs, and were all built partly to house royal tombs. **Poblet**, a few kilometres west of Montblanc, was founded as a royal residence as well as a monastery in 1151 by Ramon Berenguer IV, who created the joint Catalan-Aragonese monarchy and gave generous grants of land to the Cistercian order. The remarkable complex includes a 14th-century **Gothic royal palace**, the 15th-century **chapel of Sant Jordi** and the main **church**, housing the tombs of most of the Count-Kings of Barcelona. The monastery can be visited only on a guided tour.

Santes Creus, founded in 1158 and perhaps still more beautiful than Poblet, grew into a small village when families moved into abandoned monks' residences in 1843. Fortified walls shelter the **Palau de l'Abat** (abbot's palace), a monumental fountain, a 12th-century church and a superb Gothic cloister and chapterhouse. Visits to Santes Creus now include an audiovisual presentation, though only one a day is in English; call ahead to confirm the time.

Vallbona de les Monges, the third of these Cistercian houses, was, unlike the others, a convent of nuns. It was particularly favoured by Catalan-Aragonese queens, especially Violant of Hungary (wife of Jaume I), who was buried here. It has a fine part-Romanesque cloister, but is less grand than the other two.

Note that all three monasteries still house religious communities.

Monestir de Poblet
977 87 02 54. **Open** *Mar-Sept* 10am-12.30pm, 3-6pm Mon-Fri; 10am-12.30pm, 3-5.30pm Sat, Sun. *Oct-Feb* 10am-12.30pm, 3-5.30pm daily. **Admission** €4.20; €2.40 concessions. **No credit cards.**

Monestir de Santa Maria de Vallbona
973 33 02 66. **Open** *June-Sept* 10.30am-1.30pm, 3.30-7pm Tue-Sat; noon-1.45pm, 4.30-7pm Sun. *Oct-May* 10.30am-1.30pm, 3.30-6pm Tue-Sat; noon-1.45pm, 4.30-6pm Sun. **Admission** €2.40; €2 concessions. **No credit cards.**

Monestir de Santes Creus
977 63 83 29. **Open** *Mid Mar-mid Sept* 10am-1.30pm, 3-7pm Tue-Sun. *Mid Sept-mid Jan* 10am-1.30pm, 3-5.30pm Tue-Sun. *Mid Jan-mid Mar* 10am-1.30pm, 3-6pm Tue-Sun. **Admission** €4; €2.50 concessions. Free Tue. **No credit cards.**

Where to stay & eat

In Montblanc, **Fonda Colom** (C/Civaderia 3, 977 86 01 53, set lunch €12) is an inn behind the Plaça Major. You can eat and also stay at the highly recommended **Fonda dels Àngels** (Plaça dels Àngels 1, 977 86 01 73, closed dinner Sun, closed 3wks Sept, set lunch €10.50-€16.10, rates €35.50). If this is full, try the large **Hotel Ducal** (Francesc Macià 11, 977 86 00 25, rates €39-€45.40).

In L'Espluga de Francolí, on the way to Poblet, you'll find the **Hostal del Senglar** (Plaça Montserrat Canals, 977 87 01 21, rates €45-€53), a wonderful country hotel that serves great Catalan food (mains €12). There is also accommodation in Poblet's neighbouring village of Vimbodí in the **Fonoll** (C/Ramon Berenguer IV 2, 977 87 03 33, rates €33). Santes Creus has the equally cheap **Hostal Grau** (C/Pere El Gran 3, 977 63 83 11, rates €36). Good Catalan food can also be had here (mains €10) or at the **Restaurant Catalunya** (C/Arbreda 2, 977 63 84 32, closed Wed, set lunch €9) further down the hill.

Getting there

By bus

Hispano Igualadina (93 430 43 44) runs daily services to Montblanc from C/Europa (behind the branch of El Corte Inglés on Avda Diagonal). There are more buses running from Valls and Tarragona.

Fine vines

The recent arrival of powerful Priorat reds at the top end of the wine market has cemented Catalonia's reputation as a leading European wine-producing area. Monks were growing wine in the Priorat as long ago as the 11th century, but the area had been all but abandoned when young winemaker Alvaro Palacios set up a tiny vineyard here in the late 1980s. He battled against steep hills and a sceptical wine industry, but within a few years he was winning international acclaim and his wines were fetching some of the highest prices ever reached by Spanish wines.

The other big success story is, of course, cava. Phenomenal amounts of this light sparkling wine are made in the tiny town of Sant Sadurní d'Anoia, home to the cava giants of **Freixenet** and **Codorniu** (the first company to make cava). Manuel Raventos, heir to the Codorniu estate, worked in Champagne in the 1870s and returned to Catalonia with the brilliant idea of making sparkling wine using French methods and local grapes. His simple concept has spawned a massive company, now housed in lavish *Modernista* cellars designed by Puig i Cadafalch. Tours also visit the underground cellars, all 26 kilometres (16 miles) and five floors of them, on a train. Nearby Freixenet, which distributes some four million cases of cava to 140 countries each year, also makes for a fascinating tour.

In the nearby town of Vilafranca del Penedès, the region's largest winemaker, **Torres**, runs tours at its headquarters on the outskirts of town (not to be confused with its offices opposite the train station). Miguel Torres has long been one of Spain's most influential winemakers, responsible for introducing modern winemaking practices to the region.

Vilafranca also has a wine museum, the **Museu del Vi** (93 890 05 82, closed Mon, admission €3) in a medieval palace in the middle of town. The best place to try the local wines is **Inzolia** (C/Palma 21, 93 818 19 38, closed Mon morning, Sun), a small, cosy wine bar with an excellent list of wines available by the glass, good tapas and a well-priced shop with a great range of local wines.

Catalonia has several other *denominació d'origen* wine regions. The small Alella, just east of Barcelona, is best known for whites. More important is Terra Alta, near the Priorat in Tarragona and also renowned for its heavy reds; Gandesa is the capital. Look out too for the Bodega Cooperativa in Falset, designed by Gaudí's disciple César Martinell, and the splendidly weird Cooperativa Agrícola in Gandesa, two more great *Modernista* contributions to the wine trade.

Most of the main wine towns have festivals to celebrate the grape harvest (*verema*). In Alella it takes place around the first weekend in September. Much larger are events in Vilafranca on the first Sunday in October, and Sant Sadurní, usually held a week later. The Reina del Cava, the Cava Queen, is crowned in Sant Sadurní. For more details, ask at the Palau Robert tourist office in Barcelona (*see p321*) or local tourist offices.

It is essential to book ahead for the vineyards, and best to have a car as public transport is infrequent.

Cellars

Can Soniol del Castell

Masia Grabuac, Ctra de Vilafranca a Font Rubí (BV2127) km 6, Font Rubí (93 897 84 26). **Open** by appointment.
A limited quantity of very fine cava is made at this vineyard, centred on a historic *masia*.

Caves Codorniu

Avda Codorniu, Sant Sadurní d'Anoia (93 818 32 32). **Open** 9am-5pm Mon-Fri;

By car

For Montblanc, Take the A2, then A7, then back on the A2 to exit 9; or take the toll-free N340 to El Vendrell, then the C51 for Valls, and the N240 for Montblanc (112km/70 miles).

For Poblet, take the N240 west from Montblanc and turn left in L'Espluga de Francolí.

For Vallbona de les Monges, take the C14 north from Montblanc towards Tàrrega and turn left on to a signposted side road.

For Santes Creus, turn off the C51 or A2 before Valls, following signs to Vila-rodona.

By train

RENFE trains leave from Sants or Passeig de Gràcia to Montblanc. There are five trains a day. Journey takes about 2hrs.

Tourist information

Oficina de Turisme de Montblanc

Antiga Esglesia de Sant Francesc (977 86 17 33). **Open** 10am-1.30pm, 3-6.30pm Mon-Sat; 10am-2pm Sun.

Caves Codorniu.

9am-1pm Sat, Sun. **Admission** free Mon-Fri; €1.50 (incl free champagne glass) Sat, Sun. Tour includes a short film, a mini-train ride through the cellars and a tasting.

Caves Freixenet

C/Joan Sala 2, Sant Sadurní d'Anoia (93 891 70 00). **Tours** 10am, 11.30am, 3.30pm, 5pm Mon-Thur; 10am, 11.30am Fri. **Admission** free.
The cellars are directly opposite the station.

Scala Dei

Rambla de la Cartoixa, Scala Dei (977 82 70 27). **Open** by appointment. **Admission** free. Housed in a 12th-century monastery. Great reds, in particular the Cartoixa Scala Dei.

Torres

Finca El Maset, Pacs del Penedes (93 817 74 87/www.torres.es). **Open** 9am-5pm Mon-Fri; 9am-6pm Sat; 9am-1pm Sun. Tours on the hour. **Admission** free.

Getting there

Alella By bus Autocars Casas (93 798 11 00) from corner of Gran Via and C/Roger de Flor.

By car NII north to Montgat, then left turn to Alella (15km/9 miles).

Alt Penedès By car A2, then A7 to Sant Sadurní (44km/27 miles) and Vilafranca (55km/34 miles), or A2, then toll-free N340 from Molins de Rei, which is much slower. By train RENFE from Sants or Plaça Catalunya; trains leave hourly 6am-10pm (journey time 45min). Torres and Cordorniu are both a taxi ride from Vilafranca and Sant Sadurní stations.

Falset, Scala Dei & Gandesa By car A2, then A7 to Reus, and right on to N420 for Falset (143km/89 miles) and Gandesa (181km/112 miles). For Scala Dei take T710 from Falset, then turn right at La Vilella Baixa. By train RENFE from Sants or Passeig de Gràcia to Marçà-Falset. Six trains daily (journey time 2hrs). For Gandesa continue to Mora d'Ebre (20min) and catch a local bus.

Tourist information

Falset Avda Catalunya 6 (977 83 10 23); **Gandesa** Avda Catalunya (977 42 06 14); **Sant Sadurní d'Anoia** Plaça de l'Ajuntament 1, baixos (93 891 12 12); **Vilafranca del Penedès** C/Cort 14 (93 892 03 58).

Trips Out of Town

Paradors

If you're looking for a luxurious night's accommodation with a truly local flavour, book into one of Catalonia's paradors. The Spanish government established the Paradores de Turismo network, which now has nearly 90 hotels, in the 1920s to promote regional tourism. It has focused on saving Spain's castles, palaces and convents from falling into disrepair by converting them into hotels, but has also led to the creation of new hotels in particularly beautiful natural settings.

Catalonia has a interesting range of paradors. The ancient town of **Tortosa** was originally built around its parador, an imposing castle up on a hill (Castell de la Suda, 977 44 44 50, rates €82.80-€91.90). While the Romans first created this fortress, it was the Moors who gave the castle its current shape and built the massive internal well (*suda*) fed by the Ebre river. The castle was later converted into a royal palace and the parador retains a regal feel. It has wonderful views over the Ebre delta and Beseit mountains and overlooks the town's magnificent Gothic cathedral.

The closest parador to Barcelona is set in a medieval castle in **Cardona** (Ducs de Cardona, 93 869 12 75, rates €98.40-€114.80). The ninth-century walls enclose a second-century tower and an 11th-century Romanesque church, along with moats and a lush garden. Cardona is not Catalonia's prettiest town, but the parador's vaulted ceilings, thick stone walls and antique furniture transport you back to another era.

One of the more modern paradors in Catalonia is the sparkling white structure on a headland in **Aiguablava** (Platja d'Aiguablava, 972 62 21 62, rates €76.60-€119.50). The views of the Mediterranean and the wooded cove below are matchless. The **Parador de Vic** (Paraje el Bac de Sau, 93 812 23 23, rates €86.80-€91.90) is also in a stunning location, set in the Guilleries mountains above the Sau reservoir. A modern farmhouse, typical of the area, it has a pool set in beautiful gardens. The restaurant is famous for its regional cooking, including hearty stews and, of course, the celebrated local sausages.

The Ebre delta

About an hour down the coast from Tarragona is the **Parc Natural del Delta de l'Ebre** nature reserve, an ecologically remarkable 320-square kilometre (125-square mile) protected area. It's home to almost 300 species of birds (60 per cent of all species found in Europe), including flamingos, great crested grebes, herons, marsh harriers and a huge variety of ducks. The towns of the delta are nothing special, but the natural beauty of the place – the immense, flat, green expanse of wetlands, channels, dunes and still productive rice fields – makes it fascinating all year round.

The town of **Deltebre** is the base for most park services. From there it's easy to make day trips to the bird sanctuaries, especially the remote headland of **Punta de la Banya**. The delta's flatness makes it ideal for walking or cycling (for bicycle hire, check at the tourist office in Deltebre). Small boats offer trips along the river from the north bank about eight kilometres (five miles) east of Deltebre.

Where to stay & eat

In Deltebre you can stay at **El Buitre** (Ctra de Riumar, 977 48 05 28, rates €30); the restaurant serves very good delta rice dishes (€15). The **Delta Hotel** (Avda del Canal, 977 48 00 46, rates €66-€86.70) is a new, ecologically friendly hotel.

An excellent restaurant is **Galatxo** at the mouth of the Ebro (Desembocadura Riu Ebre, 977 26 75 03, closed Mon-Fri Jan, main courses €9.90), which serves paella and local fish specialities. **Riomar** campsite (Urbanització Riomar, 977 26 76 80, rates €12 for two people) between Deltebre and the river mouth has a pool.

Getting there

By car
Take the A2, then A7 via Vilafranca; or the toll-free N340 (Molins de Rei exit from A2).

By train & bus
RENFE from Sants or Passeig de Gràcia every 2hrs to L'Aldea-Amposta (2hrs 30min), then bus (HIFE 977 44 03 00) to Deltebre.

Tourist information

Centre d'Informació Delta de l'Ebre
C/Doctor Marti Buera 22 (977 48 96 79).
Open 10am-2pm, 3-6pm Mon-Fri; 10am-1pm, 3.30-6pm Sat; 10am-1pm Sun.

Girona &
the Costa Brava

There's plenty more to it than suncream and sangria.

Girona

Its location on a hilltop at the branching of two rivers has provided Girona with a spectacularly diverse historic legacy. Over the years, countless invasions have seen the city reborn in numerous guises, including stints as a major Roman trading town and a flourishing Arab centre. Its treasures include a vast Gothic and Romanesque **cathedral**, labyrinthine **Jewish quarter** and the **Banys Àrabs**, a 12th-century Muslim/Jewish bathhouse. Nowadays, this is a vibrant, sophisticated city with a thriving arts scene and strong local traditions.

The cathedral, built between the 11th and 15th centuries on the site of an ancient mosque, dominates the city skyline. A magnificent

Romanesque cloister, a soaring Gothic nave (the world's widest), a Renaissance façade and a five-storey tower provide an eclectic mix of styles to create a stunning whole. The cathedral museum houses the wonderfully preserved 11th-century **Tapestry of the Creation**.

Heading uphill from the cathedral you'll find spectacular views from the **Torre de Gironella**, Girona's highest point, where the Jewish community fled during the wave of pogroms in 1391. The downhill walk from the cathedral is even more spectacular – a flight of steps leads to the river **Onyar**, lined with tall, colourful houses, and traversed by the iron bridge, **Pont de les Peixateries**, designed by Eiffel. This vast structure cuts through the houses and on to the riverside **Rambla**. This

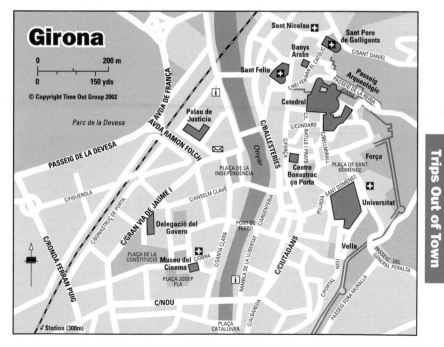

Trips Out of Town

elegant promenade is the social hub of the city and has a string of cafés, bars and galleries.

Just off the cathedral square, **C/Força** (once part of the Roman Via Augusta that stretched between Rome and southern Spain) leads to the atmospheric **Call**, the medieval Jewish quarter. Before the Jews were expelled in 1492, Girona was home to one of Spain's largest Jewish communities and the excellent Jewish museum in the **Centre Bonastruc ça Porta** (C/Sant Llorenç, 972 21 67 61), built where there was once a 15th-century synagogue, tells their story.

Another interesting walk is along the **Passeig Arqueològic**, the remains of the old city walls. The walk passes through pretty landscaped gardens and offers panoramic views of the city. The **Banys Àrabs** are also worth seeing; wonderfully preserved, they have a *mudéjar* blend of Romanesque and Moorish influences in their design. Over on the other side of the river is the **Museu del Cinema**, a fascinating journey through the history of cinematography. The city is at its finest in May, when a weeklong Corpus Christi festival of flowers fills the city's parks and public spaces.

Banys Àrabs
C/Ferran el Catòlic (972 21 32 62). **Open** *Apr-Sept* 10am-7pm Mon-Sat; 10am-2pm Sun. *Oct-Mar* 10am-2pm daily. **Admission** €1.50; 75¢ concessions. **No credit cards.**

Museu del Cinema
C/Sequia 1 (972 41 27 77). **Open** *May-Sept* 10am-8pm Tue-Sun. *Oct-Apr* 10am-6pm Tue-Fri; 10am-8pm Sat; 11am-3pm Sun. **Admission** €3; €1.50 concessions; free under-16s. **Credit** MC, V.

Where to stay & eat
The **Apartments Historic Barri Vell** (C/Bellmirall 4A, 972 22 35 83, rates €60) are fully equipped apartments with kitchens, with original fourth-century stone walls still visible downstairs. **Pensión Bellmirall** (C/Bellmirall 3, 972 20 40 09, rates €56) is a charming and friendly *hostal* with a small garden. The four-star **Hotel Carlemany** (Plaça Miquel Santaló, 972 21 12 12, rates €99.10) is a modern, comfortable hotel, while **Hotel Peninsular** (C/Nou 3 and Avda Sant Francesc 6, 972 20 38 00, rates €53-€58) is good value.

Le Bistrot (Pujada Sant Domenec 4, 972 21 88 03, set lunch €10) is a Parisian-style café-restaurant in a wonderful setting. For top-quality dining in a historic building, try the **Albareda** (C/Albareda 7, 972 22 60 02, closed Mon dinner, Sun, closed first 3wks Aug, main courses €28.30). Cheaper and simpler are **Casa Marieta** (Plaça Independéncia 5, 972 20 10 16, closed Mon, mains €11.40) and **El Pou de Cell**

(C/Força 14, 972 22 37 74, closed Sun dinner, closed 2wks Feb, set lunch €11.90), which has traditional soups and stews. **La Crêperie Bretonne** (Cort Reial 14, 972 21 81 20, closed Sun lunch, Mon, mains €5.10), has excellent crêpes served from an old French school bus.

Getting there

By bus
Barcelona Bus (93 232 04 59) from Estació del Nord.

By car
A7 or toll-free NII.

By train
RENFE from Sants or Passeig de Gràcia (1hr 15min). Trains leave hourly approx 6am-9.15pm.

Tourist information

Oficina de Turisme de Girona
Rambla Llibertat 1 (972 22 65 75). **Open** 8am-8pm Mon-Sat; 9am-2pm Sun.

From Girona to the coast

The village of **Peratallada**, just off the C66, 25 kilometres (15½ miles) east of Girona, is particularly beautiful – the medieval walls are surrounded by a moat and the castle has been converted into an upmarket hotel. The village is also well known for its food – the succulent *galtes* (pigs' cheeks), are a local speciality. Around here are dotted several other well-preserved medieval villages, many within walking distance. Heading west from Peratallada, a left turn takes you to pretty **Vulpellac**, or turn right to **Ullastret**, which has the fascinating ruins of an Iberian settlement from the third century BC and a small **Museu d'Arqueologia** (Puig de Sant Andreu, 972 17 90 58, closed Mon, €2).

Further towards the coast is the medieval village of **Pals**, with fine views and superb buildings, but now seemingly filled with second homes. From here **Begur** is the gateway to the coast; a pretty old town set below the remains of a 14th-century castle, with magnificent views. From there it's a steep three-kilometre (two-mile) walk down to the coast.

Where to stay & eat

In Peratallada, the luxurious hotel option is the 11th-century **Castell de Peratallada** (Plaça del Castell 1, 972 63 40 21, rates €180.30 with breakfast), or try the charming **Ca l'Aliu** (C/Roca 6, 972 63 40 61, rates €48-€52 including breakfast). Pals has the **Barris**

(C/Enginyer Algarra 51, 972 63 67 02, rates €31.90). In Begur, try the **Hotel Rosa** (C/Pi i Rolló 19, 972 62 30 15, closed mid Oct-mid Mar, rates €51.10-€73.30) in the centre of town.

Peratallada has several well-regarded restaurants, including **Restaurant Bonay** (Placa de les Voltes 13, 972 63 40 34, closed mid Oct-Nov, main courses €8); try the house speciality, *oca con nabos* – goose with turnips. In Begur, **Els Patis de Begur** (C/Pi i Rallo 9, 972 62 37 41, closed Mon, mains €13.80) specialises in paellas, and is one of the few places open over the winter. In Pals, **Restaurant Sa Punta** (Urbanizacion Sa Punta, 972 66 73 76, mains €21.30), set by a pool, serves excellent Mediterranean dishes.

Getting twitchy

Spain is one of Europe's most popular birdwatching destinations and Catalonia's mountains, forests and wetlands offer ample opportunities for those whose idea of fun is to spend their holidays skulking through the undergrowth with a pair of binoculars. The wetlands of the **Parc Natural del Delta de l'Ebre** are particularly rich in birdlife – nearly 300 of the 600 bird species found in Europe have been sighted here. The area is a vital breeding ground for birds who rest and feed in the delta during the winter migratory season. The flocks of flamingos make a particularly spectacular sight, and the wetlands are inundated with different species of herons, egrets, waders, gulls, ducks and terns. Even non-birdwatchers could hardly fail to be enthused by the evocatively named whiskered tern, moustached warbler, lesser short-toed lark and the red-necked nightjar.

The **Reserves Naturals del Delta del Llobregat**, between Casteldefells and Sitges, also have a remarkable range of birdlife, despite pollution problems in the Llobregat river. Some 350 species of birds live in the unusual mix of salt water marshes, pine groves, lagoons and beaches. Many endangered birds nest here and species include black-winged stilts, scoops owl, little egret and purple heron. In winter, the area is swamped with lapwings and golden plovers.

Another important refuge for migrating birds are the marshes of **Parc Natural de l'Aiguamolls de l'Empordà**, near Girona. More than 300 species have been recorded, almost 100 of which nest here, including the stone curlew, kingfisher, moustached warbler and bee-eater. In spring, when icy northern winds make the Pyrenees impassable for birds, more than 100 species have been seen here in a single day.

The Pyrenees themselves are home to several spectacular species of forest and mountain birds. The massive griffin vultures and bearded vultures are truly extraordinary-looking, while other interesting

species that have been spotted here include the peregrine falcon, wallcreeper, golden eagle and snow finch.

Tourist information

Parc Natural de l'Aiguamolls
The information centre (972 45 42 22) is at El Cortalet. To get there by car, take the A7 or N11 from Barcelona, then the Figueres exit to Roses, go through Castelló d'Empuries and turn off to Sant Pere Pescador and follow the signs to the information centre.

Parc Natural del Delta de l'Ebre
The park's information office (*see p288*) can point you in the direction of boat tours, which leave daily.

Reserves Naturals del Delta del Llobregat
The park's office (93 658 67 61) is off the Autovia de Castelldefel (C31). Go past the airport and after about 2km (1.2 miles) follow the signs to Toro Bravo's campsite. The information office is next door.

The bay at **Aiguablava**.

Getting there

By bus
Barcelona Bus (93 232 04 59) to Girona from Estació del Nord. Sarfa (93 265 11 58) has nine daily buses to Palafrugell; some continue to Begur.

By car
A7 or toll-free NII to Girona. For Peratallada, Pals and Begur take exit 6 from A7 or leave NII after Girona and take C66.

Tourist information

Oficina de Turisme de Begur
Plaça de l'Església 8 (972 62 40 20). **Open** 10am-1pm, 4-7pm Tue-Sat.

Oficina de Turisme de Pals
Plaça Major 7 (972 63 73 80). **Open** 9am-2pm, 4-8pm Mon-Sat; 10am-2pm Sun.

Costa Brava

The Costa Brava ('wild' or 'rugged' coast) was named by journalist Ferran Agullo in the early 1900s, just as the rest of the world was beginning to discover the beauty of this wild stretch of the Mediterranean. Visitors often wrongly assume the Costa Brava is the cluster of heavily touristed towns – **Calella**, **Lloret de Mar**, **Tossa** around the local hub of **Blanes**. Oddly enough, this is not the Costa Brava proper, for which the name was coined. Agullo was referring to an area that lies 50 kilometres (30 miles) further north in the Baix Empordà. This is still a relatively unspoiled area: there are no big sandy beaches and public

transport is limited, so, with the exception of the unlovely resort of **Roses**, the area has largely escaped mass tourism.

Accommodation facilities are relatively small-scale (it's essential to book in advance), as are nightlife and organised activities for children and families. This does not mean the area is undiscovered, however. In summer it's best to visit midweek to avoid the crowds.

The first town of interest in the *comarca* (district) is **Sant Feliu de Guíxols**, for centuries the principal port for Girona and the cork industry. Sant Feliu has some stunning *Modernista* buildings along the **Passeig Marítim**, a handful of fine Gothic buildings and a spectacular collection of ancient ceramics in the town museum. The curved sandy beach gets crowded, but offers respite from an otherwise rocky coast. A less-visited beach lies three kilometres (two miles) north at **Sant Pol**. Heading north about 20 kilometres (12 miles) and avoiding the more built-up tourist areas of **Platja d'Aro** and **Palamós**, you arrive at the main inlets on the peninsula. The northern ones (**Sa Riera**, **Sa Tuna**, **Aiguablava**) are most accessible from Begur, while those further south (**Tamariu**, **Llafranc** and **Calella de Palafrugell**) are best reached from Palafrugell.

Tamariu is a charming town in a small bay, with hotels and bars known for excellent seafood. You can swim from the rocks, and hire boats for exploring, water-skiing or fishing (call Paco Heredia on 972 30 13 10 or 607 29 25 78). Tamariu and nearby **Llafranc** are easily accessible by public transport, with regular buses from **Palafrugell**, the peninsula's transport hub. Just south of Begur, a narrow road takes you to **Fornells** and **Aiguablava**, both in a larger bay. Aiguablava has a beautiful white sandy beach, a small yacht harbour, an old, luxurious hotel and a modern parador.

Sa Riera, at the end of the road from Pals to the coast, is the northernmost cove of the peninsula, with one of its largest sandy beaches. There's a popular nudist beach, the **Illa Roja**, between Sa Riera and **La Platja del Racó**. From Sa Riera a road leads south to **Sa Tuna**, a picturesque fishing village with a stony beach. From there a 40-minute walk along a coastal path takes you northwards through **Aiguafreda**, a small wooded cove, to a spectacular building cut into the promontory beyond. Steps lead down to swimming pools cut into the precipitous cliff-face.

Leaving the Costa Brava outcrop, further up the coast is the small town of **L'Estartit**, a water-sports centre situated opposite the islands known as the **Illes Medes** (Catalonia's only underwater nature reserve and a popular scuba-diving spot). Glass-bottomed boats leave

L'Estartit regularly in June to September, and according to demand in April, May and October, to tour the now rare coral deposits for which the rocky islets are renowned. The more adventurous can go diving. A little inland is the **Castell de Montgrí**, an unfinished but imposing 12th-century castle with fine views.

Water sports

In L'Estartit, for diving around the Illes Medes, try the **Diving Center La Sirena** (C/Camping La Sirena, 972 75 09 54), **Unisub** (Ctra Torroella de Montgrí 15, 972 75 17 68), or **Quim's Diving Center** (Ctra Torroella de Montgrí, km 4.5, 972 75 01 63). In Calella de la Costa, catamarans, kayaks and windsurfing equipment can all be hired at **Club Nàutic Calella** (Passeig Platja, 93 766 18 52).

Where to eat

In Sant Feliu de Guíxols try the **Nàutic** (Port Esportiu, 972 32 06 63, closed Mon, set lunch €9) in the Club Nàutic sailing club, with great views and superb seafood. In Tamariu, try the seafood, particularly the sardines, at the **Royal** on the beachfront (Passeig de Mar 9, 972 62 00 41, mains €9). In Aiguablava, the **Hotel Aiguablava** (Platja de Fornells, 972 62 20 58, closed Nov-Feb) also has an excellent restaurant (set lunch €24.50).

Where to stay

In Sant Feliu de Guíxols, the **Hotel Les Noies** (Rambla del Portalet 10, 972 32 04 00, closed late Oct-early June, rates €34.30) has reasonably priced rooms. The small, friendly **Hotel Plaça** (Plaça Mercat 22, 972 32 51 55, rates €64.30-€96.50) is close to the beach and open all year. The **Casa Rovira** (C/Sant Amanç 106, 972 32 12 02/972 32 48 57, closed mid Oct-mid May, rates €43.90) is a rambling, bohemian *hostal* surrounded by gardens. Just north of Sant Feliu, in S'Agaró, is the nearest luxury option. The **Hostal de la Gavina** (Plaça de la Rosaleda, 972 32 11 00, rates €155.70-€264.50), an antique-filled five-star. Llafranc has the **Hotel Llafranc** (Passeig de Cipsela 16, 972 30 02 08, rates €79-€123 with breakfast), or try the friendly **Hotel Casamar** (C/de Nero 3-11, 972 30 01 04, rates €31.50-€51). Tamariu is home to the relaxed **Hotel Tamariu** (Passeig de Mar 2, 972 62 00 31, closed Nov-Mar, rates €75-€95). In Aiguablava, there's the local parador (*see p288* **Paradors**) or the stately, family-run **Hotel Aiguablava** (*see above*, rates €90), one of the coast's grand hotels. Choose from standard rooms or almost

self-contained villas. Sa Tuna has the **Hostal Sa Tuna** (Platja Sa Tuna, 972 62 21 98, closed Nov-Feb, rates €90.20), with five rooms in a perfect spot by the sea. In Sa Riera is the **Hotel Sa Riera** (Platja de Sa Riera, 972 62 30 00, closed mid Oct-mid Mar, half-board €47.60-€54.70). In L'Estartit is the **Santa Clara** (Passeig Marítim 18, 972 75 17 67, rates €42.10).

Getting there

By bus

Sarfa (93 265 11 58) has 15 buses daily to Sant Feliu from Estació del Nord (journey time 1hr 20min), and nine to Palafrugell (2hrs); some continue to Begur. Change in Palafrugell or Torroella for L'Estartit.

By car

A7 north to exit 9 on to C35/C65 for Sant Feliu de Guíxols, then C31 for Palafrugell (123km/76 miles); or A7 exit 6 for Palafrugell and Begur via La Bisbal.

Tourist information

Oficina de Turisme de L'Estartit

Passeig Marítim (972 75 89 10). **Open** *May* 9am-1pm, 4-7pm Mon-Fri; 10am-2pm Sat. *June, Sept* 9.30am-2pm, 4-8pm Mon-Sat; 10am-2pm Sun. *July, Aug* 9.30am-2pm, 4-9pm Mon-Sat; 10am-2pm Sun. *Oct-Apr* 9am-1pm, 3-6pm Mon-Fri; 10am-2pm Sat.

Oficina de Turisme de Palafrugell

C/Carrilet 2 (972 30 02 28). **Open** *Apr-June, Sept* 10am-1pm, 5-8pm Mon-Sat; 10am-1pm Sun. *July, Aug* 9am-9pm Mon-Sat; 10am-1pm Sun. *Oct-Mar* 10am-1pm, 4-7pm Mon-Sat; 10am-1pm Sun.

Oficina de Turisme de Sant Feliu de Guixols

Plaça Monestir (972 82 00 51). **Open** *Mid June -mid Sept* 10am-2pm, 4-8pm daily. *Mid Sept-mid June* 10am-1pm, 4-7pm Mon-Sat; 10am-2pm Sun.

Figueres to France

The centre of the northern Costa Brava and the *comarca* of **Alt Empordà** is **Figueres**. The Tramontana wind regularly sweeps this area, allegedly leaving the locals slightly touched (read crazy), a fact apparently borne out by two of Figueres' best known sons: Narcís Monturiol, the utopian socialist and inventor of the first submarine, and Salvador Dalí.

Don't be put off by the hideous urban sprawl around Figueres; the centre has some interesting pockets with a lively, tree-lined Rambla and one of Catalonia's most visited attractions, the **Teatre-Museu Dalí** (*see p294* **Surreal estate**). Also worth visiting is the **Museu de l'Empordà** (972 50 23 05) on the Rambla, for a good overview of the area's art and history.

Trips Out of Town

Surreal estate

Since Salvador Dalí's death, Figueres has become an obligatory visit for anyone curious about the great masturbator's special universe. The **Teatre-Museu Dalí**, in Figueres' former theatre, was designed by Dalí, complete with music and bizarre installations, and contains his tomb. During the summer the museum stays open into the evening, with Dalí's own choice of lighting and music. Part of the museum complex is the **Torre Galatea**, Dalí's egg-topped residence (*pictured*).

Along with the two other Empordà properties associated with the great man, this forms the 'Dalí Triangle' (*triangle dalinià*) for aspiring surrealists to disappear into. Dominating the cove of Port Lligat just outside Cadaqués is the artist's own favourite house, the **Casa-Museu de Port Lligat**, a Dalí image in itself with two giant cracked heads on the top wall seen against the rocky hillside and azure sea. The house, designed by Dalí with many strange features, was all but abandoned for years and is in very poor condition. Only eight people are allowed in at a time, so booking is essential.

In Púbol, about 35 kilometres (22 miles) south of Roses in the Baix Empordà, is the 12th-century castle, **Castell de Púbol**, which Dalí bought for his wife and muse, Gala. Here she entertained a string of young men, while Dalí himself was not allowed to visit without an appointment.

Casa-Museu de Port Lligat

972 25 10 15. **Open** *15 Mar-14 June, 16 Sept-6 Jan* 10.30am-6pm Tue-Sun. *15 Jun-15 Sept* 10.30am-9pm Tue-Sun. Closed 7 Jan-14 Mar. **Admission** €8; €5 concs. **No credit cards**.

Castell de Púbol

Info: Teatre-Museu Dalí (972 67 75 00). **Open** *15 Mar-14 June, 16 Sept-1 Nov* 10.30am-6pm Tue-Sun. *15 Jun-15 Sept* 10.30-8pm Tue-Sun. Closed 2 Nov-14 Mar. **Admission** €5.5; €4 concs. **No credit cards**. Púbol is best reached via Girona, not Figueres. Take a train to Girona or Flaçà, and then a Sarfa bus to La Bisbal, which stops at Púbol village. By car, take the NII north from Girona, and then the C66 towards La Bisbal.

Teatre-Museu Dalí

Plaça Gala-Salvador Dalí 5, Figueres (972 67 75 00). **Open** *July-Sept* 9am-7.45pm Tue-Sun. *Oct-June* 10.30am-5.45pm Tue-Sun. **Admission** €9; €6.5 concs. **No credit cards**.

East of Figueres, **Roses** is the area's largest tourist town. A fairly unattractive place, it has a glut of hotels, discos and (often overpriced) restaurants. It also has a 16th-century citadel; perhaps its only redeeming feature. To the south are the **Aiguamolls de l'Empordà**, a nature reserve and birdwatcher's paradise in the wetlands at the mouth of the Fluvià river (*see p291* **Getting twitchy**). It's home to many types of fish and amphibians – and mosquitoes, so take insect repellent.

From Roses the road climbs through spectacular switchbacks with fabulous views to take you to **Cadaqués**, which sits in splendid isolation at the end of the **Cap de Creus** peninsula. Picasso painted some of his best cubist works here around 1910, but the once

remote fishing village became best known around a decade later when Dalí and his surrealist circle flocked here. The town later became the favourite summer resort of Barcelona's cultural elite, yet in the tourist-boom years high-rise hotel-building was barred from Cadaqués, so it has kept its narrow streets and whitewashed houses. The village's cultural season includes a summer classical music festival. Thanks to its chic rating, Cadaqués is relatively expensive, but still strikingly beautiful. The peninsula around it is an extraordinary mass of rock, lined by tiny coves (many reachable only by boat) that offer the chance for complete relaxation. A short walk and you're in **Port Lligat**, the tiny bay where Dali built his main home. Beyond it a road continues to Cap de Creus, with its lighthouse, nature reserve and unique, pock-marked rock formations used as a location in many science-fiction movies. **Port de la Selva**, on the cape's north side, towards the border with France, has never received the accolades showered on Cadaqués, yet is also unspoilt, quieter and closer to the magnificent Romanesque monastery of **Sant Pere de Rodes**, often lost in clouds on the mountain above the town. Sant Pere was founded in 1022, and large sections of it are still intact.

Alternatively, south of Figueres are the well-preserved remains of the ancient city of **Empúries**, founded in 600 BC by the Phoenicians, recolonised by the Greeks and finally by the Romans in AD 2. Ruins from all three periods, as well as the layout of the original Greek harbour, are clearly visible. It's a picturesque and atmospheric ancient site, and right next to a beach. The nearest town, **L'Escala**, has an attractive beach and port, and is noted for its fine anchovies.

Sant Pere de Rodes

No phone. **Open** *June-Sept* 10am-7pm Tue-Sun. *Oct-May* 10am-1.30pm, 3-5pm Tue-Sun. **Admission** €1.80; 90¢ concessions. **No credit cards.**

Water sports

In Cadaqués, **Sotamar** (Avda Caritat Serinyana 17, 972 25 88 76) has 25 diving sites, while further south in L'Escala **Kayaking Costa Brava** (C/Enric Serra 42, 972 77 38 06) gives kayaking courses and guided trips from Tamariu to Aiguablava. Half-day trips are €36. For diving from Roses, try **Poseidon** (C/Bernd i Barbara Mörker 972, 25 57 72/972 25 44 07)

Where to stay & eat

In Figueres, the **Hotel Duran** (C/Lasauca 5, 972 50 12 50, rates €59-€64) is a comfortable place with lots of interesting mementoes from Dalí's visits, while the **Hostal Bon Repòs** (C/Villalonga 43, 972 50 92 02, rates €24) is a good budget option. Restaurants in C/Jonquera are cheapish, with tables outside in summer. **Presidente** (Ronda Firal 33, 972 50 17 00, closed Mon, set lunch €12) offers good, solid Catalan fare and excellent seafood. Near Roses is legendary restaurant **El Bulli** (*see p141*), for those who can afford it.

Further north in Cadaqués, there are not many hotels for the summer demand, and smaller *hostals* may be closed out of season, so always book. Try **Hostal Marina** (C/Riera 3, 972 25 81 99, closed Jan-Easter, rates €48.20) or the **Pension Vehí** (C/Església 6, 972 25 84 70,

rates €31.60). **Playa Sol** (Playa Pianc 3, 972 25 81 00, closed Dec-Feb, rates €138-€175 including breakfast) has lovely sea views. The **Misty** (C/Nova Port Lligat, 972 25 89 62, rates €58-€72) has a pool, or try the **Llane Petit** (C/Doctor Bartomeus 37, 972 25 10 20, closed 2nd wk Jan-Feb, rates €69.60-€108.30).

The best-known restaurant in Cadaqués is **La Galiota** (C/Narcís Monturiol 9, 972 25 81 87, closed Nov-Easter, set lunch €15.10). **Casa Anita** (C/Miguel Roset, 972 25 84 71, mains €12) is a long-running, very popular, family-owned place with excellent seafood and long queues; cheaper but also good is **Pizzeria Plaza** (Passeig Marítim 10, no phone, mains €10). At Cap de Creus, the **Restaurant Cap de Creus** (972 19 90 05) specialises in fresh fish and Indian curries (€9-€18). Rooms can also be rented in this stunning position on the wild headland jutting out into the sea.

In Port de la Selva, the **Porto Cristo** (C/Major 59, 972 38 70 62, closed Jan & Feb, rates €70.90-€120.50) is the luxury option. Near Empúries, if you have a car, the best place to stay is the village of Sant Martí d'Empúries, which has the comfortable situated **Riomar** (Platja del Riuet, 972 77 03 62, rates €56-€74).

Getting there

By bus

Barcelona Bus (93 232 04 59) has several buses daily to Figueres from Estació del Nord (2hrs 30min). Sarfa (93 265 11 98) has two buses daily to Roses and Cadaqués (2hrs 15min), and services to Roses, Port de la Selva, Cadaqués and L'Escala from Figueres.

By car

A7 or NII to Figueres (120km/74 miles). For Roses, take the C260 from Figueres.

By train

RENFE from Sants or Passeig de Gràcia to Figueres (journey 2hrs). Trains leave every hour.

Tourist information

Oficina de Turisme de Cadaqués

C/Cotxe 2A (972 25 83 15). **Open** *Easter-Oct* 10am-7pm Mon-Sat; 10am-1pm Sun. *Nov-Easter* 10am-1pm, 4-7pm Mon-Sat.

Oficina de Turisme de L'Escala

Plaça de les Escoles 1 (972 77 06 03). **Open** 10am-1.30pm, 4-7pm Tue-Fri; 10am-2pm Sat.

Oficina de Turisme de Figueres

Plaça del Sol (972 50 31 55). **Open** *Mar-June, Oct* 9am-3pm, 4.30-8pm Mon-Fri; 9.30am-1.30pm, 3.30-6.30pm Sat. *July, Aug* 9am-8pm Mon-Sat; 10am-3pm Sun. *Sept* 9am-8pm Mon-Sat. *Nov-Feb* 9am-3pm Mon-Fri.

Trips Out of Town

Vic to the Pyrenees

Inland lie medieval villages surrounded by spectacular mountain scenery.

Vic, Rupit & Les Guilleries

The lively town of **Vic** is surrounded by the spectacular mountain nature reserves and ideal walking territory of **Montseny**, **Les Guilleries** and **Collsacabra**. The town began life as the capital of the Ausetian tribe, became a Roman city, and later fell briefly to the Moors, who lost it to Wilfred the Hairy in the ninth century. Since then it has remained a religious, administrative and artistic centre.

If possible, visit Vic on a Saturday, when the market brings the medieval Plaça Major to life, or come during the **Mercat del Ram** (livestock market), held the week before Easter. Vic's other famous event is a three-day music festival in September. At other times of the year, monuments worth seeing are the **Temple Romà** (Roman temple), now an art gallery, and the neo-classical **Catedral de Sant Pere**, which has a perfectly preserved 11th-century bell tower and a set of sombre 20th-century murals by Josep Lluís Sert. In a corner of the Plaça Major is the 14th-century **Casa de la Ciutat**. Vic is also famous for its *embotits* (charcuterie), and shops selling *botifarres*, *llonganisses* and other kinds of sausages can be found in almost every street.

The district of **Osona**, of which Vic is the capital, is full of interesting villages, and can be recommended to anyone with limited time who seeks a taste of the Catalan countryside at its best. The most rewarding route is up the C153 road towards Olot into **Les Guilleries**, stopping at **Rupit**, an extraordinarily beautiful and ancient village built against the side of a medieval castle, with a precarious hanging bridge crossing a gorge. An 11th-century sanctuary, **Sant Joan de Fàbregues**, and massive farmhouses such as **El Bac de Collsacabra** and **El Corriol** (which has a collection of ceramics and historical artefacts), are all within walking distance.

Where to stay & eat

The luxury option for hotels is the relatively modern **Parador de Vic** in a fabulous location overlooking the Ter gorge (*see p288* **Paradors**). **Can Pamplona** (Crta de Vic a Puigcerdà 10, 93 883 31 12, rates €77-€84.30) is cheaper. In Tavèrnoles, just off the C153 from Vic,

Mas Banús (93 812 20 91) is a giant old *masia*. Self-contained accommodation for six for the weekend costs €220. In Rupit, there's the delightful *hostal*-restaurant **Estrella** (Plaça Bisbe Font 1, 93 852 20 05, closed Jan-Easter, rates €77.30, set lunch €13).

Vic has good medium-price restaurants. **Basset** (C/Sant Sadurní 4, 93 889 02 12, closed Sun, set menus €10.50-€14.50), has great Mediterranean dishes. **Ca l'U** (Plaça Santa Teresa 4-5, 93 889 03 45, set lunch €11) is a more traditional inn with pork and seafood dishes. For something special, take the N152 Ripoll road and before Sant Quirze de Besora turn on to a short road signposted to the **Rectoria d'Oris** (C/Rectoria, 93 859 02 30, closed Tue, main courses €19). One of the best restaurants in the area, it also has a great view.

Getting there

By bus
Empresa Sagalès (93 231 27 56) from the corner of Passeig Sant Joan and C/Diputació to Vic. For Rupit, take a local bus from Vic.

By car
Take the C17, signed for Puigcerdà, to Vic (65km/ 40 miles). For Rupit, take the C26 out of Vic (signposted to Olot).

By train
RENFE from Sants or Plaça Catalunya to Vic. Trains leave about every 90min. Journey time is 1hr 20min.

Tourist information

Oficina de Turisme de Vic
Plaça Major 1 (93 886 20 91). **Open** 9am-8pm Mon-Fri 9am-2pm, 4-7pm Sat; 10am-1pm Sun.

Besalú & Olot

Besalú, 25 kilometres (15½ miles) north of Girona, is a gem, with a medieval centre that is wonderfully peaceful out of season. The whole town centre has been declared a monument and, with few modern buildings, seems suspended in time. Of special interest are the streets of the old Jewish *call* and the *mikveh* (Jewish baths), the two main squares and the church of **Santa Júlia**, but most eye-catching of all is the intact, 12th-century fortified bridge with a gatehouse

Modernista buildings in **Olot**.

in the middle that spans the Fluvià. The
N260 road continues west to **Olot**, passing
extraordinary villages, such as **Castellfollit
de la Roca**, which looks spectacular, perched
atop a precipitous crag, but is perhap better
from a distance. The medieval town of Olot
was destroyed in an earthquake in 1427, but
it has imposing 18th-century and *Modernista*
buildings. In the last century it was home to a
school of landscape painters; the local **Museu
de la Garrotxa** (C/Hospice 8, 972 27 91 30,
closed Sun afternoon, admission €1.80) has
works by them and Ramon Casas, Santiago
Rusiñol and other *Modernista* artists.

Olot's most unusual feature, though, is
its 30-odd extinct volcanoes and numerous
lava slips, sometimes no more than green
humps in the ground, that surround it to form
the **Parc Natural de la Zona Volcànica
de la Garrotxa**. Just south of the town
on the Vic road you'll find a museum and
information centre, the **Casal dels Volcans**
(Ctra Santa Coloma 43, 972 26 67 62, closed
Mon, admission €1.80). This is a spectacular
place for walking, with many marked routes –
ask at the tourist information centre for maps.

On the pretty back road south-east to
Banyoles (G1524) is a delightful beech forest,
La Fageda d'en Jordà, made famous by
poet Joan Maragall.

Where to stay & eat

The **Venència** (C/Major 6, 972 59 12 57,
rates €30) is a decent hotel in Besalú, or try
the riverside **Siqués** (rates €51.60), which is
above the **Fonda Siqués** restaurant (Avda
Lluís Companys 6-8, 972 59 01 10, closed Sun
dinner, Mon, closed Christmas Eve-Jan, set
lunch €9 Mon-Fri). In Olot, **La Perla** (Avda
Santa Coloma 97, 972 26 23 26, rates €49.10)
is a large hotel with a good restaurant.

Restaurants in Besalú include the **Cúria
Reial** (Plaça de la Llibertat 15, 972 59 02 63,
closed Mon dinner, Tue, closed Feb, mains
€14.50) for good traditional cooking. In Olot,
Can Guix (C/Mulleres 3-5, 972 261 040,
closed Sun, closed 2wks July-Aug) has great,
cheap, local dishes (mains €6), or there's the
Restaurant Les Cols (Crta de la Canya,
972 26 92 09, closed Sun, closed 3wks July-
Aug, mains €22.90) set in a picturesque
masia with a garden. Restaurant **Hostal
de Sant Salvador** (Carretera de Camprodon
14, Sant Salvador de Bianya, 972 19 51 54,
closed Tue dinner, Wed, mains €12), around
12 kilometres (eight miles) north of Olot, is
one of the finest restaurants in the area – try
the *menu degustación*.

Getting there

By bus
TEISA (972 20 48 68) to Besalú and Olot from the
corner of C/Pau Claris and C/Consell de Cent.

By car
For Besalú and Olot, take the C66 from Girona.

Tourist information

Oficina de Turisme de Olot
C/Bisbe Lorenzana 15 (972 26 01 41). **Open**
9am-2pm, 5-7pm Mon-Fri; 10am-2pm, 5-7pm Sat;
11am-2pm Sun.

Ripoll to the Vall de Núria

Ripoll, north of Vic, grew up around the
unique church and monastery of **Santa Maria
de Ripoll**. Known as the 'cradle of Catalonia',
the church has a superb 12th-century
Romanesque stone portal. This valley was
the original fiefdom of Wilfred the Hairy before
he became Count of Barcelona. He is buried
in Santa Maria, which he founded in 879.
Wilfred also founded the monastery and
town of **Sant Joan de les Abadeses**, ten
kilometres (six miles) east up the C26 road,
and worth a visit for its Gothic bridge as well
as the 12th-century monastery. The monastery

Trips Out of Town

A house in the country

The mountains and other remote pockets of countryside offer some of Catalonia's most beautiful scenery, and there are now hundreds of *casa rurales*, also known as *casa de pagès*, open to visitors. This allows people to stay in far-flung areas and offers a peaceful alternative to hotels in the busier regions.

Many of these houses are beautifully restored *masies* (manor farmhouses), which, along with opening new areas up to tourism, allow visitors to gain a sense of local life, explore the countryside and even take part in farm life. Facilities vary enormously: some offer very simple B&B or self-contained accommodation, some provide meals and self-catering annexes, others offer real hotel service and luxuries such as pools.

The Generalitat's annual guide, *Residències: Casa de Pagès* (€4.80), lists over 500 houses and is available from bookshops or the Palau Robert information centre (*see p321*). The Catalan Farmers' Union also has a very helpful *agroturisme* website, in English, at www.agronet.org/agroturisme.

Mas Ardèvol

Carretera de Porrera a Faset, 43739 Porrera (tel/fax 977 82 80 21,/mobile 630 324 578,/ www.terra.es/personal2/ruraltur). By car A2, then A7 towards Tarragona, then N420 to Falset and turn right on the road to Porrera. **Rates** double €79. **Credit** MC, V.
This 19th-century farmhouse has three completely renovated bedrooms, plus a garden and terrace with views of the Montsant mountains and the vineyards of the Priorat. Dinner can be arranged, as can tours of the local wineries. Gemma Peyre also runs two award-winning self-contained apartments (sleeping four and seven) in nearby Porrera; they are available for weekends for €120.20 and €210.40.

Mas La Garganta

17814 La Pinya, Olot (972 27 12 89/www. turismerural.net/garganta). By car A7 or NII to Girona, then C66 to Olot, then C26 Vic road, and before reaching Les Presses turn right to La Pinya. By bus Olot or Les Presses (3km/2 miles). **Rates** €44 per person, incl breakfast & dinner. **Credit** V.
A 18th-century *masia* (*pictured*) offering B&B or self-catering in the hills of La Garrotxa, with magnificent views. There are seven double rooms, and local cheeses, liqueurs and meats are for sale. The *masia* also runs walking tours with two *masies* nearby, so you can stay in one place and walk, without bags, to the next.

Mas Salvanera

17850 Beuda, Girona (972 59 09 75/ www.salvanera.com). By car A7 to Girona, then C66 to Besalú, then N260 to Figueres and turn off to Maià de Montcal. Closed 1wk early Jan, last wk June, 1wk mid Sept. **Rates** double €84 B&B. **Credit** AmEx, MC, V.
This immaculately restored 17th-century *masia* is surrounded by a pretty garden with orchards and a large pool. Set in the foothills of the Pyrenees, near the lovely town of Besalú, it has everything from fireplaces and barbecues to toys and swings for children. There are eight comfortable en suite rooms.

Masia Can Cardús

08775 Torrelavit, Alt Penedès (93 899 50 18). By car A2, then A7 to Sant Sadurní d'Anoia, then north-west to Torrelavit. By bus or train Sant Sadurní (4km/2.5 miles). **Rates** double €36.10. **No credit cards.**
This giant *masia*, a working farm and vineyard in the Penedès wine country north of Sant Sadurní, is a former 11th-century Benedictine monastery. Six rooms sleep two, three or four.

El Molí

17469 Siurana d'Empordà, Alt Empordà (972 52 51 39/www.spain-farmhouse-holidays. com). By car A7 to Figueres (exit 4), then C31 towards L'Escala and right turn to Siurana. By bus local service from Figueres. **Rates** double €48 B&B; suite €61. **Credit** MC, V.
Amid a big garden full of medicinal herbs, this is a beautifully restored large *masia* with six rooms. The owners speak English and French and can provide ready-prepared cycle and walking routes in the area. There is also a *masia* to rent, sleeping up to ten.

museum (972 72 00 13, open 10am-2pm Mon-Fri, 10am-2pm, 4-6pm Sat, Sun, admission €2) covers a thousand years of local life.

From Sant Joan the road leads towards **Camprodon**, on the river Ter, home to a fine Romanesque church, and from there a local road veers left up the main Ter valley to the mountain village of **Setcases**, a famous beauty spot now, sadly, taken over by holiday homes. By now you are into the Pyrenees; the valley road comes to an end at **Vallter 2000** (972 13 60 75), the easternmost ski station in the mountains. As with all ski resorts in the area, the best way to visit is to book a package, available at any travel agent in Barcelona.

Ribes de Freser, the next town on the N152 north of Ripoll, is an attractive base from which to travel to the pretty if slightly gentrified villages of **Campelles** and **Queralbs**. Ribes is also the starting point for the *cremallera*, the FGC's narrow-gauge 'zipper train', which runs via Queralbs along the Freser river up to the sanctuary of **Núria**. Núria itself nestles by a lake on a plateau at over 2,000 metres (6,500 feet).

Home to the second most famous of Catalonia's patron virgins, a wooden statue of the Madonna carved in the 12th century, Núria was a refuge and place of pilgrimage long before then. The mostly 19th-century monastery that surrounds the shrine is not especially attractive, but its location is spectacular. The zipper train offers incredible views and makes Núria an accessible place to try relatively light high-mountain walking or skiing (you can get maps and information from the tourist office).

Where to stay & eat

In Ripoll, the cheap option is **Ca la Paula** (C/Pireneos 6, 972 70 00 11, closed Oct, rates €33). **La Trobada** (Passeig Honorat Vilamanya 4, 972 70 23 53, rates €58), is more comfortable. For meals, **El Racó del Francés** (Plà d'Ordina 11, 972 70 18 94, closed Sat lunch, closed 3wks Aug, set lunch €14.70) serves French dishes. In Sant Joan de les Abadesses, the best beds are at **Janpere** (C/Mestre Andreu 3, 972 72 00 77, rates €37). The attached restaurant, **Sant Pere** (closed Mon) offers local food at reasonable prices (set lunches €8-€9).

In Ribes de Freser, very comfortable rooms can be had at **Catalunya Park Hotel** (Passeig Salvador Mauri 9, 972 72 70 17, closed winter, rates €36.5 half-board, €44 full-board). **Hostal Porta de Núria** (C/Nostra Senyora de Gràcia 3, 972 72 71 37, closed May, rates €25.80) is cheaper. In Queralbs, try **Calamari**

Dramatic **Rupit**. *See p296.*

Hostal l'Avet (C/Major 5, 972 72 73 77, closed Mon-Thur; rates €22). The one good place to eat in Queralbs is **De la Plaça** (Plaça de la Vila 2, 972 72 70 37, closed Tue, closed ten days Sept-Oct, set menu €12.60), which has regional specialities.

In Núria, there's the three-star **Vall de Núria** hotel (C/Santuari Mare de Dèu de Núria, 972 73 20 20, closed 4-29 Nov 2002, rates €53.20-€76.90). You are required to stay for a minimum of two nights.

Getting there

By bus
TEISA (972 20 48 68) from the corner of C/Pau Claris and C/Consell de Cent to Ripoll, Sant Joan de les Abadesses and Camprodon.

By car
Take the C17 direct to Ripoll (104km/65 miles). For Sant Joan de les Abadesses and Camprodon, take the C26 out of Ripoll.

By train
RENFE from Sants or Plaça Catalunya, approx one train every 2hrs (journey time to Ripoll 2hrs). For Queralbs and Núria, change to the *cremallera* train in Ribes de Freser.

Tourist information

Oficina de Turisme de Núria
Estaciò de Montanya del Vall de Núria (972 73 20 20/www.valldenuria.com). Open *July-Sept* 8.20am-8pm daily. *Oct-June* 8.20am-6.15pm daily.

Oficina de Turisme de Ribes de Freser
Plaça del Ayuntamiento 3 (972 72 77 28). **Open** *Sept-July* 10am-2pm, 5-8pm Tue-Sat; 11am-1pm Sun. *Aug* 10am-2pm, 5-8pm Mon-Sat; 11am-1pm Sun.

Trips Out of Town

Berga & Puigcerdà

Some 50 kilometres (31 miles) west of Ripoll on the C26 is **Berga**, capital of the *comarca* (district) of the **Berguedà**. Just north from there the giant cliffs of the **Serra del Cadí**, one of the ranges of the 'Pre-Pyrenees' or Pyrenees foothills, loom above the town, making you feel that you're really in the mountains. Berga also has a medieval castle, **Sant Ferran**, with a suitably storybook air, and a charming old centre, with a Jewish quarter dating back to the 13th century.

It's famous for the frenzied festival of **La Patum**, held in May, and the annual mushroom-hunting competition in the Pla de Puigventós on the first Sunday in October. Great baskets of different wild mushrooms (*bolets*) are weighed in before an enthusiastic public. Anyone interested in participating should contact the tourist office.

Heading north along the C16, uphill into the Cadí, you'll come to the small town of **Bagà**, with partially preserved medieval walls around a pretty old quarter and a central square with Romanesque porticos. It marks the beginning of the **Parc Natural del Cadí-Moixeró**, a gigantic mountain park of 159 square miles (410 square kilometres) containing wildlife and forest reserves and some 20 or so ancient villages. All retain some medieval architecture, and many offer stunning views. Picasso stayed and painted in one village, Gósol, for several weeks in 1906. Rugged and austerely beautiful, the Cadí is rich in wildlife, and can feel more like the American West than the Mediterranean. Chamois, roe and red deer roam the slopes, and there are golden eagles, capercaillies and black woodpeckers.

Above Bagà the C16 road enters the Túnel del Cadí to emerge into the wide, fertile plateau of the **Cerdanya**. Described by writer Josep Pla as a 'huge casserole', the Cerdanya has an obvious geographical unity, but since a treaty signed in 1659 the French and Spanish frontier has run right across its middle, with one Spanish village, Llívia, left stranded in French territory. The fortified church in Llívia is worth visiting for its stunning acoustics.

The snow-capped peaks that ring the valley are laced with ski resorts, including **La Molina** (972 89 20 31), and **Masella** (972 14 40 00). The capital of the area (on the Spanish side), **Puigcerdà**, is a sizeable town heavily touristed by Catalans and French, where discos and après-ski bars mix with remnants of things medieval. Other places of interest in the Cerdanya are the cross-country ski centre of **Lles**, which has a Romanesque church, and **Bellver de Cerdanya**, a hilltop village on the edge of the Cadí-Moixeró that was the unlikely scene of a battle during the Civil War. The village has a park information centre.

Where to stay & eat

In Berga, try the **Estel Hotel** (C/Sant Fruitos 39, 93 821 34 63, rates €45.10-€51.60) or the **Queralt Hotel** (Plaça de la Creu 4, 93 821 06 11, rates €48.30) in the medieval centre. Puigcerdà has plenty of hotels in the town centre, including the small and charming **Avet Blau** (Plaça Santa Maria 14, 972 88 25 52, rates €60.10-€90). The **Hotel Alfonso** (C/Espanya 5, 972 88 02 46, rates €45.10) is more moderate. A little further out in Bolvir, the sumptuous **Torre del Remei** (C/Camí Reial, 972 14 01 82, rates €225.60) also has one of the best (and most expensive) restaurants in the area (main courses €66.30). Cheap, very friendly and dead central is the **Cerdanya** (C/Ramon Cosp 7, 972 88 00 10, mains €15). Excellent regional food, moderately priced, is served at **Casa Clemente** (Avda Dr Puiguillem 6, 972 88 11 66, closed Mon, closed first 2wks July, set lunches €12-€16.60). A pizzeria that also offers good regional dishes is **La Tieta** (C/Dels Ferrers 20, 972 88 01 56, closed Mon-Wed, closed mid June-mid July, pizza €9).

Getting there

By bus

ATSA (93 873 80 08) runs five buses daily to Berga from the corner of C/Balmes and C/Pelai. Journey time is about 2hrs. Alsina Graëlls (93 265 68 66) has daily buses to Puigcerdà from Estació del Nord; journey time is 3hrs.

By car

Take the C55 via Manresa, then C16 to Berga (118km/73 miles) and Bagà. From Bagà continue on the C16 through Túnel de Cadí (toll) for Puigcerdà; a scenic alternative is the C17 and N152 through Vic and Ripoll. Lles and Bellver are off the N260 west from Puigcerdà.

By train

RENFE from Sants or Plaça Catalunya to Puigcerdà. About one train every 2hrs; journey takes about 3hrs.

Tourist information

Oficina de Turisme de Berga

C/Angels 7 (93 821 13 84). **Open** 9am-2pm Mon-Thur; 9am-2pm, 5-8pm Fri, Sat.

Oficina de Turisme de Puigcerdà

C/Querol, baixos (972 88 05 42). **Open** *Mid June-mid Sept* 9am-2pm, 3-8pm Mon-Sat; 10am-2pm Sun. *Mid Sept-mid June* 9am-1pm Mon; 9am-1pm, 4-7pm Tue-Fri; 10am-1.30pm, 4.30-8pm Sat.

Directory

taxidermista...cafè restaurant
Plaça Reial 8   08002 Barcelona   tel. 93 412 45 36

Directory

Getting Around

Barcelona is a compact city and much of it is easy to explore on foot. For longer journeys, an efficient metro (underground) system and buses will get you to most places within half an hour. Bicycles are great for moving about the old city and port, while motorbikes can be handy in traffic; a car is usually more of a liability, and only comes into its own for trips out of town. For details of transport outside Barcelona, *see p276*.

Arriving & leaving

By air

Barcelona's airport is 12 kilometres (seven miles) south of the city in El Prat de Llobregat. Each airline is allocated to one of the two main terminals – A or B – for all its arrivals and departures. In both terminals there are tourist information desks, cash machines and exchange offices (open 7am-11pm daily). For airport info, call 93 298 38 38, or check website www.aena.es/ae/bcn/homepage.htm, which includes updated flight info.

Aerobús

This special bus service is usually the best way of getting into the city. Buses run from outside each terminal, via Gran Via, to Plaça Catalunya. Buses to the airport go from Plaça Catalunya via C/Aragó, and also pick up at Sants railway station and Plaça Espanya. Buses leave the airport every 15min from 6am to midnight Mon-Fri (6.30am-midnight Sat, Sun); and in the opposite direction from Plaça Catalunya, 5.30am-11.15pm Mon-Fri (6am-11.20pm Sat, Sun). The trip takes about 30min; a single ticket costs €3.15. Two local buses, the 105 and 106, also run between the airport (all terminals) and Plaça Espanya;

they take longer, but the 106 runs late (last departure from the airport 3.20am; from Plaça Espanya 3.50am; single ticket €1).

Airport trains

To get to the airport train station, take the long overhead walkway that starts between terminals A and B. Trains stop at four stations in Barcelona: Sants, Plaça Catalunya, Arc de Triomf and Clot-Aragó, all of which are also metro stops. Trains leave the airport at 13 and 43 minutes past each hour, 6.13am-10.43pm Mon-Fri. Trains to the airport leave Plaça Catalunya at 8 and 38 minutes past the hour, 5.38am-10.08pm Mon-Fri (5min later from Sants). Weekend timings vary slightly, but there are still trains every 30min. The journey takes 20-25min and costs €2.10 one way. Tickets are only valid for 2hrs after purchase.

Taxis from the airport

The taxi fare to central Barcelona should be about €12-€18 (depending very much on traffic), including a €1.90 airport supplement. Fares are about 20% higher after 10pm and at weekends. There is a minimum charge for trips to/from the airport of €10.20, and an 80¢ supplement for each large piece of luggage placed in the car boot. Ignore any cab drivers who approach you inside the airport; use the ranks outside the terminal.

Airlines

The appropriate terminal is shown in brackets.
Air Europa (B) 902 401 501/ www.air-europa.com
British Airways (B) 902 111 333/ www.british-airways.com
Easyjet (A) 902 299 992/ www.easyjet.com
Go (A) 901 333 500/www.go-fly.com
Iberia (B) 902 400 500/ www.iberia.com
Virgin Express (A) 900 467 612/ www.virgin-express.com

By bus

Most long-distance coaches (national and international) stop or terminate at **Estació d'Autobusos Barcelona-Nord** at C/Alí Bei 80, next to

Arc de Triomf rail and metro station (map p341 E5; general information 93 265 65 08). The **Estació d'Autobusos Barcelona-Sants**, by Sants rail station and Sants-Estació metro stop, is only a secondary stop for many coaches, but some international Eurolines services (information 93 490 40 00) stop only at Sants.

By car

Approaching Barcelona from virtually any direction, the most direct car access to the Old City area is by getting on to the Ronda Litoral (the coastal half of the ring road), and then taking exit 21 (Paral.lel) if you're coming from the south, or exit 22 (Via Laietana) from the north. Motorways also feed into Avda Diagonal, Avda Meridiana and Gran Via, which all provide straightforward, though sometimes congested, connections with the heart of the city. Tolls are charged on most of the city's main approach routes, payable in cash or by credit card.

By sea

Balearic Islands ferries dock at the **Moll de Barcelona** quay, at the bottom of Avda Paral.lel; **Trasmediterránea** (902 45 46 45/www.trasmediterranea.es) is the main operator. There is also a ferry three times a week between Barcelona and Genoa in Italy, from the **Moll de Ponent**, a few hundred metres further south (Grimaldi Lines; for information, phone its agent Condeminas on 93 443 98 98). Cruise ships use several

Directory

berths around the harbour; when cruisers are in port, a PortBus shuttle service transports passengers on shore leave to the foot of the Rambla.

By train

The giant **Barcelona-Sants** station (map p339 A4) is the stop or terminus for most long-distance trains run by Spanish state railways RENFE. It's about three kilometres (two miles) from the centre, but has a metro stop (Sants-Estació) on line 3 (green, the most direct for the centre) and line 5 (blue). Some international services from France do not go to Sants, but terminate at the 1920s **Estació de França** (map p343 C4), near Ciutadella park and Barceloneta metro. Other trains stop at both stations, and many also stop between the two at **Passeig de Gràcia** (map p336 D4), which can be the handiest for the city centre.

RENFE

902 24 02 02/www.renfe.es.
Open 5am-11.50pm daily.
Credit AmEx, DC, MC, V.
Some English-speaking operators. RENFE tickets can be bought or reserved by phone and delivered to an address or hotel for a small extra fee. For information on non-Spanish European trains, call 93 490 11 22 (open 7am-10pm daily).

Maps

Metro and central area street maps are included at the back of this guide. Tourist offices provide a reasonably detailed free street map, and the Ajuntament tourist offices also have a better map for €1.20. Metro maps are available free at all metro stations (ask for '*una guia del metro*') and city transport information offices (*see below*), which also have free bus maps. Metro and bus maps also indicate access points for the disabled on to public transport. You can find an interactive Barcelona street map at www.bcn.es/guia.

Public transport

The metro is generally the quickest, cheapest and most convenient way of getting around the city, although buses operate all night and cover some 'holes' in the underground network – notably around Plaça Francesc Macià. Public transport, although now highly integrated, is still run by different organisations. Local buses and the metro are run by the city transport authority (TMB). Two underground train lines (from Plaça Catalunya to Reina Elisenda, Les Planes or Avda Tibidabo; and from Plaça Espanya to Cornellà) connect with the metro, but are run by Catalan government railways, the Ferrocarrils de la Generalitat de Catalunya (FGC, often just called '*els Ferrocarrils*'), which also has suburban services.

For transport information call the 010 information line. For details of the Barcelona Card, which gives unlimited travel on public transport, and guided tours, *see p305* **Just the ticket**.

FGC information

Vestíbule, Catalunya FGC station, Eixample (93 205 15 15/www.fgc. catalunya.net). **Open** *Sept-June* 7am-9pm Mon-Fri. *July, Aug* 8am-8pm Mon-Fri. **Map** p342 B1.
Branches: FGC Provença (open 9am-7pm Mon-Fri, closed Aug); FGC Plaça Espanya (open 9am-2pm, 4-7pm Mon-Fri).

TMB information

Main vestíbule, Metro Universitat, Eixample (93 318 70 74/www.tmb. net). **Open** 8am-8pm Mon-Fri. **Map** p342 A1.
Branches: Vestíbule, Metro Sagrada Família; vestíbule, Metro Sants Estació (both open 7am-9pm Mon-Fri; 10am-2pm, 3-6pm Sat, Sun); vestíbule, Metro Diagonal (open 8am-8pm Mon-Fri).

Metro & FGC

The five metro lines are identified by a number and a colour on maps and station signs. At interchanges, lines in a particular direction are indicated by the names of the stations at the end of the line, so you should know which they are when changing between lines. On FGC lines, note that some suburban trains do not stop at all stations.

The metro currently operates from 5am to 11pm (lines 2, 3 and 5 till midnight) Monday to Thursday; 5am to 2am Friday and Saturday; 6am to midnight Sunday. Weekday hours on all metro lines are to be extended until midnight during 2002. The FGC has roughly similar hours.

Buses

City bus stops are easy to find: many routes originate in or pass through Plaça Catalunya, Plaça Universitat and/or Plaça Urquinaona. Because of the many one-way streets, buses often do not follow exactly the same route in both directions, but run along parallel streets.

Most bus routes operate between 6am and 10.30pm, Monday to Saturday, although many begin earlier and finish later. Usually there is a bus at least every 10 to 15 minutes, but they are less frequent before 8am, after 9pm and on Saturdays. On Sundays, buses are less frequent still on most routes, and a few do not run at all. You board buses at the front, and get off through the middle or rear doors. Only single tickets can be bought on board; if you have a *targeta* (*see p305* **Just the ticket**), insert it into the machine just behind the driver as you board.

Useful routes

Buses that connect Plaça Catalunya with popular parts of town include:
22 via Gràcia to the Tramvia Blau on Tibidabo and the Pedralbes monastery
24 goes up Passeig de Gràcia and is the best way to get to Parc Güell
41, 66 and **67** go to the Plaça Francesc Macià area, which is not served by the metro

Just the ticket

With a standard fare of €1 for any urban-area journey, the ticket system on Barcelona public transport sounds straightforward. It is, but after just a few rides it becomes more convenient and cheaper to use a multi-journey ticket or *targeta*. The basic ten-trip *targeta* is the T-10 (*Te-Deu* in Catalan). It cuts the cost per trip by more than 40 per cent, and can be shared by any number of people, so long as one trip is cancelled on the card for each person travelling.

The T-10, along with the other 'integrated' *targetes* listed below, lets you on to any of the four main transport systems (local RENFE and FGC trains, the metro and buses), and you can transfer between them for free for 75 minutes after the initial validation. In most cases, when transferring you have to insert your card into a machine a second time, but another unit will not be deducted. A single ticket does not allow free transfers.

A T-10 can be bought all over town – in newsagents, lottery shops and Servi-Caixa machines – as well as on the metro and train systems, but you can't buy one on a bus. There are also more expensive versions of all *targetes* used for travelling to the outer zones of the metropolitan region, but the zone 1 prices listed below will get you anywhere in Barcelona city's urban area – except to the airport.

Integrated *targetes*

All are available at metro and FGC ticket counters, and some at ticket vending machines and Servi-Caixas (currently the T-10, T-50/30 and T-Mes).

T-10 Valid for ten trips; can be shared by two or more people. €5.60.

T-Familiar Gives 70 trips in any 30-day period; can be shared. €34.30.

T-50/30 Gives 50 trips in any 30-day period; for one person only. €23.40.

T-Día Unlimited travel for one person only, for one day. €4.20.

T-Mes Unlimited travel for one person only, for any 30-day period. €36.30.

T-Trimestre Unlimited Travel for one person only, for three months. €100.

Other *targetes*

3 Dies and **5 Dies** Unlimited travel for one person for three (or five) days on the metro, buses and FGC trains. Also sold at tourist offices. €10.20 and €15.60.

Aerobús + Bus + Metro Unlimited travel for one person on the metro and buses (not FGC), including a return trip to the airport. Three-day (€13.80) or five-day (€18) pass. Sold on board the Aerobús.

Barcelona Card This tourist discount scheme also gives unlimited travel for one, two or three days.

---

41 also goes to Ciutadella and the Vila Olímpica
45 stops in Plaça Urquinaona and goes down to the beach near Port Olímpic.

Three good crosstown routes:
50 goes from north-east Barcelona past Sagrada Família, along Gran Via and then climbs Montjuïc from Plaça Espanya to Miramar
64 goes from Barceloneta beach, past Colom, Avda Paral.lel, Plaça Universitat to Sarrià and Pedralbes
7 runs the length of Avda Diagonal, from the Zona Universitària to Diagonal Mar, but deviates in the centre (along Passeig de Gràcia and Gran Via to Glòries).

Night buses

There are 16 urban night bus (Nitbus) routes, most of which run from 10.30pm-4.30am nightly, with buses every 20 to 30min. Most pass through Plaça Catalunya. Fares and *targetes* are as for daytime buses. Plaça Catalunya is also the terminus

for all-night bus services linking Barcelona with more distant parts of its metropolitan area.

TombBus

A special shoppers' bus service (the spooky-sounding name actually means 'round trip') that runs only between Plaça Catalunya and Plaça Pius XII on the Diagonal (7.30am-9.38pm Mon-Fri; 9.30am-9.20pm Sat). Normal *targetes* are not valid on the bus, and single tickets cost €1.20.

Local trains

For trips into the suburbs and surrounding towns, there are (as well as buses) regional rail lines run by the FGC and RENFE. From FGC Plaça Catalunya (the same station as for the Sarrià and Tibidabo lines), trains go to Sabadell, Terrassa and other towns

beyond Tibidabo, and from FGC Plaça Espanya, to Hospitalet and Montserrat. All trains on the RENFE local network (signed Rodalies/Cercanías at mainline stations) stop at Sants, but many lines also converge on Plaça Catalunya (for Vic and the Pyrenees, Manresa, the Penedès and Costa del Maresme) or Passeig de Gràcia (for the southern coastal line to Sitges and the Girona-Figueres line north). Fares vary according to zones. For a map of local RENFE lines, *see p347*.

Taxis

Barcelona's 10,500 black and yellow taxis are among its most distinctive symbols, and are usually easy to find. Taxis can be hailed on the street when they show a green light on the roof, and a sign saying 'Lliure/Libre' (free) behind the windscreen. There are also ranks at railway and bus stations, main squares and other locations throughout the city. Fares are reasonable.

FARES

Current official rates and supplements are shown inside each cab (in English). The current minimum fare is €1.80, which is what the meter should register when you set off. The basic rates apply 6am to 10pm Monday to Friday; at all other times (including midweek public holidays), the rate is about 20 per cent higher. There are also supplements for each item of luggage and for animals (€1), and a waiting charge. Taxi drivers are not officially required to carry more than €12 in change, and very few accept payment by credit card.

RECEIPTS & COMPLAINTS

To get a receipt, ask for '*un rebut, si us plau/un recibo, por favor*'. It should include the fare, the taxi number, the driver's NIF (tax) number, the licence plate, driver's signature and the date; if you have a complaint of any kind about a cab driver insist on all these, and the more details the better (time, route). Call transport information on 010 to explain your complaint, and follow their instructions.

RADIO CABS

The companies listed below take bookings 24 hours daily. Only some operators speak English, but if you are not at a specific address give the name of a street corner (ie Provença/ Muntaner), or a street and a bar or restaurant where you can wait. Note that phone cabs start the meter as soon as a call is answered.

Barnataxi 93 357 77 55
Fono-Taxi 93 300 11 00
Ràdio Taxi 93 225 00 00
Ràdio Taxi '033' 933 033 033
Servi-Taxi 933 300 300
Taxi Groc 93 322 22 22
Taxi Miramar 93 433 10 20

Driving

Driving in Barcelona can be wearing. There's seldom enough driving space, let alone parking space. Within the city limits a car is rarely a time-efficient form of transport, and it's only out in the country that one becomes an asset. If you do drive while here, bear these points in mind:

● Tourists can drive in Spain with a valid licence from most other countries. An international driving licence or EU photo licence can be useful as a translation/credibility aid.
● Keep your driving licence, vehicle registration and insurance documents with you at all times.
● It is compulsory to wear seat belts and carry warning triangles, spares (tyre, bulbs, fanbelt) and tools to fit them.
● The speed limit is 50kmph in towns, 90kmph on most highways and 120kmph on motorways – although it is true that most drivers ignore these maximums.
● Legal alcohol limits for drivers are low, similar to those in most EU countries.
● Children under 12 may not travel in the front of a car except in a child car seat.
● Do not leave anything of value, including car radios, in your car, nor bags or coats in view. Foreign numberplates can attract thieves.
● Many drivers ignore speed limits, and it's common to race through lights changing from amber to red (so don't brake suddenly in this situation, or you may be hit from behind).
● When oncoming or following drivers flash their lights at you, this usually means they want to get past,

although it can be a helpful warning of a speed trap or other traffic problem.
● Be on your guard against thefts at motorway rest areas, or thieves who may try to make you stop and get out, perhaps by indicating you have a flat tyre. Sometimes they can be violent. Keep your car doors and boot locked when travelling, and be wary of 'helpful' fellow motorists.

Car & motorbike hire

Car hire is relatively pricey, but it's a competitive market so shop around. The key is to check carefully what's included: ideally, you want unlimited mileage, 16 per cent VAT (IVA) included and, especially, full insurance cover, rather than the third-party minimum (*seguro obligatorio*). You will need a credit card, or a large cash deposit. Most companies also have a minimum age limit and require you to have had a licence for at least a year. Larger companies often advertise special offers on their websites.

EasyCar

Passeig Lluís Companys, 2nd level of underground car park (no phone/ www.easycar.com). Metro Arc de Triomf/39, 41, 51, N11 bus. **Open** 7am-11pm daily. **Credit** MC, V. **Map** p341 E6.
Online-only booking and payment. Basic rates for their Mercedes A-Class hatchbacks can be low (for example, two days for €64.90), but check the conditions carefully – such as only 100km of free mileage per day, and possible supplements for insurance or late return.

Europcar

Plaça Paisos Catalans, Sants (93 491 48 22/www.europcar.com). Metro Sants Estació/30, 44, 100, 109, N0, N7 bus. **Open** 7.30am-10.30pm Mon-Fri; 8am-1pm Sat. **Credit** AmEx, DC, MC, V. **Map** p339 A4.
A large international agency with several offices in Barcelona. A Renault Clio costs €112.45 for two days; a Seat Toledo €472 for a week (both include IVA, full insurance and 500km per day).
Airport branch: 93 298 33 00.

Vanguard

C/Viladomat 297, Eixample (93 439 38 80/93 322 79 51/www.vanguard rent.com). Metro Hospital Clínic/41, 54, N3 bus. **Open** 8am-2pm, 4-8pm Mon-Fri; 9am-1pm Sat, Sun. **Credit** AmEx, DC, MC, V. **Map** p339 B4. Scooter and motorcycle hire, as well as cars at good rates. All-inclusive three-day weekends from €73.90 (50cc Honda) to €174.30 (Yamaha 600). You must be 19 to hire a small bike and have had a licence a year; 25 and three years for larger bikes.

Parking

Parking is never easy in central Barcelona. The Municipal Police readily give out tickets, or tow away cars. Don't park in front of doors with the sign 'Gual Permanent', indicating an entry with 24-hour right of access. In some parts of the Old City, notably La Ribera and the Barri Gòtic, access is limited to residents for much of the day.

Pay & display areas

Many streets in the central area and the Eixample are pay-and-display areas (*Zones Blaves*, Blue Zones), with parking spaces marked in blue on the street. Parking restrictions apply 9am-2pm, 4-8pm Mon-Sat, when you can park for up to 2hrs; in the centre, the rate is €1.70/hr, less in other districts. If you overstay by no more than an hour, you can cancel the fine by paying an additional €3; to do so, press *Anul.lar denúncia* on the ticket machine, insert €3 and take the receipt that comes out. Machines accept credit cards (MC, V), but do not give change.

Car parks

Car parks (*parkings*) are signalled by a white 'P' on a blue sign. The main parking companies – private SABA and public SMASSA – both charge around €1.60/hr. You are especially advised to use a car park if you have foreign plates. The car parks below are central and open 24hrs daily:

SABA: Plaça Catalunya, Plaça Urquinaona, Arc de Triomf, Avda Catedral, Passeig de Gràcia, C/Diputació-C/Pau Claris.
SMASSA: Plaça dels Àngels-MACBA, Moll de la Fusta, Avda Francesc Cambó, Avda Paral.lel.

Metro-Park

Plaça de les Glòries, Eixample (93 265 10 47). Metro Glòries/7, 56 bus. **Open** 5am-11pm Mon-Thur; 5am-11.30am Fri, Sat. **Credit** AmEx, DC, MC, V. **Map** p341 F5. Park-and-ride facility recommended for anyone coming in to Barcelona with a car for the day. The €4.40 ticket gives unlimited travel for one day on the metro and city buses (but not the FGC). The car park is at the junction of three traffic arteries (the Diagonal, Meridiana and Gran Via), a short metro ride from the centre.

Towing away

Information 93 428 45 93/5.
Credit AmEx, DC, MC, V.
If the Municipal Police have towed away your car, they will leave a triangular sticker on the pavement. Call the number on the sticker or the 24hr one above to be told which pound it has gone to. Staff do not usually speak English. It will cost €97.70 to recover the vehicle during the first 4hrs after it was towed, plus €1.60 for each hr after that, plus (probably) a parking fine.

Petrol

Most *gasolineres* (petrol stations) have unleaded fuel (*sense plom/sin plomo*), regular (*super*) and diesel (*gas-oil*).

Cycling

Recreational bike-riding in Barcelona is on the increase, and there is an incomplete but growing network of bike lanes (*carrils bici*) along major avenues and the seafront. Mass bicycle commuting is a long way off, though, for in weekday traffic cyclists still face daunting risks – and tourists are not advised to try it, unless they're experts at home. Rollerblading is also popular. Tourist offices (*see p320*) have route details.

Al punt de trobada

C/Badajoz 24, Poblenou (93 225 05 85/bicipuntrobada@hotmail. com). Metro Llacuna/36, 92 bus. **Open** *Apr-Sept* 9am-3pm, 5-9pm daily. *Oct-Mar* 9am-2pm, 4-8pm Mon-Sat; 9am-5pm Sun. **Credit** AmEx, MC, V.
Near the beach. Mountain bikes and rollerblades cost €3.60/hr, €10.80/half day and €16/day. There are also tandems, baby seats, bike tours and other services.

Stepping out

The best way to let Barcelona seduce you is to get out for a stroll. With lively streets, short distances and a labyrinthine old town that is largely pedestrian only, most of the city's delights are best discovered on foot. But just make sure you get off on the right step:
● Take a map with you, then try not to look at it – ask for directions instead.
● Be alert and on your guard against street theft (*see p318* **Safety**).
● Don't expect cars to stop for you at pedestrian crossings, even if you have a green signal.
● In summer, time your urban exploration to avoid the hottest part of the day (2-5pm or so).

Walking times

This is how long popular walks should take, at an easy walking speed; allow extra for stops and diversions.
● La Rambla, from Plaça Catalunya to Colom: 20 minutes.
● Around the harbour, from the Rambla (Colom end) to Barceloneta beach: 25 minutes.
● Along the beach, from Barceloneta to the Port Olímpic: 25 minutes.
● From Plaça Catalunya to La Pedrera, up Passeig de Gràcia: 15 minutes.
● From La Pedrera to the Sagrada Família, along C/Provença: 20 minutes.
● Up Montjuïc, from Plaça Espanya via the escalators to the stadium: 20 minutes.

Resources A-Z

Addresses

Most apartment addresses consist of a street name followed by a street number, floor level and flat number, in that order. So, to go to C/València 246, 2n 3a, find number 246; go up to the second floor and find the door marked as 3 or 3a (the letter after the number merely shows that it's an ordinal number – like '3rd' in English). Ground-floor flats are usually called *baixos* or *bajos* (often abbreviated *bxs/bjos*); one floor up, the *entresol/entresuelo* (*entl*), and the next is often the *principal* (*pral*). Confusingly, numbered floors start here, first, second, up to the *àtic/ático* at the top.

Age restrictions

In Spain, you have to be 18 to drive a car, 16 to smoke and drink and 18 to have sex.

Business

Anyone wanting to set up shop in Barcelona needs to be aware of the intricacies of local, Spanish and EU regulations. It's a waste of time trying to deal with this system single-handed. A visit to the **Cambra de Comerç** (*see p309*) is a must; some consulates can also refer you to various professionals, and a *gestoria* (*see below*) will save you time and frustration.

Admin services

The *gestoria* is a very Spanish institution, the main function of which is to lighten the weight of local bureaucracy by dealing with it for you. A combination of book-keeper, lawyer and business adviser, a good *gestor* can be very helpful in handling paperwork

and pointing out shortcuts, though local *gestoria* employees rarely speak English.

LEC

Travessera de Gràcia 96, 2º 2ª, Gràcia (93 415 02 50). Bus 27, 31, 32. **Open** 9am-2pm, 4-7pm Mon-Fri. Closed Aug. **Map** p336 D3.
Lawyers and economists as well as a *gestoria*. Some English speakers on the staff.

Tutzo Assessors

C/Aribau 226, Eixample (93 209 67 88/tutzoass@fononegocio.com). Bus 31, 58, 64. **Open** 8.30am-2pm, 4-7pm Mon-Fri. Closed July, Fri pm Aug. **Map** p336 C3.
With years of experience, Tutzo offers legal, fiscal, accounting, social security, contracts and other services. Some English is spoken.

Conventions & conferences

Barcelona Convention Bureau

C/Tarragona 149, Eixample (93 423 18 00). Metro Tarragona/27, 30, 109, 215 bus. **Open** Sept-June 9am-2.30pm, 4-7pm Mon-Thur; 9am-3pm Fri. *July, Aug* 8am-3pm Mon-Fri. **Map** p336 D4.
Specialised arm of the city tourist authority that assists organisations and individuals holding conferences or similar events in the city.

Fira de Barcelona

Avda Reina Maria Cristina, Montjuïc (93 233 20 00/www. firabcn.es). Metro Espanya/bus all routes to Plaça Espanya. **Open** *Mid Sept-mid June* 9am-2pm, 4-6pm Mon-Fri. *Mid June-mid Sept* 9am-2pm Mon-Fri. **Map** p339 A5.
The Barcelona 'trade fair' is one of the largest permanent exhibition complexes in Europe. In addition to the main area at Plaça Espanya, it includes a huge site, Montjuïc-2, towards the airport, and administers the Palau de Congressos conference hall in the Plaça Espanya site, which can be let separately.

Courier services

Estació d'Autobusos Barcelona-Nord

C/Ali Bei 80, Eixample (93 232 43 29). Metro Arc Triomf/19, 39, 40, 41, 42, 55, 141, N4, N11 bus. **Open**

7am-10.30pm Mon-Fri; 7am-12.45pm Sat. **No credit cards**. **Map** p341 E5.
Inexpensive service at the bus station for sending parcels on scheduled buses to towns within Spain.

Missatgers Trèvol

C/Antonio Ricardos 14, La Sagrera (93 498 80 70/www.trevol.com). Metro Sagrera/bus 96. **Open** 8.30am-7pm Mon-Fri. **No credit cards**.
Cycle couriers who also have vans and motorbikes. Delivering a package (up to 6kg/13lb) by bike within the central area costs €2.80, plus tax, unless you have an account.

UPS

C/Miguel Hernández, at C/Indústria, Polígon Industrial Zona Franca, L'Hospitalet de Llobregat (freephone 900 10 24 10/fax 93 263 39 09/ www.ups.com). FGC Ildefons Cerdà/ 65 bus. **Open** 7am-8pm Mon-Fri. **Credit** AmEx, MC, V.
Next-day delivery to many destinations, both Spanish and international. Call three hours before required pick-up time. The depot is at Avda Diagonal 511 (open 8.30am-8.30pm Mon-Fri, Metro Maria Cristina); parcels dropped there before 7.30pm leave that evening.

Office & computer services

Centro de Negocios

C/Pau Claris 97, 4º 1ª, Eixample (93 304 38 58/www.centro-negocios. com). Metro Passeig de Gràcia/ 7, 50, 54, 56, bus. **Open** *Sept-July* 8am-9pm Mon-Fri. *Aug* 9am-3pm Mon-Fri. **Map** p340 D5.
Office space, desk space in shared offices, mailboxes, meeting rooms, secretarial services and a wide range of administrative services for hire.

GeoMac

606 30 89 32/geomac@terra.es. **Open** by appt. **No credit cards**.
Experienced US technician George Cowdery offers maintenance and trouble-shooting for Macs.

Microrent

C/Rosselló 35, Eixample (93 363 32 50/fax 93 322 13 57/ www.microrent.es). Metro Sants Estació or Entença/bus 27, 30, 32, 43. **Open** 9am-6pm Mon-Fri. **No credit cards**. **Map** p339 B4.
Computer equipment of all kinds for rent: PCs, Macs, laptops, peripherals, faxes and photocopiers.

Directory

Picking Pack Megaservice

C/Consell de Cent 276, Eixample (93 505 45 05/www.pickingpack.es). Metro Universitat/bus all routes to Plaça Universitat. **Open** 9am-8pm Mon-Fri; 9am-2pm Sat. **Credit** AmEx, MC, V. **Map** p340 D5. Computers, Internet access, fax, design, printing, mail-outs, meeting rooms and so on.

Translators

DUUAL

C/Ciutat 7, 2º 4ª, Barri Gòtic (93 302 25 85/fax 93 412 40 00/ duual@costacatalana.com). Metro Jaume I/17, 19, 40, 45 bus. **Open** *Oct-May* 9am-2pm, 4-7pm Mon-Thur; 9am-2pm Fri. *June-Sept* 8.30am-3pm Mon-Fri. **Map** p343 B3. Services in many languages and excellent desktop publishing facilities. Good rates.

Teodora Gambetta

C/Escorial 29-31, escala C, àtic 2ª, Gràcia (tel/fax 93 219 22 25/ teogam@menta.net). Metro Joanic/39, 55 bus. **Open** by appointment only. **Map** p337 E3. Translation of foreign-language documents by legally certified translators (*traductores jurados*); from or into English, French or Spanish. Rates are higher than for conventional translators.

Useful organisations

Ajuntament de Barcelona

Plaça Sant Miquel 4-5, Barri Gòtic (93 402 70 00/www.bcn.es). Metro Jaume I/17, 19, 40, 45 bus. **Open** *Sept-June* 8.30am-5.30pm Mon-Fri. *July, Aug* 8.15am-2.15pm Mon-Fri. **Map** p343 B3. The City Council. Permits for new businesses are issued by the ten municipal districts.

Borsa de Valors de Barcelona

Passeig de Gràcia 19, Eixample (93 401 35 55/www.borsabcn.es). Metro Passeig de Gràcia/22, 24, 28 bus. **Open** *Information* 9am-6pm. *Library* 9am-noon Mon-Fri. **Map** p340 D5. The Stock Exchange.

British Society of Catalunya

Via Augusta 213, Zona Alta (tel/fax 93 209 06 39). Metro Diagonal/16, 17, 22, 24, 28 bus. **Map** p336 C2. Keep in touch with fellow ex-pats in monthly get-togethers and other events. Membership is €9 a year.

Cambra de Comerç, Indústria i Navegació de Barcelona

Avda Diagonal 452-454, Eixample (93 688 08 66/www.cambrabcn.es). Metro Diagonal/FGC Provença/ 6, 7, 15, 16, 17, 33, 34 bus. **Open** 9am-5pm Mon-Thur; 9am-2pm Fri. **Map** p336 D4. The most important institution for business people, the Chamber of Commerce offers a wealth of information and advice.

Generalitat de Catalunya

General information 012/business development 93 476 72 00/ new businesses 902 20 15 20/ www.gencat.es. The Catalan government provides a range of consultancy services.

Complaints

If you have a complaint can't clear up on the spot, ask for an official complaint form (*hoja de reclamación/full de reclamació*), which many businesses are required to have available (in English). Fill out the form, and leave the pink copy with the business. Take this, and any receipts, guarantees and so on, to an official consumer office.

Oficina Municipal d'Informació al Consumidor

C/Ferran 34, Barri Gòtic (93 402 78 41/www.omic.bcn.es). Metro Liceu/14, 38, 59, 91 bus. **Open** *Mid Sept-mid June* 9am-2pm Mon, Wed, Fri; 9am-2pm, 4-6pm Tue, Thur. *Mid June-mid Sept* 9am-2pm Mon-Fri. **Map** p343 A-B3. Municipally run offical centre for consumer advice and complaint follow-up. You can also present a complaint in English through the website if you like.

Telèfon de Consulta del Consumidor

901 30 03 03. **Open** *Sept-June* 9am-6pm Mon-Fri. *July* 9am-5pm Mon-Fri. *Aug* 9am-3pm Mon-Fri. Generalitat-run line for consumer advice. Can provide addresses of other consumer offices in Catalonia.

Consulates

A full list of consulates in Barcelona is in the phone book under 'Consolats/Consulados'. Outside

office hours most have answerphones that give an emergency contact number.

Australian Consulate

Gran Via Carles III 98, Zona Alta (93 330 94 96/fax 93 411 09 04/ www.embaustralia.es). Metro Maria Cristina or Les Corts/59, 70, 72 bus. **Open** 10am-noon Mon-Fri. Closed Aug. **Map** p335 A2-3.

British Consulate

Avda Diagonal 477, Eixample (93 366 62 00/fax 93 366 62 21/ www.ukinspain.com). Metro Hospital Clínic/6, 7, 15, 33, 34. **Open** *End Sept-mid June* 9.30am-1.30pm, 4-5pm Mon-Fri. *Mid June-mid Sept* 9am-2pm Mon-Fri. **Map** p336 C3.

Canadian Consulate

C/Elisenda de Pinós 10, Zona Alta (93 204 27 00/fax 93 204 27 01/ www.canada-es.org). FGC Reina Elisenda/22, 64, 75 bus. **Open** 10am-1pm Mon-Fri. **Map** p336 D4.

Irish Consulate

Gran Via Carles III 94, Zona Alta (93 491 50 21/fax 93 411 29 21). Metro Maria Cristina or Les Corts/ 59, 70, 72 bus. **Open** 10am-1pm Mon-Fri. **Map** p335 A3.

New Zealand Consulate

Travessera de Gràcia 64, 2º, Gràcia (93 209 03 99/fax 93 202 08 90). Metro Passeig de Gràcia/22, 24, 28 bus. **Open** *Sept-June* 9am-1.30pm, 4-6.30pm Mon-Fri. *July, Aug* call for reduced hours. **Map** p336 C3.

US Consulate

Passeig Reina Elisenda 23, Zona Alta (93 280 22 27/fax 93 205 52 06/ www.embusa.es). FGC Reina Elisenda/22, 64, 75 bus. **Open** 9am-12.30pm, 3-5pm Mon-Fri. **Map** p335 A1.

Customs

Customs declarations are not usually necessary if you arrive in Spain from another EU country and are carrying only legal goods for personal use. The amounts given below are guidelines only; if you approach these maximums in several categories, you may still have to explain your personal habits.

● 800 cigarettes, 400 small cigars, 200 cigars and 1 kilogram of loose tobacco
● 10 litres of spirits (over 22 per cent alcohol), 20 litres of

fortified wine or alcoholic drinks with under 22 per cent alcohol, 90 litres of wine and 110 litres of beer.

Coming from a non-EU country, you can bring:
● 200 cigarettes or 100 small cigars or 50 cigars or 250 grams (8.82 ounces) of tobacco
● 1 litre of spirits (over 22 per cent alcohol) or 2 litres of any other alcoholic drink with under 22 per cent alcohol
● 50 grams (1.76 ounces) of perfume.

If you enter from Andorra, some of these limits are a little higher. Visitors can also carry up to €6,000 in cash without having to declare it. Non-EU residents can also reclaim VAT (IVA) paid on some large purchases when they leave Spain; for details, see p184.

Disabled

Transport facilities and access in general for disabled people still leave a lot to be desired, despite steady improvements. For wheelchair users, buses and taxis are usually the best public transport options. There is a special transport information phoneline, and transport maps, which you can pick up from transport information offices (see p304), indicate wheelchair access points and adapted bus routes.

Access to sights

Newer museums such as the MACBA have good access, but the process of converting older buildings is slow and difficult. Phoning ahead to check is always a good idea even if a place claims to be accessible: access might depend, for example, on getting a lift key in advance. Below are listed wheelchair-friendly venues.

Museum and galleries

La Capella
CCCB
Col.lecció Thyssen-Bornemisza (Monestir de Pedralbes)

Col.legi d'Arquitectes
Fundació Joan Miró
Fundació Antoni Tàpies
MACBA
MNAC
Museu d'Arqueologia de Catalunya
Museu d'Art Modern
Museu de les Arts Decoratives
Museu de la Ciència
Museu d'Historia de Catalunya
Museu de Zoologia
Palau de la Virreina

Institut Municipal de Persones amb Disminució

Avda Diagonal 233, Eixample (93 413 27 75). Metro Glories/ 7, 56 bus. **Open** *Mid Sept-mid June* 9am-2pm, 4-6pm Mon-Thur; 9am-2pm Fri. *Mid June-mid Sept* 9am-3pm Mon-Fri. **Map** p341 F5.
The city's organisation for the disabled has info on access to theatres, museums, and restaurants.

Transport

Information 93 486 07 52/fax 93 486 07 53. **Open** *Sept-July* 9am-9pm Mon-Fri; 9am-3pm Sat. *Aug* 9am-9pm Mon-Fri.
English speakers are sometimes available; if not, call the 010 information line (see p321).

Buses

Aerobús airport buses and the Bus Turístic are fully accessible to wheelchair users. Similar fully adapted buses also alternate with standard buses on all Nitbus services and most daytime routes. Transport maps and bus stop signs indicate which routes use adapted vehicles.

Metro & FGC

Only line 2 (Paral.lel-La Pau) has lifts and ramps at all stations; on lines 1 and 3, some stations have lifts. The Montjuïc Funicular is adapted for wheelchairs. FGC stations at Provença, Muntaner and Av Tibidabo are accessible, as are many FGC stops further out of town: Sant Cugat, Sabadell and others.

RENFE trains

Sants, França, Passeig de Gràcia and Plaça Catalunya stations are accessible to wheelchairs, but trains are not. At Sants, if you go to the Atenció al Client office ahead of time, help on the platform can be arranged.

Taxis

All taxi drivers are officially required to transport wheelchairs (and guide dogs) for no extra charge, but their cars can be inconveniently small, and in practice the willingness of

drivers to co-operate varies widely. Special minibus taxis adapted for wheelchairs can be ordered from the Taxi Amic service.

Taxi Amic

93 420 80 88. **Open** 7.30am-11pm Mon-Fri; 9am-10pm Sat, Sun.
Fares are the same as for regular cabs, but numbers are limited, so call well in advance to request a specific time.

Drugs

Many people smoke cannabis very openly in Spain, but you should be aware that its possession or consumption in public places is illegal. In private places, the law is contradictory: smoking is OK, but you can still be nabbed for possession. In practice, enforcement is often not the highest of police priorities, but you could receive a hefty fine and a lot of inconvenience. Smoking in bars is also prohibited; proprietors can be strict on this issue because it could cost them their licence.

Electricity

The standard current in Spain is now 220V. A diminishing number of old buildings still have 125V circuits, and it's advisable to check before using electrical equipment in old, cheap hotels. Plugs are all of the two-round-pin type. The 220V current works fine with British-bought 240V products with a plug adaptor (available at El Corte Inglés). With US 110V equipment you will also need a current transformer.

Gay & lesbian

Ca la Dona (see p322), is the main centre for women.

Casal Lambda

C/Verdaguer i Callis 10, Barri Gòtic (93 319 55 50/www.lambdaweb.org). Metro Urquinaona/17, 19, 40, 45 bus. **Open** 6-9pm Mon-Sat. **Map** p342 B2.
Gay cultural organisation that is the focus for a wide range of activities and publishes the monthly magazine *Lambda.*

Coordinadora Gai-Lesbiana

C/Buenaventura Muñoz 4, Eixample (900 601 601/fax 93 218 11 91). Metro Arc del Triomf/39, 41, 51 bus. **Open** 5-9pm Mon-Fri. **Map** p341 E6.
This gay umbrella organisation works with the Ajuntament on issues of concern to the gay community.

Front d'Alliberament Gai de Catalunya

C/Verdi 88, Gràcia (93 217 26 69). Metro Fontana/22, 24, 28, ND, NG bus. **Open** 5-8pm Mon-Fri. **Map** p338 D-E3.
FAG is a vocal multi-group that produces the Barcelona Gai information bulletin.

Teléfon Rosa

900 60 16 01. **Open** 6-10pm daily.
The phoneline of the Coordinadora Gai-Lesbiana gives help or advice on any gay or lesbian issue.

Health

Visitors can obtain emergency care through the public health service (Servei Catalá de la Salut, often referred to as the Seguretat Social/Seguridad Social). EU nationals are entitled to free basic medical attention if they have an E111 form (if you can get one sent or faxed within four days, you are exempt from charges). Many medicines are charged for.

For non-emergencies, it's usually quicker to use private travel insurance rather than the state system. Similarly, non-EU nationals with private medical insurance can also make use of state health services on a paying basis, it will usually be simpler to use a private clinic. If you are a resident registered with the Seguretat Social, you will be allocated a doctor and a local clinic. Information on health services is available from the 010 phoneline (*see p321*).

Accident & emergency

In a medical emergency the best thing to do is go to the casualty department (*Urgències*) of any of the main

---

---

public hospitals. All those listed below are open 24 hours daily. The Clinic or the Perecamps are the most central. If necessary, make an emergency call to 112 (all services) or 061 (ambulance).

Centre d'Urgències Perecamps

Avda Drassanes 13-15, Raval (93 441 06 00). Metro Drassanes or Paral.lel/14, 20, 36, 38, 57, 59, 64, 91 bus. **Map** p343 A4.
Located near the Rambla, this clinic specialises in primary attention for injuries and less serious emergencies.

Hospital Clínic

C/Villarroel 170, Eixample (93 227 54 00). Metro Hospital Clínic/14, 59, 63 bus. **Map** p336 C4.
The main central hospital. The Clinic also has a first-aid centre for less serious emergencies two blocks away at C/València 184 (93 227 93 00; open 9am-9pm Mon-Fri, 9am-1pm Sat).

Hospital de la Creu Roja de Barcelona

C/Dos de Maig 301, Eixample (93 507 27 00). Metro Hospital de Sant Pau/15, 19, 20, 25, 35, 45, 47, 50, 51, 92 bus. **Map** p337 F4.

Hospital del Mar

Passeig Marítim 25-29, Barceloneta (93 240 30 00). Metro Ciutadella-Vila Olímpica/45, 57, 59, 157, N8 bus. **Map** p341 E7.

Hospital de la Santa Creu i Sant Pau

C/Sant Antoni Maria Claret 167, Eixample (93 291 90 00). Metro Hospital de Sant Pau/15, 19, 20, 25, 35, 45, 47, 50, 51, N1, N4 bus. **Map** p337 F4.

AIDS/HIV

The actual death rate from AIDS is falling in Spain, but the HIV virus continues to spread in many groups, among them young heterosexuals. Many local chemists take part in a needle-exchange and condom-distribution programme for intravenous drug users. Antiretroviral drugs for HIV treatment are covered by Social Security in Spain. Free, anonymous blood tests for HIV and other sexually transmitted diseases are given at **CAP Drassanes** (*see p312*).

Actua

C/Gomis 38, baixos, Zona Alta (93 418 50 00/www.interactua.net). Bus 22, 73, 85. **Open** 9am-2pm, 4pm-7pm Mon-Fri.
Support group for people with HIV.

AIDS Information Line

900 21 22 22. **Open** *Mid Sept-May* 9am-5.30pm Mon-Fri. *June-mid Sept* 8am-3pm Mon-Fri.

Complementary medicine

Integral: Centre Mèdic i de Salut

Plaça Urquinaona 2, 3º 2ª, Eixample (93 318 30 50/www.integralcentre medic.com). Metro Urquinaona/bus all routes to Plaça Urquinaona. **Open** *Information* 9am-9pm Mon-Fri (call for an appointment). Closed Aug. **Map** p342 B1.

Directory

Acupuncture, homeopathy, and many other forms of complementary medicine are offered by a team of 20 professionals at this well-established clinic. Some speak English.

Contraception & abortion

All pharmacies sell condoms (*condons/condones*) and other forms of contraception; the contraceptive pill can be bought without a prescription. Condom vending machines can also be found in the toilets of many night-time bars and clubs, and in petrol stations.

Although abortion is legal during the first 12 weeks of pregnancy for those aged 18 or over, it is usually easier to obtain at a private clinic than at a public hospital.

Centre Jove d'Anticoncepció i Sexualitat

C/La Granja 19-21, Gràcia (93 415 10 00/www.centrejove.org). Metro Lesseps/24, 31, 32, 74 bus. **Open** *Oct-May* 10am-6.30pm Mon; noon-6.30pm Tue-Thur; 10am-2pm Fri. *June-Sept* noon-2pm Mon-Fri, with extended hours on some days. **Map** p337 E2.
A family planning centre aimed at young people (officially, under 23).

Dentists

Not covered by EU reciprocal agreements, so private rates, which can be costly, apply.

Centre Odontològic de Barcelona

C/Calàbria 251, Eixample (93 439 45 00). Metro Entença/41, 54 bus. **Open** *Sept-July* 9am-9pm Mon-Fri; 9am-2pm Sat. *Aug* 9am-1pm, 3-8pm Mon-Fri. **Credit** DC, MC, V. **Map** p339 B4.
Well equipped clinics providing a complete range of dental services. Several of the staff speak English. **Branch**: Institut Odontològic de la Sagrada Família C/Sardenya 319, baixos, Eixample (93 457 04 53).

Doctors

A Centre d'Assistència Primària (CAP) is a lower-level local health centre where you can be seen by a doctor and, if necessary, sent on to a hospital. They are open 8am to 9pm Monday to Friday and 9am to 5pm on Saturday. Alternatively, there are private healthcare specialists.

CAP Casc Antic

C/Rec Comtal 24, Barri Gòtic (93 310 14 21/93 310 50 98). Metro Arc de Triomf/39, 40, 41, 42, 51, 141 bus. **Map** p342 C2.

CAP Doctor Lluís Sayé

C/Torres i Amat 8, Raval (93 301 24 82/93 301 27 05/emergencies 93 301 25 32). Metro Universitat/ bus all routes to Plaça Universitat. **Map** p342 A1.

CAP Drassanes

Avda Drassanes 17-21, Raval (93 329 44 95). Metro Drassanes or Paral.lel/14, 20, 36, 38, 57, 59, 64, 91 bus. **Map** p343 A4.

CAP Manso

C/Manso 19, Poble Sec (93 325 28 00). Metro Poble Sec/38, 57, 157 bus. **Map** p339 B5.

CAP Vila Olímpica

C/Joan Miró 17, Vila Olímpica (93 221 37 85). Metro Ciutadella-Vila Olímpica/14, 41, 71, 92 bus. **Map** p041 F0.

Centre Mèdic Assistencial Catalonia

C/Provença 281, baixos, Eixample (93 215 37 93/mobile 620 808 476). Metro Diagonal/6, 15, 22, 24, 28, 33, 34 bus. **Open** 8am-8pm Mon-Fri. **No credit cards. Map** p336 D4.
Dr Lynd is a British doctor who has practised in Barcelona for many years. She is at this surgery 3.30-7pm Wed; at other times, leave a message at the office or on her mobile and she will ring you back.

Dr Mary McCarthy

C/Aribau 215, pral 1ª, Eixample (93 200 29 24/mobile 607 220 040). FGC Gràcia/58, 64 bus. **Open** by appointment. **Credit** V, MC. **Map** p336 C3.
An internal medicine specialist from the US. Also treats general patients.

Opticians

See p209.

Pharmacies

Pharmacies (*farmàcies*), are signalled by large green and red crosses, usually in flashing neon, and are plentiful. Most are open from 9am to 1.30pm and 4.30 to 8pm Monday to Friday, and 9am to 1.30pm on Saturdays. There are around a dozen 24-hour pharmacies around the city, and many more with permanently extended hours; some of the most central are listed below. Other pharmacies also open for out-of-hours duty (*guàrdia*) according to a rota.

The full list of all chemists open late (usually till 10pm) and overnight on any given night is posted daily outside every pharmacy door, and also given in the day's papers and on the 010 and 098 phonelines. At night, duty pharmacies often appear to be closed, and it's necessary to knock on the shutters to be served.

Farmàcia Alvarez

Passeig de Gràcia 26, Eixample (93 302 11 24). Metro Passeig de Gràcia/7, 16, 17, 22, 24, 28 bus. **Open** 24hrs daily. **Credit** MC, V. **Map** p340 D5.

Farmàcia Clapés

La Rambla 98, Barri Gòtic (93 301 28 43). Metro Liceu/14, 59, 91 bus. **Open** 24hrs daily. **Credit** MC, V. **Map** p343 A3.

Farmàcia Vilar

Vestíbule, Estació de Sants, Sants (93 490 92 07). Metro Sants Estació/30, 56, 57, 215, N2, N14 bus. **Open** 7am-10.30pm Mon-Fri; 8am-10.30pm Sat, Sun. **Credit** AmEx, MC, V. **Map** p339 A4.

Alcoholics Anonymous

93 317 77 77. **Open** 10am-1pm, 5-7pm Mon-Fri; 7-9pm Sat, Sun; answerphone at other times.
Among the local AA groups there are several that have dedicated English-speaking sections.

Telèfon de l'Esperança

93 414 48 48. **Open** 24hrs daily.
A local helpline that offers a listening ear. Staff here can also consult an extensive database to put you in touch with other specialist help groups, from psychiatric to legal. English sometimes spoken, but not guaranteed. A private foundation.

ID

From the age of 14, Spaniards legally have to carry their DNI (identity card). Foreigners are also meant to carry a national ID card or passport, but in practice it's usually OK to carry a photocopy of your passport, or a driving licence.

Insurance

For health care and EU nationals, *see p311*. Some non-EU countries have reciprocal healthcare agreements with Spain, but for most travellers it's usually more convenient to have private travel insurance – which will also, of course, cover you in case of theft and flight problems.

Internet

Internet access options will keep on evolving, but the basic choice is between Internet Service Providers (ISPs) that offer free basic access, such as Eresmas (902 501 501/www.eresmas.com), and those that charge perhaps €75 a year for better service – such as Cinet (93 502 03 39/www.cinet.es). In both cases, you still pay for your Internet time in your phone bill, but a *tarifa plana* (flat rate charge) of around €16 for two months to cover the phone costs for your off-peak Internet use (weekdays 8am-6pm is not included) is offered by phone companies such as Telefónica (information 1004) and Retevision (015).

Internet access

There are now Internet centres all over Barcelona. Some libraries (*see below*) provide Internet access, while cybercafés include **La Idea, Over the Game** and **Travel Bar** (for all, *see chapter* **Cafés & Bars**). For other computer services, *see p308*.

Change & Transfer

Estació d'Autobusos Barcelona-Nord, C/Ali Bei 80, Eixample (93 232 81 87). Metro Arc Triomf/19, 39, 40, 41, 42, 55, 141, N4, N11 bus. **Open** 8.30am-10pm Mon-Fri; 9am-5.30pm Sat, Sun. **Credit** AmEx, DC, MC, V. **Map** p341 E5.
Combined Internet centre and currency exchange office. The first 30min costs €1.20.

Ciberopcion

Gran Via de les Corts Catalanes 602, Eixample (93 412 73 08/www.ciberopcion.com). Metro Universitat/all routes to Plaça Universitat. **Open** 9am-1am Mon-Sat; 11am-1am Sun. **No credit cards. Map** p336 D4.
Cheap and fast Internet connection in a central location, with 150 terminals. It costs 60¢ for each 30min online.

easyEverything

La Rambla 31, Barri Gòtic (93 318 24 35/www.easyeverything.com). Metro Liceu/14, 38, 51, 91, N9, N12 bus. **Open** 24hrs daily. **No credit cards. Map** p343 A3.
There are 380 terminals here and 300 at Ronda Universitat 35 (93 412 10 58). Prices vary according to demand: €1.20 can get you as much as 3hrs if it's empty, but only about 20min when it's busy (usually from around noon-9pm). Connection is slow.

Inetcorner

C/Sardenya 306, Eixample (93 244 80 80/www.inetcorner.net). Metro Sagrada Familia/19, 33, 34, 43, 44, 50, 51 bus. **Open** 10am-10pm Mon-Sat; noon-8pm Sun. **No credit cards. Map** p337 F4.
Small centre next to the Sagrada Familia; iMacs are available. First 20min costs €1.80, then 4¢ a min.

Left luggage

Aeroport del Prat

Terminal B. **Open** 24hrs daily. **Rates** €3.75 per day.

Estació d'Autobusos Barcelona-Nord

C/Ali Bei 80, Eixample. Metro Arc de Triomf/19, 39, 40, 41, 42, 55, 141, N4, N11 bus. **Open** 24hrs daily. **Rates** €1.80, €2.40, €3.60 per day. **Map** p341 E5.

Estació Marítima (Balearics Ferry Terminal)

Moll de Barcelona, Port Vell. Metro Drassanes/14, 20, 36, 38, 57, 59, 64, 91, 157, N6, N9 bus. **Open** 8am-11pm daily. **Rates** €1.80, €3 per day. **Map** p340 C7.

Train stations

There are lockers at Sants and Passeig de Gràcia (both open 5.30am-11pm daily) and França (6am-11pm daily), but not at the smaller stations. Rates are €3 and €4.20 per day.

Legal help

Servicio d'Orientació Jurídica

C/València 344, Eixample (93 567 16 44). Metro Verdaguer/6, 15, 19, 33, 34, 43, 44, 50, 51, bus. **Open** 9am-2pm Mon-Fri. **Map** p337 E4.
Legal consulting service run by the Justice Department, where you can get free legal advice, and those who qualify through low income and savings can be appointed a legal-aid lawyer. Arrive before midday, and be prepared to wait.

Libraries

Barcelona has more than 20 municipal public libraries; among their many services some offer novels in English and free Internet access. Call 010 for the address of the nearest or click on to www.bcn.es/icub/biblioteques.

Ateneu Barcelonès

C/Canuda 6, Barri Gòtic (93 343 61 21/www.ateneu-bcn.org). Metro Catalunya/bus all routes to Plaça Catalunya. **Open** 9am-10.45pm daily. **Map** p342 B2.
This venerable cultural and philosophical society has the best private library in the city, open nearly every day of the year, plus a peaceful interior garden patio and bar. Initial membership costs €120 (payable in instalments), and the subsequent fee is €13.2 per month.

Biblioteca de Catalunya

C/Hospital 56, Raval (93 317 07 78/www.gencat.es/bc). Metro Liceu/14, 38, 59 bus. **Open** 9am-8pm Mon-Fri; 9am-2pm Sat. **Map** p342 A2.
The Catalan national collection is housed in the medieval Hospital de la Santa Creu and has a wonderful stock reaching back centuries. Readers' cards are required, but one-day research visits are allowed (take your passport). The library has Internet terminals, and the catalogue is online. On the ground floor are the city's most central public libraries, the Biblioteques de Sant Pau i Santa Creu (Sant Pau for adults, Santa Creu for kids).

Directory

British Council/ Institut Britànic

C/Amigó 83, Zona Alta (93 241 97 11). FGC Muntaner/14, 58, 64 bus. **Open** Oct-June 9.30am-9pm Mon-Fri; 10.30am-1.30pm Sat. July, Sept 9.30am-2pm, 4-8.30pm Mon-Fri. Closed Aug-early Sept. **Map** p336 C2. UK press, English books, satellite TV and a big multimedia section oriented towards learning English. Access is free; borrowing costs €48.10 a year (€96.20 with Internet access included).

Mediateca

CaixaForum, Avda Marquès de Comillas 6-8, Montjuïc (902 22 30 40/www.fundacio.lacaixa.es). Metro Plaça de Espanya/13, 50 bus. **Open** 11am-8pm Tue-Fri; 11am-3pm Sat. Closed Aug. **Map** p339 A5. A high-tech art, music and media library in the arts centre of Fundació la Caixa. Most materials are open-access; borrowing needs €6, and you will need to provide your ID card or passport.

Lost property

Airport & rail stations

If you lose something land-side of check-in at El Prat Airport, report the loss immediately to the Aviación Civil office in the relevant terminal, or call airport information on 93 298 38 38. There is no central lost property depot for the RENFE rail network: if you have mislaid anything on a train, look for the Atención al Viajero desk or Jefe de Estació office at the nearest main station to where your property has gone astray, or call ahead to the destination station of the train. To get information by phone on lost property at main railway stations, call their information numbers and ask for Objetos Perdidos.

Municipal Lost Property Office

Oficina de Troballes, C/Ciutat 9, Barri Gòtic (lost property enquiries 010). Metro Jaume I/17, 19, 40, 45 bus. **Open** 9am-2pm Mon-Fri. **Map** p343 B3. All items found on city public transport and taxis, or picked up by the police in the street, should eventually find their way to this office near the Ajuntament. If an item is labelled with the owner's name or a serial number, the 010 phone information service will be able to tell you if it has been handed in. Within 24hrs of the loss you can also try ringing the city transport authority on 93 318 70 74, or, for taxis, the Institut Metropolità del Taxi on 93 223 40 12.

Media

Most of Barcelona's main print and broadcast media are young, like Spain's democracy. But that doesn't mean they're innocent: the worlds of journalism and politics tend to overlap. The language factor is also important, with Catalan strong in broadcasting, and now gaining ground in print.

Daily newspapers

Two slim but informative free daily papers, Barcelona@Más and Metro, are handed out to commuters every weekday morning. As in most of Spain, regional, rather than national, dailies lead the market.

Avui

For many years this was the city's only Catalan-language newspaper; though decent, it's predictably pro-Generalitat.

El País

This rigorous, socialist-leaning paper is Spain's only real national daily. Good entertainment and arts supplements, on Friday and Saturday respectively.

El Periódico

Populist, with a tabloid look but fairly solid content. It's a close second in the circulation race, with 40% of its sales from a Catalan-language version.

La Vanguardia

Barcelona's top-selling daily. Traditionally conservative, but now a lively, well-designed paper, in Spanish, but with a good Catalan-language listings magazine on Fridays.

English language

Foreign newspapers are available at most kiosks on the Rambla and Passeig de Gràcia.

Barcelona Business

A monthly newspaper combining business news with a more general focus on Catalonia.

Metropolitan

A monthly city magazine aimed at English-speaking Barcelona residents, distributed free in bars and Anglophone hangouts.

b-guided

Quarterly bilingual style magazine for bars, clubs, shops, restaurants and exhibitions, sold at hip venues.

Listings & classifieds

The main newspapers have daily 'what's on' listings, with entertainment supplements on Fridays. For monthly listings, see Metropolitan and music/scene freebies such as Mondo Sonoro, AB, and Go (found in bars and music shops). Of the dailies, La Vanguardia has the best classified section, especially on Sundays.

Anuntis

Largest of the classified-ad magazines, it's published on Mon, Wed and Fri (phone 902 50 85 08 to place a free ad).

Guía del Ocio

A weekly listings magazine. Its pocket-sized format and availability in any kiosk make it convenient but not always complete.

Television

Spanish TV takes some getting used to: endless ad breaks, unreliable programme start times and, most irritating of all, out-of-sync voices on the mass of dubbed US and British programmes. For undubbed films look for 'VO' in listings or, on 'dual' TVs, the dual symbol at the top of the screen.

TVE1 (La Primera)

The Spanish state broadcaster, with news that can be heavily pro-government.

TVE2 (La Dos)

Also state-run, La 2 offers less commercial fare with some good late-night movies.

TV3

Regional Catalan television – entirely in Catalan, with mainstream programming.

Canal 33

Also regional and in Catalan, but with documentaries and extra sports.

Antena 3

A private channel with an emphasis on family entertainment and late-night salaciousness.

Hearts and clubs

Barcelona's newspapers come in a tabloid size, but tabloids they are not. UK *Sun*-style sensationalist dailies have never taken root here, but rather the market for soft news has been well served for more than half a century by two of the great Spanish media phenomena: the *prensa de corazón* (literally, 'the heart press'), and the *prensa deportiva* – based almost exclusively on the massive pulling power of the largest football clubs. Corazón culture completely dominates the huge magazine market: the six biggest gossip weeklies are the six top-selling mags in the country. Pick up a copy of *¡Hola!*, *Lecturas* or *Pronto* from a kiosk and you will recognise the Hollywood actors and European aristocrats who are international sensation-fodder, but the interesting bit is the collection of stars you don't know. Fifty years of Spanish gossip has created a living soap with an incredible momentum of its own. Regular characters such as 'actress' Ana Obregon and 'model' Mar Flores have 'careers', but

in reality are much better known (and paid) because of their non-stop appearances in the magazines, cavorting with landed gentry, bullfighters, actors and musicians in Malaga or Mallorca (and from time to time, Barcelona).

Most blokes, of course, don't really go for such garbage. Scandals, sure – but for the male market they have to be accompanied by scoreboards, which is just what the powerful sports dailies offer. Madrid-based *Marca* is Spain's most-read newspaper (bar none), while big sellers in Catalonia are *Mundo Deportivo* and *Sport*, both of which devote about 20 pages a day to 'news' of one sports team: Fútbol Club Barcelona. Keeping that up on a daily basis can require an approach not terribly different to that of the gossip mags – particularly in the July off-season, when the slightest rumour of a player transfer can fuel weeks of claims and bitter counterclaims, candid holiday snaps, potted biographies and quasi-statistics. Oh, and they also throw in a little coverage of the Tour de France.

Tele 5

Also private. A version of *Big Brother* has been the biggest drawcard over the past two years.

Canal +

A subscriber channel based around movies and sport, although its news and other programmes are shown unscrambled.

BTV

Most innovative of all, but also the hardest to receive in some areas, the Ajuntament's city channel features a lot of student-produced programmes.

City TV

A private channel, cloned from a Toronto city station. Repeated movies, and a few local programmes.

Satellite & cable

Digital satellite TV has taken off, with two providers, Via Digital and Canal Satélite Digital. There is one digital terrestrial company, Quiero TV, to be joined by two more in 2002. Cabling of the city is still incomplete: the main provider is Menta.

Radio

Local radio dials – especially FM – are packed, and Catalan has a strong presence.

Catalunya Mùsica (101.5 FM) is mainly classical. **Rádio 3** (98.7 FM) is a good Spanish station, with rock/roots. On shortwave, the **BBC World Service** can be heard on 15485, 12095, 9410 and 6195 KHz, depending on the time.

Money

Spain's currency is now the euro (*see p317* **Welcome to Euroland**). Notes and coins in the old currency, the peseta, ceased to be legal tender on 28 February 2002, although if you've got them they can still be cashed in – at any bank until 30 June 2002, and after that at the Banco de España. The exchange rate is 1 euro = 166.386 pesetas.

Banks & foreign exchange

Banks (*bancos*) and savings banks (*caixes d'estalvis/cajas de ahorros*) readily accept

travellers' cheques (you must show your passport), for a commission, but usually refuse to cash any kind of personal cheque except one issued by that bank. Some foreign exchange bureaus (*cambios*) don't charge commission, but these generally offer you a lower rate; it's worth shopping around. Obtaining money through an ATM machine – which are everywhere – with a debit or credit card is often the easiest option despite the fees charged for withdrawals.

BANK HOURS

Banks are normally open from 8.30am to 2pm Monday to Friday, and from 1 October to 30 April most branches also open on Saturday mornings from 8.30am to 1pm. Hours vary a little between banks: some open slightly earlier or later. Savings banks, which offer the same exchange facilities as banks, open from 8am to 2pm Monday to Friday, and from October to May are

Directory

also open on Thursdays from 4.30pm to 7.45pm. Savings banks never open on Saturday. Both close on public holidays.

OUT-OF-HOURS SERVICES

Outside normal hours there are foreign exchange offices open at the airport (Terminals A and B, open 7am-11pm daily) and Barcelona-Sants station (open 8am-9.30pm daily). There's a *cambio* at the Estació d'Autobusos Barcelona-Nord (open 8.30am-10pm Mon-Fri; 9am-5.30pm Sat, Sun), and more in the city centre. Some in the Rambla are open until midnight (3am from July to September). At the airport, Sants and outside some banks there are automatic cash exchange machines that accept notes in major currencies.

American Express

C/Rosselló 261, Eixample (93 255 00 00). Metro Diagonal/FGC Provença/ 7, 16, 17, 31, 67, 68 bus. **Open** 9.30am-6pm Mon-Fri; 10am-1pm Sat. **Map** p336 D4.
All the usual AmEx services, an ATM for AmEx cards and 24hr money transfers anywhere in the world (charges paid by the sender). **Branch:** La Rambla 74 (93 301 11 66).

Western Union Money Transfer

Loterías Manuel Martín, La Rambla 41 (93 412 70 41). Metro Liceu or Drassanes/14, 38, 59, 91 bus. **Open** 9.30am-11pm Mon-Sat; 10am-midnight Sun. **Map** p343 A3.
The quickest, although not the cheapest, way of having money sent from abroad.
Branch: **Mail Boxes** C/València 214, Eixample (93 454 69 83).

Credit cards

Major credit and charge cards are widely accepted in hotels, shops, restaurants and many other services (including metro ticket machines, and pay-and-display parking machines in the street). With major cards you can also withdraw cash from most bank cash machines, which provide instructions in different

languages at the push of a button. Banks also advance cash against a credit card, but prefer you to use the machine. Don't forget that interest will be charged.
Note: you will need photo ID (passport, driving licence or similar) when using a credit/debit card in a shop, but not usually in a restaurant.

Lost/stolen credit cards

All lines have English-speaking staff and are open 24hrs daily.
American Express 902 37 56 37
Diners Club 901 10 10 11
MasterCard 900 97 12 31
Visa 900 99 12 16

Tax

There are different rates of sales tax (IVA): for hotels and restaurants, the rate is 7 per cent; in shops, it's most commonly 16 per cent, but 4 or 7 per cent on many items. IVA is generally included in listed prices – if it's not, the expression *mas IVA* (plus sales tax) must be stated after the price. Be careful of this when getting quotes on expensive items. In shops displaying a 'Tax-Free Shopping' sticker, non EU-residents can reclaim tax on large purchases (*see p184*).

Opening times

Most shops open from 9/10am to 1/2pm and 4.30/5pm to 8/9pm, Monday to Saturday, but many do not reopen on Saturday afternoons. Markets open earlier, at 7/8am, and most smaller ones are closed by 2/3pm. Major stores, shopping centres and a growing number of shops open all day, from 10am to 9pm Monday to Saturday. Larger shops are also allowed to open some Sundays and holidays, mostly around Christmas.
In summer, staggered holidays have become more common, but many restaurants

and shops still close up for all or part of August. Many businesses work a shortened day from June to September, from 8/9am till 3pm. Most (but not all) museums close one day each week, usually Monday. For banking hours, *see p315*.

Police

Barcelona has several police forces. The **Guàrdia Urbana** wear navy and pale blue, and are concerned with traffic and local regulations, but also help to keep general law and order in the city. The **Policía Nacional**, in darker blue uniforms and white shirts (or blue, combat-style gear), patrol the streets as well, and are responsible for dealing with more serious crime. The Catalan government's police, the **Mossos d'Esquadra**, in navy and light blue with red trim, are gradually expanding their role, and are now responsible for traffic control in Barcelona province, although not in the city itself. A fourth body is the **Guàrdia Civil**, who wear military green uniforms and watch over many Spanish highways, customs posts and some government buildings, but are not often seen within Barcelona.

REPORTING A CRIME

If you are robbed or attacked, report the incident as soon as possible to the nearest police station (*comisaría*). In the centre, the most convenient is probably the Guàrdia Urbana station in the Rambla, which often has English-speaking officers on duty. In other areas, contact the Policía Nacional (the 24-hour operator on 93 290 30 00 can connect you to the closest *comisaría*).
If you report a crime you will be asked to make an official statement (*denuncia*). It is frankly unlikely that anything you have lost will be recovered, but you need the

denuncia to make an insurance claim. For emergency phone numbers, *see p311*.

Guàrdia Urbana Ciutat Vella

La Rambla 43, Barri Gòtic (93 344 13 00). Metro Liceu or Drassanes/14, 38, 59, 91 bus. **Open** 24hrs daily. **Map** p343 A3.

Postal services

Letters and postcards weighing up to 20g cost 25¢ within Spain; 45¢ to the rest of Europe; 70¢ to the rest of the world. Mail to other European countries generally arrives in three to four days, and to the USA in about a week. Aerograms (*aerogramas*) cost 54¢ for all destinations. It's usually easiest to buy stamps for cards or letters at *estancs* (*see below*); postboxes in the street are yellow with a white horn insignia. Postal information is on 902 197 197 or at www.correos.es.

Correu Central

Plaça Antoni López, Barri Gòtic (93 486 83 02). Metro Jaume I or Barceloneta/14, 17, 19, 36, 40, 45, 57, 59, 64, 157 bus. **Open** 8.30am-9.30pm Mon-Sat; reduced service 9am-2pm Sun. **Map** p339 B4. Take a ticket from the machine and wait your turn. Apart from the typical services, fax sending and receiving is offered at all post offices (more expensive than at fax shops, but with the option of courier delivery in Spain). To send something express, say you want to send it *urgente*. Postal Exprés is a reliable way of sending small packages within Spain and guarantees next-day delivery to provincial capitals and 48hr delivery elsewhere. On Sundays, not all services are available and entrance is via a door on the Vía Laietana side. Some post offices close in August. **Branches:** Ronda Universitat 23, Eixample; C/Aragó 282, Eixample. **Open** *Both* 8.30am-8.30pm Mon-Fri, 9.30am-1pm Sat.

Estancs/Estancos

The tobacco shop, usually known as an *estanc/estanco* and identified by a brown and yellow sign with the words *tabacs* or *tabacos*, is a very important Spanish institution. First and foremost, they supply cigarettes and tobacco, but they are also the main places to buy postage stamps, as well as many official forms demanded by Spanish state bureaucracy. They also sell public transport *targetes* and phonecards.

Poste Restante

Letters sent Poste Restante should be addressed to Lista de Correos, 08070 Barcelona, Spain. Pick-up is from the main post office, and you'll need your passport to collect them.

Welcome to Euroland

From the Arctic to the Mediterranean, wallets and cash registers are now jangling with the same shiny, new coins. The euro, the common European currency, became everyday reality for 300 million Europeans in 12 countries on New Year's Day 2002. The Spanish peseta, along with 11 other currencies, has been consigned to the dustbin of history.

It's been a long time coming. The push towards a union of European states and peoples began in the aftermath of World War II and has always been economically led, with the proposal for a common currency on its wish-list. This began to take on real form with the European Community's initiation of Economic and Monetary Union (EMU) in 1986 and the Treaty on European Union (1992). In 1999 came the permanent fixing of exchange rates among the initial 11 participating states: Spain, Portugal, France, Italy, Germany, Austria, the Netherlands, Belgium, Luxembourg, Ireland and Finland. Greece became the 12th member of the euro club in 2001.

One euro (€) is made up of 100 cents (¢). Watch for local variations in naming: you will see one euro written as 1€ in Spain, cents are often called *céntims/ céntimos*, and British/US practice on decimal points and commas is reversed (so 1.000€ means one thousand euros, while 1,00€ is one euro).

The seven, rather blandly designed banknotes depict doorways and bridges from different periods of European architecture. They are: €5 (grey; classical period), €10 (red; Romanesque), €20 (blue; Gothic), €50 (orange; Renaissance), €100 (green; baroque and rococo), €200 (yellow-brown; iron and glass architecture), €500 (purple; 20th-century).

One side of each coin shows the value and a map of Europe. The other side features a country-specific design, but all coins can be used in any participating state. The two largest coins are a combination of gold and silver coloured metal: €2 (gold centre, silver rim) and €1 (silver centre, gold rim), both with King Juan Carlos on the reverse side of the Spanish-minted version. Then there are three gold-coloured coins (50, 20 and 10 cents; the Spanish version shows Cervantes) and three copper-coloured coins (5, 2 and 1 cent; the Spanish version features Santiago de Compostela cathedral).

Queuing

Catalans, like other Spaniards, have a highly developed queuing culture. In small shops and at market stalls, although people may not stand in an orderly line, they are generally very well aware of when it is their turn.

Directory

Common practice is to ask when you arrive, '¿Qui es l'últim/la última?' ('Who's last?'); see who nods back at you, and follow after them. Say 'jo' ('me') to the next person who asks the same question.

Religion

Anglican: St George's Church
C/Horaci 38, Zona Alta (93 417 88 67/www.stgeorge-church.com). FGC Av Tibidabo/22, 64, 75 bus. **Main service** 11am Sun. A British church with a multicultural congregation.

Catholic Mass in English: Parròquia Maria Reina
Carretera d'Esplugues 103, Zona Alta (93 203 41 15). Metro Zona Universitaria/63, 78 bus. **Mass** 11am Sun. **Map** p335 A1.

Jewish Orthodox: Sinagoga de Barcelona
C/Avenir 24, Zona Alta (93 200 61 48). FGC Gràcia/58, 64 bus. **Prayers** call for times. **Map** p336 C3. A Sephardic, Orthodox synagogue.

Jewish Reform: Comunitat Jueva Atid de Catalunya
C/Castanyer 27, Zona Alta (93 417 37 04/www.atid.freeservers.com). FGC El Putxet or Av Tibidabo/17 bus. **Prayers** call for times. Reform synagogue.

Moslem: Mosque Tarik Bin Ziad
C/Hospital 91, Raval (93 441 91 49). Metro Liceu/14, 38, 59, bus. **Prayers** 2pm Fri; call for other times.

Safety

Pickpocketing and bag-snatching are rife in Barcelona, and tourists are a prime target. Be particularly careful around the Rambla and Barri Gòtic area, as well as on public transport and at stations; but thieves go where tourists go, even to quieter areas such as the parks and beaches. Police and authorities have put more resources into the problem recently, but it remains to be seen whether they have turned

the tide. Most street robberies are aimed at the unwary, and could be avoided if you take a few simple precautions:
● Avoid giving invitations to thieves: wallets in easily accessible pockets, or bank notes flashed in public. Bags should be well closed, and pulled to the front. When you stop, only put bags down right beside you, where you can see them constantly and where a passer-by couldn't easily snatch them.
● In busy streets or crowded places, watch for who's moving around you. If you're at all suspicious of someone, simply move somewhere else.
● Barcelona street thieves tend to use stealth and surprise rather than violence. However, muggings and knife-threats do sometimes occur. Avoid deserted streets if you're on your own at night.
● Despite precautions, sometimes you can just be unlucky. It's best not to carry more money and valuables than you have to, and to take out travel insurance.

Smoking

People in Barcelona still smoke – a lot. Non-smoking areas are rare in restaurants, although smoking bans in cinemas, theatres and on trains are generally respected. Smoking is banned throughout the metro and FGC, but many people take this to mean on trains only, not station platforms. For places to buy tobacco, see p210.

Study

Catalonia is ardently Europhile, and its universities lend enthusiastic support to EU student exchange programmes. The vast majority of foreign students in Spain under the EU's Erasmus scheme are enrolled at Catalan universities. The main

language used in universities is usually Catalan, although lecturers (and students) are often relaxed about using Castilian in class for the first few months with non-Catalan speakers. Foreign students, including EU nationals, who stay for more than three months are officially required to have a residence permit.

Centre d'Informació i Assessorament per a Joves (CIAJ)
C/Ferran 32, Barri Gòtic (93 402 78 00/fax 93 402 78 01/www.bcn.es/ciaj). Metro Liceu/14, 38, 59, 91 bus. **Open** 10am-2pm, 4pm-8pm Mon-Fri. Closed afternoons Aug. **Map** p343 A-B3. City council youth info centre, with advice and information on work, study, travel and more. Also small ads, noticeboards and free web terminals (not for email).

Secretaria General de Joventut – Punt d'Informació Juvenil
C/Calabria 147-C/Rocafort 116, Eixample (93 483 83 83/93 483 83 84/www.bcu.cesca.es). Metro Rocafort/41 bus. **Open** 9am-2pm, 3-5.30pm Mon-Fri. Closed afternoons June-mid Sept. **Map** p339 B5. Generalitat-run centre hosting a range of services: 'youth information' on work, work and study and Internet access. Other services include **Habitatge Jove** (93 483 83 92/www.habitatge jove.com) an under-35s accommodation service, and travel information centre **Viatgeteca** (93 483 83 81).

Language classes

In bilingual Barcelona, many who come to stay for a while will want (or need) to learn some Catalan, but this is also a hugely popular location for people studying Spanish. For full lists of course options, try the youth information centres listed above.

American-British College
C/Guillem Tell 27, Zona Alta (93 415 57 57/www.ambricol.es). FGC Plaça Molina/16, 17, 22, 24, 25, 27, 28, 31, 32 bus. **Open** Oct-May 9am-9pm Mon-Fri; 10am-1pm Sat. June-Sept 9am-9pm Mon-Fri. **Map** p336 D2.

An established school offering reasonably priced intensive Spanish courses. Accommodation can be arranged either with families or in student residences.

Consorci per a la Normalització Lingüística

Central office: C/Mallorca 272, 8ª, Eixample (93 272 31 00/ www.cpnl.org). Metro Passeig de Gràcia or Diagonal/20, 22, 24, 28, 43, 44 bus. **Open** *Sept-mid June* 9am-2pm, 3-6.30pm Mon-Fri. *Mid June-Aug* 8am-3pm Mon-Fri. **Map** p336 D4.

The official Generalitat organisation for the support of the Catalan language has centres around the city offering Catalan courses at low prices from beginners' level upwards, with intensive courses in summer, and self-study centres.

Escola Oficial d'Idiomes

Avda Drassanes (93 324 93 30/ www.eoibd.es). Metro Drassanes/14, 38, 59, 91 bus. **Open** *Info* 10.30am-12.30pm Mon, Thur, Fri; 10.30am-12.30pm, 4-7pm Tue, Wed. Closed afternoons June-Sept. **Map** p339 A4.
The 'official school' has semi-intensive three-month courses at all levels in Catalan, Spanish and other languages. It's cheap, and has a good reputation, so demand is high and classes are big. It also has summer courses, a self-study centre and a good library. For some courses, it may be easier to get a place in the Escola Oficial, located at Avda del Jordà 18, Vall d'Hebrón (93 418 74 85).

International House

C/Trafalgar 14, Eixample (93 268 45 11/www.ihes.com/bcn). Metro Urquinaona/bus all routes to Plaça Catalunya. **Open** 8am-9pm Mon-Fri; 10am-1.30pm Sat. **Map** p342 C1.
Intensive Spanish courses all year. IH is also a leading Barcelona centre for TEFL teacher training.

Universities

EU programmes: Socrates, Erasmus, Lingua

The Erasmus student exchange scheme and Lingua project (specifically concerned with language learning) are the main parts of the EU's Socrates programme to help students move between member states. Interested students should approach the Erasmus co-ordinator at their home college. Information is available in Britain from the UK Socrates-Erasmus Council, R&D

Building, The University, Canterbury, Kent CT2 7PD (01227 762712/fax 01227 762711/ www.ukc.ac.uk/erasmus/erasmus).

Universitat Autònoma de Barcelona

Campus de Bellaterra, 08193 (93 581 10 00/student information 93 581 11 11/www.uab.es). FGC or RENFE Universidad Autonoma/by car A18 to Cerdanyola del Valles. **Open** *Information* 10am-1.30pm, 3.30-4.30pm Mon-Fri.
A rambling 1960s campus outside the city at Bellaterra, near Sabadell, with frequent FGC train connections.

Universitat de Barcelona

Gran Via de les Corts Catalanes 585, Eixample (student information 93 403 54 17/www.ub.es). Metro Universitat/bus all routes to Plaça Universitat. **Open** Information office (Pati de Ciències entrance) *Sept-June* 9am-6pm Mon-Fri. *July, Aug* 9am-2pm Mon-Fri. **Map** p340 C-D5.
Barcelona's oldest and biggest university with faculties in the main building on Plaça Universitat, in the Zona Universitària, as well as in other parts of town.

Universitat Pompeu Fabra

Student information 93 542 22 28/ www.upf.es. Information offices: La Rambla 30-32, Barri Gòtic; C/Ramon Trias Fargas 25-27, Vila Olímpica. **Open** *Both* 9am-9pm Mon-Fri.
Founded in 1991, this social sciences-based university has faculties in various parts of central Barcelona, many of them in the Old City.

Universitat Ramon Llull

C/Claravall 1-3, Zona Alta (93 602 22 00/www.url.es). FGC Av Tibidabo/22, 58, 73, 75, 85 bus. **Open** *Information* 9am-2pm, 4-6.30pm Mon-Fri. Closed 2wks Aug.
Private, expensive university bringing together a number of previously separate institutions owned and/or run by the Jesuits, including the ESADE business school (93 280 2995/www.esade.edu); there is no strong religious presence in teaching.

Telephones

Thanks to competition in the Spanish phone market, prices are coming down and new options are constantly appearing. Former state operator Telefónica still has a

virtual monopoly on local calls and most calls from public phones, but this is slowly changing. International calls now cost the same whatever the day or hour. Some phone cards and phone centres give cheaper rates than Telefónica.

Dialling & codes

All normal Spanish phone numbers have nine digits, as the area code (93 in Barcelona and its province) must be dialled with all calls, local or long-distance. Spanish mobile phone numbers begin with 6. Numbers beginning 900 are freephone lines; other 90 numbers are special-rate services – in general, the higher the third digit, the higher the rate.

International & long-distance calls

To make an international call, dial 00 and then the country code, followed by the area code (omitting the first zero in UK numbers) and number. To call Barcelona from abroad, dial the international code (00 in the UK), then 34 for Spain.
Australia 61
Canada 1
Irish Republic 353
New Zealand 64
United Kingdom 44
USA 1

Public phones

The most common model of payphone accepts coins (from 2¢ up), Telefónica phonecards and credit cards, and has a digital display with instructions in English and other languages. For the first minute of a daytime local call, you'll be charged around 15¢; to a mobile phone around 50¢; to a 902 number, around 20¢. This type of phone also gives you credit to make further calls without having to reinsert money. Most bars and cafés also have phones for public use, but they often cost 50 per cent more than regular booths.

Post offices, newsstands and *estancs* sell €6 and €12

Directory

Telefónica phonecards. Also on sale at newsstands and shops are cards from many other companies, which offer cheaper rates than Telefónica on all but local calls. The cards give you a toll-free number to call; an operator or automatic system then connects you with the number you want and can also tell you how much you have left on the card.

Phone centres

Phone centres (*locutorios*) can also bring down call prices, and avoid the need for change. Most private centres offer international call rates that are cheaper than Telefónica's for all countries. There are many phone centres along Raval side streets, such as C/Sant Pau, or along C/Carders-C/Corders in La Ribera. Many also offer other services such as international money transfer, currency exchange and Internet access.

Cambios Sol
Vestibule, Estació de Sants, Sants (93 491 45 37) Metro Sants Estació/30, 56, 57, 215, N2, N14 bus. **Open** 8.30am-9pm daily.
Map p339 A4.
Branch: C/Colom 7, Barri Gòtic (93 310 60 65).

Oftelcom
C/Canuda 7, Barri Gòtic (93 342 73 70). Metro Catalunya/14, 38, 59, 91 bus. **Open** 11am-11pm daily.
Map p342 B2.

Operator services

Usually, operators will speak Catalan and Spanish only – except for international operators, most of whom speak English.

National directory enquiries
1003
International directory enquiries 025
National operator 1009
International operator Europe & North Africa 1008; rest of world 1005
Telephone faults service 1002
Telegrams 933 222 000
Time 093
Weather 906 365 365

Wake-up calls 096. You key in the time at which you wish to be woken, in the 24hr clock, in four figures: for example, punch in 0830 if you want to be called at 8.30am.
General information 098. A local information service provided by Telefónica. Less comprehensive than the 010 line (*see p321*), but open 24hrs.

Mobile phones

Every second Spaniard now has a *móvil*. You pay either with a monthly bill or by using easily rechargeable pre-paid cards. Call costs vary greatly according to contract options; in 2001 a very general average was around 25¢/minute. Many mobile phones from other countries can be used in Spain with a 'roaming' system, but you will probably need to contact your operator to set it up before you leave home. However, this can be expensive and it may well be cheaper to buy or rent a Spanish mobile.

Rent a Phone
C/Numància 212, Eixample (93 280 21 31/www.rphone.es). Metro Maria Cristina/7, 33, 63, 67, 68 bus. **Open** 9.30am-2pm, 4-7.30pm Mon-Fri.
Credit AmEx, MC, V. **Map** p335 B2.
Mobile phones and accessories for rent, either for use in Spain or to take to other countries. Daytime Spanish calls are charged at 90¢-€1.20/min.
Branch: Maremàgnum, Moll d'Espanya, Port Vell (93 225 81 06).
Open 11am-10.30pm daily.

Time

Local time is one hour ahead of GMT, six hours ahead of US Eastern Standard Time and nine ahead of Pacific Standard Time. So, when it's 6pm in Barcelona, it's 5pm in London and noon in New York. Summer Time operates in Spain from late March to late October, with the same changeover days as the UK.

Tipping

There are no fixed rules, nor any expectation of a set ten per cent or more, and locals tip very little. It is common to leave around five per cent for a waiter in a restaurant, and people may also leave a small tip in a bar. It's also usual to tip hotel porters and toilet attendants. In taxis, the norm is around five per cent, more for longer journeys, or if the driver has helped with bags.

Toilets

Public toilets are not common: the main railway stations have clean toilets, and in some places there are pay-on-entry cubicles that cost 15¢. Generally, it's best to pop into a bar or café; proprietors usually don't mind. Major stores or fast-food restaurants are, of course, staple standbys.

Tourist information

The city council (Ajuntament) and Catalan government (the Generalitat) both run tourist information offices, and the City of Barcelona also has an efficient information service for local citizens that's useful to visitors. Information on what's on in music, theatre, galleries and so on can be found in local papers and listings magazines (*see p314*).

City tourist offices sell multi-journey transport tickets, tourist bus (Bus Turístic) tickets and the Barcelona Card discount card. The City and Generalitat also have useful websites (in English).

Oficines d'Informació Turística
Main office: Plaça Catalunya, Eixample (906 30 12 82/from outside Spain 93 368 97 30/ www.bcn.es/www.barcelona turisme.com). Metro Catalunya/ bus all routes to Plaça Catalunya. **Open** 9am-9pm daily.
Map p342 B1.
The main office of the city tourist board (Turisme de Barcelona) is underground beneath the Corte Inglés side of the square (look for big red signs with 'i' in white). It has a information, money exchange, a

shop selling souvenirs and books, a hotel booking service and coin-in-a-slot Internet access.

Branches: Plaça Sant Jaume (in Ajuntament building, side entrance), Barri Gòtic; Barcelona-Sants station; Palau de Congressos (Trade Fair office), Avda Reina Maria Cristina, Montjuïc; A7 (or E15) Motorway, Montseny-Sud service area, km 117.

Temporary office & 'Red Jackets'

Information booth located at Sagrada Familia. **Open** *Late June-late Sept* 10am-8pm daily. Closed late Sept-late June. **Map** p337 F4.

In summer, Turisme de Barcelona opens this temporary booth (no hotel booking service). 'Red Jacket' information officers (in red uniforms) also roam the Barri Gòtic and La Rambla during the summer, ready to field questions in a heroic variety of languages from 10am-8pm daily.

Palau Robert

Passeig de Gràcia 107, Eixample (93 238 40 00/www.gencat.es). Metro Diagonal/22, 24, 28 bus. **Open** 10am-7pm Mon-Sat; 10am-2pm Sun. **Map** p336 D4.

The Generalitat's lavishly equipped information centre is at the junction of Passeig de Gràcia and the Diagonal. It has maps and other essentials for the city itself, but the speciality is a huge range of information in different media on other parts of Catalonia. It also hosts interesting exhibitions.

Branches: Airport Terminal A (93 478 47 04); Airport Terminal B (93 478 05 65). **Open** 9am-9pm daily.

Centre d'Informació de la Virreina

Palau de la Virreina, La Rambla 99, Barri Gòtic (93 301 77 75). Metro Liceu/14, 38, 59, 91 bus. **Open** 10am-2pm, 4-8pm Mon-Fri. **Ticket sales** 11am-8pm Tue-Sat, 11am-2.30pm Sun. **Map** p342 A2.

The information office of the city's culture department, with details of exhibitions, concerts and special events. Also the best place to buy tickets for the Grec summer festival (*see p217*), and some other city-sponsored events. In the same building is the Botiga de la Virreina bookshop, with a wide choice of books on Barcelona, some in English.

010 phoneline

Open 8am-10pm Mon-Sat.
City-run information line aimed mainly at local citizens, but which does an impeccable job of answering all kinds of queries. You may have to wait for an English-speaking operator. From outside Barcelona, call 93 402 70 00.

Visas & immigration

Spain is one of the European Union countries covered by the Schengen agreement, with many shared visa regulations and reduced border controls (with the exception of the UK and Ireland, the Schengen zone now takes in the entire EU, and also extends to Norway and Iceland). To travel to Schengen countries, British and Irish citizens need full passports; most EU nationals need carry only their national identity card. Passports, but not visas, are needed by US, Canadian, Australian and New Zealand citizens for stays of up to three months. Citizens of South Africa and many other countries need visas to enter Spain, obtainable from Spanish consulates and embassies in other countries (or from those of other Schengen countries that you are planning to visit). EU citizens intending to work, study or live long-term in Spain are required to obtain a residency card after arrival; non-EU nationals have a different procedure and should get a special visa in their home country before entering Spain. For more on the formalities of living in Spain, *see p322*.

Visa requirements can change, so always check the latest information with your country's Spanish embassy.

Water

You can drink Barcelona tap water, though it is heavily chlorinated and tests have recently detected a carcinogenic agent, which may make long-term consumption questionable. In any case, bottled water tastes much better, and if you ask for water in a restaurant you will automatically be served this unless you specifically request otherwise.

When to go

There's no best time to come to Barcelona. The city is at its liveliest for the many *festes* (*see chapter* **By Season**), while the weather ranges from mild to glorious. Temperatures are rarely extreme, although the high humidity summer can be debilitating.

Climate

Spring is unpredictable, and warm sunny days can alternate with cold winds and showers; May and June temperatures are perfect, and the city's streetlife is at its most vibrant. The real summer heat, sticky and humid, hits during July and August and many locals leave town. Autumn weather is generally warm and fresh, with sporadic downpours. Crisp sunshine is common from December to February. Snow is rare. *See p322* **Average monthly climate**.

Public holidays

On public holidays (*festes/fiestas*), virtually all shops, banks and offices, and many bars and restaurants, are closed. Public transport runs a limited service on Christmas and New Year's Day. When a holiday falls on a Tuesday or Thursday, some people take the intervening day before or after the weekend off as well, in a long weekend called a *pont/puente* (bridge).

Women

The Catalan capital is in many ways a female-friendly city. Sexism can certainly be found – as some shocking cases of domestic violence have recently shown, but women tourists can have a drink in a bar or go out alone without anyone making much of it, and probably feel safer in general than in many other large cities.

Average monthly climate

	Max temp (C°/F°)	Min temp (C°/F°)	Rainfall (mm/in)	Rain (days/month)
Jan	13/56	6/43	44/1.7	5
Feb	15/59	7/45	36/1.4	6
Mar	16/61	8/47	48/1.9	6
Apr	18/64	10/50	51/2	7
May	21/70	14/57	57/2.2	7
June	24/76	17/63	38/1.5	5
July	27/81	20/67	22/0.9	3
Aug	29/84	20/67	66/2.6	5
Sept	25/78	18/64	79/3.1	6
Oct	22/71	14/57	94/3.7	6
Nov	17/63	9/49	74/2.9	6
Dec	15/59	7/45	50/2.5	6

Ca La Dona

C/Casp 38, pral, Eixample (93 412 71 61/caladona@pangea.org). Metro Catalunya or Urquinaona/22, 28, 39, 45 bus. **Open** *Office* 10am-2pm, 4-8pm Mon-Thur. Closed Aug. **Map** p342 B1.
Women's centre hosting several political, artistic and social groups, and a good place for info. It also has a magazine with event listings.

Centre Municipal d'Informació i Recursos per a Dones

Av Diagonal 233, 5ª, Eixample (93 413 27 22/93 413 27 23/ www.cird. bcn.es). Metro Monumental/ 7, 56, 62 bus. **Open** *Oct-June* noon-2pm Mon-Fri, 4-7pm Tue, Thur. *July, Sept* noon-2pm Mon-Fri. Closed Aug. **Map** p341 F5.
The Ajuntament's women's resource centre. Its publications include a monthly events guide, *Agenda Dona*.

Institut Català de la Dona

Head office/library: C/Viladomat 319, entresol, Eixample (93 495 16 00/icd@correu.gencat.es). Bus 41, 54. **Open** 9am-2pm, 3-5.30pm Mon-Thur; 9am-2pm Fri. **Map** p335 B3.
Information centre: C/Portaferrissa 1-3, Barri Gòtic (93 317 92 91/ icdcentredoc@correu.gencat.es). Metro Liceu/14, 38, 59 bus. **Open** 9am-2pm, 4-6pm Mon-Fri. Reduced hours June-Sept. **Map** p342 A2.
The women's affairs department of the Catalan government.

Working

Barcelona attracts ever-growing numbers of foreign residents and working visitors. Not many from developed countries, however, are drawn here by money, for Barcelona can be a difficult place to find well-paid work, although it is still a not-too-painful place to live cheaply. Common recourses for English-speakers are jobs in the tourist sector (often seasonal and outside the city), bar work and language teaching – still the best chance of finding work quickly.

For a contract in a school, a recognised English-teaching qualification such as TEFL is useful, though not always essential (for courses, *see p319* **International House**). There is also demand for private classes, which are generally much better paid. If you are contracted from your country of origin, legal papers should be handled by your employer. Otherwise, the quickest way to deal with all the form-filling and bureaucracy is to resort to a *gestoria* (*see p308*).

EU CITIZENS

All EU citizens have the right to live, work and study in Spain, but must become legally resident if they stay for more than three months. If you have a job or study course lined up, you are ready to make an appointment to present your residency application. In Barcelona, you do this at the foreigners' office (Oficina de Extranjeros) at the Delegación del Gobierno (*see below*).

NON-EU CITIZENS

While immigration laws have relaxed for EU nationals, they have tightened for people from the rest of the world. First-time applicants officially need a special visa, obtained from a Spanish consulate in your home country, although you can start the bureaucratic ball rolling in Spain if you don't mind making at least one trip home. This, combined with the length of the process, means that good legal advice from a *gestor* (*see p308*) is especially important. There is also a sizeable undeclared, under-the-table labour market in Spain and many people manage to postpone the bureaucratic paper chase, although this can become counterproductive, even if you don't get caught.

Delegación del Gobierno – Oficina de Extranjeros

Avda Marqués de l'Argentera 2, Barceloneta (93 482 05 44/ appointments 93 482 05 60 8am-3pm Mon-Fri). Metro Barceloneta/ 14, 39, 51 bus. **Open** 9am-2pm Mon-Fri. **Map** p343 C4.
Arrive early. There are various queues; make sure you're in the right one before you start. You can expect shorter waits on Fridays.

Catalan Vocabulary

Over a third of Barcelona residents use Catalan as their predominant everyday language, around 70 per cent speak it fluently, and more than 90 per cent understand it. If you take an interest and learn a few phrases, it is likely to be appreciated.

Catalan phonetics are significantly different from those of Spanish, with a wider range of vowel sounds and soft consonants. Catalans use the familiar (*tu*) rather than the polite (*vosté*) forms of the second person very freely, but for convenience verbs are given here in the polite form. For food and menu terms, *see p160* **What's cooking?**

Pronunciation

In Catalan, as in French but unlike in Spanish, words are run together, so *si us plau* (please) is more like *sees-plow*.

à at the end of a word (as in Francesc Macià) is an open **a** rather like **ah**, but very clipped
ç, and **c** before an **i** or an **e**, are like a soft **s**, as in **s**it; **c** in all other cases is as in **c**at
e, when unstressed as in *cerveses* (beers), or *Jaume I*, is a weak sound like cen**tre** or comfor**t**able
g before **i** or **e** and **j** are pronounced like the **s** in plea**s**ure; **tg** and **tj** are similar to the **dg** in ba**dg**e
g after an **i** at the end of a word (Puig) is a hard **ch** sound, as in wa**tch**; **g** in all other cases is as in ge**t**
h is silent
ll is somewhere between the **y** in **y**es and the **lli** in mi**lli**on
l.l, the most unusual feature of Catalan spelling, has a slightly stronger stress on a single **l** sound, so para**l.l**el sounds similar to the English paral**l**el
o at the end of a word is like the **u** sound in fl**u**; **ó** at the end of a word is similar to the **o** in tom**ato**; **ò** is like the **o** in h**o**t
r beginning a word and **rr** are heavily rolled; but at the end of many words is almost silent, so *carrer* (street) sounds like *carr-ay*
s at the beginning and end of words and **ss** between vowels are soft, as in **s**it; a single **s** between two vowels is

a **z** sound, as in la**z**y
t after **l** or **n** at the end of a word is almost silent
x at the beginning of a word, or after a consonant or the letter **i**, is like the **sh** in **sh**oe, at other times like the English e**x**pert
y after an **n** at the end of a word or in **nys** is not a vowel but adds a nasal stress and a y-sound to the **n**

Basics

please *si us plau;* **very good/great/OK** *molt bé*
hello *hola;* **goodbye** *adéu*
open *obert;* **closed** *tancat*
entrance *entrada;* **exit** *sortida*
nothing at all/zilch *res de res* (said with both s silent)
price *preu;* **free** *gratuït/de franc;* **change, exchange** *canvi*
to rent *llogar;* **(for) rent, rental** *(de) lloguer*

More expressions

hello (when answering the phone) *hola, digui'm*
good morning, good day *bon dia;* **good afternoon, good evening** *bona tarda;* **good night** *bona nit*
thank you (very much) *(moltes) gràcies;* **you're welcome** *de res*
do you speak English? *parla anglès?;* **I'm sorry, I don't speak Catalan** *ho sento, no parlo català*
I don't understand *no entenc*
can you say it to me in Spanish, please? *m'ho pot dir en castellà, si us plau?*
how do you say that in Catalan? *com se diu això en català?*
what's your name? *com se diu?*
Sir/Mr *senyor (sr);* **Madam/Mrs** *senyora (sra);* **Miss** *senyoreta (srta)*
excuse me/sorry *perdoni/disculpi;* **excuse me, please** *escolti* (literally 'listen to me');' **OK/fine** *val/d'acord*
how much is it? *quant és?*
why? *perquè?;* **when?** *quan?;* **who?** *qui?;* **what?** *què?;* **where?** *on?;* **how?** *com?;* **where is...?** *on és...?;* **who is it?** *qui és?;* **is/are there any...?** *hi ha...?/n'hi ha de...?*
very *molt;* **and** *i;* **on** *amb;* **without** *sense;* **enough** *prou*
I would like... *vull...* (literally, 'I want');' **how many would you like?** *quants en vol?;* **I don't want** *no vull;* **I like** *m'agrada;* **I don't like** *no m'agrada*
good *bo/bona;* **bad** *dolent/a;* **well/badly** *bé/malament;* **small** *petit/a;* **big** *gran;* **expensive** *car/a;* **cheap** *barat/a;* **hot** (food, drink) *calent/a;* **cold** *fred/a*
something *alguna cosa;* **nothing**

res; **more** *més;* **less** *menys;* **more or less** *més o menys*
toilet *el bany/els serveis/el lavabo*

Getting around

a ticket *un bitllet;* **return** *d'anada i tornada;* **card expired** (on metro) *títol esgotat*
left *esquerra;* **right** *dreta;* **here** *aquí;* **there** *allí;* **straight on** *recte;* **at the corner** *a la cantonada;* **as far as** *fins a;* **towards** *cap a;* **near** *a prop;* **far** *lluny;* **is it far?** *és lluny?*

Time

In Catalan, quarter- and half-hours can be referred to as quarters of the next hour (so, 1.30 is two quarters of 2).

now *ara;* **later** *més tard;* **yesterday** *ahir;* **today** *avui;* **tomorrow** *demà;* **tomorrow morning** *demà pel matí*
morning *el matí;* **midday** *migdia;* **afternoon** *la tarda;* **evening** *el vespre;* **night** *la nit;* **late night** (roughly 1-6am) *la matinada*
at what time...? *a quina hora...?*
in an hour *en una hora*
at 2 *a les dues;* **at 8pm** *a les vuit del vespre;* **at 1.30** *a dos quarts de dues/a la una i mitja;* **at 5.15** *a un quart de sis/a las cinc i quart;* **at 22.30** *a vint-i-dos-trenta*

Numbers

0 *zero;* **1** *u, un, una;* **2** *dos, dues;* **3** *tres;* **4** *quatre;* **5** *cinc;* **6** *sis;* **7** *set;* **8** *vuit;* **9** *nou;* **10** *deu;* **11** *onze;* **12** *dotze;* **13** *tretze;* **14** *catorze;* **15** *quinze;* **16** *setze;* **17** *disset;* **18** *divuit;* **19** *dinou;* **20** *vint;* **21** *vint-i-u;* **22** *vint-i-dos, vint-i-dues;* **30** *trenta;* **40** *quaranta;* **50** *cinquanta;* **60** *seixanta;* **70** *setanta;* **80** *vuitanta;* **90** *noranta;* **100** *cent;* **200** *dos-cents, dues-centes;* **1,000** *mil;* **1,000,000** *un milló*

Date & season

Monday *dilluns;* **Tuesday** *dimarts;* **Wednesday** *dimecres;* **Thursday** *dijous;* **Friday** *divendres;* **Saturday** *dissabte;* **Sunday** *diumenge*
January *gener;* **February** *febrer;* **March** *març;* **April** *abril;* **May** *maig;* **June** *juny;* **July** *juliol;* **August** *agost;* **September** *setembre;* **October** *octobre;* **November** *novembre;* **December** *desembre*
spring *primavera;* **summer** *estiu;* **autumn/fall** *tardor;* **winter** *hivern*

Spanish Vocabulary

Generally referred to as *castellano* (Castilian) rather than *español*. Although many locals prefer to speak Catalan, everyone in the city can speak Spanish, and will switch to it if visitors show signs of linguistic jitters. The Spanish familiar form for 'you' – *tú* – is used very freely, but it's safer to use the more formal *usted* with older people and strangers (verbs below are given in the *usted* form).
For food and menu terms, *see p160* **What's cooking?**

Spanish pronunciation

c before an i or an e and **z** are like **th** in **th**in
c in all other cases is as in **c**at
g before an i or an e and **j** are pronounced with a guttural h-sound that doesn't exist in English – like **ch** in Scottish lo**ch**, but much harder;
g in all other cases is as in **g**et
h at the beginning of a word is normally silent
ll is pronounced almost like a **y**
ñ is like **ny** in ca**ny**on
a single **r** at the beginning of a word and **rr** elsewhere are heavily rolled

Stress rules

In words ending with a vowel, n or s, the penultimate syllable is stressed: eg *barato, viven, habitaciones*.
In words ending with any other consonant, the last syllable is stressed: eg *exterior, universidad*.
An accent marks the stressed syllable in words that depart from these rules: eg *estación, tónica*.

Useful expressions

hello *hola;* **hello** (when answering the phone) *hola, diga*
good morning, good day *buenos días;* **good afternoon, good evening** *buenas tardes;* **good evening** (after dark), **good night** *buenas noches*
goodbye/see you later *adiós/ hasta luego*
please *por favor;* **thank you (very much)** *(muchas) gracias;* **you're welcome** *de nada*
do you speak English? *¿habla inglés?;* **I don't speak Spanish** *no hablo castellano*
I don't understand *no entiendo*
can you say that to me in Catalan, please? *¿me lo puede decir en catalán, por favor?*
what's your name? *¿cómo se llama?*
speak more slowly, please *hable más despacio, por favor;* **wait a moment** *espere un momento*
Sir/Mr *señor (sr);* **Madam/Mrs** *señora (sra);* **Miss** *señorita (srta)*
excuse me/sorry *perdón;*
excuse me, please *oiga* (the standard way to attract someone's attention, politely; literally 'hear me')
OK/fine/(to a waiter) **that's enough** *vale*
where is...? *¿dónde está...?*
why? *¿porqué?;* **when?** *¿cuándo?;* **who?** *¿quién?;* **what?** *¿qué?;* **where?** *¿dónde?;* **how?** *¿cómo?* **who is it?** *¿quién es?;* **is/are there any...?** *¿hay...?*
very *muy;* **and** *y;* **or** *o;* **with** *con;* **without** *sin*
open *abierto;* **closed** *cerrado;* **what time does it open/close?** *¿a qué hora abre/cierra?*
pull (on signs) *tirar;* **push** *empujar*
I would like *quiero;* **how many would you like?** *¿cuántos quiere?;* **how much is it** *¿cuánto es?*
I like *me gusta;* **I don't like** *no me gusta*
good *bueno/a;* **bad** *malo/a;* **well/ badly** *bien/mal;* **small** *pequeño/a;* **big** *gran, grande;* **expensive** *caro/a;* **cheap** *barato/a;* **hot** (food, drink) *caliente;* **cold** *frío/a*
something *algo;* **nothing** *nada*
more/less *más/menos;* **more or less** *más o menos*
do you have any change? *¿tiene cambio?*
price *precio;* **free** *gratis;* **discount** *descuento;* **bank** *banco;* **to rent** *alquilar;* **(for) rent, rental** (en) *alquiler;* **post office** *correos;* **stamp** *sello;* **postcard** *postal;* **toilet** *los servicios*

Getting around

airport *aeropuerto;* **railway station** *estación de ferrocarril/ estación de RENFE* (Spanish railways); **metro station** *estación de metro*
entrance *entrada;* **exit** *salida*
car *coche;* **bus** *autobús;* **train** *tren;* **a ticket** *un billete;* **return** *de ida y vuelta;* **bus stop** *parada de autobus;* **the next stop** *la próxima parada*
excuse me, do you know the way to...? *¿oiga, señor/señora/etc, sabe cómo llegar a...?*
left *izquierda;* **right** *derecha*
here *aquí;* **there** *allí;* **straight on** *recto;* **to the end of the street** *al final de la calle;* **as far as** *hasta;* **towards** *hacia;* **near** *cerca;* **far** *lejos*

Accommodation

do you have a double/single room for tonight/one week? *¿tiene una habitación doble/para una persona/para esta noche/una semana?*
we have a reservation *tenemos reserva;* **an inside/outside room** *una habitación interior/exterior*
with/without bathroom *con/sin baño;* **shower** *ducha;* **double bed** *cama de matrimonio;* **with twin beds** *con dos camas;* **breakfast included** *desayuno incluido;* **air-conditioning** *aire acondicionado;* **lift** *ascensor;* **pool** *piscina*

Time

now *ahora;* **later** *más tarde;* **yesterday** *ayer;* **today** *hoy;* **tomorrow** *mañana;* **tomorrow morning** *mañana por la mañana*
morning *la mañana;* **midday** *mediodía;* **afternoon/evening** *la tarde;* **night** *la noche;* **late night** (roughly 1-6am) *la madrugada*
at what time...? *¿a qué hora...?;* **at 2** *a las dos;* **at 8pm** *a las ocho de la tarde;* **at 1.30** *a la una y media;* **at 5.15** *a las cinco y cuarto;* **in an hour** *en una hora*

Numbers

0 *cero;* **1** *un, uno, una;* **2** *dos;* **3** *tres;* **4** *cuatro;* **5** *cinco;* **6** *seis;* **7** *siete;* **8** *ocho;* **9** *nueve;* **10** *diez;* **11** *once;* **12** *doce;* **13** *trece;* **14** *catorce;* **15** *quince;* **16** *dieciséis;* **17** *diecisiete;* **18** *dieciocho;* **19** *diecinueve;* **20** *veinte;* **21** *veintiuno;* **22** *veintidós;* **30** *treinta;* **40** *cuarenta;* **50** *cincuenta;* **60** *sesenta;* **70** *setenta;* **80** *ochenta;* **90** *noventa;* **100** *cien;* **200** *doscientos;* **1,000** *mil;* **1,000,000** *un millón*

Date & season

Monday *lunes;* **Tuesday** *martes;* **Wednesday** *miércoles;* **Thursday** *jueves;* **Friday** *viernes;* **Saturday** *sábado;* **Sunday** *domingo*
January *enero;* **February** *febrero;* **March** *marzo;* **April** *abril;* **May** *mayo;* **June** *junio;* **July** *julio;* **August** *agosto;* **September** *septiembre;* **October** *octubre;* **November** *noviembre;* **December** *diciembre*
spring *primavera;* **summer** *verano;* **autumn/fall** *otoño;* **winter** *invierno*

Further Reference

Reading

Guides & walks

Amelang, J, Gil, X & McDonogh, GW: *Twelve Walks through Barcelona's Past* (Aj de Barcelona) Well thought out walks by historical theme. Original, and better informed than many walking guides.
Güell, Xavier: *Gaudí Guide* (Ed. Gustavo Gili) A handy guide, with good background on all the architect's work.
Pomés Leiz, Juliet, & Feriche, Ricardo: *Barcelona Design Guide* (Ed. Gustavo Gili) An eccentrically wide-ranging but engaging listing of everything ever considered 'designer' in BCN.

History, architecture, art & culture

Burns, Jimmy: *Barça: A People's Passion* The first full-scale history in English of one of the world's most overblown football clubs.
Elliott, JH: *The Revolt of the Catalans* Fascinating, detailed account of the Guerra dels Segadors and the Catalan revolt of the 1640s.
Fernández Armesto, Felipe: *Barcelona: A Thousand Years of the City's Past* A solid, straightforward history.
Fraser, Ronald: *Blood of Spain* A vivid oral history of the Spanish Civil War and the tensions that preceded it. It is especially good on the events of July 1936 in Barcelona.
Hooper, John: *The New Spaniards* An incisive and very readable survey of the changes in Spanish society since the death of Franco.
Hughes, Robert: *Barcelona* The most comprehensive single book about Barcelona: tendentious at times, erratic, but beautifully written, and covering every aspect of the city up to the 1992 Olympics.
Kaplan, Temma: *Red City, Blue Period – Social Movements in Picasso's Barcelona* An interesting book, tracing the interplay of avant-garde art and avant-garde politics in 1900s Barcelona.
Orwell, George: *Homage to Catalonia* The classic account of Barcelona in revolution, as written by an often bewildered, but always perceptive observer.
Paz, Abel: *Durruti, The People Armed* Closer to its theme, a biography of the most legendary of Barcelona's anarchist revolutionaries.

Solà-Morales, Ignasi: *Fin de Siècle Architecture in Barcelona* Large-scale and wide-ranging description of the city's *Modernista* heritage.
Tóibín, Colm: *Homage to Barcelona* Evocative and perceptive journey around the city: good on the booming Barcelona of the 1980s, but also excellent on Catalan Gothic, Gaudí and Miró.
van Hensbergen, Gijs: *Gaudí* A thorough account of the life of the architect.
Vázquez Montalbán, Manuel: *Barcelonas* Idiosyncratic but insightful reflections on the city by one of its most prominent modern writers.
Zerbst, Rainer: *Antoni Gaudí* Lavishly illustrated and comprehensive survey.

Literature

Calders, Pere: *The Virgin of the Railway and Other Stories* Ironic, engaging, quirky stories by a Catalan writer who spent many years in exile in Mexico.
Català, Victor: *Solitude* This masterpiece by woman novelist Caterina Albert shocked readers in 1905 with its open, modern treatment of female sexuality.
Marsé, Juan: *The Fallen* Classic novel of survival in Barcelona during the long *posguerra* after the Civil War.
Martorell, Joanot, & Martí de Gualba, Joan: *Tirant lo Blanc* The first European prose novel, from 1490, a rambling, bawdy, shaggy-dog story of travels, romances and chivalric adventures.
Mendoza, Eduardo: *City of Marvels* and *Year of the Flood* A sweeping, very entertaining saga of Barcelona between its great Exhibitions in 1888 and 1929; and a more recent novel of passions in the city of the 1950s.
Oliver, Maria Antònia: *Antipodes and Study in Lilac* Two adventures of Barcelona's first feminist detective.
Rodoreda, Mercè: *The Time of the Doves* and *My Cristina and Other Stories* A translation of *La Plaça del Diamant*, most widely read of all Catalan novels. Plus a collection of similarly bittersweet short tales.
Vázquez Montalbán, Manuel: *The Angst-Ridden Executive, An Olympic Death* Two thrillers starring detective and gourmet extraordinaire Pepe Carvalho.

Food & drink

Andrews, Colman: *Catalan Cuisine* A mine of information on food and much else (also with usable recipes).

Casas, Penelope: *Foods and Wines of Spain* A useful general handbook, which contains over 400 recipes.

Music

Angel Molina Leading Barcelona DJ with an international reputation and various remix albums released.
Estopa Two brothers from the Barcelona suburbs who have taken the local pop scene by storm, with two hit albums, sung in Spanish.
Lluís Llach An icon of the 1960s and early '70s protest against the fascist regime combines a melancholic tone with brilliant musicianship. One of the first to experiment with electronic music.
Maria del Mar Bonet Though from Mallorca, del Mar Bonet always sings in Catalan and specialises in her own compositions, North African music and traditional Mallorcan music.
Pep Sala Excellent musician and survivor of the extremely successful Catalan group Sau. Sala now produces his own music, much of which shows a rockabilly and country influence.
Els Pets Kings of Catalan language pop, led by the highly charismatic Lluis Gavald.
Quimi Portet Former guitarist for (and creative force behind) legendary Spanish pop band Ultimo de la Fila, now just as respected for his mature solo work.
Raimon Has put some of the greatest Catalan language poets, such as Ausiàs March, to music.

Barcelona online

www.barcelonareview.com Online literary review.
www.barcelonaturisme.com Tourist information from the city's official tourist authority.
www.bcn.es The city council's information-packed website.
www.catalanencyclopaedia.com Comprehensive English-language reference work covering Catalan history, geography and 'who's who'.
www.diaridebarcelona.com Local online newspaper with good English content.
www.mobilitat.org Generalitat's website on transport in Catalonia.
www.timeout.com/barcelona The online city guide, with a select monthly agenda.
www.vilaweb.com Catalan web portal and links page; in Catalan.
www.vanguardia.es Online version of Barcelona daily paper *La Vanguardia*.

Index

Advertisers' Index

Section sponsored by

Place of interest and/or entertainment	
Hospital or college	
Pedestrianised zone	
Railway station	
Metro station, FGC station	Ⓜ 〰
Area name	**BARRI GÒTIC**
History walk pp8-9	● ● ●
Walk 1: The Chino pp80-1	● ● ●
Walk 2: La Ribera pp94-5	● ● ●
Walk 3: Modernisme pp114-5	● ● ●

Maps

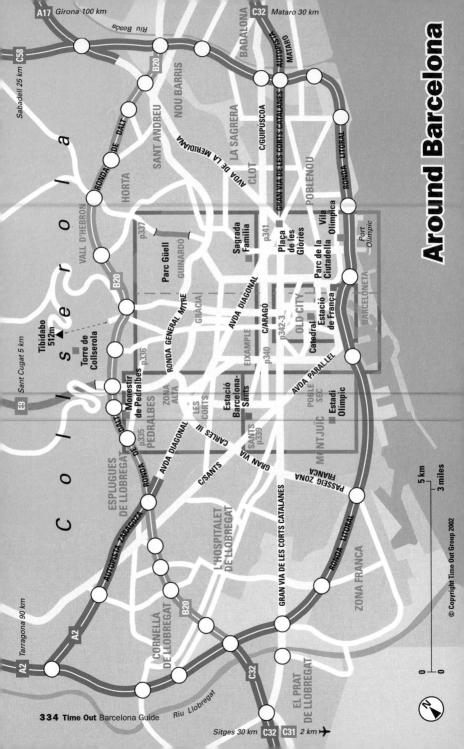

Around Barcelona

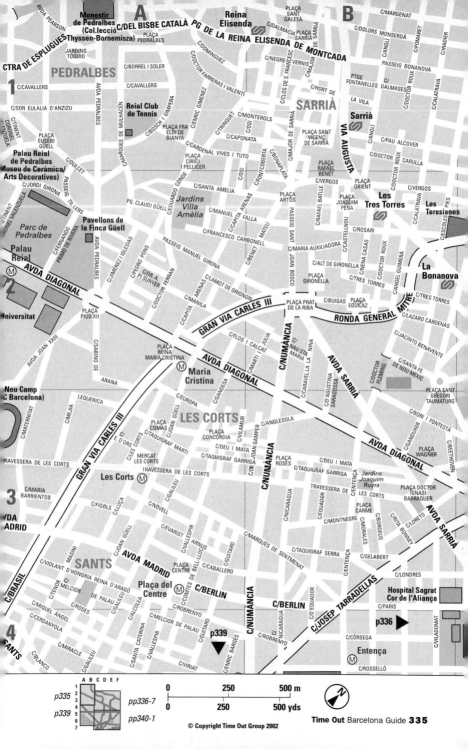

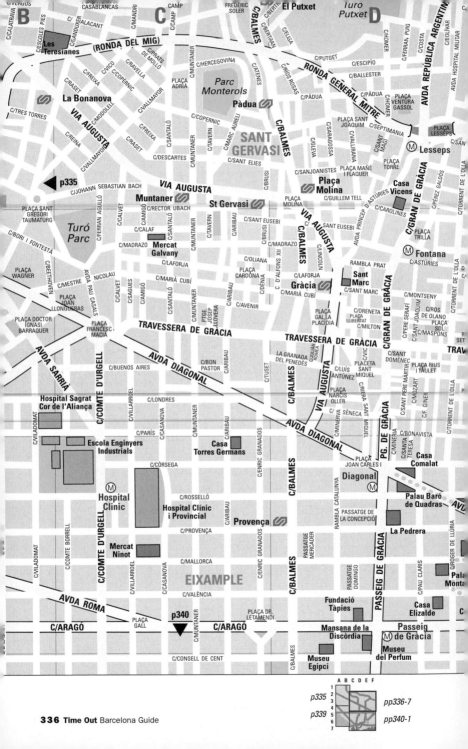

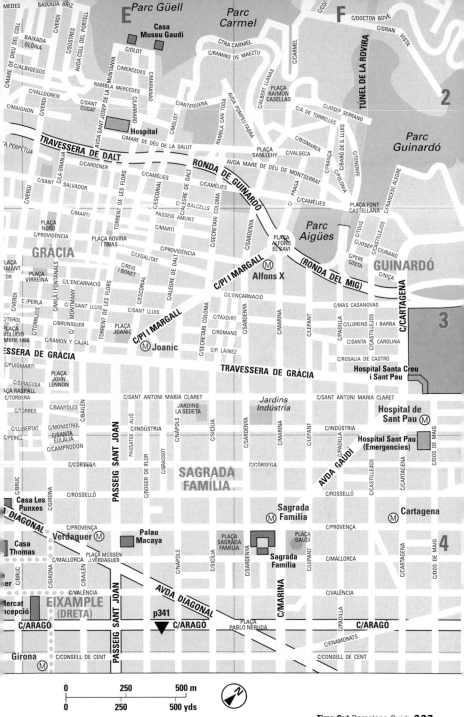

A world of services.

Targasys is always with you, ready to assure you all the tranquillity and serenity that you desire for your journeys, 24 hours a day 365 days a year.

Roadside assistance always and everywhere, infomobility so not to have surprises, insurance... and lots more.

To get to know us better contact us at the toll-free number **00-800-55555555**.

...and to discover Targa Connect's exclusive and innovative integrated infotelematic services onboard system visit us at:

www.targaconnect.com

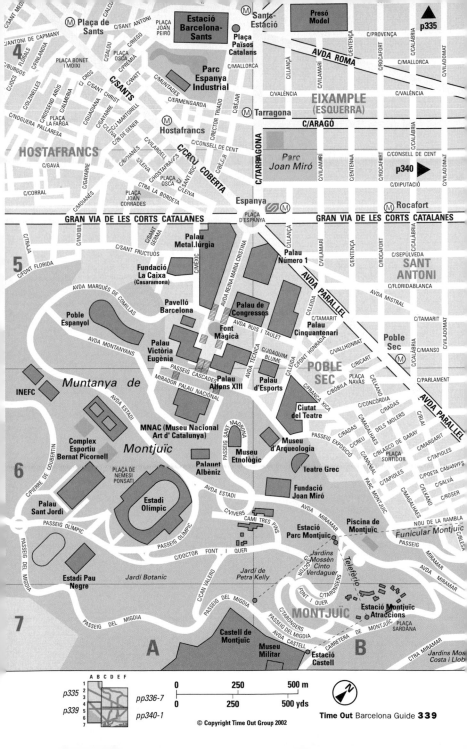

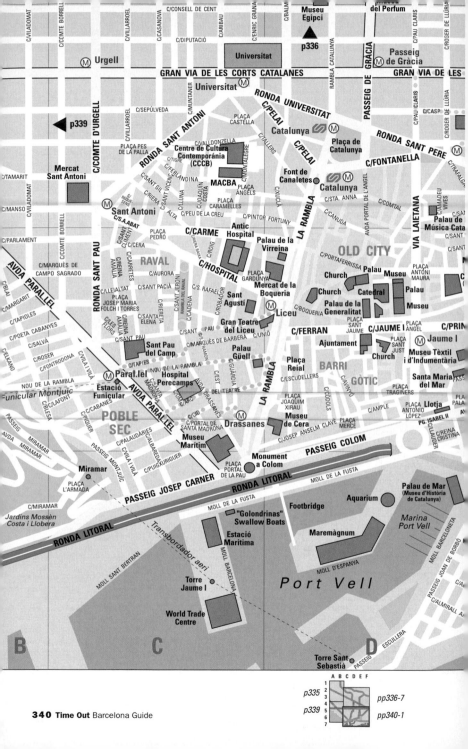

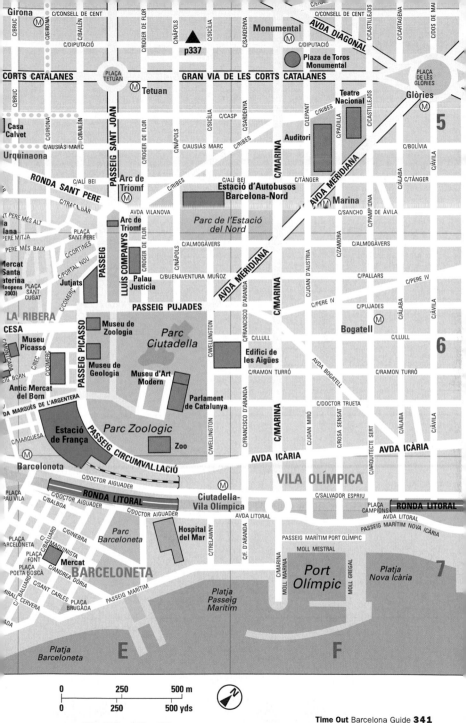

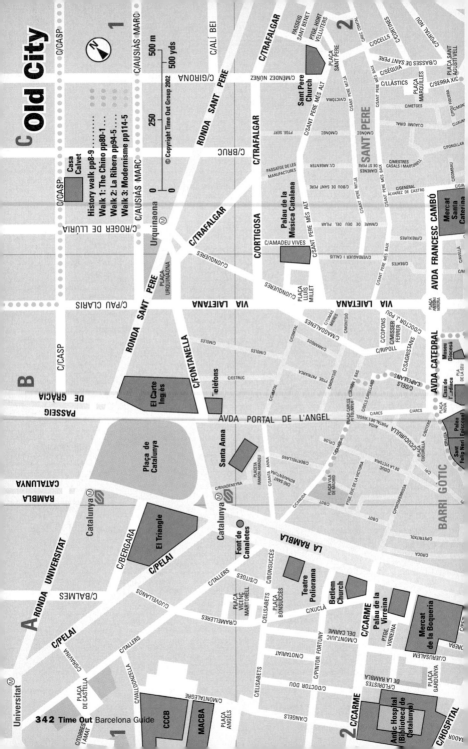

Street Index

p335   pp336-7

p339   pp340-1

References in **bold** *refer to the detailed Old City map on pages 342-3.*

Street Index

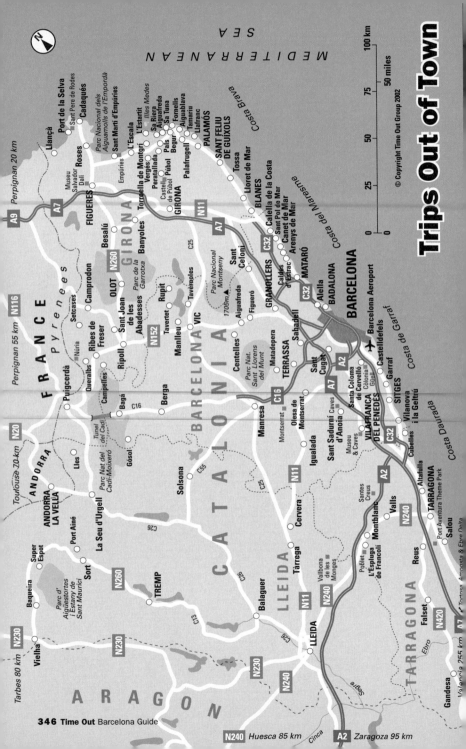

Trips Out of Town

MEDITERRANEAN SEA

Costa Brava

Costa del Maresme

Costa de Garraf

Costa Daurada

© Copyright Time Out Group 2002

346 Time Out Barcelona Guide

N240 *Huesca 85 km*   A2 *Zaragoza 95 km*

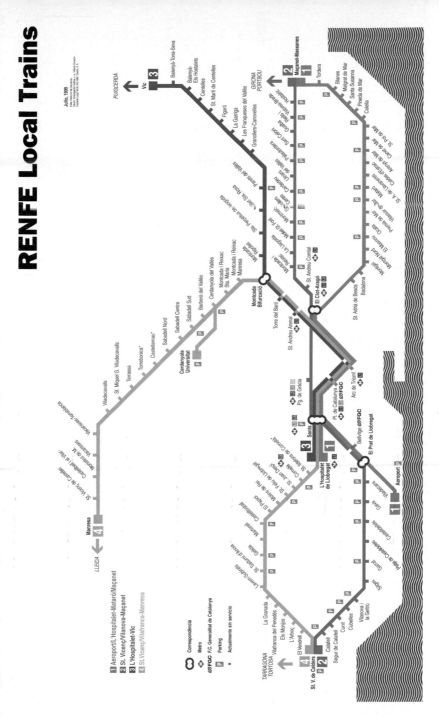